65.00

D0163380

Managers and
National Culture

Managers and National Culture

A GLOBAL PERSPECTIVE

Edited by
RICHARD B. PETERSON

Q

QUORUM BOOKS
WESTPORT, CONNECTICUT • LONDON

Library of Congress Cataloging-in-Publication Data

Peterson, Richard B.
  Managers and national culture : a global perspective / edited by Richard B.
Peterson.
      p. cm.
  Includes bibliographical references and index.
  ISBN 0–89930–602–0 (alk. paper)
  1. Industrial management—Cross-cultural studies.   2. Personnel
management—Cross-cultural studies.   3. International business
enterprises—Personnel management.   4. Executives.   I. Title.
HD31.P387   1993
658′.049—dc20   92–1747

British Library Cataloguing in Publication Data is available.

Library of Congress Catalog Card Number: 92–1747
ISBN: 0–89930–602–0

First published in 1993

Quorum Books, 88 Post Road West, Westport, Connecticut 06881
An imprint of Greenwood Publishing Group, Inc.

Printed in the United States of America

The paper used in this book complies with the
Permanent Paper Standard issued by the National
Information Standards Organization (Z39.48–1984).

10 9 8 7 6 5 4 3 2 1

CONTENTS

FIGURES AND TABLES

FIGURES

PREFACE

Why do we academics write books? I suspect that there are almost as many reasons as there are authors. Let me share with the reader some of the reasons for my going ahead with this project.

I developed a strong interest in traveling overseas after completing my M.A. in industrial relations at the University of Illinois in the mid–1950s. The hope was there that I might be assigned outside the United States while serving in the U.S. Army, but that didn't happen. The closest I got to another country was Fort Bliss, Texas, which is across the border from Juarez, Mexico. Periodic trips across the bridge whetted my appetite for more foreign travel.

The next four and one-half years found me working in the field of personnel and industrial relations for a private firm in the greater Chicago area. Once again I found the chance of going overseas somewhat remote. It would have been better had I been trained in finance or engineering, if working overseas was to be a reality.

The return for a doctorate at the University of Wisconsin finally allowed me to reach the goal. I made a conscious choice to pursue a dissertation that would provide a reason for going overseas. The summer of 1965 found my family and me living in Stockholm, Sweden. That summer was spent collecting dissertation data on managerial rights in Swedish collective bargaining. An added attraction was the opportunity to become acquainted with all my Swedish relatives. My four grandparents had immigrated to the American Middle West in the latter part of the nineteenth century. Thus, I was returning to my ancestral roots.

The time spent in Sweden spurred me to find a way to return to Europe for a longer stay. Thus, we found ourselves in Bergen, Norway, during the 1971–72 academic year where I was on leave to teach at the Norwegian School of Economics and Business Administration. There was also time to carry out research on organizational climate in separate samples of Norwegian and Swedish companies. There were even side-trips to give papers at the International Institute of Management in West Berlin, the University of Tel Aviv (Israel), and Ege University (Izmir, Turkey), the latter two visits being funded by the Fulbright Commission.

That wasn't enough exposure. Three years later I was back in Sweden and Norway looking at job design experiments at Volvo and other Scandinavian firms while on sabbatical leave. Shorter trips in 1977 and 1980 gave me the opportunity to meet with faculty at the London Business School, the London School of Economics, and the Netherlands School of Business (Nijenrode).

The fall of 1982 found my wife and me spending six weeks at the Industrial Relations Research Unit at Warwick University near Coventry, England, learning more about English industrial relations. We were also fortunate to spend some time in Athens and Thessaloniki, Greece, where I gave presentations sponsored by the International Communications Agency of the U.S. government.

Two years later brought me back to Sweden to conduct interviews with employers and union officials concerning what had happened to the Swedish Model of Industrial Relations in the intervening years. There was even time to visit the university cities of Groningen, Heidelberg, and Tubingen, Germany, and to hike in the majestic Swiss Alps at Wengen and Murren.

My international interests were not limited to Western Europe. Starting in the late 1960s, I became intrigued with the developing literature on Japanese management. How could the Japanese be successful with their strange lifetime employment system in their large companies at a time when the American and Western European management models were at the forefront? Looking back, we now realize that there is no universal model of management—whether of American, European, or Japanese origin. I still find it difficult to foresake reading the latest book or article on Japanese management or industrial relations.

Another sabbatical quarter in 1988 found the two of us exploring the land "down-under" in Australia and New Zealand. The time spent at the Australian Graduate School of Management in Sydney provided the opportunity to read extensively about managerial behavior in such countries as South Korea, Taiwan, Singapore, Thailand, Malaysia, Indonesia, and the territory of Hong Kong. Some of these countries represent the newly industrialized countries (NICs), while others aspire to that status in the coming years.

The fall of 1989 was spent in Western and Eastern Europe. Interviews in Brussels, Paris, Geneva, and Vienna provided insights into the likely impact of the 1992 Common Market (EEC) integration on national industrial relations systems within the community. Visits to Budapest, Prague, Wroclaw, and East Berlin gave me an appreciation for the challenges facing their governments and business and union leaders as former Eastern Bloc nations find their own path to democracy and the market-based economy. During this research leave we once again were back in Sweden and Norway, winding up the journey.

The summer of 1990 found me back in Japan for a joint conference of the Western Academy of Management and the Japanese near Mount Fuji to share some of the insights about management in the international context.

Then in the Summer of 1992 I attended the second WAM international Conference in Leuven, Belgium, where North American and European academics were once again exposed to internationalization issues. This was followed by conducting interviews with personnel officials in very large German multinational companies regarding their policies and practices in dealing with expatriate staff. Later interviews were to be carried out with comparable officials in British, Japanese, and American multinationals.

Finally our family has been internationalized in many ways. Our two children joined us in Stockholm (1965) and Bergen (1971–72). They attended Norwegian schools in Bergen. My wife, Barbara, was fortunate to spend a summer on the Experiment in International Living in Vienna and a Fulbright year in West Berlin before we were married. In the fall of 1981 she taught English as a second language to Russian teachers in Kiev, Russia.

Our daughter, and her family, spent almost four years in Tokyo while her husband was stationed at Yakota Air Force Base. Finally, our son went a step further by marrying a young woman from East Berlin whom he had met while studying Russian at the Pushkin Institute in Moscow. They had to wait for almost three years to gain permission from the East German authorities to marry and for her to leave the country. Today she could just walk across anyplace where the Berlin Wall stood until November 1989.

The other reason for writing this book derives from a realization that the internationalization of business is proceeding at a rapid pace. Thus, students and business practitioners must have an understanding of the important role that national culture plays in explaining managerial behavior across a variety of countries. It is most likely in the area of human resource management (HRM) that national culture will play an important role in how managers are recruited, selected, appraised, compensated, and trained and developed. The earlier books in this field gave us a good understanding of national and regional cultural values in business organizations, but most of them were written twenty to thirty years ago. This book gives us a current understanding of culture and HRM practices in many countries.

I want to thank a number of people for their role in internationalizing my way of thinking, especially to the late Everett Kassalow who opened my eyes to the study of international industrial relations in both the developed and developing countries. This "opening up" was strengthened by reading many of the books and articles published under funding by the Ford Foundation for the Inter-University Study of Labor Problems in Economic Development. The University of Wisconsin experience gave me the benefit of a solid interdisciplinary training that has been beneficial through the years.

Other people and organizations that I wish to acknowledge for their contributions include Alton Johnson; Robben Fleming; Erik Fostadius; the late Olav Harald Jensen; Dag Coward; Bulent Himmetoglu; Arie Shirom; the late Gerard B.J. Bomers; Willy Brown; B. C. Roberts; Dexter Dunphy; Tohr Yamaguchi; Don Turkington; David Smith; the Research and Travel Committee of the Schools of Business Administration at the University of Washington; the University of

Wisconsin; the Fulbright Commission; the International Communications Agency; and the Swedish government.

I also wish to thank the capable staff of Patricia Payne, Grace Lee, and Michael Dixon for typing some chapters of the book.

Finally, special thanks to my colleagues on the project who volunteered to write individual chapters on management in the fifteen countries included in this volume. This book would not have been possible if one of us had attempted to cover management in all the diverse countries included here. I am only sorry that restrictions on book length prohibited including management in other parts of the world. People have contacted me to cover management in Hungary, Argentina, Brazil, Chile, selected African nations, the Philippines, and Indonesia. Perhaps a second edition can include one or more of these countries. I also want to thank Eric Valentine and his staff at Quorum for their interest and professional handling of the publication of this book.

Managers and
National Culture

1

MANAGEMENT: AN INTERNATIONAL PERSPECTIVE

Richard B. Peterson

The study of management and managerial behavior is largely a phenomenon of the post–World War II period, although academicians and practitioners have been writing on the subject at least since the late nineteenth century. Some of the better known earlier writers included Emile Durkheim, F. W. Taylor, Henri Fayol, Max Weber, Alfred P. Sloan, Elton Mayo, and Chester Barnard. This chapter begins with a brief historical overview of the literature on management since the end of World War II. The second section discusses three important current developments that are likely to shift our attention even further toward an appreciation of the internationalization of the field of management. Finally, we outline the remaining chapters in the book.

HISTORICAL OVERVIEW

Most of the pre–World War II writers on management were associated with one of three schools of management thought: the scientific, the classical, and human relations. Frederick Winslow Taylor was the father of the Scientific Management School, which assumed that the principles of industrial engineering could be applied to create the most efficient methods of organizing work and jobs. Taylor and his colleagues gave prime attention to the management of the factory floor.

The Classical School of management grew out of the early studies by Emile Durkheim, in France, and Max Weber, in Germany. The study of bureaucracy by Weber led later writers such as Henri Fayol and Alfred P. Sloan to develop prescriptions about how management should perform its job. Various principles of management were formulated that were assumed to have universal application rather than be limited to the experience in one country.

Elton Mayo and his colleagues developed the School of Human Relations based on their early work at Western Electric's Hawthorne plant outside Chicago. Mayo focused on the need for managers to consider their employees' social and psychological needs if the firm was to be successful. Some of these early management writers were academicians, but many of those in the United States based their thoughts on their own experiences as executives or consultants.

The Early Postwar Years

The management literature greatly expanded in the two decades following World War II. Some of the best known writers in the field included Herbert Simon, Peter Drucker, Michael Crozier, James March, Rensis Likert, Talcott Parsons, William F. Whyte, Joan Woodward, and members of the Ashton Group. The overwhelming number of management scholars were full-time academics rather than practitioners or consultants. Some of them assumed that managerial and employee behavior were fairly universal, so that studies done in one country could be applied to other countries as well.

Most of the major works were done in the United States, although not all of their authors were native-born. Peter Drucker, for example, was born and raised in Europe, before he moved to the United States. French-born Michel Crozier gave us an understanding of behavior in French organizations. John Childs, and other members of the Ashton Group in England, aided our understanding of variables related to organizational structure and function. An English academic, the late Joan Woodward, introduced the importance of type of technology in understanding management practice.

Much of the literature on management and managerial behavior was written in the United States for several reasons. First, the United States came through World War II relatively unscathed economically. With some 2 percent of the world's population in the 1950s, it owned about 40 percent of the world's wealth. The nation poured large amounts of money into its colleges and universities in the forms of grants, loans, and other expenditures as enrollments increased rapidly owing to the returning GIs and, later, the baby-boom generation who reached college age beginning in the mid–1960s. The number of faculty expanded considerably to meet the student demand. Graduate students and faculty were drawn overseas to do research in other countries.

Second, the Ford, Rockefeller, and other foundations channeled considerable amounts of money into various overseas projects, running the gamut from agriculture to general encouragement of economic development in the industrialized and developing nations alike. The years 1950 to 1965 were the "glory years" for federal and private funding of international research projects. Perhaps the best known economic development project was the Inter-University Study of Labor Problems in Economic Development, largely funded by the Ford Foundation. This project was headed by four eminent economists—Clark Kerr, John Dunlop, Frederick Harbison, and Charles Myers. While much of their focus was on the study of the role of the actors (labor, management, and government) in contributing to economic development (Dunlop, 1958; Kerr et al., 1964), management received much attention in several books published under the umbrella of the Inter-University Study. Some of the more prominent volumes covered managerial ideology (Bendix, 1956), management in France (Ehrman, 1957), West Germany (Hartmann, 1959), and Britain (McGivering, Matthews, and Scott, 1960), and a broader look at management in many countries (Harbison and Myers, 1959).

Harbison and Myers (1959) argued that the process of industrialization led countries to adopt similar ways of managing enterprises, even if the underlying cultures were dissimilar. Thus, two countries at the same stage of industrialization would have common organizational structures, management processes, and ways of managing employees. Convergence theorists argued, and still do, that economic forces overwhelm cultural factors over time. Today, over thirty years later, this debate between the convergence theorists and cultural relativists continues to be played out. Later research by Haire, Ghiselli, and Porter (1966), Cole (1979), and Clark (1979) provides some evidence in support of both schools of thought.

Finally, the field of management was not as well developed in Western Europe and Japan as it was in the United States at the time. Researchers were likely to have been trained in the underlying disciplines of sociology or economics rather than business. The devastation of World War II delayed the expansion of higher education enrollments by at least a decade or so. Research monies were limited as well.

Comparative international management developed in the 1960s as a separate area dominated by academicians trained largely in business schools who focused on international business, organization theory, organizational behavior, human resource management, or business policy. The early work of Farmer and Richman (1965) set a conceptual model for the field. The Haire, Ghiselli, and Porter study (1966) of managerial attitudes in thirteen countries pointed out both similarities and differences across these nations.

During most of the 1960s, however, a number of writers argued in favor of a universal "best way" of managing people, processes, and technology. The assumption was that the best of American managerial practice was the desired model since the United States was both the most advanced industrial nation at the time and the wealthiest in terms of per capita income. Such a viewpoint was reinforced by Servan-Schreiber's *The American Challenge* (1968) when he stated that, although Western Europe represented the second strongest economic force in the world at that time, the U.S. domestic economy was first, and America's multinational corporations (MNCs) represented abroad the third largest economic power. U.S. management know-how and technology raised the specter of a weakened Western European and Common Market. Servan-Schreiber believed that only Sweden and Japan could offer much real competition to the United States and only in a limited number of industries. He was, of course, resoundingly wrong about Japan.

Recent Developments in Internationalizing Management

By the early 1970s, there was a growing consciousness that managerial behaviors varied both within and across nations and regions. Illustrating this shift away from universal managerial behavior was the publication of such books by Davis (1971) and Massie and Luytjes (1972) chronicling managerial behavior in a large number of countries. Davis and Goodman (1972) edited a volume on employees and managers in Latin America. Grosset (1970) informed us about European management styles and values that varied from our knowledge of the dominant American style and values of management. However, what really turned the idea of universal managerial behavior upside down were reports coming out of Japan. Abegglen (1958) had earlier shared his insights into the behavior of large Japanese companies with Western readers, but even then, as industrialization proceeded, he thought that the Japanese lifetime employment system would change from its feudal foundations to Western models. By 1973, Abegglen was less sure that consensus decision making, pay and promotion based primarily on seniority, generalist training, enterprise unions, and noncontractual continued employment obligation for the permanent staff would be sacrificed in the name of modernization.

Dore (1973) went one step further after completing his study of British General Electric and Hitachi. He concluded that Japan, not Britain or the United States, offered the prime model for later developing economies. Dore saw important advantages of the internal labor market mechanism in large Japanese companies like Mitsui and Mitsubishi. Taira (1970) and Koike (1988) recognized the competitive advantages of the Japanese employment system for use with its permanent staff.

Clark (1979) provided the field of comparative management with an in-depth look at the development of the lifetime employment system in a medium-size Japanese company. He showed that some of its features are culturally linked with the old household system of Tokugawa times. American executives were inclined to see that the Japanese employment system created inflexibilities by not allowing layoffs of permanent staff when business declined in volume. Pay increases and promotions based on seniority were also seen as an impediment, since the most meritorious employees and managers would not receive their due returns. However, outsiders did not recognize that the temporary staff in these firms provided the firms with sufficient flexibility to handle most business downturns (Peterson and Sullivan, 1990).

The literature on comparative management has not been confined to academic treatment of the subject. Consultants like Harris and Moran (1979) emphasize the need for better selection and training of managers who are called on to supervise employees located in countries other than the MNCs' worldwide headquarters. Copeland and Griggs (1985) provide the American expatriate manager with valuable ideas about culture and its link with appropriate managerial behavior in a variety of countries outside the United States.

Our knowledge of managerial behavior has been enhanced in recent years by the publication of three important books. Ronen (1986) provides an academic treatise of the main research literature in comparative and international management. Adler (1991) offers important lessons in consciousness-raising for students and managers alike. Dowling and Schuler (1990) cover important topics like selection, training, compensation, and labor relations implications for firms operating internationally. There is also a growing literature on managing the multinational company (e.g., Vernon and Wells, 1986).

In fact, there is a growing awareness in the United States of the cultural diversity of the workforce. An American manager today may be supervising a domestic workforce made up of native-born Caucasians, Blacks, Hispanics, Native Indians, East Indians, Southeast Asian refugees, and Europeans. Copeland and Griggs make use of a set of seven films to educate managers about domestic cultural diversity. Their films go beyond their earlier "Going International" series that educates American managers about issues relating to expatriate cross-cultural awareness selection, training, and reentry.

The Internationalizing of Management

International business operations have changed rather dramatically in the latter years of the twentieth century. The first international presence of a German, American, or Japanese firm may have been through exporting a product or establishing a sales operation in another country. Later, the company may have established an international division to manage operations in a variety of countries. More recently, the same firm may be operating on a regiocentric basis like Unilever. Some day in the not too distant future, the company may be operating globally as Nestlé does. Nestlé's world headquarters is located in Switzerland, but it does not consider itself to be a Swiss company in terms of the thinking of its managers. Its managers are drawn from many countries.

During the early postwar years U.S. firms considered themselves as primarily domestically driven, even given the number of firms that established manufacturing, sales, and service operations in Western Europe and other parts of the world in the 1950s and 1960s. Ford and General Motors may have established auto plants in England and West Germany for sales to European customers, but top management at Ford and GM still thought of themselves as running a largely domestic auto company.

Until recent years, most American 500 companies manufactured the vast majority of their products in the United States for American consumption. This situation was even truer for smaller and medium-size companies. Prior to the 1970s, U.S. firms, in large part, had a fairly captive audience for their sales. The international part of the company's operation was merely the "extra pudding on the cake" for most firms. Relatively few Western European or Japanese firms had established manufacturing plants in the United States. The situation was far different for such countries as Sweden or West Germany where economic prosperity depended on exporting approximately 35 to 40 percent of their goods. For instance, for companies like Sweden's SKF a very small percentage of their total workforce is located in the headquarters' country.

The situation is far different in the early 1990s as we move into the global economy. No longer can countries afford a situation where the vast majority of CEOs of American Fortune 500 companies never had have a foreign assignment before they reached their present position. The manager of the future will likely have different training than that provided in the past. He or she may still be educated in engineering or business, but foreign language training, as well as an undergraduate degree in international studies, may complement the MBA. These changes in the United States will only bring us up to the level of most European managers, who have been raised to be at least bilingual for decades. We now turn to important developments that are likely to challenge our understanding of management in the international context.

CURRENT INTERNATIONAL DEVELOPMENTS

The present era represents a very dynamic time in terms of human history. We are in the midst of many events that are changing our way of thinking and doing. Some of the most profound changes include (1) the breakup of the economic and military Eastern Bloc nations, and their subsequent move toward the market economy; (2) the integration of the EEC (Common Market) in 1992; (3) the possibility of a North American free trade zone that would include Canada, the United States, and Mexico; and (4) possible integration in East Asia.

The Opening Up of Eastern Europe

No one would have predicted the major realignment of the Eastern Bloc countries that began in 1989. During the fall of 1989, Hungary and Poland had already taken the first steps toward independence when my wife and I visited Budapest and Wroclaw in October. But events in Czechoslovakia and East Germany were still unexpected. I can remember asking an acquaintance in Prague one afternoon when he thought his country would disengage from the Cold War politics of the postwar period. He said it would take at least ten years to break free of the Soviets. Five days after our leaving Prague, the large demonstrations in Wenceslaus Square in Prague began. The same happened in East Germany. We asked two East Berliners when their country would start to break from the Soviet Union, COMECON, and the Warsaw Pact. They said it would be well into the twenty-first century before the Berlin Wall came down. A week later East and West Germans were celebrating on the Wall. Rumania and Bulgaria joined the parade within a month. The former Soviet Union has moved slowly toward political pluralism and a market economy. The most vivid example is the opening of the largest McDonald's restaurant in the world in Moscow.

The scenario is still being played out in these countries in different ways. Poland, Czechoslovakia, and Hungary are moving more quickly toward a Western-style market economy than the other former Eastern Bloc nations. Poland, in particular, has taken the position that "biting the bullet" now in shifting toward a truly functioning market economy, however difficult in the short term, will prove to be the wisest choice to free the nation from its economic malaise. However, in the fall of 1991 the Polish government was slowing the speed of change because of the pain of restructuring.

The rest of the former Eastern Bloc nations seem, at the present time, to be moving more gingerly away from socialistic programs and structures. Private business, as we know it in the West, has had few opportunities to flourish in these nations since World War II. There is a real shortage of professional managers who can operate effectively in the global market economy. Thus, massive programs in management development will be needed to provide the necessary expertise if their economies are to succeed. The challenge is a formidable one but one well worth seeking.

The Common Market Integration in 1992

The proposed integration of the European Common Market on December 31, 1992 is a significant event bringing together twelve nations and a consumer population of over 325 million people. Free trade, an open labor market, and the possibility of a common currency will have a profound impact on economic growth, the standard of living, and political and economic muscle in the world scene of these countries. No longer will Western Europe be a "weak sister" compared to the Japanese and U.S. economies. Looking ahead, the Common Market may even be stronger if Austria, Sweden, or other European Free Trade Association countries, Turkey, and some of the Eastern European nations gain admittance in the coming years.

The North American Free Trade Zone

In response to the integration of the Common Market, the United States and its neighbors are moving toward closer economic integration. Canada and the United States already have an agreement to eventually drop all tariffs and duties affecting trade between them. There followed discussion with Mexico for trilateral agreements. In August 1992 representatives of the three countries agreed on the elements of the North American Free Trade Agreement. If this agreement is ratified, the per capita gross national product (GNP) of these countries would be 7.7 percent larger than the GNP of the EEC at the present time. The population of these three countries presently exceeds 350 million.

East Asian Union

Finally, Japan and the "Four Dragons" (South Korea, Taiwan, Hong Kong, and Singapore), may be compelled to form some economic union or association, for they are feeling the nascent impact of competition from the newest Asian countries to industrialize, notably Thailand, Malaysia, Indonesia, and the Philippines. How Australia and New Zealand will fit in is still an open question. Although culturally they are much closer to England, Canada, and the United States, their location would better fit them to enter an Asian coalition.

SIGNIFICANCE OF SUCH DEVELOPMENTS

The significance of these events for the study of managers in the international arena lies in the increasing recognition by national leaders of the crucial role that managers and all other employees will play in the coming years in the global economy. The declining birth rate in most of Western Europe, Japan, and the

United States will mean fewer entrants into the labor force in the coming years compared to the baby-boom entrants of the mid–1960s to mid–1980s. Thus, the supply of potential managers in those countries will be limited in the early part of the twenty-first century. Another problem is that of the inadequate training and experience of managers in Eastern Europe with operating in a market economy. No matter how bright and enthusiastic they might be, managers need to go through a learning process in order to be effective in carrying out their role. Most, if not all, of the former communist nations lack training centers like INSEAD (France), IMEDE (Switzerland), the International Institute of Studies and Training (Japan), and the American Management Association (United States). The management and executive development programs in Dalian and Beijing, China, for instance, do not begin to meet China's economic and management development needs.

The West and Japan will need to transfer their know-how, technology, and management systems to other parts of the world, if those countries are not to be left behind in terms of economic development and per capita standard of living. It is a mighty challenge for both the giving and the receiving nations. For the giving nations improved economic performance by the poorer nations will, in turn, open new consumer markets for the developed world's products and services. This possibility is especially important now, given the relative saturation of domestic markets in a number of industrialized countries. As the developing nations turn in a better performance, they will, no doubt, prod the developed countries to improve their own competitiveness. Thus, recruiting, selecting, compensating, training, and motivating managers will take on even more importance as the length of the product life cycle shortens even more. The countries that do the best job of managing human resources effectively are also likely to be among the top economic performers.

The Western European countries are most likely to concentrate on helping their Eastern European neighbors, whereas Japan will focus its attention on Asia. The United States and Canada will direct their energies more broadly, although one should not rule out their commitment to strengthening the economic infrastructures and human resources of Central and South American countries.

In the 1960s, we could speak primarily about a nation's domestic economy. Most nations, with the exception of such countries as the United States, England, West Germany, Switzerland, Belgium, the Netherlands, and Sweden, were not heavily involved in international operations. Today we find many players in the global economy; the new entrants, largely drawn from Asia, include South Korea, Taiwan, Hong Kong, and Singapore. But even some smaller Western European countries are operating more actively in the world economy. It is no longer unusual today to hear about an American firm, for example, drawing basic resources from a variety of developing countries, assembling the final product in Hong Kong, and then marketing it in the United States, Europe, and Asia.

The United States is still the largest economy in the world with a gross domestic product of $5.6 trillion (*Fortune*, July 27, 1992, p. 68). The figure is a good deal higher, if we include its overseas investments. However, in the past few years Japan's direct overseas investment has exceeded U.S. investment on a yearly basis by a good margin.

Another dramatic change is the increasing penetration of foreign-owned firms in the United States. *Fortune* magazine (July 31, 1989) reported that total foreign investment in the United States in 1988 was $329 billion. Britain, Japan, the Netherlands, Canada, and West Germany head the list. The united Germany passed Canada in total direct foreign investment in 1990 according to the June 1991 issue of *Survey of Current Business* (p. 32). The United States, in turn, had $327 billion invested in other countries at the same time. Slightly over one-half of the U.S. total was concentrated in Canada, Britain, West Germany, Bermuda, and Switzerland. Even so, direct foreign investment as a share of total tangible wealth of the United States represents only 5 percent, although it is 10 percent in manufacturing. The U.S. Department of Commerce (1989, 1981) reports that between 1980 and 1989 U.S. direct investment abroad increased from $213,468 billion to $373,436 billion. Foreign direct investment in the United States over the same period increased dramatically from $65,483 billion to $400,817 billion. Even so, in 1990 America led the world in direct foreign investment, with England a distant second.

These statistics make it abundantly clear that managers will be required to think more globally in the future. Anyone who visits Geneva, Switzerland, notes the multilingual, multinational populace. The same can be said of London, Paris, Frankfurt, or New York. According to a *Fortune* article (February 12, 1990), 360 American electronics firms in Japan employ more than 72,000 people. That compares to about 68,000 employees of Japanese-owned firms in the United States.

The difficulties that some Japanese managers have encountered in supervising a non-Japanese workforce reinforces the need for flexible education, training, and exposure to other cultures of tomorrow's internationally oriented managers. The fact that several Japanese firms have been charged with employment discrimination by the EEOC (Equal Employment Opportunity Commission) (e.g. the Itoh Trading Company case) shows the difficulty of operating internationally. Research on Japanese plants and offices in Southeast Asia tells a similar story (Stening and Everett, 1984). There is also evidence that some of the same problems presently exist in maquiladora firms owned by the Japanese on the Mexican border with the United States.

The U.S. and Western European-based firms have made plenty of blunders. For example, some American MNCs that established operations in Western Europe in the 1950s and 1960s assumed that they could implement their corporate labor relations policies. They found that the trade unions, employers, and governments in selected countries made it clear that local policies and practices would apply (e.g., Sweden). For this reason most multinational corporations now hire citizens of the country where the subsidiary or joint venture is located to cover personnel and labor relations. Local staff are aware of the legal and commonly acceptable norms of human resource management in their country.

Western European firms at one time suffered in the developing world because of their past colonialistic practices, notably in India, Southeast Asia, the Middle East, Africa, and Latin America. More recently, the behavior of the leaders of their overseas operations have become more sensitive to local practices. In the past one could talk about international operations and international business. Developments in the 1990s make clear the reality of globalization of the economy as more and more actors enter the world competition for ideas, products, technologies, and services. Twenty years ago the United States could have been described as an economic island where the fruits of its production could satisfy the diverse needs of its citizens. Foreign-owned products were a small blip in its economy. Today it is estimated that more than 85 percent of American industries are impacted by products made by foreign-owned companies.

OUTLINE OF THIS BOOK

As mentioned earlier, some of the previous work in international/comparative management has taken an institutional perspective. Massie and Luytjes's *Management in an International Context* (1972) is a good example of this approach to the field. The institutional perspective made sense since many of the non-American contributors were economists. It appears that few sociologists, anthropologists, or psychologists were interested in studying management behavior at the time. The Boddewyn et al. volume (1972), *World Business Systems and Environment*, took a somewhat more behavioral viewpoint in stressing the role of dominant cultural values in helping to explain managerial behavior in different areas of the world.

More recently, we find two books on managers across nations that take a labor market perspective. Myron Roomkin's *Managers as Employees* (1989) consists of individual chapters on Britain, the United States, Australia, New Zealand, West Germany, Sweden, France, Italy, and Japan.

Our book takes a somewhat different approach. We will stress the evolution of the managerial class in fifteen different countries; identify the dominant cultural values that influence the way most managers behave in each of the countries; and elaborate on the human resource management (HRM) functions that apply to managers in the respective nations.

Each author begins his or her chapter by defining how the term *manager* will be used in treating the particular country. This definition is followed by a brief presentation of the postwar growth of the specific nation's economy and employment trends for the managerial cadre. Each author then discusses the evolution of the managerial class in that country, giving specific attention to the status of managers in the society; the ideology of the managerial group as an elite; and the bases of the legitimacy of managers and business in general over the postwar years. Next, the authors discuss the dominant cultural values that influence the way managers behave in the particular country. Each author links the societal value with actual managerial behavior. We fully recognize that in most countries there is variance within the culture as well. Proof of this fact is the growing recognition by U.S. management of the rich cultural diversity of the American workforce (e.g., blacks, Hispanics, Orientals).

Where political considerations play an important part in how managers behave (e.g., the Commonwealth of Independent States), party ideology and power will be discussed in this section. Its importance in the future (e.g., Eastern Europe) remains to be seen. The ethnic diversity in such countries as Rumania and Czechoslovakia may create political problems that impact the role of managers in those countries.

A major part of each chapter is devoted to human resource management functional activities as they apply to managers in the particular country. Specifically, each author provides the reader with information regarding selection, compensation, management development, and performance appraisal of managers in the country he or she covers. If labor relations is a factor in the particular country, that topic is also addressed. The concluding section of each chapter summarizes postwar shifts in the status, ideology, and legitimacy of the managerial class; looks at recent trends in professionalizing the managerial group; addresses emerging economic and social developments that may affect the managerial cadre in the future; and raises any questions that need to be answered in the future about managers in the particular nation.

A number of chapters go beyond the original outline to include information and issues that provide us with greater understanding about culture, organizational behavior, and other areas that they felt it was important to include in their discussion of the particular country. The elaboration takes advantage of the particular interests and expertise of the author(s) in those countries. The editor believes that the reader will gain from this broader focus.

We do not try to cover the voluminous research literature on managers in or across countries. Part of that research literature is found in Ronen's *Comparative and Multinational Management* (1986). The domestic treatment of managerial behavior in such countries as the United States, Germany, Britain, and Japan is overwhelming.

ORDER OF REMAINING CHAPTERS

We lead off our discussion of managers in specific countries with the treatment of the United States, since it has played a leading role in the world economy during much of the twentieth century.

Chapters 3 through 7 focus on the Western European nations, specifically, Great Britain, France, Germany, Sweden, and Austria because of their commonalities. The first three countries are already members of the Common Market, whereas Austria and Sweden have applied for membership. Both Austria and Sweden are presently members of the European Free Trade Association (EFTA).

Chapters 8 and 9 provide the reader with insights on the former Soviet Union and Poland. Until recently both were members of the Eastern Bloc. The very recent changes in this part of the world raise the strong possibility that what is said about the past forty-five years may have less meaning by the year 2000.

Poland is presently moving briskly toward a free market economy and independent institutions (pluralism), but the road is not an easy one. The Commonwealth of Independent States is experiencing major difficulties in strengthening its economy.

The next two chapters look at managers in two very different Middle East nations. Chapter 10 focuses on Israel, a country with many cultural influences. Chapter 11 provides a look at managers in Saudi Arabia, a conservative Muslim nation that has experienced profound changes since the ascendancy of the Ibn Saud royal family and the nation's control over the production of its rich petroleum fields.

The following five chapters give us a perspective on managers in the Asian part of the Pacific Rim. We lead off the discussion with Japan, the most industrially advanced of the Asia nations and the second strongest economy in the world today. Chapter 13 takes us to South Korea, one of the newly industrialized countries (NICs) of Asia. Chapter 14 describes management in the territory of Hong Kong, one of the so-called Four Dragons, where Chinese influence is strong. We then turn to Mainland China, a country of some 1.1 billion people. The post–Mao period (since 1978) has seen major steps toward strengthening the Chinese economy, but the reverberations of the Tiananmen Square massacre in early June 1989 continue to raise serious questions about the future. We wind up our discussion of management in Asia in Chapter 16 by looking at managers in Malaysia. Malaysia, along with Thailand and Indonesia, seems primed to follow the path of the earlier Asian NICs in the coming years.

The book closes with an integration of both the common and divergent themes that emerge from our discussion of managerial behavior in these fifteen countries.

REFERENCES

Abegglen, J. 1958. *The Japanese Factory: Aspects of Its Social Organization*. Glencoe, Ill.: Free Press.

Abegglen, J. 1973. *Management and Worker*. Tokyo: Sophia University Press.

Adler, N. J. 1991. *International Dimensions of Organizational Behavior*. Second Edition. Boston: PWS-Kent.

Bendix, R. 1956. *Work and Authority in Industry*. New York: John Wiley and Sons.

Boddewyn, J.; Engberg, H.; Fayerweather, J.; Ness, W., Jr.; Franck, P.; and Kapoor, A. 1972. *World Business Systems and Environments*. Scranton, Pa.: Intext.

Clark, R. 1979. *The Japanese Company*. New Haven, Conn.: Yale University Press

Cole, R. E., 1979. *Work, Mobility, and Participation: A Comparative Study of American and Japanese Industry*. Berkeley, Cal.: University of California Press.

Copeland, L., and Griggs, L. 1985. *Going International: How to Make Friends and Deal Effectively in the Global Marketplace*. New York: Random House.

Davis, S., and Goodman, L., eds. 1972. *Workers and Managers in Latin America*. Lexington, Mass.: D.C. Heath.

Davis, M. 1971. *Comparative Management: Organizational and Cultural Perspectives*. Englewood Cliffs, N.J.: Prentice-Hall.

Dore, R. 1973. *British Factory-Japanese Factory*. Berkeley, Cal.: University of California Press.

Dowling, P. J., and Schuler, R. S. 1991. *International Dimensions of Human Resource Management*. Boston: PWS-Kent.

Dunlop, J. 1958. *Industrial Relations Systems*. New York: Henry Holt.

Ehrmann, H. W. 1957. *Organized Business in France*. Princeton, N.J.: Princeton University Press.

Farmer, R. N., and Richman, B. M. 1965. *Comparative Management and Economic Progress*. Homewood, Ill.: Irwin.

"Where Global Growth Is Going." *Fortune*. July 31, 1989, pp. 80–81.

"You Can Make Money in Japan." *Fortune*. February 12, 1990, pp. 85–92.

"How the Nations Rank." *Fortune*. July 27, 1992, p. 68.

Grosset, S. 1970. *Management: American and European Styles*. Belmont, Cal.: Wadsworth.

Haire, M., Ghiselli, E. E., and Porter, L. W. 1966. *Managerial Thinking: An International Study*. New York: Wiley.

Harbison, F., and Myers, C. 1959. *Management in the Industrial World: An International Analysis*. New York: McGraw-Hill.

Harris, P. R., and Moran, R. T. 1979. *Managing Cultural Differences*. Houston, Tx.: Gulf Publishing.

Hartmann, H. 1959. *Authority and Organization in German Management*. Princeton, NJ: Princeton University Press.

Kerr, C., Dunlop, J., Harbison, F., and Myers, C. 1964. *Industrialism and Industrial Man*. New York: Oxford University Press.

Koike, K. 1988. *Understanding Industrial Relations in Modern Japan*. New York: St. Martin's Press.

Massie, J. L., and Luytjes, J. 1972. *Management in an International Context*. New York: Harper and Row.

McGivering, I., Matthews, D., and Scott, W. H. 1960. *Management in Britain*. Liverpool, England: Liverpool University Press.

Peterson, R. B., and Sullivan, J. 1990. "Japan's Lifetime Employment: Whither It Goest?" In S. B. Prasad, ed. *Advances in International Comparative Management*. Volume 5. Greenwich, Conn. JAI Press, pp. 169–194.

Ronen, S. 1986. *Comparative and Multinational Management*. New York: John Wiley and Sons.

Roomkin, M. J., ed. 1989. *Managers as Employees*. New York: Oxford University Press.

Servan-Schreiber, J. 1968. *The American Challenge*. Trans. R. Steel. New York: Atheneum.

Stening, B. W., and Everett, J. E. 1984 (May). "Japanese Managers in Southeast Asia: Amiable Superstars or Arrogant Upstarts?" *Asia Pacific Journal of Management*. pp. 171–180.

Taira, K. 1970. *Economic Development and the Labor Market in Japan*. New York: Columbia University Press.

Vernon, R., and Wells, L. T., Jr. 1986. *Manager in the International Economy*. Fifth Edition. Englewood Cliffs, N.J.: Prentice-Hall.

2

UNITED STATES

Richard B. Peterson and Jane George-Falvy

We begin our treatment of national managerial behaviors by looking at the American experience, since much of the literature on management comes from academicians and practitioners in the United States. In fact, during the so-called golden days of the 1960s, some writers assumed that the type of managerial behavior practiced by successful U.S. managers should be the model for other countries (Servan-Schrieber, 1968). Study teams visited the United States in the 1950s and 1960s to learn from the experts, much like they are now going to Japan.

The meaning of the word "manager" in the United States is not easy to pin down. Roomkin (1989) presents various definitions of American managers, including legal, organizational, and statistical approaches. For example, the Wage and Hour Law states that the term "manager" includes the broad category of executive, administrative, and professional personnel who are not subject to the requirement of being paid overtime wages and salaries for work beyond eight hours per day and forty hours per week. Some analysts use the term narrowly to identify those members of an organization who supervise one or more employees. Others are likely to lump executive, administrative, and professional staff into the broad category of manager. For our purposes, we think of managers as those personnel above the first level of supervision (e.g., foremen) who act in executive, administrative, or professional capacities. However, we do not include executives at the very top policy-making level of the organization.

In the next section we examine the growth of the U.S. economy since 1950, followed by a report on employment trends for managers since 1975. Next we address the evolution of the managerial class in the United States. Then we go into some depth on the role of American cultural values in shaping their behavior.

Table 2.1

GNP in the United States, 1950–1990 (in billions of dollars)

Year	GNP
1950	308.1 *
1960	513.0 *
1970	1,015.5
1980	2,372.0
1990	5,521.3

*Fourth quarter only.

Sources: U.S. Department of Commerce, Bureau of Economic Analysis, *National Income and Product Accounts of the United States: Statistical Tables* (Washington, D.C.: U.S. Government Printing Office, September 1986), pp. 2–4; and *Standard and Poor's Statistical Service: Current Statistics* (New York: Standard and Poor's Corporation, February 1991), p. 7.

THE GROWTH OF THE ECONOMY AND MANAGERIAL EMPLOYMENT

The American economy experienced impressive growth during the postwar period. Table 2.1 reports the gross national product (GNP) from 1950 to 1990 based on ten-year intervals. It can be seen that the GNP grew from $308 billion in 1950 to over $5.5 trillion forty years later. This roughly eighteenfold growth in GNP is far in excess of inflation during that period. Therefore, it is not surprising that the managerial ranks also grew quickly.

Table 2.2 shows employment data for managerial and professional employment as reported by the Bureau of Labor Statistics for the years 1975, 1980, 1985, and 1990. Employment in the broad category of managerial and professional specialty grew 70 percent over the fifteen-year period. Most of the overall growth benefited women who traditionally had not been well represented at this level of organizations. The statistical subcategory of most interest to us under the managerial and professional specialty is entitled executive, administrative, and managerial.

Table 2.3 reports the employment data from the Bureau of Labor Statistics for the years 1982 through 1990. We were unable to use employment data from earlier years, because different titles were used in reporting statistics for this group. The table shows that managerial employment grew from almost 11 million in 1982 to somewhat less than 15 million eight years later. This represents a growth of almost 35 percent in the executive, administrative, and managerial category. Note in Table 2.2 that executive, administrative, and managerial employment represented almost 50 percent of the Managerial and Professional Specialty in 1990. Unfortunately, the Bureau of Labor Statistics does not single out the managerial subcategory.

Table 2.2
Employment in Managerial and Professional Jobs in the United States, 1975, 1980, 1985, and 1990 (in millions)

Category	Year 1975	1980	1985	1990
Managerial and Professional Specialty	17,996	22,038	25,851	30,657
Executive, Administrative, and Managerial	8,105	10,215	12,221	14,839
Professional Specialty	9,891	11,823	13,318	15,818

Source: U.S. Department of Labor, Bureau of Labor Statistics, *Labor Force Statistics Derived from the Current Population Survey, 1948–1987*, Bulletin 2307, August 1988, pp. 664, 681. Update in U.S. Department of Labor, Bureau of Labor Statistics, *Employment and Earnings*, January 1991, p. 183.

Table 2.3
Executive, Administrative, and Managerial Employment in the United States between 1982 and 1990 (in millions)

Year	Executive, Administrative, and Managerial (Average)
1982	10,994
1983	11,168
1984	11,892
1985	12,550
1986	12,979
1987	13,666
1988	14,216
1989	14,848
1990	14,839

Source: U.S. Department of Labor, Bureau of Labor Statistics, *Labor Force Statistics Derived from the Current Population Survey* (Washington, D.C.: U.S. Government Printing Office, Bulletin 2307, August 1988), p. 183. Update in U.S. Department of Labor, Bureau of Labor Statistics, *Employment and Earnings*, January 1991, p. 183.

Table 2.4
Employment for Executive, Administrative, and Managerial Workers in the United States, 1986, and Moderate Growth Projection for 2000 (in thousands)

Projected Occupational Group	1986		2000		Percent Change 1986-2000
	No.	Percent	No.	Percent	Percent
Executive, Administrative, and Managerial Workers	10,583	9.5	13,616	10.2	28.7
Total Labor Force	111,623	100.0	133,030	100.0	19.7

Source: "Projection 2000: Overview and Implication," *Monthly Labor Review*, September 1987, pp. 6, 47 (modified).

Employment and Earnings (January 1991) reports that the average weekly salary for executive, administrative, and managerial staff in 1990 was $608 or approximately $31,600 yearly. This figure understates the situation, because it includes low-, medium-, and high-level managers from firms ranging from very small to Fortune 500 corporations.

What is the employment outlook for U.S. managers until the year 2000? Table 2.4 reports employment from 1986 to the year 2000. While total U.S. employment is expected to grow by almost 22 million people (19.7 percent), executive, administrative, and managerial staff will increase by more than 3 million (28.7 percent). It is one of five occupational categories projected to experience faster than average employment growth over the fourteen-year period. Bishop and Carter project that between 1988 and 2000 the number of managers will increase by 34.8 percent (unpublished table provided by John Bishop). By the year 2000, executive, administrative, and managerial employees will constitute 10.2 percent of the labor force (up from 9.5 percent in 1986). This growth in managerial employment is explained by the increasing complexity of business operations and the large employment gains likely in the service and trade industries where, because of small company size, a higher than average proportion of employment is in managerial occupations.

EVOLUTION OF THE MANAGERIAL CLASS

The United States has experienced considerable changes in its labor force since its founding. For example, in 1790 some 90 percent of the population was associated in one way or another with agricultural pursuits. Many farmers were self-employed, relying on other members of the family or close neighbors to help in the farming chores. Rapid industrialization after the Civil War resulted in employment shifts away from self-employment toward working for someone else for a wage or salary. The vast majority of the nonagricultural workforce were in blue-, rather than white-collar, jobs.

Public attention during the late-nineteenth century was riveted on the titans of American industry like Andrew Carnegie and John D. Rockefeller, or financial power wielders like J. P. Morgan. Most firms at the time did not need a large number of managers and supervisors to run the business (Cavanaugh, 1990).

The rise of the great corporations began to take place in the early twentieth century with the formation of such business enterprises as U.S. Steel, but the real managerial revolution is a product of the post–World War II period. James Burnham (1941) was one of the first people to forecast the emergence of the managerial class, to be found principally in the large private corporations like AT&T, General Motors, and Standard Oil Company of New Jersey (now EXXON).

The increase in size of firms, coupled with the need for technical expertise and administrative staff, led companies tô employ a growing number of line and staff managerial personnel. By 1957, white-collar employees outnumbered their blue-collar counterparts for the first time. Middle management also became a real presence on the company's organizational chart. By the 1980s some company executives decried the fact that there were too many managers and staff personnel. Corporate decision making became slow and unwieldy in many American companies. What are the bases for the legitimacy of managers? Do they share a common ideology? What is the status of managers in American society?

Managerial Legitimacy

The legitimacy of managers is imbedded in the concept of private property that derives from the English legal system (Bendix, 1956). In the modern U.S. corporation the owners (stockholders) give power to the executives to run the day-to-day operations of the enterprise. The executives, in turn, hire managers to handle the specialized line and staff functions of the organization. Where ownership and management are synonymous, the rights of private property are even more firmly based. Hence, managers have responsibility for accomplishing specific goals and are given formal authority to see that the goals are reached.

Managerial Ideology

Most American business leaders share a common ideology or value system. College graduates who aspire to managerial careers are often socialized to accept many of the key organizational values and principles. These include the values of individualism, the rights of private property, the primary role of the market, the right to accumulate individual wealth and company profits, and the preference for a laissez-faire role of government in business activity.

Managerial Status

Most opinion polls show that managers have considerable status in American society based on both the power they wield and their incomes. Business is one of the most popular career paths. Some 20 to 25 percent of entering college freshmen identify business as their expected college major. These figures are much higher than in the earlier postwar years. An MBA is seen as an advantage for those aspiring to managerial careers.

Roomkin (1989) states that managers gained considerable status in the 1980s. Managerial salaries today compare very favorably with those of most other career choices of college graduates. Managers employed in Fortune 500 companies may receive salaries ranging from $40,000 to as much as $120,000 per year. In addition, managers in some firms are included in bonus pools based on exceeding department, division, and/or company performance goals. These salary figures are much higher, on average, than those of college graduates who enter such fields as public school teaching, nursing, and social work. Some managers may eventually be promoted to executive-level positions that provide even greater status and financial rewards. Salaries for chief executive officers (CEOs) of major firms often exceed $1 million per year in salary and bonuses. This does not even include stock options and a variety of other benefits that accrue to the policy-making staff. The salaries given above, however, are not representative of most small and medium-size firms in the United States where managerial salaries are lower.

The behavior of American managers is explained in large part by the values they absorb from the broader society, as well as their specific experiences in the company. The following section addresses both the values of the broader society and managerial values themselves.

AMERICAN SOCIETAL VALUES AND MANAGERIAL VALUES

We will begin by identifying some of the common features of American society that have shaped managerial values. However, most of the discussion will concentrate on the dominant value system of managers themselves.

Societal Values
American society has been heavily influenced by Judeo-Christian tenets, basic postulates of the Protestant Reformation, the ideals of the American Revolution, and the economics of the Industrial Revolution (e.g., Bartels, 1982; Cavanaugh, 1990). These movements advocated beliefs in the ideals of brotherhood, stewardship, a sense of calling, democracy, liberty, equality of people, self-fulfillment, and the right to association. Perhaps the best known characterization of Americans remains that of Alexis de Tocqueville, a French nobleman, who visited the United States in the mid to late 1830s. His characterization of the American people in *Democracy in America* is surprisingly consistent with similar writings in recent years. De Tocqueville listed the following values as widely shared by Americans: the valuing of facts over consistent ideals; pragmatism in preference to an ideology; individualism of thought; belief in the virtue of working hard; and individualism in the sense of ''enlightened self-interest'' (de Tocqueville, 1946).

Dominant Managerial Values

A number of writers have commented over the past few decades on the dominant values of American managers (e.g., Baida, 1990; Cavanaugh, 1990; DeBettignies, 1973; Lodge, 1987; Newman, 1972). There is a fair amount of commonality across their lists.

Achievement and success. Managers share a common belief that being successful is a worthwhile pursuit. Success is best measured by the ability to move upward through the organization, with increasing financial rewards being the most tangible evidence of personal achievement.

Hard work. Managers often justify their success in terms of their personal willingness to be task-oriented. They believe they have earned the extra status and financial returns associated with "moving up the ladder" by being willing to work beyond the normal forty-hour work week.

Efficiency and pragmatism. Managers are inclined to seek out more efficient methods of organizing work that lead to decreased per unit costs. Most of them have a practical orientation. Rarely do they give much time to contemplation in their work routine. They see the organizational advantages of technological progress, based on improved methods or equipment. Efficiency is often defined as a time consciousness—time is not to be wasted.

Optimism. On the whole, successful American managers emphasize the positive and deemphasize the negative in their daily business dealings. The emphasis is on progress and not failure. Managers are likely to share a favorable view of the future rather than dwell much in the past.

Puritanism. The Puritan work ethic is usually accepted; that is, the manager accepts individual responsibility and accountability, as contrasted with the responsibility taken by the group as in Japan. In recent years some American companies have shifted their focus toward teamwork in carrying out organizational missions, but clearly, most managers continue to be evaluated largely on the basis of individual rather than group performance.

Scientific orientation. American managers have a clear preference for empirically based scientific and rational thinking as opposed to nonlinear or intuitive reasoning processes. The emphasis in managerial decision making is on identifying viable options and then choosing the "best one" available.

Impersonality in interpersonal work relationships. Many American managers deal with their superiors, peers, and subordinates in a spirit of friendliness and informality. However, such interchanges are often conducted at a surface level. Managers frequently feel more comfortable maintaining a certain impersonality and distance between themselves and other company staff than forming close working relationships.

Equality of opportunity for upward mobility. Most managers are uncomfortable with promotions that are based on such factors as personal connections, attendance at Ivy League universities, or other factors not justified on the basis of merit and performance. The assumption is that qualifications and past performance are the key criteria for advancement in the firm.

Acceptance of competition as a fact of life. American managers learn to accept the fact that competition from other employees and firms is an inevitable fact of life, whether they like it or not. Monopolistic behavior, when compared to the situation in some other countries, is deplored.

These factors help to explain both the fact and fiction of American managerial values. While some of these values have changed over the past century or more, it is surprising how many of them continue to be mentioned over and over. American managers do not have a monopoly on these values, but managers in other countries rarely hold most of these values to the same degree as in the United States. Foreign business leaders and managers often identify many of these factors as generalizable to American management (Nimgade, 1989; Whitehill, 1989).

Table 2.5 provides a link between American cultural characteristics and associated managerial values and behavior. It is based on a broad reading of the literature on both societal and managerial values.

HUMAN RESOURCE MANAGEMENT

This section covers the major functions of human resource management as they relate to managers in the United States. Many of the human resource functions are not applied differently to American managers than they are to lower level employees, but some differences are noteworthy. Attention is given to the following topics: recruitment, selection, compensation, benefits, performance appraisal training and development, and labor relations.

Recruitment

Although some managers and even CEOs have worked their way up from the bottom of their organization in the manner of Horatio Alger, far and away most managers in U.S. companies are college educated. They begin in a management track entry-level position and, if successful, are brought into the managerial force through internal promotion. The larger U.S. firms devote a significant portion of their personnel energies to recruiting on the campuses of U.S. colleges and universities.

Just what businesses hope to find among job-seeking graduating seniors has as many answers as there are businesses. Throughout the 1980s, some business leaders touted oral communication and writing skills as well as the intellectual rigor of liberal arts graduates as a solution to lagging U.S. eminence in the world economy. Paradoxically, the heated business environment favored graduates with specialized business and engineering majors from the larger universities, the perception being that they were more employment-ready as well as already committed, personally, to the aims of business.

It is difficult to generalize about the cultural background of U.S. managers. In the brief history of this country, business has been fostered by a laissez-faire attitude. As a result, the values of business—those of competition, risk taking, the utility of technological progress, and advancement—are widely held. Similarly, postsecondary education has become available to an ever increasing por-

Table 2.5
Cultural Links to American Managerial Behavior

Cultural Characteristics	Managerial Behavior
Individualism	Focus on individual contribution and benefit to self or dept.
Self-reliance (responsibility)	Willingness to take on personal responsibility
Efficiency	Stress on bottom-line cost consideration.
Favorable view of future (optimism)	Favorable outlook toward success of future projects and greater likelihood of reaching them
Pragmatic	Tendency to make fairly simple judgments of whether a particular project worked.
Rationality	Emphasis on logic and rationality in reaching decisions
Contractual relationships	Emphasis on impersonality in work behavior
Puritanism	In some cases, overemphasis on work, but also strong moral commitment
Humanitarianism	Sympathy for subordinates and peers, but usually directed toward non-work situation
Materialism	Heavy reliance on economic motivation to spur work force-equating value of project with profitability
Time consciousness	Short-term perspective on output
Equality	Rewards based more on what one does rather than who one is. Worth in organization predicated on ability to deliver
Competitive	Pressure to strive to do better
Openness and direct behavior	Telegraphing clearly where one stands
Moralism	Commitment bordering on ideology
Loyalty	More often directed toward self, section, department than entire enterprise

tion of the population. While the potential exists for managers to arise from every socioeconomic segment, it is not necessarily the case that they do.

Whatever the background of a potential manager, it appears clear that because most management positions require a bachelor's degree, colleges and universities are and will continue to be the source of those in the management track. At the same time one should not underestimate the influence of connection within the business community on the activities of business. The so-called old boys network has in many cases served to place the well-connected son (or, only recently, daughter) with a firm he (or she) might otherwise have failed to impress.

Managers may likewise be recruited away from other companies. These employees are prized for their proven success, their business contacts, and their experience. The 1980s saw a growth in the practice of head-hunting and a boom for consulting agencies devoted to seeking and acquiring experienced managers and executives. Nevertheless, in-house manager development remains the most popular form of recruitment in U.S. companies. Its main advantages are a lower start-up time for the employee, a higher probability of on-the-job success, and a lower recruitment cost. Table 2.6 lists responses to a survey asking businesses about their preferred recruitment sources. In descending order, companies preferred promotion from within, newspaper advertisements, employee references, search firms, and, finally, private employment agencies as their five most useful recruitment sources. Whether potential management stock is recruited internally or externally, each candidate will be subjected to some type of screening procedure to enable the company to make a hiring decision.

Selection

In staffing an organization, two often contradictory goals are sought: (1) to maximize the chance of hiring the best applicants for each position and (2) to minimize the chance of an Equal Employment Opportunity (EEO) lawsuit. Many selection procedures are subject to legal regulation and scrutiny by federal, state, and local agencies. As such, it is important to examine the legal framework surrounding employee selection in the United States.

Legal Issues   Most selection activities are federally regulated under the Civil Rights Act of 1964, subsequent amendments to the act, Supreme Court rulings, and related legislation. Title VII of the Civil Rights Act, as amended, makes it illegal to use an individual's age, race, sex, national origin, or religion as a basis for making a hiring decision. From subsequent case law, any selection procedure should, at face value, appear *job relevant*; it should in some way reflect the nature of the work performed on the job (Arvey and Faley, 1988; Gatewood and Field, 1990). In addition, any selection procedure must not violate something called the *four-fifths rule*, in which a selection procedure must not select fewer minority applicants for a job than four-fifths of the nonminority job applicants who are selected.

Case law interpreting Title VII of the Civil Rights Act has encouraged a practice known as affirmative action, which attempts to increase the number of members of protected classes (minorities, women, older workers, and the dis-

Table 2.6
Use of Various Recruitment Sources by U.S. Firms

Recruitment Source	% of companies using
Internal	
Promotion from within	95
Employee reference	64
Walk-in	46
Advertising	
Newspaper	85
Journals/Magazines	50
Direct Mail	8
Radio/TV	2
Outside References	
Colleges/Universities	45
Professional Societies	37
Community Agencies	9
Vocational/Technical School	8
High Schools	2
Unions	1
Employment Services	
Search Firms	63
Private	60
State	23
U.S. Employment Service	7
Computerized resume services	2
Video interview services	1
Special Events	
Career conferences	19
Open houses	7

Source: BNA PPF Survey no. 146, *Recruiting and Selection Procedures*, Personnel Policies Forum Survey No. 146, pp. 7, 17 (May 1988). Copyright 1988 by The Bureau of National Affairs, Inc. (800–372–1033).

abled) in the workforce. Affirmative action programs can include steps such as trying to recruit or encourage more members of protected classes to apply for a particular job. In what are sometimes called quota practices, a company mandates that a certain number of job hires must belong to one or more of the protected classes. Affirmative action plans that make use of quotas are often criticized for producing reverse discrimination. While these laws have been in place for over twenty-five years, their effect on the composition of the labor force, particularly managerial positions, has not been substantial.

In 1987 roughly 38 percent of the ranks of executive, administrative, and managerial positions were comprised of women, and only about 10 percent were minorities (Bureau of Labor Statistics, 1988). However, these percentages are misleadingly generous in that they include administrative positions with the executive and managerial classification. Administrative positions are often largely secretarial or clerical in nature, making the true percentage of women and minorities holding actual managerial positions smaller.

There is a massive body of legislation and case law pertaining to selection procedures (which, of course, are beyond the scope of this volume). In addition, many of these regulations are under constant scrutiny by the courts. Of late, the U.S. Supreme Court has challenged and significantly lessened the impact of the existing twenty-five years of civil rights legislation, which may have a dramatic effect on selection procedures. Those with a strong interest in selection issues are encouraged to consult texts such as Arvey and Faley (1988) and Gatewood and Field (1990).

A wide variety of selection methods are utilized in the United States, all subject to the legal regulations described previously. New case law can change the extent to which a practice is legally defensible, and subsequently the extent to which it is used. The most common techniques for selecting managers include interviews and pre-employment tests.

Interviews   The interview continues to be the most popular selection method across all positions (Bragg, 1981; BNA Survey no. 146, 1988). In 1965, Ulrich and Trumbo reported that 99 percent of all firms in the United States used interviews as a selection technique. Since the early 1960s, many researchers (e.g., Hunter and Hunter, 1984) have demonstrated that interviews are poor predictors of subsequent employee success on the job. In spite of the frequent and strong attacks, Hennneman, et al. (1980) reported that the interview was still the most commonly used selection method. A 1988 survey conducted by the Bureau of National Affairs indicated that most outside applicants were given at least two interviews before being hired (BNA Survey no. 146, 1988). In response to the vehement criticism of the validity of interviews as a selection method, many companies (one-third, as reported by BNA Survey No. 146, 1988) have adopted a structured or semistructured interview approach rather than the more common unstructured interview. A structured interview consists of developing questions that reflect job-relevant items as determined by a job analysis, anticipating interviewee answers and determining point values for each reply, asking all candidates the same questions, and using multiple raters (Scarpello and Ledvinka, 1988). While one-third of the companies queried by the Bureau of National Affairs reportedly use structured interviews, another one-fifth indicate that their interviews are becoming more structured (BNA Survey no. 146, 1988).

Pre-employment Tests   A variety of pre-employment tests are given to potential managers, including ability tests, personality assessments, performance tests, honesty tests, and assessment center performance. Table 2.7 indicates the prevalence of the most common types of pre-employment tests used by U.S. companies. While this table suggests that testing is not widely used in managerial selection, the number of companies employing some sort of testing procedure for their managerial staff does appear to be increasing.

Ability tests are conducted in three domains: mental or cognitive abilities,

Table 2.7
Types of Pre-Employment Tests Given to U.S. Managers and Supervisors

Type of Test	% of Companies Using
Ability	
Cognitive/Mental	9
Job Knowledge	5
Physical	1
Personality	13
Performance Test/Work Sample	3
Assessment Center	10
Honesty	
Written	3
Polygraph	2
Other	
Medical Exam	45
Drug Test	21
Genetic Screening	1

Source: BNA PPF Survey no. 146, *Recruiting and Selection Procedures*, Personnel Policies Forum Survey No. 146, pp. 7, 17 (May 1988). Copyright 1988 by The Bureau of National Affairs, Inc. (800–372–1033).

special abilities, and physical abilities. Mental or cognitive ability tests assess such traits as intelligence, verbal aptitude, numerical aptitude, spatial abilities, form perception, and motor coordination. Special ability tests focus on job-specific aptitudes such as mechanical ability, clerical motor dexterity, and sensory abilities. Physical ability tests measure a person's capacity to perform job-specific physical tasks. In general, ability testing has come under a great deal of scrutiny as being an avenue toward possible discrimination, and has been the issue in numerous Equal Employment Opportunity (EEO) court cases. As indicated in Table 2.7, ability tests of each kind are not widely used in managerial selection.

Personality tests consist of the use of various clinical methods to evaluate managerial effectiveness. Techniques such as graphology (handwriting analysis) and achievement motivation analysis fall under the rubric of personality testing. As shown in Table 2.7, 13 percent of the sampled companies in a BNA survey do use some sort of personality inventory as a pre-employment screen for their managerial or supervisory staff.

Assessment centers are a more complex form of performance testing/work samples that are more appropriate for managerial level positions. Assessment center testing consists of putting a job candidate through a series of realistic, demanding, and intensive exercises, usually lasting at least three days, which simulate managerial situations and predict a person's future success as a manager. The use of assessment centers appears to have reached its zenith and is now experiencing a decline. The technique is enormously expensive, and companies are beginning to realize that other methods do a better job of predicting managerial success at a much lower cost (Schneider and Schmitt, 1986).

Honesty tests are being touted as a reliable, valid technique to screen out persons who are likely to engage in some sort of illegal activity (Sackett and Harris, 1984). They may increase in popularity as employee theft and fraud continue, and as the polygraph declines in popularity. The validity of the polygraph is questionable (Sackett and Harris, 1984), and in many states, its use as a selection device has been made illegal. More states are expected to enact similar legislation, making honesty tests (with demonstrated validity) more attractive to employers, even for managerial positions.

Medical exams are given to managerial/supervisory level applicants by about 45 percent of the respondents to the BNA survey. The tests are usually given on a pass/fail basis, with those who fail excluded from further consideration. The guidelines for what constitutes failing a medical exam are not clearly established.

Application blanks are almost universally used in the selection of lower level positions, but are not widely used in managerial selection. However, a person's background may be assessed by training and experience evaluations.

Some kind of training and experience evaluations are almost always conducted, though often the process is informal. It can consist simply of examining the candidate's résumé or vita to determine whether education and experience requirements are met. As such, training and experience evaluations are typically used as a first step in managerial selection, and not as the primary basis of a selection decision.

Reference checks, once extremely popular, are not being used to the same degree for two major reasons. First, several court-ordered judgments have been made against companies giving poor recommendations when they cannot document the basis for the poor reference. Employers are being warned by legal counsel only to verify periods of employment to persons who request references. Furthermore, many job candidates are seeking new employment without their current employer's knowledge of their attempts to find another job, making a current job reference difficult to obtain.

In general, much the same process is used for the selection of managers in the United States as for other employees, with less emphasis on initial documents such as applications and letters of recommendation. A good résumé is essential to gain an initial audience, and then interviews tend to be given substantial weight.

Compensation

Compensation of managers in the United States is subject to many factors, including governmental regulation. Most employers are concerned about establishing internally equitable compensation plans, as well as externally equitable rates of pay to attract and retain valued employees.

Legal Issues   The U.S. government regulates compensation through (1) Fair Exchange laws, (2) Income Continuity programs, and (3) Retirement Security programs.

Fair Exchange laws pertain to the fair exchange of compensation for labor as regulated under the Fair Labor Standards Act (1938), which specifies a minimum wage, provides for payment of overtime, and requires that employers keep records of their compensation practices. However, most executive, administrative, and professional positions are exempt from both the minimum wage and overtime pay provisions. The Equal Pay Act of 1963 placed an additional regulation on compensation, mandating that no pay differences could be made on the basis of an employee's sex.

Income Continuity laws regulate the taxation of wages in the United States to provide funding for such programs as Social Security, which provides income to the retired and dependents of retired persons; Workers' Compensation, which provides income to persons injured on the job; and Unemployment Insurance, which provides income to persons who are temporarily unemployed.

Retirement Security programs are also funded through taxation of wages. These programs provide income (Social Security) and medical coverage (Medicare and Supplemental Medical Insurance) to retired persons and their dependents.

Compensation Ranges   Nearly all U.S. managers (92 percent according to BNA Survey no. 147, 1990) are salaried, only 6 percent are paid by the hour, and 3 percent are salaried with commissions. The survey indicated that only about 22 percent of middle managers receive overtime compensation for hours worked beyond a standard work week (typically set at forty hours). Of that 22 percent, 44 percent are given compensatory time off, and 33 percent are paid their normal salary for the extra hours worked.

The range of compensation for U.S. managers can more accurately be described as a gulf. Salaries are higher in the United States than in other nations in the world, but the range of compensation is perhaps the largest. Salaries differ 20 to 50 percent even within the same job (Milkovich and Newman, 1990). Entry-level managers at franchise operations can make as little as $22,000 a year. The median salary for executive, administrative, and managerial positions in 1987, as reported by the U.S. Bureau of Labor Statistics, was about $30,000 per year. However, the median for men was $36,000 but only $22,000 for women. These figures are likely to be low because they include administrative positions that are often secretarial or clerical in nature. Other studies echo the pay differential that exists between men and women. One study indicated that female managers make 36 percent less than their male counterparts (Lumpkin and Tudor, 1990). The fantastic increases in executive pay in recent years are slowly spreading even into the nonexecutive levels. One periodical reported that middle managers can expect to earn only one-tenth of what their senior-level counterparts make, but that this ranged from $75,000 to $150,000 per year (Weiss, 1989).

Downsizing is eliminating middle management positions. This factor, coupled with the glut of baby boomers who are now progressing into the ranks of middle management, has produced stiff competition for jobs and fewer salary increases. Middle managers beginning a career in 1975 could expect to triple their income in ten years, but today's middle managers will be lucky to double their income in the next ten (Weber, Driscol, and Brandt, 1990).

Compensation Issues   Three main issues are at stake when determining compensation for managerial jobs: the internal equity of the system to compensate different jobs fairly within an organization; the external equity or equivalence of the pay system compared to other organizations; and the extent to which pay practices and policies are kept secret within an organization.

Internal equity involves the fair distribution of pay among jobs within an organization. To pay jobs equitably, organizations conduct job analyses to determine the tasks and responsibilities for each job, and then a job evaluation to determine the worth of the managerial job to the organization. According to a BNA survey (no. 147, 1990), 89 percent of responding companies had written job descriptions, 75 percent performed job evaluations, and 67 percent performed job analyses to help develop job descriptions and a compensation plan that equitably pays between the various jobs within their organization. Job analysis and evaluation can be cumbersome tasks, and many methods exist. Outside help is available from consulting agencies such as the Hay Group, as well as many of the large accounting firms that have consulting services. For analyzing managerial jobs, the Hay method is the most commonly used technique (Milkovich and Newman, 1990).

Through external equity salaries are comparable to what other organizations offer. About 94 percent of the companies surveyed by BNA (Survey no. 147, 1990) indicated that they used wage and salary surveys to determine whether their pay was on a par with that of other organizations. The survey reported that for compensation of middle managers, 22 percent of the responding companies paid higher than market wages, 11 percent lower, and 59 percent about the same as the market, with 8 percent not responding to the question.

Pay secrecy is a popular topic in the compensation literature as it relates to the design of compensation systems that appear fair to employees (Greenberg, 1987). A hypothesized component of perceived fairness is the extent to which pay practices are communicated to the employees. Table 2.8 describes the amount of information provided to various classifications of employees by their employer (BNA Survey no. 147, 1990). Most managerial employees are made aware of the ranges of compensation available to them as well as others in the organization, but are not given specific information concerning other individuals.

Adjustment of Compensation   According to the Hay Group report (1988) on compensation and benefits, employers are increasingly turning to variable compensation plans that provide more performance-based awards granted contingent

Table 2.8
Pay Information Communicated to Employees

Information Communicated	% of employees provided with info[*]	
	Non-Management	Management
Employee's Current Job		
pay grade and range	71	69
midpoint of wages	49	58
All Jobs		
grades and ranges/non-mr.gt	20	39
grades and ranges/mngt	7	23

[*] Percentages do not add to 100 as many employers reveal multiple pay practices.

Source: *Wage and Salary Administration*, June 1990. Personnel Policies Forum Survey No. 147, pp. 13, 19 (June 1990). Copyright 1990 by The Bureau of National Affairs, Inc. (800–372–1033).

on improved business results. While largely an incentive for managerial performance, these awards are becoming available to employees further down in the organization hierarchy. Although performance-based awards are more typically used in larger organizations, an increasing number of smaller businesses are adopting such plans. Table 2.9 lists the most prevalent forms of adjustments to base compensation given to U.S. middle managers.

An interesting trend in the adjustment of employee salaries concerns the way in which an adjustment is paid. More and more companies (23 percent within the last two years) are beginning to give employees a lump-sum payment in lieu of a base pay increase (BNA Survey no. 147, 1990) to contain labor costs, increase employee satisfaction with pay, and more strongly link performance contingent pay to annually assessed performance.

Table 2.9
Types and Prevalence of Base Pay Increases Given to U.S. Middle Managers

Type of Pay Increase	Prevalence Among Middle Managers (%)[*]
Merit	86
General **	26
Skill or Knowledge Increase	15
Length of Service	8

[*] Percentages do not sum to 100 as many companies employ multiple base pay increase plans.

** General pay increases are typically based on a rise in the cost of living as determined by the Consumer Price Index.

Source: *Wage and Salary Administration*, June 1990. Personnel Policies Forum Survey No. 147, pp. 13, 19 (June 1990). Copyright 1990 by The Bureau of National Affairs, Inc. (800–372–1033).

Merit pay involves basing pay increases on successful job performance. The 1980s brought a shift from seniority-based pay increases to merit-based systems. Today, the majority of U.S. employers make use of a merit pay system. While the programs are often difficult to administer, companies that have merit pay programs generally experience decreased turnover, and the remaining turnover is usually comprised of poor performers (Lawler, 1981). When companies abandon a merit pay program, negative outcomes such as decreased employee satisfaction and turnover among high performers often result (Lawler, 1981).

General increases are also called across-the-board increases and are designed to adjust wages to keep up with increases in the cost of living. These adjustments are declining in favor of merit payments.

Skill or knowledge increases are adjustments made according to the acquisition of new skills or knowledge, and their use is fairly prevalent across U.S. employers. However, they are not as applicable to managerial level employees. Length of service increases are still quite prevalent, in spite of the trend toward basing pay increases on performance or merit.

Recognition awards are very common in American businesses. Magnus (1981) reports that two-thirds of American companies have recognition award programs that provide employees with both monetary and nonmonetary awards for outstanding contributions and/or performance.

Benefits

In addition to base pay, a variety of benefits are available to American managers. Benefits available to managers do not differ dramatically from what is available to those lower in an organization, but when an employee jumps to the executive level, the benefits provided increase considerably. Like most other human resource functions, the bestowal of benefits on employees is subject to governmental influence.

It is an employer's responsibility to fund all or part of Worker's Compensation programs, Unemployment Insurance, Social Security, as well as pension plans (Ledvinka, 1982). To urge employers to submit to these regulations, the government provides favorable tax benefits for those employers who provide health care and pension plans. The Employee Retirement Income Security Act of 1974 (ERISA) regulates how employers fund their retirement benefit plans. Specifically, ERISA defines (1) participation requirements (who must be covered by a pension plan), (2) vesting requirements (how long a person must be employed to access his or her retirement benefits), and (3) how much the employer must contribute to the plan (Schmitt, 1981).

Nearly all companies offer their managerial employees health insurance, life insurance, vacations, paid holidays, and retirement income. The Hay Group (1988) reports an increase in flexible benefit plans in which employees are allowed to choose their benefits or to some extent vary the level of funding of each benefit to a predetermined company funding limit. A BNA survey (no. 137, 1984) indicates that benefits cost U.S. companies an average of $29,053 per employee, each year. Rising health care costs are a primary recipient of benefit

Table 2.10
Prevalence of Employee Health Care Benefits for Management and Exempt Employees

Heath Care Benefit	% of Organizations Providing Benefit
Comprehensive Medical Plan	74
Base Medical Plan	37
Supplemental Major Medical	37
Dental Plan	76
Prescription Drugs	48
Vision	21
Sickness & Accident	49
Long Term Disability	91

Source: Health and Life Insurance Benefit Plans, March 1984. Personnel Policies Forum Survey No. 137, pp. 3 (May 1984). Copyright 1984 by The Bureau of National Affairs, Inc. (800–372–1033).

dollars, which lead one-third of the companies responding to the BNA survey to undertake cost-containment measures such as instituting or raising deductibles.

The United States, unlike all other Western nations, does not provide government-funded health care coverage to all persons. Health care coverage is funded primarily by employers for those persons of working age and their"dependents. Health insurance coverage is almost universally provided to managerial-level employees by large U.S. employers. Table 2.10 details the prevalence of the most common types of health benefits offered. While the strong majority of managers are provided with hospital or medical coverage, most have annual deductibles of $100, and 46 percent have higher deductibles (Hay Group, 1988).

Life insurance is offered to managerial-level employees and above by 100 percent of the firms responding to a BNA survey (no 127, 1984).

Vacation benefits are available to most exempt employees, which includes managers. Most companies offer two weeks of paid vacation per year across all industries and company sizes. It takes approximately five years of service to gain an extra week of vacation, and about ten years to get a fourth week. Vacation accruals are designed as an incentive for employees to remain with the company.

Nearly all companies provide paid holidays to their salaried personnel. The total number of paid holidays allowed includes regularly designated holidays, personal floating, and companywide floating. About 95 percent of all companies offer between eight and thirteen paid holidays per year, with an average of about eleven (BNA Survey no. 142, 1986). The Hay Group (1988) notes that the allotment of floating holidays is on the rise.

Retirement funding is moving away from sole reliance on a defined benefit retirement plan. The Hay Group (1988) reports that the number of companies

Table 2.11
Percentage of Managerial Employees Appraised

Percentage of Companies (across industries)

Supervisors
Appraise   91
Do not appraise   9

Middle Managers
Appraise   87
Do not appraise   13

Top Management
Appraise   67
Do not appraise   33

Source: Performance Appraisal Programs, Personnel Policies Forum Survey No. 135, pp. 4, 6, 12 (February 1983). Copyright 1983 by the Bureau of National Affairs, Inc. (800–372–1033).

that have only a defined benefit plan decreased from 91 percent to 78 percent in just four years (1984 to 1988). Capital accumulation plans are gaining in popularity, especially plans defined under Section 401(k) of the Tax Reform Act of 1987, in which employees can contribute to their retirement account with pre-tax income (up to a regulated limit), often with their company making a matching contribution.

Performance Appraisal

Traditionally, American managers were exempt from performance evaluation (Whistler and Harper, 1962). This, along with several other factors, has changed in the last thirty years. According to one survey, 92 percent of responding firms that had some type of performance appraisal system (BNA Survey no. 135, 1983) conducted appraisals of their managerial staff (supervisors and above). Table 2.11 presents the percentage of American managers working for companies with an appraisal system, who were given some form of performance appraisal.

Researchers (BNA Survey no. 135, 1983; Cleveland, Murphy, and Williams, 1989; DeVries et al., 1986) have identified three trends in use of performance appraisals: (1) the methods used to appraise performance have undergone substantial evolution, with the older methods of appraisals gradually being replaced by newer methods, which have been shown to be more valid measures of performance; (2) the number of uses for performance appraisal data has increased (Table 2.12 indicates various uses of performance appraisal data and the extent to which companies utilize each application); and (3) changes such as more training of evaluators and form revisions are prevalent. The increased number

Table 2.12
Uses of Performance Appraisal Data

Use	Percent of Companies who use on each group		
	Supervisors	Middle Managers	Top Managers
Determine wage/salary adjustments	87	87	87
Promotion	80	80	80
Communication	72	71	71
Determine training & development needs	72	72	70
HR Planning	40	42	44
Development of skills, inventories or other employer information systems	20	20	21
Determine order of layoff	13	13	13
Other	3	4	2

Source: Performance Appraisal Programs, Personnel Policies Forum Survey No. 135, pp. 4, 6, 12 (February 1983). Copyright 1983 by The Bureau of National Affairs, Inc. (800–372–1033).

of uses of performance appraisal data is noteworthy. No longer just a method to determine wage and salary adjustments, performance appraisal has become an important part of counseling and development of the managerial employee.

Legal Issues   Title VII of the Civil Rights Act of 1964 gave employees the right to challenge performance appraisals if they demonstrated adverse impact (a violation of the four-fifths rule) on a protected class. Thus, if a performance appraisal system in a particular company is used for making promotion decisions, and the promotion rate of a minority group is less than four-fifths or 80 percent of the promotion rate of the highest nonminority group, adverse impact is said to occur, and the performance appraisal system is open to legal attack. Various court cases have demonstrated that performance appraisal systems that appear discriminatory are legally defensible. Successful defenses against suits brought by employees have occurred when (1) the performance appraisal is based on a job analysis and, as such, the evaluation form accurately reflects job characteristics; (2) supervisors have been properly trained to give evaluations; (3) a formal appeal process has been established; (4) the procedure is well documented; and (5) assistance is provided to poor performers (Scarpello and Ledvinka, 1988).

Performance Appraisal Techniques   Table 2.13 presents the most commonly used performance appraisal techniques and the extent to which they are employed for the various levels of management.

Essays, though still fairly prevalent for managerial positions, are decreasing in use as appraisal instruments. Essay or narrative evaluations can range from a simple summary of a supervisor's thoughts about the subordinate's performance

Table 2.13
Common Performance Appraisal Techniques

Technique	Supervisors	----- Percentage Used by Managment Group[*] ----- Middle Management	Top Management
Essay	59	63	46
Rating Scale	56	5	46
MBO	44	49	56
Checklists	28	25	21
Critical Incidents	19	18	19
Ranking	7	8	7
Other	3	4	4

[*] Percentages do not sum to 100 as many companies employ multiple rating techniques.

Source: Performance Appraisal Programs, Personnel Policies Forum Survey No. 135, pp. 4, 6, 12 (February 1983). Copyright 1983 by The Bureau of National Affairs, Inc. (800–372–1033).

to a rich, complex description of performance that is useful to both employer and employee. The major problems with this technique are the variability between and within raters as to the quality of the finished product, the accuracy of the performance assessment, and the tendency of raters to focus on traits that the candidate possesses or lacks (i.e., leadership ability, initiative, creativity), instead of specific behaviors that are more under the candidate's control. The continued use of essay evaluations for managerial positions is likely due to the difficulties in developing specific behavioral criteria for managerial positions.

Rating scales are by far the most researched appraisal technique, which has resulted in the creation and validation of numerous scales. The scales are grouped into various forms, including graphic scales and behaviorally based scales. Graphic rating scales are used to rate managers on traits such as their leadership ability, initiative, and interpersonal competence. Assessments are also made of the manager's quantity and quality of work. These trait-type scales are easy to create and administer, but they have rather poor psychometric properties. The extent to which they yield accurate descriptions of performance, as well as the tendency for multiple raters to give different ratings to the same person, have led to sharp criticisms of graphic rating scales.

Behaviorally based rating scales were created to answer some of the criticisms levied against graphic scales. Behavioral rating scales fall into one of three predominant forms: Behaviorally Anchored Rating Scales (BARS, Smith and Kendall, 1963), Behavioral Expectation Scales (BES, Campbell et al., 1973), or Behavioral Observation Scales (BOS, Latham and Wexley, 1981). BARS and

BES are basically identical scales in which a rater checks off on a form behaviors that could be expected on the part of the candidate. BOS scales eliminate the rater's subjective judgments by asking the rater to recall specific behaviors they have seen the candidate perform. The goal of all forms of behavioral rating scales is to make the rating process as accurate and reliable as possible, to help free the rater of subjective judgments, and to ensure that as wide a range of employee behaviors are rated as possible. However, all are based on prior job analyses that determine the behaviors appropriate and necessary for successful job performance, which often is difficult to describe for managerial positions. Thus, behavioral rating scales are not as widely used on managers as they are on lower level positions.

Management By Objectives (MBO) has become quite popular and seems particularly suited for making managerial ratings. MBO, in a nutshell, consists of setting specific performance goals for each employee (Ordiorne, 1965). These goals may be participatively set by the individual being appraised and his or her supervisor. The goals are highly individualistic, which is appropriate for managerial positions, for job descriptions may differ quite radically even between two managers at approximately the same level in an organization.

Timing of Performance Appraisals   Performance appraisals tend to be conducted annually for most American managers. For managers whose performance is appraised, annual intervals appear most common according to the results of one survey. Appraisals are given annually to 85 percent of first-level supervisors, 86 percent of middle managers, and 89 percent of top-level management (BNA Survey no. 135, 1983). The same survey indicated that semiannual reviews were given to 9 percent of first-level supervisors, 8 percent of middle managers, and 6 percent of top-level management.

Training and Development

The training and development of a manager begins with some form of education. Collegiate schools of business came under fire in the late 1950s as being too narrow and vocational in their curricula. Since that time, a more rigorous academic approach as well as the growth of postgraduate business education have increased the efficacy and prestige of business schools. Between 1965 and 1985, MBAs increased from 6.3 percent to 22.5 percent of all master's degrees awarded (Smith et al., 1987).

Unfortunately, business leaders often denigrate this educational background of many managers, which might be considered their pretraining training. The business schools themselves have often been at a loss to define their mission. Although business schools strive to supply employers with what it is perceived that they want, the requirements of businesses have broadened and changed in response to stiffer international competition. As Clarence Brown of the U.S. Department of Commerce put it:

[Business Education] has felt the pressure for highly training people who can master massive but discrete technical and managerial skills: finance, engineering, accounting, marketing, production, distribution, personnel management, labor relations, research, and so on. At the same time, it has seen the need for men and women who have the breadth, perspective, and flexibility of mind to cope with a social environment that is rapidly becoming more fragmented and complex. (Smith et al., 1987, p. 65)

Managerial training and development can take a variety of forms. Training that is done within the company is called in-house training; other training and development activities are conducted external to the organization. Since the majority of medium- to large-sized companies recruit managerial-level employees from colleges and universities and expect to invest a substantial amount of training in their recruits, most employ their own internal training staff. Another variable dimension is the formality of the training provided. Formality is defined by the extent to which the activities are structured and uniform across all employees.

Internal Training Programs   Most companies give their managers some in-house training. Of the companies that responded to a BNA survey (no. 140, 1985), 88 percent provided their middle managers with formal, in-house training. Only about 1 percent of responding companies provided informal training programs. The topics covered by in-house training programs usually include orientation to the organizational climate and practices. Beyond this, the amount and nature of training offered is quite variable across organizations.

External Training Programs   The amount and extent of external training programs offered to managers in the United States is staggering. The training and development of employees is an industry of its own on which employers spend an estimated $100 billion annually according to Kelly, 1982. Many organizations vie for what appear to be plentiful dollars earmarked for training activities. Universities offer MBA degrees for which many companies will sponsor employee enrollment by providing time off to attend classes, tuition reimbursement, and full or partial salary while enrolled. For employees who cannot be given time off, universities offer evening and weekend degree programs. Also offered by universities and management associations are shorter special executive and managerial development programs. Private companies offer training in every area from customer service to leadership enhancement to interpersonal sensitivity. Training and development fads grip U.S. businesses with amazing frequency. When private training companies claim to offer new and better training in an attempt to increase their market share, corporations worry that they are going to miss out on a new revolution and so they quickly soak up all that is offered to them.

Labor Relations

The Wagner Act of 1935 (also known as the National Labor Relations Act) gave employees the right to organize into unions. In addition, Title VII of the Civil Service Reform Act of 1978 extended this right to persons employed by the federal government. The Bureau of Labor Statistics (1988) reported that only about 7 percent of all managerial- and professional-level employees in the United States belong to unions, and about 9 percent are represented by unions. The reality is that the National Labor Relations Act, as amended, provides no legal obligation for American private sector employers covered by the act to recognize or negotiate with their managerial staff. Not surprisingly, few American companies have extended collective bargaining to their managers. The same holds true, in most cases, for grievance rights. Firms like Federal Express and Northrop represent exceptions to this rule. Nonmanagerial employees in many firms have access to a nonunion grievance procedure not provided their superiors. On the other hand, professional staff, such as engineers at Boeing and nurses and public school teachers in some hospitals and school districts, are represented by unions or associations for the purpose of bargaining over pay, hours, and working conditions. More choice is provided lower managerial personnel in various levels of governmental employment than is true in the private sector.

CONCLUSIONS AND FUTURE TRENDS

What can be said about American managers? First, they are a small but growing sector of the total labor force. By the year 2000 they are expected to comprise over 10 percent of all labor force membership. Second, for the most part they share a common ideology and values, and have very high status in American society. Third, if we were to stereotype a typical American manager in terms of how he or she saw his or her job and life in general, we would likely use the following values: the legitimacy of achievement and success; belief in hard work; efficiency and pragmatism; optimism; puritanism; commitment to a scientific, rational orientation; impersonality in work settings; belief in equality of opportunity; acceptance of competition as a fact of life; and individualism. Perhaps no other country in the world holds all these values as strongly as do American managers.

Finally, as the "home" of much of what we know as professional human resource management today, American managers are recruited, selected, appraised, and trained using techniques and approaches largely developed first in the United States. Given managers' socialization and the strong resistance of employers to managerial organizing efforts, private sector managers, with few exceptions, do not belong to unions for the purpose of collective bargaining.

With regard to the future of American managers, labor force trends show continued growth, but that growth will largely be concentrated in small firms in the service sector. The trend in large firms is toward downsizing or eliminating whole levels of management. Competition and improvements in technology have resulted in large numbers of corporate managers being laid off or encouraged to take sweetened or unsweetened early retirement. Managers are no longer as immune from job loss as was true during earlier postwar recessions. Some of them are no longer as crucial to the firm's success. During the 1980s, many firms were no longer willing to keep all their managerial staff on the payroll during economic downturns, as had been the case in earlier years. Managers, like other employees, were seen as a variable cost. This trend continued with the recession that began in about August 1990 and continued into 1992. Not surprisingly, corporate and managerial loyalty has suffered in the process. Being a manager has perhaps lost some of its aura. What this holds for the future competitiveness of the U.S. economy is not yet clear. However, a continuation of this trend may bode poorly for American managers and companies in the world economy.

REFERENCES

Arvey, R. D., and Faley, R. H. 1988. *Fairness in Selecting Employees*. Reading, Mass.: Addison-Wesley.

Baida, P. 1990. *Poor Richard's Legacy: American Business Values from Benjamin Franklin to Donald Trump*. New York: William Morrow and Co.

Bartels, R. 1982. "National Culture-Business Relations: United States and Japan Contrasted." *Management International Review* 22 (2):4–12.

Bellah, R, et al. 1985. *Habits of the Heart*. New York: Harper and Row.

Bendix, R. 1956. *Work and Authority in Industry*. New York: John Wiley and Sons.

Bragg, A. 1981. "Recruiting's Finest Hour: The Interview." *Sales and Marketing Management* 127:57–63.

Bureau of Labor Statistics. 1988. *Labor Force Statistics Derived from the Current Population Survey, 1948–1987* (Bulletin 2307). Washington, D.C.: U.S. Department of Labor.

Bureau of National Affairs. 1990 (June). *PPF Survey No. 147: Wage and Salary Administration*. Washington D.C.: Bureau of National Affairs.

———. 1988 (May). *PPF Survey No. 146: Recruiting and Selection Procedures*. Washington D.C.: Bureau of National Affairs.

———. 1986 (November). *PPF Survey No. 142: Paid Holiday and Vacation Policies*. Washington D.C.: Bureau of National Affairs.

———. 1985. (September). *PPF Survey No. 140: Training and Development Programs*. Washington D.C.: Bureau of National Affairs.

———. 1984 (March). *PPF Survey No. 137: Health and Life Insurance Benefit Plans*. Washington D.C.: Bureau of National Affairs.

———. 1983 (February). *PPF Survey No. 135: Performance Appraisal Programs*. Washington D.C.: Bureau of National Affairs.

Burnham, J. 1941. *The Managerial Revolution: What Is Happening in the World*. New York: John Day Co.

Campbell, J. P.; Dunnette, M. D.; Arvey, R. D.; and Hellervik, L. V. 1973. "The Development and Evaluation of Behaviorally Based Rating Scales." *Journal of Applied Psychology* 57:15–27.

Cavanaugh, G. F. 1990. *American Business Values*. 2nd ed. Englewood Cliffs, N.J.: Prentice-Hall.

Cleveland, J. N.; Murphy, K. R.; and Williams, R. E. 1989. "Multiple Uses of Performance Appraisal: Prevalence and Correlates." *Journal of Applied Psychology* 74:130–135.

de Bettignies, H. C. 1973. "Japanese Organizational Behavior: A Psychocultural Approach." In Desmond Graves, ed., *Management Research: A Cross-cultural Perspective*. San Francisco: Jossey-Bass.

de Tocqueville, A. 1946. *Democracy in America*. New York: Alfred A. Knopf.

DeVries, D. L.; Morrison, A. M.; Shullman, S. L.; and Gerlach, M. C. 1986. *Performance Appraisal on the Line*. Greensboro, N.C.: Center for Creative Leadership.

Gatewood, R. D., and Field, H. S. 1990. *Human Resource Selection*. 2nd ed.. San Francisco. Dryden Press.

Greenberg, G. 1987. "Reactions to Procedural Injustice in Payment Distributions: Do the Means Justify the Ends?" *Journal of Applied Psychology* 72:55–61.

Grimsley, G., and Jarret, H. 1975. "The Relation of Past Managerial Achievement to Test Measures Obtained in the Employment Situation: Methodology and Results II." *Personnel Psychology* 28:215–231.

Hay Group. 1988. *Compensation and Benefits Strategies for 1989 and Beyond*. Philadelphia: Hay Group.

Henneman, H. G.; Schwab, D. P.; Fossum, J. A.; and Dyer, C. D. 1980. *Personnel/ Human Resource Management*. Homewood, Ill.: Irwin.

Hunter, J. E., and Hunter, R. F. 1984. "Validity and Utility of Alternative Predictors of Job Performance." *Psychological Bulletin* 96:72–95.

Kelly, J. B. 1982. "A Primer on Transfer of Training." *Training & Development Journal* 36: 102–106.

Latham, G. P., and Wexley, K. N. 1981. *Increasing Productivity Through Performance Appraisal*. Reading, Mass.: Addison-Wesley.

Lawler, E. E., III 1981. *Pay and Organizational Development*. Reading, Mass.: Addison-Wesley.

Ledvinka, J. 1982. *Federal Regulations of Personnel and Human Resource Management*. Boston: Kent Publishing.

Lodge, G. C., and Vogel, E. F., eds. 1987. *Ideology and National Competitiveness: An Analysis of Nine Countries*. Boston: Harvard Business School Press.

Lumpkin, J. R., and Tudor, R. K. 1990. "Effect of Pay Differential on Job Satisfaction: A Study of the Gender Gap." *Journal of Purchasing and Material Management* 26(3):25–29.

Magnus, M. 1981. "Employee Recognition: A Key to Motivation." *Personnel Journal* 60:103–107.

Milkovich, G. T., and Newman, J. M. 1990. *Compensation*. 3rd ed. Homewood, Ill.: Irwin.

Newman, W. H. 1972. "Cultural Assumptions Underlying U.S. Management Concepts." In J. L. Massie and J. Luytijes, eds. *Management in an International Context*. New York: Harper and Row.

Nimgade, A. 1989. "American Management as Viewed by International Professionals." *Business Horizons* 32(6):98–105.

Ordiorne, G. S. 1965. *Management By Objectives: A System of Managerial Leadership*. Belmont, Calif.: Fearon.

Roomkin, M. J. 1989. "United States." In Myron J. Roomkin, ed., *Managers as Employees*. New York: Oxford University Press.

Sackett, P. R., and Harris, M. M. 1984. "Honesty Testing for Personnel Selection: A Review and Critique." *Personnel Psychology* 37:221–246.

Scarpello, V., and Ledvinka, J. 1988. *Personnel/Human Resource Management*. Boston: PWS-Kent.

Schmitt, R. 1981. *Private Pension Plan Reform: A Summary of the Employee Retirement Income Security Act of 1974 (ERISA)*. Congressional Research Service, Report No. 81-247 EPN.

Schneider, B., and Schmitt, N. 1986. *Staffing Organizations*. 2nd ed.. Glenview, Ill.: Scott, Foresman and Co.

Servan-Schreiber, Jacques. 1968. *The American Challenge*. New York: Atheneum.

Smith, K. R.; Albrect, P. A.; Delbecq, A. L.; Miles, R. E.; and Reinmuth, J. E. 1987. In J. R. Evans, ed., *Proceedings 50th Anniversary Conference, Hofstra School of Business*. Hempstead, N.Y.: Hofstra University.

Smith, P. C., and Kendall, C. M. 1963. "Retranslation of Expectations: An Approach to the Construction of Unambiguous Anchors for Rating Scales." *Journal of Applied Psychology* 47:149–155.

Ulrich, V., and Trumbo, D. 1965. "The Selection Interview Since 1949." *Psychological Bulletin* 63:100–116.

Weber, J., Driscol, L., and Brandt, R. 1990 (December 10). "Farewell Fast Track." *Business Week*.

Weber, M. 1958. *The Protestant Ethic and the Spirit of Capitalism*. Trans. T. Parsons. New York: Scribner's.

Weiss, S. 1989 (October). "Locked Out: Why Middle Managers May Never Find the Key to the American Dream." *Business Month*, 39–49.

Whistler, T. L., and Harper, S. F., eds. 1962. *Performance Appraisal: Research and Practice*. New York: Holt, Rinehart and Winston.

Whitehill, A. M. 1989. "American Executives Through Foreign Eyes." *Business Horizons* 32(16):42–48.

3

GREAT BRITAIN

Moshe Banai and
Dennis John Gayle

Under English common law, a corporation is a juridical person. Members of the board of directors possess a fiduciary responsibility to their stockholders. Managers report through the corporate hierarchy to the managing director, who is elected by the board of directors. We use the term *manager* to include professionals who play specific formal roles in corporate organization and direction, excluding supervisory personnel, except for our discussion of managerial training and development. In England, first-line supervisory workers are considered a distinct occupational group. Furthermore, their background, training, and work environment are rather similar to those of their subordinates. This approach yields a group that comprised only some 3.1 percent of the country's labor force in 1968 (International Labor Organization, 1969).

Within the public sector, the formal concentration of power in cabinet government encouraged the emergence of a civil service staffed by some 700,000 permanent public managers, who were not governed by administrative statutes that related their responsibilities and status to any accepted concept of the public interest (Wright, 1977:299). A subgroup of senior public managers, amounting to about 3,000, exercises substantial if anonymous influence over ministerial decisions (Norton, 1984:188–193). Within the private sector, Britain had about 350,000 senior and 800,000 middle managers by 1987 (*Economist*, 1989:26–28). Definitional differences persist: by another count, there were some 784,000 managers and administrators in 1986, a total projected to increase to 935,000 by 1995 (Sisson, 1989).

This chapter summarily describes the British business environment and examines managerial behavior in Britain. We begin by reviewing the structure and performance of Britain's economy, with an emphasis on the period since 1970. We then discuss the national labor market and industrial relations in Britain, as well as the evolving public policies that have underpinned the nation's business environment. Successive sections examine managerial values, recruitment, selection, performance evaluation, and compensation. These are followed by an assessment of managerial training and development.

EVOLUTION OF MANAGERIAL CLASS, CULTURE, AND MANAGERIAL BEHAVIOR

During the 1970s, Britain was often characterized as a land of mediocre management, adversarial industrial relations, declining industries, education policy drift, inadequate marketing, insufficient research and development, and widespread disdain for business (*Economist*, 1989:5). Growth in the annual average gross domestic product (GDP) fell from 2.8 percent in 1965–73 to only 1.0 percent in 1973–84. Between 1971 and 1981, manufacturing employment fell by 24.0 percent. This contributed to a total official unemployment count of 3.33 million people, or 13.0 percent of the labor force, at the beginning of the 1980s.

Table 3.1 details British economic structure and performance during the 1960–87 period. It presents selected data dealing with gross domestic product, investment, and sectoral growth, as well as Britain's external balances. Only during the 1980s did GDP growth equal or exceed the level of 5 percent achieved in the 1960s. Yet, annual GDP growth averaged between 2.1 and 2.9 percent throughout the period reviewed. The manufacturing sector, which stabilized at about a quarter of the country's domestic product, achieved the least sectoral growth. By contrast, the services sector, which expanded from 53 to 60 percent of GDP, maintained annual average growth rates exceeding 2 percent. Britain experienced recurrent trade (and occasional current) account deficits, as exemplified by the years 1976, 1984, and 1987, but these became increasingly less significant as a proportion of gross national product (GNP).

Table 3.2 displays GNP and GDP per capita indicators, as well as GDP distribution, trade, and current account balances, from 1950 to 1989, using data from the British Central Statistical Office, in pounds sterling. This data series further documents the rapid expansion of the services sector relative to manufacturing and agriculture, particularly during the 1980s. To be sure, during the Thatcher era, GNP per capita increased by approximately 217 percent, between 1980 and 1989, but this record must be compared with growth of 440 percent during the 1970s, 181 percent during the 1960s, and 186 percent during the 1950s. Such outcomes suggest that the domestic product was most evenly distributed in the 1970s, when the Labour party governed the country. Table 3.2 also indicates that British GNP per capita more than doubled between 1980 and 1989 (in current prices), when explosive growth in the size of Britain's trade and current account deficits also occurred.

Services exports first exceeded exports of manufacturers in 1980, and this became a continuing trend. Since 1963, imports of manufactures have risen at an annual rate of 6 percent. By 1988, the manufacturing sector generated less than 22 percent of British GDP, compared with a level of 29 percent in Japan and 33 percent in West Germany. During that year, Britain's visible external

Table 3.1
British Economic Growth, 1960–87

Years	GNP/Cap US$	GDI (%)	GDP $m	Trade Bal $m	C/A Bal $m	GDP Growth (Percent)	GDP Distribution Agr	Man	Serv (%)	Sectoral Growth Agr	Man	Serv (%)
1960-70	4,020[a]	5.0	71,360[b]	-9,715[a]	-2,502[a]	2.9	4	32	53	2.3	3.4	2.7
1970-79	6,320[c]	0.8	401,380[c]	816[d]	12,634[d]	2.1	2	25	62	0.8	0.6	2.4
1965-80	9,660[e]	0.6	473,220[e]	-11,382[f]	1,417[f]	2.4	3	24	51	1.6	-1.2	2.2
1980-87	10,420[g]	5.3	575,750[g]	-23,260[g]	-2,621[g]	2.6	2	25	60	3.2	1.3	2.6

Notes: GDI = gross domestic investment; GDP = gross domestic product; Trade Bal = merchandise trade balance; C/A Bal = current account balance; Agr/Man/Serv = agricultural/manufacturing/service sectors.
[a]1976; [b]1970; [c]1979; [d]1981; [e]1982; [f]1984; [g]1987.

Source: IBRD, World Development Reports, 1981–89 (New York: Oxford University Press, 1981–89).

Table 3.2
British Economic Growth, 1950–89 (million pounds sterling)

YEAR	GNP/Capita [Pounds Sterling @ Current Prices]	GDP/Capita [Pounds Sterling @ Current Prices]	GDP Distribution Agr	Man	Serv	Trade Balances	C/A
1950	236	228	682	4148	687	-51	+307
1955	338	335	791	6124	1034	-313	-155
1960	441	437	912	8164	1595	-406	-255
1965	588	580	1056	10747	2464	-237	-49
1970	802	791	1246	14212	5296	+12	+681
1975	1717	1702	2530	26256	13914	-3257	-1524
1980	3534	3538	4197	53095	30169	1357	2843
1985	5464	5420	5553	72615	73088	-3345	2750
1989	7672	7601	6561	97380	129175	-23840	-19126

Sources: Central Statistical Office: *Economic Trends*, London, United Kingdom, 1986, 1990; *The Central Statistical Office Blue Book 1990: United Kingdom National Accounts*, London, United Kingdom, 1990; *The Pink Book, 1990: United Kingdom Balance of Payments*, London, United Kingdom, 1972, 1990; *Annual Abstract of Statistics, 1960, 1968*, London, United Kingdom, 1960, 1968; *National Income and Expenditure 1979*, London, United Kingdom, 1979.

trade was dominated by one sector: machinery and transport equipment. This sector accounted for nearly 40 percent of all exports and imports, with a sectoral trade deficit of over 8 billion pounds sterling (about U.S.$12.48 billion), more than double the 1987 outcome (Harverson, 1989:11).

Meanwhile, the value of acquisitions and mergers soared from 3.68 billion pounds in 1972 to 22.1 billion pounds in 1988 (Waller, 1989:14). In 1989, Britain's current account deficit amounted to a record 20.30 billion pounds sterling (about $34 billion), or 4 percent of the country's gross domestic product (Carrington and Toman, 1990:1, A14). Central government expenditure expanded from 32.7 percent of GNP in 1972 to a level of 41.4 percent in 1983 (World Bank, 1986:183). This expansion was not financed by increased revenue: the public sector deficit, or Public Sector Borrowing Requirement, grew by 18.6 percent during 1979, and again by 13.6 percent in 1980 (Pollard, 1983:431). However, following the elimination of exchange controls in 1979 (initially imposed as a wartime measure in 1939), Britain's net external assets expanded rapidly, to peak at 112 billion pounds sterling in 1986 (Norman, 1989:18).

The Labor Market and Industrial Relations

As in many other countries, in Britain trade unionism began with the local organization of skilled workers, during the nineteenth century. Trade union leaders sought to improve the terms and conditions of employment for their members by limiting labor supply. The ability of such leaders to do so was eventually undermined by technological change, the growth of mass markets and large industrial enterprises, the development of employer organizations, and the implementation of improved management techniques. In reaction, trade unions evolved into much larger organizations, with more heterogeneous memberships. In turn, this led to more centralized decision making, larger numbers of full-time union officials, and more bureaucratic union administration.

British unions have traditionally sought to establish standard job rates and have often opposed links between pay and performance appraisal. Nonetheless, most unions have accepted performance appraisal and job evaluation, while in many cases seeking representation on job evaluation panels. This situation has led to Britain's hybrid system of public sector pay, which is determined by a mix of indexation, independent pay review boards, and collective bargaining. A comparable hybrid system may also be found in major private sector organizations.

Between 1942 and 1970, Britain enjoyed virtually full employment, and the proportion of male manual workers in the labor force declined from almost 70 percent to 58.8 percent, as a fundamental change in occupational, ethnic, and economic structure ensued (Harrison, 1984:380–381). The proportion of minorities in the labor force has increased appreciably since 1942. Asians constitute the largest nonwhite ethnic group (about 2 percent of the population), and West Indians the second largest (some 1 percent), trailed by Africans, Arabs, Chinese, and others (another 2 percent approximately).

Some 22 percent of whites were members of professional, managerial, or employer categories, compared to 20 percent of Asians and only 6 percent of West Indians (Barber, 1985). Meanwhile, British employment trends have been changing with particular rapidity in the southeast, where the financial sector employed 10 percent more people in 1989 than the manufacturing sector. This was in complete contrast to 1980, when twice as many workers were engaged in manufacturing than in finance.

On the other hand, manufacturing has been expanding in the north, where it accounted for one-third of the region's gross domestic product, while service sector employment has been increasing more briskly in Wales than in Britain as a whole (Cambridge Econometrics, 1990). The revival of the manufacturing sector has been substantially driven by a decade of Japanese investment, which has been moving increasingly into research and development, partly in response to the declared concerns of union leaders (Murray, 1991:17). Across the country, the range of annual pay for entry-level university and polytechnic graduates continued to widen in 1990, from about 9,000 pounds for secondary school teachers to 21,000 pounds for consultants, while the number of young people entering the labor market began to decline (*Economist*, 1990a:57).

Until the 1970s, British trade unions were offered only marginal forms of consultation with government. In the mid–1970s, a "social contract" was signed between the Trade Union Congress (TUC) and the Labour party, dealing with a range of economic and social policies. This agreement produced more favorable labor legislation and larger union representation in state agencies. It eventually collapsed, however, because the TUC was both unable to attain as much influence over government economic policy as it desired and unwilling to play a role in implementing policies oriented toward increased productivity.

The trade unions were almost completely excluded from the political process of the Conservative government after 1979, as it restricted union power by legislation. This legislation required full ballots of labor union members before any strike action could be taken; called for the direct election of officials; made parent unions liable for the actions of their branches; and banned the closed shop, as well as industrial action in firms unrelated to a given dispute. In partial consequence, the number of working days lost per thousand employees declined sharply, from almost 1,300 in 1983 (when over 3 million workers were unemployed) to 150 in 1988. At that point, the proportion of Britain's employed labor force that belonged to a union had fallen to some 42 percent, from 54 percent in 1979 (*Economist*, 1989:7–8).

Although the unemployment level declined substantially from a peak of 11.2 percent in 1986 to 5.8 percent, or 1.67 million people, in 1989 (compared to a European Community average of 9.5 percent), the nation's inflation rate remained much higher than the rates of competing industrial countries, at almost 8 percent, and wage settlement increases were running at more than 9 percent by the fall of that year (Mathewson, 1990:57–58). Britain's hybrid system of public sector pay, which is determined by a mix of indexation, independent pay review boards, and collective bargaining, tended to encourage both industrial unrest and inflation.

In the winter of 1990, the Trades Union Congress estimated that collective bargaining decided the pay of 15 million people (half the nation's workforce), including many ununionized workers, despite former Prime Minister Thatcher's assault on the unions. Indeed, unit labor costs in the manufacturing sector rose by 9.7 percent during the year to August 1990, while average corporate earnings increased by 10.3 percent. Although the number of strikes per year steadily declined from 2,500 in 1978 to approximately 650 during the year to August 1990, Britain's average wages and prices remain substantially higher than those of any other EEC country within the Community's Exchange Rate Mechanism (ERM) (*Economist*, 1990f:61).

Yet for the first time in eight years real wages have been falling, whereas such wages have been rising in every other ERM country except Spain. At the same time, skilled workers remained scarce everywhere in Britain, except in Northern Ireland, and one-third of all Confederation of British Industry members reported that the need to recruit or retain workers was a key factor in unit labor cost expansion. A September 1990 survey by Industrial Relations Services of 300 businesses, employing some 670,000 workers, revealed that almost 70 percent of companies with wage settlements due that autumn intended to offer larger pay increases than they did one year earlier (*Economist*, 1990d:66). In addition, pay bargaining has become increasingly decentralized. For instance, since the collapse of centralized negotiations in the winter of 1989, the pay of 450,000 manual engineering workers has been set locally; British Rail has offered signal technicians a rise of up to 25 percent in areas such as southern London, where up to half such jobs remain unfilled.

In summary, unions in Britain have been traditionally allied with the Labour party, thus helping to draft social legislation. In addition, they have continued to engage in collective bargaining with employers. As a result, the relative strength of unions has waxed and waned, with perceptible lags, according to the economic health of the country and the political ascendancy of the Labour party. At the beginning of the 1990s, a combination of economic recession and a comparatively weak Labour party resulted in the dwindling power of the unions in Britain.

Public Policy

The Labour and Conservative parties dominate Britain's political system. For most of the twentieth century, the Labour party attracted the bulk of its supporters from the working class, whereas the middle classes were typically affiliated with the Conservative party. The Labour party was founded in 1900 to secure the election of working-class members of Parliament and to promote greater equality of opportunity.

The 1942 Beveridge Report on Social Welfare, together with John Maynard Keynes's Full Employment White Paper and the Butler Education Act of 1944, led to the creation of a comprehensive British welfare state. In turn, if classical Conservatives extol nineteenth-century free market principles, most practicing Conservative politicians have readily accepted incremental (and occasionally, radical) policy changes in order to preserve existing institutions and values. By 1970, there were an estimated 350,000 individual Labour party members, compared to 1.6 million Conservative party members (Rose, 1974:141, 190).

The present Conservative party emphasizes the need to create an "enterprise culture" capable of generating a "property-owning democracy." Accordingly, the Conservative platform consistently encouraged entrepreneurship, shareownership, homeownership, and free market competition in three successive winning electoral platforms. In 1945, a quarter of the country's population consisted of homeowners. By 1988, this proportion had grown to almost 60 percent. The post–1979 Conservative party government, which until spring 1991 was led by Prime Minister Margaret Thatcher, reduced the basic income tax rate from 33 to 25 percent, while increasing the maximum capital gains tax rate from 30 to 40 percent, with the intention of encouraging productivity and discouraging speculation (*Economist*, 1988a: 13–14).

During the decade to 1987, the British government implemented the world's most extensive privatization program, creating thirteen new companies with a market capitalization of almost 60 billion pounds, or US$93.60 billion (Veljanovski, 1990:107–108). By the end of 1989, only 25 percent of all workers remained in the public sector. Meanwhile, the bulk of Conservative party supporters became increasingly concentrated in the south of England, whereas most Labour party supporters were to be found in the north of England, Scotland, and the inner cities. By spring 1990, however, a *Daily Telegraph* poll indicated that electoral support for the Conservatives had fallen to 18.5 percent, its lowest in nineteen years, compared with a level of 49.6 percent for the Labour party, led by Neil Kinnock (*El Nuevo Herald*, 1990:9A). Although electoral support for the Conservatives recovered somewhat, after John Major became prime minister, the governing party was still five points behind the Labour party in midsummer 1991, enough to give Kinnock a secure parliamentary majority of fifteen to twenty seats.

Even so, the reawakened strength of market capitalism was indicated by the Labour party's revised industrial policy, as summarized in *Industry 2000*. If this policy document restated the traditional Labour themes of regional banking and the "social ownership of utilities," it also emphasized the importance of public–private sector partnership, effective management training, and the creation of a "one-stop" business development service for small firms, in place of some forty existing schemes run by five government departments (*Economist*, 1990c: 63–64). This policy statement continues to influence the debate concerning the evolution of Britain's business environment.

Managerial Education

The structure of Britain's educational system is fundamental to an understanding of managerial behavior. Students are admitted to secondary schools at the age of eleven, after completing their primary education. Most pupils remain in secondary school for five years and graduate at the age of sixteen with an Ordinary Level General Certificate of Education. They then search for a job. Those pupils who are interested in securing a higher education complete a further two years of high school education and graduate with an Advanced Level General Certificate of Education. Under the 1988 Education Act, a national curriculum that emphasizes vocational subjects such as design and technology was put in place. In addition, after April 1, 1990, schools were funded according to the number of pupils enrolled, on the basis of local financial management.

This legislation was intended to encourage improvement in the quality of all educational programs, on the basis of the premise that good schools would attract larger numbers of students and consequently receive more funding. However, British students remain behind their EEC counterparts in both mathematical achievement and vocational preparation (Keep, 1988:28–31). At the same time, the educational process continues to evidence a sharp distinction between the 60 percent of pupils who leave school at the age of sixteen for employment or limited vocational training, and those who remain in full-time education for an additional two years at schools or colleges of further education (Prowse, 1989:18). Successful members of this group graduate with an Advanced Level General Certificate of Education. They then apply for entry to one of the country's forty-seven universities, or a college of education, polytechnic, or adult education program. Britain's rate of full-time participation in education for sixteen to eighteen year olds (32 percent) is much lower than comparable ratios in France (58 percent), Japan (69 percent), and the United States (79 percent) (Keep, 1986).

There are essentially two social classes in Britain, the middle and the working classes. The upper middle class consists of higher managerial and professional persons, whereas the middle class includes lower managerial and administrative groups and the lower middle class contains skilled or supervisory nonmanual workers (Halsey, 1981:47–54). Another important and relevant distinction is between privately funded or "public" grammar schools, and schools funded by the public. The high cost of attendance at privately funded schools limits attendance to members of the middle and upper classes, whereas publicly funded schools are available to the lower classes.

There remains a strong correlation between public school education and membership in the social and educational elite (Fox, 1985:54–55). By 1980, 1,200 privately funded grammar schools were producing more than a quarter of all university entrants, while educating less than 6 percent of the total secondary school population. Meanwhile, 15 percent of all British youths were entering a university (Gayle, 1989:148–149). Thus, the British education system tends to reinforce class divisions at a young age, with clear implications for managerial development. Many higher level managers received their education at private schools and later went on to Oxford or Cambridge.

In contrast, most middle-level managers were educated at comprehensive schools and went to ordinary red-brick, technologically oriented universities (Granick, 1972). This practice created two types of managers: those who were designated to assume chief executive and top management positions, and those who could aspire to reach only upper middle-level management positions. However, the percentage of Oxbridge graduates who have become managers fell steadily from 28 percent in 1954 to 13.8 percent in 1980 (Poole et al., 1981:47). Whereas eighteen of the chairmen of the top fifty British companies, in terms of annual turnover, came from publicly funded schools in 1979, ten years later, thirty-five such chairmen were educated at state institutions (Hannah, 1990:1). However, the higher management jobs still tend to go to people who have not been educated to understand the technical details of corporate operations. Consequently, they may need to rely on the second-tier managers to help them in their decisions. Important decisions may be repeatedly deferred, since higher level managers are rarely technically competent to appraise entrepreneurial opportunities.

If British managers, as a group, are better educated than the general population (Poole et al., 1981:48), they also tend to be less educated than managers in several other comparable countries. A 1989 survey indicated that only some 25 percent of senior managers had earned university degrees, compared to 85 percent in the United States and Japan, as well as 65 percent in Germany and France (*Economist*, 1989:26–28). In particular, Britain also lags behind competing countries in the number of engineering and technology graduates in management (Mant, 1979:106). For instance, over the years one of the most consistent difficulties faced by the Ford Motor Company in Britain has been "finding an adequate number of middle managers and line workers, capable of keeping assembly lines running in a reasonably efficient manner" (Griffiths, 1989:12). At an economywide level, during the winter of 1988, some 28 percent of all companies reported skill shortages, compared with less than 5 percent in 1980 (Confederation of British Industry, 1990).

At least since the 1850s, business has been widely viewed as a pursuit unfit for gentlemen (Wiener, 1981). If the number of new small-company registrations almost doubled annually during the decade to 1989, it remains indicative that the proportion of Cambridge University graduates embarking on manufacturing and civil engineering careers declined from 16 to 9 percent between 1979 and 1988. To be sure, the proportion of such graduates commencing careers in stockbroking, other financial services, advertising, and management consultancy rose from 8 to 13 percent. Nonetheless, the combined graduate total turning to business rather than the professions and the civil service fell marginally (*Economist*, 1989:28, 30). Even so, cooperation between British universities and foreign as well as domestic corporations has become increasingly common. For example, Hitachi Limited and Toshiba Corporation have contributed funds for the construction of a research facility at Cambridge University's Cavendish Laboratory, and Eisai Corporation has committed more than 50 million pounds to a fifteen-year research program concerning neurological disorders at University College, London (Murray, 1991:17).

Managerial Values

In 1980 Hofstede identified and measured four operational dimensions of culture: *power distance*, or the extent to which an unequal distribution of power is accepted by less powerful members of society; *uncertainty avoidance*, or threat perception as a modal response to ambiguity within a given society; *individualism*, or the extent to which members of a cultural group define themselves primarily as individuals; and *masculinity*, or the presence of dominant social values that emphasize assertiveness and the acquisition of material wealth. When Hofstede measured these dimensions within the subsidiaries of one multinational company across forty countries, including Britain, he found that British managers scored low to medium on both power distance and uncertainty avoidance (35 on a 100-point scale), moderately high on masculinity (66), and high on individualism (89).

This study was limited to a single subsidiary of an American company involved in information-processing technology. Accordingly, it does not represent the population of British managers. Nevertheless, a replication of Hofstede's study by Banai (1985), using seven British banks, yielded very similar results. These managers appeared more oriented toward challenge, advancement, and skill application than either leisure time or training. Such findings are also supported by those of Sirota and Greenwood (1971), who ranked managerial concerns in fourteen countries, including Britain.

The results of the Hofstede study which showed high levels of individualism were very similar to Graves's (1973) findings that British managers typically view authority as vested in the person rather than the organization. Success is based on the strength of an individual personality rather than on teamwork. This strong and potentially dangerous requirement for individual autonomy and achievement is held in check by managers' keen sense of fair play and loyalty to corporate goals. Bendix (1956) reports that British managers are influenced by concepts of entrepreneurship that were conceived during the Industrial Revolution. As a result, they focus on maximizing the profitability of their particular unit rather than that of the organization as a whole.

As Cooper and Cox (1989) contend, distinctive British traditions and value orientations have strong implications for organizational management. During the 1980s, many of the traditional symbols of division between worker and manager were dismantled. Single-status canteens were substituted for corporate dining rooms. Segmented car parks were eliminated. Regular workforce briefings became common, and managers were more frequently seen on the shop floor. However, British cultural traditions continue to emphasize stability and to encourage rather authoritarian styles of management. Such orientations appear natural because managers and workers frequently have quite divergent social, cultural, and educational backgrounds.

The ideal manager is seen as the classically educated and cultured generalist who is able to cope with any contingency; specialists are often met with suspicion. Social and political skills are emphasized, combined with limited amounts of accounting and economics (*Economist*, 1988b:88–90). In actuality, the prototypical manager epitomizes caution, waiting until a competitor has successfully embarked on a new venture before following suit and then minimizing risk by sharing it with others, without explicitly acknowledging this risk-aversion. To be a manager is often to belong to a social class rather than a professional group. Such an orientation naturally limits the need for management education and training.

British managers tend to be more production than market-oriented. Many seek short-term profits at the expense of long-run market positions, failing to recognize the dynamics of competition. By contrast, French managers, for example, tend to be oriented more toward model building and the development of long-term perspectives (Adler, 1991). British managers are less likely to communicate with colleagues in other departments than their North American counterparts, while also frequently ignoring the potential for intraorganizational conflict (Fiedler, 1981; *International Business Chronicle*, 1991:6). For example, a decision to withhold dividend payments might be described as an opportunity for reinvestments and expanded future profits rather than as a loss for stockholders. Poor quality goods may represent an opportunity for experimentation, intended to improve future production standards, rather than a loss of consumer satisfaction. Public inconvenience associated with pollution may be reinterpreted to mean reduced costs and prices.

When discussing managerial values, it is essential to consider the effect of Britain's class system. Despite the declared concern of Prime Minister John Major to create a "classless society," Britain continues to be a monarchy, fostering an hereditary peerage with law-making powers. An elaborate system of titles and decorations persists. This emphasis on inherited legitimacy partly explains why social origin can be more instrumental for promotion than technical competence. Fiedler (1981) reports that the majority of managers have been promoted from white-collar positions. Norburn (1987) finds that a much larger percentage of British managers have parents from white-collar backgrounds (62 percent) than is the case with American managers (45 percent). Management styles also tend to be more formalized than in the United States. For instance, an American executive in England described how visitors to his office were successively screened by a secretary, a receptionist, and an office manager. Efforts to develop a more streamlined approach were seen as inconsistent with English culture (Adler, 1991).

In thinking about worker motivation, managers tend to draw on relatively complex cognitive and psychoanalytical models of organizational behavior. Any effort to increase productivity is typically treated as more an issue of organizational development than individual employee training. Indeed, a 1989 study by Deloitte, Haskins and Sells found that, although British employers had increased the total number of training days by some 15 percent, between 1984 and 1987, two-thirds of all employees surveyed had not undergone any training at all during the preceding three years.

HUMAN RESOURCE MANAGEMENT

Recruitment

Managerial recruitment involves preparing candidate pools for management positions. The characteristics of the British education system influence the phi-

losophies and principles that underpin the process of recruiting college undergraduates in Britain. Some British corporations recruit college undergraduates
as part of their management training programs. They are recruited to serve in
entry-level posts that may otherwise be occupied by employees with a high
school education. However, these positions are considered to be temporary, and
trainees are typically rotated through a small number of entry-level posts as part
of their training in order to prepare them for assignment to an assistant post,
before they can be considered for appointment to management positions in their
own right.

This method of recruitment provides the organization with good quality employees and lower level managers for comparatively little cost. But it creates
two major problems. First, many of the graduates like to examine several jobs
before making a commitment to any one organization. Hence, many trainees
leave their first employer after the initial training program has been completed,
thereby depriving the organization of the chance to benefit from its investment.
Second, the rapid promotion of undergraduate trainees, as compared to the slow
promotion of high school graduates, creates a two-tier system that encourages
dissatisfaction among the second group of employees. Despite these disadvan-
tages, more and more corporations recruit university undergraduate trainees (Adams and Meadows, 1985).

The recruitment process is different for business school graduates. The prerequisites for admission into an MBA program in England include several years
of corporate experience. Thus, after the completion of their MBA degree, graduates may return to the organization that had employed them before they started
their graduate studies, or join another one. In any case, depending on the extent
and scope of their previous corporate experience, as well as the market demand
for their type of specialization, they opt for immediate lower or even middle
management positions. They are introduced into their management positions
through a short orientation program.

Other methods of external recruitment are applied to upper middle and higher
level management positions. These methods include advertisements in national
newspapers such as *The Financial Times* and *The Economist*. For lower and
middle management the local press is widely used, and its use increases with
company size. For specialist posts the main source of applicants can be found
in professional and trade journals. The government professional and executive
recruitment agency (PER) is not widely used. When these methods are not
fruitful, organizations resort to private employment agencies, "head-hunters"
(who may charge up to one-third of the manager's annual salary as commission
fees), or personal contacts.

Many British organizations have a stated policy of internal recruitment where
possible. Employees join organizations in entry-level positions, as apprentices,
trainees, or simply workers, and gradually, over many years, they make their
way into the higher echelons of management. Even today, it is not unusual to
find British managers who started out in entry-level positions and gradually made
it to the top of their corporation. Internal advertisements may be used at junior

and middle management levels, while for more senior levels appointments tend to be made on the basis of some form of internal assessment and personal contact. Standard criteria for the promotion of employees into management positions will be described later in this chapter.

In most companies no single individual has overall responsibility for recruitment. The two individuals who are most involved in executive recruitment are the managing director and the head of personnel (Robertson and Makin, 1986). Although British employment laws are very similar to those existing in the United States, there are two major differences. First, Britain has no legislation concerning age discrimination, although more than half the nation's managers are over forty (Skapinker, 1989: 10). Consequently, older managers may be forced into early retirement, and those who are laid off may never be able to regain a managerial position. Second, Britain does not have an affirmative action policy, which aims at enhancing the employment of protected groups. Minority groups comprise only a small portion of the British workforce, and British women are not as legally assertive as American women in their demands for equal employment opportunities. Thus, British companies devote only very limited organizational resources to recruitment policies and controls; greater effort is directed to selection (Thompson, 1978).

Managerial Selection

The goal of managerial selection is to find the best person for the job: to match individual qualifications and job requirements. The single most used selection method is the interview. A survey by Gill (1980) found that over 90 percent of the companies surveyed relied almost exclusively on interviews to select managers. The survey also found that panel selection boards were used by 15 to 20 percent of companies, but that this ratio rose to one in three corporations with over 5,000 employees. Group selection methods were used by 5 percent of the companies, mostly for recent college trainees.

Tests were little used at managerial levels by British industry. Where general intelligence and aptitude tests were used, they were applied mostly to computer staff. Personality tests were more often used for sales and marketing posts, but even then the use of these tests was very limited. Graphology (handwriting) tests were used in only a handful of British companies and subsidiaries of European companies in Britain. Medical exams were applied in almost all corporations, as the final test, before an invitation was issued to join the organization.

The widespread adoption of the assessment center method for selection in the United States has not been mirrored in Britain, despite the pioneering work of the civil service (Fletcher and Dulewicz, 1984). An Institute of Personnel Management survey found that only 4 percent of organizations sampled used this technique (Gill, 1977). British managers remained unconvinced that the results obtained by this method were worth the high costs in time and money. Almost without exception, personality and other factors not directly related to ability were critical to the executive assessment process (Gill, 1980). The three most valued qualities were motivation, job performance, and ability to get along with colleagues. Such qualities are most difficult to assess during the course of an interview; yet most executives are selected on the basis of an interview alone (Robertson and Makin, 1986).

Applicants for managerial jobs usually submit their résumé, which the employing organization uses for initial screening purposes. In many cases, the résumé is accompanied by letters of recommendation from two or more people who are familiar with the candidate. They may be previous employers, community leaders, professors at educational institutions, bankers, or others. Although the validity of references as predictors of work success has been found doubtful, corporations continue to use them as indicators of the social contacts and ties that a manager may have. References may indicate membership in the managers' social class, a factor that is still considered important at top-level managerial positions. As the selection process moves toward its final stages, there is an increase in the involvement of line managers, who are responsible for the final selection of candidates at lower and middle management levels (Robertson and Makin, 1986).

Performance Appraisal

Managers in Britain are assessed on the basis of both their performance and personality (Cox and Cooper, 1989). A wide breadth of experience involving many functions, and often several different industries, is a key element in executive success. British managers tend to believe that, in order to become a chief executive, a manager must be familiar with the various aspects of his organization, and that this familiarity is best achieved through intraorganizational rotation and experiential learning of top management functions.

Another characteristic of a successful management career is risk aversion. Managers are encouraged to take only carefully calculated risks, within the limits of their skills and abilities. This goes hand in hand with the phenomenon that we mentioned earlier: frequently, senior British managers do not have enough technical knowledge to assess new opportunities, and therefore, they avoid innovative ventures.

High achievement, human relations skills, and the need for power and influence are additional characteristics of successful senior managers. This drive for power is well established in the literature as a characteristic of successful management (Bower, 1966; McClelland and Boyatzis, 1982). However, such motivations cannot be directly expressed (Cox and Cooper, 1989:242). The explicit acceptance of power distances between managers and their subordinates is foreign to British culture (Hofstede, 1980). Consequently, British managers prefer to relate to their power need as ''power to influence and control events'' rather than power over people, despite having little sense of the lives of blue-collar workers.

In summary, the skills characteristic of successful managers in Britain include an analytical ability to define the core problem elements and ignore irrelevancies; a capacity to make and implement unpleasant decisions; strong communications skills; and a long time-horizon. Communication skills are all the more important because the managerial process itself may be more important than the end results, or bottom line. In accordance with the principle of fair play, a basic British social norm, honesty and integrity, predictability, and a reputation for honoring commitments and generating trust are core values in management. Managers also expect their subordinates (who usually belong to a different social class) to display these characteristics, while accepting a paternalistic style of management and trusting their superiors to look after their interests.

Most companies apply some kind of formal performance appraisal system to managers. This is comprised of structured or semistructured questionnaires, completed by direct supervisors once or twice annually and before promotions. Some organizations conduct such performance appraisals across the board, usually a few months before the annual salary increase, whereas others complete these appraisals on the individual employee's birthday or employment anniversary.

These appraisal systems are based on specified job descriptions together with performance measures. Some organizations, including the civil service, use short-term objectives as partial criteria for job performance (Erban, 1989). In some cases, behavioral skills are also assessed during this evaluation (Mumford and Buley, 1988). However, comprehensive Management By Objectives systems (Ordiorne, 1965) are normally used only by the subsidiaries of American companies in Britain. Employees may be provided with either written performance appraisals, in full or in part, or with verbal summaries only. In most cases, performance appraisals are used as a means of determining compensation levels.

Managerial Compensation

Managers in Britain have traditionally made less money than most of their Western counterparts (Curnow, 1986). In 1989, managing directors of medium-sized British companies, with an annual turnover of 30 million pounds, continued to earn less than their counterparts in other advanced industrial countries. Such directors were in ninth place, behind countries such as the United States, France, Germany, Italy, and the Netherlands, when their pay was adjusted for cost of living (P-E Inbucon, 1989). During that year, the average gross salary and bonuses of British managing directors amounted to 39,243 pounds sterling (US$61,219), compared with 20,470 pounds sterling (US$31,933) in the case of middle managers and 15,090 pounds sterling (US$23,540) for junior managers (Dixon, 1989:14). By 1990, however, British managerial compensation was roughly in line with EEC averages, and whereas overall earnings from employment rose by some 10 percent, in 1989–90 increases for the highest paid directors in the nation's seventy-eight top companies averaged 22.3 percent (Incomes Data Services, 1990). Table 3.3 demonstrates that, in 1989–90, at ten major companies there was no correlation (except in the case of British Airways) between the highest level managerial compensation and corporate earnings per share during the preceding year.

During the 1960s and 1970s, it was assumed that older workers with more experience would always earn more than younger employees and that managers working alongside each other should earn roughly the same salaries. Job scope

Table 3.3
British Managerial Compensation, 1989–90

Company	Pay {1}	Increase % {2}	EPS % {3}
Lonrho	1,317,257	29.8	16.3
Burton Group	899,000	-9.7	16.1
Marks & Spencer	619,961	46.1	5.7
British Airways	515,818	19.5	15.7
Imperial Chemical Industries	514,000	7.5	14.2
Trafalgar House	480,000	62.7	15.8
Barclays Bank	470,283	47.2	259.8
British Telecom	374,152	32.2	9.7
British Steel	308,451	79.1	36.6
Courtaulds	250,792	24.5	-12.7

[1] Highest paid director's compensation (pounds sterling).

[2] Percentage increase on year earlier.

[3] Rise in corporate earnings per share during previous year.

Source: Incomes Data Services (Company Accounts for Years Ending Between September 1989 and March 1990) (London, 1990).

was the principal determinant of relative pay within an organization. In addition, a gradual career-earning progression was considered equitable. This approach mitigated the salary differences among managers in various hierarchical positions. Meanwhile, general salary levels were decided by reference to market surveys and government incomes policies.

During the 1980s, however, an additional set of factors began to be taken into account. These included individual characteristics, such as age, experience, qualifications, skills, contribution to the company, as well as current and potential performance. Salary adjustments were also made on the basis of the employer's cost structure, industry position, prospective earnings, and organizational philosophy. Accordingly, traditional restrictions on salary differentials, based on the principle of equity, are giving way to the premise that individual pay should be linked to the achievement of defined objectives. More and more corporations link their pay reviews to their business, market, and management planning cycles rather than sticking to the confines of the union negotiating year. An increase in individual choice and more personalized salary arrangements has resulted from attention to factors such as the treatment of surpluses in pension schemes, portable pensions, profit-sharing, and short-term contracts (Wood, 1985).

In addition, severe skill shortages in many sectors, including computers and finance, have led to stiff competition in the recruitment market. In the past, executive rewards came largely through promotion and a lifetime earnings progression. Managers are now demanding more cash in advance because future rewards are uncertain. Changes can be seen, not only in the large bonus awards given to top executives, but also in the increasing use of merit pay systems, variable cash bonuses, and employee share options (Curnow, 1986). Other techniques used by employers to attract and retain highly skilled managers and specialists are golden parachutes, key contributor schemes, extended vacations, and variable frequency salary reviews. However, many managers opt for fringe benefits rather than cash, because of the associated tax advantages. Since the mid–1970s, the most common such benefit has been a company car: over 90 percent of senior British managers are allocated such automobiles, more than anywhere else in the world. Some managers have even accepted pay cuts in order to join corporations that offer the use of more prestigious cars (Lublin, 1990:R29).

Managerial unionization is more common in Britain and other European countries than it is in the United States. However, the ratio of union membership is much lower among managers than among their subordinates. Traditionally, managerial terms and employment conditions have been determined by employers on an individual basis. Between 1940 and 1980, however, collective bargaining became increasingly common, particularly within the public sector. By 1980, nearly 40 percent of managers were covered by collective agreements (Poole et al., 1981).

Union membership among managers is a function of three conditions: the presence and institutional recognition of a union within an organization; the location of an organization in the public or private sector; and the willingness of individual managers to endorse collective principles (Poole et al., 1981). Thus the impact of managerial unionism has generally been confined to the public and cooperative sectors and some large private sector corporations, such as Imperial Chemical Industries.

A study by Green, Hadjimatheou, and Smail (1985) found that two-thirds of British workers enjoy some entitlement to sick pay. All workers are entitled to holidays, but the holiday entitlement is more extensive for higher paid and long-tenured employees. Some 50 percent of the managers studied enjoyed private pension entitlements, and some younger managers also benefited from job-linked accommodation.

When it comes to pensions and lump-sum gratuities, professionals and managers may expect an annual pension that is 22 percentage points higher, as a ratio of final salary, than that received by an unskilled worker. Similarly, lump-sum gratuities will be 63 percentage points higher, on average. Finally, medical insurance is also gaining momentum as an important fringe benefit, despite the existence of the National Health Service.

Training and Development

The training and development of the workforce begins as early as high school. The process therefore involves public policy and resources. The British government is less involved than the governments of other advanced industrial countries in training and developing the national workforce. Furthermore, the formal management education system in Britain is very small in size and does not satisfy the country's needs. During the nineteenth century, the nation's economic growth was not accompanied by the corresponding development of a formal management education system.

The belief was that "British managers, like British gentlemen, are born rather than made" (Whitely, Thomas, and Marceau, 1981: 31). It was only after World War II that business courses were developed at the undergraduate level. It was not until the mid–1960s that the need for state-supported postgraduate management education was realized, with the establishment of the London and the Manchester Business Schools. These and other universities are producing about 1,250 MBAs per year (Warner, 1987), a mere drop in the ocean of the 1.5 million managers in Britain, and about 12 percent of the desired annual output of 10,000 MBAs (*Financial Times*, 1985:14). Indeed, neither Oxford nor Cambridge University offered MBA degrees until the early 1990s.

In addition, Britain lacks a coherent system of vocational education and training, or an equivalent of the West German Chambers of Commerce, which are concerned *inter alia* with training, education, and management development (Evans, 1987; Keep, 1986). Although a National Council for Vocational Qualifications (NCVQ) was established in 1987, with the mission of ranking jobs and their required qualifications systematically, the Council's efforts have yielded extraordinarily limited results (*Economist*, 1990e:65–66). This phenomenon also helps to create a serious shortage of management skills in the British labor market. Since 1987 the Confederation of British Industry, the Association of British Chambers of Commerce, and the Manpower Services Commission have all cooperated in the establishment of local employer networks (LENs), which aim at coordinating training on a cross-sectional basis and at local levels. This move has shifted the responsibility for skill development from the Engineering Industry Training Board to the British Chambers of Commerce. It is too early to assess whether this move has the potential to solve the acute shortage of management skills within British industry.

The most common type of management training program is the supervisory training program, which aims at helping employees move into their first supervisory position. This type of training is sometimes entitled "training the trainers," and is designed to enhance the first-level managers' ability to train their subordinates on the job. This program may be run internally by a given corporation or by external training agencies such as the Institute of Personnel Management, the British Institute of Management, or private consultants.

Middle-level managers may enjoy functional training programs that help them update themselves in their own organizational functions, such as finance, production, and personnel. These programs are run by business schools, management associations, research groups, and international organizations, such as the European subsidiary of the American Management Association. Some large organizations run their own residential training centers (Barry, 1988). Top-level managers would typically not participate in any formal training program at all. Managers at this level would participate in conferences or social meetings during which a keynote professional speaker might provide them with new knowledge. However, the purpose of these meetings is mostly social and not functional.

In some cases of planned organizational change, top management becomes involved in the development of in-house training programs that include the whole population of the organization (Furtado, 1988). However, these are rare occasions. The top managers perceive themselves as policy-makers, who are supposed to formulate change in corporate objectives rather than as trainees, and are expected to change skills, attitudes, or behavior.

Training programs for lower and middle-level managers use a range of modern training techniques, including off-the-job methods such as lectures and seminars, role playing, simulations, case studies, and critical incidents (Smith, 1988). But the most commonly used techniques of managerial training in Britain are still the traditional on-the-job methods, such as coaching or apprenticeship, "assistant to" positions, role modeling, rotation, understudy assignments, and task force assignments.

Formal management career planning programs have been introduced into the British human resources systems by subsidiaries of American companies in Britain. Career planning programs involve the training of managers and their consequential promotion according to a long-term human resources plan, which is linked to the corporation's strategic objectives. Some British corporations offer promotion ladders to new university graduate recruits, up to the level of middle management. However, career planning programs are mostly available to only a limited number of managers and usually lack the potential to carry them over to upper level positions. The main reason is that human resources planning in Britain has not reached the professional level that could allow formal career planning programs for all the managers in the organization throughout every stage of their careers (Burgoyne, 1988).

From a career development perspective, there are four main routes toward upper level management positions for ambitious British middle managers. The "evolutionary" route involves expanding the scope of a functional division by innovative problem solving: managers grow in stature along with their division and move on to progressively more important responsibilities. In the "command-centered" route, managers typically progress by managing increasingly important branches or divisions, while doing essentially the same work. Managers who adopt the "constructional" route become highly skilled manipulators of internal corporate politics and procedures, securing promotion in rapid succession. Finally, managers who adopt the "turnaround" route actively seek postings in failing operations, with the specific assignment of reversing their decline (Gunz, 1989).

Senior managers often designate "high flyers" at a relatively young age: junior managers who are intended for fast promotion to upper management. Whereas middle-level managers metaphorically enter a regular elevator, proceeding slowly from floor to floor, the potential top-level managers enter express elevators, stopping briefly along the way to the penthouse. If they do not remain in intermediate positions long enough to see the consequences of their actions, such managers are exposed to many facets of their company in a manner that introduces them to a greater number of multifunctional problems than their counterparts in the United States. Meanwhile, other middle managers frequently complain of insufficient responsibility and motivation.

CONCLUSIONS AND TRENDS

Within the British business environment, the services sector dominates, accounting for 60 percent of GDP, although the premier external trade sector consists of machinery and transport equipment. Since 1960, annual GDP growth has been relatively stable, despite substantial variance in domestic investment. Employment in the financial sector has been expanding, particularly in the southeast. Although the overall unemployment level fell to 5.8 percent in 1989, the nation's inflation rate has remained relatively high, at almost 8 percent.

Since 1980, the governing Conservative party has sought to create an enterprise culture capable of generating a property-owning democracy. Britain has embarked on the world's most extensive privatization program. Severe skill shortages in sectors such as computers and finance have led to sharp competition in the recruitment market. Managerial pay is now more closely linked to individual characteristics and to the achievement of defined corporate objectives rather than seniority. In the course of managerial selection and recruitment, the three most valued qualities are usually declared to be individual initiative, potential job contribution, and collegiality. Interviews and references remain the prime instruments for managerial selection, even though these qualities are not easily assessed by such methods.

Even more paradoxically, British cultural traditions continue to include the modal belief that managers are born, not made. Such an attitude helps to limit the perceived need for formal management education and training. Despite a declared orientation toward challenge and skill application, the typical manager remains risk-averse, preferring to limit potential losses rather than to maximize corporate gains. At the same time, the structure of Britain's education and managerial selection systems still tends to produce senior managers who are rarely technically competent to appraise entrepreneurial opportunities.

Two major factors affect managerial behavior in Britain: tradition as a dominant and positive social value, and an unchallenged class system. British society values tradition: the sense that behavioral codes that have worked well in the past should be preserved and that change should only be introduced when unavoidable. Although such attitudes seem to restrain development and innovation, some advantages are apparent. First, to minimize experimentation is to limit the possibility of losses from inappropriate projects. The typical British manager waits for others to demonstrate the merits of a new venture. If a new system, such as a local area network, is introduced, such a step will be taken only in order to minimize potential losses from competitors, who might succeed in generating benefits from the use of such systems.

Second, when implementing a new project, managers minimize risk by collaborating with others, so that any associated losses are widely distributed. Third, unsuccessful managers admit their mistakes and pay the consequences, thereby allowing their successors to reap the benefits of successful policy changes. As a corollary, unionization among managers has not been a significant factor in compensation arrangements, although some 40 percent of managers are formally affiliated with such unions, particularly in the public sector.

These attitudes contrast with those prevailing in the United States, where managers face strong pressures from shareholders to take risks in their decision making, so as to maximize the possibility of short-term gains. Consequently, mistakes are not freely admitted. When the admission of failure is inevitable, U.S. managers evade sole responsibility, as far as is possible. Such behavior makes it difficult for the Board of Directors, or for shareholders, to identify errors at an early stage. In addition, it may be difficult to alter erroneous decisions when managers make obscure mistakes or relate their actions to external factors.

To be sure, the conservative cast of typical British managers is one reason for the country's sluggish economic growth, as documented earlier in this chapter. Yet resistance to change buttresses the class system, so that management becomes a status rather than a profession. Managers who were not born into the appropriate class face major obstacles when seeking promotion. At the same time, since management is a social class, there is limited emphasis on management education and training. Intuitive judgments based on experience and wisdom are preferred to scientific assessment. Whereas management is considered a profession in the United States and university degrees are usually required for advancement, social class is the most common "pass" required of new entrants in Britain. Although this orientation is most evident within the public sector, it significantly influences managerial career development within the private sector as well.

On October 8, 1990, Britain became a member of the European Monetary System's Exchange Rate Mechanism, eleven years after the government first began to consider such an action. Three weeks later, EEC leaders agreed to surrender control over national monetary policy on January 1, 1994, and to move toward the creation of a European political union, despite the objections of former British Prime Minister Thatcher. The more pragmatic approach of her successor,

John Major, toward the evolution of the European Community makes it more likely that a single European currency and central bank system will be in place before the end of the twentieth century.

Meanwhile, business is shifting from a multinational to transnational structure, with blurring distinctions between parent and subsidiary. For example, in 1990, at least forty-five manufacturing companies, with a minimum of $3 billion in annual sales (such as Nestlé, Hoffmann-La Roche, Volvo, Gillette, and Xerox), derived at least 40 percent of these sales from markets other than their home country, while customizing products and services, and deploying a distinctive identity within each major market. In reaction to these developments, European companies have increasingly engaged in cross-border deals. For instance, Siemens of Germany and Britain's GEC have jointly acquired Plessey; France's Carnaud and Metal Box of Britain have merged to form CMB Packaging; and Italy's FIAT has announced plans to swap shares and some business with France's Alcatel-Alsthom.

Such changes will substantially alter the environment within which British managers are trained, recruited, selected, compensated, and assessed. Education Secretary Kenneth Clarke's recent white papers on further (sixteen to eighteen years old) and higher (eighteen-plus) education foreshadow some of the transformations in managerial training and development that will be initiated as a result. By the end of the 1990s, Britain may have some thirty new universities in place, as polytechnics are allowed to award their own degrees. Meanwhile, a new set of school-based vocational examinations, set by the Business and Technical Education Council, as well as the City and Guilds Institute, will be taken at the same time as Advanced Level General Certificate of Education examinations by further education students (including sixth formers), who are subject to national rather than Local Authority control. The prime purpose of these changes is to increase the number of students who remain in further and higher education after age sixteen without imposing an intolerable burden on the Treasury.

The recent establishment of business schools by Oxford and Cambridge also suggests that managerial recruitment and selection, as well as performance appraisal, will become even less oriented toward traditional practice and more professional. Formal career planning programs are likely to become more prevalent in managerial training. Merit pay systems, variable cash bonuses, and employee share options will probably assume more importance in managerial compensation. Competitiveness within the EEC and across defined global market niches will become increasingly explicit objectives for British corporations. In turn, this implies that the structure of Britain's managerial education and selection systems will continue to come under growing pressure. Incremental changes, which were only reluctantly put in place during the 1990s, will more and more clearly reveal the imperative need to alter established managerial attitudes and values in such a way as to increase the fit between rhetoric and performance.

REFERENCES

Adams, M., and Meadows, P. 1985 (September). "The Changing Graduate Labor Market." *Employment Gazette*, pp. 343 ff.

Adler, N. 1991. *International Dimensions of Organizational Behavior*. Boston: Kent Press.

Ascher, K. 1986 (January). "Mastering the Business Graduate." *Personnel Management*, pp. 28–30.

Banai, M. 1985. "Cultural Adaptation of Expatriate Managers in Foreign Banks in London." Unpublished Ph.D. diss., London Business School, England.

Barber, A. 1985 (December). "Ethnic Origin and Economic Status." *Employment Gazette*, pp. 467 ff.

Barry, A. 1988 (September). "Whatever Happened to Company Training Centres?" *Personnel Management*, pp. 42–46.

Bendix, R. 1956. *Work and Authority in Industry*. New York: John Wiley and Sons, 1956.

Bower, M. 1966. *The Will to Manage*. New York: McGraw-Hill.

Burgoyne, J. 1988 (July). "Management Development for the Individual and the Organization." *Personnel Review*, pp. 40–45.

Cambridge Econometrics and Northern Ireland Economic Research Center. 1990. *Regional Economic Prospects*, 21 St. Andrew's Street, Cambridge, CB2 3AX, England.

Carrington, T. and Toman, B. 1990 (February 7) "Britain's Big Increase in Interest Rates Stirs Fears of a Recession." *Wall Street Journal*.

Child, J. 1969. *British Management Thought*. London: George Allen and Unwin.

Confederation of British Industry. 1990. *Quarterly Industrial Trends Survey*. London: CBI, March.

Cooper, C. L., and Cox, C. J. 1989. "Applying American Organizational Sciences in Europe and the United Kingdom. In C.A.B. Osigweh, ed., *Organizational Science Abroad: Constraints and Perspectives*. New York: Plenum Press, pp. 57–65.

Cox, C. J., and Cooper, C. L. 1989. "The Making of the British CEO: Childhood, Work Experience, Personality, and Management Style." *The Academy of Management Executive* 3 (3): 241–245.

Crockett, G., and Elias, P. 1984. "British Managers: A Study of Their Education, Training, Mobility and Earnings." *British Journal of Industrial Relations* 22 (1): 34–46.

Curnow, B. 1986 (October). "The Creative Approach to Pay." *Personnel Management*, pp. 70–75.

Dixon, M. 1989 (September 20). "What Managers' Pay Buys in Different Lands." *Financial Times*, p. 14.

Economist, The. 1988a (April 9). "Growing Rich Again." Pp. 13–14.

———. 1988b (October 15). "European Management: Discordant National Anthems." Pp. 88–90.

———. 1989 (May 20). Special Survey. "The End of the Beginning: A Survey of British Business." Pp. 1–30.

———. 1990a (January 13). "Gotta Lotta Jobs." P. 57.

———. 1990b (January 20). "Swept with Confused Alarms." Pp. 57–58.

————. 1990c (February 17). "Off the Ropes." Pp. 63–64.

————. 1990d (September 22). "The Sin of Wages," P. 66.

————. 1990e (September 29). "Vocational Fudge." Pp. 65–66.

————. 1990f (October 27). "Can't Pay, Will Pay." Pp. 61–63.

————. 1990g (November 17). "Business This Week." P. 81.

El Nuevo Herald. 1990 (March 3). "Margaret Thatcher Pierde Popularidad." P. 9A.

Erban, P. 1989 (February). "How They Manage Performance in Windsor." *Personnel Management*, Pp. 42–45.

Evans, J. 1987 (November). "Can LENs Provide a Focus for Local Training Needs?" *Personnel Management*, pp. 36–40.

Fiedler, J. 1981. *The British Business Elite.* London: Routledge and Kegan Paul.

Fletcher, C. A., and Dulewicz, V. 1984. "An Empirical Study of a UK-Based Assessment Center." *Journal of Management Studies* 21(1): 83–97.

Fox, I. 1985. *Private Schools and Public Issues: The Parents' View.* London and Basingstoke: Macmillan.

Furtado, T. 1988 (March). "Training for a Different Management Style." *Personnel Management*, pp. 40–43.

Gapper, J. 1989 (November 17). "Survey Reveals Poor State of Training in British Companies." *Financial Times*, p. 11.

Gayle, D. J. 1989. "Education Policy in the United Kingdom." In F. N. Bolotin, ed., *International Public Policy Sourcebook: Education and Environment*, pp. 137–158. Westport, Conn.: Greenwood Press.

Gill, D. 1977. *Appraising Performance: Present Trends and the Next Decade.* IPM Information Report 25. London: Institute of Personnel Management.

————. 1980 (September). "How British Industry Selects Its Managers." *Personnel Management*, pp. 49–52.

Granick, D. 1972. *Managerial Comparison of Four Developed Countries.* London: MIT Press.

Graves, D. 1973. "The Impact of Culture upon Managerial Attitudes, Belief and Behavior in England and France." In D. Graves, ed., *Management Research—A Cross Cultural Perspective.* London: Elsevier.

Green, F., Hadjimatheou, G., and Smail, R. 1985 (July). "Fringe Benefit Distribution in Britain." *British Journal of Industrial Relations.* 23 (2): 261–280.

Griffiths, J. 1989 (August 25). "The Illiteracy That Undermines Engineering Management." *Financial Times*, p. 12.

Gunz, H. 1989. *Careers and Corporate Cultures.* Oxford: Basil Blackwell.

Halsey, A. H. 1981. *Change in British Society.* Oxford: Oxford University Press, pp. 47–54.

Hannah, L. 1990. "The Class Origins of British Managers." Occasional Paper, London School of Economics and Political Science.

Harrison, J.F.C. 1984. *The English Common People: A Social History from the Norman Conquest to the Present.* Beckenham, Kent: Croom Helm, pp. 380–381.

Harverson, P. 1989 (October 12). "Producers Fail to Meet Demands of Consumers." *Financial Times*, p. 11.

Hofstede, G. 1980. *Culture's Consequences: International Differences in Work Related Values.* Beverly Hills, Calif.: Sage Publications.

Incomes Data Services. 1990. *British Managerial Compensation in 1989–1990.* London: IDS.

International Business Chronicle. 1991 (March 4–17). "Management Style: United States vs. European." P. 6.

International Labor Organization. 1969. *1968 Yearbook of Labor Statistics.* Geneva: ILO Secretariat.

Keep, E. 1986 (August). "Can Britain Build a Coherent Vocational Training System?" *Personnel Management,* pp. 28–31.

Lublin, J. 1990 (April 18). "The Continental Divide." In *Wall Street Journal Report,* "Executive Pay: Looking Abroad," pp. R28–R29.

Makin, P., and Robertson, I. 1986 (November). "Selecting the Best Selection Techniques." *Personnel Management,* pp. 38–41.

Mant, A. 1979. *The Rise and Fall of the British Manager.* London: Pan.

Mathewson, W. 1989 (October 5). "Warning for Britons." *Wall Street Journal,* October 5, p. A24.

———. 1990 (January 20). "Swept with Confused Alarms." *The Economist,* pp. 57–58.

McClelland, D. C., and Boyatzis, R. E. 1982. "Leadership Motive Pattern and Long Term Success in Management." *Journal of Applied Psychology* 67 (6): 737–743.

Mumford, J., and Buley, T. 1988 (December). "Rewarding Behavioral Skills as Part of Performance." *Personnel Management,* pp. 33–37.

Murray, G. 1991 (March 11–17). "Britain Becoming a Base for Japanese Companies R&D." *The Japan Times Weekly,* International Edition, p. 17.

Norman, P. 1989 (October 23). "Going over the Cliff." *Financial Times,* p. 18.

Norton, Philip. 1984. *The British Polity.* New York: Longman Inc., pp. 188–193.

Odiorne, G. S. 1965. *Management By Objectives: A System of Managerial Leadership.* Belmont, Calif.: Fearon.

P-E Inbucon. 1989. *Survey of International Taxation and Living Costs.* Park House, Wick Road, Egham, Surrey TW20 OHW, Britain.

Pollard, S. 1983. *Development of the British Economy, 1914–1980.* London: Edward Arnold, p. 431.

Poole, M., Mansfield, R., Blyton, P., and Frost, P. 1981. *Management in Focus: The British Manager in the Early 1980s.* Aldershot: Gower.

Prowse, M. 1989 (November 29). "The Need to Stay the Course." *Financial Times,* p. 18.

Robertson, I. T., and Makin, P.J. 1986. "Management Selection in Britain: A Survey and Critique." *Journal of Occupational Psychology* 59.

Rose, R. 1974. *Politics in England: An Interpretation.* Boston: Little, Brown and Co., pp. 141, 190.

Saunders, C., and Marsden, D. 1979. "A Six-Country Comparison of the Distribution of Industrial Earnings in the 1970s." *Background Paper 8,* Royal Commission on the Distribution of Income and Wealth, London: Her Majesty's Stationery Office.

Sirota, D., and Greenwood, M. 1971 (January–February). "Understand Your Overseas Work Force." *Harvard Business Review,* pp. 53–60.

Sisson K. 1989. "Personnel Management in Transition." In K. Sisson, ed., *Personnel Management in Britain.* Oxford: Basil Blackwell, pp. 22–54.

Skapinker, M. 1989 (October 2). "Skills of Older Staff Ignored." *Financial Times,* p. 10.

Smith, R. 1988 (October). "Training by Simulation." *Personnel Management,* pp. 66–71.

Thompson, G. F. 1978. *A Textbook of Personnel Management*. 3rd ed. London: Institute of Personnel Management.

Veljanovski, C. 1990. "Privatization: Progress, Issues and Problems." In D. J. Gayle and J. N. Goodrich, eds., *Privatization and Deregulation in Global Perspective*. Westport, Conn.: Greenwood Press, pp. 107–108.

Waller, D. 1989 (October 23). "Merger Mania Comes under the Microscope." *Financial Times*, p. 14.

Warner, M. 1987 (January). "Industrialization, Management Education and Training Systems: A Comparative Analysis." *Journal of Management Studies* 24(1): 91–112.

Whitely R., Thomas, A., and Marceau, J. 1981. *Masters of Business? Business Schools and Graduates in Britain and France*. London: Tavistock.

Wiener, M. 1981. *English Culture and the Decline of the Industrial Spirit, 1850–1980*. Cambridge: Cambridge University Press.

Wood, D. 1985 (November). "Life after Pay Policy." *Personnel Management*, pp. 31–35.

World Bank. 1986. *World Development Report 1986*. New York: Oxford University Press, p. 183.

Wright, M. 1977. "Ministers and Civil Servants: Relations and Responsibilities." *Parliamentary Affairs* 30: 299.

4

FRANCE

Jacques Rojot

In this chapter the term *managers* is not to be understood solely in the American sense, for the exact role it describes is not well defined in French business circles, custom, and law. France has a close approximation of the American "executives," which consists of *cadres dirigeants*. However, executives are a subset of the relatively restricted and well-defined U.S. category of managers, whereas *cadres dirigeants* are a subset of the much more all-encompassing cadres. The category of cadres, of course, includes managers and excludes foremen or the first level of supervision. But it also includes many other categories of employees, which in the United States would be qualified not as managers, but as professional employees, higher ranking salesmen, or senior technical staff.

Intermediate between the cadres and the white- and blue-collar employees in France is the category of technicians and *agents de maitrise*, which includes supervisory staff of the first rank and technical staff with lower qualifications. The legal definition of cadres has been discussed elsewhere (Rojot, 1989a), but, for an understanding of what follows, a cadre can be defined as an employee who holds one or several of the following characteristics: (1) the power of command over other employees by delegation of the employer, above the first rank of supervision; (2) a graduate degree in given fields from given schools or universities; (3) formal or informal training granting knowledge equivalent to the one resulting from a graduate degree; (4) a great amount of initiative and responsibility in the performance of one's work; (5) the ability to reach certain pay levels fixed in collective agreements; and/or (6) the performance of certain tasks in the enterprise such as traveling salespersons representing the company on their own.

France's gross domestic product (GDP) in 1989 was over 5.600 billion French francs. It represented 20 percent of the European Economic Community's (EEC's) GDP, second behind the Federal Republic of Germany (25.5 percent).

The 1980s were characterized by four district periods. First, growth slowed down to a little more than 1 percent per year in 1980 and 1981. Second, a spur to 2.5 percent occurred in 1982 as a consequence of policies designed to stimulate consumption after the left came to power. Third, after 1984, the return to equilibrium after drastic policy changes in view of the disastrous consequences of the 1982 policies (namely, the worsening rate of inflation and balance of payments), brought a slow return to growth up to about 3.5 percent in 1988. According to statistics from the Organization for Economic Cooperation and Development (OECD), it appears that a slowdown of growth took place during the second half of 1989 and that, for 1990, a 1.5 percent increase of GDP was all that was expected, with projections of a return to a 2.5 to 3 percent growth rate in the following years.

The labor force in 1988 totaled 21.7 million people, that is, 59 percent of the population between fifteen and sixty-four years of age. After continuously decreasing from 1980 to 1985 to a low of 21.45 million, the total is slowly picking up again, but it still remains below the 21.9 million reached in 1980. In 1988, 18.3 million or 83.5 percent of the labor force were wage earners. Conversely, unemployment increased consistently between 1980 and 1986 (and actually since 1973), from 6.3 to 10.4 percent, and it now seems to have stabilized: the annual figure was 10.1 percent for 1988. The highest rates of unemployment are found among youth and women. The rate for people under twenty-five was 25 percent, up to 40 percent for those who held no high school diploma or vocational degree. The present unemployment figure is 13 percent for women against 9 percent for men.

EVOLUTION OF THE FRENCH MANAGERIAL CLASS

Status

Historically, the notion of cadre appeared around the group of graduate engineers, who, as early as the late 1920s and early 1930s, defended a modified version of the emerging division between ownership and management (Berle and Means, 1932). It was never as clearly defined as the U.S. version because of the characteristic features of the French society of the times (Boltanski, 1982:118), and it was colored by corporatism and Catholicism. Nevertheless, it proposed the idea of a group intermediate between employers, owners, and simple wage earners. The number of engineers had steadily grown with the industrialization of the country. After 1945, new categories of administrative cadres which appeared in increasing numbers began to gather around this core. Moreover, with the growing influence of Taylorism, many engineers came to believe that they were the sole owners of technical knowledge (Groux, 1983). They maintained that this role allowed them to determine scientifically not only how work should be organized, but also how profit should be allocated between owner-employers and workers. The engineer was thereby put into the role of referee between social partners. That way of thinking found some ideological roots in the thought of Saint-Simon, formulated in the preceding century, which allocated a special role in society to those who would come to be known as technocrats. It became instrumental in the shaping of the ideology of a value system based on competence and merit, efficiency and objectivity. This common glue cemented many cadres around a common feeling of belonging to a separate social group.

By the 1960s, the group of cadres was institutionalized and well recognized in French society (Boltanski, 1982: 232). Witness to it are the institutions devoted specifically to the cadres (retirement system, placement system, and specific addenda to collective agreements). Cadres are now so much a part of French society that it has become the consumer's role model. The weekly periodicals built around the model of the U.S. news magazines advertise products of which the cadres are the model consumers. However, the group of cadres, far from being neatly defined, is a "fuzzy set" with permeable borders. Within it very different occupational or earnings careers can be identified, depending on the cumulative influence of the individual's educational degree, social origin, and family connections (Boltanski, 1982:373). Even though the cadre entails very different types of profiles, it retains its cohesiveness, for two possible reasons.

First, social and economic modernization demands that an increasing and different category of employees fulfill its needs and expectations, and these needs and expectations are no longer either those of the traditional working class or those of the small-size employer-owner. Second, each member of the group has a vested interest in defining himself as a cadre (Boltanski, 1982:477). By being referred to as cadres, those individuals with a working-class background and no formal degree acquire accession to a highly valued reference group, often at the price of hardships such as night school and personal privations. At higher levels, membership in cadres legitimates the power of top-ranking executives in terms of the merit ethic prevalent in the cadre value system. They are at that level because, in the eyes of all the cadres, they deserve it. In addition, it insures the active solidarity of a large mass of midlevel employees behind the goals of the enterprise and its directors. It also veils statistically their high wages and privileges by aggregating them with the much less privileged but numerically larger category of midlevel employees.

Depending on the exact definition retained and while maintaining a relatively restrictive concept, the number of cadres may be estimated to total 1 to 1.9 million in the private sector and probably less than 0.9 million in the public sector. If the managerial class is considered an elite, it is therefore in a quite extended sense in a labor force of 21.7 million people. This is even more the case given the wide differences between the various types of cadres we have described. However, it should be remembered that the model around which the "fuzzy set" of cadres identifies is extremely elitist. It is the model, so aptly described by Suleiman (1979), of the self-reinforcing effect of the *grandes écoles* and of the *grand corps*. The model can be summarized as follows. The system of higher education in France has traditionally been a monopoly of the state. It is divided between the universities, which are oriented toward the pursuit of knowledge, questioning, and inquiry, and the *écoles* which focus on a more practical-oriented training. The *écoles* were created by the successive governments of France, predating the Revolution and the Napoleonic era, For example, in the eighteenth century, the Ecole des Mines and the Ecole des Ponts et Chauseées trained engineers to build roads and quarry mines; under Napoleon the Ecole Polytechnique was charged with training artillery officers; under the Fourth Republic the Ecole Nationale d'Administration trained qualified civil servants, and so on.

The goals of the *écoles* have consistently been to attract young people who would become the elite of the nation and hold the highest positions in the state. Their teaching was always practical and applied, with the possible exception of the *école* initially designed to train teachers for the lycées (Ecole Normale Supérieure). Many such *écoles* have been created. Of course, defining which among them were truly the *grandes écoles* remains controversial. It may safely be proposed that the three top-ranking ones are the Ecole Normale Supérieure, Ecole Polytechnique, and Ecole Nationale d'Administration.

By definition, an elite who graduated from these *grandes écoles* favored the status quo. The *grandes écoles* were based on the secondary school system of lycées, which would select the best students after a grueling process of training in preparatory special classes and highly selective competitive exams. The universities, open to all holders of a baccalaureate, were at best the object of benign neglect on the part of government and at worst the object of hostility, because of their theoretical orientation and their opposition to the established powers.

This basic division persists to this day, with subtle gradations. On the one hand, the number of *écoles* has multiplied; not all of them give access to public service, and not all of them were created by the state. There are even more subtle gradations between the true *grande* and the "quite grand" or the "not so grand." In engineering, for instance, the gradation between the Ecole Polytechnique, Ecole Centrale, Ecole des Arts et Métiers, and the several regional institutes of engineering (INSA) is a well-known fact. On the other hand, the universities have developed more professionally oriented curricula in business, computer science, engineering, and so on. Even so, at least in very general terms, the *école* model is still valid today.

Suleiman (1979) has carefully detailed the functioning of this model. The two most prestigious *écoles* (the Ecole Polytechnique and the Ecole Nationale d'Administration) give access, for only a few of their own top graduates, to what is called the *grands corps* of the state. Those corps are categories of civil servants who are initially attached to a given governmental institution with high prestige, manned by only the top graduates of one of the two schools. After a few years in the service of the institution of origin, however, the members are seconded into career paths consisting of a succession of jobs toward the most prestigious positions. Those positions were originally in government and in public sector firms, but today they extend into politics, industry, and business. The *grands corps* recruit only the best graduates of these best schools (with the exception of the discretionary appointment of a small percentage of individuals at the disposal of the president of the Republic) and are legitimized because only the best apply. The seniors in each corps guide the careers of the juniors in most branches of government, politics, nationalized industry, and, more and more often, private industry. Only some sectors of the elite do not follow this pattern, such as the university, the law and the judiciary (except, however, for the administrative branch), medicine, science, and large parts of the private sector (which may nevertheless recruit among the graduates of lesser ecoles).

As a result, the system of elite formation is more institutionalized in France than in most other countries (Suleiman, 1979). Before joining ranks of the elite, in France the individual must demonstrate considerable competence. Once this is done at an early age, it is never questioned again. Besides, no alternative paths are open to a considerable number of key positions in French society. The system is now institutionalized to the point that no government is without its high proportion of ministers who are former members of the *grands corps*. For instance, it is virtually impossible to become a director in the Finance Ministry or a private or public large bank chief executive officer without having been a member of a specific given corps.

Of course, not all members of the *grands corps* have such exalted careers, but, more and more, membership in them is becoming necessary. In addition, the system seems to be quite independent of the social origin of its members, even if, because of the "social and cultural capital" (Bourdieu, 1979; Gouldner, 1979) acquired in their family environment, most of the *grand corps* members themselves are members of the upper class.

In 1979, Suleiman correctly forecast that the system would not change with a different political orientation of the government. He foresaw that the predominance of the *grands corps* graduates in politics as well as in government and industry would not be challenged by the coming of a leftist government. With the Socialists back in government for more that ten years, after twenty-five years away from power, it appears that the power of the *grands corps* is stronger than ever, all campaign promises of democratization notwithstanding.

Clearly, only a very small proportion of the cadres are members of this ruling elite, or even directly in touch with some of its members. However, its existence is well publicized, and it plays the part of a role model and sets the dominant pattern of behavior among cadres at lower levels.

The ruling elite spreads naturally from the public to the private sector. Chairmanships and directorships of the nationalized companies are a preserve of the *grands corps*. But more and more of the graduates of the three top *grandes écoles*, whether or not they reached the *grands corps*, move into the private sector after a few years of public service. Many of them reach executive positions and extend a far-reaching network.

INFLUENCE OF DOMINANT CULTURAL VALUES ON MANAGERIAL BEHAVIOR

A fully satisfactory answer to the question of how cultural values influence managers' behavior would demand (1) an agreed upon definition of culture and (2) demonstrated evidence that culture affects managerial behavior. A discussion of these two points is beyond the scope of this chapter; nevertheless, there is agreement neither on what constitutes culture and its definition (Kroeber and Kluckholn, 1952) nor on the idea that cultural differences influence managerial behavior (Farmer and Richman, 1965; Haire, Ghiselli and Porter, 1966; Gonzales and McMillan, 1961; Harbison and Myers, 1959; Negandhi and Estafen, 1965) Whatever the theoretical problems raised by both points, it has long been intuitively felt that men and societal customs influence the way work is carried out, as is illustrated by Montesquieu's theory of the influence of climates and Pascal's famous saying "Vérité en-deça des Pyrénées, erreur au-delà" (What is held to be true on this side of the Pyrenees Mountains is held to be wrong on the other).

More recently, several observers examined the influence of culture on management and included France in their samples. Hofstede (1980) has probably done one of the more extensive studies based on an international survey in a multinational corporation. He defines culture as the "collective mental programming of people in an environment." At the national level these cultures differ on four criteria:. First is power distance, which is the degree of social acceptance of the unequal distribution of power in organizations and institutions. Second, uncertainty avoidance is the degree to which a society tries to avoid ambiguous and uncertain situations which it views as threatening. Consequently, it provides greater stability, more formal rules, is less tolerant of deviant ideas and behaviors, and believes in the attainability of absolute truths and expertise. It is correlated with a higher degree of anxiety and agressiveness, of which one of the by-products is a strong inner urge to work hard. Third, a continuum of individualism collectivism extends from a loosely knit framework of social relations where people take care of themselves toward a network of tight groups where people look after each other and to which they owe absolute loyalty. Fourth, a continuum goes from "masculinity" toward "femininity" of the dominant social values— that is, encompassing the values on which men scored relatively higher than women, whatever the global score for the society itself.

With regard to the power distance criterion, France ranked sixteenth out of fifty-three (with a score of 68 out of a potential 110); on uncertainty avoidance it ranked tenth with a score of 86 out of a possible 120); on individualism it ranked eleventh (with a score of 71 out of a 100); and finally, on masculinity it ranked thirty-sixth (with a score of 43 out of 100).

Michel Crozier (1963) provided the basic elements of an analysis of French culture. What follows is our own interpretation of his insights. It is all the more interesting to review because Crozier's later work implicitly raises the problem of combining his very influential theory (elaborated later; see Crozier and Friedberg, 1977) of strategic analysis of organizations with the notion of national cultures. The theory of strategic analysis considers organizations as systems in which individuals act strategically—that is, toward the fulfillment of their own immediate material interests. But if culture has a role in motivating individual behavior, then, presumably, something other than their own immediate material interests influences the individual's behavior in organizations.

According to Crozier, French organizations consist of clearly differentiated levels in which the members of a given level have a clear understanding of the rights and duties appropriate to an employee or manager at his or her own level of the hierarchy. However, there is little communication, or sharing of understanding, across hierarchical levels. Furthermore, a strict egalitarianism exists among members of a given level or stratum of the organization. This behavior is based on a wider understanding of French culture itself in which social status is clearly delineated.

These characteristics are explained by two observable cultural traits specific to the French: (1) the French have a basic difficulty facing conflict, particularly when it is face to face; and (2) the French have difficulty developing group leadership. These two traits are facets of the relationship to authority and are presumably shared by managers as well.

The French attitude toward authority is determined by basic cultural values that are closely linked to institutional patterns such as class relationships and the educational system. The French conception of authority is absolutist, omnipotent, and universalist. The holder of authority knows no limits to his power and no constraints in exerting it, beyond narrowly interpreted legal ones that in any case are difficult to enforce in a relationship of subordination. Because of its absolute nature, authority cannot be shared or compromised and must remain sovereign, both actually and symbolically. Procedural rules are unnecessary because the authority is absolute and concepts of fairness are as irrelevant as concepts of commutative justice. The idea of checks and balances, of due process, as well as of institutionalized countervailing power or substantive limitations is foreign to it.

This concept of absolutism is both offensive and defensive: offensive because the person who has authority has boundless authority over others, and defensive because authority confers total autonomy and freedom of interference from others. The person who has authority owes no one an account of his or her actions. Individual isolation within strata and isolation between strata allow some defensive power to anyone. Within one's own little sphere of isolation, one can act from one's own will and not by submission to authority of somebody else. Some positive aspects of absolute authority are also retained, although to a lesser degree in lower strata. They consist in the ritualistic aspects linked with belonging in a strata and the social status that it confers.

Seen from below, such a mode of authority is threatening, and exposure to it is to be avoided at any cost. Contact with authority can mean only either abject submissiveness or total conflict. Combined with the other French cultural values of independence, individual autonomy, and search for security, absolute submission is unacceptable and total conflict too risky because of the unequal balance of power. Therefore, subordinates will avoid having to deal directly with the superior in order to avoid face-to-face conflict. Not to do so is to acknowledge one's total dependence on another person. The only other alternative to avoidance is total conflict, which is completely destructive and a losing proposition because of the superior's omnipotence.

Seen from the top, the risk of face-to-face conflict must also be avoided. Since the superior's authority is absolute, it cannot conceivably be challenged, and it is impossible to run even the risk of such a challenge. This has been illustrated by employers' attitudes to unions (Rojot, 1986). For the superiors, it is combined with the other French cultural value of rationality, which implies that people in positions of authority will seek to bring about order, symmetry, and harmony over the environment that they rule and will therefore seek to apply an identical regulation for everyone.

The organizational solution to the dilemma of avoiding face-to-face conflict rests on the creation of rules. From below, a person obeys the rules and thus does not submit to the absolute authority of an individual, thereby protecting his or her independence. From the top, where rules are issued, they confirm higher management's capacity of sovereign power. Those rules are impersonal, which from below reinforce the sense of following an abstract order and not bowing to absolutism; from above follows the rational model of a "one best way" of ruling absolutely over one's domain without having to be bothered to make unnecessary allowances for individual peculiarities. Impersonal rules by necessity imply that people who decide must remain far above those who are affected by their decisions, for they cannot possibly know them well and take their specific needs into account without favoritism. Thus, power is centralized at the top, and below, the impersonal rules define strata of subordinates with precisely defined borders and specific rights and duties.

The end result is Crozier's classic model of the bureaucratic vicious circle, which presents the following features: impersonal rules; centralized decisions; isolated strata of employees; and parallel power relationships, which we have illustrated elsewhere (Rojot, 1990).

Theoretically, the central power is all powerful, but in each stratum, under the conditions of observing the formal behavior prescribed by the impersonal rules, individuals enjoy total protection and independence. Of course, impersonal rules cannot foresee every possible case requiring a specific behavior, the more so in a complex environment. The only possibility to act from the standpoint of the central power is to issue additional rules, which also provide additional shelter inside strata. The rules need to be impersonal; therefore, the power recedes more and more, putting more distance from the knowledge of the elements necessary to take decisions. Men at the top must decide without knowing what the real situation is, for they have no primary knowledge of information, and it is in the interest of the subordinates to hide or manipulate such information. The power of those at the top is therefore useless, and, unavoidably, parallel informal power relationships develop.

Amado, Faucheux, and Laurent (1990) contrast the American and French models of management. Unlike the American model, the French is personalist and social: a system of individuals organized in a social hierarchy that must be managed. The French manager bases his authority on a superior degree of knowledge and competence and therefore centralizes authority and responsibility. The model relies on hierarchical dependence.

Schneider (1985) reviews the literature on the categories defined by Hofstede and by Kluckholn and Strodbeck (1961): relationship to nature, human relationships, truth and reality, human nature, human activity, and attitudes toward time and change. Schneider finds that compared with the U.S. national culture the French national culture has had a larger impact on strategy formulation by enterprises. French culture is characterized along the following dimensions: passive instead of active monitoring of the environment; preference for qualitative over quantitative information; preference for sources of information that are subjective and personal, or that emanate from authorities; preference for a logical analytical approach over mathematical decision models; different sets of priorities that will be developed in terms of importance, urgency, and certainty; and an internal rather than external focus.

Maurice, Sellier, and Silvestre (1982), studying similar enterprises within the same industries in France and Germany, noted intriguing differences between the two nations. The average wage for a blue-collar worker compared to that for a white-collar employee was lower in France than in Germany. White-collar employees were not only better paid but also proportionally more numerous in France. Only 40 percent of French workers against 75 percent in Germany hold a vocational degree. The German foremen were also less numerous than the French. Such differences were explained by the role of continuing education in Germany, based on the alternate system of training between school and plant for "meisters." The German system allows workers to accumulate degrees up to the level of graduate engineer throughout their professional lives. This scale of degrees is a condition for promotion, whereas in France the promotion is granted more as a function of the individual's seniority and potential or initial training. The French training system is narrowly related to mobility and firm specific skills, whereas the German system, with its life-long vocational training, gives access to nationally recognized degrees. It allows interentreprise mobility at various levels of technical job ladders. Conversely, in France, because the training is enterprise specific, inter-enterprise mobility is hampered. Promotion is therefore dependent more on change of status than on moves on a technical ladder. The German foreman, as holder of a technical degree, enjoys more autonomy and prestige than his French equivalent. In turn, both training and mobility are related to organizational features, with a larger span of control for foremen and more multi-skilling for workers in Germany.

Rojot (1981, 1988) has attempted to explain the differences between collective agreements in the United States and in France by the national cultural traits that permeate the legal systems of the two countries. He notes that the differences in the regulation of collective agreements can be explained by the primacy of the individual contract of employment over the collective agreement, the absence of a duty to perform replaced by a duty to pay damages, and the presence of a minimal extended floor of statutory protection in the case of France. Those factors can themselves be traced back to cultural values: In France reigns the absolute primacy of the formal rights of the individual. The only allowable limits to these rights can issue from public policy that is embodied in compulsory provisions for the equal good of all citizens, as imposed by an interventionist central government.

According to Trepo (1975) efforts to introduce Management By Objectives (MBO) in France have failed because of the French fear of face-to-face conflict, the way they view authority, and the way top managers are selected. He demonstrates that even though subordinate managers may vocally ask for more responsibility, in fact they remain passive, looking for protection from above and avoiding a committal to specific objectives. Reciprocally, top managers, who rule autocratically, see the company as a kind of elite school, where to be the boss means to be the most intelligent one and therefore consider that subordinates cannot conceivably have valid ideas to offer. Of course, this does not mean that Management By Objectives or evaluation of performance according to a similar system is not practiced in France—far from it. However, in many cases, the system of MBO as it is applied in practice in companies is only remotely linked to the objectives assigned to it by its original promoters and takes a wholly different meaning, even if its form is apparently respected.

In conclusion, the best way to sum up the influence of culture on management in France is perhaps to quote an experienced personnel manager, editor-in-chief of the *Journal of the Personnel Managers' National Association* (Laurioz, quoted by Rojot, 1989). He attributes the following characteristics to French management: "A quite individualistic national temperament. . . . A style of management which is fairly authoritarian and intuitive, preferably cultivating hierarchy and a pyramid shaped organization. . . . the great length enjoyed by the original degree." However, national culture cannot be confused with automatic behavior conditioning. Cultural reality is complex (Amado, Faucheux, and Laurent, 1990). On the one hand, culture is a central model evolving alternately by a movement of identification and reproduction opposed to a movement of reaction and distancing relative to it. On the other hand, each individual has not only his personality but also his goals and strategies. Culture constitutes a more or less conscious constraint on these strategies, but it will impact different individuals in different ways. There is a big gap between the characteristics of the French culture and the behavior of a given individual French manager in given circumstances.

HUMAN RESOURCE MANAGEMENT AND MANAGERS

Selection

As has been discussed elsewhere (Rojot, 1989a), given that the above definition of cadres is far from being a neatly discriminating one, the question of the number of cadres is also widely debated. For the purposes of this chapter, we retain the concepts used by the Association Générale des Institutions de Retraite des Cadres (AGIRC) and the Association pour l'Emploi des Cadres (APEC), if only because these two organizations issue most of the available recent statistics. AGIRC is the compulsory pension system to which all cadres (and cadres' employers) contribute, beyond the basic Social Security retirement contribution.

Table 4.1
Cadres by Economic Sector as a Percentage of All Employees (APEC-AGIRC definition)

Sector of the Economy	Percentage of Cadres in 1986
Construction	09
Industry	11
Trade	14
Transportation	09
Services	24

Source: Association pour L'Emploi de Cadres, 1991. *Quid des Cadres*, Paris.

APEC is the countrywide placement system for unemployed cadres. Other data that we occasionally use in this chapter come from the National Institute for Statistics and Economic Studies (INSEE), the surveys carried out by the Ministry of Labor (Enquête Structure des Emplois, Enquête Emploi), or private institutes. Therefore, the following figures may not be similar, for the sources may use different definitions of cadres or may not include organizations with less than ten employees or may include the public sector, which is normally out of the scope of the present analysis.

According to the AGIRC figures available for 1989, France's private sector had 1,898,870 cadres. This figure includes a few individuals who technically belong to the categories of supervisory and technical staff and are not granted the status of cadres by collective agreements but are allowed to contribute to the cadres' retirement system.

Unless otherwise mentioned, the figures below are AGIRC or APEC (Association for the Employment of Cadres) figures, used by courtesy of APEC, and are issued mostly from the *Quid des Cadres*, edited by the APEC and published in 1991.

Even though the labor force as a whole decreased during the 1980–85 period, the number of cadres increased during this period, at an average annual rate of slightly above 2 percent a year. Therefore, the cadres now represent 15.5 percent of total employment in the private sector against 12.5 percent in 1982. Cadres are present in unequal numbers in enterprises with important sectoral differences as illustrated in Tables 4.1 and 4.2.

These figures, however, average out some wide discrepancies. For instance, within services, the ratio of cadres to all other employees averages out at 24 percent but is much higher than average in banking, insurance, and consulting

Table 4.2
Percentage of Cadres Employed by Major Economic Sector in 1986

Sector of the Economy	Percentage of All Cadres in 1986
Construction	06.0
Industry	33.5
Trade	18.5
Transportation	07.0
Services	35.0

Source: Association pour L'Emploi de Cadres, 1991. *Quid des Cadres*, Paris.

and engineering firms and much lower than average in consumer-oriented services. In the same way, in high-technology industries, it is much higher than the 11 percent average. Moreover, this ratio is lower in medium-size enterprises than in both small and large enterprises (Table 4.3). Presumably, this reflects economies of scale that increase up to a certain limit with size and then decrease while size still increases because of specialization, decentralization, and growing functional and research and development departments (Blau and Schoenherr, 1971). The fact that about 38 percent of all cadres are employed in small-size enterprises reflects the important part played by small enterprises in the French economic structure (Table 4.4). Finally, there is also a geographical influence. Cadres are overrepresented in the Paris area where 37 percent of them are located; this reflects the high degree of centralization of the French society. Presumably many headquarters of companies, where a large number of cadres are employed,

Table 4.3
Cadres as a Percentage of All Employees by Size of Enterprise for Enterprises above Ten Employees

Number of employees	Percentage of Cadres in 1986
11 - 49	14.5
50 - 499	11.0
>500	13.5

Source: Association pour L'Emploi de Cadres, 1991. *Quid des Cadres*, Paris.

Table 4.4
Percentage of All Cadres Employed According to Size of Enterprise above Ten Employees, 1986

Number of Employees in Enterprise	Percentage of All Cadres
11 - 49	38
50 - 499	36
>500	26

Source: Association pour L'Emploi de Cadres, 1991. *Quid des Cadres*, Paris.

are established near the central political and administrative locus of power (APEC, 1991).

The APEC study also records the allocation of cadres within the main functions of the enterprise. Two effects are notable: a concentration of research and development cadres in the Paris area, probably reflecting a concentration of high-technology and consulting firms; and a size effect as illustrated in Table 4.5 (APEC, 1991).

The cadre population is older than the labor force in general, with 42 percent of the employed cadres aged less than forty years against 55 percent of the labor force (Table 4.6). This is due to at least two factors. First, cadres have a longer schooling before entering the labor force, to which must be added the compulsory year of national service for males. Second, many individuals do not enter the labor force as cadres but are later promoted into this status after a variable number of years of service in other positions.

The trend over the past ten years has been toward an increase in the number

Table 4.5
Distribution of Cadres by Functional Area and Size of Undertaking in 1986 (percentage)

	Size of Undertaking			
	<50	50 - 500	>500	All
General Management	16.0	06.5	02.0	11.0
Technical	28.0	34.0	57.0	34.0
Administrative	31.0	27.0	21.5	28.5
Marketing, Sales	25.0	32.5	19.5	26.5

Source: Association pour L'Emploi de Cadres, 1991. *Quid des Cadres*, Paris.

Table 4.6
Percentage of Cadres by Age and Gender in 1986

Age	Men	Women
< 30	10	16
30 - 34	13	16
35 - 39	17	18
40 - 44	19	18
45 - 49	15	12
50 - 54	13	09
55 - 59	09	07
> 60	04	04

Source: Association pour L'Emploi de Cadres, 1991. *Quid des Cadres*, Paris.

of cadres below the age of thirty and between forty and fifty. Retirement can now legally occur at sixty and can actually be taken at this age under certain conditions related to earlier contributions into the system. Forced early retirements before sixty, under workforce restructuring social plans, have taken place in large numbers, although they have probably had less impact on cadres than on the labor force in general. These factors probably help explain why the average age of cadres, which now stands at forty-two, has changed little over the past ten years, despite the increase in younger cadres (APEC, 1991).

The number of women among cadres increases consistently but slowly and remains low when compared with their labor force rate of participation in general. The total labor force participation rate of men decreased from 55.6 to 51.0 percent from 1970 to 1987, while the total activity rate for women increased from 29.4 to 35.9 percent. During the same period, the average rate of participation moved up slightly from 42.2 to 43.3 percent, resulting in women representing 43.5 percent of the civilian working population in 1987 and 42.1 percent of wage earners (Eurostat, 1989). Nevertheless, women represented only 22 percent of the cadres in 1988 (21.5 percent in 1987), up from 17 percent in 1980.

As shown in Table 4.7 the average level of education of cadres has steadily increased. The older generations, where the percentage of self-educated was relatively high, have been replaced by younger individuals who are more likely to be holders of formal degrees. This trend has been stimulated in recent years by lowering the retirement age to sixty and by the consequences of social plans in case of economic restructuring.

Until a few years ago, up to 50 percent of cadres were self-educated, with,

Table 4.7
Initial Education of the Cadre Population (percentage)

Initial Training	1982	1985	1988
Grandes Ecoles	21	21	21
University's Master or higher	21	23	26
Baccalaureate plus 2 years	09	10	11
Baccalaureate alone	16	15	13
Other (less schooling)	33	31	29

Source: Association pour L'Emploi de Cadres, 1991. *Quid des Cadres*, Paris.

of course, an indeterminate amount of continuing education provided during their careers. This is probably no longer true. Moreover, direct access to the level of cadre for new entrants in the labor force with a higher education has generally become more restricted (Rojot, 1989a).

The French educational system is relatively complex. It can be characterized by the parallel existence of several systems of post-baccalaureate educational tracks. In terms of number of years of schooling, the French baccalaureate is generally considered to be the equivalent of an American high school degree. However, it is granted not by acquiring credits over the years, but by passing an examination in the final year of schooling. Success in that examination conditions access to higher education.

In principle, universities are open to all holders of the baccalaureate, and the selection occurs at the end of the first-year exam. Selection for the *grandes écoles* occurs through competitive exam, prepared in special post-baccalaureate classes. However, the actual picture is even more complex, for some pre-baccalaureate institutions (lycées) and the Institutes of Technology grant degrees in technology to those who have had two years of schooling after the baccalaureate.

In general, cadres show a higher degree of initial training in large enterprises. The percentage of cadres with initial training below a level equivalent to the baccalaureate plus two years remains quite high in middle- and small-size enterprises, whereas it falls to 37 percent only in enterprises that employ more than 500 employees. The latter seek to recruit graduates from the *grandes écoles*. They represent 50 percent of all their cadres, whereas only 13 percent are university graduates. The comparable figures for all enterprises (above ten employees) were, respectively, 21, 26, and 53 percent. There were also wide variations according to the sectors of the economy concerned. The percentage of self-educated cadres was still significantly higher in trade and services (47 percent) than in industry (33 percent). Not surprisingly, holders of an engineering degree represented almost 50 percent of the cadres in industry against 14 percent in other sectors. Conversely, graduates of business schools represented 25 percent of the cadres in trade and services against 5 percent in other sectors (APEC, 1991).

Most of those who become managers receive an initial training in fields that are not necessarily related to management, but may instead be in engineering, law, public administration, and so on. Although vastly improved and having made headways, both in the universities and in the *écoles* system, some, funded by the Chambers of Commerce, have reached a certain degree of prominence. Nonetheless, training in management per se still has ground to gain in France (Rojot, 1989a).

In terms of family background, cadres are predominantly sons of cadres. A 1977 study (Groux, 1983) reports the following figures, using a broader definition of cadre than the one given above, notably because it encompasses the public service and in particular includes teachers. In all, 72.4 percent of cadres were sons of cadres on the average. In the more restricted category of *cadres superieurs* (upper level of cadres), 52.4 percent were sons of *cadres superieurs* themselves, 8 percent sons of employer-owners, 20 percent of *cadres moyens* (with lower status than *cadres supérieurs*), 6.9 percent of white-collar employees, and 8.7 percent of workers. Among the *cadres moyens*, out of 100 sons of *cadres moyens*, 29.9 percent were *cadres moyens*, 34.9 percent were *cadres supérieurs*, 5.7 percent employer-owners or self-employed employed professionals, 8.2 percent white-collar employees, and 17.3 percent workers. Groux (1983) adds that in 1975 30.4 percent of students in the universities were sons of *cadres supérieurs* against 12 percent of sons of manual workers. For the same year and according to the same definitions of the socioeconomic groups, *cadres supérieurs* and workers represented, respectively, 6.7 percent and 43.7 percent of the labor force. A son of a cadre was 12.5 times more likely to become a student than the son of a worker; this differential tended to increase with time. The same phenomenon was accentuated at the level of the *grandes écoles* where, in the top nine engineering schools between 1962 and 1975 the percentage of the sons of *cadres supérieurs* had increased from 40.9 to 57 percent and the percentage of sons of workers had decreased from 5 to 2 percent. It is added (Groux, 1983) that the universities and the lower strata of small *grandes écoles* insure the reproduction of the social group of *cadres moyens*, whereas the top *grandes écoles* insure the reproduction of the social group of the *cadres dirigeants* (the top stratum of *cadres supérieurs*).

Dominant Selection Techniques

Before reviewing the common selection techniques, let us note that the APEC study shows interesting data on the pool out of which cadres are recruited. Out of every 100 cadres hired in 1988, 26 were becoming cadres by internal promotion and 74 were hired on the labor market as cadres, while 22 percent were new entrants with a higher education degree.

Relatively little is known about the selection techniques used by companies.

A wide-ranging survey has not been carried out recently on the subject. From the table of contents of the numerous textbooks on personnel management published recently as well as from small nonrepresentative surveys carried out by trade publications, some generalities can be made. However, it is clear that the sophistication of the tools used depends largely on the size of the enterprise concerned, as is reported elsewhere (Rojot, 1989a). A surprising factor is a high use of graphology (the "scientific" analysis of handwriting to predict personality and performance).

A 1985 APEC study of a sample of eighty enterprises concludes that each enterprise constitutes a specific case, although it points toward an ideal type of selection process, characterized by a set of successive steps initiated by the decision to proceed to external recruitment. A first elimination of the candidates, either spontaneous, presented by the state placement system, or resulting from an ad published in a general or trade newspaper, occurs at the stage of reading the curriculum vitae. A second filter results from a graphological analysis. The candidates are then submitted to tests (aptitude, personality, or intelligence), resulting in an additional elimination. Then those who remained under consideration are convened again for filling a biographical questionnaire and interviews. At this stage very few candidates remain. The final decision occurs on the basis of an additional "in-depth" graphological analysis and top-level interviews as well as reference checks.

Apparently, campus recruitment and job conventions are rarely used. Headhunters, assessment centers, and the like are reserved for the top managers positions.

Compensation

In 1988, according to a survey by a weekly magazine carried out in enterprises with over 100 employees (APEC, 1991), cadres between forty and forty-five years of age earned a yearly average of 450,000 FF (US$90,000 at November 1990 rates and US$78,947 at April 1991 rates). For the convenience of computation, the November 1990 rates are henceforth used in this chapter. The average pay of graduates of the fifteen top *grandes écoles* was 340,000 FF (US$68,000). For other *grandes écoles* or holders or a university master's degree (or above), the pay was 260,000 FF (US$52,000). The effect of the degree seems to increase with age and not the opposite, as would be expected. The pay differential between the two extreme categories is 30 percent at twenty years of age and reaches 80 percent at retirement.

On the average, a chief executive officer in the same sample earned 1 million FF (US$200,000), a division manager 492,000 FF (US$98,400), and a production engineer 271,000 FF (US$54,200). For a similar job title and degree, both seniority and the size of the enterprise have a very significant effect. However, the wage spread is quite wide for individual cases. Some chief executive officers of large firms earn several million francs, but in terms of the great majority of cadres wages are within a narrow range. In all 56 percent of them earn between 120,000 and 240,000 FF (US$24,000 to 48,000), and 81 percent earn below

Table 4.8
Yearly Pay of Cadres by Gender in 1986

Yearly Wage	Men	Women
<120,400	08	20
120,400 - 160,500	16	27
160,500 - 200,600	21	24
200,600 - 240,700	17	13
240,700 - 361,000	24	12
361,000 - 481,400	08	03
>481,400	06	01

Note: Pay in French francs.

Source: Association pour L'Emploi de Cadres, 1991. *Quid des Cadres*, Paris.

300,000 FF (US$60,000). The median wage for 1988 was 199,686 FF (US$39,937).

According to another study with a different sample, new graduate entrants recruited as cadres in large enterprises (which recruit mostly *grandes écoles* graduates commanding higher entry wages) earned on the average 134,000 FF, which reflects the relative lack of some highly qualified cadres in specific sectors.

There is a notable differential owing to sex (see Table 4.8). This differential is partly explained by the fact that women cadres are on the average younger than men and tend to congregate in jobs with lower pay. If the public sector was added, the effect would be even more marked, for there are more women cadres than men cadres in the public sector and pay is noticeably lower.

A debate has arisen concerning the alleged loss (or increase) of the purchasing power of cadres (Rojot, 1989a). Data from APEC tends to show, on average, that purchasing power has remained stable over a ten-year period. In 1979 the median pay for cadres was 100,808 FF: in 1987, it reached 192,242 FF, an increase of 91 percent. Over the same period inflation was estimated at 90 percent. Therefore, the real level of pay decreased slightly for cadres, whereas it increased slightly for blue-collar workers and more markedly for white-collar employees over the same period. Other data (Rojot, 1978, 1989a) tend to reveal that, in the longer run, cadres have noticeably lost ground to other wage earner categories.

These figures reflect only averages, however. Data provided by the Hay Group (Rojot, 1990) show that, in 1987, 37 percent of the companies sampled granted only individualized pay increases to their cadres, up from 24 percent in 1986 and 18 percent in 1984. However, the trend seemed to stabilize in 1988 and 1989. Companies that have already adopted a system of individualization of cadres' pay keep it, but few new ones adopt it. Among companies sampled, 63 percent granted a mix of general and individualized increases and 75 percent gave bonuses linked to objectives in 48 percent of cases.

Finally, after the reform of 1986, gain-sharing plans have become increasingly popular (Rojot, 1991). In 1985, 1,303 gain-sharing plans were in effect against, respectively, 2,162, 2,630, and 4,600 for 1986, 1987, and 1988. Their number is expected to grow again. The average share of gains was 4,989 FF, representing 4.1 percent on the average of the wage bill. Cadres were allocated 2.32 and 2.25 times more than blue- and white-collar employees, respectively.

Managerial Performance Appraisal

Performance appraisal does not exactly follow the traditional pattern of objectives jointly and contractually set with clear rules to be applied. However, this does not mean that performance appraisal will not follow a useful purpose. Bypassing the formal communications structure, establishing personal relationships, or providing information used for self-guidance, for example, constitute positive side effects of such a system. From the negative standpoint, however, the system can be manipulated and become a stake in a game where one tries to avoid the other's influence and to acquire power by subtly storing materials for building up a case to be used when needs arise. Finally, the performance appraisal instrument is powerful enough that, in a number of cases, under the influence of the dominant managerial theories, it is applied to some degree according to its initial purpose.

An APEC survey (APEC, 1991) notes that 80 percent of the large enterprises that answered the survey had formalized appraisal procedures, with the appraisal most often taking place during a meeting between superior and subordinate. Therefore, the range can go from the highly formalized MBO with forms filled and stored, to a simple meeting with a very general discussion. According to the same survey, the criteria used to appraise cadres were very diversified, as can be seen in Table 4.9.

Management Development

Continuing education is important in France. It constitutes an essential feature of modernization, by facilitating occupational mobility and therefore decreasing unemployment. Complex legislative provisions allow individuals to take paid educational leave for their own purposes. In addition, there is a statutory obligation, that enterprises must allocate 1.2 percent of their wage bill to training, under penalty of being taxed in the same amount. The actual amount spent by enterprises is now about twice the compulsory minimum.

Multiple institutions provide this training, most often under the guise of short programs with specific skills improvement and no degree granted. However, innovative experiments exist. These institutions include the universities; the *écoles* of all types; consultants and private "schools"; or the enterprises themselves organizing in-company training. The quality of the programs varies from excellent to fraudulent. Several governmental efforts have yet to bring clarity to what remains a very profitable quasi-jungle.

Table 4.9
Criteria for Cadres' Performance Appraisal

Criteria	Percent of Cases Used
Ability to command	60
Ability to decide	60
Speed of intervention	60
Capacity to fulfill commitments and timeliness	60
Sense of the enterprise	50
Capacity to convince	50
Quality of contact	70
Creativity-Proposals	60
Competence	45
Net income	40

Source: Association pour L'Emploi de Cadres, 1991. *Quid des Cadres*, Paris.

Labor Relations

Cadres, as any wage earner in the private sector in France, enjoy the full protection of the extensive labor law, including a full right to join or not to join unions, a right that is constitutionally protected (Despax and Rojot, 1987). In practice, however, this right often seems more theoretical than actual, at least in the private sector.

The unionization of cadres has been discussed in more detail elsewhere (Rojot, 1978, 1989a). The general trend has been aptly summarized by Groux (1983) who notes that a cadre who wants to be active in the union movement will appear as a "strange being" to his fellows cadres. The situation can be outlined in the following propositions: The rate of unionization among cadres grew slowly between the 1960s and the late 1970s. It remains markedly lower than the general rate of unionization, which is itself among the lowest in the EEC (Rojot, 1989b)— between 9 and 12 percent of all wage earners. Unionization is concentrated in the public sector or among low-ranking cadres, or cadres "who do not have much to expect from their company" (Groux, 1983) in the private sector. Cadres can be members either of a union center restricted to cadres or technical staff (CGC) or to the cadre organizations within the four main employee unions (UCC-CFDT, UGICT-CGT, UGICA-CFDT, UCI-FO). For many reasons (Rojot, 1978, 1989a), cadres' strikes are not practical; cadres' unions show little militancy beyond statements issued at the national level and collective bargaining at the industry level.

Cadres are covered by collective agreements. As mentioned earlier, as employees they enjoy the full protection of labor law; therefore the collective agreements signed by the employers' associations as well as with individual employers apply fully to them. Furthermore, specific cadres-level collective agreements may grant them supplementary benefits.

CONCLUSIONS AND TRENDS

In the period between the end of World War II and the 1960s, cadres became a social group with distinct features and a privileged status around a role model of competence and elitism. They still constitute such a group, though not a well-limited one. However, as their number has increased, the differential in wage and nonwage benefits which existed to their profit has narrowed. They have also been hit by unemployment, though less so than other categories of wage earners. Finally, the divisions within their group seem increasingly visible in terms of status.

Crozier (1978) had noted that the "malaise des cadres" much talked about in the 1970s was in fact the result of the passage from a model of the role of cadre "based on loyalty, compromise, and especially a tendency to limit communication that guaranteed the manager both security and power" to a model "based on rapid exchange of information, competition and collaboration." By the mid-1980s the passage was obviously made and more or less willfully accepted by the cadres, probably under the acknowledgment of the effects of the 1973 and 1979 oil crises. Employers had ceased trading unquestioned loyalty for high status and full job security and now demanded performance in addition to loyalty in a competitive environment where unemployment was a possibility (Rojot, 1989a).

What are the trends for the 1990s? A surge in unionization is unlikely (Rojot, 1989a). It also seems unlikely that the "fuzzy set" of cadres will explode because of the role that the group plays in French society and the vested interests of its members to its continuation. Finally, it seems very unlikely that the *grandes écoles* model will become less dominant. The two determining factors in the emergence of a new model are likely to be top management strategies in the area of human resources management regarding the cadres' involvement in elaborating and implementing policies, and the impact of new technologies and new methods of work organization on the jobs of the cadres and all other employees (Rojot, 1989c). Both elements are indeterminate at the present time.

REFERENCES

Amado, G., Faucheux, C., and Laurent, A. 1990. "Changements organisationnels et réalités culturelles," In J. F., Chanlat, ed., *L'individu dans l'organisation, les dimensions oubliées.* Québec: Laval University Press.

Association pour l'Emploi de Cadres. 1991. *Quid des Cadres*, Paris: APEC.

Berle, A. A., and Means, G. C. 1932. *The Modern Corporation and Private Property.* New York: Macmillan Co.

Birnbaum, P. et al. 1977. *Les sommets de l'Etat: Essai sur l'élite au pouvoir en France.* Paris: Seuil.

Blau, P. M., and Schoenherr, R. A. 1971. *The Structure of Organizations.* New York: Basic Books.

Boltanski L. 1982. *Les cadres.* Paris: Les éditions de Minuit.

Bourdieu, P. 1979. *La distinction.* Paris: Les editions de Minuit.

Crozier, M. 1963. *Le phénoméne bureaucratique.* Paris: Editions du Seuil.

———. 1978. "Attitudes of French Managers Regarding the Administration of Their Firms," *International Studies of Management and Organization* 8 (3).

Crozier, M., and Friedberg, E. 1977. *L'acteur et le système.* Paris: Editions du Seuil.

Despax, M., and Rojot, J. 1987. *Labour Law and Industrial Relations in France.* Deventer: Kluwer.

d'Iribarne, P. 1989. *La Logique de l'honneur.* Paris: Editions du Seuil.

Farmer, R. N., and Richman, B. M. 1965. *Comparative Management and Economic Progress.* Homewood, Ill.: Richard D. Irwin.

Gonzales, R. F., and McMillan, C., Jr. 1961. "The Universality of American Management Philosophy," *Journal of the Academy of Management* 4(1): 33–41.

Gouldner, A. W. 1979. *The Future of Intellectuals and the Rise of the New Class.* London: Seabury Press.

Groux, G. 1983. *Les Cadres.* Paris: Editions La Découverte/Maspero.

Haire, M., Ghiselli, E. E., and Porter, L. W. 1966. *Managerial Thinking: An International Study.* New York: John Wiley and Sons.

Harbison, F., and Myers, C. A. 1959. *Management in the Industrial World.* New York: McGraw-Hill Co.

Hofstede, G. H. 1980. *Culture's Consequences. International Differences in Work Related Values.* Beverly Hills, Calif.: Sage Publications.

———. 1980. "Motivation, Leadership and Organisation: Do American Theories Apply Abroad?" *Organizational Dynamics* (Summer).

Kerr, C., Dunlop, J. T., Harbison, F. H., and Myers, C. A. 1960. *Industrialism and Industrial Man.* Cambridge, Mass.: Harvard University Press.

Kluckholn, F. R., and Strodtbeck, F. L. 1961. *Variations in Value Orientations.* Evanston, Ill.: Row, Peterson.

Kroeber, A. L., and Kluckholn, C. 1952. *Culture: A Critical Review of Concepts and Definitions.* Peabody Museum Papers 47 (1). Cambridge, Mass.: Harvard University Press.

Laurioz, J. "Specificities of the French Socio-Economic Scene." *Personnel,* 76–79.

Maurice, M., Sellier, F., and Silvestre, J. J., 1982. *Politique d'Education et Organisation Industrielle en France et en Allemagne.* Paris: Presses Universitaires de France.

Negandhi, A. R., and Estafen, B. D. 1965 (December). "A Research Model to Determine the Applicability of American Management Know-How in Differing Cultures and/or Environments." *Academy of Management Journal* 8 (4).

Rojot, J. 1978 (Fall). "Evolutionary Trends among the French Managerial Group." *International Studies of Management and Organisation* 7 (3).

———. 1981. "L'influence de Principes issus du Contexte Social Général sur la Réglementation des Accords Collectifs en France et aux Etats-Unis." In *Systèmes de Relations Industrielles, Thèse soutenue pour l'obtention du Doctorat d'Etat.* Université de Rennes.

———. 1986, (January). "The Development of French Employers' Policies Towards Unions." *Labour and Society* 11 (1).

———. 1988. "Droits collectifs et droits individuels, les situations françaises, américaines et anglaises." In R. Blouin et al., eds., *La Charte des droits et les Relations Industrielles*. Quebec: Laval University Press.

———. 1989a. "France." In M. J. Roomkin, ed., *Managers as Employees*. Oxford: Oxford University Press.

———. 1989b. "The Myth of French Exceptionalism." In Barbash J. and Barbash K., eds., *Theories and Concepts in Comparative Industrial Relations*. Columbia: University of South Carolina Press.

———. 1989c. "National Experiences in Labour Market Flexibility." In OECD, ed., *Labour Market Flexibility, Trends in Enterprises*. Paris: OECD.

———. 1990. "Human Resources Management in France." In R. Pieper, ed., *Human Resources Management: An International Comparison*. Berlin: Walter de Gruyter and Co.

———. Forthcoming. "*L'Intéréssement*." Communication of the Second Annual Congress of L'Association Française de Gestion des Resources Humaines.

Schneider, S. C. 1985 (July). "Strategy Formulation: The Impact of National Culture: The Case of France." *Pace University Working Papers*, no. 48.

Suleiman, E. 1979. *Les Elites en France, Grands Corps et Grandes Ecoles*. Paris: Editions du Seuil. Translated from *Elites in French Society; the Politics of Survival*. Princeton, N.J.: Princeton University Press, 1978.

Trepo, G. 1975, (March). "Mise en place d'une D.P.O.: Le rôle crucial de la direction." *Direction et Gestion*, 1, and "Participation: un douloureux constat d'échec, *Entreprise*, no. 1020.

5

GERMANY

Rick Molz

Management in Germany today reflects the history and cultural values of the German people, as well as modern management theory. Because of the rapid and unforeseen unification of the former states of East and West Germany in October 1990, this chapter is limited to the study of managerial behavior in the former West Germany. The unification of the German states has created a new economic superpower that is composed of two disparate halves. The half made up of the former West Germany has flourished within the free market and capitalistic Western alliance, while the Eastern half has struggled to achieve even moderate success by Western standards, although it has traditionally led the Eastern European economies.

The economic and managerial changes resulting from the unification of Germany are difficult to forecast with any degree of accuracy. Minor squabbles are already emerging over repatriation of property confiscated forty years ago by the former communist government in East Germany, alternate methods of privatization of enterprise, and protection of private assets. These are primarily macro-level changes and are unlikely to affect the fundamentals of organizational behavior and management in the former West Germany. The same is not true of the former East Germany. Since the former East German economy is widely expected to be absorbed and undergo a basic transformation toward the standards of West Germany, the current managerial practices, behavioral norms, and human resource approaches of East German firms are likely to undergo fundamental changes. The degree to which East German managerial practices will continue is unknown. It is anticipated that the West German practices will become more prevalent in the former East German nation.

Germany is one of the leading industrialized nations of the European Common Market. The Deutsche Bundesbank is generally considered to be one of the strongest central banks in the world, which has led to a very strong deutsche

Table 5.1
GNP, West and East Germany (billion U.S. dollars)

	1960	1970	1980	1985	1990
West Germany	379.8	592.7	771.4	809.2	
					1,170.0
East Germany	99.0	134.9	179.4	197.1	

Source: 1960–85: Central Intelligence Agency, *Handbook for Economic Statistics*, 1989; 1990: *The Economist* Intelligence Unit, World Outlook, 1991.

mark. This core economic strength, combined with traditional German excellence in engineering and manufacturing, has put Germany in a very favorable position among the world's economies. Table 5.1 shows changes in gross national product since the end of World War II, while Table 5.2 presents the same information as percentage changes. Comparative data are also shown for the former East German state. Total employment in 1990 in the united Germany stood at about 38,270,000 full-time positions (*New York Times*, October 23, 1990), although the country has experienced periods of relatively high unemployment. Table 5.3 shows the percentage changes of the workforce unemployed since 1960.

This study was performed through database and literature review. In addition, on-site field interviews with managers in eleven West German firms were conducted to enrich and provide current case examples. The firms were from a variety of industries, including private, public, and mixed ownership. They ranged in size from only a few hundred employees to over 200,000. Table 5.4 presents complete information on the field research panel that was included in the study. For reasons of both preserving confidentiality and facilitating candor, quotes are not directly attributed. The field research portion of the study took place between October 1989 and January 1990. Each individual was interviewed in person.

The interviews focused on entry-level, midlevel, and senior managers of the

Table 5.2
GNP, Average Annual Growth Rate, West and East Germany (percentage)

	1961-70	1971-80	1981-85	1990
West Germany	4.6%	2.8%	1.3%	
				4.0%
East Germany	3.1%	2.8%	1.9%	

Source: 1961–85: Central Intelligence Agency, *Handbook for Economic Statistics*, 1989; 1990: *The Economist* Intelligence Unit, World Outlook, 1991.

Table 5.3
Unemployment by Percentage of Labor Force, West Germany

1960	1970	1980	1985	1990
1.1	0.6	4.0	9.3	7.9*

* Unified Germany, including those classified as employed but not working.

Source: 1960–85: Central Intelligence Agency, *Handbook for Economic Statistics*, 1989; 1990: *New York Times*, October 23, 1990.

firms. Managers are defined as individuals who control either human, physical, or capital resources. Entry-level managers are those who were hired directly for managerial training programs or who were expected to begin working under the guidance of a more senior manager. Entry-level managers also included individuals who were promoted into management from a nonmanagerial position. These descriptors are consistent with Roomkin's (1989) definition of managers.

German law and tradition have a formal definition of upper level managers, which fits into the above definitions. The top level is the *Spitzenfuehrungskrafte*, which is composed of top or senior managers who sit on the managing board, or *Vorstand*. The second level is the *Leitende Angestellte*, which is made up of upper and middle managers. This group includes vice-presidents and department heads (Witte, 1989).

This chapter includes sections on the cultural values and evolution of management in Germany, human resource management, and projections for the future of management in Germany.

CULTURAL VALUES AND THE EVOLUTION OF MANAGEMENT IN GERMANY

This section discusses the history of cultural values in Germany and their importance in the evolution of management.

Cultural Values

In a study conducted in the early 1950s, Heinz Hartmann analyzed the transition of German values through the period beginning with the Nazi ascension to power to the beginning of the rebirth of the German economy. Hartmann (1970) believed that three key values survived the devastation of the German socioeconomic system: the *Beruf*, or professional calling; a strong belief in the sanctity of private property; and the existence of a social elite. He also described the disappearance of an important element of the German economy, that of the *Unternehmer* or procurator, who was legally responsible for representing the company and its judicial entry into the public registry. The *Unternehmer* held

Table 5.4
Participants in Research Study

	INDIVIDUAL	TITLE	COMPANY
1.	Rolf Strauss	General Manager	Cascan GMBH
2.	Hans-Wolfgang Pfeifer	Vortsitzender Instandsetzungs-betriebe	Frankfurter Allgemeine Zeitung
3.	Alexander Bautzmann	Geschaftsfuhrer	Deutsche Service-Gesellschaft der Bahn GMBH
4.	Rainer Wolf	Vice President	Citibank AG
5.	Richard Meister	Director of Personnel	Deutsche Bundesbahn
6.	Gundolf Praast	President	Deutsche SPAR
7.	Werner von Swietochowski	Manager of Sales	Landesbank Rheinland-Pfalz
8.	Bruno Broking	Geschaftsfuhrer	MIP Instand-setungsbertiebe
9.	Othmar Christ	Fuhrungskrafteen-wicklung	Hoechst
10.	Gottfried Langenstein	Director, International Relations	ZDF Zweites Deutsches Fernsehen
11.	Clemens von Arnim	Sprecher	Chemetall, GMBH

Table 5.4 (continued)

	LOCATION	INDUSTRY	# OF EMPLOYEES
1.	Wiesbaden	Pharmeceutical Marketing	450
2.	Frankfurt	Publishing, Informational Databases	1300
3.	Frankfurt	Railroad services	3350
4.	Frankfurt	Investment and commercial banking	550
5.	Frankfurt	National railroad	235,000
6.	Frankfurt	Supermarket cooperative	40 direct 30,000 in franchises
7.	Mainz	Savings Bank	330
8.	Mainz	Heavy industrial and military equipment refurbishing	5000
9.	Frankfurt	Chemical Manufacturing	165,000
10.	Mainz	Television broadcasting	4000
11.	Frankfurt	Specialty chemical manufacturing	1400

an important paternalistic role in the formulation and growth of companies prior to the Nazi period. This official was personally responsible for molding the enterprise to benefit the public good and to be sensitive to the workers' rights. The *Unternehmer* was effectively replaced in the postwar era by the managing board (*Vorstand*) below. According to Hartmann, three German managerial values emerged in the early 1950s; pride in work, paternalism, and service to the commonweal.

The discussions with the research panel confirmed an evolution from Hartmann's 1950 assessment of cultural values. Traditional German cultural values have found their way into many aspects, of industry and management. There are frequent symbolic references in the history of the German people to the German Folk and the responsibility of the greater society for the common man. This responsibility has come to be shared by the German state, government, and social institutions. These social institutions include, among others, industry, churches, and educational organizations. In many instances the line between these institutions and the state is ambiguous. For example, many churches receive direct financial support from the state, because the churches actively implement government social programs, such as basic education and child care. Industry has many responsibilities for the common man, and these values have been institutionalized in workers' rights. Industry also has the responsibility to implement or administer certain social programs, which in other societies might be left to the government. Since these programs reflect core German values, the expectation of the commercial and private sector to carry out these tasks is not viewed as an imposition, as might be the case in some other market economies. This reciprocal responsibility for the common good between the common man and various social institutions is termed service to the commonweal.

German society places a strong value on the rights of workers and the guarantee of certain social benefits for the workers. These concepts are consistent with Hartmann's view of paternalism (James, 1989). Today, these social benefits include the right to an education, health care, liberal annual paid vacations, retirement pensions, disability programs, and others. The necessity for these programs is not viewed as an unwarranted imposition on managerial prerogatives, but as the accepted manner of delivering benefits to the German Folk. These social values are held by managers as well as workers, and represent a paternalistic commitment to the commonweal as identified by Hartmann.

Hartmann also identified pride in work as an emerging value. This concept has found its way into the workplace as a personal emphasis on professionalism and quality. German workers are viewed as skilled artisans. As such, they study the theoretical and practical aspects of their work. Most will undertake a long apprenticeship, and after several years they will become recognized as "masters" in their chosen profession or skill area. This long and arduous path to full membership in a craft has several outcomes. First, workers take great pride in their work. Even workers on a factory assembly line undertake this kind of training, and take pride in the product they assemble. Second, workers tend to stay in their profession, not moving around from one profession to another.

Third, the concept of the master craftsman legitimizes the position of both workers and management as having a professional commitment to their area of expertise. This encourages respect for individual contributors to the enterprise.

Two cultural values, as Hartmann states, survived the war and the rebirth of the German economy: a strong emphasis on private property and the existence of a social elite. No members of the research panel identified these values.

Respect for privacy parallels a respect for law in Germany. Within this context, respect for property continues but in a communitarian view of property tempered by the commitment to the commonweal. Within the context of respect for privacy and the law, if the commonweal requires that an individual forsake private property, than such sacrifice is expected (Allen, 1987).

The research panel agreed that Germany has a less important social elite than any other nation with an Anglo-Saxon heritage. While this elite may have existed and been influential prior to the rise of the Nazis, it was so completely coopted by the National Socialists to be discredited after the war, and was effectively shut out from further influence as the economy was rebuilt.

The concept of the *Beruf*, or a calling in a profession, continues to be important in the context of German management. Many of the members of the research panel stressed the dignity and an individual's honor of life-long commitment to the profession of management and administration.

Another important evolutionary element that Hartmann failed to predict was the significant influence of American values on German management. The impact of the Marshall Plan and the presence of hundreds of thousands of U.S. troops on German soil cannot be overlooked. Since many American companies developed commercial contacts in the postwar rebirth of the German economy, the American influence on postwar Germany is undeniable (Berghahn, 1986; James, 1989).

The Evolution of Management

Following World War II, Germany was a defeated, occupied, devastated country. The economy was rebuilt through the efforts of the German people, with help from the Marshall Plan. During this period, the power of today's managers and industrialists became institutionalized. This emerging managerial power and influence became specialized and focused on the task of rebuilding the nation's economy and industrial capacity. Managers have had less influence in the postwar years, being restricted today to the development of the economy, export and import policies, and the nature of the workplace.

Currently, management is considered one of many influential groups in West Germany. Among the few prominent business leaders of recent years was Alfred Herrhausen, the former head of Deutsche Bank AG. Herrhausen, who was a close friend of Chancellor Helmut Kohl, was assassinated by a terrorist group in November 1989 and was allegedly targeted because of his influence over national economic policy.

German enterprise and managers are often stereotyped as being bureaucratic and authoritarian. In a comparative study of British, French, and German firms,

Lawrence (1980) reported that the German firms were the least bureaucratic, as measured by compartmentalization and hierarchy. They placed relatively less significance on the administrative aspects of enterprise, focusing more on engineering and production. In essence, the German firms kept administration "in its place," as a support to the real mission of the firm, producing goods or services that consumers wished to purchase.

The Germans themselves, and not just outsiders, consider German managers and enterprises to be authoritarian. Lawrence's study found, however, that individual managers would almost universally accept this assessment of German management in general, but deny it applied to their own managerial behavior. This finding was supported by the research panel. Lawrence argues that the German value of striving to attain the commonweal is manifested in the readiness of individuals to accept and carry out legitimate directives from above. As a result, managers carry out orders from a central authority, which can easily be defined as authoritarian, while the individual manager may see himself as merely making decisions to contribute to the betterment of the commonweal.

In 1973 the West German Federal Economics Ministry commissioned the American consulting firm Booz, Allen and Hamilton to prepare a report on German management. Not surprisingly, the report was critical of many aspects of German management that did not conform to American practices. The most basic criticism was that German companies tended to be person- rather than system-oriented (Lawrence, 1980). This is consistent with the cultural history of the *Unternehmer*.

The *Unternehmer*, and its successor, the *Vorstand*, or managing board, bear a personal responsibility for the firm. The supremacy of the *Unternehmer* or the *Vorstand* is the source of the authoritarian image and reality of German management, but the authority is based on a paternalistic championing of the German values of the commonweal and the rights of the workers (Child and Kieser, 1981). As such, the *Unternehmer*, or *Vorstand*, is active in overseeing the operations of the firm. This person-oriented approach also explains the lesser importance of managerial systems than one would expect to find in similar sized American firms.

Management Status

A typical high-level manager commands respect for his knowledge of industry, management, and the economy, but is not thought to have specialized insights on other aspects of society. The scope of managers' influence has become more constrained over the last few years, as the news media have become increasingly critical of managerial decisions and as political groups such as the Green party have raised awareness of environmental and other issues, challenging managerial decisions in these areas.

Perhaps a more important area relating to the scope of managerial influence is the German tradition of workers' rights. Although this tradition is related to labor unions, the two issues are not identical, and workers' rights are generally considered separately from those of organized unions. In the German culture, management has a moral and legal obligation to be sensitive and responsive to workers' rights. The functional relationship between management and workers legitimizes the role of each in society. Although the influence of workers as a group has risen and fallen, just as has occurred with management, workers in West Germany are generally granted greater legitimacy and rights as a group than in most other societies, thereby balancing and constraining the influence of managers (James, 1989; Thimm, 1980).

The status of managers in West Germany is a complex issue. Prior research has shown that management and industry are accorded high status in Germany, for they contribute to the commonweal and the people's quality of life (Lawrence, 1980). The research panel agreed that managers are accorded high status in narrow fields, specifically, the area of commerce and economic development.

Management Ideology

Ideologically, managers are conservative and committed to free market economics. This ideology is largely independent of politics, and managers actively support both the conservative Christian Democratic party and its frequent coalition partner, the Free Democratic party. Managers as a group are less likely to affiliate with the liberal Social Democratic party or the environmental Green party.

Many large enterprises in West Germany have direct ties to the government. These include those in transportation, such as the Deutsche Bundesbahn Railroad, and Lufthansa Airlines, churches, savings and loan institutions, and radio and television. Although West Germany has a free market economy with large-scale private ownership, the national and regional governments often hold large ownership positions in private concerns. In some instances this has led to politicization of the upper levels of management.

HUMAN RESOURCE MANAGEMENT

This section discusses managerial staffing, recruiting, selection, organizational entry, training and development, performance appraisal, career development, compensation, and labor relations.

Managerial Staffing

The managerial group in West Germany has few striking demographic characteristics. Entry-level managers are generally in their twenties or early thirties, while midlevel managers are generally in their midthirties to their sixties. Senior-level managers are in their fifties or older, although most will retire in their late fifties or early sixties. A few younger people may enter senior management on a fast track. Since Germany is not an ethnically diverse country, the vast majority of managers are ethnic Germans, although there has been a recent influx of foreign nationals recruited specifically as managers. This is largely a result of the growth of the European Economic Community and the "one Europe" market that was expected to be implemented at the end of 1992.

Both men and women are represented in all levels of management in West

Germany, although there are many fewer women. None of the executives on the research panel expressed any reservations about having women in midlevel or senior-level positions. One midsized company had no women in midlevel management, but one of the three senior executives was a woman. Several companies reported that between 5 and 10 percent of their midlevel managers were women, and at least one had a specific target of increasing the percentage of midlevel women managers to 20 percent. Others had already exceeded this proportion of midlevel managers who were women.

Managers come from all classes of society; none of the interviewees identified any class constraints on a person entering management. The most important factors in identifying potential new managers were education or work experience. Opportunities for these experiences are not limited by class.

The German educational system offers two routes to advanced education in technical fields. One is the traditional German university program, which is similar to the university in the British-based educational system. The other route is through the *Fachhochschule*, which also offers a tertiary-level education, with programs similar to those found in the universities, with two exceptions. The *Fachhochschule* is usually based on a specific skill, such as management, accounting, or engineering and does not offer doctoral-level degrees.

No distinct pattern of education exists for midlevel or senior-level managers. It is not uncommon for managers to have doctoral-level degrees, and in West German industry the attainment of a doctorate is considered an important indication of a person's ability, motivation, and career potential. At the same time, a significant percentage of successful midlevel and senior-level managers do not have either a university or *Fachhochschule* education.

Recent trends, however, reveal the rising expectation that entry-level and midlevel managers have tertiary education, either from a university or the *Fachhochschule*. In all cases, however, those workers who lack such an education can move into management. In some cases the enterprise had special programs to send highly qualified workers to an appropriate *Fachhochschule*.

The research panel did not point to any single educational institution in West Germany that could be identified as an elite institution. As one manager expressed it: "There are good and less good institutions. Some are known for particular areas of study, but there is not one elite institution." Various *Fachhochschulen* and universities were identified for different programs in technical areas. In the area of management and economics, the University of Cologne and the Free University in Koblenz were identified as having strong programs. The European Business School, a *Fachhochschule* in the Rhine Main-Frankfurt area, was the most commonly identified tertiary institution. No institutions were identified outside of Germany. These findings are generally consistent with those presented by Lawrence (1980). Management education was found to be less developed in Germany than in Anglo-Saxon nations.

Sources of Recruitment

Today the university or the *Fachhochschule* are the most common source of entry-level managers. Entry-level people may be attracted to the firm either through direct response to a newspaper advertisement or through a professor acting as an intermediary. On-campus recruiting is not common in West Germany. More often, students interested in a firm will respond to an advertisement placed in national newspapers. Some firms have an active program to recruit in universities, having developed a network of contacts, including ongoing working relationships with professors, use of research grants, or having executives serve as adjunct professors.

Recruitment of midlevel managers is handled largely in accord with the firm's recruitment policies. Under German labor law, all nonentry-level positions must be posted internally, and internal candidates are given a preference in selection. Although the law may require such internal postings, the level of commitment to promote from within varies from company to company. As one manager explained: "We do promote from within. However, it is also important to have new blood. This means we often have to write job descriptions for the new position such that none of the existing people can fill it. This may be subverting the system, but it is important to have new ideas." When a firm goes outside for new midlevel managers, it is likely to advertise in newspapers, to use networking among professionals in the industry, or to employ search firms. The use of search firms is not universally approved. Several managers suggested they would hire a search firm under certain circumstances, but none was enthusiastic. The shortage of Euro-managers and managers with significant cross-national experience is forcing an increase in the use executive search firms (Tully, 1990).

Posting management jobs also has the effect of requiring that nonmanagerial employees have the opportunity to move into entry-level management positions. Although this option may be required under German labor law, the degree to which firms work with the concept varies. Some firms find 40 percent of their entry-level managers among the workers, while others rarely move a worker into management. Several firms have special programs to facilitate this internal movement. One firm that routinely uses an assessment center for managerial evaluation will allow well-qualified nonmanagerial workers also to participate in the assessment center evaluation. This firm adds the workers who perform well in the assessment center to a pool of qualified entry-level managers; it has developed about 15 percent of its entry-level managers through this program.

Selection of Entry-Level Managers

Entry-level managers are selected based on individual qualifications and skills, which are evaluated in a variety of ways. The most commonly cited qualifications are based on ability. The research panel identified descriptors such as brilliance, specialized knowledge, experience, foreign language skills, and comfort with modern technology. In addition, the panel placed heavy emphasis on personal attributes such as character, self-presentation, interpersonal relations, personality, fit with the organizational culture, flexibility, orientation toward action, and general managerial capabilities.

West German firms seek out people with the technical and interpersonal skills normally associated with management, but in some ways they expect more. As one manager explained:

We look for evidence of leadership quality and a total way of life. The way of life we want shows stability and direction, and a commitment. We might shy away from people who seemed to be drifting or unclear about what they wanted to do. On the other hand, we do not hold drifting against people, if they have shown themselves to have moved to a more stable and goal directed lifestyle. The entire way of life is important.

The selection methods used in assessing potential entry-level managers are typical of those used in most developed Western nations. A strong emphasis is placed on letters of recommendation, university and *Fachhochschule* records, and talks with individuals who know the potential employee. None of the firms participating in this research used psychological testing. Interviews are an important part of the selection process with almost all organizations using interviews in some form. A typical approach was to schedule a day-long interview during which the candidate might meet several line and staff people, participate in a group discussion, and be asked some nondirective probing questions.

Assessment centers are widely used in evaluating employees for promotion and development. Some firms use small-scale assessment centers to aid in the hiring of entry-level managers.

Organizational Entry

Different firms have different approaches to integrating the new manager into the organization. Programs for organizational entry ranged from simply placing the new employee in his work assignment for on-the-job training to a two-year orientation program. Typical experiences for those in a company with a formal orientation program included a series of short rotational assignments for exposure and experience, and alternation between the work assignment and time in field or operational units. In some cases, formal technical training was part of the orientation, depending on the job the new person was assigned. Some companies encouraged mentoring, although most did not have a formal mentoring program.

Training and Managerial Development

All the firms interviewed had some form of advanced training for professional development. For some, the opportunity for training was based on the employee initiating a request for a specific type of training. In other firms, special training offices were dedicated solely to employee developmental training programs. Most of the firms used a combination of in-house training and external training. The external training could be done through specialized institutes, such as INSEAD in France or the International Business School in Germany. Other external training was done through industry associations that offered training programs specifically oriented toward that industry.

Another form of development and training was through job rotation. These assignments were often multicultural and developed a manager's ability to work effectively in a global economy. Developing language skills and multicultural sensitivity were the objectives of these programs. Another approach to development of multicultural skills was used by a firm with operating units in about a dozen nations. The head of the West German Division explained:

We are very oriented toward advanced training. We have programs on all aspects of the management of the enterprise. We also sponsor international meetings semi-annually for employees with similar tasks. The purposes of these meetings are to build a sense of belongingness, but also to share ideas and innovative approaches.

Managerial Performance Appraisal

Managerial performance appraisal in West Germany is an ongoing process, with both formal and informal aspects. The criteria for performance appraisal take three forms. First, performance is based on quantifiable objectives, usually set in terms of balance sheet responsibilities or a level of sales performance. Second, annual goal-setting meetings are common for managers dealing with less quantifiable programs; these meetings link the employee's objectives with the overall corporate plan. These agreed-upon goals become the criteria for the employee's performance evaluation. Third, less formal criteria are usually worked out in routine interaction between manager and supervisor. In these cases, the criteria for a manager's performance are the accomplishment of the specific tasks assigned by the supervisor. The actual performance appraisal process can be formal or informal. In many cases, the informal performance appraisal is the more critical and meaningful of the two.

Informal performance appraisal is carried out in the daily interaction between manager and supervisor. This relationship can be characterized as one of candid communication and interaction. When a manager is not performing adequately, the supervisor speaks with the manager directly and immediately. This type of communication is not viewed negatively; rather the employee regards such a session as positive criticism. To some extent it may be seen as a type of coaching that goes on between supervisor and employee, although it is more directive and critical than most forms of coaching. This interaction becomes an important part of the performance evaluation process in West German firms.

More formal performance appraisals are done through periodic written evaluations, assessment centers, or performance review commissions. Not all large, sophisticated organizations use a formal written performance appraisal. Several of the firms participating in this research used formal appraisals only every three to five years. In many cases, this formal, written performance appraisal was viewed as somewhat of a bureaucratic exercise to supplement the more important and frequent informal performance appraisal sessions. Assessment centers were also used by several firms in the research sample. Two used small-scale centers to assist in selecting candidates for entry-level positions, and four firms relied heavily on the centers for the performance appraisal of managers.

Career Development and Planning

The performance appraisal system works best for managers who are performing well; managers who do not perform well are dealt with separately. Entry-level managers are usually hired for a one-year probationary period. Those whose performance is not satisfactory at the conclusion of their probationary period are asked to leave the company. Once employees have completed their probationary period, they are relatively secure in their position. After ten years, a person cannot be fired from a position under normal circumstances. If the employee is convicted of fraud against the organization, he or she will be terminated. But termination based solely on poor managerial performance is difficult. One manager describes the sequence of actions a supervisor would take when dealing with a poor performer.

First, the employee would be counselled to improve performance. If this is not successful, the employee would be advised that his future in the firm is not good. This is usually enough to get him to look elsewhere for a job. In some cases the employee would be demoted, but not by title. It is difficult to demote or fire someone, because the works council can intervene on the employee's behalf, and the disciplined employee will often take the firm to court. It is just not worth the trouble.

A manager at another firm addressed the issue in more detail.

It is very difficult to fire anyone after ten years with a company. Some of these people are no longer productive, and will create impediments to organizational effectiveness. You may see these people on an organization chart off by themselves, where they appear to supervise no one and be responsible for some unimportant task. They have been shunted off to the side to get them out of the way.

Other managers stressed that they would terminate poorly performing managers, because to keep them on the payroll was not good for the company or fair to other managers. When these poor performers were fired, the legally mandated severance costs to the company were significant.

Poor performance is less of a problem with top-level senior managers. These managers, defined here as those sitting on the *Vorstand*, or managing board, are usually on limited fixed-term contracts. These contracts, which are commonly for five years, are intended to create flexibility within the company and to keep senior managers responsive to corporate objectives.

Compensation of Managers

Compensation of managers in Germany is influenced by how much competition for managerial skills exists in the labor market, whether the firm is privately owned or affiliated with the state, whether the firm is unionized, and the individual managerial performance. West Germany has a competitive labor market for managers. Many firms determine the base range for managerial compensation from salary surveys that indicate the normal salary appropriate for managers holding a particular position. These salary surveys become an input into the

Table 5.5
Average Pay of Managing Directors of Manufacturing Firms

Switzerland	$230,000
West Germany	180,000
France	176,000
Great Britain	116,000

Source: *Wall Street Journal*, May 24, 1990.

firm's overall compensation strategy, which determines whether the firm will offer high or low salaries within the range. As a result of the Common Market, the labor market for managerial skills is rapidly becoming a European-wide market. With the coming of the 1992 unified product market, nations that have traditionally had lower managerial salaries are experiencing rapid increases in salary levels. West Germany has traditionally had one of the higher managerial salary scales in the Common Market, and West German firms have been able to attract qualified managers from other Common Market nations. The average salaries for managing directors of manufacturing firms in Western Europe are shown in Table 5.5.

Managerial salaries are also determined on the basis of whether the firm is affiliated with the government. Many firms are linked with the government in some manner; such firms are more likely to have a bureaucratic salary system, with identified professional wage grades, step increases, and requirements for time in grade before promotion. In these firms the manager's salary is constrained by the regulations governing salary administration. Firms that are not affiliated with the government have greater flexibility in salary determination.

Firms that are unionized frequently tie changes in managerial salaries directly to changes in union wage scales. In this case the salary administration process for managers begins with tying the normal increase in nonunion salary directly to the increase in union negotiated salary.

The competition in the managerial labor market, the effects of government affiliation, and the ties to union contracts become constraints that affect the overall determination of a manager's salary. After these constraints are satisfied, the salary determination is related primarily to individual performance. Take, for example, a firm that is not tied to the government, is not unionized, and draws managers from the European labor market. In this firm, we would expect to see a high degree of flexibility in determining managers' salaries, with the primary determinant being individual performance. In a firm that obtains its managers primarily from the West German labor market, is affiliated with the government, and is unionized, we would expect a manager's individual performance to play a less important role in determining the salary. In these cases salary is only loosely linked to performance. In extreme cases, salary may only be linked to performance in the length of time a person may have to wait for a within-grade step increase. At the other end of the spectrum, salary may be directly linked to performance through on-the-spot bonuses of several thousand deutsche marks (DM) or sizable end-of-year bonuses. In the firms making up the research panel, salaries quoted for middle managers ranged from 50,000 DM (approximately $33,000) to 200,000 DM (approximately $133,000). Salaries for entry-level managers were correspondingly lower, and salaries for top-level managers were quoted up to 300,000 DM (approximately $200,000).

Annual bonuses would be added to these base salaries. These bonuses include a variable Christmas bonus, which is tied to seniority and base salary, and an annual bonus. This annual bonus is almost always one month's pay, except in government-affiliated firms, where bonuses may be restricted through regulation. In private firms the annual bonus will be more directly associated with individual performance and may be several months' pay. The use of stock options is not common in Germany (Witte, 1989).

West Germany has a large program in mandated fringe benefits, funded primarily through payroll taxes. These payroll taxes were approximately 36 percent in 1988 (U.S. Department of Labor). One firm quoted the combined cost of mandated fringe benefits and other nonmandated specific fringe benefits as totaling 83 percent of the base salary.

Supplemental compensation was largely within the overall compensation package described earlier in this chapter. In some firms, midlevel and high-level employees were provided automobiles, although this perquisite was more common for high-level employees. Midlevel managers would receive a car when it was required to perform their job. In several firms, an employer-funded pension plan was offered to supplement the state-administered plan. None of the firms participating in the research panel provided any form of personal services as supplementary compensation.

Labor Relations

The three principal actors in labor relations of the typical West German firm are the management of the firm, the works councils, and the labor unions. Industrial relations in Germany are defined under a series of laws passed in 1952, 1972, and 1976. Specifically, they detail the relationship between labor unions, works councils, owners, the supervisory board, and the managing board. They define and develop the concept of codetermination, under which contributors of both capital and labor will theoretically work together for the commonweal (Thimm, 1980).

Management The management structure of the German firm consists of the supervisory board (*Aufsichtsrat*) and the managing board (*Vorstand*). The supervisory board is the rough equivalent of the American corporation's board of directors, and the managing board is similar to a management committee in the

American corporation, where the chief executive officer (CEO) and senior executives would oversee the operations of the firm.

As mandated in industrial relations legislation, the supervisory board comprises representatives of shareholders (including government-appointed representatives in the case of firms partly owned by the federal or state governments), labor unions, and the works councils. The board is responsible for strategic decisions and the financial performance of the firm. It appoints the managing board, but in Germany no member of the supervisory board may also be a member of the managing board. The supervisory board does not participate in the normal managerial decision making or operations of the firm. The board's formal influence is felt through the naming of the managing board. Senior managers regard the supervisory board as a source of advice and support, not as a shareholder's watchdog (Hartmann, 1970; Thimm, 1980).

The managing board, or *Vorstand*, is responsible for the overall management of the firm, and under German industrial relations law, the managing board (not the supervisory board) is recognized as the legal entity representing the firm. This has the effect of giving the managing board more power vis-à-vis the supervisory board, particularly in the area of industrial relations. The industrial relations laws require representatives of shareholders, works councils, and unions on both the supervisory board and the managing board. The law specifically recognizes the members of the managing board as professionals who are individually and collectively responsible for the overall management of the firm and the implementation of the industrial relations policies. The managing board is further strengthened under the industrial relations laws in that when a supervisory board does not support the managing board, the managing board may appeal directly to the stockholders for a special meeting to review the disagreement (Hartmann, 1970; Thimm, 1980). The professional management structure functions as the staff of the managing board.

Works Councils   Under German labor law, the employees of the firm are protected from unilateral decisions by management. This protection is institutionalized through the use of works councils, or *Betriebsrat*. The works council is an instrument designed to facilitate employee participation in the economic and social decisions affecting the individual's workplace. As an agent of social cooperation, it is not intended to undertake adversarial actions. The works councils have the legal right to approve or reject all business decisions affecting workers. These include hirings, firings, transfers, promotions, and relocations. Each works council is elected every three years by the employees it represents. Any given firm may have more than one works council, with each representing a different class of employees. The council has legal standing in the firm; management does not have an option to accept the presence of a works council. The management must provide resources for the council and must collaborate with the works council on all personnel matters.

The existence of works councils was not viewed negatively. One manager explained:

The relationship between the works council and management need not be adversarial, although it is on some issues. The works councils can be a positive collaborative force, although on some issues there is deep disagreement, and the works councils can be very effective in thwarting managerial plans. But they do a lot to reduce conflict by acting as an intermediary and they tend to be flexible in solving problems. They can also be helpful in getting around an individual that has been blocking things from happening.

Managers may or may not be represented by a works council. In many firms the middle and entry-level management will be represented by the works council, although it may be separate from the works council that represents the nonmanagerial workers.

Works councils function as a mechanism to implement a centrally held value in West Germany: that employees and the firm are in a unique relationship to contribute to the commonweal. This requires mutual understanding and commitment.

Unions   Labor unions in West Germany are generally considered to be powerful groups, although the degree of power varies by company and industry. Membership in unions is voluntary and at the discretion of the individual employee. In 1988, there were approximately 9.4 million labor union members, or about 41 percent of the eligible workforce (U.S. Department of Labor, 1988–89). Since the unification of the two Germanies, unions have experienced considerable labor growth by enrolling workers from the eastern part of the unified nation (Business Europe, June 8, 1990).

Labor unions work hard to have their members elected to works councils, and the 1976 industrial relations legislation made this task much easier (Thimm, 1980). Unions are generally considered to have significant influence over the policies and approaches of the works councils. One manager explained:

Unions and works councils are not the same, although they are closely related. An analogy would be political parties and government. The works council is a legally recognized body that has legally defined rights and responsibilities. Both the union and the works council members are elected by the workers, although the election processes are independent. The union always puts up a slate of candidates for the works council, but nonunion members are also nominated.

Unions are recognized as carrying out the adversarial role that has been generally seen as inappropriate for the works councils. The unions negotiate the collective bargaining agreements, whereas the works councils monitor its implementation. Although only a minority of workers are union members, the influence of unions is enhanced through their ability to elect members to the works councils, their political power in state and federal legislatures, and their capacity to negotiate favorable collective bargaining agreements. Unions have and are willing to use work stoppages, strikes, and slowdowns to achieve their ends, and the presence of union representatives on supervisory and management boards always gives them a voice at the highest levels of the enterprise. The federal labor ministry can, and often does, declare that collective bargaining agreements apply to nonunion employees of the same firm, or the agreement can be made applicable to other firms in the same industry (Thimm, 1980).

Unions view their role as protecting the rights of their members and seeking to expand the legitimate agenda over which they have influence. But unions also view their role professionally. One manager commented: "Unions in West Germany not only represent their members, but they also emphasize professionalism among their members. They strive to instill a sense of professionalism and responsibility, and to assure that members are trained to fully understand the implications of their job."

Another organization represents managerial employees in different industries. The organization, die Union der Leitende Angestellten (the Union of Managerial Employees), is an umbrella association for nine independent member associations operating in specific industries. The Union of Managerial Employees addresses issues concerning the rights of managerial employees in relation to labor and social security regulations, compensation, protection against dismissal, and retirement provisions. Although it positions itself alongside labor unions, it has always considered itself a professional league, not a labor union. It represents only about 8 percent of the managerial employees that would fall within its defined target population (Witte, 1989).

PROJECTIONS FOR THE FUTURE

The future of management is probably less certain in Germany than in most nations. On one level, the future should be stable. Here is a nation with a strong economy, an excellent export/import ratio, a high standard of living, and general harmony among government, business, and labor. These strengths should reduce any environmental pressures for significant change in the way management works in the western part of the country.

But this success has itself created a paradox that may lead to change. The unification of East and West Germany may have an impact on the management of West German firms. Had West Germany not been so economically successful, the interest of the East German people in joining West Germany may have been much weaker. As the reality of the unification develops, we can only speculate on how the intermeshing of the managerial cultures of the two nations will affect the future of management. East Germany has a long history as a wasteful centrally planned economy, with inefficient employment policies to assure full employment. East German management was responsive to a central planning committee rather than market pressures, and had a highly politicized management structure. Since both sectors have had a significant number of firms that are affiliated with the state in some way, we can only speculate how unification will impact managerial culture.

This situation extends to forecasting the future of human resource management in Germany. Following unification, industry in the former East Germany has undergone a fundamental transformation, with thousands of enterprises closing and hundreds of thousands of workers losing their jobs. The patterns of human resource management described in this chapter seem to be inoperative in the transitional phase of the unified German economy.

Human resource management in the western section of Germany is likely to continue to evolve toward a modern systems approach. More formalized systems approaches to performance appraisal, employee selection, identification of training needs, and career development are likely to emerge. Women are likely to continue to make inroads in the management hierarchy. The personal and paternalistic characteristic of the German managerial culture is not likely to change significantly. The recognition of the master craftsman, and the importance of both individual and commonweal responsibility and accountability, will continue to be central to German management. The personal approach to recruiting, appraisal, and selection will probably continue to make German management uniquely German. There is likely to be a continued growth of a sense of professionalism in German firms, and this is likely to be seen at both the managerial and worker level.

Yet within all of these projections, the unknown impact of the integration of East Germany makes it difficult to forecast the future. It is unclear how much of the economic security, lack of emphasis on productivity, subsidized food and housing, and guaranteed job (regardless of worker performance) the former East German citizens will be willing to forsake. This tradeoff may influence how management functions in unified Germany.

Germany is a prosperous, modern, and democratic state. It will be challenged to integrate the former East German state. The western half has had one of the strongest economies in the world and has achieved a successful integration of balancing managerial prerogatives, economic efficiency, and workers' rights. The role of management in this evolution has been both as a leader in using modern management techniques and as a compliant social group that recognizes its responsibilities within the state. Management in Germany is not only responsible for efficiency, profit, and production of goods or services, but it is also held responsible by the broader society for implementing certain social programs that are expected of the productive enterprise.

REFERENCES

Allen, C. "Germany: Competing Communitarianisms." In *Ideology and National Competitiveness: An Analysis of Nine Countries*, ed. G. C. Lodge and E. F. Vogel. Boston: Harvard Business School Press, 1987.

Berghahn, V. *The Americanisation of West German Industry, 1945–1973*. Cambridge, England: Cambridge University Press, 1986.

Business Europe. *German Labor Goes East* (June 8, 1990): p. 6.

Child, J., and Kieser, A. "Organization and Managerial Roles in British and West German Companies: An Examination of the Culture-free Thesis." In *Organization and Nation*, ed. D. J. Hickson and C. J. McMillan. Westmead, England: Gower Publishing, 1981.

Central Intelligence Agency. *Handbook of Economic Statistics, 1989*. CPAS 89–10002. Langley, Va.: Central Intelligence Agency, 1989.

The Economist Intelligence Unit. *World Outlook, 1991*. London, 1991.

Hartmann, H. *Authority and Organization in German Management*. Westport, Conn.: Greenwood Press, 1970.

Hartmann, H., Bock-Rosenthal, E., and Helmer, E. *Leitende Angestellte: Selbstverstaendnis und Killektive Forderungen*. Neuwied, Germany: Luchterhand Verlag, 1973.

James, H. *A German Identity, 1770–1990*. New York: Routledge, 1989.

Lawrence, P. *Managers and Management in West Germany*. New York: St. Martin's Press, 1980.

New York Times. *Slowing Economy Predicted for United Germany* National Edition (October 23, 1990): p. C. 20.

Roomkin, M. *Managers as Employees: An International Comparison of the Changing Character of Managerial Employment*. New York: Oxford University Press, 1989.

Thimm, A. *The False Promise of Codetermination: The Changing Nature of European Workers' Participation*. Lexington, Mass.: Lexington Books, 1980.

Tully, S. "The Hunt for the Global Manager." *Fortune 121*: 11 (May 21, 1990): pp. 140–144.

U.S. Department of Labor. *Foreign Labor Trends, Federal Republic of Germany 1988–89*. FLT 89–55. Washington, D.C.: Government Printing Office.

Witte, E. "Germany." In *Managers as Employees: An International Comparison of the Changing Character of Managerial Employment*, ed. M. Roomkin. New York: Oxford University Press, 1989.

Wall Street Journal. *Executive Pay in Europe* (May 24, 1990): p. A10.

6

SWEDEN

Jan Selmer

It is the Swedish management style that is unusual, not the style of other countries.

Hedlund and Aman, 1984: 154

The concept of manager is given various interpretations in different parts of the world. It is sometimes reserved exclusively for private sector organizations. In the case of Sweden, however, that would be too limited a handling of the topic since the public sector comprises a considerable part of organizational life. Furthermore, there is no sharp demarcation line between these two sectors, since a significant part of the state-owned companies are competing on the open market and are expected to make a profit, as for example, the Swedish Railways, Telecom, and the Postal Service. Moreover, there is a considerable amount of movement of managerial staff, especially at the top levels, between private and public sector organizations. Consequently, this chapter considers both public and private managerial behavior and differentiates between them when appropriate. Given the special egalitarian atmosphere in Swedish organizations, however, it is not always relevant to distinguish between different positions of managers, since their managerial behavior is generally similar. Hence, hierarchical differentiation between managerial behavior will be done only when explicitly required.

GENERAL FACTS ON SWEDEN

With an area of 450,000 square kilometers, Sweden is the fourth largest country in Europe. Half of its land surface is covered with forests, and less than 10 percent is farmland. Lakes dot the Swedish countryside, which is relatively flat. A long mountain chain in the northwest reaches heights of up to more than 2,100 meters. There are thousands of islands along the jagged coastline. Sweden is located so far north in Europe that the Arctic Circle slices through its most northern province, Lappland. But it is not an Arctic country. Thanks to the winds that blow from the warm Gulf Stream in the Atlantic, Sweden has a rather mild climate considering its location. Since the country is quite long, however, the distance between the northern and southern tip of the country is nearly 1,600 kilometers. Thus, its natural features and climate are quite varied. Far northern Sweden has long, dark, cold winters, but in June and July the never-setting "Midnight Sun" gives rich compensation (Swedish Institute, 1989).

Sweden has a population of 8.5 million, with over 85 percent living in the southern half of the country. Like other industrialized countries, Sweden has a low birth rate and a high life expectancy. Since World War II, a net immigration of approximately 700,000, mostly from neighboring Scandinavian countries but also from elsewhere in the world, has accounted for more than half of the population growth. Statistically speaking, each inhabitant of Sweden has 54,000 square meters to move around in. People are accustomed to plenty of space and to access to a rather unspoiled nature. Most of the population lives in cities and towns, especially in the three major urban regions of Stockholm, Gothenburg, and Malmö (Swedish Institute, 1988).

Popular government in Sweden rests on old traditions. The Swedish Parliament stems from the Ting (tribal courts) and the election of kings in the Viking Age. It became a permanent institution in the fifteenth century. Today, Sweden has a parliamentary government built on a multiparty system. The monarchy is constitutional, and the king's authority is of a purely formal nature as head of state (Swedish Institute, 1986). The parliamentary ombudsmen investigate suspected abuses of authority by civil servants. Other ombudsmen protect the public by keeping a watchful eye on business practices, consumer rights, ethnic and sex discrimination, and press ethics. With few exceptions, government documents are open to inspection by the public and press at any time (Swedish Institute, 1986, 1988).

Table 6.1 depicts the growth of the Swedish economy since 1946. In the immediate postwar years, Sweden experienced an export-led growth. The Korean War inflation, succeeded by the cyclical downturns of 1953–54 and 1957–58, pulled down average annual growth during the 1950s to 3.4 percent. However, the 1960s became the golden decade for Sweden as well as many other industrialized countries, with an average annual GDP growth of 4.6 percent. During the same period, however, a gradual stiffening of international competition was in the making, and the 1970s turned out to be a decade of slow growth and rising economic and social discontent. The average annual increase in gross domestic product (GDP) was only 2 percent, which was below the average rate for the Organization for Economic Cooperation and Development (OECD) countries. Unfortunately, the 1980s proved to be even worse with a meager average annual growth rate in GDP of 1.9 percent (Swedish Institute, 1989).

Table 6.2 shows the contribution to GDP from the various economic sectors. In 1988, services accounted for a larger share than in 1970—61 percent compared

Table 6.1
GDP Volume Growth, 1946–88 (annual averages, percent)

1946 - 50	4.8
1951 - 60	3.4
1961 - 65	5.3
1966 - 70	3.9
1971 - 75	2.7
1976 - 80	1.3
1981 - 85	1.9
1986 - 88	1.9

Source: Swedish Institute, 1989.

with 57 percent. Mining and manufacturing, agriculture, forestry and fishing, and construction are sectors with diminishing shares of national output. On the other hand, energy production increased in relative importance, reflecting an expansion of nuclear power. The GDP share of wholesaling, retailing, hotels, and restaurants decreased slightly, while that of other private and business services increased. Another conspicuous trend has been the steady increase of local government as a share of GDP, not broken until 1983 (Swedish Institute, 1989).

Shortly after the end of World War II, virtual full employment was established, and the adjustment to peacetime conditions was completed by the early 1950s. The "golden 1960s" were characterized by full employment, and even during the problematic 1970s, Sweden managed to keep the registered unemployment at just about 2 percent on the average; it was a better performance than most OECD countries. During the 1980s, total unemployment was still relatively low, although the rate became higher in the youngest age group (Swedish Institute, 1989). See Table 6.3 for specific 1970 and 1988 data.

Table 6.4 displays the distribution of the labor force by sector, showing distinct long-term trends, such as an expanding public, in particular, local government sector and a declining industrial sector. The service sector, except trade, is also

Table 6.2
Contribution to GDP by Various Sectors, 1970 and 1988 (percent, constant 1980 prices)

	1970	1988
Agriculture, fishing and forestry	4.6	3.4
Mining and manufacturing	27.1	24.2
Electricity, gas and water works	1.9	3.7
Construction	9.5	7.7
Wholesaling, retailing and restaurants	12.9	12.4
Other private and business services[a]	22.3	24.7
Central government	6.4	5.2
Local governments	15.3	18.5

[a] Transport, communications, banking, insurance, property management, and so on.
Source: Swedish Institute, 1989.

growing rapidly. Noteworthy too, is the decrease in employment in agriculture, fishing, and forestry (Swedish Institute, 1989).

THE INTERNATIONAL SWEDISH ECONOMY

When industrialization, which started in Great Britain in the mid-eighteenth century, spread to the rest of Europe in the nineteenth century, Sweden supplied the iron and wood that were in demand as raw material for building factories, machines, and housing. The early industries in Sweden grew from domestic natural resources. Swedish industry did not really begin to grow until the 1890s, although it then developed very rapidly between 1900 and 1930 and transformed Sweden into one of Europe's leading industrial nations after World War II. Over

Table 6.3
Human Resources, 1970 and 1988

	1970	1988
Mean population, 000s	8,040	8,438
Labor force, 000s	3,910	4,471
Participation rate, ages 16-64, %	73.3	84.0
Total open unemployment, %	1.5	1.6
Unemployment, ages 16-24, %	2.8	3.3

Source: Swedish Institute, 1989.

the past 100 years, Sweden's industrial growth rate has been second only to Japan's (Lawrence and Spybey, 1986:35).

Optimism and an entrepreneurial spirit prevailed in Swedish industry during the late nineteenth and early twentieth centuries. The structural transformation of Swedish industry toward a growing share of manufactured goods began in the period from 1880 to World War I. During these decades numerous companies were formed, often based on Swedish inventions or refinements of foreign designs. Among them were pulp production, foundry steel processes, electric power transmission technology, the gas-driven refrigerator, automatic lighthouse, table telephone, centrifugal separator, modern ball-bearing, zipper, safety match, and adjustable spanner. A common feature of all these product inventions was their high value-added potential and their suitability for exporting. During those decades, Swedish industry laid the economic foundations for the contemporary society and well-being. Today, internationally well-known companies such as AGA, Alfa-Laval, ASEA, Electrolux, Ericsson, Sandvik, and SKF are all examples of this development (Swedish Institute, 1987).

A distinguishing feature of Swedish industry was its rapid internationalization. The new industrial companies formed during the turn of the century almost immediately became international exporters, exploiting the global opportunities of their products. The expertise of these companies was in production and technology rather than in the Swedish market, making foreign operations crucial to these companies from the start. For example, Ericsson, the Swedish telephone

Table 6.4
Employment by Sector, 1970 and 1988 (percent of labor force)

	1970	1988
Agriculture, fishing and forestry	8.2	3.8
Mining and manufacturing	26.6	22.0
Electricity, gas and water works	0.7	0.8
Construction	9.3	6.2
Wholesaling, retailing and restaurants	14.5	14.0
Other private and business services[a]	8.9	20.8
Central government	6.2	6.4
Local governments	14.1	24.4

[a] Includes transport, communications, banking, insurance, property management, and so on.
Source: Swedish Institute, 1989.

company, was well established in Russia long before the Revolution of 1917, and all its large factories were accordingly confiscated. Alfa-Laval established a subsidiary in the United States immediately after it had been formed in Sweden. Contributing to the rapid internationalization and development of Swedish industry was the fact that industrialization in Sweden occurred late and during the growth phase of the industrial societies. Swedish industry specialized in technological and product fields that were emerging, rather than in those that were maturing and soon to be outdated. Hence, Swedish industry could concentrate on international expansion, and demands of domestic modernization came much later, as compared to other countries that had been industrialized earlier (Hedlund, 1989; Hedlund and Aman, 1984:18).

Today industry accounts for about 85 percent of Sweden's exports. There has been a gradual shift from the traditional emphasis on raw materials to advanced manufactured products with sophisticated technology, such as transportation equipment, electronics, electrical equipment, and chemicals. Whereas these industries may be characterized as growth sectors, the ailing industries are in such traditional areas as textiles and apparel, iron and steel, shipbuilding, and parts of the forest product sector (Swedish Institute, 1989).

The early internationalization of Swedish industry developed into a heavy external dependence. Swedish exports comprise more than one-third of GDP, making Sweden the fifth most export-dependent country in the world (Swedish Institute, 1989).

EVOLUTION OF THE MANAGERIAL CLASS

This section deals with the societal status of the Swedish managerial class, its ideological background and social legitimacy.

Societal Status

An inquiry into the status of industry in Sweden would elicit contradictory answers, for this question pertains to choices of careers among well-qualified people. In countries where the status of industry is high, management will be the first career choice of the able and ambitious, as in the United States, Japan, or Germany. Where the status of business is low, national talent will prefer the service of the state or the free professions, such as one finds in Britain. In this sense, Swedes disagree whether civil service or industry has more status. There is no doubt that industry has a high standing in Sweden, but civil service employment also carries high prestige though for different reasons (Lawrence and Spybey, 1986).

The broader consideration that surrounds the notion of the status of industry is that of the place of industry and industrialization in the popular mind. In some countries, these concepts are nearly "dirty words" as they are in Great Britain, for example. There has been no equivalent tendency in Sweden; indeed, the reverse has been the case. In Swedish folk memory, industrialization is a national success story that goes something like this: "Once upon a time there was an isolated and poor country in the north of Europe; then industrialization came along and everything started to get better; then barely a hundred years later we found ourselves just about the richest country in the world." Hence, the industrialization of Sweden is unavoidably connected to a swift economic upgrading of the whole nation, and certainly it is nothing to abhor or to be ashamed of. On the contrary, Swedish national pride is inextricably linked to this achievement (Lawrence and Spybey, 1986).

So, on the whole, managers in Sweden enjoy considerable prestige and respectability. This general tendency has, however, varied somewhat in recent decades. As in many other European countries affected by the wave of political leftism originating with the student radicalization in the late 1960s, managers, and what they stood for, became suspect or even despicable in the eyes of public opinion during most of the 1970s. This was the age when "profit" became a dirty word and many companies on the brink of bankruptcy, or even beyond that, were taken over by their employees. In the beginning of the 1980s, however, a new era dawned, when making money became not only legitimate again, but also highly respectable and definitely an activity beneficial to society. Obviously, this trend has developed even further in the international arena where widespread privatization campaigns and the recent demise of communism constitute a completely new paradigm. Needless to say, this worldwide phenomenon has also had its impact in Sweden, both politically and economically, and not the least, when it comes to further reestablishing the status and esteem of the business executive as the bearer of the key to continued wealth for Sweden.

Managerial Ideology

It is doubtful whether a unified Swedish managerial ideology exists. The concept of ideology might be too comprehensive to describe what guides managerial thinking and behavior. Nevertheless, the basic egalitarian value, pervasive in Swedish society as well as managerial life, is a major determinant of managerial behavior. Much of Swedish managerial life would appear to be totally incomprehensible without such an explanatory factor.

Another essential determinant of managerial behavior is the authority of competence and the attachment to act correctly, which have replaced autocratic or hierarchical bases of authority and leadership, made irrelevant by the advent of egalitarianism. It promotes competent leadership and hard work in managers and induces them to do the right thing for the right reasons.

> To insist upon "management" as a profession, rather than the natural and rational way good men conduct themselves anyway, is in a way to degrade the activity (Hedlund, 1989).

Although Swedish managers are usually specialists rather than generalists, the very notion that management should be a *profession* is cast in serious doubt in Sweden. Even in business schools, the students hardly think that they are in school to learn a profession of management; rather, they are given a well-rounded training, but "the tricks of the trade" are gained in subsequent employment (Hedlund, 1989). Besides, the English word *profession* does not have an exact translation into Swedish. The word used in Swedish is *yrke*, which is a closer equivalent of the English word *occupation*. Hence, everybody has an *yrke*. In fact, a house painter or a plumber has more of an *yrke* then a lawyer, priest, or an executive. The implication is that the more skill-oriented the work, the more the term *yrke* is appropriate (Hedlund, 1989). Furthermore, there is not even an accurate translation of the word "manager" into Swedish, the nearest perhaps being *direktor*, which refers to a top executive or a president rather than to a manager.

The reverence for technology among Swedish managers, and the fact that engineers are very well represented among their ranks, suggest a solid base for design, quality, and product innovation and for the development of manufacturing methods. The fact and record of punctual delivery is another Swedish managerial strength. They not only do it well, but, more important, they are also *known* to do it well (Lawrence and Spybey, 1986).

The strong export orientation of Swedish managers in general is another essential feature. It also appears that in a sense successful exporting is "all in the mind." Exporting takes place because people believe in it and do the things consequent on that belief. Swedish managers also have a high degree of product-mindedness. Generally, they have knowledge and understanding of their company's products and an interest in their functioning and application, as well as an awareness of how the products were derived and how they will be further developed. Another corresponding characteristic is the persistent search for new markets and business opportunities, as is their interest in new applications. This concerns not only new products, but also new uses for existing products (if necessary, modified) or new applications for existing systems or competencies (Lawrence and Spybey, 1986). Egalitarianism lubricates the codetermination system and facilitates communication. It contributes to the relative lack of status-mongering among Swedish managers, and it promotes good interdepartmental relations, efficient teamwork, successful implementation of new policies, and respect for agreements, both on the intraorganizational level and with respect to customers and clients. Moreover, there is a relative absence of politicking, intriguing, and maneuvering among Swedish managers (Lawrence and Spybey, 1986).

The participative decision-making system preferred by Swedish managers may be slow, but there are compensating benefits. If it is slow and participative, it will also be integrative; fewer people will be alienated, and more people will be carried along with the decision. Besides, the obverse of slow decision making is fast implementation. Hence, most of the time, Swedish reasonableness and the inclination to avoid conflict and the willingness to compromise are beneficial to the organization. Even if it takes time, it saves energy and ensures outcomes (Lawrence and Spybey, 1986).

On the other hand, it could be argued that a general lessening of motivation and involvement has become evident among Swedish managers. First, there appears to be a diminished concern with promotion—not every young Swedish manager wants to get to the top. With regard to their objectives, they are more likely to pursue a balance between work and family satisfactions, without work necessarily dominating family satisfactions (Lawrence and Spybey, 1986).

Second, there is a related tendency to avoid line jobs in management, that is, posts where the manager is manifestly responsible for performance, often with a large number of subordinates. Such positions are typically in sales, production, and general management. Indeed, apparently exposed line positions are often occupied by managers who appear to be younger than their counterparts elsewhere. Possibly, only the young are willing to accept the irritation of such positions (Lawrence and Spybey, 1986).

Third, the transfer to sheltered staff positions often takes place through a "sideways" (i.e., lateral) slide. In the relative absence of a monetary drawback, managers are sometimes prepared to give up increments of power for the prospects of a quieter life. Hence, managerial "decolonization" is at least as common as building empires (Lawrence and Spybey, 1986).

In addition, a marked reluctance to work long hours, an aversion to engage in business travel, especially trips that take up the weekend, and a widely held attitude that holidays are sacrosanct have become widespread. In July, Sweden literally closes down, and it is virtually impossible to get anything done in the business world. Another related aspect is a lack of enthusiasm for business entertaining, which is felt to be either an unreasonable demand on the (working) wife of the manager or an imposition on leisure time. Finally, there is a reluctance to move (geographically) among Swedish managers, both domestically and to a foreign assignment (Lawrence and Spybey, 1986).

All of these manifestations of deficient motivation and involvement on the part of Swedish managers are not merely indicative of their relatively modest material rewards, but also reflect the equality of the sexes, the general importance attached to family life, and the Swedes' enthusiasm for nature, scenery, and their summer houses in the country. Hence, Swedish managers seem to be less likely to be diverted from these alternative leisure-family-equality values by crude financial incentives than are managers in the United States, for example (Lawrence and Spybey, 1986).

In conclusion, there might be a case for the "purity of motive" of Swedish top managers. Those who do accept promotions and who do fill exposed line posts are rather less likely to do so out of pecuniary reasons than their colleagues in other countries. Those who get to the top must want to be there for intrinsic rather than extrinsic reasons. At the same time, it could be argued that the lower financial rewards constitute a loss in dynamism since they largely defuse the fight for promotion. However, there is a corresponding gain in efficiency through less politicking, fewer power struggles, and more cooperation between functions and different hierarchical levels (Lawrence and Spybey, 1986).

Social Legitimacy

Sweden's unique mix of dynamic free enterprises, low unemployment, heavy redistribution of income, and close labor-management cooperation has conditioned the minds of managers as well as the general public as to the base of managerial legitimacy. Needless to say, it is the private, free market system and world-beating industrial companies that have supported the lavish Swedish welfare system. Although this blend of capitalism and socialism has encountered severe problems recently, the original vision of creating *folkhemmet*, a people's home where workers would be highly taxed but are guaranteed employment and universal welfare, has for many decades influenced attitudes toward industry. While the state took care of the people, private industry was allowed to flourish. In the manufacturing sector of the Swedish economy, government ownership amounts to only about 7 percent, well below the average of Western European countries. Sweden's free trade record is also more liberal than that of most countries in Western Europe (Ellis, 1990; Pedersen, 1990).

Consequently, the political base of legitimacy of private sector management has been firmly established for a long time. However, political radicalism in Sweden, as well as in many other countries, during the late 1960s and 1970s, brought discredit to business managers in general and profit making in particular. That has all changed today, and the worldwide admiration for private economic management and its efficiency has also made a deep impression in Sweden.

The public sector is one of the largest in the world. If transfer payments such as pensions, sick pay, and child allowances are included, nearly 60 percent of GDP passes through the public sector today, against 30 percent a few decades ago (Swedish Institute, 1989). Therefore, public servants are far from scarce in Sweden. Besides, the legitimacy of public sector managers is firmly rooted in historic traditions and Swedish attitudes toward the state administration. Historically, the Social Democratic party ruled Sweden during the period 1932–76 and returned to power 1982. Hence, its ideology has left its mark on the Swedish society during a longer period than in any other country. This includes the conviction that "collective" decisions, that is, decisions made by central authorities, guarantee the fairest order of things. Interesting evidence to this effect can also be found much farther back in history. The centrally controlled state seems to have already emerged during the early sixteenth century, established by the Swedish King Gustav Vasa. Besides, the Swedish peasants were never suppressed to the extent that they were in most other countries in Europe. They were mostly owners of their land, under the Crown. Thus, they were consistently represented in the parliaments called by the king. It is not a far-fetched guess to say that this background contributed considerably to the extensive level of enthusiasm for government, engendering an ingrained respect for the law and central authorities. Hence, it seems to be a cultural pattern to respect the authority of the government and the state. People simply believe in the benevolence of the state authorities and trust in their goodwill (Daun, 1989; Lawrence and Spybey, 1986). But this image of the state and authorities seems to have also been enhanced through the Swedish peoples' ingrained matter-of-factness and belief in rationality (Daun, 1989).

CULTURE AND MANAGERIAL BEHAVIOR

This section discusses the cultural values of Swedish managers and their behavioral implications. Common stereotypes are reviewed, as well as fundamental managerial characteristics such as equality and informality, consensual decision making, and the authority of knowledge. The last-named is also known as the cult of competence.

Stereotypes

Most Swedes have both positive and negative stereotypes about themselves. On the positive side, many Swedes think of themselves as having a good general education and being well organized, kind, dependable, rational, efficient, honest, willing to compromise, punctual, taciturn, and *lagom*—not too much, not too little, just right (Daun and Phillips-Martinsson, 1986). There is nothing negative about these characteristics in the Swedish context; on the contrary, Swedes are proud of these traits. Although their tendency to remain silent doesn't make them great sociable persons, their silence is also included in their self-image of their efficiency; they don't waste time talking nonsense (Daun and Phillips-Martinsson, 1986).

When observed and interpreted by people from other cultures, however, these positive character traits may be perceived as more problematic than the negative stereotypes that Swedes have about themselves. For example, when Swedes regard themselves as well organized, honest, efficient, and punctual, they consider discipline and orderliness as morally loaded values, as outstanding personal qualities. But just because it is self-evident to Swedes it is far from clear that this emphasis also has a positive image in other cultures. For example, to Swedes, punctuality is a virtue that offers many benefits, one advantage being that one's work day can be planned in detail and meetings can both be planned to start and end at a certain time. To Swedes, this is an example of efficiency and rationality, but to a foreigner, it might seem that Swedes practice an unsympathetic and impractical inflexibility in their human relations (Daun and Phillips-Martinsson, 1986).

Among the Swedish negative self-stereotypes are lack of social talents, narrowmindedness, shyness, self-complacency, stiffness, enviousness, and fear of making fools of themselves. Since these stereotypes are perceived as negative, Swedes either accept the negative consequences resulting from these character traits or try to compensate for them (Daun and Phillips-Martinsson, 1986).

Equality and Informality

A strong commitment to egalitarianism is rooted in the Swedish culture at large. Differences between people, groups, classes, and even sexes are less noticeable than they are in many other Western societies. Not only is Swedish society undifferentiated in many respects, but also there is a widespread feeling that this lack of differentiation is morally right as being the normal way of things. The Swedish vernacular is exuberant with sayings such as *en man ar lika god som en ann* (a man is as good as anyone else). Hence, it is considered bad manners to act "uppity" or to set oneself apart from others (Lawrence and Spybey, 1986). A revealing example of the extent and degree of egalitarianism in Swedish organizations is that the boss's coffee is made by the boss himself, as opposed to most other countries. During coffee breaks, there is no secretary serving coffee and cakes, not even when the boss has guests in his office (Laine-Sveiby, 1987).

Informal behavior is highly valued in Sweden, and it is absolutely necessary if one wants to be an effective manager. The trick is to earn respect despite this informal image. This is a subtle art that appears to be natural to Swedish managers: They seem to be world champions in "management by winks and nods"; often another Swede is needed to perceive and correctly interpret such indirect signals (Hedlund and Aman, 1984).

A company's most important resource is its employees, but the well-being of the employees is not the company's ultimate goal. Swedish managers seem to be able to distinguish between the people-centered approach toward employees and at the same time use people as tools. To Swedes there is no incompatibility in this duality. Hence, a Swedish manager defines modern leadership accordingly as to "create such prerequisites in an organisation that everybody should be happy to give their utmost to produce a result as good as it ever can be" (Laine-Sveiby, 1987:132; Olson, 1989).

An American who had lived several years in Sweden still could not understand how Swedish organizations worked: "It is something strange with Swedish workplaces. There does not seem to be anybody in charge. And yet the work gets done. How do they do it?" (Laine-Sveiby, 1987:23). The Swedish leadership style has frequently been described as extremely "soft" by foreign observers. Charismatic and dominant leaders are considered scarce in Sweden. But after prolonged exposure to Swedish management, foreigners might detect that beneath the low-key, pliable surface, Swedish steel lays hidden. Hence, there is a distinction between *form* and *content*. Although the form could be soft and unpretentious, the content is quite tough; hence, the expression "iron fists in kid gloves" is quite an adequate description of the Swedish leadership style (Laine-Sveiby, 1987:57).

Contributing to the misconception of the extreme softness of Swedish managers is their inconspicuous appearance. It is difficult to distinguish Swedish managers from other employees, since dress code and behavior are generally nondistinguishing features. And they have neither executive lifts nor their own dining room. To a foreigner it might seem to be a competition in humility when the Swedish bosses avoid all external symbols of their status (Laine-Sveiby, 1987).

Informal channels of communication are common and important; vertical as well as horizontal communication links penetrate the organization; and the familial and egalitarian communicative style is pervasive. The telephone is a very popular mode of communication in Sweden. Managers consider it a waste of time to write memos or letters to their colleagues or subordinates; instead, they just talk to them over the telephone (Forss, Hawk, and Hedlund, 1984). Besides, the Swedish executives usually make their telephone calls themselves. No intermediaries or secretaries are needed at each end of the line to try to connect the bosses at the same time. It is perhaps only in Sweden that the director general for the National Labour Market Board (AMS) with over 20,000 employees makes his telephone calls himself and introduces himself to a stranger with the words, "yeah, well, hi, my name is Allan Larsson," with no direct indication of his status and position (Laine-Sveiby, 1987).

Yet another facet of the informal style is the manner by which Swedes address people. Most people insist on being on a first-name basis with everybody, from workmates to bosses and from juniors to seniors. Hence, titles are seldom used in Swedish workplaces. Since everybody is on a first-name basis, titles sound strange and pretentious. But even when a third person is spoken of in a conversation, that person's first name, and not title, is used. Furthermore, Swedish bosses usually refer to their subordinates as *mina medarbetare* (my collaborators) instead of *min personal* (my staff).

Although this egalitarian approach is relatively recent, it is a quality of which Swedes are now militantly proud. Egalitarianism has clear implications for Swedish management; for example, it facilitates internal communication and favors upward communication from the shop floor, reduces interpersonal friction between ranks, and constitutes a work value that appeals to everyone (Lawrence and Spybey, 1986).

Teamwork is a pervasive feature in Swedish organisational life. There are blue-collar autonomous groups on the shop floor, an array of white-collar project groups at the office level, and various task forces or special interest groups at the management and executive level. Most important to a Swedish manager is the ability to select a good team and develop knowledge of how to lead it. The project group or program structure, invariably connected to the matrix organization, totally dominates the service and professional sectors in Sweden such as banking, brokerage, accounting, advertising, and law. Matrix structures can be found in all sectors of the Swedish economy, and even incorporated into other types of organizational structures (Forss, Hawk, and Hedlund 1984).

Consensual Decision Making

There is generally a strong concern for consensus-building procedures in decision making in Swedish organizations. Decision making in Sweden is normally participative. It is therefore natural for a Swedish manager to consult his subordinates, and not just cosmetically, for he or she relies on subordinates' initiatives. The subject matter is carefully investigated and discussed in committees. This committee system is not only prevalent in the private sector, but it is even more frequent within the public sector. Committee work is especially pervasive within government agencies and departments; it is a common joke that committees are sometimes formed not to solve problems but to bury them (Forss, Hawk and Hedlund, 1984).

There is a definite tendency to avoid unilateral action, and it is rare that decisions are based only on formal authority. Instead, there is a general preference for informal, implicit, consensual decision making. In Sweden anything that the boss does may be challenged; and management prerogatives are not easily accepted. A Swede is not easily impressed by anybody or anything: That makes him a dangerously skilled negotiator, this is a necessary ability in a Swedish consensus-based decision-making system. One advantage of this organic system is that once the decision is formally made, it has been sanctioned and shared by all affected parties. The obvious disadvantage is, of course, that it takes time. But the obverse side of slow decision making is fast implementation (Forss, Hawk, and Hedlund, 1984; Laine-Sveiby, 1987).

This participatory consensus-building is not just a matter of Swedish character or cultural values. Since 1977, Sweden has had codetermination legislation that makes widespread consultation mandatory in many decision-making situations

(MBL), and employee representation on boards of directors was introduced in 1973 (Rubenowitz, Norrgren, and Tannenbaum, 1983).

> Swedish management seems to lack clear decisions; it seems as if a decision
> isn't made until it has been executed (Larsson, 1986).

Thus, outsiders recognize the Swedish consensus-based decision-making system as being very slow as well as fussy and implicit. Hence, Swedish managers are often accused of a certain degree of indecisiveness: Swedes seem to prolong the decision-making process, if they do not try to avoid decisions altogether. The latter proposition has seriously been forwarded by researchers studying organizational behavior in Swedish organizations. Following basically a phenomenological approach, some researchers have suggested that Swedish organizational behavior includes "talk" and "action," with the two functions seeming to blend into each other without any intermediary step, as for example, decision. It is a well-known fact that Swedish management is action-oriented, and a favorite managerial expression is *att vidtaga atgarder*: to adopt measures (Czarniawska and Wolff, 1986).

Difficult and embarrassing situations are avoided, sometimes at high cost. In Sweden it is considered very immature not to be able to cope with an inclination to contradict one another. The person who wants to show respect will never dream of engaging another in a real discussion where the other's opinion might really be scrutinized (Laine-Sveiby, 1987).

This norm of conflict avoidance is expressed in many ways when staff-management conflicts arise in a Swedish company. In most cases all parties prefer to close their eyes, hoping that the problems will go away in the meantime. To an external observer, it could even be difficult to detect that conflict resolution is in progress. One example is the lack of reprimands against employees who do not perform well. Top management does not seem to do anything overt about it. But that does not imply that the Swedish executives disregard the real problems; rather, only solutions to the problems are sought along lines acceptable to Swedish values. Transfer to another post or retraining is perhaps the most common mechanism of Swedish conflict resolution. Often solutions cannot be implemented immediately, for it might take some time to find a solution that could benefit both parties. Although the Swedish way of conflict resolution can be slow, no open conflict need ever occur. The embarrassment of open confrontation is avoided, and the parties may retreat with their dignity intact. There are no losers (Laine-Sveiby 1987).

Sometimes, however, potential conflicts can stay unresolved for a long time, continuing to smoulder but not allowed to burst into a head-on confrontation. The Swedish way of administering such situations would be to break all contacts and communication with the other party, rather than to risk an open conflict. This breakdown of all communication is a security valve that makes it possible to go on and live with conflicts, sometimes year after year (Forss, Hawk, and Hedlund, 1984).

A factor contributing to conflict avoidance and consensus-seeking activities is the willingness to compromise. Swedes never give way; instead, they compromise. The compromise is a rational and attractive course of action, the behavioral expression of Swedish reasonableness and moderation. Even when Swedes think that they are completely in the right, they might be willing to meet halfway. The compromise is used with the pragmatic intent of proceeding without further delay to be able to make a decision; yet, in other situations, the compromise is probably a way of avoiding the embarrassment of overt conflict (Daun, 1989).

Swedish companies usually have very flat organizational hierarchies that to a large extent are decentralized. Lower organizational levels usually have a substantial influence on decisions, and, more often than not, they have their own budgetary resources to develop expertise and make their voices heard, and they can often implement projects of their own. At higher organizational levels, it is typically believed that decisions should be taken close to sources of information and daily operations (Forss, 1987; Forss, Hawk, and Hedlund, 1984).

Authority of Knowledge

In Sweden, the practical solution is regarded as superior, and when there is a conflict between this and other interests, the practical solution will prevail. One advantage of this cool, nonemotional attitude toward problems is that it helps prevent a lot of argumentation. When intelligent people meet to make decisions and everybody is focused on the facts, there is no real reason to disagree (Jenkins, 1968). Although this observation is a little bit exaggerated, it is interesting as a contrast to what could be the case in many other countries.

> There is no other country in the world with so many "experts" as Sweden (Laine-Sveiby, 1987:124).

One base of authority within Swedish organizations is the claim to an area of knowledge or expertise. A person's image and the respect he or she can demand from others basically rests on that person's own competence in a specific area. Specialization is very important in Swedish society where it is highly developed. As noted earlier, this phenomenon has been called a cult of competence. In Sweden there is no amateur point of view: people do not speak when they do not know, leaving it to those who do know. It could be argued that the cult of competence is but a facet of Swedish egalitarianism. Competence is, at least in principle, something that everybody can acquire; as such, in the Swedish context, it is a much more acceptable discriminator than some kind of ascribed status (Lawrence and Spybey, 1986).

In the Swedish view, there is generally one best way of making, doing, solving, or arranging any challenge, task, or problem. To reach this optimum stage, competence, patience, and a readiness to compromise are necessary. However, it must be pointed out that competence is action-oriented: All abstract knowledge must be transformable in skill and expertise that allows for the practice of the

Swedish principle of "management by letting people perform" (Laine-Sveiby, 1987:65; Lawrence and Spybey, 1986:62).

Accordingly, Sveiby and Risling (1986) define leadership as based on knowledge. A leader should be one stage ahead of the staff, giving him the power of the initiative. A leader must have not only narrow expert knowledge, but also the ability to keep track of the whole field of knowledge that is represented within his or her company. A leader must be able to dig in where it is needed and not hesitate to work all night if necessary, leading with the power of good example. Above all, a leader in Sweden has sufficient acumen to see the organization behind the individual persons, reaping benefits from the knowledge of individuals to contribute to the well-being of the total organization. On the other hand, the leader might also use the organization to allow the staff to develop their individual knowledge.

The described style of leadership fits perfectly well with the Swedish way of thinking. With its orientation toward rationality and its concrete logic, all of Sweden is one great knowledge company. People are seen as conveyors of different types of necessary competence. Hence, the task of the business executive is to transfer this abstract competence into concrete results (Laine-Sveiby, 1987).

The formal position in the organizational hierarchy is not enough to determine a person's authority. Moreover, authority cannot be gained by being talkative. On the contrary, to be silent has never been perceived as a negative trait among Swedes. A famous Swedish proverb goes: *Att tala ar silver, men tiga ar guld*: to speak is silver, but silence is golden. Neither is it advisable to try to keep a position of strength by power-play or pressuring others (Laine-Sveiby, 1987).

Hence, in this egalitarian and nonassertive organizational environment where patience, restraint, moderation, and emotional control are highly valued, there is only one way to gain personal authority. A Swedish manager must claim his own area of expertise and stick to it. Competent knowledge and hard work are the only way to earn the respect of subordinates (Laine-Sveiby, 1987).

HUMAN RESOURCE MANAGEMENT

This section provides certain demographic characteristics of Swedish managers. Then we cover how these managers are recruited, selected, compensated, appraised, developed, and affected by union organization.

Demographics

The managers' general level of qualifications in Sweden seems to be higher than that in many other countries. At least a college background seems to be the rule, and most middle and top management are university graduates. Moreover, double degrees with, for example, one in engineering and the other in business, are not uncommon. However, there is a relative absence of managers with a doctorate, although some people with higher education go into industry more than they did so before, due to a lack of opportunity of an academic career (Lawrence and Spybey, 1986).

Swedish managers tend to be specialists rather than generalists, in contrast to American managers, who typically appear to believe that they can "manage anything" or the typical British manager, who is proud to count himself as "a bit of an all-rounder" (Lawrence and Spybey, 1986:52).

Swedish managers generally seem to be most qualified in engineering, business, and law, in that order. Production managers and managers in other technical positions tend to be engineers, with either a technical college diploma or a university degree in engineering. Commercial managers have qualifications in business, since they have either graduated from a commercial college or they have the university degree in business, *civilekonom*. Personnel managers tend to have either a law, sociology, or business university degree (Lawrence and Spybey 1986).

Since most big companies are in engineering, it is preferred that a Swedish top executive have an engineering degree. Indeed, if all managerial ranks are considered and not just the top, engineers are still predominant in Swedish industry. At the top, however, there has been a definite change. Starting in the 1960s, it has been increasingly more common to appoint sales or marketing people as managing directors. One of the more prominent examples of this trend is Percy Barnevik of ABB (formerly ASEA). Currently, most of the larger companies are headed by an executive with a business degree, although there are still some engineers in top positions, and occasional lawyers, like Pehr Gyllenhammar, the head of Volvo (Lawrence and Spybey, 1986).

During the decades of growth following World War II and until the beginning of the 1970s, the immigration of foreign labor was encouraged as a way of meeting the needs of Swedish industry. Today, foreign citizens make up about 5 percent of the country's workforce. However, this has had little effect on the ethnic structure of the ranks of Swedish managers, since this foreign reinforcement comprises mainly blue-collar workers (Swedish Institute, 1989).

Women currently make up about half of the total labor force, and since the early 1970s a series of laws have been enacted in Sweden aimed at promoting sexual equality. However, the real problem in Sweden, as elsewhere, is how to make society change, since it largely seems to ignore the legislative approach (Lawrence and Spybey, 1986). Sweden has, however, achieved a higher degree of sexual equality than many other countries. Swedish women tend to defer and compromise less, marry later, have greater claims to independent careers, and are more likely to work outside their home. A very high percentage of women work outside the home in Sweden—85 percent in 1989—although half of them were in part-time jobs (Statistiska Centralbyran, 1990a).

Needless to say, as in most other countries, most managers are men, but there has been a rapid infusion of women into the executive world. Today, young Swedish women, who are as thoroughly prepared for a business career as their male counterparts, frequently prefer a career, at least temporarily, over marriage and children. Women are amply represented in business schools and faculties at universities, to the extent that they sometimes make up the majority of the business students. However, women managers are less visible in the private sector than in the public sector, with fewer women having top positions in private than in public sector organizations. As yet, none of the leading Swedish industrial corporations is headed by a woman. Nevertheless, on the whole, more career opportunities are open to women in Sweden than in most other countries, and Sweden even has a female equality ombudsman (*JamO*) to look after the legislated equal rights of women (and men) in the job market.

As to the distribution of age of managers, a recent investigation of Scandinavian top managers found that one of seven was under forty years of age, one of eight was over sixty years, one of fifty over sixty-five years, and more were over fifty than between forty and fifty years of age. Hence, to reach a top position might take at least thirty years for most managers (Sjoborg, 1986).

Recruitment and Selection

Nine years of schooling are compulsory for all children starting at age seven. Over 90 percent go on to at least two years of upper secondary school, choosing from among numerous vocational or academic study lines. Furthermore, an extensive system of municipal adult education enables adults to acquire the same primary and secondary education as young persons. Schools are run by municipalities and provide free instruction, books, and lunches. Altogether Sweden has more than thirty institutions of higher education, operated by the state and providing free instruction. Slightly more than half of the students in higher education are women, and a large number of students are people over twenty-five taking advantage of liberalized admission rules for those with work experience (Swedish Institute, 1988).

Despite the egalitarian Swedish society and its lack of differentiation, there are some informal status ratings in the Swedish higher educational system. Degree courses in engineering are offered primarily at the technical universities. However, two of these are more prestigious than the others; first, the Royal Technical University in Stockholm, closely followed by the Chalmers Technical University in Gothenburg. Both were founded in the second quarter of the nineteenth century and are enormously prestigious (Lawrence and Spybey, 1986).

With regard to the business degree, the *civilekonom*, there is also a ranking according to prestige. Originally, this degree was only awarded by the Stockholm School of Economics (*Handelshogskolan*), founded at the turn of the century, but later another *Handelshogskola* was founded in Gothenburg, which also awarded the *civilekonom* (Lawrence and Spybey 1986). Although these two are probably preeminent, during the last two decades the business degree *civilekonom* has been awarded by all major universities as well as some of the more newly created regional universities.

In Sweden, there is a much greater interchange between universities, industry, and the state administration than in many other countries. It is fairly common to transfer from a university post to business or to the civil service and, in many cases, back again. That constitutes a Swedish equivalent of the "old boys network.'' Hence, a select group of individuals from the universities circulate in government, the civil service, industry, and the trade unions (Lawrence and Spybey, 1986).

In the managerial selection process, most employers still use appraisal of educational background and formal competence as a traditional ingredient, at least as a screening device. However, it is seldom the exclusive basis for a decision on employment outside the public sector, which still seems to hold formal merits in high regard (Engelbert, 1989).

Interviews with applicants, on the other hand, are quite common. Most employers agree that the interview with the applicant is essential, but frequently it is conducted merely to check whether one can get along on the interpersonal level. Although personal relations are important, a short meeting is hardly ideal in assessing future trustful interpersonal affinity (Engelbert, 1989).

Employment consultants are becoming increasingly more popular in Sweden as well as in many other countries. Unfortunately, that line of business has a reputation of fortune-hunting and is strewn with people who are much better in selling themselves than in assessing applicants. Hence, it is natural for the consultant to favor such a talent among the applicants. Unfortunately, an ability to sell oneself has little to do with leadership capability, competence, creativity, and a willingness to cooperate—qualities appreciated in the Swedish management culture. However, in pure head-hunting cases, one's own staff can be utilized since they know the company and its business well. However, this option is seldom used in Sweden, where the slightest hint of nepotism or similar irregularities is taken extremely seriously (Engelbert, 1989).

The written tests used in Sweden are of two different types: performance tests, which try to measure talent or skills and knowledge; and tests that deal with personality, interests, and attitudes. This type utilizes questionnaires or projective tests, with projective tests handled only by specialists. Today a number of testing firms offer a variety of these tests, on a consulting basis or through direct sale of the test to the client company to be used by their own employment staff. The direct sale approach usually involves some kind of certification to make sure the client company staff members can handle the test in a correct way (Engelbert, 1989).

Generally, selection techniques are used in much the same way and to the same extent in Sweden as in many other Western industrialized countries. Typical for Sweden in this respect, however, is a positive basic attitude to people, which sometimes results in a hiring decision against one's better knowledge. A countervailing force to that overoptimistic attitude is the strict employment legislation, which makes it virtually impossible to fire anybody, except under extraordinary circumstances.

Compensation

Sweden has avoided pursuing a state income policy. The trade unions and the employer organizations are considered strong enough to reach their own agreements on salaries and other work conditions. These conditions have traditionally been regulated by nationwide collective bargaining agreements. But as a result of government taxation policies, the high inflation rate, and the shrinking space for salary increases in real terms, there has recently been a growing degree of consultation with the government on salary and income issues (Swedish Institute, 1989).

Collective bargaining covers both privately and publicly employed white- and blue-collar workers, except in the case of chief executive officers (CEOs) who negotiate directly with their employers on an individual basis.

Base Salary and Indirect Compensation   In Sweden, there is relatively little differentiation as to net earned income. It is not only that wage differences between various skill grades of blue-collar workers, or between shop floor workers and first-line supervisors, are quite narrow; the wage span for the whole occupational structure is narrower than that in many other Western countries. Consequently, the differences between managerial and worker salaries, between salaries of various managerial grades, between graduate and nongraduate salaries, are all considerably less than those elsewhere (Lawrence and Spybey, 1986).

Swedish managers are poorly paid by international standards. Table 6.5 presents salaries for some private and public sector categories of managers. Furthermore, an income tax system that is more sharply progressive than that in most West European countries further reduces the net income of the Swedish manager. However, this system has recently been revised, so that instead of marginal taxation rates of 60 to 80 percent, which were common among middle-class income earners, the new marginal rate maximum is about 50 percent. In addition to salaries, employers also pay fees for pensions and other statutory social benefits under labor-management agreements, amounting to 42.9 percent of gross wages during 1988 (Swedish Institute, 1989).

Traditionally, the managerial wage structure in Sweden leaves very little allowance for individual performance incentives, perhaps reflecting the egalitarian basic values. Besides, fringe benefits are less common in Sweden than in many other countries since everyone is taxed without exception (Lawrence and Spybey, 1986:64–65). However, recently signs of modest changes have been detected in this entrenched policy, even in the public sector where the previously totally dominant principle of seniority has been supplemented with performance and market demand criteria in adjusting salaries.

Since 1978, the minimum paid vacation has been five weeks per year, but managers frequently enjoy longer vacations than that. All residents in Sweden are covered by national health insurance. If a person is ill or must stay home to take care of sick children, that person receives a taxable daily allowance, equal, in most cases, to 90 percent of lost income. Except for modest fees, the health insurance pays all hospitalization costs, prescribed drugs, laboratory fees, and visits to doctors and public outpatient clinics. This insurance also covers a large proportion of private doctors' fees and about 40 percent of dental care costs.

When a child is born, the parents are legally entitled to a total of twelve months of paid leave from work, which can be shared between them, with an option of saving six of these months for use during the child's first four years.

Table 6.5
Management Base Salaries, 1988 (arithmetic mean, SEK[a])

	Top Managers	Other Managers
Private Sector		
Mining and manufacturing	20,579	
Wholesaling and retailing	19,469	
Commercial and savings banks	22,882	14,020
Insurance companies	20,350	
Pharmacies	17,771	
Public Sector		
Government:		
Inspector of police		11,756
Head of department	18,687	
Principal assistant secretary		13,403
Local governments:		
Librarian		10,362
County councils:		
Head physician	28,052	
Assistant physician		15,510

[a] 1 SEK = US$ 0.16 in 1988
Source: Statistiska Centralbyran, 1990b:231.

They also receive tax-free child allowances, equal for everyone, until the child's sixteenth birthday. Children who then continue their education are entitled to study allowances. At the university levels, these consist mainly of repayable loans. Municipalities provide a growing number of children with day-care and after-school activities at low cost. Low-income families and pensioners are eligible for housing allowances.

The basic old-age pension financed by tax revenues is payable to everyone from the age of sixty-five. The state also pays an income-related supplementary pension (ATP) financed from employer payroll fees. The two types of pension, both of which rise automatically with inflation, are designed to provide two-thirds of a pensioner's average real earnings during his fifteen best paid years (Swedish Institute, 1988). In addition, supplemental private pension schemes became increasingly popular until the tax-exempt status of the policy was suddenly revoked.

Nonmonetary Compensation A satisfying job, in terms of work that the individual finds interesting, is extremely important to a Swede and is a powerful motivator in the Swedish context. Such attitudes might somewhat compensate for the relative lack of material rewards available to Swedish managers (Lawrence and Spybey, 1986). Consensual decision making is an integral part of Swedish managerial behavior, and a long series of changes and innovations in employee participation have taken place in Swedish companies. Developments have occurred regarding three different levels of participation: shop floor participation, company participation, and financial participation. Shop floor participation affects lower and middle management in redefining their leadership roles. Company participation refers to employee influence over their workplace through union representation at various company levels and affects managers at both ends of the representative channel. Finally, financial participation focuses on the question of who should own companies and does not directly affect managerial functions.

Performance Appraisal

Performance appraisal techniques go very much against the grain of Swedish managerial culture, and formal systems are not very common in Swedish organizations. Typically, employees are expected to adhere to more or less explicitly stated goals, but without much systematic performance evaluation and feedback. The tendency is to favor the developmental and training part of the performance appraisal function over the evaluative/judgmental element with its potential conflicts. Instead, information on individual job performance is usually brought about through informal and personalized control and communication in Swedish organizations, suited to basic cultural managerial values. However, a recent tendency has been toward more standardized and mechanistic control systems in Swedish companies, especially in large multinationals, manifested through greater reliance on financial reporting and control as well as more coordination between headquarters and subsidiaries (Hedlund, 1989; Hedlund and Aman, 1984).

Furthermore, Sweden has shown a growing interest in *Personalekonomi* (human resource accounting). However, the focus is on human capital investments, human asset statements, costing of human resources, and so on, rather than on individual staff performance appraisal (Grojer, 1990; Johanson and Nilson, 1990).

Labor Relations

Industrial relations are usually identified with reasonableness and compromise. Unlike most countries, Sweden has separate trade unions for white-collar and blue-collar workers. The founding of the Social Democratic Labor party in Sweden in 1889 preceded the establishment of an umbrella organization uniting a number of different manual-worker trade unions in 1898 into the Swedish Trade Union Confederation (LO). White-collar workers were not represented by LO. Instead, white-collar workers' unions established their own umbrella organizations like the Central Organization of Salaried Employees (TCO). Formed in 1944, TCO represents both private sector employees and civil servants, with over 1 million members or about 75 percent of all white-collar workers at the present time. The Swedish Confederation of Professional Associations (SACO/ SR), which is for professionals and civil servants, has another 10 percent of the white-collar workforce, most of whom have university-level training (Lawrence and Spybey, 1986). Union membership is very high in Sweden; about 85 percent of the country's white-collar workers and 90 percent of its blue-collar workers belong to a trade union (Swedish Institute, 1989). Only CEO's and ministers of government departments are barred from union membership, for these are considered as employers or their representatives.

Most private sector employers belong to the Swedish Employers' Confederation (SAF), which has more than 42,000 affiliated firms employing more than 1.2 million people. There are also employers' organizations representing central and local governments, public corporations, cooperatives, banks, newspaper publishers, shipping, and a few other industries (Swedish Institute, 1989).

As a consequence of the high degree of unionization, there is a high level of support for unions and attitudes toward them are positive. A survey study of union attitudes found that 52 percent of Swedish respondents believed that the unions were responsible for improvements in living standards. The corresponding figure for the United Kingdom was only 6 percent (Scase, 1978). However, the pervasive power of the unions has also been questioned in Sweden. Their traditional focus on monetary compensation, resulting in increased inflationary pressures, instead of emphasizing other qualities in the work situation, has come under heavy criticism recently.

CONCLUSIONS AND TRENDS

Most Swedish managers would explicitly deny that they have very much power at all, and, contrary to many other countries where managers issue such statements as lip service, they would probably be correct. The Swedish egalitarian society and, hence, management culture, makes any manager more of a *primus inter pares* than a center of organizational dominance. The idea of relatively equal and strong men united in a battle under a commander who is merely the first among these equals indeed already had roots in the Viking Age (Forss, Hawk, and Hedlund, 1984).

Generally, the influence Swedish managers can exert within the organization is contingent on their respectability based on their competence and knowledge, as explained earlier. Of course, the extent of that influence is also to a certain degree based on rank, but much less so than in many other countries. Managers' organizational influence is also alleviated by the high degree of unionization and the elaborate participative decision-making system, evoked by culture and imposed by legislation. External managerial influence on social or political issues is usually channeled through the unions or employers' organizations. Societal influence on a more personal basis is also regularly wielded through the considerable amount of interchange of senior staff between public and private sector organizations. Occasionally, celebrated top managers like Jan Carlzon (SAS), Pehr Gyllenhammar (Volvo), and Hans Werthen (Electrolux) have so successfully mustered public support for their personal opinions that they might have influenced political decisions. In most countries, this situation would not raise any eyebrows, but in a Swedish context, it is something remarkable.

Private market capitalism has recently experienced a global thrust that has affected Sweden as well. Consequently, the status of private sector managers in Sweden has increased considerably, whereas the status of public sector management stands to lose even further from such a development.

There are signs of emerging changes in managerial behavior in Sweden. The management culture prevalent at the time of Swedish industrialization barely 100 years ago, could hardly be described as egalitarian, participative, and "soft." Rather, it was firmly based on authoritarian and patriarchal values. Once again, there are some contemporary signs of tougher and more autocratic attitudes in Swedish managerial behavior. Strong leadership is now again acclaimed, and there could be a return to a more charismatic and assertive leadership pattern.

A crucial point, however, is what will happen in the Swedish society at large, since managerial culture merely reflects the national culture. In that respect, it has been suggested that in the future Swedes will be more superficially extroverted and more indifferent toward strangers, accepting cultural variety but at the same time appreciating the Swedish way of life. Swedes will increasingly try to realize themselves at work, giving them less leisure time. The current trend of more informal relationships between people will continue, and there will be fewer restraints on emotional expressions. Cynicism might become more common, substantiated as less respect for politics and authorities, less belief in the natural goodness in human beings, and an increased challenge to the blind belief in reason implicating decreasing expert power in the future (Selmer, in press). Although most of these proposed cultural changes seem to be in accordance with international developments, basic cultural values appear to be quite resilient in the face of quick changes, which would also inhibit sudden transformations of the Swedish managerial culture (Forss, Hawk, and Hedlund, 1984; Hedlund, 1989).

There are several significant challenges in the near future. The deteroriation of the economy's competitive position is an acute problem. The devaluations of the Swedish crown in 1981 and 1982 had a strong favorable impact on the Swedish economy, and the competitive position of Swedish industry improved substantially. During the last years, however, capacity constraints have been a growing bottleneck, and, combined with a shortage in labor, costs and prices have been pushed up. Hence, the competitive edge has largely been exhausted, and the relative cost and price deteriorations have resulted in increasing losses in the market shares of exported manufactures.

Ultimately, there is a need for more permanent cost and structural adjustments. The future of Swedish industry no longer lies in manufacturing products with low production costs for sale at low prices in markets with a high demand. Sweden must instead sell high-valued products of superior technical quality in extremely severe international competition in markets where Sweden constantly has to compete with countries that have a similar industrial structure. This strategy is contingent on the relatively low pay level for well-educated as opposed to salaries for low-educated personnel, which in an international perspective are high. Hence, it is advantageous to develop products that require a high degree of engineering skills, whereas sheer routine manufacturing for the same reason is distinctly undesirable.

In the long run, Swedish business will have to enter an era of development, where universities and technological centers become generators in developing new products, some of which will be manufactured elsewhere. There are already clear signs of such a novel trend. The selling of know-how rather than the products themselves is becoming an increasingly common feature in the Swedish internationalized business world (East Asia Project, 1987; Swedish Institute, 1989).

On the other hand, because of the very rapid advancements in robot techniques, wage levels are becoming less pertinent to manufacturing than the ability to develop and fully utilize all the possibilities provided by industrial robots. Because of the relatively high level of unskilled labor costs in Sweden, the level of industrial robotization is extremely high. In the industrial sector that manufactures electrical and electronic equipment, the number of robots per 10,000 workers is the highest in the world. This development implies that it will be possible in the future to retain high-quality manufacturing in Sweden and maybe even some fully automated, lower grade mass production (East Asia Project, 1987; Swedish Institute, 1989).

Another complementary way of strengthening Swedish industry is through improved productivity. During the 1960s, real industrial output per hour worked increased by an annual average of 7.5 percent, perhaps an all-time Swedish record. In the 1970s, productivity rose by 3.5 percent per year, but the 1980s was characterized by ups and downs resulting in an annual average increase of 3 percent (Swedish Institute, 1989).

The concept of productivity should be applied in a "total" sense to include the output of all human resources, including all staff and support functions in an organization. The development of total productivity is, however, dependent on a number of factors beyond the performance of each individual employee. When we look back, it seems obvious that productivity improvements have been due largely to increased capital inputs and the resultant upgrading of production techniques. Therefore, the capacity for productivity improvements of the human resource itself is not yet fully utilized in Sweden today. Although productivity is also influenced by many political, legal, and economic considerations on the national level, all companies must have a productivity increase each and every year (Sjoborg, 1986).

The importance of the productivity concept for the future of the national economy in general, and its business organizations in particular, seems to be widely acknowledged by managers today. A recent investigation of Scandinavian top managers found that 80 percent of them agree that productivity will be more important as a means of competition in the future and that productivity is one of the few variable factors that managers will also be able to influence in the future. Moreover, 90 percent of them agree that productivity escalation will save the industry in the future (Sjoborg, 1986).

Consequently, these discernible current tendencies and speculated future developments constitute formidable challenges for Swedish managers. Fundamental changes in industry, regarding both structure and activities, require extraordinary efforts in education and research as well as a wholehearted commitment to high technology. The importance of the educational level of the labor force as a whole will be a decisive factor in the competition between countries. Needless to say, future managers have to be even better trained than before and probably less specialized than earlier owing to the volatility of the future business environment. Furthermore, a continuing internationalization of the already highly international Swedish economy can be expected, with subsequent increased requirements of special skills and knowledge necessary to do business on a global scale.

The internationalization of the system for higher education has already begun, and most institutions have special units promoting international cooperation and exchange of experience as well as organizing student and staff interchanges. Furthermore, academic courses are to an increasing extent being given in English, and several institutions for higher education are currently selling their educational services in the international market, something that was not possible just a few years ago.

This endeavor coincides with ongoing discussions of the deficient quality of some areas of the higher education system in Sweden and how to improve the situation. So far, dwindling state funding has mostly induced the institutions for higher education to open up to private industry for financial support, also approved of and supported by the government. In many cases, this has resulted in close collaboration and the establishment of applied research centers and technological "villages." Hence, a foundation has been laid to develop a new type of Swedish manager to cope with the challenges of the future.

REFERENCES

Czarniawska, B., and Wolff, R. 1986. "How We Decide and How We Act: On the Assumptions of Viking Organization Theory." *Research Paper* 6304. Stockholm: Economic Research Institute, Stockholm School of Economics.

Daun, A. 1989. *Svensk Mentalitet* [Swedish Mentality]. Stockholm.

Daun, A., and Phillips-Martinsson, J. 1986. "Hur Djupt Sitter Svenskheten?" [How Deep is the Swedishness?], *Forskning och Framsteg*, No. 6.

East Asia Project. 1987. *Made in Sweden*. Gothenburg.

Ellis, R. 1990 (March 11). "Swedes' Good Life Turns Sour." *The Sunday Times*,.

Engelbert, B. 1989. "Ta Tillvara Det Du Ser och Hor" [Take Advantage of What You See and Hear]. *Personal*, No. 1.

Forss, K. 1987. *Arbete Utomlands* [Work Abroad]. Lund.

Forss, K., Hawk, D., and Hedlund, G. 1984. "Cultural Differences—Swedishness in Legislation, Multinational Corporations, and Aid Administration." *Research Paper* 84/5. Stockholm: Institute of International Business, Stockholm School of Economics.

Grojer, J-E. 1990, *Det Personalekonomiska Bokslutet* [The Human Resource Annual Statement], Vallingby.

Hedlund, G. 1989. "Managing International Business: A Swedish Model." Unpublished manuscript.

Hedlund, G., and Aman, P. 1984. *Managing Relationships with Foreign Subsidiaries*. Stockholm.

Jenkins, D. 1968. *Sweden and the Price of Progress*. New York: Coward.

Johanson, U. and Nilson, M. 1990. *Personalekonomi: en Litteraturstudie* [Human Resource Accounting: A Literature Review]. Personalekonomiska Institutets skriftserie, no. 90:1, University of Stockholm, Stockholm.

Laine-Sveiby, K. 1987. *Svenskhet som Strategi* [Swedishness as Strategy]. Stockholm.

Larsson, K. 1986. *Det Stora Klivet* [The Big Step]. Stockholm.

Lawrence, P., and Spybey, P. 1986. *Management and Society in Sweden*. London.

Likert, R. 1961. *New Patterns of Management*. New York.

Olson, F. 1989 (February 15). "Entusiasm och Kampanda Ledarens Mal" [Enthusiasm and Fighting Spirit Are the Goals of the Leader]. *Svenska Dagbladet*.

Pedersen, D. 1990 (March 5). "The Swedish Model." *Newsweek*,.

Rubenowitz, S., Norrgren, F., and Tannenbaum, A. S. 1983. "Some Social Psychological Effects of Direct and Indirect Participation in Ten Swedish Companies." *Organization Studies* 4(3).

Scase, R. 1978. "Social Democracy and Workers' Conceptions of Power in England and Sweden." In S. Giner, & M. S. Archer, eds. *Contemporary Europe: Social Structures and Cultural Patterns*. London.

Selmer, J. In press. *Vikings and Dragons: Swedish Management in Southeast Asia*. Singapore.

Sjoborg, E. 1986. *Skandinaviskt Management* [Scandinavian Management]. Malmö.

Statistika Centralbyran. 1990a. *Lathund om Jamlikhet 1990* [Summary about Equality]. Stockholm.

————. 1990b. *Sveriges Officiella Statistik* [Statistical Abstract of Sweden]. Stockholm.

Sveiby, K. E., and Risling, A. 1986. *Kunskapsforetaget—Seklets Viktigaste Ledarut-maning?* [The Knowledge Company—The Most Important Leader] Challenge of the Century?. Stockholm.

Swedish Institute. 1986 (March). "Sweden." *Fact Sheets on Sweden.*

————. 1987 (December). "Swedish Industry." *Fact Sheets on Sweden.*

————. 1988 (March). "General Facts on Sweden." *Fact Sheets on Sweden.*

————. 1989 (July). "The Swedish Economy." *Fact Sheets on Sweden.*

7

AUSTRIA

Peter R. Haiss and
Werner Schicklgruber

In Austria two basic groups form what is familiarly known as a manager: (1) small companies, which are mostly family-owned businesses—their owner-managers are by their very definition managers; and (2) medium and large companies which are led by employed managers who are responsible to one of three types of owners: private domestic, foreign, or public, including direct or indirect governmental control. The large nationalized sector emerged in the postwar period out of the need to prevent enterprises that had been declared "German property" from being appropriated by the occupation forces after World War II. Thus, there is a close tie between actual managers in companies and "public" managers in governmental bodies.

THE ECONOMY

Austria accounts for only 0.15 percent of the world population, and it produces 0.8 percent of the world's social product. A share of 1.2 percent of world foreign trade makes Austria highly dependent on foreign markets (in the order of 70 percent of gross domestic product [GDP]). Out of the third of Austrian businesses that are under foreign influence, about 60 percent are under German ownership. Compared with that of other industrialized countries, Austria's economic performance has been quite impressive in the last three decades. On the basis of purchasing power parities, the Austrian growth rate was one percentage point above the average figure for member countries of the Organization of Economic Cooperation and Development (OECD) in terms of real GDP per capita. This reflects a positive growth differential against nearly all industrialized countries including Germany and the United States, the only exception being Japan.

GENERAL EMPLOYMENT TRENDS

According to the 1988 governmental population survey, 67 percent of Austria's resident population were employable, that is, fifteen to sixty-five years of age. Out of these 3.4 million residents, 14 percent were self-employed. By sectors of the economy, 8 percent of employed persons belonged to the primary sector, 37 percent to the secondary sector, and 55 percent to the services sector. Because of Austria's characteristic business structures with its high share of small- and medium-sized companies, 42 percent of the total number of employees work with companies employing one to forty-nine employees, another 32 percent belong to companies with a staff of 50 to 499, and 26 percent work in companies with a workforce of 500 or more. The Austrian unemployment rate is about 5 percent, which is well below the OECD average. In the 1980s, the potential labor supply was growing. This statistic has to be viewed in the context of the quite large number of foreigners leaving the Austrian labor market.

EVOLUTION OF THE MANAGERIAL CLASS IN AUSTRIA

The renowned Austrian economist, Joseph A. Schumpeter, stressed the central role of the so-called pioneer-type entrepreneur for economic development. However, as many researchers have pointed out, the status of entrepreneurship in Austria is poor compared to that of Western Europe generally. Economic restrictions on entrepreneurship have led to a severe scarcity of capital formation. In England industrial companies developed autonomously from preindustrial entities by internal financing during the Industrial Revolution. In Austria, however, the second wave of industrialization took place as late as the second half of the nineteenth century. It was stimulated by banks, which founded new companies or transformed conglomerates of small firms into industrial joint-stock companies. Thus, usually risk-averse bankers had to assume an entrepreneurial role within Austrian society. With the development of capital markets, however, the entrepreneurial role was removed from internal (dealing with staff) to external (dealing with customers) bank managers. Thereby, accountant and lawyer-type managers were replaced by more marketing-oriented managers, reflecting a societal value change. The current trends are toward self-employment, a fair number of management buyouts, and an attitude that no longer regards profits as evil.

Culture and Managerial Behavior

There is not a great deal of literature on Austrian cultural values and managers. However, Hofstede (1980) reported the results of a large-scale study involving employees and managers in forty countries working for a large American multinational corporation. Austria showed the lowest power distance. This finding translates into consultative decision making, solidarity, hierarchy as a means of convenience, and a stress on expert power. The Austrian social partnership system, that is, the institutionalized approach to solving social and economic problems through compromise and consensus rather than through confrontation, nicely mirrors this low power distance. In this way, conflict tends to be pragmatic rather than fundamental. Unions in countries low in power distance tend to be more pragmatic about earnings, employment security, and working conditions—which is exactly the case in Austria.

The relatively high uncertainty avoidance in Austria leads to a greater dependence of citizens on authorities, more elaborate legal systems, standardization, structuring of activities, emphasis on details and rituals, and risk aversion. As a result of this high uncertainty avoidance, in Austria Management by objectives has become "management by joint goal setting." This mitigates some of the risk and favors the team approach, which is also in line with the medium emphasis on individualism present in Austria. Goals are not imposed down the ranks but are agreed upon through discussion. However, the reliance on experts and the importance of regularity, mechanisms, and rituals are impediments toward change and progress. Thus, little is invested into research and development. There is also a commitment to preserving existing jobs. It has been argued that, while allowing for stability, the timely reallocation of capital and labor out of declining industries may have been retarded.

The interaction of low power distance and high uncertainty avoidance leads to the fact that the idea of openly disagreeing with lawful superiors simply does not occur. Therefore, the superego (a concept developed by an Austrian, Sigmund Freud) is internalized. Dissenters within companies are usually ousted, and seniority (i.e., well-fitted behavior within the company for several years) becomes an important mechanism in enabling employees to rise within Austrian companies. While information is dealt with in secrecy, it is important to use the grapevine.

Conflicts are not dealt with directly, but through the formation of working groups, whereby the topics are subdivided for subworking groups that develop rituals for mutual understanding of the other party's point of view. This in turn leads to a breaking up of the ingroup versus outgroup definition for the members of the so-called inner circle of both political parties and companies, for these inner groups overlap with one another. Therefore, networking among inner circles is of utmost importance for successful managerial behavior. While there often is a democratic leadership style on the surface, in reality it is the intertwined hierarchical cores where decisions are made in silence. The effort to reduce the complexity of "either-or" decisions to "both-and" thereby often results in "neither-nor" decisions.

Inherent in these findings are many issues that pertain to human resource management: industrial democracy as a way of bridging different interest groups; codetermination in decision making; structuring of activities; types of compensation; and managerial selection and recruitment. Although some of the arguments presented earlier may sound overstated, they contain some truth, as patterns of institutions within the Austrian society with particular structures and ways of functioning developed over time. These patterns served the country well as a stabilizing framework along the Iron Curtain. The close relation between business and labor on the one hand, and the strong personal link of both with the gov-

Table 7.1
Attempt to Estimate the Number and Gender of Austrian Managers
(Microcensus, 1988)

	Total 000's	Male Shares in%	Female Shares in%
Self-employed persons excl. family members and excl. agrucultural sectur	194.6	69	31
High-ranked employees: Executives	41.2	90	10
High-qualified occupation	113.3	80	20
Total	349.9	75	25
ad memoriam: Main occupation "managing" or "running the business" 1)	302.6	79	21

1) Sample of the microcensus predicted for the total number of employed persons.

Source: Austrian Central Office of Statistics, Vienna.

ernment as well as a reduced capitalism by the large public sector (i.e., nationalized banks and industry), constitute a framework that helps reduce risks and stabilize expectations.

HUMAN RESOURCE MANAGEMENT AND AUSTRIAN MANAGERS

Managers as a Sample

We used figures from two different sources to come up with a meaningful number of managers. First, the agricultural sector and family members assisting company owners are eliminated from the number of self-employed persons. This leaves us with 194,600 owner-managers. Second are employees with leadership functions (41,200 people) and those who fall in the category "high-qualified occupation" (113,300 persons). While the female share of self-employed persons is rather high (31 percent), it is only 20 percent among employees in "high-qualified leading occupations." (See Table 7.1.)

Self-employed persons are concentrated in the owners of rather small firms (22 percent), while 21 percent of the employees' group are in leading positions, probably in large companies. Thus, these two groups have a completely different social status. A rather high share of managers work for governmental institutions or for companies under governmental influence.

The General Educational System

Nearly 40 percent of managers have finished primary school as well as an apprenticeship, reflecting the large number of manager-owned small companies. Another 40 percent of Austrian managers have earned high school degrees. Roughly 13 percent of Austrian managers are university graduates.

This stratification is also the result of Austria's nonelitist, dual educational system with its strong emphasis on public schools. During the eighth grade, the duality of the educational system comes into play. First, students can choose to continue with high school and college, respectively, from the ninth to twelfth grade. This leads to a comprehensive final school-leaving examination, which is somewhat similar to a baccalaureate and grants the right to enroll in university graduate programs. Second, secondary school graduates (ninth grade) can choose to take only one more compulsory year of intermediate school and then start working full time as an apprentice with a company. However, usually over a three-year period, each apprentice has to attend regular school about one day a week. Thus, every Austrian has at least nine years of compulsory education, with a foreign language (usually English) being taught from the third grade on.

The educational system is based on a very egalitarian approach, with public support for books and bussing, and no tuition for schools or universities. Private schools, like the Theresian Academy, offer campuslike environments for the wealthy. The emphasis is on longtime evaluation of achievements and grades. Even those who went through the apprenticeship route can gain the right to attend university by passing special examinations and providing proof of practical work experience. Because of the historical development of universities, there is no campus system. A particular difference lies in the fact that doctoral graduates usually go into nonuniversity jobs. The links between business and the universities are less firm.

Recruitment

Managers at Austria's largest 500 companies stay with the same company for an average of about seven years. Compared to the United States, where managers remain for about three years on the same job, this would constitute low mobility. This seven-year stay is especially true for the top management layer. However, for about one-third of Austria's managers, the shortest time span with one company is only one year. When switching jobs, about 90 percent of Austrian managers generally accept and internalize the company's central norms and values. However, a recent study (Rottmann, 1987) revealed that these managers also keep some positive critical distance from their company. When moving upward in the hierarchy through switching jobs, about one-third of the managers go to companies of equivalent size, and one-third move up from smaller companies. Slightly more than half of all managerial positions are filled from the outside. About 10 percent of the companies in Austria only recruit from within.

This is not surprising, given the often intertwined interest groups and personal adherence to the collectivity as discussed earlier.

The usual route to an entry-level managerial position with a larger company starts from a commercial high school or a domestic business university. There also has been a trend toward recruiting MBAs from U.S. business schools. Recruiting from companies with strong management development programs is increasingly being done to fill positions. For example, all managers who made inroads onto the managing board of Austrian banks below the age of forty are an offspring of Girozentrale's prominent management development program. A large number of managers in governmental and government-related positions started their careers at bodies that form the Social Partnership System (e.g., Chamber, Union).

Selection

Austrian companies usually require very detailed curricula vitae that are different from U.S.-style résumés. Selection normally starts with an interview covering the applicant's goals, experience, and background. Case studies are included in these interviews. Many companies also require the successful completion of some psychological test. This is the case for only entry-level positions, however. Although detailed written job descriptions are widely used for white-collar jobs, this is only applies to 20 percent of managerial jobs. Increasingly, assessment centers are used for both selection and personnel development. Stringent laws tightly regulating the circumstances (e.g., advance notice) under which a person can leave for another job and strong unionization are supportive of job security, but not managerial mobility. Interestingly, the trend is toward the use of head-hunters. Whereas in the early 1980s only about 20 percent of job openings were filled with the assistance of head-hunters, this figure rose to about 30 percent in 1990, with 85 percent of Austrian companies using such services.

Evaluation, testing, and screening of candidates and the search for them are usually done by personnel service companies, while 70 percent of top management positions are filled through direct contact and executive calls. Job advertisements in daily newspapers account for about 70 percent of newly filled, lower ranked positions. Of specific sensitivity in terms of job search is the question of payment. Austrians are very secretive about their salary and earnings.

Prominent Management Development Centers

Out of the roughly 10,500 master's and doctoral graduates at Austrian universities, about 1,550 graduate in business administration and economics every year. There has also been an influx of graduates in law, technical studies, and agrobusiness into management. The Vienna University of Economics provides the largest number of graduates in business administration (about 805 a year, equivalent to Harvard), with a rather high dropout rate of 63 percent. This screening is the result of low-entry barriers and a demanding curriculum. Through joint study programs, it cooperates with forty outstanding universities from both Western and Eastern European countries. Although the Vienna University of

Economics offers the largest variety of areas of concentration, a couple of universities offer some kind of double-degree programs, for example, chemistry and business administration. A recent student poll about universities that offer business curricula showed the University of Linz as winner, with Graz, Klagenfurt, and Innsbruck also highly ranked (Mayer, 1990). All these public universities have the right to grant master's and doctoral degrees of about the same value, for Austria has no elitist "*grande écoles*" system as is the case in France. Although a large number of exchange programs have been established, only a small minority of students goes abroad. Among those, Fulbright students are very prominent.

As mentioned above, a variety of public commercial colleges and high schools are an important source of managerial education. Their areas of specialization mirror the Austrian sectoral and industry structure, for example, with special tourist colleges. Annual public spending per student amounts to about $5,000 each for about 80,000 students in business-related fields.

Other important management development centers for both public and business administration are private institutions run by the largest political parties, for example, the Political Academy of the conservative Austrian People's party or the Karl Renner Institute of the Socialist party. Institutions that form the Social Partnership System referred to earlier also provide massive business training, which is usually open to the public. This pertains to the Chamber of Commerce's *Wirtschaftsförderungsinstitut*, the Export Academy, the Industries' Management Institute, the Chamber of Labor's *Berufsförderungsinstitut*, and union institutions. Other privately run management development centers open to the public are the Hernstein Institute in Vienna (specializing in strategic management and organizational behavior) and the Austrian Academy for Advanced Management (ÖAF) for the broadest array of business-related fields. In-house management development programs are widespread among banks and larger companies.

Compensation of Managers

Productivity in Austria rose by 2.9 percent and 1.9 percent per annum in the periods 1970–80 and 1980–88, respectively. Real wages lagged behind the productivity gain adjusted by changes in the terms of trade by 0.5 percent per year in the 1980s, owing to more difficult labor market conditions and stronger international competition. Since the Austrian schilling (AS) was revaluated effectively against a currency basket of Austria's main trading partners, the unit labor costs adjusted by exchange rates rose 3.5 percent per annum in 1980–88, one percentage point above the average for those basket countries. Distribution imbalances within the wage brackets rose from 1970 on. The tax reform of 1988 brought a new tax scale with a lower marginal tax rate and fewer brackets than before in income tax as well as in corporate tax.

Against the background of a per capita income per employee of roughly AS250,000 (or $20,000) per year in 1988, there are clear differences by managerial level, function, and industry. While members of the board, for instance, CEOs, tip the AS2 million mark, the income of division heads generally ranges from AS 0.4 to 1.4 million. To receive above-average compensation, a manager should work in a growing industry with a joint-stock company that has more than 500 employees and that is located either in Austria's capital, Vienna, or in the western districts. He should have a specific qualification, for instance, be a university graduate, be forty years old, and have spent least at five to ten years with the company.

Bonuses and Fringe Benefits

Bonuses and other supplementary income play a significant role in the total compensation of Austrian managers. On average, fringe benefits (company cars, life insurance coverage, etc.) make up roughly a quarter of the total earnings of upper level managers. The base salary consists of fourteen payments (twelve months plus holiday and Christmas). Besides these fixed monthly salaries, more than 30 percent of the managers receive a further variable income quota. This usually amounts to a range of 12 to 28 percent of total compensation. The importance of employee stock ownership plans is growing. Bonuses are common for board members and division heads.

The most prominent example of an individual component of compensation is a regular contractual monthly overtime payment. Managers' fringe benefits also include insurance premiums paid by the company. (About 60 percent of all managers receive this benefit.) More than 70 percent of division heads and basically all board members have company cars. With about one-fifth of board members living in company residences, company housing is of less importance.

In addition to the public pension system, individual pensions are very prevalent among managers. More than 70 percent of the managing board members and about 50 percent of division heads receive such company pensions. Labor contracts in Austria specify that employees, and thereby managers, have the right to receive a lump-sum payment of about two to four monthly salaries upon termination of the working contract by the company. In a few cases, this even extends to managers who leave voluntarily.

Austrian managers rank in the middle in terms of direct compensation among European managers (Ploner, 1990). The CEOs' gross income per year was AS1.65 million (or about $135,000) in Austria. This total amounts to only 64 percent of the highest ranking Swiss managers. More or less the same imbalance holds true for the compensation of board members or division heads occupied in specific functional sections of the company. Austrian managers rank even lower, if allowance is made for taxes and social insurance, and for differences in the purchasing power of the individual countries. The net income of Austrian CEOs at purchase power parities can be found in the lower third of the respective samples.

Managerial Performance Appraisal

Performance appraisal, usually based on some management by joint goal-setting system, is taken very seriously in Austrian companies. What may be included is legally codified. In larger companies, usually there also exists a contract between the company and its employees (including managers) about both parties' duties and rights, which specifies how such performance appraisal must be done. Generally, the criteria are explicitly stated and available to those evaluated. Such performance appraisals are usually done on an annual basis. It is normally only a one-way activity, however; that is, superiors evaluate the efforts, achievements, and potential of further development of their subordinates, not the reverse. Upward performance appraisal feedback is usually done only in subsidiaries of U.S. companies. These performance appraisal ratings are typically accomplished via interviews, following an evaluation guideline. Evaluations are made available to the person evaluated; in most instances, the form is even countersigned. Thus, performance appraisal serves more of an evaluation than a development purpose.

Although performance appraisal is based on the individual's achievements, for managers it usually also covers an evaluation of the manager's team. These performance appraisals seriously influence a manager's further pay and subsequent career as long as he or she stays with the same company. However, as mentioned earlier, this formal and (at least on the surface) objective part of performance appraisal is usually accompanied by an old boys network, for example, people who know one another from common interest groups, clubs, and the like. In addition, knowing and interacting with your direct competitors (be it on the company, private, or political level) is relatively easy in a country with the population size of greater Chicago.

Labor Relations

Economic arrangements that reduce instability cannot be achieved by government policy alone. Labor relations also have to rely on specific interactions between economic and social groups. The Social Partnership is considered to be Austria's solution of such a stabilizing framework. On the business side, the members of the partnership are the Federal Economic Chamber, with obligatory membership for all employers, and the Association of Industrialists, a voluntary organization representing large companies (Table 7.2). Of lesser importance are the agricultural chamber for farmers' interests and smaller chambers representing specific groups of liberal professions. The labor side is represented through the Chamber of Labor, with obligatory membership for all employees and the Association of Trade Unions with voluntary membership. Nearly 60 percent of all employees are members of a trade union, although there has been a downward trend during the last few years. Because unions are organized along industrial sectors, no separate union represents managers. Although neither the business nor the labor side is technically partisan, elections within the various organizations yield a more or less clean political split and consequently a high degree of overlapping personnel across private and public institutions representing the respective side.

The Social Partnership system embodies the Austrian approach to economic and social problems, which is to seek solutions through compromise and consensus rather than through confrontation. The central body is the Parity Com-

Table 7.2
Structure of Employers' and Employees' Organizations

	Legal public law entities (membership compulsory)	Entities under private law (membership voluntary)
Business (general)	Federal Economic Chamber	Association of Industrialists
(agricultural)	Chamber of Agriculture	Annual Meeting of Agro-Chamber
(liberal professions)	different chambers	different institutions
Labor	Chamber of Labor	Federation of Trade Unions

mission for Wages and Prices. Made up of the chancellor, the minister for economic affairs, two representatives from each chamber and from the union association, the Parity Commission was intended to regulate wage and price increases. Currently, it acts more as a forum in which political and economic leaders regularly get together to discuss economic and social policy without the pressure of public exposure. More broadly, the social partners act as a second parliament, introducing policy initiatives, negotiating the details of legislation, and ensuring implementation, as well as negotiating wage rounds and resolving industrial disputes.

Within the Social Partnership, three working groups are of specific importance: the Price Subcommittee, the Economic and Social Advisory Board, and the Wage Subcommittee. The Wage Subcommittee oversees the wage-bargaining process in which highly centralized negotiations establish base wages. The committee does not determine the outcome but mainly influences the timing of the wage adjustment. The annual process is kicked off by a proclamation of separate guidelines formulated by the central employers' and employees' organizations. The technical orientation of the unions for wage adjustments is, generally speaking, the productivity gain of the overall economy. The process relies crucially on the self-discipline and self-restraint of the trade unions.

The price-setting process reduces the dangers of demand-pull inflation. The wage-setting process decreases the probability of cost-push inflation. Thus, the Austrian Social Partnership can be considered an institution that reduces risk costs by stabilizing expectations and that reduces adjustment costs by providing orientations and support for structural change. A closely related approach views the Social Partnership as a constitutional contract between business and labor. The basic consensus was established in a period of uncertainty (World War II and shortly afterward); the unanimity rule—which is the only fixed regulation—prevents both sides from exploiting short-run advantages.

The system is not all-encompassing, however. Apart from constitutional objections (Social Partnership is neither provided for nor formally established in Austria's constitution) and the missing representation of some economic and social groups, economic objections stem from the commitment to preserve existing jobs. The Social Partnership system tends to preserve existing structures. On the one hand, employers' associations are not particularly enthusiastic about new or progressive enterprises that logically do not fit into traditional patterns. On the other hand, union representatives are also unwilling to extend their solidarity to new vocational or professional groups whose ambitions and mobility make it difficult to fit them into established structures. This is especially important because of Austria's large nationalized sector. The timely reallocation of capital and labor out of declining industries may thus be retarded.

An understanding of two main factors constituting the social climate in Austria (i.e., the intimacy of the acting persons and groups in a very small country and the Social Partnership system incidental to these circumstances) leads to conclusions about specific managerial attitudes in this context. Managers in Austria are highly incorporated into the actual system of business/labor relationship. Owner-managers experience the relations to their workforce not only directly, but also against the background of agreements that their own association has made with the relevant labor union. Within single companies, some leeway is left for negotiations only in case of individual, probably day-to-day problems—certainly not for topics like general wage increases, working hours, and general working conditions.

CONCLUSIONS AND FUTURE TRENDS

The shifting attitudes and behavior of the Austrian population as well as a change in its formation will result in subtle alterations. For example, managers need to give more thought in the future to ecological and ethical considerations. Although there is a convergence in trends across countries, no convergence has yet occurred in what exactly these considerations are (e.g., what is ethical business behavior?). On the other hand, the aging of the population poses further challenges and opportunities to management. It will become more difficult for many family-owned businesses to find somebody to step in when the owner-founder retires. The rising average age of managers may lower their mobility. Life will be characterized by a longer time span of active work, requiring more frequent retraining and continued learning. All this has numerous implications for human resource management. Companies will increasingly have to compete for good managers, reemphasizing company-internal management development. Similarly, the new restriction for politicians to accept only one paid political function at a time will change the networking function of the Social Partnership system as much as the inclusion of new societal movements into it.

What does this mean for human resource practices? Certainly, organizations

Table 7.3
Future Issues for Personnel Management

Function	Issue
Selection & Recruiting	- more women in higher managerial ranks - stronger international competition for high-quality managers - higher mobility - sellers' market due to aging population
Training	- increasing importance of company-internal management development, programs to attract & keep managers - cross-cultural training for international teamwork - information-technology - retraining of elder managers
Compensation	- seniority of lesser importance - rising retirement age, thereby changing social security and pension system - more employee ownership plans - performance-based pay for non-sales positions possible through technology - more flexible shop and work hours
Labor Relations	- looser-coupled systems - integrate green and grey political movements, foreign "guest" workers and immigrants - decreased job security - rising influence of multinational companies and international bodies, falling influence of national governments

will become flatter as responsibility becomes decentralized. Austrian managers will have to think European, not only regionally. The generation of young managers is more apt to job-hop. Seniority will become of less importance for growth. But with the lack of enough young managers to fill up the ranks, older managers will be given second chances. Management teams will become increasingly international. Old boys networks will still exist, but their composition and role may change. Where there is a more market-driven economy, there are also fewer entry and exit barriers. It will be easier to start companies and do management buyouts. Job security in Austria will become less stable. See Table 7.3 for a summary of future issues for personnel management.

Many of these factors will lead to the greater influence of multinational companies and the relatively diminished influence of national governments in general. Thus, a small economy like Austria without large conglomerates will lose some of its sovereignty. There will also be an increased foreign stake in Austrian businesses, with resulting development opportunities for Austrian managers. On the other hand, this will open new chances inherent in the industry structure in

Austria. We must not undervalue small and start-up companies, because they play an important role in a market economy in innovation and in the process of gaining individual entrepreneurial skills. The possibilities these firms can offer for the overall economy are closely connected with their ability to grow and form symbiotic alliances. It is exactly this symbiosis, this bridging between different interests, this close networking which is often regarded as a prerequisite for flat organizations, joint ventures, entrepreneurship, and competitive alliances. These are inherent in Austrian's current management methods, thereby reinforcing underlying cultural values and behavior.

REFERENCES

Almond, G., and Powell, G. 1986. *Comparative Politics.* Princeton N.J.: Princeton University Press.

Bayer, K. 1990. *"Remuneration und Anreiz in der Öst. Industrie."* WIFO-Monatsberichte 2/90:81–90.

Crawford, J., Garland, B. and Schweiger, G. 1987. "Austrian, German, and Swiss Product Quality Perceptions of Foreign Goods." *Werbeforschung & Praxis* 2:29–34.

Drennig, M. 1988. "Wirtschaftliche & pychologische Voraussetzungen für offene Märkte." In M. Stadlinger, ed., *Österreich 2000.* Vienna: Deutsch, pp 125–136.

Guger, A. 1990. "Einkommens- und Produktivitäsgefälle erringert." *WIFO-Monatsberichte* 2/90:74–78.

Haiss, P. 1988. "Headhunting in Österreich: Für ein paar Prozente mehr." *Gewinn* 7/1:46–48.

———. 1990. *Cultural Influences on Strategic Planning.* Heidelberg/New York: Physica Publishing Co.

Hamid, S. 1988. *Die Suche nach Führungskräften in Österreich.* Vienna: Boyden International.

Hofstede, G. 1980. *Culture's Consequences.* Beverly Hills, Calif.: Sage Publications.

Holzmann, R., and Wickler, G. 1983 (February). "Austrian Economic Policy." *Empirica,*: 183–204.

Kaase, M., and Marsh, A. 1976. *Matrix of Political Action.* 10th Political Science Congress, Edinburgh.

Kennedy, P. 1987. *The Rise and Fall of the Great Powers.* New York: Random House.

Knapp, H. 1990. "Besen, Besen, seid's gewesen?" *Finanznachrichten* 15/16:1–14.

Lynn, R., and Hampson, S. "National Differences in Extraversion and Neuroticism." *British Journal of Social and Clinical Psychology* 14:223–240.

McClelland, D. 1961. *The Achieving Society.* Princeton, N.J.: Van Nostrand Reinhold.

Mayer, T. 1990. "Image & Wirklichkeit." *Standard* 6 (19):10.

Millendorfer, J. 1988. "Grenzen des Wachstums." In Stadlinger, M., ed., *Österreich 2000.* Vienna: Deutsch.

Moormann, J. 1988 (June). "Strategische Planung in Geschäftsbanken." *Die Bank*:309–315.

Nowotny, E. 1989. "Institutionelle Grundlagen und Entscheidungsverhältnisse in der öst. Wirtschaftspolitik." In H. Abele et al., ed., *Handbuch der öst. Wirtschaftspolitik.* Vienna: Manz, pp. 44–54.

Ploner, F. 1990 (July-August). "Unterm Strich schaut es anders aus. Gewinn." pp. 36–
    38.
Ringel, E. 1987. *Zur Gesundung der österreichischen Seele.* Vienna: Europaverlag.
Rottmann, J. 1987. "Senkung der Personalfluktuation." Ph.D. diss., University of Eco-
    nomics, Vienna.
Rule, J., and Sedgwick, M. 1986. "The Next Ten Years in Banking." *Journal of Retail
    Banking* 1/2:41–47.
Schneider, P., and Schneider, A. 1971. "Social Mobilization." *Comparative Political
    Studies* 4:69–90.
Schulze, G. 1990. "Ein CI-Bild von Unternehmen." *Industrie* 17:18–21.
Schumpeter, J. 1934. *Theory of Economic Development.* Cambridge, Mass.: Harvard
    University Press.
Tannenbaum, A., Kavcic, B., Rosner, M., Vianello, M., and Wieser, G. 1974. *Hierarchy
    in Organizations.* San Francisco: Jossey-Bass.

8

COMMONWEALTH OF INDEPENDENT STATES

Vladimir S. Rapoport, Valeria Ryssina,
Stuart A. Umpleby, and
William E. Halal

Like other countries in both the East and the West, the political system in the former Soviet Union has experienced cycles of reform and retrenchment. The War Communism of 1917–21, the first five-year plan of 1928–32, World War II, the late 1950s, and the 1970s were periods of centralization; and the New Economic Policy of 1921–28, the mid–1930s, the immediate post–Stalin period, the second half of the 1960s, and the last few years were periods of decentralization. The magnitude of the reforms in each cycle have varied greatly (Aslund, 1989).

In the late 1980s, rapid and far-reaching political and economic changes occurred in the Soviet Union. The conception underlying the nation's economic development changed fundamentally. In the 1990s, the assumptions and institutions of a planned economy are being replaced with those of a regulated market. The new economic policies presuppose the development of a variety of forms of property, including private property, greater independence of state-owned enterprises, and development of securities and credit markets.

Since the failure of the attempted coup in August 1991, the political system has changed fundamentally. The old Soviet Union has broken up and has been replaced by a Commonwealth of Independent States. Each republic is now debating methods for changing to a market economy, the new role of the republics, and the means for protecting the social security of the population. Much new legislation is being written.

One of the most important problems to be solved, before the new concept of economic development can be realized, is how to train managers who will be able to implement the economic reforms and to raise the national economy to a new level of productivity. Human resource management is one of the weakest and most obsolete features of the management system in the former Soviet Union.

Table 8.1

Basic Indicators of Economic and Social Development, 1960–88 (1940 = 1.0)

	1960	1970	1980	1985	1987	1988
Gross national product	4.2	8.1	13.6	16.1	17.4	18.4
National income	4.4	8.7	14.1	16.8	18.2	18.9
Production capital (all sectors)	3.2	7.4	16.0	21.8	24.4	
Industrial products	5.2	12.0	24.0	25.0	28.0	28.0
Means of production	6.6	16.0	29.0	35.0	38.0	
Consumer goods	3.2	6.5	11.0	13.0	14.0	15.0
Gross agricultural output	1.6	2.2	2.4	2.7	2.9	2.9
Involvement of capital resources	6.3	12.7	21.7	25.1	28.3	27.9
Capital investments	6.3	12.3	20.1	24.0	26.8	29.0
Productivity of public labor	4.0	7.4	10.8	12.6	13.6	
Labor productivity						
in industry	3.0	4.9	7.7	9.0	9.7	
in agriculture (public)	2.0	3.3	4.0	4.6	5.2	
in construction	2.9	4.5	6.4	7.3	7.9	
on railway transport	2.1	3.5	4.4	4.7	5.1	
Real per capita income	2.5	3.5	4.4	4.7	5.1	

Source: *Narodnoye Khoziaystvo* (Moscow: Finansy i Statistika Publishers, 1987 and 1989).

It has not changed for decades. Naturally, many problems have accumulated which need to be solved in the course of economic reform.

This chapter describes human resource management in the Commonwealth of Independent States in the context of the economic development of the country since the end of World War II, the economic situation at the beginning of the 1990s, the new demands on executives as a result of the economic reform process, and previous efforts at managerial reform. We present data on managerial personnel, describe the current system of human resource management and the problems to be solved there, and describe the government program of managerial personnel development that is now being drawn up. Statistics refer to the fifteen republics of the USSR rather than the eleven or twelve republics (minus the three Baltic republics and perhaps Armenia) of the Commonwealth of Independent States. "Russia" refers to the Russian Republic which was the largest and most influential republic in the former Soviet Union.

ECONOMIC DEVELOPMENT IN THE POSTWAR PERIOD

Throughout the postwar period in the USSR, the management of the economy emphasized extensive development. The results of the strategy of extensive development are presented in Table 8.1. In the 1940–88 period, gross national product (GNP) and national income increased more than eighteen times. The volume of industrial output grew twenty-eight-fold. Capital investments were twenty-nine times higher than before. However, the volume of consumer goods output increased more slowly (fifteen times the 1940 level). Agricultural output

Table 8.2
Mean Annual Growth of Final Indexes of National Economic Development of the USSR, 1961–85 (percent)

Indexes for	1961-1961	1966-1970	1971-1975	1976-1980	1981-1985
Increment of national income in physical terms	5.7	7.2	5.1	3.8	3.1
Increment of real per capita income	3.6	5.9	4.4	3.4	2.1
Increment of aggregate efficiency of per resource utlization			2.0	1.0	0.6

Source: S. S. Shatalin, "Social Development and Economic Growth," *Kommunist*, No. 14 (1986):60.

grew only 2.9 times, whereas the real per capita income of the population grew about fivefold. In this period the number of people engaged in the USSR economy doubled (from 62.9 million to 128.9 million). The number of workers and clerks grew rapidly (from 33.9 million to 117.2 million), while the number of collective farmers declined to less than half the 1940 number (from 29 million to 11.7 million) (*Narodnoye Khoziaystvo*, 1987 and 1989).

By the early 1980s, the extensive development of the economy had been exhausted. The results that had been achieved up to then could be accounted for by the use of increasing amounts of resources. Very little attention had been paid to improving efficiency.

In the 1970s, there was a trend toward lower capital productivity (see Table 8.2) primarily because of low rates of technological innovation. Agricultural yields and animal husbandry also improved more slowly in the 1970s than earlier. Growth rates at large fell drastically. The decline in growth rates was associated with the fact that the rate of adding resources to the economy declined while the costs of producing them rose.

In the late 1970s and early 1980s, attempts were made to change the strategy of economic development—to orient it more than before toward intensification of production. More attention was also paid to consumer goods. But the attempts failed to achieve the desired results (see Table 8.2). Delays in reorganizing the economy and in orienting it toward intensification, combined with high resource consumption in production processes, aggravated the problems of supplying raw materials, fuel, and the latest technology, which was needed for further economic development. Delays in reorganization also substantially encumbered the opportunities for increasing exports and for earning hard currency. The structure of the national product and of foreign trade continued to be dominated by raw

Table 8.3
Labor Productivity Growth Rates by Sectors, 1960–88

	(1940 = 100)			(1980 = 100)			
	1960	1970	1980	1985	1986	1987	1988
Industrial total	156	182	190	117	122	126	132
Heavy industry	172	204	214	119	124	130	138
energy	156	160	164	102	105	110	116
metallurgy	139	150	157	108	113	117	138
engineering	204	264	281	129	138	146	124
chemical/forestry	172	210	221	122	129	138	156
construction materials	139	156	160	110	117	122	145
Light industry	142	156	160	110	113	115	128
food processing	131	153	162	117	124	120	121

Source: *Narodnoye Khoziaystvo* (Moscow: Finansy i Statistika Publishers, 1987 and 1989).

materials and fuels. The use of these materials for trade contributed to slower economic development.

The changes in economic policy proved to be insufficient to compensate for the reduced growth rates in the production of resources. This was another factor contributing to lower rates of economic growth in general. Labor productivity growth rates also decreased (see Table 8.3).

THE ECONOMIC SITUATION IN THE LATE 1980S AND EARLY 1990S

Another attempt to overcome these undesirable trends was made in 1987, when the Plenum of the Communist party of the Soviet Union (CPSU) adopted the program outlined in The Guiding Principles of Radical Reorganization of Economic Management and when the Law on State Enterprises was adopted. This program emphasized greater independence for enterprises in planning production and in spending earned income. It also called for greater participation of workers' collectives in decision making about operations. The program envisaged the development of contractual relations between enterprises and the right to fix contract prices. According to the program, the role of the central economic bodies and ministries was to change. They were supposed to concentrate on formulating research and development policies and economic strategies, while abandoning administrative command of enterprises and shifting to economic methods of management.

Flexible credit and favorable tax policies were to play important roles among the economic incentives for improved management. The banks were to extend credit to enterprises to help them modernize their technology, thereby stimulating investment and reducing government subsidies to enterprises. Introduction of a single-tax policy for all enterprises was intended to put them on an equal footing and to encourage them to raise their efficiency. Enterprises were granted more freedom in foreign economic activities.

The proposed measures were far from comprehensive, however. They were also not sufficiently coordinated with each other. Many of them were never implemented. Some decentralization of management led to higher prices and wages and greater disparities in production. Since there were no markets to set prices, the revenues of enterprises had nothing to do with either efficiency or competitiveness. The reins of power remained in the hands of central agencies, which controlled credit and investment. Enterprises whose performance was below breakeven continued to receive subsidies.

The Law on State Enterprises (Associations) turned out to be incomplete and declarative. Many of its articles were only wishful thinking, with no one responsible for enforcement. In 1990, only two and a half years after the adoption of this law, a new law was passed on the enterprise in the USSR. The new law was a modified version of the old law with respect to permitting market relations and pluralism in forms of property. But, in addition, it gave greater freedom to business units.

The period after 1987 was characterized by one substantial achievement: development of a cooperative movement. Cooperatives were supposed to saturate the economy with consumer goods. But uncertainty surrounding the legislation concerning cooperatives, preferences (relating to equipment and raw materials) given to state-owned enterprises, the tight credit situation, higher prices for resources sold to cooperatives, scarce equipment, and a number of other factors handicapped the development of cooperatives, forcing them to fix higher prices for their products, to "eat up their profits," and even to go out of business.

The expected new forms of property did not develop in agriculture either. The new law on leasing agricultural land did not yield the desired results owing to the fuzziness of the legislation; high taxes; problems in procuring agricultural machines, fodder, and other needed materials; and restrictions imposed on lessors by the collective farms and local authorities.

On the whole, the reforms of 1987 turned out to be inadequate. They did not stimulate the use of accumulated reserves. Government spending increased, while budget revenues decreased. The large deficit was financed by increasing the money supply, which produced inflation. In 1989 the consumer goods market was completely out of balance. The growing inflation and the concomitant increased demand aggravated the deficit. Since 1989 a number of industries had been lowering their volumes of production. The trend continued in 1990.

In November 1990 the Supreme Soviet of the USSR adopted the Concept of National Economic Stabilization and Transition to a Market Economy. This general statement was a combination of the government program and several more radical alternative programs for pulling the country out of the economic crisis. It was the third (and, at the time, the most radical) plan for economic development of all those adopted since 1987.

The economic development program adopted in late 1990 aimed at creating all the necessary conditions for transition to a real market. The idea that a market is necessary is not doubted by any side in the debate. The program's most important goals are privatizing enterprises and creating a mixed economy, giving impetus to market mechanisms, strengthening the ruble and providing the preconditions for its convertibility, loosening prices, and creating special guarantees for the population.

THE NEW ECONOMIC ENVIRONMENT AND DEMANDS ON MANAGERS

With the development of a market and the emergence of new forms of property and economic relations, the managers' external environment changed drastically. Under the old system managers had limited autonomy. All the decisions regarding incentives, prices, investment, and supplies were made outside the firm. The result was a high degree of administrative dependency in which the risks of innovation without political support were high and in which managers adapted to the inordinate external demands by pursuing the immediate goal of fulfilling the plan rather than the larger goals of the organization (Beissinger, 1982: 463). A change to a market economy alters the nature of the uncertainties and risks that managers encounter, and the period of transition is particularly stressful. As managerial functions become technically rather than politically complex, greater demands are made on the manager's professional expertise (Gvishiani and Milner, 1987; Kitov, 1985).

Until very recently, the Russian executive's expertise was based on operating in an environment of centralized distribution of resources and products. Inefficient firms were subsidized in order to prevent unemployment. Resources were allocated by a central ministry. To cope with possible shortages, managers requested and stockpiled more resources than they needed. If shortages occurred nonetheless, managers resorted to barter. They did not have to market their goods; distribution was handled by the central ministry. Often the best quality goods were withheld from state distribution for use in barter arrangements, either to obtain resources needed to meet the plan or to obtain goods for the manager's personal use.

In the United States one frequently hears the claim that Russians can understand a market economy because there is a black market in Russia which, it is assumed, operates on free market principles. But the shadow economy in Russia is not like a black market—a market in illegal goods—in a Western country. Consider the following description by Vladimir Shubkin.

A certain amount of leather brought to a state factory is enough to make ten pairs of shoes. But the leather is well "stretched" and, as a result, twenty pairs are made. The whole batch is sold through state shops. The money received from the sale of the illicit goods goes to pay second salaries to officials at the ministry and the central department (they supply factories with the right quotas and "stretchable" leather), factory workers involved in the business, and shop assistants selling those goods. That second salary is much higher than the official one and is given without any pay lists or signatures—people in that business do not like to leave any traces behind. So, it turns out that two enterprises are operating under one signboard, a state-owned one and a shadow concern. And this is common not only in the consumer goods and food industries, but also in Group A (the production of the means of production). (Shubkin, 1988: 16)

As the current reforms take effect, managers will have to learn how to operate in a market economy. Whereas in a centrally planned economy managers are preoccupied with obtaining resources, in a market economy managers focus on making products of sufficient quality that people will want to buy them. Hence, in a centrally planned economy managers focus on problems of supply, but in a market economy managers try to increase demand. Purchasing, pricing, marketing, investing, and responding to legal requirements are just some of the new skills managers will have to master.

These new tasks will make it mandatory for managers to be more concerned with strategic thinking. They will have to learn the methods for making long-term forecasts and for optimizing production decisions. Managers will also need to acquire skills in organizing the diffusion of new technology, motivating creativity, conducting market research, and promoting new products. With greater involvement of business organizations in the global economy, business managers will have to master a large body of knowledge about the world market and international business law.

The activities of managers will also be affected by employees' more active participation in operational management and the development of democracy and openness both within the enterprise and in society at large. The manager has to be prepared to operate in an environment featuring collective forms of work and his work team's constant assessment of his performance.

MANAGERIAL PERSONNEL

Russian managers today are struggling to cope with a political and economic environment that could easily be called revolutionary. They are being required to learn new skills and to operate in fundamentally different ways. One positive trend is that the value of their work is recognized more now than in the past.

The Ideology of Managers

From 1917 to 1991, the ideology in the Soviet Union was Marxism-Leninism, which claimed the superiority of a party-state for building a "worker's paradise." Until the 1987 reforms, no distinction was made between public and private sector managers. All managers who were not criminals were managers of state-owned enterprises. Business and government were not separate activities within the society. The state was one huge pyramid. All organizations—government agencies, manufacturing firms, labor unions, Young Pioneers (similar to Boy Scouts), hospitals, universities, marriage bureaus, apartment houses, and vacation resorts—were under one government. All organizations had two sets of managers—functional managers and party secretaries. The party secretaries served as a shadow cabinet in each organization. They participated in management and ensured Communist party control of all sectors of society.

After the initial revolutionary enthusiasm associated with building a new society, the climate within Soviet organizations became similar to that in post offices and other state-owned organizations in Western countries, except that in the Soviet Union there was an added climate of fear. Under Joseph Stalin, millions of people were killed or sent to concentration camps. More recently, under Leonid Brezhnev, during what is now called the period of stagnation, one could lose one's job, housing, or even citizenship for challenging the state. Speech and the press were rigidly controlled. There was no opportunity legally to start a small business, and suggestions for innovations within organizations were not rewarded by the monopoly economic environment.

Attitudes Toward Managers

After the 1917 Revolution, the Soviet leadership, the public, and official economic science developed a negative attitude toward managers in general. Communist ideology maintained that the capitalist class was a parasite on society. Russian citizens have seen many cartoons of fat, greedy capitalists cruelly exploiting downtrodden workers. Some of this image carried over to managers. Managers were regarded as an undesirable addition to production. Their work was viewed as unproductive. Improvement in efficiency was associated with reducing managerial costs to a minimum. The 1961 Program of the Communist party of the Soviet Union is an example of this attitude toward managers: "One should strive for reduction in administrative staff and involvement of wider masses in the process of mastering the skills of management, so that in the future management ceases to be a profession."

Enterprise managers and professionals were regarded as ordinary employees authorized by ministries and agencies to carry out on a lower level the functions associated with managing the national economy. This view led to regarding enterprise managers as functionaries of state administrative bodies. The role of the managers of ministries was basically to redistribute the revenues earned by enterprises.

In the late 1960s, Russian economists came to recognize the productive character of managerial work. However, the manager's role in improving the quality and efficiency of production was severely underestimated, and in some cases simply ignored. No decisive steps were made toward changing personnel policies and the public image of managers.

In the mid–1980s an unprecedented campaign of criticizing the bureaucratic nature of managerial staff rose on the tide of glasnost or openness (Azarov, 1988). Many of the critics completely forgot the constructive role of managers.

The Number of Managers

What have been the results of the long-standing attitude toward managers? With regard to the number of managerial staff, no doctrine or prevailing sentiment

Table 8.4
Number of Managerial Staff of Enterprises by Sectors of the National Economy

	Thousand people	% of total
Total	14 890	12.7
Managerial staff of enterprises and organizations (November 15, 1990)	13 205	11.4
Manufacturing	4 796	11.7
Agriculture and forestry	1 016	7.7
Transport and communications	1 004	10.0
Construction	2 038	15.7
Trade, public catering, material supply, procurement	1 333	13.7
Communal services and non-production units of public services	485	14.6
Health care, physical education, social security	382	5.4
Education, culture and arts, science and science-supporting organizations	1 525	10.2
Crediting and state insurance organizations	314	45.5
State administration, agencies and ministries, managerial personnel of cooperatives and public organizations (January 1, 1989)	1 685	100

Source: *Narodnoye Khoziaystvo* (Moscow: Finansy i Statistika Publishers, 1987 and 1989).

could overcome actual needs. As the amount of managerial work increased, the number of managerial personnel increased. Unfortunately, the statistics employed for estimating the number of managerial personnel are far from perfect. The latest comparable statistical data on the number of managerial personnel in the USSR are for 1985. At that time, the number of managerial staff was slightly over 17.7 million people. The percentage of managerial personnel among the total number of those employed amounted to 14.9 percent. Despite the enormous effort aimed at reducing the number of managerial personnel, the number actually grew by 20 percent since 1960. The number of staff people supporting managers grew almost 2.5 times, or by about 10 million people (see Tables 8.4 and 8.5).

In 1988, the Committee for Statistics registered managerial staff using different (compared to 1985) criteria. People such as messengers, typists, stenographers, guards, and other supporting staff were not included in the more recent figures. According to the new classification, in 1988 the managerial corps in the USSR amounted to 14.962 million people. However, if this figure were computed in the previous manner, the 1988 level could be assessed as 17.8 million people (Alov, 1990). Actually, then, the figure remained unchanged, despite the fact that since 1985 several ministries and agencies were liquidated, and the personnel of the remaining industries were substantially reduced. One reason for the lack

Table 8.5

Number of Employees of Economic Ministries and Agencies, Public Administration, Cooperatives, and Informal Organizations, 1970–88 (thousands)

	1970	1980	1985	1986	1987	1988
Total managerial personnel	1724	2231	2376	3266	1981	1831
Ministries and agencies	1217	1531	1623	1604	1216	1080
Personnel in all-Union ministries and agencies	88	104	107	108	103	85
Personnel in Union-Republic ministries and agencies	116	134	140	135	133	108
Other	1013	1293	1356	1361	970	887
Staff of presidiums of supreme councils and their executive bodies	261	297	312	314	319	311
Court and legal organizations	70	84	92	95	97	99
Managerial personnel of cooperatives and informal organizations	176	319	349	353	349	341

Source: Narodnoye Khoziaystvo (Moscow: Finansy i Statistika Publishers, 1987 and 1989).

of change in the number of managers is that some part of the central bodies' managerial personnel simply withdrew from those structures and moved to specially established business organizations where they engaged in the same type of work.

In 1989, an attempt was made to reduce the number of managerial staff in business organizations via an increase in taxes for each person in that staff, but this program was ignored. The managerial staff of enterprises and organizations grew by 667,000 people.

When we analyze the factors operating in 1989 and 1990, we find reason to believe that in 1990 in the USSR the number of those engaged in managerial and management support work amounted to no less than the same 18 million people as in 1985. How many managers are among them? If we assume that this category includes those who make managerial decisions or bear responsibility for their support, we can speak of 9 or 10 million people. Thus, this category of employees is becoming larger and is now second only to the number of workers. Is this figure large or small? We can answer this question by analyzing the relevant data provided by the United States. Their statistics regard as managerial personnel not only managers on various levels, but also clerks, technicians, and even specialists, or engineers engaged in operations. In the U.S. economy, this category amounts to about 41 million people.

We should also bear in mind that many engineers and technicians, who are classified by Russian statistics as managerial staff, in fact perform the functions characteristic of those performed by skilled workers. Thus, the real number of those engaged in management in the former USSR (if we use the American approach) will be far below 18 million people. Hence, the size of the managerial staff in Russia is relatively small.

The small number of managers in Russia may be explained by the fact that the Russian economy is not as highly developed as the economies in the United States, Western Europe, and Japan. Western nations have almost fully completed the primary and secondary stages of development marked by agriculture and manufacturing, and they are now well into the tertiary stage of service and knowledge industries, which are more management intensive. In contrast, Russia is still struggling to develop an effective agricultural and manufacturing infrastructure that can provide adequate consumer goods. The early stages of development are more labor intensive.

Trade Unions

Until recent years independent labor unions were illegal. They were thought to be unnecessary because the party operated in the interests of the workers. There were official labor unions, but they were controlled by the party rather than by the workers. Since 1988 independent labor unions have been permitted. But the leaders of these unions still have little experience in organizing and negotiating to obtain benefits for their members. Unions of miners are the most well organized so far and have already achieved some concessions. Unionization is expected to increase, perhaps dramatically.

Regarding their attitudes toward unions, most managers are reluctant to share power. Independent labor unions represent a loss of power for the party bureaucracy. However, there is a recognition by the reform leaders that unions are a necessary part of the growth of democracy. Currently negotiations do not take place within a well-developed legal and historical framework. Labor-management relations are roughly comparable to those in the United States in the early years of this century. Negotiations sometimes occur not between labor and management but rather between workers and the central government.

Grievance systems assume a recognized authority to report a grievance to. But currently there is a struggle for power in the Soviet Union. Western-style grievance systems have not yet been established.

Table 8.6

Distribution of the Population Engaged in the National Economy by Sectors, 1940–88 (percent)

	1940	1960	1970	1980	1985	1986	1988
Total engaged	100	100	100	100	100	100	100
Industry and construction	23	32	38	39	38	38	39
Agriculture and forestry	54	39	25	20	20	19	19
Transport and communication	5	7	8	9	9	9	8
Trade and public catering, material supply, sales and procurement	5	6	7	8	8	8	8
Health care, social security, education, culture and art, science and science supporting activities	6	11	16	17	18	18	19
State administration	3	2	2	2	2	2	2
Crediting, insurance, other sectors (municipal services)	4	3	4	5	5	6	5

Source: *Narodnoye Khoziaystvo* (Moscow: Finansy i Statistika Publishers, 1987 and 1989).

RUSSIAN MANAGEMENT IN CULTURAL PERSPECTIVE

Many of the characteristics of the economic environment described above are unfamiliar to Western readers. Westerners can perhaps more easily understand the society by comparing it to a Western society at an earlier stage of industrial development. Although sectors such as military weapons and space technology have been carefully cultivated, the former USSR lags far behind industrially developed countries in such important areas as the productivity of labor, the technological level of production, and the quality of goods produced. The consumer goods manufacturing and distribution systems of the economy are primitive; the bulk of the workforce remains employed in blue-collar jobs (see Table 8.6), and per capita income is a small fraction of that enjoyed in advanced nations. The result is a relatively simple state of management development, often noted in the data, and a small number of managers relative to workers.

The region's less developed economy helps to explain the current crisis. The dramatic changes in the communist world since 1989 can perhaps be understood as roughly comparable to the transition the United States experienced during the Great Depression of the 1930s. The Great Depression occurred because of a failure in the free market system that called the viability of capitalism into question, but it was corrected with insured savings, unemployment benefits, and various other social welfare programs that stabilized the American economy.

The development of the domestic economy of Russia lags the United States by about fifty years, and it is making a similar transition at roughly the same point in its development. Just as Franklin D. Roosevelt led the American people through a painful adjustment to correct the flaws of capitalism, Mikhail Gorbachev presided over an unprecedented period of confusing change that shook the ideological foundations of socialism. And just as the United States did not abandon capitalism but improved it by adopting elements of socialism, socialist states may with time evolve into what some have proposed as an advanced form of socialism that incorporates Western ideals of democracy and free markets— a "democratic, market socialism" (Halal, 1988).

A cultural idiosyncrasy of Russian management is the way authority is used. Although in recent years socialist countries have made a strong move toward democracy, the manner in which decision-making power is shared differs from the participative leadership gaining ascendancy in Western economies like the United States.

Russian culture embodies two main principles: (1) a communitarian, egalitarian ethic that favors democratic decision making (the word "soviet" comes from a Russian word for a community council); and (2) an authoritarian ethic that favors strong centralized control. Russian management has reconciled these two principles through the concept of democratic centralization. Members of an organization discuss and agree on major policy decisions, including the appointment of leaders, and the leader is then accorded the legitimacy to carry out these jointly decided policies in a firm, authoritarian manner in order to expedite action. Thus, two opposing principles are united into a dynamic tension by moving alternately between democratic and centralized modes of power (Lawrence and Viachoutsicos, 1990).

U.S. corporations operate differently. In U.S. corporations, top managers tend to set goals in an autocratic fashion, while the means to achieve the goals have been determined in an increasingly democratic manner through quality circles and total quality management.

Cultures have historical roots. The Russian historical experience has been a series of wars and lesser conflicts between national groups. Russian citizens tend to be loyal to family and friends but distrustful of outsiders.

In individualist cultures people define the ingroup as "people who are like me in social class, race, beliefs, attitudes, and values." This is a huge group. In collectivist cultures people share and show harmony within ingroups, but the total society may be characterized by much disharmony and nonsharing, because so many relationships are individual–outgroup relationships. Relationships with merchants, policemen, and bureaucrats are outgroup relationships. (Triandis et al., 1988)

The United States, on the other hand, was settled by people fleeing oppressive regimes in Europe. Americans, distrustful of central authority, developed methods for working together while limiting the role of government. If people believe that human beings in general are trustworthy, honest, generous, and inclined to compromise, then the role of government can be limited. But if people assume that human beings generally are dishonest, not generous, and inclined to be confrontational, then they are likely to assume that a strong government is necessary to resolve conflicts and to provide for the less fortunate (Umpleby, 1991). Some Russian citizens today still believe that strong government is necessary to prevent chaos. The reform of the Russian political and economic system will require major changes in the values and beliefs of the people if the new institutions are to work as intended.

HUMAN RESOURCE MANAGEMENT AND MANAGERS

At a time when radically new demands are being placed on Russian managers and when more people with management training are needed to build a more advanced economy, the system of management training and development is, unfortunately, not prepared to meet the challenge.

Previous Efforts at Managerial Reform

The current wave of interest in managerial reform has been made possible by dramatic political changes. Carrying out the proposed managerial reforms will help make the political reforms irreversible. To understand how managerial reforms will change the system, it is useful to understand how the previous managerial system served the one-party political system and how previous managerial reforms were altered by the political system. Mark Beissinger has studied the diffusion of Western management ideas in Russia prior to 1982.

One of the major tools, if not the major tool, by which the Party has been able to maintain its control over the enterprise (and over society as a whole) has been through its control over personnel recruitment and socialization. These personnel weapons included the education of personnel, setting the criteria used to select personnel, and participation in the selection process itself. (Beissinger, 1982:16)

In the early postrevolutionary period, political control of managerial selection opened avenues for social advancement for the lower classes by defining recruitment and training in a political rather than a social manner. However, as new elites became established, the political nature of the selection process permitted a new set of well-connected families to become entrenched. Establishing more objective methods of selection will reward competence and improve productivity and will also tend to weaken the power of the party.

Before 1930 Russia had relatively progressive managerial recruitment and training policies. The borders were open to new ideas. However, during Stalin's revolution from above, research on management was halted, and instruction for executives was limited to ideology and to technical subjects. Executive selection became largely a matter of political and personal loyalties:

These developments were an integral part of a larger political and economic system created by Stalin whose purpose was to maintain strict control over the lives and activities of its managers while fostering a break-neck pace of industrial growth. Western management thought, with its focus on efficiency, represented a threat to the legitimacy of a system which was founded upon the idea of economic growth without regard to the human or economic costs. (Beissinger, 1982: 86)

Stalin's policy of forced industrialization led to the isolation of the USSR from Western management thought. During the 1960s an effort was made to reform Soviet management by importing Western management ideas. At first, these imports were intended to help managers learn how to use more efficiently the greater operational authority that was supposed to be granted to them as a result of economic reform. Management development was viewed as part of economic reform. But in the late 1960s and early 1970s management development came to be embraced by some of the more conservative members of the party leadership as an alternative to systemic change. Rather than using training as a way of helping managers adapt to a competitive economic environment, after the early 1970s the party tried to use training as a way of improving economic performance without changing the centralized nature of the economic system (Beissinger, 1982: 170).

This shift of emphasis was justified on the grounds that a centrally planned economy was inherently superior. Advocates of this view claimed that the efficiency of market economies could be explained not by the market mechanism, but by the superior techniques and skills of capitalist managers. The assumption behind this shift was that education, not reform, was sufficient to improve the efficiency of the Russian economy. It was thought that professionalism without operational autonomy could bring Russian industry into the era of the scientific-technological revolution. But during a period of more than two decades, this strategy had little impact on the efficiency of Russian industry (Beissinger, 1982: 463).

Selection and Assessment of Managers

Currently, formal assessment of executives is carried out in all organizations in conformity with a special regulation, once every three years. But in most cases this highly important instrument of personnel management does not have any significance for a number of reasons.

First, the purpose of assessment is, as a rule, purely administrative—to confirm that the manager meets the position requirements and to find out if it is necessary to change the level of his or her work compensation. Neglected are such important purposes of assessment as management development (by identifying gaps in knowledge and arranging the needed training) and improvement of the management system as a whole (by identifying the quality of performance of managers and recommending improvements in management techniques) (Bizyukova, 1984).

Second, in most situations the assessment is not based on careful analysis of the manager's work, and the entire procedure is reduced to a written essay that is submitted to an assessment commission. Absence of adequate job descriptions and regulations adds to the difficulty of making a detailed analysis of the manager's activity.

Third, so far the results of a manager's assessment have had only limited influence on the career and work compensation of the person assessed. The important factor is the criteria for assessment and selection of personnel. Up to now, the demands on managerial personnel have tended to be described at a general and rather abstract level rather than being focused on specific job requirements. Although each organization—government or business institution—has job descriptions, in most cases they are quite formal and are not employed as an effective instrument of personnel management (Shakhovoi, 1985). In fact, the only criteria for selecting a person from outside the organization have been that person's curriculum vitae and the last position he or she occupied. The criteria for selecting managers for promotion within the organization have been their accomplishments while in the earlier position.

There are several reasons for such a simplified approach. First, an employee who can manage one kind of job is commonly believed to be capable of coping with a different one. Second, there is a lack of unbiased methods for predicting the employee's performance in a new position. Third, there has been a lack of personnel services able to employ sophisticated assessment techniques.

Personnel departments, which are less numerous than similar departments in the West, have traditionally been staffed by retired military officers and party functionaries whose responsibilities included mostly technical operations of employment, such as job rotation and changes in work compensation. In the 1980s, large-scale enterprises developed sociopsychological centers that invited participation by specialists. However, these centers, as a rule, acted independently of the personnel departments and did not have any influence on the personnel policies in organizations. The weakness of the personnel departments to a large degree accounts for the fact that no valid instrument, such as personnel assessment, is used to motivate, control, and promote managerial personnel.

Recently, in individual industries and regions there have been changes for the better. For example, in the Estonian Republic, as well as in the all-Union Ministry of Energy, in the Ministry of Shipbuilding, and in a number of other industries, managerial assessment has begun to take its proper place in human resource management. These organizations have developed an original methodology for a comprehensive analysis of managerial activity and for preparing detailed requirements for each manager. The assessment itself has become a decisive factor in personnel decision making, somewhat like a Western assessment.

Despite these few promising developments, the increased attention given to managerial assessment is mostly verbal. So far there is not a single center of managerial assessment in the Commonwealth of Independent States. The reasons are the narrow objectives that were formulated for assessment (assessment centers are needed only where management development is not neglected), as well as lack of appropriate methodologies. Currently, several centers train candidate managers; to a certain degree, the centers perform the functions of assessment centers in that they give references based on how the trainees fulfill their training tasks. They conduct tests on personal qualities. Such centers can be found in the power industry, in shipbuilding, and in a number of industries in the Estonian Republic.

Compensation of Managers

An important factor affecting the development of the managerial personnel of the state administrative system is the comparatively low level of managers' salaries, which tends to undermine their motivation. In industry, for instance, in the period between 1940 and 1988 the share of managerial staff in the industrial production labor force increased by 20.7 percent, whereas its share in the total wage fund decreased by 32 percent.

In the 1940s the average salary of the personnel employed in economic management bodies was 18 percent higher than the average throughout the national economy, while in 1987 it was 9 percent lower. In 1986, in thirty-five branches of industry, construction, and agriculture, the share of enterprise managers' salaries in the wage and salary funds of enterprises was from 8 to 31 percent lower than the share of their number in the total number of employees (Hrutsky, 1990). Monetary bonuses were given to managers who fulfilled the plan, but there were no stock options because there was no stock.

Quite naturally, such a low compensation level for the managerial staff, both absolutely and relatively, led to an inferior quality of work, less initiative, brain drain, and a general deterioration of managerial and professional competence. The low compensation level was also the main reason for corruption, bribery, extortion, and disregard of national and public interests in favor of self-interest. However, the situation is changing. The new economic development program envisages eliminating the old work compensation rules. These changes will undoubtedly have a positive impact on the performance of managers.

Management Development

The nonrecognition of the productive character and special professional status of managers, the relatively low compensation level, as well as relatively narrow goals and objectives set for managers (i.e., implementation of objectives formulated by people at a higher level and fulfillment of "directive" plans) were all reflected in the qualifications of managers and the approach taken to their training.

Currently, in industry only 42 percent of managers and 36 percent of staff specialists have had some higher education (see Table 8.7). A rather large share (46 percent managers and 50 percent staff employees) have secondary technical education. Ten percent of work superintendents, 19 percent of foremen, 26 percent of shop managers, team leaders, and managers of subsidiaries and farms

Table 8.7

Educational Level of Managers and Staff Specialists by Sectors of the Economy (percent)

	Managers		Staff specialists	
	Higher educa-tion	Secondary profes-sional education	Higher educa-tion	Secondary profes-sional education
Total for the national economy	45	41	41	46
Industry	42	46	36	50
Agriculture	36	40	22	60
Transport and communications	32	41	21	51
Construction	44	47	30	51
Sales and public catering	25	53	20	64
Social amenities	28	51	21	50
Health care, sports, and social insurance	38	57	27	68
Culture and education	55	31	61	31
Science and scien-tific services	80	15	66	23
Administration, credit, and insurance	58	31	41	42

Source: *Narodnoye Khoziaystvo* (Moscow: Finansy i Statistika Publishers, 1987 and 1989).

do not have even secondary technical education. Among the managerial staff that have higher education, engineers predominate. Only a minor part of the managerial staff have special management training.

In the former Sovier Union, as in other East European countries, postgraduate management development is more common than basic management education. Because for a long time management had not been regarded as a profession, specialized higher education institutions for training managers appeared only in the last decade. At present there are only three such colleges (Ryssina, 1989). Because the majority of Russian managers have a technical background, most engineering colleges include in their programs courses on production engineering. However, these courses cannot qualify as specialized management training.

Postgraduate Management Education Long postgraduate courses can be found, but only in a small number of higher education institutions. The longest one is a two-year program at the Academy of the National Economy of the USSR Council of Ministers and the School of Commerce that became affiliated with it just recently. The Academy provides training for the upper echelon of managers in the national economy.

Middle-level managerial personnel get their postgraduate education at special departments of economic and engineering colleges. At present there are twelve such departments. These departments admit managers of enterprises, organizations, and institutions who are under forty years of age, have a higher education, and have no less than five years post-diploma experience with a positive evaluation as managers. The major and most common form of education for middle-level managers is provided by the sectoral management development institutes (SMDIs). Currently, there are over 80 SMDIs with 130 subsidiaries. The SMDIs train managers whose positions range from enterprise managers to shop managers.

There are also seven Republic intersectoral institutes of management development that are largely oriented toward training personnel for their own Republics. As a rule, they perform management and methodological research and also act as consultants for the region's organizations. Management development for middle- and lower-level managers is also carried out in management development courses organized by 220 engineering and economics colleges.

According to the USSR Statistical Agency, the total number of those who update their knowledge in this country annually includes 13 percent of managers of enterprises, institutions, organizations and their deputies, 12 percent of chief specialists and their deputies, 7 percent of accountants and their deputies, 11 percent of heads of structural units and their deputies (shop managers, team leaders, heads of laboratories), and 6 percent of foremen and work superintendents. Thus, with the present scale of management development, managerial personnel can undergo retraining on the average of once in ten years.

The system of training executives relatively late in life has a number of important consequences. When training is conducted by a ministry, it tends to focus on technical competence in dealing with matters of concern to that ministry. In addition, individual ministries can insist on their own requirements, specify their own ranking systems, and refuse to cooperate in attempts to standardize assessment. Personnel flows between organizations are minimized. The development of a common language among managers in different organizations is impeded. Consequently, the diffusion of management science has generally occurred more effectively in interbranch training institutions (Beissinger, 1982:308).

Problems in Management Education   The management development system is plagued by a host of problems. There are serious weaknesses in the content of management development programs. In the majority of training centers, the level of teaching is inadequate. In addition, the training centers operate with mostly obsolete methods of instruction.

The management development system suffers from a shortage of qualified instructors. This shortage stems from a lack of programs for training the teachers for the system. Furthermore, there is inadequate involvement of teachers in research and consulting activities.

The primary cause of the poor quality of management training is the low level of management research in the theory of production management, as well as applied research in management problems. Thus, the management education system is not yet able to provide a highly skilled managerial corps.

CONCLUSIONS AND TRENDS

Currently, there is a high demand for managers who can adapt to a new environment and particularly for managers who can engage in joint ventures with Western firms. The current organizational restructuring is occurring in an environment of great political uncertainty, a worsening economic situation, and changes in social values. Moral beliefs are changing and are creating stress both for those who served the now delegitimized administrative system and those who would condemn those who served the earlier system. There are also problems in adjusting to an information society.

The human resource management problem has attracted serious attention as part of the ongoing economic reorganization. In order to develop the needed managerial personnel, a special department on managerial personnel problems was set up in late 1989 in the State Commission on Economic Reform of the USSR Council of Ministers. Previously, no organization had the task of addressing the problems of managerial personnel. The department began its work with an analysis of the situation and an elaboration of a concept for a national program on training and utilizing managerial personnel in the new economic environment.

The basic concept is that the weakness of the managerial corps is one of the problems of perestroika and requires radical change of the entire human resource management system. The goal is that no manager will be appointed to his or her post without first proving that he or she has the required abilities, and, if not, getting the necessary training, confirmed by an appropriate certificate.

The emphasis will be on post-diploma training in the system of national, sectoral, and intersectoral training centers whose network is to be substantially expanded. Increasingly, a larger number of managers will undergo training in the network of self-supporting cooperative or state-owned training centers (business schools). These schools will admit not only managers nominated and supported by their organizations but also those who come there at their own expense.

Recently, about thirty such centers and schools for training managers were established in Moscow alone. They range from large schools (e.g., a state-owned center affiliated with the Plekhanov National Economy Institute providing both off-the-job and on-the-job training and giving a higher education diploma) to small cooperative schools (courses that last from one to two weeks). There are now presumably several hundred such centers operating throughout the country. There is a high demand for managerial training. The prices are high, but unfortunately the quality is also not high.

In the near future, managerial training will also be undertaken by various professional foundations and associations that have begun emerging since 1989. One such professional association is the Union of Managers. Under its auspices a foundation called Manpower for Reform has been established. Its objective is to select promising candidates to be trained abroad. These people undergo a strict professional trial and preliminary training. The money for the foundation comes from contributions by Russian companies and foreign companies operating in Russia, for whom it is cheaper to train and employ a Russian citizen than to invite a manager from their own country.

To improve the quality of training, it will be necessary to develop courses to improve teachers' qualifications and internship programs for teachers at the leading research and higher education institutions. Considerable effort will be required to create adequate textbooks, including audiovisual tapes for training managers. Given the scarcity of teachers, great importance is attached to creating materials for self-instruction, such as computer-based textbooks and films.

A significant role in building the qualifications of managers belongs to special literature, especially professional periodical publications. Until recently, there has been no professional publication for managers. Since 1989 the situation has changed; magazines addressed specifically to managers have been founded (*Commersant*, *Business in the USSR*, *Manager*, etc.). These publications will also help form a corps of qualified and well-informed managers.

Performance assessment will have to play an important role in selection, promotion, and placement of personnel. It is planned to set up a network of self-supporting research and consulting centers that will develop procedures for assessment and provide assistance in using them. The end product of assessment activities should be detailed references for the persons assessed.

Of course, in order to implement these ideas, it will be necessary to strengthen the personnel departments of organizations and reinforce them with qualified specialists, which will require resolving a number of organizational, legal, training, and methodological problems.

ACKNOWLEDGMENT

Travel associated with preparing this chapter was supported by the Soros Foundation, Commonwealth of Independent States.

REFERENCES

Alov, V. 1990. "How Many Managers Have We Got?" *Manager* 1:19–21 (in Russian).
Aslund, A. 1989. *Gorbachev's Struggle for Economic Reform*. Ithaca, N.Y.: Cornell University Press.
Azarov, N. 1988. *Bureaucrats on Public Trial*. Moscow: Novosti Press Agency Publishing House.
Beissinger, M. R. 1982. *The Politics of Convergence: The Diffusion of Western Management Ideas in the Soviet Union*. Ann Arbor, Mich.: University Microfilms.

Bizyukova, I. 1984. *Managerial Manpower: Selection and Assessment*. Moscow: Moskovsky Rabochy Publishers (in Russian).

Gvishiani, J., and Milner, B. 1987. *Organization of Management: Problems of Perestroika*. Moscow: Ekonomika Publishers, pp. 254–290 (in Russian).

Halal, W. E. 1988. "Political Economy in an Information Age." In L. Preston, ed., *Research in Corporate Social Policy and Performance*. Greenwich, Conn.: JAI Press.

Hrutsky, V. 1990. "The Paper Tiger Myth." *Manager* 1:31–32 (in Russian).

Kitov, A., ed. 1985. *Formation of Business Managers' New Economic Mentality*. Moscow: Academy of the National Economy (in Russian).

Lawrence, P., and Viachoutsicos, C. 1990. *Behind the Walls: Decision-making in Soviet and U.S. Enterprise*. Cambridge, Mass.: Harvard Business School Press.

Narodnoye Khoziaystvo. 1987 and 1989. Moscow: Finansy i Statistika Publishers.

Ryssina, V. 1989. *Management Education and Development in European Socialist Countries*. Geneva: ILO Press.

Shakhovoi, V. 1985. *Manpower in Management Systems*. Moscow: Mysl Publishers (in Russian).

Shubkin, V. 1988. "Bureaucracy." *Bureaucrats on Public Trial*. Compiled by N. Azarov. Moscow: Novosti Press Agency, pp. 7–22, originally published in *Znamya*.

Triandis, H. C., Bontempo, R., Villareal, M. J., Asai, M., and Lucca, N. 1988. "Individualism and Collectivism: Cross-cultural Perspectives on Self-ingroup Relationships." *Journal of Personality and Social Psychology* 54 (2):323–338.

Umpleby, S. A. 1991. "A Preliminary Inventory of Theories Available to Guide the Reform of Socialist Societies." *Cybernetics and Systems* 22 (4):389–410.

9

POLAND

Józef Koziński and Tadeusz Listwan

In this chapter managers are mainly people who hold managerial posts at middle and higher levels in state-owned industrial enterprises. There are several reasons why we define managers in this way:

1. Predominance of the state-owned sector in the national economy; apart from agriculture, the importance of private business is marginal in respect of the number of employees and production output,

2. Dominant contribution of industry to the national income (over 50 percent); it should also be noted that industry was always treated as something more than the fundamental base of the socialist order but rather its core (Szczepański, 1969),

3. Accessibility to representative research findings regarding managers of industrial enterprises, which allows more cognitive plausibility of conclusions and judgments presented below.

The discussions and research findings presented in this chapter refer, in principle, to the period of the centralized, command system in the postwar economy. At present Poland is in a transition between the command- and market-oriented economy. Occurrences since the revival of Solidarity in 1989 are also indicated insofar as they have an impact on managerial behavior. It should be stressed that a number of statements given below are merely hypotheses because of the lack of representative research information about the subject under study. Data used in this chapter were derived either from official statistical yearbooks of Poland or sample research carried out by various authors. Research can hardly be generalized, but it seems useful to illustrate some trends with sample results, for the officially published statistical data do not provide information about the total population of managers.

Table 9.1
Poland's Net Material Product (NMP)—Index Numbers and Composition, 1950–88 (1970 = 100.0)

	1950		1960		1970	1980		1980	
	Index Number	Compo- sition	Index Number	Compo- sition	Compo- sition	Index Number	Compo- sition	Index Number	Compo- sition
Total NMP	26.8	100.0	55.5	100.0	100.0	169.1	100.0	182.3	100.0
Industry	17.1	24.3	44.9	34.5	44.0	189.5	50.2	202.9	49.1
Con- struction	21.5	8.2	52.3	10.3	11.7	139.4	13.3	131.3	12.0
Agricul- ture	74.1	60.3	89.4	34.5	22.7	71.9	12.0	89.4	13.0
Other Acti- vities of the Material Sphere	18.2	7.2	59.1	20.7	21.6	205.6	23.6	225.4	25.9
Per capita	35.1	X	61.1	X	X	154.7	X	156.8	X

In countries with centrally planned economies, the Material Product System (MPS) was commonly used for standardizing the national account data. The MPS includes only production of goods and material services (those directly linked to the production of goods). All other services are excluded. Since 1980, the data on gross domestic product (GDP) have been accessible in Poland, but they are not comparable with previous periods.

Source: Poland, Statistical Data (Warsaw, 1989), pp. 8–15; Rocznik Statystyczny, 1988 (Warsaw, 1988), pp. xxxii–xlvii.

EVOLUTION OF THE POLISH MANAGERIAL CLASS

Poland's Economy After World War II

The postwar growth of Poland's economy is shown in Table 9.1. After World War II, Poland was a less developed country that had been damaged by war operations. In its Net Material Product (NMP) structure, the dominant role was played by agriculture (accounting for almost 65 percent of the total NMP). By the late 1940s, major economic sectors were socialized (except agriculture, which remained mostly private over the whole postwar period). The collectivized and centrally planned economy started the process of industrialization, which, in general, was successful until the late 1970s. Beginning in 1960, industrial output became more dominant than agriculture. Nonagricultural sectors developed more rapidly.

Poland's economic development, however, was marked by steady market disequilibria. Because prices of production factors and consumer goods were not real market categories, the extensive growth reached its limits by the end of the

1970s. It resulted in a general economic crisis, with a production decrease in all economic sectors. Social disturbances at the beginning of the 1980s, together with the economic crisis, forced the ruling Communist party to introduce limited economic reform, which was a combination of centrally planned and market systems. The shortcomings of that mixed economy soon became apparent, as economic progress proved insufficient in the 1980s. The general level of economic development measured per capita at the end of the 1980s was about the same as at the beginning of the decade.

The inefficiencies of the collectivized economy in Poland were also shown by the nation's relative closedness and extremely high indebtedness. Foreign turnover per capita never exceeded $1,000. Total debts amounted to about $40 billion in 1989. That year a peaceful political revolution took place in Poland. Henceforth, the nation's economy will follow a market orientation, but it will take time to transform the planned system into a market economy.

After 1989, economic depression resulted from the process of reforming the system. The costs of transforming the economy in terms of decreasing the national income, both total and per capita, and production output of major economic sectors are very high.

Employment

In spite of the shortcomings of the economic system and policy and of disturbances in economic growth, Poland has made a real effort to use its workforce (see Table 9.2). The share of employed people in the labor force shows a generally increasing trend and is relatively high in comparison with that in Western economies. As in other socialist countries, in Poland there was practically no unemployment, although it could only partially be attributed to economic development. Other important reasons for the very low unemployment were the social employment of people and the ineffective use of the labor force. However, almost two years of market experiments (1990–91) resulted in a new phenomenon for Poland—unemployment. Table 9.3 shows the dramatic development of unemployment the 1990s.

The expansion of the state-owned sector was accompanied by its increasing share in total employment. By the end of 1989, approximately 90 percent of employees in the private sector worked in agriculture. Employment in nonagricultural private business was always marginal under the command system. The privatization process that started in Poland in 1990 slightly changed that proportion in favor of the private sector.

Two other facts are worth noting. First, the ratio of workers (manual employees) to nonworkers remains practically unchanged in postwar Poland. The share of workers in the total employment is relatively high. Second, considering employment by kinds of activities, it should be noticed that the proportion of people working in services is rather low. The above indices are rather typical for centrally planned state-owned economies in which the "working class" in manufacturing sectors is dominating, the reason for it being the Marxist ideology and resulting economic policies of governments.

Table 9.2
Employment in Poland, 1950–88

	1950	1960	1970	1980	1988
Labor Force (millions)	14.5	16.3	18.3	21.2	21.9
Employment (millions)	10.2	12.4	15.2	17.3	17.2
Labor Force Participation Rate (percent) *	70.3	76.1	83.1	81.6	78.5
Employment by Major Kinds of Activities (percent):					
– Industry	20.7	25.5	29.3	30.3	28.5
– Agriculture	53.6	43.3	34.3	29.7	28.2
– Services	n.a.	n.a.	7.8	9.1	11.2
Employment by Job Catergories (percent):					
– Workers	n.a.	67.0	65.1	66.6	64.2
– Non-workers, of which:	n.a.	33.0	34.9	33.4	35.8
– Top management	n.a.	n.a.	n.a.	n.a.	1.4
– Technicians and engineers	n.a.	n.a.	n.a.	n.a.	9.7
– Economic and financial staff	n.a.	n.a.	n.a.	n.a.	9.4
– Support staff	n.a.	n.a.	n.a.	n.a.	3.8
Employment in Collectivized Sectors (percent)	43.1	58.1	67.8	73.4	71.5

*Labor Force Participation Rate-Employment: Labor Force.

Source: Data derived from Poland, Statistical Data (Warsaw, 1989), pp. 9, 10 and 25; Rocznik Statystyczny, 1987 (Warsaw 1988), p. 62.

Employment of Managers

Statistical data about managers are not easily accessible in Poland because of the way jobs are classified there. Among nonworkers, only top management executives are identified as managers. This narrow subcategory includes only directors and vice-directors of business organizations. Hence, its share in the total employment amounted to only 1.4 percent of the labor force in 1989. Middle- and low-level managers are hidden in other subcategories of nonworkers. For 1973–83 we have some more detailed data on the proportion of managers to other nonworkers (Table 9.4).

Two trends are notable here. First, the relationship of managers to nonworkers (about 25 percent) and to all employees (about 6 percent) remains relatively constant and is consistent with the constant share of nonworkers in the total employment. These data witness the low role of nonmanual jobs in Poland, which, in turn, is connected with the rather low prestige of managers (the problem being discussed below). Second, as might be expected, the largest category

Table 9.3
Unemployment in Poland, 1990–91

	1990			1991	
	Jan.	June	Dec.	March	May
Number of Unemployed Persons (thousands)	55.8	568.0	1,126.0	1,322.0	1,434.0
Ratio of Unemployed Persons to Employed Population (%)	0.3	3.1	6.1	7.1	7.7

Source: Biuletyn Statystyczny GUS (June 1991), pp. 26–28.

Table 9.4
Distribution of Job Categories among Polish Nonworkers, 1973–83 (numbers in thousands)

	Year					
	1973		1977		1983	
	Number	Percent	Number	Percent	Number	Percent
Non-workers	3,177.4	100.0	3,785.2	100.0	3,859.6	100.0
Managers	801.6	25.2	981.6	25.9	984.3	25.5
Specialists					1,959.9	50.8
	2,375.8	74.8	2,803.6	74.1		
Executive non-workers					915.3	23.7

Source: Rocznik Statystyczny Pracy, 1986 (Warsaw, 1987), p.146.

Table 9.5
Distribution of Polish Managers by Levels of Management in 1983

Management levels	x
Top management (directors and vice-directors)	17.5
Middle management (managers of departments and similar internal units)	65.4
Foremen	17.1

Source: Rocznik Statystyczny Pracy, 1986; Warsaw, 1987, p. 168.

among all managers are those from the middle level (see Table 9.5). The category includes such posts as chief accountants and heads of financial or similar departments, chief manufacturing engineers and managers of manufacturing sections, managers of construction, process and design departments, and managers of administrative departments or sections. A well-developed hierarchy of managerial jobs is a firmly rooted tradition in Central European nations. Holders of posts who are just below top management are usually called chiefs (chief process engineer, chief project designer, chief accountant, and the like). Jobs from the next hierarchical levels are simply managers, though in fact they are also differentiated by the status of the organizational units they manage. Relatively small units are called sections, while larger ones are called departments. Thus, a manager of a sales department has a higher hierarchical rank than a manager of a wage section. Another criterion of differentiation of managers is whether organizational units perform line or staff tasks. Managers working in line positions enjoy higher prestige than those belonging to the staff. It also manifests itself in compensation differentiation. All this corresponds with organizational structures of enterprises, which are predominantly functional (departmentization by functions) and tall (consisting of many hierarchical levels) at the same time.

Social Status of Managers

In relation to managers in Poland, we can say that the social status of managers is not high and that it has not essentially changed in the postwar period. Nevertheless, we can observe some differences in separate time periods regarding prestige.

Immediately after the war (i.e., prior to 1949), respect for managers seemed to be relatively high for two reasons. First, the selection criteria used were managerial proficiency and skills. The enterprises were still independent to a limited extent. War damage and loss of qualified staff were enormous. At that time, the managerial job was extremely difficult and required much talent and entrepreneurship. Second, intellectual professions enjoyed high esteem that carried over from the prewar period. The people performing managerial jobs were educated and trained before the war.

The next subperiod, 1949 to the early 1960s, was characterized by the growth of manufacturing, a larger number of managerial posts, concentration of management, and expansion of the Marxist ideology—all accompanied by the visible decrease in prestige of managers. People with a low social position, without necessary professional experience and higher education, were often appointed to managerial jobs (Najduchowska, 1984). Ideology and politics decided an appointment to managerial jobs, which were mainly confined to controlling the manufacturing processes within enterprises inasmuch as the physical output of goods was always the highest economic priority. Strategic management was performed by levels above enterprises. Hence, investigations concerning the prestige of various occupations revealed that a department head (a typical middle-level post) was ranked only sixteenth among all occupations involved in the study.

The 1960s was a decade of only small changes, although managers became better educated than in previous periods. In terms of public opinion, however, the prestige of directors was lower than before, while the respect for manual workers increased (Sarapata, 1985).

The 1970s were characterized by some attempts to reform the economy, although these reform efforts did not go beyond the dogma of the collectivized economy. The reforms were expressed in a limited decentralization and more autonomy for enterprises. The economy was opened to the West, including the purchase of modern technologies. As a result, the need for vigorous and innovative managers emerged. The mass media often presented directors as heroes. Use of political criteria in selecting managers was slightly weakened. The percentage of directors with higher education increased to 81 percent, and people from higher social positions were appointed to directorships (Najduchowska, 1984). More attention was paid to development of managerial skills. Under these general conditions, the prestige of managers increased, including that of directors (Sarapata, 1985). However, the social status of managers remained rather low. The research findings concerning social values are indirect proof of this statement. Among values under study, that is, education, income, managerial job, and cultural compensation, the managerial job ranked fourth (Koralewicz-Zębik, 1974).

The situation worsened at the end of the 1970s. Under conditions of an increasing economic crisis and later under martial law of December 1981, the government strongly insisted on political criteria while selecting managers. In state-owned enterprises almost all higher posts, and a considerable number of middle-level posts, came within the so-called party's nomenclature (the system of recruitment, selection and appointment to managerial jobs from among the people who were politically loyal to the Communist party). This lasted until 1989. We have no extensive research findings for that period, but it may be reasonably assumed that this system meant a further decrease in the prestige of managers. It manifested itself in the reluctance of employees to assume managerial duties.

Discussing the causes of that generally low respect for managers in Poland, Sarapata (1985) states that respect for a profession is a result of the evaluation of work output of people who do the job; of the characteristics of people belonging to the profession; and of benefits the managers reap from the job. Sarapata concludes that, in Poland the society's respect for managers is an outgrowth of the assessment of professional skills and moral qualifications of people holding managerial posts. Access to material goods, power, and other related values seems to be of less significance in gaining the public's respect. Moreover, the essential factors imposed on the people being selected for managerial jobs were doctrinal assumptions regarding production work and the leading role of the working classes.

Until 1989 Poland had no real labor market. Appointment to managerial posts and promotions were not based on objective selection criteria, but on the wishes of the party, government agencies, and local authorities. Finally, the level of compensation for managerial work was also a factor that discouraged managerial careers and reduced workers' desires to be promoted.

Another specific factor influencing the selection and prestige of managers is the unclearly defined legal status of managers, especially directors. Who, based on what criteria, appoints and assesses directors? What is the proper way to dismiss directors? It was difficult to answer these questions. Legal regulations that were in force and practice often diverged from each other. As a result, sudden removals would occur, with no possibility of appeal. Quite a different matter was the so-called staff-roundabout rule, according to which a person who was loyal to the political system could never be reduced in rank once appointed to a managerial post. He or she could only be appointed to another post of the same rank in another firm as long as he or she remained loyal to the party. In light of these circumstances, let us try to answer the question concerning legitimacy, ideology, and other characteristics of the managerial class in Poland.

Most managers (approximately 90 percent) were members of the Communist party and at least formally accepted the communist ideology and its resultant policies. That is why ideological and political reasons had priority over economic efficiency. A considerable number of managers, particularly among directors, were people actively engaged in party politics. It is hard to state clearly to what extent this attitude resulted from internal conviction. It may be reasonably assumed that, as the years went by and the economic crisis appeared and deepened, pure opportunism played an increasingly important role. It is very likely that prior to the early 1970s a significant proportion of managers performed their duties in the belief that they served ''the revolutionary transformation of the socioeconomic order and construction of socialism.'' They felt their mission in life was to build a better social and economic order. In this period, however, another ''ideology'' was also observable, which should be imputed rather to medium- and lower-level managers. It was a conservative, lower middle-class ideology that consisted in efforts to retain the humble position and material goods that this category of managers had earned (Koralewicz-Zębik, 1975).

Considering this state of affairs, it is open to doubt whether managers in Poland can reasonably be treated as an elite distinguished by power, talent, privileges, and enterpreneurship. Instead, we should speak about a social class distinguished by its place in the social division of labor (a group of people earning their living through performing defined duties by means of acquired knowledge and skills). However, it should be emphasized that Polish managers, particularly those from higher management levels, are increasingly aware that they constitute a distinct profession with their own values, habits, behavior modes, and measures of success. This awareness, though not widespread, is constantly rising.

DOMINANT CULTURAL VALUES

The literature does not contain extensive and representative research studies concerning the system of values of managers in Poland. Hence, the statements and judgments expressed below are hypotheses framed on the basis of a few research findings that have been published and on reflections on the historical experiences of the Polish people.

As mentioned earlier, aspirations for promotion, career, and success are not common among Polish managers. Nevertheless, we can assume that the need for success among managers is higher than it would be in other occupational groups. This assumption is supported by some research findings (Kottas, 1979) which indicate that, in comparison with managers from the United States, Italy, and Turkey, Polish managers are second, in terms of their need for success, after Americans.

Numerous investigations carried out by means of Bass's Orientation Inventory prove that Polish managers are primarily task-oriented and that the higher the management level the stronger the task orientation (Dobruszek, 1976; Kostecki, 1979). Attitudes emphasizing efficiency and pragmatism of action were moderate and reduced for ideological and political reasons. Poles, including Polish managers, can attempt big projects and achieve big results. This occurs, however, in extremely difficult situations and, of course, only when they are convinced of the purposefulness of action. Under normal conditions, they seem to be lacking in endurance and enthusiasm. Poles also have a strong feeling of dignity and seek independence and autonomy. Therefore, they painfully feel any restrictions in these fields.

Research findings concerning the satisfaction of managers from Haire, Ghiselli, and Porter's questionnaire was done over several years (1966). In this research, a typology of needs similar to Maslow's classification was used. The findings point out that Polish managers displayed a high level of aspiration for all needs and that the level of dissatisfaction was highest in relation to safety, autonomy, and self-actualization needs (Listwan, 1974; Sarapata, 1970; Szaban,

1983; Zebrowska, 1989). The research studies under discussion suggest that the lower the level of management, the lower the level of satisfaction of needs.

Poles are recognized as individualists, and we can suppose that their experience with collectivized economy—over forty years of it—has not significantly reduced this characteristic. The postwar political and social order has probably had stronger repercussions on their feeling of egalitarianism since an egalitarian point of view is a rooted feature of postwar Poles. At the same time, it seems that the higher the level in the social hierarchy, the lower the level of egalitarianism.

The set of features and cultural values outlined here is, as it is in all societies, a result of the influence of natural, demographic, cultural, and other factors. In the postwar period, two factors have apparently been most important: historical conditions and an "experiment" of infecting the nation with a social and political order that was alien to Christian traditions and values. The Poles characteristically identify themselves with small social groups (e.g., family, friends) and the nation. Intermediate groups of identification have not developed: the world of work organizations is not too attractive for them (Nowak, 1979).

A systematic review of the Poles' societal values, and managers' behaviors and attitudes is presented in Figure 9.1. It includes those characteristics of Polish managers which, in our opinion, are of great significance for the development of a market economy in Poland. They represent both weak and strong points of people who, to a large extent, will assume responsibility for the depth, pace, and scope, and, finally the success of necessary economic adjustments in the future.

These research findings do not, of course, exhaust the question of the societal and cultural values of Polish managers. In order to present them more comprehensively, we should consider the Polish historical experience over the last two centuries. A methodological problem always arises when contemporary occurrences are explained by historical data. Linkages between the past and present are often constructed in ways that vary from author to author. Therefore, the point of view presented here is our own interpretation, although the validity of a historical explanation of managerial behavior in Poland is beyond doubt.

The last years of Poland's monarchy, in the late eighteenth century, was marked by the predominance of the aristocracy and gentry, while townspeople and peasants had very little influence. Central and Eastern Europe, east of the Elbe, were agricultural societies, serving essentially as a granary for Western Europe. The dominant position of the Polish gentry resulting from this grain monoculture had strong repercussions on the Poles' societal and cultural values. The gentry developed a system of values, the most important being extreme individualism, a strong feeling of dignity, and the equality of all "gentlemen" in the political sphere. In the economic sphere, the gentry developed a contempt for manual work and town business activity (manufacturing, trade, commerce). The "well-born" did not have much respect for pragmatism of action, which was necessary among townspeople. The only career they considered appropriate was in politics, the priesthood, and the military. These values cultivated by the Polish gentry were inherited by a very particular social class, typical for Slavic

Figure 9.1

Link between Societal Values and Behavior and Attitudes Preferred by Polish Managers

VALUES	PREFERRED MANAGERIAL BEHAVIOR AND ATTITUDES
Dignity	Emotional way of action Aspiration for formal authority Attachment to formal ranks and degrees Predominance of formal knowledge over practical skills
Individualism	Resistance to uniform, standardized patterns of action Particularism of action, putting interests of internal units before interests of enterprises Reduced ability for teamwork Reduced awareness of linkages between own career and enterprise's success Good performance of "one-man" activities
Independence and autonomy	Tendency toward ignoring formal rules Tendency toward ignoring abilities and knowledge of higher levels Positive reaction to the increase of freedom for units under command
Egalitarianism	Lack of acceptance of material disparities (characteristic for lower management levels) Reduced tolerance for different behavior of others
Moderate efficiency and pragmatism	Low flexibility in action Aversion to risky decisions and activities Insufficient cooperation in organized activities Aversion to development of managerial skills and knowledge (once acquired education treated as sufficient for the whole duration of the professional activity)
Moderate aspiration for success and career	Need for employment safety Moderate optimism in action Moderate aspiration for promotion Caution in action Aversion to duties requiring sacrifice in personal life Immobility (aversion to change of an employer and occupation)

Figure 9.1 (continued)

VALUES	PREFERRED MANAGERIAL BEHAVIOR AND ATTITUDES
Identification with family and the nation	Loyalty to close persons Conformity Looking for esteem and friendship among collaborators Activity in informal groups Getting things done through informal contacts Persons before essence in problem solving Local or national patriotism before economic efficiency
Efficiency in extreme situations	Lack of endurance and regularity under normal conditions Good results in case of extraordinary challenges Need for fame and striking effects Enthusiasm for novelties
Creativity	Capability of solving nonroutine problems "No impossible problems" attitude

nations in Europe, called the intelligentsia. This elite derived mainly from the gentry whose significance increased immediately after the complete partition of Poland in 1796 by Russia, Prussia, and Austria. The gentry, who identified themselves with the nation, took the lead in Poland's struggles for freedom. However, during the 120 years that Poland was partitioned the gentry gradually lost their importance.

Abandonment of serfdom was the final stage of the transformation of the gentry into the intelligentsia. Some of them became landholders, running their agricultural business in the capitalistic way, but they were still considered representatives of the intelligentsia. The gentry, who were educated people, inculcated their values in the intelligentsia. These values were enriched by aspiration for political independence and strong identification with the nation. At the same time, an individual career in the service of invaders was not acceptable. Since the Poles' primary task was to fight for their nation's independence, industrial activity was of less significance. This disobedience of the German and Russian invaders deepened the Poles' dignity and individualism, and made business activity all the less important.

Industrialization was far slower in Central and Eastern Europe than in the West. Consequently, the demand for entrepreneurship emerged relatively slowly and late, and did not take root as a primary value. The emerging class of entrepreneurs and managers was recruited largely from the declassed gentry. They often understood their role as that of serving the nation, individual aspirations for wealth were either secondary or hidden. The pace of industrialization was rather slow, and when Poland finally regained its independence in 1918 it was a nation with many remnants of precapitalistic societies, both materially and psychologically.

The majority of Poles in 1918 were peasants. Their eternal dream had been to abandon serfdom and become landowners, a goal they finally achieved in the mid-nineteenth century. Their farms were small and inefficient. Because of the low level of industrialization at that time, the economy did not absorb many people from agriculture, nor was there a high demand for agricultural products in urban areas. Therefore the peasants developed attitudes of caution, limited aspirations for promotion, shrewdness, and respect for tradition. They would play a very important role in the formation of modern Poland which is considered a post-peasant society. With education, the peasants submitted to the influence of the intelligentsia. Although, modern Poles are mostly descendants of peasants, they inherited their societal and cultural values from the gentry-intelligentsia.

These circumstances also generated the cult of the family as a shelter for the Polish spirit and bolstered the role of the Catholic Church as supporter of Polish values amidst the Orthodox and Protestant invaders. Unlike Protestant beliefs, Catholic doctrine does not emphasize business activity, with its efficiency and effectiveness as criteria of success. Rather, individual piety and charity distinguish a good Christian among Catholics. Nor should the role of Polish literature be omitted in any discussion of the Poles' cultural values. The masterpieces of Polish literature focus on the problems of Poland's independence; heroes are mostly patriots who sacrifice their personal affairs, and even lives, for freedom. Thus, the literature has reflected and, at the same time, consolidated values arising from the nation's historical experience.

After gaining independence in 1918, Poland faced many difficulties, especially the problem of reintegrating the nation and state. One approach to solving this problem was to stress patriotic education among the youth. Poland now entered a new era with numerous residual elements of underdeveloped capitalism. Two decades of the ''second'' republic were not sufficient to generate pro-business attitudes. Economic progress in this period was meager and did not significantly increase the number of entrepreneurs and managers.

The almost six-year Nazi occupation during World War II was to some extent a repetition of Poland's struggles for freedom. Such values as patriotism, disobedience of the invaders, and exaltation of dignity over order, economic efficiency, and individual success again became paramount.

A Soviet-type economy was created in postwar Poland. Its main characteristics were state ownership, emphasis on heavy industry, predominance of growth over efficiency, and high centralization. In the political and social dimensions, the socialist order aimed at promoting the working classes and social justice. Despite the high rate of industrialization, it did not produce dynamic, vigorous, and enterprising managers, primarily because the highly centralized, planned economy did not need them. Rather it required that strategies and policies be worked out by the planning ministries. Industry absorbed millions of people from the agricultural sphere who moved from the countryside to urban areas, bringing with them the values and attitudes typical of the peasantry. Paradoxically and unexpectedly for the authorities, the system of values formed by the intelligentsia in previous periods became only slightly weakened. The new, atheistic, pro-Soviet oppressive regime was not accepted by the great majority of Polish people.

On the other hand, some efforts of the communist government were effective. Specifically, egalitarian ideology became widespread among the urban working classes, who stemmed mainly from the peasantry. Characteristically engineering jobs gradually became a part of intellectual occupations, and engineers and technicians were referred to as technological intelligentsia. The ideals of that professional group included technological feasibility of products and services while no attention was paid to market aspects. Generally, people who were in charge of economic organizations did not focus on the efficiency of enterprises, but rather on access to financial and material resources distributed by the state. Thus, an effective general manager was a person successful in attaining money, raw materials, equipment, energy, and workforce. Sharp competition arose among enterprises and whole industries on the input side of the production process. Thus, a false conviction that the success of industries, regions, and social groups depended on the goodwill of the state became common among the people, including managers.

The most important influences on managerial behavior in Poland can be summarized as follows:

- In the last two centuries of its existence, Poland's business problems were overwhelmed by questions of freedom and independence.
- The economic and political powers ruling the country were conceived as strangers, forced on the nation.
- In principle, Poland did not experience a developed market type economy.
- The social and cultural values of Poles were mainly generated by social classes which were not involved in business activity.

The products of these influences are the values and behaviors shown in Figure 9.1. Generally they do not favor Poland's economic transformation. (Figure 9.2 shows that these dominant cultural values arose from more than one cause.) Apart from the primary value, each of the behaviors is related to other elements of the system of cultural and societal values.

The attitudes of Polish managers sometimes seem to be inconsistent. For example, Polish managers consider themselves creative people who are called upon to and capable of solving nonroutine problems. This creativity has arisen from both the peasant's shrewdness and the gentry's heroic "fantasy" and was adopted as a value by successors of those two classes. It is often accompanied by a disregard of day-to-day, routine problems and a formal, standardized way of action. In extraordinary situations, especially in cases touching on matters of honor, the Poles' creativity can produce excellent results.

As mentioned earlier, the prestige of Polish managers was not very high in the early postwar period. The general public did not appreciate managerial work because they did not perceive its impact on their daily lives. (Much more effect

Figure 9.2
Primary and Secondary Causes of Behavior and Attitudes of Polish Managers

MANAGERIAL BEHAVIOR AND ATTITUDES (see numbers from Figure 1.)	UNDERLYING VALUES AS PRIMARY AND SECONDARY CAUSES								
	Dignity	Individualism	Independence	Egalitarianism	Moderate Efficiency	Moderate Aspiration for Success	Identification with Family and Nation	Efficiency in Extreme Situations	Creativity
1.	P	S(1)	S(2)						
2.	P				S				
3.	P	S(2)			S(1)	S(2)			
4.	P				S(1)	S(2)			
5.		P							S
6.		P	S						
7.		P	S(1)		S(2)				
8.		P	S(1)					S(2)	
9.	S(2)	P	S(3)						S(1)
10.			P	S(1)	S(2)	S(3)			
11.	S(3)	S(1)	P						
12.	S(1)	S(3	P					S(4)	S(2)
13.	S			P					
14.				P					
15.	S(3)	S(2)	S(4)		P	S(1)			
16.	S(1)				P	S(2)			
17.			S(1)		P	S(2)			
18.					P	S			
19.	S(2)		S(4)	S(3)	S(1)	P			
20.						P		S	
21.		S(1)		S(2)		P	S(3)	S(4)	
22.					S	P			
23.					S(2)	P	S(1)		
24.	S(2)		S(3)			P	S(1)		
25.							P		
26							S	P	
27.	S(3)				S(2)	S(1)	P		
28.	S(3)				S(2)	S(1)	P		
29.		S(2)					P		S(1)
30.	S(3)				S(1)	S(2)	P		
31.	S(1)			S(2)			P		
32.						S(1)	S(2)	P	
33.	S(2)	S(3)						P	S(1)
34.	S(2)	S(1)			S(3)			P	
35.		S(1)						P	S(2)
36.	S(2)	S(1)							P
37.		S							P
38.						S(2)	S(1)	P	

P = primary cause

S = secondary cause (number in brackets indicates the cause's rank)

was attributed to the state.) In addition, the common people realized that managerial careers carried a price: the necessity of loyalty to the political system. This attitude prohibited the development of aspirations for individual success and careers.

Changing undesirable attitudes and behavior will require a sophisticated approach. Whereas education can provide knowledge of the most effective managerial behavior, educational efforts may continue to be hampered by values held by managers and the public. Therefore, adoption of a market economy seems to be of decisive importance, for it can eventually lead to modification of old values and the emergence of new ones. The new government that arose from Solidarity is trying to follow that approach. It is attempting to create conditions under which the general efficiency of the business activity will use the Poles' system of values. Thus, such values as dignity and autonomy may be used as prerequisites for consolidating Poland's economic sovereignity, which, in turn, requires deep economic reforms. Still, values such as individualism and egalitarianism, may be incompatible with the general austerity program presently in effect.

HUMAN RESOURCE MANAGEMENT IN RELATION TO MANAGERS

Demographic Characteristics of Managers

Complete statistical data regarding the demographic characteristics of managers in Poland are not available. That is why the demographic description of the population of managers also requires data from sample tests. Let us first consider educational data for the total population of managers (see Table 9.6). To some extent, it is surprising that managers are not better educated than specialists. The percentage of graduates from higher and secondary schools among managers is a bit lower than among specialists. This situation may be interpreted in the context of ways and sources of recruitment and selection of managers. Over time, however, managers as a group display higher and higher levels of education. The percentage of managers with higher education is differentiated among management levels, ranging from 54 percent in top management through 27 percent in middle management to a little bit more than 11 percent among foremen. One of the formally declared goals of socialist societies was equal rights for women in terms of equal promotion and earning opportunities. The data in Table 9.7 show an increasing share of female managers, although it does not correspond with the percentage of women among all employees (about 45 percent). The sectoral distribution of female managers indicates that their share is higher in services. This reflects the fact that women constitute only 35 percent of all employees in manufacturing and about 72 percent in services. Women generally perform middle-level management duties. Even in highly feminized sectors, their share in top management is relatively low. For example, in education it is 9 percent; in health service, 17.6 percent; and in insurance and banking, 8 percent. In manufacturing, female directors do not exceed 0.1 percent of all managers (Graniewska, 1985; Najduchowska, 1984).

In 1977 and 1983, respectively, 30.9 percent and 35.6 percent of female managers had received higher education, the measure being higher than in the whole population of managers. The managerial careers of women do not, however, correspond with their educational potential. It is connected with both societal values and economic conditions. The traditional role of the woman taking care of the home and the man earning the family's living is still strong. That is why any career aspirations, including a career in management, are lower among women than among men, although this attitude has been slowly changing for

Table 9.6
Polish Managers by Level of Education, 1983

Levels of	Number in thousands			Percent		
Education	Mana-gers	Specia-lists	Other non-workers	Mana-gers	Specia-lists	Other non-workers
Graduates of higher schools	322.3	647.1	28.7	32.7	33.0	3.1
Graduates of secondary and post-secondary vocational schools	453.1	1,001.9	483.0	46.0	51.1	52.8
Graduates of general secon-dary (high) schools	155.1	235.0	229.5	15.8	12.0	25.1
Graduates of primary schools	53.8	48.9	105.0	5.5	2.5	11.5
Employees who have not finished primary schools	0.5	0.4	0.5	0.0	0.0	0.0
Total	984.3	1,959.9	915.4	100.0	100.0	100.0

Source: Same as in Table 9.4.

years. Apart from it, family and housekeeping responsibilities do not allow women to be involved in external activities on the scale exercised by the male population.

Information about age characteristics is especially scarce in Poland. Conclusions can only be reached indirectly. Common observations indicate that the majority of managers are in the forty- to forty-nine year cohort. Statistics published in 1972 show that the youngest directors were thirty-seven years old and that the dominant group was over fifty years of age (Najduchowska, 1984). Female managers showed roughly the same proportions with regard to age. Interestingly, both candidates and winners of competitions for directorial posts are relatively old. Statistical data show that the age of the dominant group of candidates was forty-five years and of winners fifty years (Kozinski, 1985; Listwan, 1974). These data confirm the prevalent notion among both theorists and practitioners that managers are too old and begin their careers too late.

Table 9.7
Female Managers in Poland, 1977 and 1983 (percentage)

	1977	1983
All managers	31.0	35.6
By management levels		
– Top management	n.a.	8.0
– Middle management	n.a.	40.5
– Foremen	n.a.	8.3
By chosen sectors		
– Industry and construction	7.8.	9.8.
– Trade	60.5	61.2
– Education	57.1	60.1
– Health service	65.5	69.6

Source: Data derived from Rocznik Statystyczny Przemyslu, 1986 (Warsaw, 1987), p. 168; D. Graniewska (1985), pp. 47–49.

In addition to equal rights for women, the socialist order strove to promote the welfare of the working classes. Table 9.8 presents data on the family background of directors and female managers in two different periods. The data confirm that social background is becoming less important in managerial careers.

Types of Careers and Sources of Recruitment

Analysis of the professional careers of directors reveals the existence of three types of pure careers and several types of mixed careers (Najduchowska, 1984). Among the pure careers are technological-engineering, administrative-financial, and political types. The first career type relates to people with engineering education who, in general, pass through the following posts: lower supervisor, middle supervisor, chief engineer, vice-director responsible for technology (manufacturing), and director. This type of career is the most frequent and is related to more than 50 percent of all careers in the last three decades. The second career type, the administrative-financial (about 20 percent) consists of promotion to subsequent management levels in administrative or financial areas of various enterprises. The political type of career includes those directors who began as active members of the political party apparatus, labor unions, army, and other public institutions and then moved to economic organizations.

These three types of careers comprise about 80 percent of directors. The remaining 20 percent are directors characterized by mixed careers in which vertical movements were intermingled with horizontal ones. Generally, the relatively low differentiation of career paths can be noted, which is accompanied

Table 9.8
Directors and Female Managers by Family Background, 1972 and 1977
(percentage)

Parents belonging to:	Directors (1972)	Female Managers (1977)
Workers	54.0	31.4
Peasants	24.0	16.0
Intellectuals	21.0	49.1
Parentage not determined	1.0	2.6

Source: D. Graniewska (1985), p. 59; Najduchowska (1984), p. 127.

by narrow qualifications for managerial tasks. One result was that people promoted to top management still concentrated on problems and areas they were
particularly familiar with.

The three types of careers and the number of people representing them were
connected with level and type of education. The considerable majority of managers, including directors, were graduates of engineering schools. Several factors
were responsible for the engineering orientation of managers: the predominance
of management posts with technical or manufacturing tasks, profiles of higher
schools that resulted in a considerable supply of graduates of technical universities
(polytechnics), and the highly centralized system of planned economy that restricted the enterprises to executive units, mainly carrying out production processes requiring technical qualifications. Most financial decisions were made
outside the enterprises. As mentioned earlier, engineering professions formed
the so-called technological intelligentsia. For some time, the percentage of managers with nonengineering education has been slowly increasing. In 1982, approximately 68 percent of directors were graduates from engineering schools
and 26 percent were from schools specializing in microeconomics, whereas in
1965 the respective figures had been 65 and 22 percent.

With regard to other questions regarding recruitment, it is interesting to consider what role social background has in managerial selection. One of the essential
factors in the low prestige of managers is the preference applied by decisive
bodies in selecting managers. In fact, apart from the period prior to 1949, political
and ideological criteria always played an important role, particularly during
1949–60. At that time, the doctrine of "proper" social background was expressed
in the mass promotion of workers to managerial posts, including directorial
positions. They were promoted after they had finished one of many courses for
workers proposed for managerial jobs and after their biographies had been carefully analyzed in order to eliminate "class-strange" people. Of course, affiliation
to the party was obligatory. In the later period, until the early 1980s, political

and ideological reasons continued to play an important role in selection, and party affiliation became the focal point.

Even so, education and professional experience have been playing a more important role since the early 1960s. Generally, one might state that the lower the managerial post the more important was the merit of the job and the less significant were political factors. A departure from the rules mentioned occurred during a short period of sixteen months in 1980–81, when, under the pressure of Solidarity, selection criteria were based mainly on merit. Generally, however, in the postwar period the basic factors impacting the mechanism of selection for managerial posts were sex, social background, and political affiliation and activity. During this period, education was not important in career-making. The situation has changed since 1989. Merit has again become the main criterion of assessment.

Methods of Selection for Managerial Posts

Two methods of selecting managers have been used. The closed method uses a set of unclear criteria with no opportunity for applicants to apply for consideration. The open method of selection involves public notification of the criteria and the right of applicants to apply for the managerial position through a competitive process.

The closed selection, especially one of its variants, the so-called selection by coordination, was used more than the open method. In the closed approach, decisive bodies (senior superiors, party representatives, and, to a lesser degree, labor union and personnel department representatives) agreed on the selection of candidates. During the selection process, personal data were analyzed, and candidates were interviewed frequently in order to gain information about them and in turn to inform them about employer expectations of them. The circle of candidates was usually very limited, and the most important characteristic of the candidates selected was loyalty. Hence, the opinion spread that managers who were thus selected were "passive, mediocre, but loyal." In addition, this selection method was time consuming, and the higher the post, the longer the procedure.

The open method of selection was through competition for managerial posts. The open selection type became widespread after the social protest in 1980. The competition was particularly applied to the selection of directors and since 1981 the law has required competition for these posts. The essence of the competition is to match up the characteristics of the candidates with the requirements of the vacancies. Thus, the primary task of organizations involved in competition is to apply investigation techniques that will allow them to rate the candidates' qualifications and to fill the vacant post according to the rule of "the right man in the right place." Among these techniques are job analysis and description as well as observing, interviewing, and testing candidates. The competitions are handled by specially formed competition committees, consisting of a few persons, each representing the staff of the enterprise and external organizations that have some impact on the enterprises. Until 1989 the committees included representatives of self-management bodies, political parties, labor unions, professional organizations, banks, and the appropriate government ministry. After 1989, the number of members was reduced because political organizations were excluded from competition. The committees were allowed to hire specialists from consulting firms and academic centers as their advisers. When competitions were properly run, this method produced good results for enterprises (Listwan, Koziński, and Witkowski, 1986). In some cases, however, competitions were only a cover for decisions made previously and thus were very similar to "selection by coordination."

The selection problem is associated with the institution of the so-called reserve managers. This group included employees who were being prepared for promotion. Formally, the reserve managers groups existed in the majority of enterprises; in reality, however, many enterprises had them on paper only. This source was seldom used to fill vacant managerial jobs. It was just one more evidence of political and ideological dominance of the personnel function and a symptom of an unreasonable personnel policy.

Training and Development

As in other former socialist countries, until recently the idea that management was a professional activity was generally rejected. Hence, preparation for managerial tasks was a supplementary activity in relation to the present occupation, and there was always a tinge of politics in management development. As the economic system became more decentralized and external conditions of enterprises more complex, it appeared obvious that short courses aiming at exposing nonmanagers to managerial duties were not sufficient. Therefore, a number of management development centers were started, particularly in the 1970s, and higher schools founded chairs or institutes of organization and management. These centers developed various forms of management training, the most important of them being postgraduate studies for practitioners from the enterprises. The training centers and institutes are concentrated mainly in or around big cities and employ qualified lecturers (e.g., Warsaw, Cracow, Wroclaw, and Lodz). In Warsaw at least three management development centers should be mentioned: the Institute of Administration and Management (formerly the Institute of Organization and Management Development); the Faculty of Management at Warsaw University; and the Central School of Commerce and Trade. In the remaining cities, academies of economics have taken the lead in management training.

As a result of Poland's economic reform, management (business) schools organized as profit-making institutions independent of universities (academies) have emerged. They offer training courses for those who want to enter upon a managerial career or to improve their managerial skills as practitioners. Some of those schools are assisted by foreign lecturers and capital.

Compensation

One problem associated with human resource management in Poland is the question of compensation of managers: whether they are rewarded according to

Table 9.9
Wages and Salaries in Poland, 1955–90

	1955	1960	1970	1975	1980	1985	1988	1990
Index numbers of average real wages (1970 = 100.0)	62.5	84.0	100.0	141.6	157.3	127.5	144.5	115.1
Average salary of non-workers as a percentage of the average wage (nominal average wage = 100.0)	130.0	118.4	107.0	114.7	100.9	106.7	102.6	n.a.
Average salary of top management as a percentage of the average wage (nominal average wage = 100.0)	n.a.	n.a.	n.a.	n.a.	n.a.	144.0	153.0	n.a.

Source: Data derived from Rocznik Statystyczny, 1989 (Warsaw, 1990), p. XXXV and 180; Rocznik Statystyczny, 1981 (Warsaw, 1982), p. 164; Rocznik Statystyczny, 1977 (Warsaw, 1978), p. 91; Rocznik Statystyczny, 1962 (Warsaw, 1963), pp. 394–396; Rocznik Statystyczny, 1990 (Warsaw, 1991), p. 167.

the responsibility and products of their work. This general question involves two aspects: whether managers are sufficiently rewarded in relation to other occupational groups and whether the compensation system encourages people to launch managerial careers.

Before proceeding to particular problems of compensation of managers, we should note that wages in general are one of the poorest results of the collectivized economy. It manifests itself in a relatively slow increase of real wages from 1955 to 1990 (see Table 9.9). In the period 1950 to 1988, real wages increased approximately 2.3 times, while the Net Material Product increased 4.4 times. In 1981, the average real wage reached its highest level and then was constantly decreasing until 1985. It increased again in the next three years, but it fell again in 1990 and 1991 as a result of efforts aiming at restructuring the Polish economy.

A comparison of the salaries of nonworkers with the average wages of workers proves that nonmanual jobs are not materially appreciated, and it corresponds with the earlier statements regarding the low prestige of those jobs. The same holds true for directorial salaries. In general, the compensation system in Poland

Table 9.10
Relative Differentiation of Salaries of Managers of Subsequent Hierarchical
Levels (Foreman's salary = 100.0)

	1960	1968	1985
Foreman	100.0	100.0	100.0
Managers of manufacturing units	135.0	129.7	110.4
Managers of staff departments	214.5	112.4	99.1
Plant managers	274.0	n.a.	n.a.
Line vice-directors	342.6	187.0	n.a.
Staff vice-directors	295.2	161.6	110.5
Directors	380.3	198.3	149.6

Source: Data derived from: Rocznik Statystyczny Pracy, 1971 (Warsaw, 1972), pp. 322–324; Rocznik Statystyczny Pracy, 1986 (Warsaw, 1987), pp. 291–294.

is characterized by a relatively "flat" structure of wages and salaries. Managerial jobs requiring professional knowledge and skills are not equally compensated either in terms of material rewards or prestige. As shown in Table 9.10, the differentiation of managerial salaries by management levels has constantly become lower and lower. This trend obviously discouraged people from aiming at managerial careers.

Characteristically, line managers earn more than staff units. In this context, the higher salaries of engineer-managers correspond with their relatively higher prestige in comparison with other groups of nonworkers. Over 60 percent of directors are engineers. Three fundamental reasons are responsible for this situation. First, in the postwar period the economy was growth oriented; production volume and annual increases were much more important than efficiency. Second, production work, that is, the work producing material goods, in accordance with the Marxist theory, was treated as the main source of the national wealth. Third, this doctrine also satisfied the public's egalitarian point of view. The "flat" structure of wages, higher pay, and esteem for those who perform production work are the consequences of those factors.

The salaries of managers are also differentiated in respect of business sectors. Basically, people.employed in services earn much less than those in manufacturing industries. Heavy and extractive industries are particularly privileged. It

Table 9.11

Relations of Salaries of Chosen Managerial Posts by Economic Sectors in 1985 (Manufacturing Industry = 100.0)

	Coal	Steel	Furni-ture	Construc-tion	Trade	Finance	Agricul-ture
			Economic Sectors				
Director	292.7	122.9	85.4	92.8	88.2	68.9	78.7
Vice-director	n.a.	n.a.	n.a.	92.0	99.0	84.1	82.4
Staff-dept. manager	n.a.	n.a.	n.a.	95.8	102.0	90.0	86.2
Line-dept. manager	n.a.	n.a.	n.a.	82.1	102.4	n.a.	80.4
Foreman	n.a.	n.a.	n.a.	80.2	79.7	n.a.	74.1

Source: Rocznik Statystyczny Pracy, 1986 (Warsaw, 1987), pp. 291–294.

is very informative to consider pay relations among peer managers in different economic sectors (see Table 9.11).

In 1986, the average wage of a coal miner was 34 percent higher than a nationwide average directorial salary. It is estimated that a graduate from a higher school entering a managerial career matches the pay level of an average worker at the age of thirty-five to forty years. The undervalued managerial salaries were, in a measure, equalized by the system of privileged sale of some deficit goods (mostly durable home appliances, cars, electronics, housing apartments). Various forms of bonds, debentures, coupons, and so on entitled receivers to buy some goods. This system constituted a form of additional, hidden compensation of managers, particularly those from the higher management levels as well as officials from noneconomic organizations.

The economic and political reorientation of 1989 has created conditions for a more objective and rational system of compensation for managers. However, whether it will be accomplished soon is in doubt because of the egalitarian mentality of the public and the poor state of economy. In private firms being established at present, the pay system is still unknown, although common observations indicate that private businesses pay managers more than state-owned firms.

The compensation system of Polish directors deserves special attention. In centrally planned economies, directors are state officials who manage state-owned enterprises on behalf of and in the name of the state. Their basic salaries were, therefore, centrally determined. Until the late 1970s, the base salaries of directors were differentiated in accordance with the industry involved. Categories of enterprises, varying in number in various periods, were determined by means of such criteria as number of employees, complexity of manufacturing technology, type of production, and its importance for the national economy. The higher the category, the higher the salary of a director. The initial economic reforms in 1981 brought about a changed approach to the compensation of directors. More attention was paid to strictly economic factors, such as financial results, value of assets, and possibility of financing the development outlays from internal resources. The new system did not, however, mean omitting the idea of categories of enterprises.

In relation to other managerial posts, the centralized economy manifested itself in the application of uniform pay scales within the same industries or occupational groups. Higher posts generally requiring higher qualifications offered higher salaries within a defined range. The decentralization of economic policy resulted in some changes in the managerial compensation system. The so-called in-company compensation systems were introduced. Enterprises were empowered, to a limited extent, to make the payment policy on their own. The in-company compensation system is an agreement between a director of an enterprise and an enterprise's labor union. The agreement is registered and approved by a ministry that checks whether legal regulations imposed on payment policy are taken into account. The most important restriction associated with the compensation system under discussion is the maximum increase of the wage fund. In comparison with previous systems, it means that financial rewards for managers depend more on enterprise success.

The typical compensation package for managers consists of base salary, supplemental salary, and bonuses. As mentioned earlier, base salary is determined either by common or in-company regulations, or both. The same regulations relate to supplemental salary and bonuses, although not as strictly. The supplemental salary has more than twenty possible components, the most important being the management supplement dependent on the number of subordinates and management level. Bonuses given to top management are dependent mainly on parameters imposed by the state, in accordance with the present economic policy (for example, profit, export sale, savings of materials, energy, environmental pollution, production quality, and others). Two types of bonuses are provided to middle- and lower-level managers. In the first group, some tasks derived from the parameters imposed on enterprises are generated by the enterprise's top management for various areas and levels of management. The second group depends on ratings of the behavior of managers and their subordinates (for example, work discipline, work accidents, training and development of subor-

Table 9.12

Structure of Average Managerial Salaries by Post, 1985 (percentage)

		Elements		
	Base salary	Supplemental salary	Bonuses	Other elements
Director	48.6	31.3	20.0	3.0
Vice-director	58.3	24.5	16.1	3.3
Line-dept. manager	56.7	24.8	16.4	3.8
Staff-dept. manager	59.5	24.5	16.3	2.7
Foreman	55.7	23.2	14.0	9.1

Source: Rocznik Statystyczny Pracy, 1986 (Warsaw, 1987), p. 291.

dinates, and the like). Bonuses provided to managers are paid in accordance with in-company bonus-rewarding systems.

As shown in Table 9.12, there are no significant differences among structures of salaries across management levels, except for directors, whose base salary does not exceed 50 percent. The director's supplemental salary (depending mainly on the category of enterprises) and bonuses (depending mainly on performance of efficiency parameters) is a little larger than those of other managerial positions. The share of base pay to total pay of nonworkers ranges from 70 to 80 percent.

Because of the dominant type of ownership in Poland, stock options are seldom used. In state-owned and cooperative enterprises, bonuses are, to a certain degree, connected with and paid from the after-tax profit. However, this kind of bonus does not usually exceed 5 percent of the total salary, and it amounts to about 15 to 25 percent of total bonuses. In contrast, at the higher management level, the share of this kind of bonus is larger. In those state-owned enterprises that are targeted to be privatized in the future, stock options for managers and workers will be applied. The privatization process in Poland has just begun.

Management Performance Appraisal

In the 1970s, management appraisal was widespread in Poland. Despite the centralized system, there was no uniform system of employee appraisal before 1970. Therefore, in practice, various appraisal systems were used, and many enterprises did not carry out any appraisal activity at all. This situation still holds true for medium-sized and small enterprises.

The most widespread method used was an annual appraisal, where performance goals were not clearly defined. Most frequently, instrumental purposes were observable (using the appraisal in compensation policy, personnel decision making, and stimulating higher effectiveness). The appraisal method used was a mixed form, with an appraisal of personal characteristics dominant. Other frequent appraisal criteria included individual performance, attitude toward the social and political system, and skills and achievements.

Formally, appraisals were performed through special questionnaires which, apart from basic data regarding the given position and holder, contained separate assessments for each criterion, total appraisal, and conclusions. With regard to appraisal techniques, rating and point scales were most often used. The appraisal work was conducted primarily by committees consisting of the senior superiors of the managers being appraised, representatives of the company's party unit, labor union officials, and the personnel department. The appraisal procedures usually also included the possibility of self-appraisal and appeal against the final appraisal (decision).

Most frequently, the appraisal forms had the following shortcomings:

• Lack of clearly defined goals.
• Short-term horizon done mostly at yearly intervals.
• Low diversification of ratings.
• Significant importance, or even domination, of political criteria and a corresponding role of party representatives among the appraising subjects.
• Excessive formalism.

The most important deficiency, however, was the weak feedback to other elements of the personnel function. Generally, the appraisal systems used were not purposeful, either for organization or for managerial career planning, and they had no influence on managerial behavior.

Labor Relations

In the postwar period, unionization in Poland, as in other former socialist countries, amounted to almost 100 percent. Labor unions were expected to serve as a transmission belt of ideas, goals, and tasks generated by the party. They were organized as nationwide sectoral unions, controlled by the central union council. Important representatives of the party played the role of leaders of labor unions. The personal identity of the party and union organizations was an expression of the class character of unions. Prior to 1980, it was taken for granted that all employees, including managers, were members of labor unions.

Partners of the collective bargaining system and other negotiation forms were the sectoral unions, and the central authorities called for the administration of economic sectors. On the enterprise level, the directors and leaders of labor unions were only carrying out tasks that emanated from central agreements.

With the rise of Solidarity in 1980, the sectoral unions collapsed. Most employees joined Solidarity (approximately 9 million); others (0.5 million) formed new, so-called autonomous unions. Only party apparatchiks and more active members of class unions kept their former union affiliation. Unionization fell to about 70 percent. These figures are very rough because all unions tended to overstate their numbers, and frequently double membership took place. In the transitional period between martial law and the revival of Solidarity, new class labor unions were founded. These new unions grouped only members of one enterprise and were confined to the activity within the respective enterprises. The degree of unionization was much lower than before, although new unions gained new members. In 1988, new unions reported membership of about 7 million (slightly over 40 percent of total employment). The new unions became official partners of collective bargaining on the enterprise level in the form of in-company compensation systems. With time, however, they tended to create sectoral union representation. Finally, they set up a nationwide union agreement. This representation of the union movement insisted on bargaining on the level of economic sectors and thus weakened the role of enterprise union leaders and the importance of in-company compensation systems.

The revival of Solidarity did not change the relationship between the enterprise's management and the labor unions, except that more than one union was now allowed in an enterprise. Some additional attempts were made to create occupation-based unions. In some regions and a few enterprises, nonworkers generally, or managers as such, founded their own unions. The overall degree of unionization among nonworkers, particularly among managers, is still lower than before the rise of Solidarity in 1980. At present, Solidarity has a little more than 2 million members, and the class unions about 5 million people (45 percent of total employment), the figure being much lower for managers. The great majority of unionized nonworkers belongs either to Solidarity or to class unions.

Apart from labor unions, managers in Poland are often members of professional societies that group people of the same education line (e.g., engineers, accountants, and lawyers). Formal or informal clubs of directors, organizers, or managers are sometimes affiliated with such societies, but they aim primarily at exchanging experiences, knowledge, and information. They also permit personal contacts among members and their families.

CONCLUSION

In the postwar period, the behavior of Polish managers was largely determined by the social and political order: namely, the domination of politics over economy, of production over efficiency, and high centralization over decentralization.

The basic deficiencies of the personnel function in the collectivized economy included:

• The lack of rational career planning.
• The predominance of political and ideological criteria of selection and promotion of managers and in managerial performance appraisal.
• The lack of rational motivational systems.
• The incomplete system of management training and development.

These deficiencies should be viewed within the framework of the national characteristics of Poles discussed earlier in the chapter. Neither the cultural and societal values inherited from previous periods and enriched in the postwar period, nor the socioeconomic order of postwar Poland favored efficient managerial behavior. The jump from underdeveloped capitalism to socialism did not create a demand for enterprising, pragmatic, success-seeking leader-managers. The poor state of the economy and the market shortages resulted in the dissatisfaction and even frustration of managers. This situation became more common with the passing years.

Only in 1989 did the social protest of 1980 impact the economy. The democratization of political life has been followed by efforts to create an economy based on market rules. The most important changes expected in the future are:

- Privatization—the process has already started and will take a long time to effect. It is the biggest challenge for the Polish economy and the people who manage it,
- Demonopolization of huge, state-owned enterprises; in many cases, 100 percent monopolies will be dissolved and divided into smaller units within the next few years. In addition, new firms will be set up, competing with hitherto monopolies, but time and capital are needed.
- Foreign capital inflow; the process has already begun and is expected to intensify in the near future,
- Expansion of new economic sectors particularly the service sectors (tourism, banking, insurance, consulting, telecommunication) and those requiring rather small business units (retail trade, repair of home appliances, cars, apartments, etc.).

These changes are expected to produce

- A demand for managers prepared to deal with a market economy in all its dimensions.
- An increase in the number of managers running more, but smaller, enterprises.
- An increase in the demand for managers with a microeconomic type of education instead of engineering.
- An increase in the demand for managers capable of coping with nonmanufacturing business activity.
- A demand for managers who have not been contaminated by a centralized, bureaucratic mode of management.
- An increase in the importance of strategic problems being faced by enterprises.
- An increased number of enterpreneurs who will also perform the roles of managers.
- A change in relationships among managers and owners. Most managers will stop being state officers running state-owned enterprises; gradually, managers will be most responsible to private owners.

At present, Poland's economy lacks a sufficient number of properly prepared managers. Therefore, the training and development of managers should be intensified. The primary objective of management schools is to educate, train, and develop new managers, released from the demands of the planned economy and capable of acting under new conditions.

Managers themselves are already undergoing radical changes. An intensive displacement of managers is taking place, partially as a result of the establishment of new firms and partially because of dismissals of managers recognized as incompetent in old firms. Another development is the emergence of private businesspeople. At present, differences between these two groups, managers and businesspeople, are not easily discerned, with the exception that clearly businesspeople run businesses on their own. However, private sector entrepreneurs have some capital, they are usually younger, and they are more dynamic and enterprising. This group is expected to grow. As yet, there are not many of them, and they face the difficulties typical of pioneers.

In light of the new expectations, many problems have to be solved. The key question is how to establish the system of education and select the best individuals who will one day generate Poland's social and economic progress. The existing business schools cannot produce enough managers. Universities and academies do not have instructors schooled in the principles of the market economy. One possible solution is foreign assistance to instruct Poland's instructors. Educational and training activity, however, are not sufficient to remedy the situation. Societal values rooted in the Polish mentality may constitute the main obstacle to change in managerial behavior. No doubt, material conditions of education, programs, and training content—even instructors—may be relatively easily changed. But radical change in managerial behavior will require a long-term experience with the managerial role in the context of the new management realities of the market.

Other questions remain. For example, is Poland to find the "golden way" between business efficiency and values arising from employee participation in management? Employee self-management in state-owned enterprises accords well with the public's egalitarian view. What process should be adopted to promote young people to higher ranks? To what extent should women be promoted to higher posts? A very important question with economic, as well as political and social, ramifications, centers on what should be done with people who performed managerial jobs in the former state-owned economy. Total removal of these managers might be dangerous for the economy, and unfair in terms of politics and social justice. On the other hand, a considerable number of them were members of the party's nomenclature, and the public believes they are primarily responsible for the present state of the economy. Their professional qualifications may also be questioned under the new conditions. Should they keep their positions or be completely removed? Removal seems to be the most inconvenient alternative from all points of view.

Similar problems have been satisfactorily solved in other countries. However, Poland has its own unique character and indiscriminately transferring the experiences of other countries to Poland is difficult, though meriting serious consideration and thought.

REFERENCES

Dobruszek, M. 1976. "Osobowość kierowników w gospodarce." *Organizacje. Socjologia struktur procesów ról*. Warsaw: PWN.

Graniewska, D. 1985. *Awans zawodowy kobiet a fazy życia rodzinnego.* Warsaw.

Haire, M., Ghiselli, B., and Porter, L. 1966. *Managerial Thinking. An International Study.* New York: John Wiley.

Koralewicz-Zębik, J. 1974. *System wartości a struktura społeczna.* Wrocław: Ossolineum.

————. 1979. "Przemiany systemu wartości społeczeństwa polskiego." *Studia Socjologiczne* 4.

Kostecki, M. 1979. *Kadra kierownicza w przemyśle.* Warsaw: PWN.

Kottas, A. 1979. "Dazenie do osiagnieć jako motyw działania kierowników gospodarczych." *Biuletyn Psychometryczny,* Vol. I.

Koziński, J. 1985. "Cechy społeczno-zawodowe wymagane od kandydatów na stanowiska kierownicze." *Doskonalenie Kadr Kierowniczych* 3.

Listwan, T. 1974. "Potrzeby i motywacje kierowników kombinatu." *Doskonalenie Kadr Kierowniczych* 3.

————. Koziński, J., and Witkowski, S. 1986. *Konkursy na stanowiska kierownicze.* Warsaw: PWE.

Najduchowska, H. 1984. *Kwalifikacje i drogi zawodowe dyrektorów.* Warsaw: PWN.

Nowak, S. 1979. "System wartości społeczeństwa polskiego." *Studia Socjologiczne* 4.

Sarapata, A. 1970. "Motywacje i satysfakcje dyrektorów. Studium Porównawcze." *Studia Socjologiczne* 3.

Szaban, J. 1983. "Motywacje dyrektorów polskich." *Przegląd Organizacji* 12.

Szczepański, J. 1969. *Przemysł i społeczeństwo w Polsce Ludowej.* Wrocław: Ossolineum.

Wasilewski, J. 1981. *Kariery społeczno-zawodowe dyrektorów.* Wrocław: Ossolineum.

Żebrowska, E. 1989. "Potrzeby i motywacje dyrektorów." *Zarządzanie* 3.

10

ISRAEL

Itzhak Harpaz and Ilan Meshoulam

This chapter describes some of the major aspects of managerial behavior in Israel. It discusses the social and culture context that affects managers and their operations, particularly regarding human resource management and industrial relations.

DEFINITION

Two main available sources were used as background material for gathering data on Israeli managers. The first source consisted of the very limited amount of published empirical data. The term *managers*, not uniformly defined in these works, usually refers to those who occupy middle- to top-level organizational positions. The second source was the *Statistical Abstract of Israel*. This publication, which provides statistical data on the country's labor force, uses a general undefined category, called administrators and managers. Hence, "manager" is used quite broadly in the discussion to follow.

LABOR FORCE CHARACTERISTICS

Israel's civilian labor force numbered 1,553,000 workers in 1988 (*Statistical Abstract of Israel*, 1989). The relatively young age of the country's population (one-third are under the age of fourteen) (*Facts*, 1985) ensures the continued growth of the labor force, even as the population increases and matures. (The percentage of workers has experienced an annual growth of about 7 percent since 1949; see Rosenstein 1984.) Table 10.1 presents statistics on the labor force distribution by sex. The table shows the steadily rising participation of women in most capacities throughout the economy. Women accounted for 40 percent of all workers in 1988. Since 1973, the number of men and women in academic,

Table 10.1
Distribution of Civilian Labor Force by Sex, 1955–88

Population			*Year*		
	1955	1960	1970	1980	1988
Total labor force					
(thousands)	631.2	735.8	1001.4	1318.1	1553.0
Men (%)	80.1	78.1	69.2	63.7	63.2
Women (%)	26.5	27.3	29.3	35.7	40.0

Source: Statistical Abstracts of Israel, 1960, 1970, 1980, 1989.

professional, and technical occupations has grown in percentage as well as total numbers, as has the number in sales, clerical, and managerial positions. Since that time, the country has witnessed a decrease in both skilled and unskilled workers in industry, building, and agriculture, although a relatively high percentage of workers in most occupations tend to remain employed in the same job for ten years or more (*Statistical Abstract of Israel*, 1982). Table 10.2 divides the labor force by economic sector.

In 1988, more than 22 percent were employed in industry, 4.6 percent in agriculture, and the rest in construction and various public and private services and utilities (*Statistical Abstract of Israel*, 1989). Unemployment levels have held relatively steady, being about 4 percent a year from 1974 to 1983, but rising to about 6.5 percent annually between 1984 and 1988 (*Statistical Abstract of Israel*, 1989). But at the end of 1989 and the beginning of 1990, unemployment experienced another jump, to about 9 percent annually.

THE ECONOMY

From 1948 (the year of its establishment) to 1973, Israel's economy grew at the rapid rate of 10 percent a year. After 1973, as a result of both the Yom Kippur War and the world economic recession of the 1970s, its economic growth slowed considerably. In 1978–79, it was half the earlier rate, it fell further to 3.2 percent in 1980–81, and it reached a low point of 1.2 percent in 1982–83 (*Facts*, 1985).

Israel's gross domestic product (GDP) consists, in round terms, of a business sector (70 percent), private ownership of dwellings (10 percent), and the services of government and nonprofit/private institutions (20 percent). The private sector's share of GDP is 50 percent; that of the cooperative Histadrut-General Federal of Labor 20 percent; and that of the public sector, 30 percent. Table 10.3 presents

Table 10.2
Division of Labor Force by Economic Sector, 1950–88 (percentage)

Economic Sector	Year				
	1950	1960	1970	1980	1988
Agriculture	17.6	17.3	8.8	6.4	4.6
Industry	21.5	23.8	24.3	23.7	22.3
Electricity	2.0	2.3	1.2	1.0	1.0
Construction	9.3	8.9	8.3	6.4	5.1
Commerce	13.5	12.3	13.0	11.7	14.3
Finance	-	-	5.2	8.2	10.2
Transportation	6.6	6.4	7.5	6.9	6.6
Public Services	21.2	22.0	24.0	29.6	29.2
Personal Services	8.3	7.5	7.7	6.2	6.7

Source: Statistical Abstracts of Israel, 1960, 1970, 1980, 1989.

data on gross national product and gross domestic product since 1950. Although gross GDP per civilian employed person has more than doubled in the past two decades (1970—$13,200; 1980—$15,800; 1988—$27,300), it lags far behind that of the United States (in 1988, $41,700; Israel Institute of Productivity, 1989).

Since 1967, Israel's economy has been rapidly transformed into a modern industrial system, whose output exploits some of the most sophisticated production processes. Generally, industry in Israel has concentrated on manufactured

Table 10.3
GNP and GDP, 1950–88 (millions US$)

Gross Product	Year				
	1950	1960	1970	1980	1988
GNP (per employee)	950	2,354	5,401	20,756	42,705
GDP	976	2,690	6,259	21,831	41,112

Source: Statistical Abstracts of Israel, 1960, 1970, 1980, 1989.

products with high added values because of the country's lack of the most basic raw materials.

The industrial sector is dynamic and widely diversified, producing for both domestic consumption and export. Using its own scientific creativity and technical innovation, Israel has developed high-technology products, and is currently a world leader in the fields of medical electronics, agrotechnology, telecommunications, chemical products, solar energy, and computer hardware.

Table 10.4 presents data on employed persons by size and type of organization. Industrial enterprises controlled by the public sector account for about 15 percent of Israel's total industrial output. Government-owned enterprises are particularly prominent in such areas as mining, heavy chemicals, transportation (including airlines), utilities, and military and aircraft industries (*Facts*, 1985). In recent years the government has tried to sell some of its ownership in various organizations; thus, there is a growth in privatization.

MANAGEMENT STYLE, CULTURE AND VALUES

Israeli management is very heterogeneous in origin, education, occupation, and background (see the description of demographic characteristics later in this chapter). Are there specific traits that can be attributed to the Israeli manager? Is there such a phenomenon as an Israeli management culture?

Managerial style in Israel is influenced by the system and culture within which it operates. Aharoni (1985) identified four central components that are typical of the Israeli style of management. First, most firms in Israel are relatively small. As a result, most organizations do not operate under a rigid structure of rules and regulations. Hence, informality in operations and in interpersonal relations, including those between managers and subordinates, is common.

Second, since many of the economic, social, and political systems operate on an informal basis, managers have to be personally involved with these systems or must be constantly updated on changes and new developments. When a manager has to be frequently on the move, solving emergencies as they develop and unable to rely on subordinates, it is very difficult to decentralize authority.

Third, because of the lack of importance attributed to systematic planning, the dynamic nature of the country's political and economic environments, and relatively frequent changes in laws and regulations, long-range planning is extremely difficult to implement. As a result, the Israeli manager must develop specific skills that are not taught in business schools—such as improvisation and ingenuity. The fact that most Israeli managers serve for three or more years in the Israeli Defense Forces, generally as officers, helps them develop the needed skill.

Fourth, the higher the position of managers, the greater the expectations placed on them. Managers have to demonstrate that they know more and that they can make decisions. This situation creates a syndrome summed up by ''You can rely upon me''—in other words, a culture claiming that successful managers are those you may depend on to solve problems. Nevertheless, in an environmental reality

Table 10.4
Number of Employed Persons, by Size and Type of Legally Registered Organization (establishments with five or more employed persons)

	Employed persons (%)	Establishments (%)	Employed Persons (thousands)	Number of Establishments
Group Size				
(Number of employed persons in establishment)				
5-9	6.7	43.9	20.0	2,985
10-14	4.4	16.6	13.1	1,132
15-19	2.9	7.6	8.7	517
20-24	3.0	6.2	9.1	422
25-29	2.5	4.1	7.5	277
30-49	6.5	7.7	19.6	523
50-99	10.2	6.7	30.6	453
100-299	18.2	5.0	54.5	338
300+	45.6	2.2	136.7	152
Type of legally registered organization				
Single Owner	4.2	19.8	12.5	1,346
Partnership	2.7	12.7	8.2	861
Private limited co.	50.6	59.6	151.6	4,051
Public limited co.	29.6	3.0	88.8	206
Cooperative society*	5.9	4.7	17.8	321
Other (incl. not known)	7.0	0.2	20.9	14

* Including kibbutz-owned establishments not registered as separate legal units.

Source: *Statistical Abstracts of Israel*, 1989.

in which uncertainty is one of the most stable elements, managers have to be courageous to express doubts. Such courage is a highly typical trait of Israel's managerial culture.

In the late 1980s the Human Resources section of the Israeli Strategic Forum (a group of leading Israeli managers from various sectors that attempted to derive conclusions about Israeli business) held a series of discussions dealing with the Israeli manager and the managerial culture. Participants, all of whom were executives or academicians, clearly called for perpetuating and fostering traditional Israeli characteristics rather than changing to the heterogeneity that characterizes Israeli managers. It was felt that two important factors produced a kind of common denominator for Israelis, and so could not be ignored: the values set by the Jewish culture and religion; and the survival mode of the state of Israel. It is important to understand some of these values and behaviors that influence Israeli management. In this regard too, Frounman's (1989) comparison of U.S. and Israeli work values is also instructive.

Israeli management tends toward teamwork, group responsibility, work involvement, and a high sense and need of belonging. On the other hand, it exhibits little appreciation for privacy, whether one's own or another's. It is common, for instance, to ask directly about one's income level and place in the salary structure. Israeli managers and workers have a strong tendency to argue simply for the sake of argument. Decision making, in fact, is often carried out through the process of open arguments. Debate, coupled with the lack of a meetings tradition, makes the decision-making process very vocal, emotional, and participative. There is much openness in the system's direct approach, mixed with friendship and common objectives, and no "code of politeness."

Leadership is achieved by natural authority; formal authority will be met by cynicism or skepticism. Consequently, the problem of discipline seriously affects the ability of Israeli organizations to control large systems. The Israeli style is informal, reflected by dress, language, and a direct approach. Yet the system is not free of status symbols, which Israel has adapted from the West. Risk taking comes naturally. The influence of Israeli environmental conditions likely contributes to this style. The average Israeli worker, and definitely the management, have a strong commitment to their organization. Israeli management still maintains the traditional set of values of high commitment to the organizations and high involvement. The low mobility of Israeli workers is probably one of the outcomes of such values.

Finally, contrary to the notion of "How to join the system" that prevails in many cultures, the Israeli manager's notion usually is, "How to beat the system." Consequently, what is promoted are improvisation, short cuts, and immediate responses—all actions that are in accord with the spirit of nondiscipline and survival. Accompanying those values are innovative problem solving and a very high degree of self-criticism. Long-range planning strategies are not emphasized; little of this work is done in most organizations. Very recently, however, that area has started to receive more attention because of poor business results, the

entrance of new, more formally educated managers into organizations, and the
environmental pressures of growing global competition.

Meaning of Work

Work values and the meaning of work for Israeli managers may be examined
from a comprehensive, eight-country comparative study conducted in the early
1980s. (An account of the development and theoretical conceptualization of that
project is beyond the scope of this chapter; the reader may refer to MOW—
International Research Team (1987) for a detailed description of the research
design, instrumentation, and procedures.) As part of the study, an ecological
method was employed to arrive at a random sample of Israel's labor force. Of
the 973 individuals composing the sample, 179 were identified as managers.
The results presented here deal only with the data from Israel pertaining to the
central variables of the meaning of work for these managers. (A detailed account
of the Israeli study may be found in Harpaz, 1990.)

The following were the highlights of the findings:

- Work clearly seems to be of considerable importance in the Israeli manager's life.

- For Israeli managers, apparently the company is of greater importance than the manager's occupation/profession; hence managers have a local rather than a universal orientation—and it is to the organization that they give greater preference.

- Israeli managers place greater importance on expressive work aspects, such as interesting
  work and autonomy, in contrast to either extrinsic work aspects or comfort aspects.

- Although managers of either sex equally find interesting work and interpersonal relations
  to be of importance, there were some distinctions between them. Men ascribe significantly more importance to autonomy and job security, whereas women focus on convenient work hours and opportunity for upgrading or promotion. Women's focus on
  promotion may reflect the recent influx of young women into lower level managerial
  positions; they aspire to more senior, male-dominated offices.

- Most Israeli managers (95.5 percent) would choose to continue working even if there
  were no longer any financial reason to do so; of the total Israeli labor force, 88 percent
  expressed such a desire. This also attests to the high centrality of work for Israeli
  managers.

In conclusion, the profile of the Israeli manager that emerged from the study
is that of a person highly committed to the job whose work is second only to
the family unit. The Israeli manager has a strong intrinsic work-values orientation. Money seems of less concern as a valued work outcome, probably because
Israeli managers are relatively well paid in relation to the average prevailing
income in the market. Finally, Israeli managers identify with their employing
organizations significantly more than with their profession. These empirical findings revealed through the Meaning of Work Project agree with the commonly
expressed belief of these traits.

Table 10.5
Distribution of Management by Sex, 1955–88

Population	Year				
	1955	1960	1970	1980	1988
All Managers (thousands)	92.1*	98.1*	165.8*	47.7	89.6
Men (percent)	78.2	73.2	62.5	92.5	85.3
Women (percent)	21.8	26.8	37.5	7.5	14.7

* These figures include clerical workers.
Source: Statistical Abstracts of Israel, 1961, 1971, 1981, 1989.

HUMAN RESOURCE MANAGEMENT AND MANAGERS

Managerial Staffing and Development

No objective, reliable data are available on all the demographic characteristics of Israeli managers. According to Bar-Yoseph (1960), when the country was in its early developmental stages, its managers were young—in their late thirties and early forties. In the 1960s, a study portrayed managers in the following age distribution: 45 percent were fifty years and over; 37 percent, forty to forty-nine years old; and 18 percent, thirty to thirty-nine years old (Peled, 1964). In the 1970s, Israeli CEOs were found to be relatively young—an average age of fifty-one years (Margalit and Weinshall, 1972). In the 1980s, it was reported that the average age of managers was 47.7 years (Caspi, 1987). Hence, the Israeli manager may be said to be relatively young. Although women's role in the labor force is increasing significantly (the proportion of women having almost doubled in the last forty years), this has had very little impact on the proportion of women in management, where the percentage of women has been on the decline in recent years as may be observed in Table 10.5.

Only in the past decade have women begun to enter the managerial ranks substantially. Izraeli (1988) attributed this development to the structural and economic changes the country underwent, affording new opportunities and therefore provoking less contention among men for managerial positions. The macro-level changes in market conditions, though affecting the absolute numbers of women managers, have been inadequate to surmount the obstacles to a woman's progression into management. Therefore, no meaningful changes have taken place in the status of women's managerial roles in Israel. Most of their gains have occurred in economic branches in which they are in any case concentrated or in which a relatively higher proportion of male managers already exists (Izraeli,

1988), such as lower level, or to a lesser extent middle-level, positions in the public and educational services.

In addition to the usual factors that hinder women's opportunities to attain important managerial positions, certain constraints can be attributed specifically to Israel. The role of the military in producing a management stratum is an Israeli idiosyncrasy (Izraeli, 1988). Although military service for women is compulsory, the tasks they perform in the military are usually secondary. As a result, women are not exposed to the intensive training and experience that men receive in the military service (Izraeli, 1988). Thus, after retirement from military service, women meet with fewer and less favorable opportunities for managerial jobs in the labor market than do men.

Additional differences between the sexes exist in relation to the meaning of work for them. For instance, work was consistently observed to be more important to men than to women. If the time devoted to work may be taken as an indicator of work involvement/centrality, men worked 48.02 hours per week, while women worked 34.10 hours. In the rankings of work goals, by a sample representing the labor force, differing emphasis was given to various aspects. Thus, such work goals as "pay," "opportunity for upgrading and promotion," and "job security" are ranked noticeably more important by men than by women. Women opted for items like "convenient work hours" and "opportunity to learn." The issue of convenient work hours represents the traditional role conflict between the time women have to allocate for work and their family responsibilities. On the other hand, the opportunity to learn may reflect the rise in the number of women in the labor force and their desire for development in order to achieve parity with men (Harpaz, 1990).

With regard to work, women in Israel possess different attitudes and expectations from men because of the "social direction" they receive through sex-role socialization from childhood to adulthood. These social influences affect the expectations of women in work development and achievement. Alternatively, these influences are expressed in the family domain and in social interaction. As a result, Israeli women gravitate toward jobs offering fewer opportunities for power, advancement, and influence. Managerial positions do not offer the flexibility that may allow women to perform dual key functions in the family and at work.

Table 10.6 presents the distribution of Israeli managers by their country of origin. As the table shows, the number of managers of Asian and African origin is small compared to those of Israeli and European-American backgrounds. There is a trend in the growth and decline in managerial birthplaces: the percentage of Israeli-born is steadily increasing in the population, while that of European-American background is decreasing.

It is interesting to compare these figures with those obtained from three earlier studies. In the 1960s, managers tended to be mostly of European origin (83 percent); 11 percent were Israeli-born and 3 percent were of Middle Eastern (Asian and African) origin (Peled, 1964). In the 1970s, the distribution was as

Table 10.6
Distribution of Managers by Country of Origin, 1970–88 (percentage)

		Year	
Birth Place	1970	1980	1988
Israeli-Born	31.9	41.3	49
Born in Asia-Africa	20.2	16.2	21
Born in Europe-America	47.9	42.5	30

Source: Statistical Abstracts of Israel, 1971, 1981, 1989.

follows: 78 percent European or American, 20 percent Israeli-born, and only 2 percent Asian or African (Margalit and Weinshall, 1972). In 1985, 58 percent of the managers were Israeli-born, 37 percent of European and American origin, and 5 percent of Asian and African descent (Caspi, 1987).

The typical Israeli manager, then, has a Western-oriented background and is from Israel, Europe, or the United States. This demographic characteristic accords with the positions which the Israeli-born or Israelis of European or U.S. background hold in the country's economy and in its society.

Table 10.7 shows trends in managers' years of schooling. The number of years a manager spends in school has increased steadily. A very small percentage of managers can obtain such a position with only eight years of schooling or less. On the other hand, academic education gained extreme importance in the 1980s, so that by 1988 more than 51 percent of all managers possessed at least thirteen years of schooling. This trend indicates the professionalization of the management field that has developed over the years.

With regard to the mobility of managers, Margalit's (1981) study of top management found that 8.1 percent never changed their organization, 17 percent experienced one change, 28.5 percent went through two changes, and 46.4 percent had worked in four or more companies. Study of a representative sample of the labor force, including 179 managers, revealed that tenure in present job averaged twelve years (Harpaz, 1990).

Recruitment Sources

During the 1950s, the average Israeli manager, generally male, did not usually start in a managerial position in his particular organization. It is difficult to argue that Israeli managers came from a specific educational or technological elite. In spite of the differences among the various types of managers, they all shared some common characteristics (Bar-Yoseph, 1960).

Most of them either arrived in Israel as pioneers or were born in the state: they were leaders of youth movements, volunteer organizations, and the under-

Table 10.7
Distribution of Managers by Years of Schooling, 1970–88 (percentage)

Years of Schooling	1970	1980	1988
1-8	15	8.7	5.5
9-12	64.7	53.1	43.3
13+	20.3	4 .5	51.2

Source: Statistical Abstracts of Israel, 1971, 1981, 1989.

ground before the existence of the state. Thus, national values were of utmost importance and were highly regarded. Their activities emanated from a single organization but were rooted in national movements; thus, they saw their job not as limited to a single organization, but in a national capacity.

Most of the managers were Histadrut members (as individuals, not as a manager's union); thus, organizationally, but not ideologically, they were associated more closely with the worker than with the owner. They did not have the prototype of a traditional Israeli industrial manager to follow, and they were not considered a defined status group.

The foregoing picture is of Israeli management throughout the 1960s. The development of business schools or management departments helped to change this pattern. The foundation for training managers in Israel was laid by the Technion in Haifa and the Hebrew University in Jerusalem. The first impetus to change came in 1953 with the establishment of the Faculty of Industrial Engineering and Management at the Technion-Israel Institute of Technology. Its graduates have been trained mainly for staff positions in management: industrial engineering, operations research, cost accounting and budgetary control, industrial economics, industrial relations, and so on. Consequently, they mainly fulfill managerial positions that require diverse quantitative methods rather than areas such as marketing, finance, and human resource management. Degrees may be obtained at all academic levels.

The country's second business department was founded in 1957 at the Hebrew University within the Kaplan School of Economics and Social Sciences. During its early years, a relatively small number of graduates staffed industrial organizations. This presumably occurred because many of the students were government officials in midmanagement positions, and the program focused on economic studies (Weinshall, 1968). The business school began to flourish in the 1970s; it now offers degrees from the baccalaureate to the doctorate level.

Currently, it is one of the country's major schools for training students in all aspects of management and accounting.

A third major academic business center opened in 1966 at Tel-Aviv University—the Recanati Graduate School of Business Administration. Focusing primarily on graduate studies, it considers its main goal to be the training of managers for Israel's middle and higher organizational levels. The school imparts managerial skills (i.e., policy-making and its application) for all organizational and managerial functions. It also offers special programs for managers from industry and the military. The size of this school and its central location in the state have made it the most influential business school in Israel and a prominent source for recruiting managers.

All the other Israeli universities—Bar-Ilan University near Tel-Aviv, the University of Haifa in the north, and Ben-Gurion University of the Negev in the south—opened departments in the 1970s that teach management or business classes. These courses are offered mainly through economic departments or faculties of social sciences.

An important major source of recruitment to managerial jobs is the military—specifically, retired senior military officers. The relative average age of officers in the Israeli military is low. So when they retire from military service they are still relatively young but have accumulated a vast amount of managerial skills and know-how through managing large-scale forces, controlling sizable budgets, and operating state-of-the art technological hardware. Moreover, they bring with them two very important assets acquired through years of service: ingenuity and improvisation (Peri, 1973).

Dominant Selection Techniques

The Israelis use various selection techniques for managerial jobs.

Interview. The interview has long been the most widely used means of selection; it is conducted at all organizational levels by the prospective employing superior, not by professional interviewers. Most of interviewers have not received specific training in the basic elements of interviewing.

Application forms. Application forms gather information that organizations find useful. Unlike the United States, Israel has no specific laws or regulations restricting the kinds of information that can be requested. Thus, questions relating to age, religion, national origin, marital status, sex, number of children, or even applicant's father's name are common elements on an application form.

Tests. Privately owned organizations specializing in recruitment and testing use a wide variety of tests, including general aptitude and skills tests, a variety of psychological tests, and personality tests. Applicants are usually sent to these privately owned consulting firms by the prospective employing organizations. No figures are available, however, regarding the proportion of organizations that use this selection method in contrast to organizations that use their own tailor-made tests. Nor are much data available on the validity and reliability of these tests.

Graphology. Handwriting analysis is a prevalent selection device. Three graphological associations, with a combined membership of up to 150 individuals, make their liv-

elihood from graphology. In addition, a few hundred "amateur graphologists" also
analyze handwriting for selection purposes (Nevo, 1986). The popularity of graphology
is evident in the number of newspaper recruitment advertisements that ask applicants
to respond in their own handwriting. Nevo (1986) also evaluated the effectiveness of
graphology as a selection tool and found it to be very poor. In spite of the criticism
of this practice, this selection device still has a strong following.

Head-hunters. In the last decade the use of head-hunters for management selection has
become popular. Larger organizations established selection methods to help organizations choose their middle- and top-level managers.

Assessment center. A relatively new method used by a limited number of large organizations is the assessment center, which is most commonly run by a specialized outside
agency and is designed mostly for selection consideration.

Except for graphology, none of these selection techniques has been subjected
to empirical research to determine their validity and reliability. In most cases,
organizations take for granted the methods they employ or those used by outside
agencies. A major reason for this lack of verification may be the lack of any
legal constraints on organizational selection practices.

On the basis of a survey of prevailing selection practices in Israel, Nevo and
Rafaeli (1987) presented the following estimate of their use:

Selection Procedure	Frequency of Use (%)
Personal interview	84
Background data	72
Previous experience	40
Knowledge (skills) test	32
Probationary period	40
Certificates/diplomas	44
Psychological testing	30
Reference letters	30
Graphology	16

Personal interview and background data seem to be the most frequently used
selection methods in the Israeli market.

Management Training and Development

With the growth and maturity of Israeli organizations, we are witnessing
increasing attention to management training and development. Large organizations are investing in "tailor-made" programs that use internal and external
resources. Smaller organizations are relying mainly on external consultants and
on training and development centers.

Various centers are available for the ongoing and advanced training and practicing managers. The most prominent centers are:

The Israeli Management Center (MIL)—jointly created in 1959 and supported by the Ministry of Commerce and Industry, Manufacturers Association, and the Histadrut. As a professional association of managers, MIL is open to middle- and high-level managers. The center operates a special women's forum to promote the advancement of women in management.

Israeli Institute of Productivity—a public institute operated by the Ministry of Labor and Welfare in cooperation with the Histadrut and the Manufacturers Association. Its activities, covering all aspects of management, are directed at all levels, from first-line to the highest ranking managers.

The Central School of Administration—operated through the general civil service office and aimed at developing and training managers in the civil service branches. The school offers courses aimed at all managerial levels within organizations.

Midreshet Rupin–Department of Training Kibbutz Managers—run by the kibbutz movement and operated under the authority of the Training Services Department of the Ministry of Agriculture and the Farmer's Association.

Universities Extension Programs—aimed at managerial training and development. Six of Israel's seven major universities offer extension programs ranging from single, one- or two-day enrichment seminars on a special theme to a full program requiring 800 hours of study spread out over three years.

The Management College—offers two types of programs. The first provides various programs aimed at practicing managers that lead to a diploma or a certificate. In 1988 the college began a second track, awarding bachelor's degrees in the fields of marketing and accounting.

In addition to the external training centers, most large organizations (500 employees or more) invest in a dedicated resource to support its management and development activities. Those activities consist of a mixture of conventional management training, organization development, and individual development programs such as rotation, individual learning, special coaching, and more. Most organizations are assisted by external consultants to carry out the work. Few consulting firms specialize in in-house training programs. In larger organizations (above 1,000 employees), it is not unusual to find internal consultants, especially in the area of organization development, who are taking an active part in management development.

Management Compensation

Various factors have made the Israeli compensation method extremely complex. First, extremely high inflation, especially in the late 1970s to the mid–1980s, forced the development of means to protect income. Second, the high level of tax on a relatively small income enticed organizations to find ways to compensate its management through avoiding taxable income. Payments in kind became a very popular method of compensation. Third is the segmentation of the Israeli economy into three distinct sectors. Each of these sectors uses different compensation methods that have mutual influence but are not equally free in their competition with one another. This situation causes both the public and the

Table 10.8
Average Monthly Salary by Management Level, March 1989

Level	Salary (NIS)
Level 1+ = V.P. or equivalent	10,574
Level 1 = Division/Functional Manager	8,024
Level 2 = Department Manager	6,030
Level 3 = Ass. Department Manager	5,001

Note: US$1 = About 2 NIS (New Israeli Shekels)
Source: Management Survey Report, May 1989.

Hevrat Haovdim sector (the economic branch of the Histadrut) to find "innovative" ways to compensate management, in order both to attract good personnel and to compete with the private sector.

Compensation Structure

Base Salary. Base salary varies from sector to sector. The private sector pays the highest, followed by the Histadrut-owned organizations, and, lastly, the government organizations. Of course, some differences exist between the various industries in a sector. In the 1970s, the banks were the highest paying organizations; later, high-technology industries paid the top salaries. Table 10.8 presents average management base salaries for 1989 according to management level based on a survey of 72 companies.

Table 10.9 presents the distribution of salaries among the various professions. At the top are research and development professionals, followed by those in the financial world. At the bottom of the list are human resource professionals at all management levels; this indicates the status of that function. The differences between professions are not great (approximately 10 percent from the top to the bottom), yet differences between organizations can be substantial. In the extreme case of human resource professionals, it is almost a ratio of 3 to 1.

The difference in gross salary between the private corporation and the Histadrut and public sectors is enormous. Histadrut management salaries are correlated with those of the public sector, which are regulated. The highest governmental professional is the ministry director-general, whose salary is equivalent to that of a member of the Knesset (or between levels 2 and 3; see Table 10.9). A newly proposed scale, recommended by a committee appointed by the government to evaluate the compensation structure in the civil service, calls for a monthly salary (at the highest grade level with the highest possible seniority) of

Table 10.9
Average Monthly Gross Salary of Managers (in NIS) by Profession (in large organizations only)

Profession	Managerial Level			
	1+	1	2	3
Finance	10848	7854	5929	4381
Marketing/Sales	10633	8441	6833	5634
Manufacturing	9996	8097	6719	4705
Human Resources	9540	7295	4910	3976
Research and Development	11239	8180	6280	5702
Engineering	10355	8822	5949	5091

Note: Data represents those firms having over 30 million in new Israeli currency in annual revenue and/or 600 employees.

Source: *Management Survey Report*, May 1989.

NIS 6,016 (approximately $3,000) a month (Recommendations of the Committee for Evaluating the Salary System in the Civil Service, 1989).

Fringe Benefits. Israel carries a high level of benefit costs. The most popular fringe benefits presented in Table 10.10, can amount to almost 55 percent of the base salary. Other similar payments, especially for the managerial workforce, can easily bring this price tag to 60 to 70 percent. Some of the more common fringes given to management include company cars, management insurance, stock options, and overtime.

The management Salary Survey (1989) points out that 100 percent of managers at levels 0 and 1+ receive a company car (fully paid for and minted by the organization); 93 percent of level 1 managers, 92 percent of level 2 managers, and 90 percent of level 3 receive a car. Israeli law demands that, when terminating an employee's service, the employer provide severance pay not less than the last base salary multiplied by the number of years of service. This policy provides the manager with both life insurance and a pension. It protects the employee's family not only in case of death or retirement, but also in case of disability. Almost all managers in the private sector enjoy this benefit. Israeli law does not distinguish between exempt and nonexempt employees. Management, therefore, is entitled to overtime payment.

Table 10.10
Fringe Benefits in Israel, 1990 (percentage)

Benefit	Tax Exempt	Non-exempt	Hourly
National Insurance*	10.5	10.5	10.5
Saving Insurance*	5	5	5
Severance Pay*	8.3	8.3	8.3
Disability Insurance**	2.7	-	-
Educational Fund*	7.5	2.0	-
Vacation*	3	3	3
Salary 13*** †	8.3	8.3	8.3
Transportation***	3.5	3.5	3.5
Subsidized Meals***	3.2	6.3	9.8
Meals Gross ups*	1.1	2.3	3.5
Miscellaneous	.9	1	2.7
Total	54.0	50.2	54.6

Notes: * regulated ** management only *** customary ∂ One additional monthly salary, making it the "thirteenth month" of pay annually.

Source: Based on applicable regulations and a sample of fifteen organizations.

Private industry customarily grants bonuses to management, especially to those at the two highest levels. Bonuses are based largely on a combination of the organization's profitability and the manager's performance. In public organizations, they are not as common except for the top level of the organization.

The use of stock options as a bonus is relatively new in Israel. Historically, only a few companies, especially in the high-tech fields, have had schemes for the allocation of an option for shares at a reduced price. In some unique cases, top management received shares as part of their income. According to the Management Salary Guide (1989), only 5 percent of management level 1 + in industry received shares, while 20 percent received options at favorable prices; 15 percent

Table 10.11
Consumer Price Index Change, 1970–88 (percentage)

Year	Percentage
1970	10.1
1971	13.4
1972	12.4
1973	26.4
1974	56.2
1975	23.5
1976	38.0
1977	42.5
1978	48.1
1979	111.4
1980	132.9
1981	101.5
1982	131.5
1983	190.7
1984	444.9
1985	185.2
1986	19.7
1987	16.1
1988	16.4

Source: Statistical Abstracts of Israel, 1989.

of those at levels 1 and 2 and none at level 3 received options. In commerce and services, none of the managers surveyed received either form of this benefit. In 1989, the managers surveyed received either form of this benefit. Also in 1989, the Knesset approved a new income tax code to encourage organizations to issue shares to their employees and enjoy a tax break (Income Tax Regulations, 1989).

Payments in Kind. Mainly because of Israel's historically high income tax rates, which reached 87.2 percent in 1975 and which currently (1991) demand a maximum marginal rate of 51 percent, a tradition developed of payments in kind. Although many of these payments are taxable, they are still offered, especially to management. These items range from home telephone perks and luxury cars to open expense accounts and international travel.

Indexation. Inflation plays a major part in Israel's compensation scheme. Table 11.11 presents the Consumer Price Index, reflecting inflation levels in the past two decades. Employees are protected against inflation through the use of an advanced indexation system. An official cost-of-living index is published monthly by the government's Central Bureau of Statistics, based on an agreed statistical "Expense Basket." This official cost of living index provides the basis for the indexation mechanism. Every time the accumulated index reaches 7 percent, a percentage of this figure (currently 70 percent) is paid to all salaried employees. However, problems for the management attach to this practice. First, the ceiling imposed on the cost of living has the effect of reducing management's compensation relative to lower income groups and closing the gap between levels. Second, the high tax brackets of most managers reduce the indexation net and quickly push managers to the highest income tax bracket. Third, the management role becomes tenuous as a major managerial tool is lost—meritocracy.

Managerial Performance Appraisal

Use of performance appraisal systems is a common practice in most Israeli organizations that exceed 100 employees. The only limited survey conducted on the subject showed that of thirty-one organizations surveyed (over 70 percent of them with a population of at least 700 employees), 80 percent claimed to have implemented a formalized system (Krausz, 1989).

The level and purpose of the application vary greatly. Many organizations use the appraisal method as a vehicle for making decisions on whether to grant tenure to new employees or to lay employees off. Krausz (1989) found that 70 percent of the organizations in the sample used performance appraisal for those purposes and 30 percent for promotion decisions. In recent years, there has been a growing trend to use performance appraisal systems for management and employee development purposes. In the mid–1980s, for example, both the Israel Defense Forces and the police force have insisted that the appraisal be discussed with the person appraised and a development program drawn. Krausz's survey also found that the system is usually developed by the personnel department (in over 80 percent of the organizations studied). However, some consultant-developed systems are still used.

Zevolun (1989) divided Israel's appraisal market into two segments. The old type of system is based mainly on the boss filling out appraisal forms, which are later filed in the employee's file. These appraisals are used only for promotion, demotion, or termination. The new type consists of systems used in a broad spectrum of usages emphasizing the betterment of the system itself: input to the training system, feedback to management on its proficiency as appraisers, and so on. According to Rogovsky (1989), three different systems are in use in Israel. First is the employee-traits approach, which focuses on appraising an employee's relevant attributes (punctuality, determination, teamwork, etc.). This methodology is widely employed and provides a common questionnaire that facilitates comparisons among employees. However, it focuses on the employee's "evaluated" personality, not on the performance.

The second system uses the behavioral approach, emphasizing performance through a list of typical job-related behavioral characteristics or cases. This method focuses on performance rather than personality, but it cannot easily create a representative list of a broad range of employees' behavioral characteristics.

Many of the newly developed appraisal systems in Israel, however, are leaning in this direction.

The third, a goal-accomplished system, focuses on the employee's achievement of a set of goals. Its advantage is that it is able to focus on relevant outputs; its disadvantage is that the format does not permit valid comparison among employees. Although this methodology is of little use in traditional industries, it is widely used in the high-technology and multinational organizations represented in Israel.

Although some Israeli organizations, especially in the high-tech industry, have been using the appraisal methodology mainly for developmental purposes, most organizations in Israel view performance appraisal as an administrative tool rather than an aid in the development and growth of their employees or managers (Krausz, 1989).

Labor Relations

Israel's industrial relations system is tripartite, consisting of workers and their unions, employers and their association, and the government.

The Histadrut   The Histadrut (General Federation of Labor) represents more than 80 percent of all salaried workers in Israel (Rosenstein, 1984). This federation has a wide organizational basis, since workers without any professional or sectoral common denominator may be included under its umbrella. The Trade Union Department of the Histadrut, consisting of approximately forty national unions, both blue- and white-collar workers (Bartal, 1978), is the organizational arm of the labor federation.

Apart from being a labor federation, the Histadrut undertakes various national tasks, such as settlement, housing, education, and productivity. In addition, membership in the Histadrut provides the worker with comprehensive health insurance through its health fund, which is the largest in the country.

The Employers   Three major sectors of employers exist in the Israeli economy: private, public, and labor (Histadrut). The private sector encompasses about 80 percent of Israel's industry and about 70 percent of all factory workers. The public sector employs about 32 percent of the labor force—a relatively high rate (Shirom, 1983)—and is the single largest employer in the state. The third employer is the Histadrut itself, which works through Hevrat Ha-Ovdim, the central holding company for all economic enterprises owned by or affiliated with the Histadrut. Histadrut firms employ about 18 percent of the Israeli labor force.

The Government   The government's participation and influence in Israeli labor relations are intensive and pervasive. Sixty percent of the capital in the Israeli economy comes from the government and is directed through its budget. As an employer, the government negotiates with representatives of the public sector. Government also exerts influence through extensive labor legislation as well as the use of arbitration and mediation procedures and labor courts for settling labor disputes. Managers who form the three sectors have to take into consideration various state and labor laws and other norms and practices, although such regulations do not affect managers as individuals or as a group. Perhaps the most important way the government makes its influence felt is through its economic policy and the economic actions it takes. The need for capital, the perennial deficit in the country's balance of payments, and continuous high inflation have required the government to try to prevent wages from rising, on the one hand, and to increase taxation, on the other. This situation naturally creates unrest in industrial relations, on the part of both employees and employers (Galin and Harel, 1978). Thus, the government's prominent role in the industrial relations system directly affects the two other sectors.

Managerial Unionization No manager's union or association exists in Israel. Managers can join the Histadrut on an individual basis, regardless of their occupation or hierarchical position. As a result, managers have no direct influence on their employees' decision to join labor unions. A very small segment of Israeli industry, mainly the high-technology sector, does have a policy to avoid unionization. However, this does not represent individual managerial attitudes in opposition to unions, as might be the situation in other countries.

For several reasons, managerial associations did not evolve in Israel. According to Shirom (1983), before the establishment of the state, neither family ties nor political relations provided the focus of support for managers. With the rise of the class of professional managers, more favorable conditions began to develop for a common managerial forum. Nevertheless, various institutional factors served to block this tendency: (1) the existence of three sectors in the Israeli economy, making it difficult to correlate managerial employment conditions or pay; (2) the Histadrut's opposition to establishing a managerial organization that would take an active role in the industrial relations system; (3) the relatively small number of managers in the labor market, which has created competition among employers as well as among the managers themselves; and (4) scanty research regarding managers in Israel, who are the least researched participants in the Israeli industrial relations system (Shirom, 1983).

CONCLUSIONS

Status of Managers

Although it is difficult to define managers as a status group, they do enjoy a relatively high status in Israel. The sources of this status vary and have changed over time. What different aspects contributed positively to the status of managers in the first two decades of the state of Israel (1950s and 1960s)?

Because Jews of European background traditionally gave respect to authority figures and power, managers are viewed favorably by the public by virtue of position. This was especially valid during the first two decades of the new state, when most of the population consisted mainly of individuals of European descent.

Another important factor contributing to the status of managers in those early years was their homogeneous demographic background. The majority were either Israeli or European-born (but long-term residents of the state), spoke fluent Hebrew, and were well established in the state. Therefore, this relatively small number was singled out as a special elite group, relatively powerful and influential. Being a manager, whether in the public or the private sector, was considered a service to society and therefore demanded respect.

Most of these factors became less important in the 1970s and 1980s, for the following reasons:

- Changes in the values of the society as a whole shifted, so that instead of being obliged to society the feeling became that one was entitled to certain benefits. Therefore, contribution to society lost some of its status-bestowing power.
- Remuneration became more pronounced as managers began to receive higher compensation; today they are among the highest paid group in the labor market. As Israeli society becomes more materialistic, people with high earnings are generally considered more successful and powerful.
- The field has became increasingly professionalized since the 1970s. With the development of business schools and management departments in universities and other management development centers, management has become a profession. Degrees, diplomas, or certificates are now required for access to managerial positions.

Professionalism of Managers

In the 1950s and 1960s, the scale of Israel's economy, labor market, and industry was relatively small. The number of managers required, as well as their skill level, was not high. The needs of industry were limited because of the nature of its restricted, unsophisticated operations, and throughout this period, managers received hardly any formal training.

As the economy developed, diversified, and became more complex, the need for professional managers grew. The specialized management training schools and institutes that emerged did more than supply the new and increasing demand for professional managers. They helped make organizations aware that professionalism may come about through systematic, formal learning.

At the beginning of the 1990s, a new breed of Israeli managers is being created. Those holding general managerial positions are most likely university graduates who studied finance. Industrial managers are generally graduates of programs (mainly academic) that concentrate on skills needed for performance in that field. Managers in the public sector receive training in public administration through political science departments at the universities. Some managers also undergo periodic development through the Central School of Administration for the public sector.

Although, generally, the professionalism of management is the growing trend, managers from the older generation may still be found in all economic sectors. Especially problematic is the situation in the public sector, in which performance criteria are very difficult to measure. Unlike the situation in the private sector or in industry, profitability is not a top priority. Compensation in public services, even for managers, is relatively low. The value of service to society, which used to be cherished in the early years of the new state, is diminishing. As a result, the highly motivated, more competent managers are not attracted to this sector. Hence, the quality and professionalism of managers in the public sector are substantially lower than those of their counterparts in other branches of the economy.

Further discouraging the entrance of skilled managers into the public services is the fact that the ''right contact'' rather than excellent performance is often needed to secure a job in this sector (Lorch, 1987).

Emerging Trends

The changes that affect the Western business world also influence Israel's managerial structure. In the past decade in particular, six main areas have been affected, and probably will continue to influence the management field: globalization, recession, women in management, job security, technology, and social standing.

Globalization As a relatively small, isolated country, Israel is dependent on international markets for many of its needs. This situation forces the country to treat globalization as a ''survival objective.'' Its dependency on the United States, its close relations with some East European countries, and its striving to become an integral part of Europe 1992—these are just a few of the reasons why management in Israel will clearly have to orient itself more globally.

Although some changes have occurred in recent years, it will take some time for the country's management to shift its attitude to create an international mindset. Among other things, the government will be required to review most of Israel's laws that are related to, or have a bearing on, international economic affairs—for example, laws of free capital (in and out of the country), investment, and working permits—and adjust them accordingly. Some trends in that direction can already be observed, such as the extension in the liberalization of currency control.

Recession In the late 1980s and into the early 1990s, Israel encountered a very difficult economic situation, with clear signs that the country was in a recession. Unemployment reached a level of 10 percent (in some areas of the country ranging as high as 14 percent). Many corporations lost money; some were on the verge of bankruptcy. Although all the predictions indicated that the economy was headed in a healthier direction, management was put on the line. In fact, the situation highlighted the weakness of Israeli management and created concern about its education, selection, and responsibility. This trend will likely continue. It will force organizations to pay more attention to management development and selection. The demand for trained managers will increase, especially those with international experience.

Women in Management The role of women in management is slowly growing, and women's recognition of discrimination is rising. The number of awareness courses and seminars on this subject is increasing. This trend will also undoubtedly continue, and Israel will have more and more women in management and in higher positions. There is a growing voice to change some legal limitations in Israeli society, in order to advance this trend.

Job Security A large proportion of Israel's economy is composed of the public and semipublic sectors, which are very protective of their workforces.

Many Israeli companies offer job security to their employees, including managers. With the relative growth of individual contracts, however, there is a trend toward meritocracy in compensation and reward for contribution rather than position or length of service. In other words, the trend is toward higher compensation and lower job protection.

Technology   The growing role of high-tech organizations in Israel has brought new understanding to the expectations of the managerial role. There is an increased realization that a different management style is required, one that is more strategy-oriented in business outlooks and more guidance-oriented in its approach to workers. The old "Boss" type does not fit the changing needs of the new environment or the values of the young generation. The management role is increasingly becoming that of bridging the organization's changing needs and the individual's changing expectations of the workplace. The rapid changes in technology and the success of some of the high-tech companies in the country are proof that managing can be done differently. To many organizations, the high-tech companies serve as a positive role model for a different breed of management.

Social Standing   As in many Western countries, managers in Israel are in the top income level. This phenomenon is relatively new, and it is not clear how it will influence Israeli society at large. We believe that Israel will follow the United States: managers will increasingly find themselves occupying a leading position in the country. To date, very few Israeli managers have taken a more public role and either joined the political system or accepted a governmental position, whether at local or national levels. Status in society and the huge difference in earnings still make such a move prohibitive. With the growing standing of management in Israeli society, more managers will probably associate themselves with the public sector, and this will benefit it greatly.

Questions for the Future

Many questions still remain unanswered. No real, extensive research has been conducted on the Israeli manager. Empirically, it is not even known whether such a term as "an Israeli manager" exists and what his or her values would be. What is the influence of the universities on the Israeli manager? What is the influence of service in the armed forces on the Israeli managerial style and values? Only further systematic studies will provide answers to these and other questions.

The Israeli environment is dynamic. For years, Israel has struggled for survival, not only in the battlefield, but also in the economic sphere. The years of stress and the need for quick reactions and improvisations still influence the Israeli manager. Should management imitate the American way or the European? Or should it create a distinct fashion? What does it mean, to create one's own style? How will this influence existing operations? How will managerial style affect individuals in the Israeli system and their environment? Another area of questions involves the Israeli educational system, at both the high school and university level. Are managers trained in the right way, and are desired outcomes obtained? In fact, are the desired outcomes known? Does Israel encourage the most competent individuals to go into managerial positions?

Since the establishment of Israel in 1948, the government's involvement in business has been extensive. As a result, politics is a major ingredient in the country's business life. Managers have been appointed, promoted, and fired on the basis of political affiliation. What will it take to change this system, and can it be changed without the need to alter, first, the whole political system of the country? Once the political system is changed—and today there are genuine attempts to do so—how would this affect management? Can management go through the transformation, and at what cost and within what time frame?

REFERENCES

Aharoni, Y. 1985 (December). "Is There an Israeli Management Style?" *Hamifal* (The Factory), 31: 6–8. (Hebrew)

Bartal, G. 1978. *Histadrut-Structure and Activities*. Tel Aviv: Histadrut-General Federation of Labor. (Hebrew)

Bar-Yoseph, R. 1960. "Contradictions in the Role of the Israeli Manager." *Administration and Management* 6. (3): 2–8. (Hebrew)

Caspi, A. 1987 (December). "Profile of the Israeli Senior Manager." *Nihul* (Management): 7–12. (Hebrew)

Comparative Data on the Israeli Economy 1960–1977. 1979. Jerusalem: Ministry of Industry and Commerce. (Hebrew)

Expansion Order Regarding Indexation. 1989 (July 2). Yalkut Hapirsumim 3675. Government of Israel. (Hebrew)

Frounman, D. 1989. "U.S. Versus Israel Working Values." Unpublished paper. Jerusalem: Intel Co.

Galin, A., and Harel, A. 1978. *Developments and Trends in Israeli Industrial and Labor Relations System*. Tel Aviv: Massada. (Hebrew)

Harpaz, I. 1990. *The Meaning of Work in Israel: Its Nature and Consequences*. New York: Praeger.

ILO-International Labor Organization. 1983. *Yearbook of Labour Statistics*. Geneva.

Income Tax Regulations. 1989 (September 9) KT5221, Paragraph 102. Jerusalem. (Hebrew)

Israeli Forum on Strategic Thinking on Israeli Economic Industrial Infrastructure Future. 1989 (July-August). Unpublished summary of discussions. (Hebrew)

Israel's Economy. 1972. Jerusalem: Ministry of Finance. (Hebrew)

Izraeli, D. N., 1988. "Women's Movement into Management in Israel." In N. J. Adler and D. N. Izraeli, eds., *Women in Management Worldwide*. Armonk, N.Y.: Sharpe.

Krausz, M. 1989 (September). "Performance Appraisal Practices in a Highly Unionized Country." *Human Resource Management*.

Lorch, N. 1987 (June). "Appointments by Contacts." *Nihul* (Management): 10–12. (Hebrew)

Management Salary Guide Co. 1989 (May). *Management Salary Guide*. (Hebrew)

Margalit, Y. 1981. "The Israeli Presidents." MBA Thesis, School of Business, Tel Aviv University. (Hebrew)

————, and Weinshall, T. 1972. *Administration and Management* 18 (6): 16–35. (Hebrew)

MOW—International Research Team. 1987. *The Meaning of Working*. London: Academic Press.

Nevo, B. 1986 (October). The Validity of Graphology in Israel.'' *Nihul* (Management), No. 52: 7–9. (Hebrew)

————, and Rafaeli, A. 1987 (August). "Selection of Workers in Israel: A Survey.'' *Nihul* (Management): 7–12. (Hebrew)

Peled, U. 1964. *Managerial Climate in Israel*. Israel Management Center and the Israel Institute of Applied Research. (Hebrew)

Peri, Y. 1973. "The First and Second Careers of Israeli Army Officers.'' *Public Administration in Israel and Abroad* 14: 106–122.

Recommendations of the Committee of Evaluation of Compensation System in the Public Sector (The Zussman's Committee). 1989 (February). Jerusalem. (Hebrew)

Rogovsky, I. 1989. Multigrade Integrated Performance Appraisal. Unpublished paper, G. R. Institute. (Hebrew)

Rosenstein, E. 1984. "The Structure and Function of the Israeli Industrial Relations System.'' *Economics Quarterly* 121: 205–208. (Hebrew)

Shirom, A. 1983. *Introduction to Labor Relations in Israel*. Tel Aviv: Am-Oved. (Hebrew)

Weinshall, T.D. 1968. "Higher Education in Business Administration in Israel.'' *Administration and Management* 14 (3): 24–31. (Hebrew)

————. 1976. "The Industrialization of a Rapidly Developing Country—Israel.'' In R. Dubin, ed., *Handbook of Work, Organization and Society*. Chicago: Rand McNally.

Work Productivity and Production in Israel from an International Perspective. 1989. Tel Aviv: Israeli Institute of Productivity. (Hebrew)

Zevolun, E. 1989 (June). On Performance Management and Appraisal—How to Operate Appraisal Systems?'' *Human Resources* (Mashaby Enosh). (Hebrew)

11

SAUDI ARABIA

Robert W. Moore

> The things that go with luxury and a life of ease break the vigor of group feeling, which alone produces superiority. When group feeling is destroyed, the tribe is no longer able to defend or protect itself, let alone press its claims. It will be swallowed up by other nations.
>
> —From the ancient *Mugaddima* by Ibn Khaldun
> cited by Balfour-Paul, 1986.

To understand managerial behavior in modern Saudi Arabia, it is important to appreciate Arab values and customs and recognize the all-encompassing influence of Islam. Because management in the Peninsula differs by industry and nation and offers so few parallels with countries outside the Gulf region, no unitary definition of Saudi or Gulf management is entirely appropriate, even though management practices in the region mirror those of the Arab world at large.

In this chapter, we will first recount the traditional forces that are present in contemporary Saudi Arabia and that guide so much of its culture and conduct. Then we will explore the emergence of a managerial class that has adapted to modern technology and speculate on what this portends for specific organizational practices.

The Arabian bedouin has long been romanticized. References to "Arab in the desert" and "Arabian in the wilderness" can be found in the third book of Jeremiah and the thirteenth book of Isaiah which date from the eighth and ninth centuries B.C. Despite a long list of presumed characteristics attributed to modern Arabs such as fatalism, pride, cunning, and shyness (Hamady, 1960; Laffin, 1975; Patai, 1973), the Arab of today should only be characterized by one constant: the use of colloquial Arabic as a primary tongue (Patai, 1973). Still, inhabitants of the Arab world share a racial, religious, and linguistic heritage that fosters a consistent set of attitudes and beliefs that are more alike than different.

The Arabic language, which Muslims respect as the language of God, has had an enormous influence on Arab culture and character. The language spread in the wake of invasions to the North and East from the Arabian Peninsula soon after the prophet Muhammad's death in 632. Less than a century afterward, the Arab sector of the Dar al Islam (House of Islam) included all the semitic nations of the North Africa Sahara as well as the present Middle East to the north.

The Saudi state is traced directly to an alliance formed in 1744 by Muhammad ibn Saud, the leader of a small tribe from the barren center of the Peninsula, and Muhammad ibn Abd al-Wahhab, a religious scholar and descendant of a long line of *quadat* (judges and interpreters of the *shari'a* or Islamic temporal/ spiritual law—including but not limited to the Qur'an). Al-Wahhab preached the Muslim message of *tawhid*, the oneness of God, and he argued for a return to orthodox Sunni practices. In keeping with early Islamic revivals, it was furthered through a *jihad* or more exactly, a *Din Muhammad bi'l-sayf*, "the religion of Muhammad with the sword."

The state was also founded as an attempt to purify Islam by restoring and extending the *shari'a* to all aspects of Muslim existence and by proclaiming once more the unity of God. (Islam arose in reaction to the polytheistic practices of the age, including the Christian notion of the trinity.) That state also took the name of *al-Muwahhidun* or "unitarian."

The eighteenth-century Wahhabi movement in Arabia is notable for its reform of heretical religious practices such as veneration for Muhammad's tomb and the worship of relics. Because the vast interior of Arabia was essentially free of Ottoman rule at the time, Muhammad ibn Saud was able to extend the scope of his kingdom without interference from Constantinople, and, by the turn of the nineteenth century, he captured the holy cities of Mecca and Medina. The Al Saud family was driven back to its ancestral home a decade later by the superior and more disciplined forces of the Ottoman viceroy of Egypt. Late in the century, the Al Saud were forced to abandon their territory altogether and, at the turn of this century, took refuge in Kuwait. From this low point in family history, Abd al-Aziz ibn Abd al-Rahman ibn Saud forcibly resurrected the Saudi state and in 1902 took the present capital of Riyadh with only forty followers. Bolstered by its identity with Wahhabism, the house of Saud overthrew the foreign Hashimite rulers and enlarged the kingdom so that by 1926 it had expanded to its present borders and in 1932 took its present name.

The Arabian Peninsula itself is a vast, largely arid, desert the size of Western Europe. If it were superimposed on a map of the United States, it would overlay an area extending from the Atlantic Coast to the Mississippi River. Like much of the rest of the Arab world, the population growth of Saudi Arabia is rapidly increasing and is growing between 2½ to 3 percent per year which means a doubling of population every twelve years (Oppenheimer, 1988).

THE SAUDI KINGDOM AND ITS POLITY

In the Western world study of organizational behavior has been intellectually separated from the economy and the culture, but in the Arabian Peninsula managerial behavior is not so easily isolated from the larger context. This is because tribal societies are tied to their past. In the case of Saudi Arabia, the political and social system remains theological and monarchical. The royal family is linked with the '*ulama*' (religious leaders and theological scholars) and the armed forces. The '*ulama*' preach the divine necessity of obedience to royal rule through their interpretation of the *shari'a*, and, if theological interpretation fails to allay potential opposition, internal security is maintained by the timeless custom of subsidies, bribes, and violence (Tibi, 1985). The gradual transformation of the house of Saud from an extended family allied with a handful of other royal families to the present semblance of a modern bureaucracy has been justified and supported by their traditional privileges as defenders of the faith, pan-Arab influence in the region, and growing ties with the United States that began with the discovery of oil in 1933.

Because tribal rule operates through personal fealty, bureaucratic mechanisms have grown slowly, yet reluctantly and inexorably. Preference for the ancient practice of *majlis* (or the right of citizens to personally petition leaders including the ministers and the king for redress of grievances and assistance) persists as an idealized concept of justice and governance, but has diminished in practice. *Majlis* originated long ago in an era when tribal cohesiveness was energized by personal relationships. Today, the privilege has been transferred to organizations of all kinds and is considered an inherent and tacit employee and membership right.

The Saudi nation looms in power and size over the other Gulf sheikdoms, emirates, and sultanates that share the Peninsula. As one might expect, there has been a history of tribal contention between the Saudi bedouin and their more worldly Gulf neighbors who before the advent of oil survived as traders. Prior to World War II, Saudi Arabia competed with Iraq and Iran for hegemony over these smaller states. But the expansionist interests of all three states were checkmated, and the lesser Gulf states have since acquired a sense of sovereignty. After World War II, the Gulf states smoothed their frictions with Saudi Arabia by paying tribute. After oil revenue made them wealthy, stability was enhanced by deference to the kingdom's leadership of the Organization of Petroleum Exporting Countries (OPEC).

The very top of the Saudi oligarchy consists of an inner circle of some 100 members, of whom half are members of the Al Saud (which must number 7,000 today). The rest come from aristocratic families and a few unrelated but outstanding '*ulama*'. In recent decades, distinguished commoners have emerged to exert influence at the top levels of government and particularly business. Initiation to membership in the ruling elite is not a public matter, but it seems to be based on the virtues of seniority, prestige, merit, and leadership qualities as well as blood. Today, the ruling class probably totals 20,000 supported by another 100,000 influential commoner families (Huyette, 1985).

Despite a history of interdynastic rivalry and the chain that links tribe–clan–family honor, the elites that rule the Peninsula are bound together today by enduring geopolitical concerns: scriptural opposition to Israel, the unresolved

Table 11.1
Gross Domestic Product of Saudi Arabia, 1970–90 (in billion US$)

Year	GDP
1970	4
1975	38
1980	115
1985	70
1990	95 (est.)

Source: *Saudi Arabia: A Country Study*, Department of Defense, and *World Fact Book*, CIA.

plight of dispossessed Palestinians (Muna, 1980), Islamic radicalism and Pan-Arabism, dependence on a workforce dominated by foreigners of more or less "temporary" status, and the anomaly of relying on Israel's ally, the United States, for its national security. With a citizen base of less than 10 million and an inability to repel potential enemies with modern weapons, Saudi Arabia's sheer size and thin population are strategic drawbacks that more than offset its enormous wealth.

THE OIL BOOM AND BUST

The Arabian Peninsula possesses at least half of the world's proven oil reserves. Oil wealth that began to trickle down to the masses in 1974 turned into a flood that lasted until 1982–83. The years since have been relatively lean. The simple logic of oil supply and world demand will dictate a resurgence of wealth to the oil-producing nations of the Saudi Peninsula by the turn of the century. In the meantime, it is important to appreciate the countervailing jolts that a decade of oil money has inflicted on a society that was virtually unchanged for thousands of years. The nation's social fabric was shaken by a sudden influx of wealth and shaken again by the recession that followed. The first jolt hit an economically primitive society; the second disrupted its rush to modernization.

Saudi Arabia was nearly bankrupt a quarter of a century ago under inept King Saud when oil-producing revenue was well below US$500 million. In 1970, revenues began to grow geometrically. From the 1974 embargo price of $2 a barrel, OPEC pressures had raised the price to almost $37 a barrel by 1980 and Saudi revenues peaked at over $100 billion in 1981 (Oppenheimer, 1988). Statistics for Saudi Arabia are notoriously inaccurate and incomplete as the *World Fact Book*, published by the Central Intelligence Agency (CIA), points out. See Table 11.1 for statistics on Saudi Arabia's gross domestic product, (GDP) since 1970.

Approximately half the $600 billion Saudi oil revenues earned during the decade following the 1974 embargo was reinvested abroad, and the rest was spent on public works and the military. All the oil-producing states of Arabia embarked on economic diversification and ambitious infrastructure programs, with particular emphasis on education and health care. Aid programs for their oil-poor Arab neighbors amounted to $5 billion or more a year, while worker remittances probably added another $3 billion (Owen, 1985).

In the 1980s, wealth strained domestic capabilities, and the demand for goods and services outstripped supply. Prices increased three to four times more than in adjacent parts of the Arab world. Rapid growth also brought enormous technical and social change. Arabs and foreigners poured into once remote regions in response to infrastructure development and the burgeoning needs of the populace. Of course, the influx of foreigners is unrelated to the 2 million pilgrims who annually visit the holy cities of Mecca and Medina for the *Hajj*. In 1975, 65 percent of the migrant workers came from other Arab countries. A decade later, this percentage dropped below 45 percent. An estimated 4 to 6 million foreigners worked in the Arabian Peninsula at the peak of the boom—more than 2 million Arabs, 3 million mostly Muslim Asians, and the balance from Africa, Europe, and the Western Hemisphere (Owen, 1986).

Although the government is reluctant to publicize the number of guest workers, they composed close to half of Saudi Arabia's workforce in the late 1970s. By official count, they dropped to 1.2 million of the total population of 9.2 million by 1980. This compares to the underreported official figures of 50 percent or more for Kuwait's foreign workers and almost 80 percent for the United Arab Emirates (Oppenheimer, 1988). Of the 1990 Saudi population, variously estimated at 9.5 to 12.5 million, at least 2 million are still foreigners. The expatriate population in Saudi Arabia is diverse. Today, there are about 85,000 Americans and British, 120,000 Turks, 550,000 Pakistanis, 250,000 Filipinos, 100,000 Thais, and 380,000 Indians, among others.

By 1985, oil production fell by two-thirds, while the price per barrel fell by almost half. Annual oil revenue dropped to 21 billion by 1987 and hovered in that range until prices rose on the heels of Iraq's invasion of Kuwait. This downturn in revenues was due to a complex of factors including a world economic recession, conservation in Organization for Economic Cooperation and Development (OECD) countries, the opening of the North Sea and Alaska oil fields, and, especially, the collapse of OPEC's effectiveness (Sayigh, 1984). King Fahd's policy of becoming OPEC's swing producer, that is, unilaterally cutting back or increasing production to stabilize price, was certainly a contributing factor, causing development projects to slow, foreign aid to be cut, and many businesses to go bankrupt. But the fall was cushioned by at least $300 billion in monetary reserves that had been built up at home and abroad. By 1983, this reserve was drawn to half that amount, and it has dropped further since. The government downsized public expectations through reduced benefits and a sizable trade and budgetary deficit. But with most of the world's oil reserves in their possession and the industrial world's complete dependence on oil for energy, a decade or two of inconvenience can be tolerated. However, the belt-tightening did not do much to reduce dependence on imported labor. According to Owen

(1985), a number of government programs encouraged private enterprise to turn from trade to industry and accelerated government sponsorship of what has since proved to be a largely ineffectual program of domestic training.

THE EVOLUTION OF A MANAGERIAL CLASS

The lean years have not been years of unremitting forbearance in keeping with bedouin values. During the 1970s, wealthier families took their highly visible holidays or vacations in Europe while observing traditional Islamic customs at home. With the acquisition of wealth, class distinctions began to intrude on the egalitarianism that marked bedouin society (Kay and Basil, 1979). The position and competence that mark managerial classes everywhere have also emerged as distinctions, even though the rewards are not so visible.

Trade has largely remained in the hands of families, and children are trained in business and language for future success. During the heady days of easy riches, families encouraged members to pursue government service as a career and often subsidized them to offset the financial loss. Family ties and old relationships are favored in all business dealings. Huyette (1985) even noted a Saudi version of the old school tie. Graduates of Victoria College in Egypt in the 1950s and 1960s acquired an influence in business and government to rival Polytechnique in France. But their sons and grandsons and sometimes their daughters are no longer sent abroad for preparatory school, to insure that they grow up thoroughly steeped in Saudi values before beginning university education at home or abroad. Since families are exceptionally close and protective, most would like to see their children completely educated within the Kingdom. However, the successes of Saudis educated in universities abroad present a dilemma for Saudis who are ambitious for their children.

Government efforts to train locals in lower level skills in order to replace foreigners have been thwarted by opportunities and high wages in the growing public and private sectors of the petroleum/petrochemical business and the basic industries that have been built in government, and in multiple public subsidies. Management is needed in all sectors of construction, retail and service industries, and other institutions that oversee the *rentier* returns of financial investments. A *rentier* state controls and receives most of its revenue from natural resources rather than capital production and depends on make-work policies to keep its citizens occupied.

All these primary domestic industries and agencies are headed by Saudi top managers by law and are increasingly staffed by middle managers under the government's drive for "Saudization," a program seeking to replace foreign workers with Saudi nationals at the management and professional levels. In their quest for industrial self-sufficiency, the government subsidized primary industries. Turnkey petrochemical and fertilizer plants were constructed to complement oil production, and iron, steel, aluminum, cement plants, and light and intermediate industries were constructed all over Arabia at great cost. The results of this development have been almost universally discouraging. Afifi (1988) observed that even joint ventures have almost all failed in terms of return on investment, training of the native population, and technological transfer. Saudi industrialization has lagged badly behind the profitable investments in the securities of developed nations by Kuwait and the smaller Gulf states. Today, gross national product (GNP) in Saudi Arabia is almost solely attributable to oil and the investments bought by oil. Only the certainty of a need for oil by an increasingly industrialized world assures Saudi Arabia's economic future.

In the course of a consulting engagement, McWhinney (1986) noted that the Saudis tend to distance themselves from productive activity. Saudis who headed organizations titled themselves directors on organization charts, while foreigners who reported to them were titled managers. The roles they performed followed the titles they were given. Saudis assumed classic bureaucratic tasks, signing documents and setting policies but rarely supervising work or allocating resources.

The notion of a management elite in a feudal society seems a contradiction in terms since management is a twentieth-century social invention and, by most criteria, Saudi Arabia and the Gulf states are far from modern. Yet skilled managers are acquiring a presence of their own. The ownership of business and the governance of most ministries have remained centralized in the ruling elites. But middle- and upper level managers have recently developed strong and frequent alliances across industries that they nurture with the frequent and friendly visits that Arabs so enjoy in order to converse over coffee and food. Until recently, such interchange would have been more inclined toward kinship and organizational lines.

The growing numbers of managers and professionals and the policy of Saudization indicates less reliance on skilled expatriates. Most managers in the flat organizations that typify Saudi industry may not always possess the university degrees or other credentials of recently hired trainees. However, their on-the-job skills and recent evidence of promotions necessitated by competence have developed a commitment to skill and power that mirrors managerial classes elsewhere. When pressures are brought to promote newly hired and better educated Saudis, foreign and national middle managers have not always welcomed the intrusion or delegated significant decisions until the newcomers have proven themselves.

The titled oligarchy of Arabia at the top of the system is not an exclusive bastion. Marriages have always been arranged with talented and educated commoners, and education has become a desired attribute in potential spouses. Royalty has coopted talent instead of relegating promising commoners to a separate bourgeoisie or intelligentsia substatum.

Saudi higher education is largely traceable to the Arabian-American Oil (ARAMCO) educational programs of the 1950s that sent talented Saudi employees to the American University in Beirut or to the United States before the opening of the University of Petroleum and Minerals in Dhahran. Higher education in Saudi Arabia switched from a British-Egyptian format to an American one in the mid–1970s. The first Saudi five-year development plan (1970–75) highlighted education as a social priority. Compulsory and almost free education cover between a third and a fourth of the population—including many who seem in no rush to complete their studies. Abir (1988) concludes that, while the expansion of education and the decline of illiteracy have been impressive (more than 90 percent of the 1950 population was functionally illiterate), the standards of education are less impressive. By 1985, the nation's seven universities and fourteen women's colleges had grown to 9,000 professors and 80,000 students. Another 15,000 to 20,000 Saudi students were believed to be attending foreign, mostly American colleges and universities. The government formerly provided all the assistance needed to acquire an education. Tuition, food and housing, books, and, until 1986, guaranteed government employment upon graduation were granted to all university graduates (except women).

The guarantee of jobs bloated the government bureaucracy by the mid–1980s. The bureaucracies in the Gulf states have not yet earned notoriety as sinecures because alternative opportunities exist in the private sector and Arabia was spared the arcane heritage of the Ottoman Empire. But a study by Palmer et al. (1989) found Saudi bureaucrats even less predisposed to innovation than Egyptian and Sudanese bureaucrats for fear of "upsetting the supervisor." The authors of this study attributed this predisposition to fatalism, social conformity, and a poorly developed work ethic. Eighty-six percent of the Saudi respondents in this study agreed that "one should be cautious in making even routine decisions." A Ministry of the Interior official has publicly expressed concern about the ad hoc structure in local administration, low educational requirements, overstaffing, and lack of coordination (Al Awaji, 1989). Other states in the region also established bureaucracies to distribute income and create employment.

By the 1985–86 budget, education allocations were reduced by a full third. The bulk of the savings came from cutting off monumental building projects and tightening admissions and graduation requirements in higher education. More demanding standards were extended to schools of medicine, business, and the sciences, which generally use English-language texts, English-language lectures, and a large number of foreign instructors. Graduates of the better secular schools (especially the former University of Petroleum and Minerals, now King Fahd University in Dhahran) will undoubtedly rise to high managerial positions in competition with less talented students born into advantaged families. They have proven their worth in the important oil, planning, and military ministries and have become leaders of the emerging managerial-bourgeois elite.

CULTURAL VALUES

The Arab culture is comparatively more pervasive than Western cultures. In Saudi Arabia especially, the Islamic religion permeates all social organizations and institutions. Employees there often spend up to two or more hours a day in prayer. To outsiders and even Westernized Arabs, Arab society can appear a seamless whole with no easy demarcation between work organizations and the sociopolitical and religious-linguistic setting in which it operates. Access to power follows a different and less linear route than a policy of advancement by merit.

Reductionist thinking may dismiss Arab tribalism as a primitive form of social organization destined to be superseded by rule of law and the impersonal canons of bureaucracy. But tribe and family are powerfully resistant organizing principles that underlie all governance. The cohesion of the tribe is built through a common language and history tied together by a web of associated customs, myths, and beliefs. This is not to say that tribal values and sentiments are associated only with developing economies; rather, they are simply more visible. Groupings such as race, nation, sect, faction, and gang all evoke the raw tribal sentiments of patriotism, honor, and brotherhood and the opposite sentiments of disgrace and rejection.

Arab Tribalism

The strength of the tribe lies in the reciprocity of favors, support, obligation and identity that extends the protection and affection of the family to its members. As Bourdieu put it from the context of an Algerian tribe,

The family is the alpha and omega of the whole system: the primary group and structural model for any possible grouping, it is the indissoluble atom of society which assigns and assures to each of its members his place, his function, his very reason for existence and, to a certain degree, his existence itself. (1962)

Family life therefore imposes tighter emotional ties than in economically oriented societies like the United States. Arabs are reared to be social, and the bedouin and trader traditions foster close personal ties. Despite an authoritarian appearance, Arabian managers today perceive their organizations as operating along the lines of Likert's System 3, that is, a "consultative" management system. However similar this may seem to prevailing North American and European practices, there were also perceptions that managers support the efforts of subordinates because they lack faith in their ability to be resourceful and mask power with benevolence (Hollingsworth and Al Jafary, 1983). Palmer et al. (1989) found that Saudis in bureaucracies were very disinclined to take risks or try new ideas.

A more recent survey found the opposite inclination among Saudis hired by Saudi-American joint ventures (Al Twaijri, 1989). They expressed dissatisfaction with the lengthy period that elapsed between the completion of their training and the assumption of managerial duties. At the same time, older Americans found their relationships with Arab friends an important benefit of their job. This turns the conventional wisdom upside down. It may be that educated Saudis who seek employment in private sector joint ventures (which by law must have Saudi majority ownership) are more ambitious than those who join government bureaucracies. It also suggests a convergence in work values and motivations between relatively younger and less experienced Saudis and older American managers.

Even with evidence of youthful ambition, the traditional obligations of the extended family lead us to believe differently. Where family ties are strong, sensibilities are strong. Behaviors and acts that might evoke little response between urban Westerners can cause serious feuds between Arabs. Cultures built on family ties as in Japan and the Arab states have developed social mechanisms such as refined manners and formalized standards of conduct to protect their members from inadvertent insult.

The ties of tribal affection are hardly egalitarian. Members who are not attractive or closely linked by blood are not accorded the affection and respect due closer relatives and cohorts. Disputes are passed up to tribal elders for resolution because disputes disrupt the equilibrium of past legacies. In the absence of a formal and impersonal legal system to which all sides can submit, conflict is never completely resolvable; dishonor that is not completely restored can erupt in violence. Hence, the path to leadership has been honed in a more or less zero-sum environment.

Tribes themselves have been an impediment to the consolidation and modernization of the Saudi state. There is evidence that Riyadh had encouraged detribalization through land allotments before oil revenue supported government employment. By 1977, approximately one bedouin family in three had at least one family member working for the government. With growing employment opportunities, the economic independence of traditional tribes has been greatly reduced. Local influence has been transferred back to the extended family and through the benefits of Saudi and other Gulf state citizenship, to the state itself (MacLachlan, 1986). Ali (1989a) found that managers with desert origins were less satisfied with their supervisor, job, and work group than urban Saudis and Kuwaitis. He suggests that by moving to the city and having to rely on his individual actions instead of kinship ties, the bedouin experiences a crisis in identity that leaves him dissatisfied with his new world and most aspects of modernity.

The Arabic Language

A word about Arabic is in order. The language and its calligraphy have a powerful hold over its speakers and readers. Hamady's seminal book (1960) on Arab character conveys the magnitude of its power and beauty. Even illiterate Arabs are conscious of its aesthetic qualities and the spiritual enrichment it imparts to their lives.

Unhappily, its richness abounds with rococo adornment that translates as excess to restrained and literal Western ears. The Arab way of choosing words and phrases for their alliteration results in equivocal meanings where logic would be more helpful. Laffin (1975) ties the language to commonly held Western observations of Arab character; that is: (1) the language is more persuasive than logical; (2) linguistic reality preempts perceptual reality; (3) words per se serve to justify or rationalize, so (4) because the Arab means what he says at the moment, dissimulation comes naturally.

Unfortunately, these perceptions arise because Arabs, as a whole, and especially the less Westernized Arabs of the Peninsula, value the person and the relationship more than the task and good manners more than verbal precision. Ali (1986–87) stresses the importance of the sociocentric dimension of doing business with Arabs and the inadvisability of getting down to business before building a friendship. Only after displaying an empathy and sensitivity for Arab rituals and beliefs is it advisable to explore the social advantages of a business proposition before getting down to crass details and the incidental possibility of profit.

Shame and Honor as Social Control and Motivation

Tribal societies use shame to educate and control their members. So-called shame cultures have been contrasted with guilt cultures, but the distinction seems faintly old-fashioned as standards of morality and conscience have diminished in much of the Western world. Shame and guilt constrain social and ethical conduct. Shame societies like the Arabs look to their social group for guidance in behavior and attitude. Hence, right and wrong are matters of circumstance and become relative terms that apply to acceptable behavior. The primacy of the family and other kinship groups are taken very seriously. From early childhood, Arabs participate in conversation and socialize with their elders, and the importance of loyalty and devotion are constantly stressed. Fear of ridicule and family disgrace force conformity, particularly in times of crisis. Because the group matters so much, Arabs find their social bearings externalized in the beliefs, customs, and expectations of their group.

A guilt society emphasizes the self (from the same root as the word "selfish") and control of the self. Much Western child rearing involves training the conscience of the individual as an arbitrator of a person's moral conduct. A tribe orientation focuses on the correctness of outcomes and the instrumentality of acts, and it cares little for good intentions gone wrong or the cognitive consistency of the individual. Members of shame societies look to environmental cues for direction, and, as a consequence, they learn to be socially adroit, socially sensitive, faultlessly sincere, and blindly loyal.

The distinction between shame and guilt is probably overdrawn because both operate concurrently, but the relative power of the group over the person is a fundamental distinction that has been observed by cultural anthropologists for decades and empirically verified in recent years (Hofstede, 1980). In Hofstede's typology of individualism and collectivism, Arabs are among the most collective of all people. This is seen not only in their ability to bargain and mediate, but also in the way they sustain grudges and devalue tasks.

The quest for honor (*sharaf*) is the other side of the coin. Most peoples seek status and power as an end, but ethnic groups follow different routes to power and the symbols of power. For most Arabs, honor, pride, and dignity are transcendental virtues (Hamady, 1960), an attitude shared by their Mediterranean neighbors. Honor is won on behalf of the family and other groups and is more apt to be based on reputation and descent than on wealth for the average Saudi. The baksheesh, kickbacks, and extortion that seem an integral part of conducting business in Saudi Arabia are largely phenomena of upper class greed; a taste for wealth is hardly confined to the Arab world.

Tribal norms impose no obligation of fairness to strangers or other outsiders. In practice, this has resulted in oligarchical rule in organizations and nations. Because the polar opposites of honor and shame are public events, all acts are subordinated to them. The quality of mercy or a public admission of error is a statement of weakness in traditional Arab society, and weakness furthers the interests of opponents. Weakness is not a manly (*muruwwa*) virtue, and failure to be manly or virtuous is to be avoided. Trust rests on consanguinity and friendship. Yet the bedouin finds room to include exquisite manners and hospitality toward strangers in his social code. A society driven by the carrot of honor and the stick of shame follows very different norms than the contractarian arrangements of Western democracies or procedural justice in the workplace.

Westerners are often confounded by what they interpret as needless lies or cheating in the course of work and commerce with the Arabs. Such acts are often intended to protect both parties, however. A refusal not to act on a request is considered a serious social affront. To openly admit one's inability not only insults the acumen of the person giving the order or request, but also causes a loss of face. As centuries of trading have proven, no arrangement is ever finalized if something is yet undone. Furthermore, Arabs assess many situations in idealized rather than factual terms (Watson, 1970). Things are communicated as they would desire it rather than with ontological certitude.

To Westerners, words have a kind of third-order meaning. First, there is an experience, then a thought, and then a spoken word. In the language of Allah, the word takes precedent over the perception. Arabs aspire to an idealized conduct that imparts what Ali (1986–87) sees as a "split personality" between the demographic person and the real person. If aspirations are not met, personal responsibility is not compromised. Accomplishment is not assessed in terms of social competition, but in developing one's own inner potential consistent with the values of the group. As sensitive observers realize, Arabs possess a deep sense of themselves under the layers of conformity that are exposed to public scrutiny (McWhinney, 1986).

Melikian (1978), who analyzed the Saudi character through a sentence completion method, concludes that their genuine concern for others through loyalty, warmth, and responsiveness is intended to enhance their own needs for succor and to allay their fear of loneliness. While they believe that an open expression of feelings is desirable, they are not prepared to betray their own feelings. In keeping with their need for an idealized public image, they hide these feelings for fear others will despise them for their weaknesses and injure their pride, dignity, and self-respect.

Time

Arabs treat time very differently than Westerners, who conceive of time in the Newtonian sense: fixed yet moving, unchangeable yet changing, unidirectional yet conceptually reversible, linear, unidimensional, and precise. To Saudis, time holds no such meaning. Edward T. Hall (1983) has argued that culture's strongest hold on the individual is at the unconscious core level to which people are acculturated or "programmed" (Hofstede, 1980). Hall suggests that time is handled differently in the monochronic and polychronic dimensions of time he uses to contrast cultures. Monochronic societies follow an ordered, exact, schedule-driven use of public time as epitomized by Americans and other Northerners. Polychronic use of time involves multiple, cyclical, unstructured, and apparently random (to monochronic eyes) acts and chance involvements that typify Mediterranean, Latin American, and especially Arab time.

In general, Arabs are oriented not toward projects or tasks, but toward people. A strong work ethic smells of exploitation and is incompatible with the sentiments of friendship (Muna, 1980). Work-oriented Westerners learn to stick to the task because of work's importance. The opposite attitude predominates in much of the Middle East. Egyptian bureaucracies, for example, are legendary for their inability to perform because of constant interruptions and interpersonal exchanges.

The influence of the predominant Saudi Arabian cultural values on selected managerial behaviors is summarized in Table 11.2.

HUMAN RESOURCE MANAGEMENT AND MANAGERS

Managerial Selection

Cultural factors considered earlier determine who is hired, who will rise in the organization, and to what level. Western and Asian multinational enterprises operating in host countries of the Arabian Peninsula follow home country practices. Foreign managers are there to do a job knowing they are in a weigh station in their work lives. In joint ventures or family-owned businesses where the family is actively involved in management, the top levels are invariably reserved for owners and those with family ties. But personnel in the middle strata of management are presumed to have attained the skills to do the job. Lower levels of management are a training ground for upper- or middle-level management as it is everywhere. Multinationals and foreign companies are legally required to have local sponsors, but it is unusual to involve these sponsors in the management of the firm.

Nationality and the university from which a candidate takes a degree are also important considerations. Graduation from a university of distinction counts. In the Saudi Peninsula, Western universities are preferred to Middle Eastern universities and prestigious universities to less prestigious universities. Degrees from Oxbridge and selective U.S. universities can be more desirable than family connections in larger firms and critical governmental agencies. Nationality also matters. Despite the egalitarian precepts of Islam, nationals from less developed countries (LDCs) such as the Indian subcontinent have little hope of rising on merit, and even a degree from a prestigious university in the West may not overcome the stigma of a nation's poverty.

Expatriate managers joining Saudi firms find that interviews are an important

Table 11.2
Selected Cultural Values and Related Managerial Behavior

Cultural Values	Managerial Behaviors
Tribal and family loyalty	Work group loyalty Paternal sociability Stable employment and a sense of belonging A pleasant workplace Careful selection of employees Nepotism
Arabic language	Business as an intellectual activity Access to employees and peers Management by walking around Conversation as recreation
Close and warm friendships	A person rather than task and money orientation Theory Y management Avoidance of judgment
Islam	Sensitivity to Islamic virtues Observance of the Qur'an and Sharia Work as personal/spiritual growth
Majlis	Consultative management A full and fair hearing Adherence to norms
Honor and shame	Clear guidelines and conflict avoidance Positive reinforcement Training and defined job duties Private correction of mistakes Avoidance of competition

An idealized self	Centralized decision making
	Assumption of responsibility appropriate to
	  position
	Empathy and respect for the self-image of
	  others

Polychronic use of time	Right and left brain facility A bias for action Patience and flexibility
Independence	Sensitivity to control Interest in the individual
Male domination	Separation of sexes Open work life; closed family life

means whereby Saudi top managers can assess the chemistry of the relationship for friendship and compatibility. Applicants for jobs in family-owned firms are seldom required to submit to psychological or occupational tests. Companies generally look at the academic discipline and institution first, the grade point average in engineering and business, and, in the case of women, her father's or husband's permission to allow her to work.

The role of family honor is seen in a young Arab's job search. He or his parents are apt to ask a well-placed clansman to carry the family's case to an employer. Given the norm of reciprocity, an owner or an official is approached where a positive balance of obligations has been built up. Upon successfully obtaining a position, the young man or his kin may assume an obligation (dare we call it a liability) to be called upon at some later time. Job qualifications do not seem to matter for Saudi nationals. Once situated, the young man is himself bound to a cycle of obligation and repayment.

In Saudi Arabia, women are barred from most occupations except traditional fields such as social work, nursing, teaching in girls' schools, or occupations where the majority of clients are women. Because religious traditionalism and hence segregation of the sexes is currently on the rise as Sunnis vie with Shi'ahs for scriptural purity, institutions have emerged to serve women only. Oddly enough, this has created considerable entrepreneurial opportunities for women. Under Islamic law, women hold wealth in their own name, and many banks are owned, staffed, and cater only to women. Obviously, this same situation applies to many other businesses that deal with women as their primary clientele.

In recent years, the tightened economy has clouded the job prospects of many university graduates. The February 15, 1987, *Washington Post* reported that most graduates of the first class of 3,000 at King Saud University in Riyadh were finding jobs hard to come by. The university, which now has a student body of 30,000 students and a library of 2 million volumes, was built by a French-American joint venture in only forty months at a cost of $4 billion. Despite a governmental policy of replacing 150,000 managerial jobs now being held by foreigners, the science and engineering skills needed for most of these jobs are not being met by Saudi graduates, 70 percent of whom pursue non-technical studies. Dr. Turki of the university was quoted as saying that graduates "want a university degree for the name of it." The desire to implement a policy of admissions and advancement by merit ran afoul of the royal family, and nepotism has once more become the norm (Murphy, 1989).

If the person under consideration for promotion in a national firm is a well-regarded and well-connected Saudi, his prospects are much greater than a foreigner who may have only competency and productivity to recommend him. Only in exceptional circumstances do particular skills and the ability to produce dictate who will be promoted. Most new managers may not find the scope of their authority expanded enough to match their new title and pay because power at the highly centralized policy level is not readily shared with middle managers.

Compensation

Compensation for management and professional positions in the Peninsula is thought to rank with the highest in the world. But unlike the Netherlands where the whole population is virtually covered by the same single compensation plan, Saudi compensation arrangements are highly fragmented and secret. There are few rigid guidelines for pay in Saudi firms, and salaries are often negotiated. Managers usually get a salary and accommodations, while foreigners also get return air fare and a month's vacation, usually during school vacation in the summer.

Company bonuses were common until 1986 when they virtually disappeared for middle managers. But with free housing, education, and other benefits, these fringe benefits may still not be enough incentive to entice Saudis or the citizens of other Gulf countries to the workplace.

Like most other management practices, the compensation equation depends on the person, his connections, the size of the company, and whether the company is domestic or foreign. Foreign multinationals like Schlumberger that are firmly entrenched in the Saudi economy use corporatewide compensation programs without having to make "cultural" adjustments. Large domestic companies like the National Commercial Bank of Saudi Arabia with 175 branches and the Al-Jaffali Group are apt to pay all managers of the same rank the same pay. Not only is this policy administratively simple, but it also meets the egalitarian preferences of middle managers steeped in a tribal ethos. Even slight differences in pay can cause dissatisfaction, and this forces management to justify the differences on some acceptable basis like seniority, responsibility, education, or experience. Pay grades are becoming common in larger firms that are affected by both internal and external labor markets. Subtle differences in the internal equity of managerial and skilled jobs are rarely recognized and formalized through job evaluation techniques. Instead, jobs are often slotted into pay grades by senior managers or owners who possess an overall knowledge of the jobs performed and are familiar with the businesses. In the recent past, foreign consultants have tailored job evaluation installations to particular industries. But the outside job market is the more meaningful side of the compensation equation because of the large numbers of foreign workers. Except for the oil industry, salaries are seldom surveyed at the national level, and the salaries offered for entry-level jobs become the base for skilled workers, supervisors, and managers above them. Smaller, family-dominated firms do not seek internal equity, and they simply pay family members more than unrelated employees.

In keeping with a practice that ARAMCO initiated when it was a joint venture, some foreign managers and professionals can enjoy an advantage over Saudis or other Gulf nationals. Foreign managers and professionals from advanced Western economies are traditionally given a 15 percent differential over the going rate for a job to attract them to the Peninsula and to offset what locals jokingly refer to as cultural deprivation. On the other hand, employees from poor Third World countries find their pay factored down to reflect rates in their own countries, plus the differential needed to make working abroad attractive. This inequality is not altogether a source of distress for employees from LDCs who appear to be more committed to their firms than their Saudi and Western counterparts. Bangladesh managers and professionals in the Gulf states earn six to eight times more than they can earn at home, while unskilled workers earn four to six times what they earn at home (Al Meer, 1989).

A recent study noted that Saudis employed in joint ventures with American firms resented what they considered the anachronistic differential paid Americans and Europeans, even though Saudis were younger and less experienced than their expatriate counterparts (Al Twaijri, 1989). The author of the study was astonished to find that the Americans surveyed were generally satisfied with their physical surroundings because "it is known that Americans are more cultured and they consider office beautification to be almost a necessity."

Another study found higher commitment toward their organizations among Asians than among Westerners or Saudis, despite pay and benefit discrimination, because Asians used their home countries as the basis for comparison (Al Meer, 1989). Beyond the pay differential, most of the Asians hired are Muslims who factor in the advantage of a free trip to Mecca and the holy places to their contract. Few Saudi managers enter into formal employment contracts, whereas all expatriates are obligated by law to do so if they work for Saudi organizations.

Because of Islamic precepts and bedouin egalitarianism, Arabs view the usual exchange of skills, knowledge, ability, and other attributes for pay and other benefits differently than members of competitive capitalist societies in the Hong Kong and U.S. mold. Money is far less important to the Arabs. As Serageldin Sherbiny, and Serageldin (1984) observed, the discipline of modern organizations patterned along Western lines includes longer working hours, hierarchy and status, productivity, and other costs that run counter to traditional Arab interests. Government agencies and enterprises are able to offset their poorer compensation with fewer restraints and controls than private employers.

In a survey of Iraqi and Saudi managers, Ali (1989b) notes that those with upper class origins have developed an appetite for material wealth. Modernization and access to material wealth have created class distinctions and different values in the once homogeneous Arab world. Saudi workers have gained a reputation for two sometimes inconsistent traits: intense loyalty to their group and resistance to authority. Saudi managers need to integrate these characteristics if employees are to be effective. They seem naturally drawn to organizational life as a result of their need for belonging. Authority (parentage at the family level) is an organizational concomitant. Saudi managers work hard to coopt or cancel out competing loyalties. In short, a work situation that mirrors the family works best. This means that rewards and work are neither instrumentalities nor an end in themselves. Work must enhance social development and personal betterment. Job challenge, autonomy, variety, or redesign are secondary to the sense of group cohesion, peer approbation, and personal esteem that fulfill an Arab's social needs.

It is not entirely correct to segment the Saudi economy into private and public sectors for compensation purposes. In theory and practice, the two sectors overlap a good deal. Oil is the source of Saudi wealth, and it is controlled by the royal elite for the general welfare. In the headier days of the oil boom, the government was generous to a fault. Every Saudi was given an annual housing allowance of $10,000, and managers were given American cars and free medical care, including overseas checkups. In 1984, these privileges were done away with.

However, $100,000 interest-free twenty-five-year loans are still available for any Saudi who wishes to buy their own home, and the inflated salaries granted some managers in the 1970s are still being paid from deficit earnings.

Management Performance Appraisal

Clearly, in Saudi Arabia the emphasis is on the person rather than the job. In his review of the literature, Ali (1989b) notes that Arab managers generally avoid responsibility or risk, prefer stability over challenge, opt for security, favor central decision making because it enhances respect, and subordinate organizational goals and performance to personal relationships. Formal appraisals are used in large foreign-dominated firms, banks, and universities. But given the Arab tendency to look at others holistically and with a halo effect, formal reviews as in the West are fraught with peril for both supervisor and employee alike. The confrontation that results is too harsh for Arab sensibilities and easily undercuts its presumed motivating purpose. Even where formal evaluations have been introduced as a bureaucratic dictate, they are not given much weight. In general, positive and timely feedback is the usual form of training and motivation for employees, in keeping with Arabic paternalism and good manners.

The case is different with foreign managers and professional employees. They possess unique skills, and the ministry that approves the employment contract expects them to groom a national as a replacement. Citizens who report to foreign managers are likely to defer even glaringly obvious decisions and tasks to the foreign manager in light of their expectations of what he is supposed to perform. Since he is effectively on a year-to-year employment contract, the foreign manager is apt to work hard or appear to work hard if he wants to renew his contract. Foreign workers generally find they must bear a disproportionate share of the work load. Organizations under government control or subsidy grant their nationals a virtual sinecure, and nationals learn to shift much of their work load sideways to foreign colleagues or upward to foreign managers for detailed decisions.

With Saudization, the pressure on foreign managers to perform has increased. With fewer foreigners to carry the burden, Saudis will be forced to become more productive. These changes make performance appraisal an increasingly important tool for organizational control. But when foreigners are involved, the process takes on a political dimension. A foreigner who receives a modest (read that as realistic) appraisal does not have his contract renewed. This places foreigners at a distinct disadvantage. Formal appraisals are an instrument of considerable power for managers, and in the West, managers are expected to exercise this power in an evenhanded way. A foreign manager in the Gulf who rates nationals as less than "excellent" raises the suspicion that he lacks the leadership skills to motivate his subordinates—ergo, a rationale for denying an extension of his employment contract. On the other hand, favorable appraisals given underperforming nationals procedurally disadvantage productive workers and create another source of discontent. It is no wonder that foreign managers are apt to avoid participating in formal performance appraisals.

Labor Relations

Unions are outlawed in all Peninsula states because they present potential threats to the ruling families and carry the scent of a heretical ideology. With a mercantilist economic system in place, the many and varied benefits and rights still available to citizens, and employment opportunities, there is little incentive for citizens to organize against employer excesses. Foreigners in Saudi Arabia hold few rights in the Western sense, and the very idea of organizing would be dealt with harshly.

Work relationships, like all other relationships in Saudi Arabia, are governed by the teachings of the Qur'an. Saudi courts and administrative agencies apply these principles to Muslim and non-Muslim and foreigner and national alike. Employers and employees are urged to work out their differences ex post and to enter into a written and evenhanded resolution. Low-status Saudis and foreigners from LDCs have complained that governmental agencies and Islamic courts seem too inclined to "signal a friendly" resolution favoring Westerners and particularly Americans. This is one instance where the litigious sophistication and penchant for formalizing relationships puts Americans in good stead. A Saudi labor code is slowly emerging that covers most ordinary workplace disputes, which in many parts of the West would be handled through collective bargaining.

The extent to which employee rights are enforced by the monarchy is illustrated by a situation reported to me by the Lebanese general manager of an air freight company owned by a very wealthy Saudi and close personal friend of Prince Sultan, the defense minister and brother of King Fahd. A laborer resigned to return to Pakistan. Upon payment of his earnings, including a prorated bonus and return air fare, he signed a standard document witnessed by a fellow Pakistani testifying that he had received what was due him. Yet he later wrote a letter from Pakistan to King Fahd alleging that he had not been paid. The office of the king gave the company three hours to produce the necessary proof and certification from the Ministry of Labor that all the Pakistani's rights had been met. The general manager relates that, even with proof, he was afraid that his company would be severely penalized. As it was, the owner suffered embarrassment in the royal court and paid the Pakistani once again.

Other Gulf states also encourage resolution of conflicts by owners. If this does not work, the Ministry of Labor offers to arbitrate. If the issue is still unsettled, civil courts are available, and more complete labor codes than in Saudi Arabia have been developed to resolve most issues.

CONCLUSION

Arabia of today is far different from the Arabia of just two decades ago. The surface divergences from Western societies are still there, but in less obvious ways, the region is forever changed. The management class that is in the forefront of change can be expected to push still further. Competition for funds and work has generated a harsher economic environment, and Saudi entrepreneurs have emerged to challenge foreign firms, particularly in construction (see Moon, 1986).

After six years of deficits, the government stopped paying stipends for study abroad and canceled foreign aid in 1989. Because 65 percent of all Saudis are under the age of twenty-five, their absorption into the workplace has become the single most critical domestic problem facing the monarchy. The promise of the early part of the decade has turned to despair for some. In an erstwhile crime-free country, a handful of university graduates were recently executed for theft, blaming their crime on their inability to find work. Murphy (1989) quotes A. M. Hasadhan, the secretary general of the Civil Service Commission, as saying that young Saudis are spoiled. They decline anything but white-collar assignments, want short shifts and Thursdays off (the day before the Saudi weekend), and complain of scrutiny at work (presumably so they can read papers in the morning and bring each other mint tea between going to and from the local mosque at least four times a day for prayer).

The schism between the ideals of Muslim totalism and modernity are not easily reconciled. Recent studies such as Ali's (1989b) point out why this is so. With work performance prized less than social conformity and spiritual purity, managers are hampered in carrying out their responsibilities. Loyalty to family, sect, tribe, and state does not transfer to the workplace, even though Arabs are favorably inclined toward their work setting and their co-workers. They do not separate work from play as Westerners do, since their primary recreation is social and discussion of politics and social issues can best be carried out in the workplace and in coffeehouses.

Ali (1989a) also surveyed 103 managers in the area and found that general managers of large and small organizations, who were less educated, higher paid, and less experienced, were more satisfied than departmental managers in larger organizations who were more educated, lower paid, and more experienced. This profile might apply to any developed country. In terms of decision style, participation was more highly prized by managers who worked in foreign companies than by those who worked in bureaucracies. These and other findings hint that perhaps more ambitious managers lean toward the private sector and seek greater organizational involvement, as opposed to the widespread reliance on immediate supervisors and the emphasis on form over function so typical of bureaucracies in LDCs.

This should be expected. Saudi Arabia's investment in Western education has been enormous. Technology transfer has neither offset a lopsided economy nor provided an economic alternative to imports. Rather than succumb to the idle comforts of a *rentier* existence, Arabian leaders have exhibited a determination to improve and diversify their economy in the face of a trader mentality and an inclination to fatalism. While the analysis of service industry strategies by Anastos, Bedos, and Seaman (1980) finds that they tend to be more reactive than innovative, prospective, or entrepreneurial, this is a rational response in a recession era and not necessarily an innate limitation.

Thus far, fundamental change has hardly been apparent. The future of the workforce and the ability of managers to operate effectively will depend on the economy. From the viewpoint of sheer potential wealth, no country is more advantageously situated than Saudi Arabia. If oil prices and production rise enough to keep ahead of the growing workforce, it is apt to remain a *rentier* state in the foreseeable future. In the highly unlikely situation of a stagnant oil market, the nation would be forced to follow the painful road to self-sufficiency. To accomplish this goal, it would need to meld Western managerial practices and thought to traditional behavior and customs. This does not mean that it is impossible to balance the two. The work ethic that marks an advanced economic system is not yet in place. A hunger for wealth and a commitment to performance are two different things. In spite of Islamic standards of conduct and trust, it is far easier for a developing state with Saudi Arabia's prospects to surrender to the former than build toward the latter.

ACKNOWLEDGMENT

The author wishes to thank Amin Jabbour, Elias Al Hajj, and Dr. Abbas Ali for their assistance. The interpretations of their remarks or writings are the author's alone.

REFERENCES

Abir, M. 1988. *Saudi Arabia in the Oil Era*. Boulder, Colo.: Westview Press.

Afifi, S. M. 1988. "Responsibility of Lack of Management and Marketing Technology for the Failure to Attain Development Objectives of Technology Transfer." *Symposium on Scopes and Efforts of Advanced and Renewed Technologies on Arab Societies*. University of Qatar and Unesco.

Al Awaji, I. 1989. "Bureaucracy and Development in Saudi Arabia: The Case of Local Administration." *Journal of Asian and African Studies* 24 (1–2): 49–61.

Al Meer, A.R.A. 1989. "Organizational Commitment: A Comparison of Westerners, Asians, and Saudis." *International Studies of Management and Organization* 19 (2): 74–84.

Al Twaijri, M. I. 1989. "A Cross-Cultural Comparison of American-Saudi Managerial Values in U.S.-Related Firms in Saudi Arabia." *International Studies of Management and Organization* 19 (2): 58–73.

Ali, A. 1986–87. "The Arab Executive: A Study in Values and Work Orientation." *American-Arab Affairs* 19: 94–100.

Ali, A. J. 1989a. "Decision Style and Work Satisfaction of Gulf Executives: A Cross National Study." *International Studies of Management and Organization* 19 (2): 22–37.

———. 1989b. "A Comparative Study of Managerial Beliefs about Work in the Arab States." *Advances in International Comparative Management*, Vol. 4. Greenwich, Conn.: JAI Press, pp. 95–112.

Anastos, D., Bedos, A., and Seaman, B. 1980. "The Development of Modern Management Practices in Saudi Arabia." *Columbia Journal of World Business* 15 (2): 51–58.

Balfour-Paul, G. 1986. "Kuwait, Qatar, and the United Arab Emirates." In I. R. Netton, ed., *Arabia and the Gulf: From Traditional Society to Modern States*. Totowa, N.J.: Barnes and Noble Books.

Bourdieu, P. 1962. *The Algerians*. Boston: Beacon Press.

Hall, E. T. 1983. *The Dance of Life: The Other Dimension of Time*. Garden City, N.Y.: Anchor Press/Doubleday.

Hamady, S. 1960. *Temperament and Character of the Arabs*. New York: Twayne.

Hofstede, G. 1980. *Cultures Consequences*. Beverly Hills, Calif.: Sage.

Hollingsworth, A. T., and Al Jafary, A. 1983. "An Exploratory Study of Managerial Practices in the Arabian Gulf Region." *Journal of International Business Studies* 14: 143–152.

Huyette, S. S. 1985. *Political Adaptation in Saudi Arabia: A Study of the Council of Ministers*. Boulder, Colo.: Westview Press.

Kay, S., and Basil, M. 1979. *Saudi Arabia Past and Present*. London: McNamara.

Laffin, J. 1975. *The Arab Mind Considered: A Need for Understanding*. New York: Taplinger.

MacLachlan, K. 1986. "Saudi Arabia: Political and Social Evolution." In I. R. Netton, ed., *Arabia and the Gulf: From Traditional Society to Modern State*. Totowa, N.J.: Barnes and Noble Books.

McWhinney, W. 1986. "Tales of Arabian Days." *New Management* 3 (4): 38–43.

Melikian, L. H. 1978. "The Modal Personality of Saudi College Students: A Study in National Character." In L. C. Brown and N. Itzkowitz, eds., *Psychological Dimensions of Near Eastern Studies*. Princeton, N.J.: Darwin Press.

Moon, C. I. 1986. "Korean Contractors in Saudi Arabia: Their Rise and Fall." *The Middle East Journal* 40 (4): 614–633.

Muna, F. A. 1980. *The Arab Executive*. New York: St. Martin's Press.

Murphy, K. 1989 (November 11). "For Saudis the Sands are Shifting." *Los Angeles Times*, p. A1.

Oppenheimer, P. M. 1988. "Arab Oil Power: Permanent or Eclipse? or Temporary Fading?" *Middle East Review* 20 (3): 9–16.

Owen, R. 1985. "The Arab Oil Economy: Present Structure and Future Prospects." In S. K. Farsoun, ed., *Arab Society: Continuity and Change*. London: Croom Helm.

———. 1986. "Migrant Workers in the Gulf." *Middle East Review* 18: 24–27.

Palmer, M., Al-Hegelan, A., Abdelrahman, M. B., Leila, A., and Yassin, E. S. 1989. "Bureaucratic Innovation and Economic Development in the Middle East." *Journal of Asian and African Affairs* 24 (1–2): 12–23.

Patai, R. 1973. *The Arab Mind*. New York: Charles Scribner's Sons.

Sayigh, Y. A. 1983. *Arab Oil Policies in the 1970's*. London: Croom Helm.

———. 1984. "A Balance Sheet for the Decade." *The Middle East* 115: 1–18.

Serageldin, I. A., Sherbiny, N. A., and Serageldin, M. I. 1984. *Saudis in Transition: Challenges of Changing Labor Market*. London: Oxford University Press.

Tibi, B. 1985. "A Typology of Arab Political Systems." In S. K. Farsoun, ed., *Arab Society: Continuity and Change*. London: Croom Helm.

Watson, O. M. 1970. *Proxemic Behavior: A Cross-Cultural Study*. Hague: Mouton.

12

JAPAN

Sully Taylor

As we move into the 1990s, Japan's position as a world economic leader is indisputable. This success has led to the incredible growth of Japanese firms over the past four decades. The Japanese managerial class has grown along with the increasing numbers of people working in companies, and consequently represents an important linchpin in the system that has propelled Japan to economic success.

Before proceeding, it is necessary first to clarify what is meant by a manager in this chapter. A manager in Japan is similar to a manager in the United States with regard to duties and role in the organization, although the characteristics of a manager specific to the Japanese situation will be discussed later in this chapter. The term *manager* as used here refers to the employee who is at or near the level of *kacho* and works for a large firm (over 1,000 employees). *Kacho* is ordinarily translated as section chief. A *kacho* can have from around 5 to over 100 subordinates, with the larger number being most typical in the production areas of the firm. However, the description of manager also includes the two positions just above the *kacho* level, the *jicho* (assistant department head) and the *bucho* (department head), as well as the one just preceding it, the *kakaricho* (assistant section chief).

EVOLUTION OF THE JAPANESE MANAGERIAL CLASS

At the end of World War II Japan was a country in ruins, with its industrial base largely destroyed and no capital to invest in rebuilding. The task of achieving sufficient economic growth to sustain the population was therefore a daunting one. Eschewing the approaches of borrowing heavily abroad or inviting heavy investment by foreign multinationals, the Japanese adopted a pay-as-you-go strategy toward economic development (McCraw, 1986). Led by the Ministry

Table 12.1
Japan's Economic Growth, 1950–90

FISCAL YEAR	REAL GNP YEN (TRILLION)	CHANGES:PERIOD TO PERIOD
1950	5.1	
1960	15	13.2%
1970	71.3	10.4%
1975	188.2	2.7%
1980	239.9	4.3%
1985	291.2	4.7%
1988	334	5.3%
1990	361	3.6%

Source: Edward Lincoln, *Facing Economic Maturity* (Washington, D.C.: Brookings Institution, 1988), p. 39.

of International Trade and Industry and the Ministry of Finance, Japan adopted an industrial policy that targeted certain industries as strategic to growth and provided a number of supports for their development. Subsidies, tax incentives, lower interest rates, and tariffs on imports were among some of the instruments used to help build such industries as textiles, shipbuilding, steel, and automobiles. By the early 1960s, the Japanese economy had recovered to the point that the nation was wealthy enough to host the Olympics in 1964, having tripled their gross national product (GNP) in a decade (see Table 12.1).

In addition to growth, the structure of the economy changed. As can be seen in Table 12.2 there was a shift of employment out of the primary sector. While at the end of the war over 50 percent of the Japanese engaged in agriculture, by the early 1960s this figure had dropped to 20 percent. These trends continued during the next two decades as Japan gradually moved into emerging industries such as electronics, computers, and semiconductors, and, more recently, into biotechnology and telecommunications—all areas in which it is either dominant or a strong competitor. In supercomputers, for example, three Japanese firms now have models that rival the vaunted Cray computer of the United States (*JEI Report*, No. 13B, 1990).

Japanese firms have become increasingly globalized as a result of their strength in a number of industries. Investment in the United States has been increasing in recent years, and it is expected that Japanese firms will employ 1 million Americans by the year 2000. Yet while economic growth has continued to be strong, with GNP expanding 5 percent in real terms in fiscal year 1989, it has also brought increasing strife with Japan's trading partners, particularly over the issues of dumping and equal access to the Japanese market (*JEI Report*, No. 15B, June 29, 1990). The bureaucratic machine set up to produce the high rates of growth has not always been able to adjust as quickly as might be desirable.

Table 12.2
Employment in Japan by Sector 1950–90

FISCAL YEAR	TOTAL EMP. (MILLIONS	PRIMARY SECTOR a	SECONDA- RY SECTOR b	TERTIARY SECTOR c
1950	35.7	51.6%	21.7%	28.6%
1955	40.9	37.6%	24.4%	38.1%
1960	44.4	30.2%	28.0%	41.8%
1965	47.3	23.5%	31.9%	44.6%
1970	50.9	17.4%	35.2%	47.3%
1975	52.2	12.7%	35.2%	51.9%
1980	55.4	10.4%	34.8%	54.5%
1985	58.1	8.8%	34.3%	56.5%
1990 (est.)	61.5	7.0%	33.0%	60.0%

[a] Includes agriculture, forestry, and fishing.

[b] Includes construction, mining, and manufacturing.

[c] Includes services and government.

Sources: Edward Lincoln, *Japan: Facing Economic Maturity* (Washington, D.C.: Brookings Institution, 1988), p. 63, and *The Japan Economic Almanac*, 1989, p. 44.

Officials within the bureaucracies in particular, imbued with the national goal of achieving economic growth at all costs, have often continued practices set up to keep foreign competitors out long after the political climate has changed.

In summary, the Japanese managers of the post–World War II era can be seen as the product of a period of incredible economic growth. They operated in a competitive environment that was shielded from foreign pressure, and they managed a workforce that vividly recalled the poverty and destitution of the immediate postwar period. There was a national consensus on the need for personal sacrifice in order to achieve economic security for the nation, a social agreement that has only recently begun to be questioned seriously. It is important to place both the way in which these managers approached the management task and the manner in which they themselves were managed in this context.

THE INFLUENCE OF SOCIAL VALUES ON MANAGERIAL BEHAVIOR

Every society has a set of basic values that influences the behavior of all members within that society, both within and outside organizations. When discussing Japanese organizational behavior, the values that are most commonly emphasized are groupism, harmony, hierarchy, *amae*, *on* and *giri*, *gambare*, and a final category that can be loosely termed uncertainty avoidance (Doi, 1973; Nakane, 1970). Each of these values will be examined for its influence on Japanese values.

Groupism

Groupism is one of the most salient characteristics of Japanese society in general. This emphasis on groupism has its roots in the agricultual and religious traditions of the country. As in most wet-paddy rice cultures, the great need for cooperation in planting and harvesting this main food staple led to a heavy emphasis on cooperation and group activities. Confucian values, imported into Japan from China starting in the seventh century, also emphasized the importance of the social organism over the individual's salvation (Reischauer, 1977). In addition to these factors, the poverty of preindustrial Japan with its lack of natural resources encouraged the commitment of the individual to the group as a means of survival in a harsh economic environment. For the modern Japanese, groupism remains a core value, consciously engendered and encouraged from kindergarten by parents, teachers, and neighbors. It is through the group that the average Japanese gains a sense of identity.

For the Japanese manager in a large modern corporation, this emphasis on the group heavily influences the way in which his job is defined and carried out. The most fundamental influence is on his sense of the purpose of his job, which in turn is derived from his concept of the firm. In many Western countries, particularly in the United States, the firm is seen as a set of assets owned by the stockholders who risk their resources in a particular undertaking. Managers within this system are seen as representatives of the stockholders, whose main job is to maximize the return on the stockholders' investment. Japanese managers, on the other hand, operate within an environment in which employees and stockholders are seen as possessing equal stakes in the survival of the firm and equal claim to the profits of the firm. In such a system, the manager becomes a mediator between the respective interests of the stockholders and employees. In order to effectively represent the interests of both groups, all three groups (shareholders, managers, and employees) must remain stable, for if the composition were constantly changing through turnover, the task of understanding their respective interests would be too onerous for the managers. Since until recently a great deal of the financing needed by Japanese corporations was raised through loans from banks, and the banks tended to be patient investors, managers were not pressured by short-term demands of stockholders as in the United States. Thus, all three groups tend to remain stable over time, which permits the manager to see himself as a mediator between groups rather than as a maximizer of stockholder value.

Harmony

Groupism plays a role not only in how a Japanese manager views his purpose within the firm, but also in the way in which he carries out his job. The Japanese manager's role and behavior is heavily influenced by both his own and his employees' group orientation. A great deal of time is spent on building group harmony and identification, often through social activities. Harmony is an important value in Japan, largely because small communities in preindustrial Japan needed to cooperate in the planting and harvesting of rice, the most important crop. Intragroup conflict would result in decreased cooperation and hence decreased yields and possible starvation. Confucian ideology, with its emphasis on the subordination of individual desire and wants to the preservation of society as a whole, reinforces the personal constraints that individuals undertake in the name of harmony. For the Japanese manager, getting to know each member of his group on a personal basis is an important component of his job. It is also important for him to understand and incorporate the concerns of each member of the group regarding any decision that is made so that strife within the group is minimized.

Hierarchy

Every Japanese has a keen sense of the order of things, whether it be the ranking of companies, positions within a company, universities, countries, or restaurants. For a Japanese manager, the sense of hierarchy is important for several reasons. First, it affects the way in which he sees his career within the firm. It represents an orderly progression from one level to another, with the learning of one level imperative to successful achievement in the next. Second, it affects his interactions with both subordinates and superiors. Behavior and language are modified according to whether the person being addressed is inferior or superior in rank, with greater curtness typifying downward communication and greater deference given superiors, both to a degree not common in the West. Such changes of behavior are seen as natural. Finally, the sense of hierarchy allows a type of interaction with subordinates that in the West could be perceived as threatening. The acceptance of the legitimacy of hierarchy by all, managers and subordinates alike, permits the subordinate to correct statements made by the manager, while the manager himself is able to openly acknowledge a lack of information concerning a topic (Dore, 1987). The manager, by virtue of having achieved the position he holds, has proven his competence, and because time rather than performance will enable his subordinate to move up to his level, he does not perceive questioning of his knowledge as an assault on his position. He cannot be overtaken by those lower on the hierarchy. This freedom to acknowledge a lack of information is particularly important in the Japanese setting because of the emphasis on producing generalist rather than specialist managers.

Amae

The word *amae* (See Mendenhall, n.d.) comes from the verb *amaeru*, which is the desire to depend on the love, patience, and tolerance of others. There is a subtle sense of obligation that those dependent on others feel toward those who encourage the dependence. The other face of *amaeru* is *amayakasu*, which is the deference to the gratification of another's desire to *amaeru*. In the West this type of dependency, which typifies the mother-child relationship, is typically cut off in childhood. Indeed, a child is constantly pushed to stand on its own two feet in preparation for the individualism of adulthood. In Japan, however, *amae* is encouraged in adult relationships such as those between husband-wife, teacher-pupil, and boss-subordinate. For the Japanese manager this social value influences his interactions with his subordinates in that he is constantly reinforcing the tendency of those below him to depend on him. This may in part explain the tendency of Japanese supervisors to intervene in a subordinate's work more often, directly, and without being requested to do so than is ordinarily found in such countries as the United States (Lincoln, 1989; Sullivan and Taylor, 1991). Moreover, this value enhances his sense of responsibility for his subordinates, expanding his scope of concerns to such matters as obtaining a spouse for the unmarried subordinate or ensuring that all his employees drive safe cars. A manager thus has a much broader view of his role in the lives of his employees than does a typical Western manager.

On and Giri

Tied in with the social value of *amae* are the concepts of *on* and *giri*. Both values revolve around the central idea of obligation and debt for favors or kindnesses received from others. *On* is the more serious, weightier sense of obligation of the two. It is owed to those who have provided significant help, such as a parent or teacher. A child owes *on* to parents for their favor of giving him birth (Zimmerman, 1985). *Giri* is a parallel sense of obligation, but it is based on the many smaller debts and obligations incurred during the normal course of life. *Giri* is closely related to *gimu*, the word for duty. *Giri* are the many small and not so small favors and kindnesses granted to others, such as easing a subordinate's heavy work load or giving a customer an extra price discount. Japanese people are always very conscious of the *giri* they owe and are owed. To ignore the *giri* one owes, or to allow personal feelings or desires to interfere in the discharge of *giri*, is to threaten the social order through the introduction of the uncertainty of spontaneous human feeling (Reischauer, 1977).

For Japanese managers the concepts of *on* and *giri* are crucial. A manager is very aware of the importance of the personal loyalty he acquires from subordinates as a consequence of granting numerous small favors. This loyalty can be of tremendous importance if, for example, the manager must ask a subordinate to perform a particularly onerous task or duty. While never directly mentioned, the subordinate has a keen sense of the duty he owes his boss, and undertaking an unpleasant task is one way of showing his appreciation and sense of obligation. Even if the boss or subordinate is transferred to another part of the company, the tie of *giri* remains strong and can be called upon at any time.

The tie is not one way, however. The boss acquires a sense of *giri* toward the subordinate as a consequence of the subordinate's daily efforts, both expected and unexpected, to perform his job as fully as possible. This sense of *giri*, combined with the manager's position of greater power, impels him to do everything he can to ensure his subordinate's well-being, both on and off the job. The paternalism with which Japanese firms have been characterized is reinforced in the interpersonal relationship between boss and subordinate by this sense of *giri*.

Gambare

No one English translation captures the subtleties of the word *gambare*. It can be variously translated as "to do your best," "to hang tough," or "to put all one's efforts into a task.'' From childhood Japanese learn that this is the most important ingredient in achieving success, more important in some ways than the individual talents and capabilities with which one is born.

For the Japanese manager this concept is important in two ways. First, as will be discussed later, the manager himself is often transferred from one unrelated department to another, such as from personnel to sales. The manager often receives little more than two weeks' notice before he must take up his new duties, and training for the position is rare. The company relies on the manager's *gambare* attitude to help him learn the knowledge and skills he needs for the new position. He will spend a great deal of extra time in the beginning familiarizing himself with his new department and job, often on his own time. The assumption is that given a certain basic intelligence and education, anyone can learn to do almost anything if he puts his mind to it. The manager in turn expects the same *gambare* attitude on the part of his subordinates, whether it be to learn new tasks that are necessary for doing the job or being willing to give extra effort and time if the work load suddenly demands them.

This reliance on *gambare* is also an important reason why on-the-job training is so prevalent in Japanese companies. A worker can be expected to rise to the challenge of learning a job from his colleagues, to put full effort into observing and learning from co-workers the skills he needs to do the job. For example, researchers can be transferred from one research project to another fairly quickly, and they are expected to do the necessary extra reading and study to get up to speed as quickly as possible.

The organizational structure in which a Japanese manager functions is greatly influenced by the values described above. Japanese organizations tend to have finely graded hierarchies and narrow spans of control. This provides a great number of status rankings, which in a hierarchical society is of obvious benefit (Lincoln, 1989). Moreover, authority and decision making tend to be centralized on a formal basis, yet in actual practice Japanese managers are expected to bring others into the decision-making process through such techniques as *nemawashi* and *ringi*. This reflects the strong emphasis on groupism and the necessity of avoiding strife. In short, a Japanese manager's role is essentially that of a counselor and confidant to the group he manages in which he encourages *amae* from his subordinates and tries to exercise direct authority as little as possible (Lincoln, 1989). While managers do use assertiveness when giving commands to their subordinates, such commands are based on a thorough knowledge of what each subordinate's position is on an issue, a learning process that takes a considerable amount of the manager's time and attention (Sullivan and Taylor, 1991).

HUMAN RESOURCE MANAGEMENT

The Japanese human resource management system as practiced in large firms has been characterized as permanent employment (Abegglen, 1958). The features of the system include hiring recent graduates only and retaining them in the organization for their careers; basing promotion and salary increase decisions mainly on seniority rather than individual performance; and having enterprise-style rather than industry-based unions. Essentially, the permanent employment system is an internal labor market system, Japanese style. The human resource management system regarding managerial personnel as described below should be viewed from this internal labor market perspective.

Managerial Selection

The overwhelming majority of Japanese middle managers in large firms are male, although in recent years some women have been accepted into the managerial tracks of large firms. Yet even today only 7.3 percent of working women have a subordinate, and none of Japan's larger and more famous companies has ever had a woman as a board member. In a survey by the Nihon Keizai Shimbun in 1988, it was found that only 1.29 percent of managers are women (*JEI Report*, No. 18A, 1989). Thus, it is still fairly safe to assume that midlevel Japanese managers are overwhelmingly male.

A Japanese management track employee reaches the *kacho* level in his early to mid-thirties, although over the last fifteen years the speed of promotion has slowed down. (See Figure 12.1.) Moreover, the slowdown differs somewhat by industry. In the more mature industries such as steel and automobiles, the lower growth rates of recent years have led to the allocation of a decreasing number of management positions to those on the management track. As a consequence, the average age at which an employee makes *kacho* in these industries is higher relative to that in the higher growth industries of telecommunications or computers. A concurrent adjustment in the mature industries is to create more levels of management, that is, more steps in the lower rungs of management, as a way of providing sufficient opportunities for promotion. At the other extreme with regard to responding to this challenge is Toyota Motor Company, which recently eliminated most of its middle-management positions in an attempt to decrease the value of a promotion as a reward and thus avoid becoming top-heavy (*Wall Street Journal*, August 8, 1989).

Because of Japan's largely homogeneous population, the management class does not tend to be dominated by any particular ethnic group. However, the few minorities that do exist in Japan are excluded. One of these is the Korean minority. Many Koreans have lived in Japan since the occupation of their country in the first half of this century, yet the majority do not hold Japanese passports even though they may have been born in Japan. This state of affairs is partially of their own volition. Yet it is safe to say that the majority of Japanese firms, particularly the larger firms, do everything possible to avoid hiring a member of the Korean minority in Japan. The same holds true for those who belong to the traditional underclass of *burakumin*, a group that performed the distasteful tasks of society, like butchering, in preindustrial Japan. One way in which some Japanese companies avoid hiring such people, who physically resemble the majority of Japanese, is to hire a private detective to investigate the family backgrounds of all serious candidates for a position. Since family records are

Figure 12.1
Average Age at Promotion of Managers, 1973–87

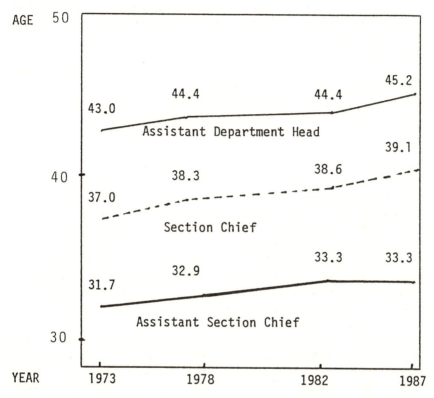

Source: *Rosei Jiho* #2875 (Labor Administration Bulletin), April 8, 1988.

on file at the city hall of a person's residence and are open to inspection by outsiders, this is a relatively easy check to make.

In large Japanese firms, managers are drawn from an internal pool of employees who enter the firm directly from university. Future managers are hired on either the administrative (*jimukei*) or the technical (*gijitsukei*) track (Pucik, 1984). The administrative track is for those employees who will be utilized largely in administrative posts such as planning, personnel, or sales, while the technical track is for those who will be involved in technical jobs, usually in research and development (R&D) or production. Both tracks have a managerial path within them that are roughly equivalent. Thus, when discussing midlevel managers in Japan it is important to keep in mind that the designation applies as much to technical personnel as to administrative personnel. One track is not considered more elite than the other. In fact, technical track people are often found in the upper management ranks of large Japanese corporations, as evidenced by the large number of engineers in those ranks. The new president of Honda Corporation, for example, is an engineer who was formerly head of R&D (*Wall Street Journal*, May 11, 1990).

In selecting young men to join the company, large Japanese firms have in the past relied on a combination of criteria: the university and major of the candidate, an interview, a test, and a background check. University grades are of little importance (Pucik, 1984). Different methods are used for selecting those who are bound for the administrative track versus those who are hired into the technical track. Those hired into the administrative track usually receive literature concerning the firm early in their senior year. If they are interested in applying for a job, they send in a postcard. The personnel department selects those most interesting to them and then finds members of the firm who have graduated from the same universities. These members are sent to interview the candidates, performing both initial screening and suasion functions.

If a candidate is found to be acceptable, he or she is invited to take a test that consists of general knowledge questions and an essay. The test tends to be a formality, with about 90 percent passing. Further interviews, held at the company itself, are then conducted. In these interviews the company tries to determine the candidate's fit with the firm. In particular, it wants to make sure that the young man is sociable and, while able to take a stand, is not too strong-minded (Pucik and Hatvany, 1983). In the process, the company is most concerned with determining the individual's potential as an employee rather than his or her present skills and knowledge. As a consequence, neither the student's courses nor grades have much weight in the hiring decision.

With the technical track employees, the situation is somewhat different. Here the present technical expertise of the potential employee is somewhat more important. The company attempts to ascertain the quality of these candidates by choosing those who have been selected to be members of the senior seminars conducted by the most famous professors at the top universities. A professor's recommendation carries a great deal of weight; in fact, it is virtually impossible to be hired without it. The professor only writes one recommendation for each student. In an attempt to allocate the graduates in a way that no major company is left without some good recruits, the professor will often influence the candidate's choice of firm. The necessity of obtaining the professor's recommendation leads the graduate to accept this guidance, in spite of the enormity of the decision due to the immobility of Japanese labor markets.

Entrance into university, and thus into a company, is based largely on the individual's intelligence and diligence rather than on family background or contacts. This is not to say that neither matters. Particularly in recent years, the ability of more wealthy families to purchase special tutoring for their children that enables them to perform better on the entrance exams has led to the greater influence of the socioeconomic variable in the composition of the student body than before. Moreover, if a family member or friend works for a firm to which a student is applying, such relationships are weighed positively. For example, if the father of a candidate is good friends with the president, and the president lets it be known to the personnel department that he favors the hiring of the candidate, then the person's chances of being hired are increased, although not to the extent of ignoring basic hiring criteria. However, it can be concluded that the selection criteria for both administrative and technical track employees are based largely on the individual competence and accomplishments of the candidate.

As stated above, management track employees are hired into large Japanese firms upon graduation from college, and it is now rare to find a Japanese manager without a university degree. Those from technical fields are often hired upon completing their M.S. degrees, with some companies paying for the additional two years in return for a promise they will join the firm upon completing the degree. In fact, 44 percent of all master's degrees awarded in Japan are given in engineering. There is a very clear hierarchy of universities with regard to recruitment of candidates. At the top of the hierarchy are the public universities such as Tokyo University, followed by Kyoto University, and Hitotsubashi University, Osaka University, the Tokyo Institute of Technology, and then by a group of private universities such as Keio, Waseda, and Sophia. Those entering the administrative track are usually drawn from the humanities, commerce, or law, which in Japan is an undergraduate degree. Graduates of the engineering track are hired in much greater numbers by Japanese firms than American firms. Thus, Japan produces twice as many engineers as the United States in spite of having only half the population (Westney and Sakakibara, 1988). The large number of people with engineering backgrounds in management has led to increased understanding of the manufacturing side of the firm across functions and levels, which often leads to better decision making regarding investment in new technology (Yonekura, 1988). The large number of people with law backgrounds is also beneficial, increasing the awareness of legal issues among those managers.

Graduates of top universities choose to join these large firms partly because of the paucity of entrepreneurship opportunities such as exist in the United States. Part of the value to the firm of having graduates from these top universities is the networking capability that the recruits have acquired along with their undergraduate degrees. Because so much business in Japan relies on personal contact, any personal characteristic, such as being fellow alumni, that helps to establish the contact is extremely valuable. A young man who joins a firm straight out of Tokyo University has two important networks already at work for him: the people already in the firm who are also graduates of his university, and the men who were in his class at the university and other fellow alumni who join a variety of firms and government offices. Having attended Tokyo makes them all part of the same group, and hence smoothes the process of establishing a relationship when needed. Within the firm, older members from the same university will often undertake a mentoring role for the new recruit, a valuable asset often denied those who graduated from universities from which the firm has not recruited in the past. At the present time, as large Japanese firms diversify into unrelated areas, they often need to recruit at universities they haven't tapped as sources previously. However, they sometimes find candidates reluctant to sign on because of the lack of older fellow graduates who can provide help and support.

Japanese firms consider the socialization of new employees to be very important, and a great deal of attention is given to the initial training of recruits into the management track (Pucik, 1984, 1988; Pucik and Hatvany, 1983; Rohlen, 1975). By the time a new recruit actually arrives at the company for his first day of work, he has met with a number of present employees, particularly those who are fellow alumni and are in his track (i.e., technical versus administrative). All new recruits join the company on the same day, usually April 1, for this date coincides with the beginning of the school year. Thus, firms carry out welcoming ceremonies throughout the country at the same time. In the initial ceremony, the new recruits are addressed by the top echelon of the company, who try to instill a sense of the corporate mission and shared purpose in the young men and women.

Immediately afterward, the recruits begin an intensive training program that lasts one to six months. The training is often carried out at the corporation's training facilities where they all live and share communal quarters. The atmosphere at these initial training retreats is similar to military boot camp training. There are lectures on corporate organization, policies, products, and history; team-building exercises; training in business and social etiquette; and often physical training to instill endurance such as zen meditation and long hikes in the middle of the night to a freezing waterfall in which all immerse themselves. In some firms a period of training "on the lines" is also incorporated into the training, the exact nature of which is largely determined by the industry to which the firm belongs. For example, in the steel industry a young recruit will often spend a few months working in a place like the hot strip mill, keeping the same shifts and performing the same duties as the blue-collar workers. In other industries such as electronics, sales experience is considered valuable in order for the recruit to learn about the products of the firm and its customers. One of the main purposes of this kind of experience is to imbue in the employee a sense of the product base of the firm and of the work of the bulk of the company's employees.

The recruits emerge from this training period with a strong network of relationships with the other recruits who joined the company with them. As mentioned previously, this network will prove invaluable in the subsequent years. They have also been inculcated with a sense of shared purpose with these cohorts, a commitment to the group which will serve as an important force in their work motivation in the future. They have a thorough grounding in all aspects of the firm, and through the endurance exercises they have strengthened the self-discipline and ability to endure hard work and long hours that was begun during their studies to pass the rigorous examinations for entrance into a prestigious university. This particular Japanese sense of work *machismo* becomes an important part of their self-identity, instilling in them a deep "fighting spirit" to better the fortunes of their firm vis-à-vis other firms.

But what the initial training does not do is give the young men a lot of skills or knowledge that are specialized to a particular job, particularly those on the administrative track (Tanaka, 1980; Taylor, 1989). In fact, only at the end of the training period do they find out their work assignments. While their desires regarding placement have been sounded out, the decision is very much at the discretion of the company and is dependent on both its needs and assessment of the candidate during the initial training. Because of the generalist nature of Japanese managers, the department to which he is first assigned is not crucially important, for he can be sure that he will eventually be moved to another department. He has joined a company rather than taken a particular job.

Japanese firms have not traditionally relied on outside schools to provide business training for their managers, either before joining the firm or subsequently. This is partially attributable to the belief that management skills are specific to the firm, and thus the firm itself is in the best position to provide them. As a consequence, one does not find in Japan the predominance of MBA programs that exists in the United States, although this picture is changing. One exception is the fairly common practice of selecting a few young management track employees each year to send abroad to study in an MBA program in the United States. The purpose of such programs is as much to acquire contacts among the other Japanese MBA students as to learn American business techniques and theory. These alumni groups are becoming another important source of networking in Japan, paralleling the network of former Fulbrighters that exists among the top management of large Japanese firms.

Some recent attempts have been made in Japan to provide more management training in academic settings. One is IIST, which was initiated by MITI and is in Fujinomiya, near Mount Fuji; another is the Nomura School of Business; and a third is the International University of Japan. These institutions offer a variety of management development programs, but they are small and have had relatively little impact on changing the traditional approach to training management track employees.

While recruiting young men from Japanese universities has been the overwhelmingly preferred source of recruits for large Japanese corporations over the last forty years, in recent years the tight labor market combined with changes in strategic direction, particularly the move toward becoming more international, has led large corporations to widen their traditional recruiting net. In addition to recruiting at what could be considered the second-tier Japanese universities, they have also begun to recruit among Japanese who have acquired their degrees from U.S. universities. One company that acts as a go-between for companies and potential overseas recruits is Recruit America.

In recruiting those with technical backgrounds, two trends have become evident in recent years. First, as mentioned earlier, the diversification into new lines of business has created the need to recruit at universities and among majors, such as those in bio-engineering, that are new for many of these large Japanese corporations. At the same time, the tight labor market, particularly among those with technical backgrounds, has led many large firms to promote the recruitment of women. Hitachi, Toshiba, and others have been actively seeking out the top science women graduates and hiring them on the same track as their male counterparts. For example, in 1985, 20 percent of the nearly 900 researchers hired by Toshiba Corporation to staff its new $88 million semiconductor lab were women (*Business Week*, February 25, 1985).

Finally, an important divergence from the past is the increasing number of midcareer hires by large Japanese firms (Taylor, 1989). Particularly in the technical fields, where firms need specialized knowledge and in high-growth industries such as investment, the need for crucial skills and knowledge to fulfill present needs has led to a willingness to break with the pattern of hiring only from new university graduates, although there is still reluctance to hire from a competitor (McMillan, 1989: 190). The net effect of the changes taking place in recruitment of future managers in Japan is a greater heterogeneity among those staffing the midlevel management positions. While these effects will not be strongly felt for about ten years, it is a trend that many personnel directors in Japanese firms have recognized and for which they are attempting to prepare.

Compensation of Managers

Salary determination in large Japanese firms is largely a function of the individual's place in the corporate hierarchy rather than the exact duties he carries out. In addition, a strong sense of egalitarianism pervades the system; that is, each employee's compensation is a function of his personal needs as well as his contributions.

A manager's salary is largely determined by the rank (*shikaku*) he has reached in his firm. Rank is separate from the position or job title (*yakushoku*) a manager holds. (For a thorough discussion of the *shikoku* versus *yakushoku* designation, see Pucik, 1984.) This system can be understood as similar to that used in the U.S. military, where it is necessary to have reached a certain rank before becoming eligible for a certain position. For example, in order to become a department head (*bucho*), it is necessary to have reached the *bucho-yaku* rank. Moreover, it has been the convention in large Japanese companies since World War II to require a certain number of years in a rank before promotion to the next level becomes possible. As a consequence, seniority becomes a de facto requirement for promotion to certain ranks, and this is why seniority plays such an important role in determining the salary a manager receives.

Merit is also used in determining the salary level of managers, far more than for those who have not yet reached the manager level. The difference in pay between those in the same rank and position is relatively small, however. For example, a *kacho* who performs exceptionally well during his first year on the job may receive a salary increase of 12,000 yen a month, while a cohort who is performing satisfactorily will receive an increase of 10,000 yen. Although the difference in increase is 20 percent, the overall effect on salary is still relatively small. (At 145 yen/dollar, the difference is equal to around $14.) More important, increases based on merit are not permitted to accumulate to the point of creating an internal equity problem. If the high-performing manager continues to perform well, he will be promoted to the next rank as soon as he has served the minimum number of years in the present position, thus putting him in a different salary class from the average performing manager. It can be safely said that merit increases are used not so much as a monetary reward as an indication to the employee that he will have high future income.

Some differences exist between industries and individual corporations regarding the relative emphasis each places on seniority versus merit in determining salary. In the declining industries such as steel and shipbuilding, greater emphasis is still placed on seniority, although some changes have taken place in recent years. In the mature industries such as automobiles and electronics, the tendency is to emphasize merit more, to have a more balanced system. In the high-growth industries such as securities, in recent years more emphasis has been given to merit as a way of dealing with the highly competitive environment and retaining the specialized employees who are so vital to success. Yet even in the high-growth industries merit is usually a significant factor in determining the bonus rather than the base salary of the employee, which allows the firms to avoid getting locked in to higher and higher salaries for their employees. The base salary remains a balance between seniority and merit.

The base salary is also partially determined by the employee's marital status, as well as the number of children he has. These special family allowances are granted to all employees and are not particular to the management level.

The bonus portion of the salary is very large in most Japanese corporations. It usually equals four to five times the monthly base salary of the employee, and it is paid twice a year, once in the summer and once in the winter. In the securities firms it can range up to eight times the base monthly salary of the employee. The average bonus amount for unionized employees is negotiated each year in the spring along with the amount of salary increase, and serves as a benchmark for determining the average bonus of management employees. While bonuses can be adjusted if a firm undergoes an extremely severe business downturn, in general bonuses tend to be sticky downward (Dore, 1986). Most Japanese employees, managers included, consider the bonus as part of their overall salary package, and the family budget is calculated on the expectation that the full amount will be received. Hence, firms are reluctant to tamper with the bonus. This is not to say that salary is not adjusted during difficult times. In fact, pay cuts do occur when necessary, starting from the top management ranks of the firm where the deepest pay cuts are made. Managerial-level employees in general are expected to absorb as much of the pay cut as possible before employees below the rank of manager are required to accept such cuts. The rationale is that managers are the better paid of the total employee group, and hence have greater ability to absorb such a loss of income.

Because seniority is such an important determinant of salary level, companies tend to underpay new employees and overpay older employees relative to their job tasks. White-collar workers in the twenty to twenty-four age bracket (i.e., those with a college degree) working in firms with over 1,000 employees are paid an average of 173,400 yen per month, exclusive of bonus. At 145 yen/

dollar, this is equivalent to $1,193 per month. As can be seen from Table 12.3, earning power peaks in the fifty to fifty-four age bracket, with the average monthly salary equal to $4,179 per month, before dropping off to $4,075 per month. This reflects the fact that until recently most large corporations set the retirement age at fifty-five. Some of the retirees are hired back, but at greatly reduced salaries. The rationale for what amounts to decreasing the salary of the oldest workers is that, since they have passed their peak years with regard to expenses, particularly with regard to putting their children through college and buying a house, their financial needs are less demanding than those of the people just behind them.

Managers in large Japanese firms are not ordinarily offered stock options as part of their compensation package. All employees are able to buy stock in the company at reduced rates, but no special stock option is available to only managers. Until recently, most employees did not utilize this privilege to any significant degree. This is partially because dividends are low or nonexistent, and are also taxable. As a consequence, most Japanese employees have elected to put their money into regular savings accounts such as the postal savings system.

Japanese companies pay pensions to all full-time employees, including managers. Whereas in the past an employee would usually receive a lump-sum payment upon retirement, in recent years the practice has been decreasing, with more employees electing to receive an annuity (see Table 12.3). The pension amount is determined by rank and number of years of service. The average lump-sum payment is equal to forty-one times the base monthly salary for a person with a bachelor's degree working in a large Japanese firm (*Chingin Tokei Soran 1990*).

Besides the base salary and bonus, a wide number of benefits are offered to Japanese managers working in large firms. Given the high cost of housing in Japan, probably the most significant benefit offered to managers (as well as to other employees) working in large corporations is subsidized housing. This usually consists of an apartment in a large apartment complex owned and managed by the firm. There are no moving-in fees such as are typical in the Japanese rental market, which often equal five times the monthly rent and are largely nonrefundable. In addition, the rent itself is highly subsidized, often equal to as little as one-sixth of the open market price for equivalent housing.

In addition to housing, managers receive a very comprehensive medical insurance package. Japan has a national health insurance program not unlike those of the United Kingdom and Canada which covers a large portion of both medical and dental costs. In recent years, because of the fiscal deficits of the central government, the portion paid by individuals has been raised to about 30 percent. Individuals can, of course, choose to see a private physician or dentist, but in that case all costs are borne by the employee.

Another way in which large Japanese firms deliver medical care to their employees, including managers, is to set up their own medical insurance unit that substitutes for the national health insurance system. The firms are usually able to negotiate better rates with providers owing to the better health of the

Table 12.3
Average Monthly Base Salaries in Japan, 1988, in Companies with More Than Ten Employees: Males with College Degrees

Age	Manufac-turing	Wholesale, Retail, and Food?	Finance and insurance	Services
18-19	132.5	131.0	133.2	127.1
20-24	152.7	154.3	169.2	150.7
25-29	190.5	199.6	227.4	186.6
30-34	237.7	247.4	320.2	235.5
35-39	280.4	307.2	381.5	283.2
40-44	338.3	364.3	459.5	346.8
45-49	386.9	409.0	522.2	422.6
50-54	425.6	436.4	543.8	452.1
55-59	385.8	466.3	424.3	417.8

Source: *Chingin Tokei Soran 1990* [An Overview of Wage Statistics, 1990], p. 120. Sogo Rodo Kenkyujo, 1989: Tokyo. Permission granted by Policy Planning and Research Department, Minister's Secretariat, Ministry of Labour.

average employee in their firm relative to the general population. For the employee, the cost of treatment is reduced to 10 percent from 30 percent of the total; yet he is able to choose among the same doctors as are available to those on the national health insurance system. In addition, many of these firms set up their own medical facilities, including both on-site clinics and full-fledged hospitals, which are used by the employees of the firm or the group of firms (*keiretsu*) to which it belongs. An employee who is feeling ill first sees one of the physicians at the on-site clinic before consulting with a noncompany doctor.

A manager enjoys a number of other indirect benefits. One of these benefits is company coverage of his travel expenses to and from the office. In most of the large cities, a manager typically commutes to work via the train and/or subway. The firm pays for the monthly passes. In addition, a clerk in the section will be responsible for obtaining the passes. Cafeterias are provided at the workplace, with meals costing about half what would be charged in a local restaurant. Vacations, when they are actually taken, can be spent at company resorts where the costs are heavily subsidized. A manager and his family can spend a few days at a first-class resort owned by his company and pay only around 10 to 20 percent of the real cost. In addition, the company often has negotiated discounts for its employees at hotels and resorts it does not own itself. Members of the management class do not receive any preference in the reservation process, however.

The desire to own a home is strong among the Japanese, and most employees who have reached the management level are ready to buy a house if they have not done so already. Typically, the company offers low-interest mortgage loans to all its employees, including managers, which in a country with such high housing costs can be a significant benefit. Once a manager has bought a home, he does not sell it even if he is transferred to another city because of the significant transaction costs that are involved. As a consequence, companies very often will take over the management of the houses of the employees it has transferred, usually renting them at very reduced rates to other employees in the firm. Very often, however, a manager who is transferred will leave his family behind in the house, particularly if his children are attending good schools in the area, in order to avoid disrupting their studies. Thus, Japan's very competitive educational system has reinforced the phenomenon of the *tanshin funin*, or unaccompanied transferee.

A final aspect of managerial compensation is his expense allowance. As mentioned previously, a Japanese manager spends a great deal of his time learning about his employees through social activities after work. In addition, he is often involved in entertaining customers and other significant business relations. Particularly if the manager is in sales or is in the construction industry or an industry with close ties to the government, the after-hours entertainment bill can be significant. Because of the small size of Japanese houses and apartments, this entertainment always takes place in a restaurant or bar and can become a significant expense for the manager.

Moreover, given the *amae* relationship between boss and employee, the manager is also very involved in all important life events of his employees, such as marriages and funerals. In Japan it is customary to give a monetary gift on such occasions, and the higher one's status the more one is expected to give. All these expenses become very heavy for a manager, the weight increasing with each additional rung up the corporate ladder he climbs. Consequently, the company often grants him a management allowance above and beyond salary and bonus which can be used for taking subordinates out drinking or for paying for the gifts for funerals and weddings. The manager is given an expense account to cover the costs of entertaining business clients.

The overall picture of the compensation package afforded to a manager in a large Japanese corporation is one of all-encompassing care for the employee and his family, combined with an egalitarian approach to the allocation of rewards. Particularly with regard to the nonsalary components of the compensation package, there is very little difference between managerial and nonmanagerial employees. It is only in the top positions, such as assistant plant manager or vice-president, that a manager no longer commutes by train and is awarded a company car and chauffeur, or that he eats in a special dining hall. In fact, if a manager is working at a production site, he is expected to change from his business suit into the same style of uniform as is utilized by all male employees within the plant, from the youngest blue-collar worker to the plant manager. Diversions from the egalitarian reward system, such as being driven to work, are usually made in order to alleviate the time and pressure demands on the manager, and thus are more a reflection of the higher value of their time rather than a reward.

A manager is rewarded in other ways beyond the compensation package. These rewards have to do with the nature of the job itself. Probably the most important reward that a Japanese manager receives as part of his job is the status of having made the rank of manager. Because hierarchy is such an important part of Japanese culture, one's place in the hierarchy relative to others is a central focus for Japanese employees. A great deal of the individual's personal identity is derived from his sense of place in the hierarchy. Thus, bestowing the title of manager on an employee is a great reward in and of itself.

Managers also acquire greater autonomy as they move up the ladder, particularly with regard to how they carry out their jobs. General performance goals for the section or department are worked out in consultation with superiors, but leeway is given on how to actually achieve those goals. This is not to say that decisions, particularly important ones, are made without consulting those above. But particularly in the day-to-day operation of the section or department, the manager is at much greater liberty to determine what he does than he has been previously. This sense of empowerment could be considered one of the nonfinancial aspects of his compensation package.

Managerial Performance Appraisal

The performance appraisal of white-collar employees in Japan has been called implicit as opposed to explicit, as in the United States, and systematic versus haphazard, again as in the United States (Pucik, 1988). The performance appraisal system in large Japanese companies is regarded as a key source of information about an employee's abilities, knowledge, and potential. Since the company will be "hiring" almost exclusively from within the firm, it has an opportunity as well as a need to know as much about each "candidate" as possible. The personnel department makes sure that the performance appraisal is actually performed and the results sent to it, for it is the personnel department that makes the determination of which position an employee will be given next. Performance appraisals are carried out at least two to three times a year (JETRO, 1983; Pucik, 1984). The forms and procedures used by managers are largely standardized. The personnel department becomes the repository of this information. In this sense the system is highly systematized.

At the same time, the system is usually implicit rather than explicit. For example, employees do not receive direct feedback. As Pucik states, "[I]n the Japanese cultural context, it is preferable to avoid one-on-one confrontations where direct criticism may imply a loss of face and claims of credit create a suspicion of unhealthy individualism" (1988:493). This lack of direct knowledge about one's performance is true at all levels of the firm. Most employees gain a sense of the quality of their performance from the small differences in bonus or pay increase relative to their cohorts that they receive and of course, from the speed of promotion into the next rank.

A typical performance appraisal form is reproduced in Appendix A. This form would be used with employees just below the level of manager. In addition to providing the information on this form, a manager's superior also gathers information on the manager's performance with regard to firm goal achievement and earnings; on cooperation both off the job and with all departments of the firm; and on the categories of decisiveness and ability to lead teams. The manager being evaluated is required to write paragraph statements in response to questions on these areas, and his superior and a second superior then add their own evaluations before forwarding everything to the personnel department (JETRO, 1983). Ordinarily, the employee does not see the evaluations of his performance his superiors write.

The personnel department uses the information in the evaluation report as a basis for determining both the employee's career development and pay and bonus. As stated previously, the actual impact on salary and bonus tends to be small, particularly at levels below manager, but it is not very significant even at the higher levels. The information also influences decisions concerning who to place on the elite track, skill and training requirements, and other career development concerns. The results of the performance appraisal thus weigh very heavily in determining an employee's career within a firm.

One purpose that is not met by the performance appraisal process is the avoidance of lawsuits over unlawful dismissal or blocked promotions. Such cases have become commonplace in the United States but are rare in Japan. As a consequence, the performance appraisal system can remain opaque to the employee since such opaqueness is not likely to be used as a basis for suing the firm. Although the implicit nature of the system surprises many American managers because of the emphasis American culture places on clarity in communication, the lack of direct feedback does not apparently bother the majority of Japanese employees. At the same time, it must be remembered that a great deal of indirect feedback is given to employees, including managers, during informal encounters with their superiors, particularly over drinks at the end of the day. Thus, while the mechanism for providing feedback may be very different from that used in the West and full of haphazardness and opaqueness, this may be preferable to many Japanese employees, for it saves face.

Labor Relations

The involvement of Japanese managers in unions and unionization, though complex, can be characterized as positive rather than antagonistic. One reason for this positive relationship has to do with the involvement of young employees who join Japanese firms in union activities, and another is the enterprise-style unions that dominate large Japanese firms. The second reason will be examined first.

Japanese industry is dominated by what is called enterprise unions, that is, by unions that are organized at each firm rather than industrywide. This system of enterprise unions is an outgrowth of the industrial relations system of the war period, during which unions were suspended and supplanted by enterprise community sharing as a means of keeping wage costs down (Taira, 1970:188). The enterprise union "commonly includes all plants in a company even though they may have different production lines or fall into different industries."

When a recruit joins a large Japanese firm, he is expected to become a member of the union. Until he reaches the level of manager, he is considered a nonexempt employee and consequently eligible to join the union. The experience helps these future managers become familiar with the concerns of the nonexempt employees and with the main leaders of the union. It also helps to increase the level of cooperation between union and company. White-collar employees often hold leadership positions in the union. However, the participation of both white-collar and blue-collar workers in the same union can lead to internal union conflicts, for the white-collar workers are not entirely sure whom they represent (Cole, 1971).

Because of the firm-level organizational structure of Japanese unions and the combined participation of white- and blue-collar workers, there is a much greater identification of the union with the firm than with an industrywide body of workers. Moreover, a great deal of information is shared between the firm and the union. The purpose of this information sharing is to persuade the other of the reasonableness of its demands with regard to wage increases, the major issue that is debated each year since employment security is guaranteed for the permanent staff. At the time the average pay hike is determined for the year, each side tries to persuade the other of the firm's "ability to pay" (Aoki, 1987; Taira, 1970). The outcome of these close relationships between firm and union is a relatively positive attitude on the part of most managers with regard to the union, although, of course, some variation exists across firms and industries (Shirai, 1983).

Managers do not tend to become involved in grievance procedures with the unions for the simple reason that few unions have formalized grievance procedures, and members tend to avoid filing grievances or even bringing grievances to the attention of their supervisors (Cole, 1971:231). Thus, the lack of a confrontational relationship between managers and workers, and the traditional submission of the Japanese worker to the authority of management, results in a lack of involvement of Japanese managers in conflicts with the union.

The extent to which Japanese managers have to deal with unions is decreasing due to a drop in the number of union members. As can be seen in Figure 12.2, the percentage of workers unionized in Japan has dropped to 27.6 percent, a decrease from the 55 percent rate of the late 1940s. This decrease is partly a reflection of the move out of secondary industries to tertiary industries, which are traditionally nonunionized (*Japan Economic Almanac*, 1989). In addition, the tight labor market in Japan of the late 1980s and early 1990s indicates that labor will be able to command increasingly better wages and conditions without the intervention of a union representative, although recent shocks in the Tokyo stock market have resulted in lower than expected wage increases (*Japan Economic Index Report B*, April 13, 1990).

In the 1990s, one issue that will figure more prominently in the Japanese manager's dealings in union negotiations is an increased demand for free time. Whereas wage increases have been the main issue on the bargaining table in the past, recent changes in Japanese values, along with the attainment of nominal wages that are now among the world's highest, have led to a desire for a decrease in the number of hours worked (*Japan Economic Almanac*, 1988:47). The chal-

Figure 12.2
Percent of Labor Force Unionized, 1970–87

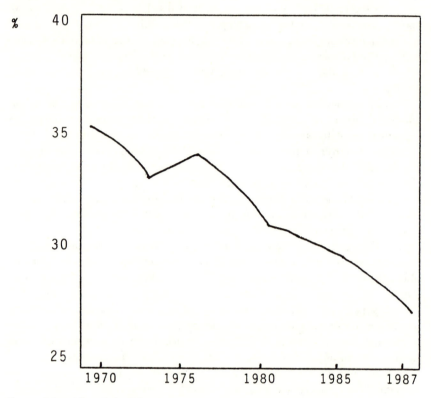

Source: Adapted from Labor White Paper, 1989, p. 89. Ministry of Labor, Tokyo.

lenge to the manager of the future will be how to maintain productivity while lowering the average work load from its present 2,111 hours per year to 1,800 as proposed in what is called the New Maekawa Report (*Japan Economic Almanac*, 1989:46). It may be that, rather than a national average wage increase set by the negotiations of the most important enterprise unions with their firms, as has been done in the past, the lead unions will now set the norm with regard to average decreases in the number of hours worked.

CONCLUSIONS

Japan is rapidly evolving economically, socially, and politically. Changes are occurring that portend significant modifications in the role, power, and prestige of Japan's managers in the future. These changes include the restructuring of the economy, changes in the labor force, and globalization of firms.

The first significant change taking place in Japan is the restructuring of the economy away from manufacturing into the service sector. According to a recent Ministry of Labor study, the ratio of workers in tertiary industries will increase from 56.9 percent in 1985 to 61.8 percent by 1995 (*Japan Economic Almanac*, 1989). In part, the lower employment in the secondary sector can be attributed to increasing automation, as evidenced by the record investment of Japanese firms in plant and equipment in 1989 (*JEI Report*, No. 44B, 1989). This shift toward a service economy has significant implications for the type of manager required in the future. Whereas the manager in a manufacturing firm is in charge of a group of permanent employees who work full time and are stable, the manager in the service sector is more apt to be dealing with part-time and temporary workers. The skills required for many jobs in the service industries, such as cashier or salesperson, will be less firm-specific and require less investment in training. More Japanese managers in the future may be managing groups of employees that include a preponderance of people who are not considered permanent. The manager's role thus shifts from one of counselor and developer of subordinates to a more controlling and directive model. More emphasis on the present performance of employees and less on building group consensus on decisions could be other results. In this sense, more midlevel Japanese managers in the future may resemble their American counterparts.

A second major change is occurring in the composition of the workforce itself. Japanese workers are aging, are in short supply, and are composed of more women and of young people with a new value system. The Japanese government has pressured large firms to retain employees past the previous retirement age of fifty-five as one way of decreasing the burden on the social welfare system. This will create at least two challenges for the midlevel manager of tomorrow. The first is to deal with the increasingly likely situation of managing work groups in which more than a few employees are older than the manager himself, for it will not be possible to provide upper level positions for this large group of older employees owing to slower economic growth. This will require skills to balance the need for directing older workers with the need to respect age. Second, managers will be dealing with the challenges of older workers such as obsolete skills and longer learning curves. In addition to requiring new skills, this also means a decrease in the need for the counselor and confidant role that played such an important part in the past.

In addition, workers are in short supply in Japan, as evidenced by a recent Ministry of Labor report. This may create a shift in the balance of power between managers and their subordinates. Whereas in the past managers could assume that workers, both blue- and white-collar, would remain with the firm at least in part owing to the difficulty of obtaining a position in another firm, in the future such an assumption may not be as correct. The increasing opportunity for employment has led young recruits to renege on acceptance of offers of employment, and is leading to increasing mobility between firms. The nearly 2,000 foreign firms in Japan also offer ample opportunity for a dissatisfied worker to jump ship. The consequence of this seller's market is that a manager may be forced to be more careful of the ways in which he interacts with his subordinates, and to incorporate the subordinate's wishes concerning job content and job rotation into personnel decisions. Beyond the traditional need to build good relationships as a way of building communication networks within the firm, the future Japanese manager will be concerned with creating a good relationship as a way of retaining the employee.

A third important change in the workforce is the increasing number of women in the workplace, particularly in nonclerical positions. With the tight labor market, and in response to the passage of an equal employment bill in 1985, Japanese employers are becoming more receptive to the idea of hiring women in both the administrative and technical tracks, particularly in areas of critical shortage such as engineering and R&D (Taylor, 1989). This change has several important effects on the way Japanese managers will carry out their jobs. First, they will need to become adept at managing work groups that have diversity, since in addition to women more and more foreigners are working in Japanese firms. They themselves will need to learn new attitudes toward women in particular and to instill these attitudes in their male colleagues. More demands will be placed on managers to accommodate family commitments by both the women employees and the spouses who are required to help out more at home than in the past. Whereas earlier a Japanese manager could assume a certain uniformity of behavior, needs, and wishes among his subordinates, the manager of the future will be faced with a greater need to accommodate his role to different types of employees and to expand his role to help build groups composed of different types of people.

A fourth and final aspect of the workforce that is changing is the shifting values of the younger generation, the so-called *shinjinrui*. The generation now entering the workforce was born into an era of economic prosperity in Japan, and they do not share the anxiety concerning the future and the commitment to work that characterizes the older generation. They are more interested in enjoying their lives now rather than waiting for future rewards, and they are not as willing to sacrifice either time or money for the greater good of their firms. This attitude may lead to a need for a different approach to leadership, more of a charismatic style than a counselor style, as the way to inspire effort (Dore, 1987).

Moreover, the *shinjinrui* may be more willing to question the authority of the manager than in the past. As management promotion slowly becomes more dependent on performance than seniority, career paths become less rigid and the possibility of bypassing one's boss opens up. Thus, the entire relationship of a manager with his subordinate is likely to be affected by the value shift represented by the *shinjinrui*.

The globalization of Japanese firms will also significantly influence the role of the Japanese manager of the future. In the United States the number of Americans working for Japanese firms will continue to climb, while the historic changes in Europe are leading to increasing investment there as well. Moreover, Japanese firms are following the general trend toward globalization experienced in all major firms today. What this means is an ever increasing number of Japanese managers working overseas, managing foreign employees.

The challenge of these assignments will force midlevel managers to learn new managing skills and to adjust to new attitudes concerning work and to different organizational behavior. When these managers return to Japan, they will form an ever growing body of employees who have adapted successfully abroad, and they will have alternative ways of managing people with regard to such things as leadership and motivation. They will probably draw on these skills and knowledge in managing their Japanese employees, which will in turn lead to new expectations for those managers who have not been abroad. For example, some managers who have spent a considerable time abroad are more adept at giving subordinates direct feedback and do so when they return to working within Japan (Taylor, 1989). Employees who grow accustomed to such feedback will begin to demand the same treatment from other managers. In this way internationalization could lead to changes in the role of Japanese managers.

With regard to the power, status, and ideology of Japanese middle managers, probably the most important change that is occurring is the shift away from the vision of the role of management that gained currency in the mid–1950s, which has infused so much of Japanese management practice since then. In the immediate postwar period, the desire to defuse the increasing radicalness of the union movement and to form a management philosophy that was radically different from that prevailing before the war led to a drafting of ideology by the influential Doyukai group (Yoshino, 1968). While the statement was not accepted completely by either the Doyukai or the business community in general, it served as an important model that has informed Japanese management since. The text of this statement is reproduced in Appendix B. The most important element within it is the setting out of an equal partnership between shareholders, managers, and laborers. Whether or not such a total equality was truly implemented is irrelevant.

What is crucial is that the welfare and interests of the employees have been major concerns of Japanese managers since World War II. Yet, because of the changes in the workforce and industrial structure, this outlook will likely be eroded. As the group of employees becomes more fluid and diverse, and loyalty to one firm decreases, the social contract with employees will change. This will place the employment relationship on a more contractual basis, which in turn informs the role of a manager. For example, the incorporation of the social value of groupism into the way managers structure their work relationships may decrease. As the commitment of both managers and employees to the ideal of sharing ownership of the firm erodes, managers will no longer be able to use the sense of group commitment to motivate employees. Nor will they be able to invest in the training or career development of employees with the assurance of retaining workers. Managers may need to learn how to improve worker productivity through more immediate motivational tools. Concurrently, the manager himself may see his career as spanning more than one firm, and as a consequence may demand greater clarity in the performance appraisal process and reward for present performance as well as clearer definition of his responsibilities and authority.

Since the manager will be carrying his skills and knowledge to another firm, he will need to be able to clearly define what his personal achievements and skills are as a way of selling these in the labor market. Other changes in the managerial role are likely from this shift in the social contract regarding the employment relationship, from greater professionalization and specialization to a decrease in the *amae* relationship. The shifts will be gradual, however, and it is unlikely they will move so far away from basic cultural values as to follow the model of U.S. management.

The power and prestige of the manager in Japan has always been great (Yoshino, 1968). Neither will likely change materially in the next decade. In fact, as careers in such bureaucracies as MITI and the Ministry of Finance become less attractive owing to the lower salaries and loss of dominance of these agencies in the economy, the business career may gain even more allure. In particular, if the Japanese economy continues its strong position in the world and Japanese firms retain their top positions in such industries as banking, semiconductors, and automobiles, the power and prestige of Japanese managers within society will remain as strong as it has been in the past.

Appendix A
Typical Performance Appraisal Form for Managers

PERFORMANCE OF WORK

Quality: Is output accurate? Is presentation satisfactory?
Volume: Is output efficient and punctual?
Originality: Makes practical improvements?
Leadership: Has the ability to lead other employees?
Comments:

WORK ATTITUDES

Obedience: Follows rules?
Cooperation: Makes suggestions? Works toward self-improvement?
Responsibility: Reliable?
Comments:

ABILITY

Basic ability: Is depth and breadth of general knowledge sufficient?
Is specific knowledge satisfactory?
Performs job with skill?
Has stamina to perform job?

Conceptual ability: Understands directions and working environment?
Has innovative ideas? Applies new methods?
Are verbal skills adequate?
Avoids mistakes?

PERFORMANCE

Goal achievement: achieved 50% above goal
         "   20% above goal
         "   goal
         "   less than goal
         "   20% under goal or less

Appendix A (Continued)

> Effectiveness of instruction to subordinates: strong positive results
> observable results
> no results

WORK ATTITUDES

Preparation: Is organization good? Has motivation?

ABILITY

Conceptual ability: Handles company's plan-do-see system?
Coordinates with people outside firm?
Makes frequent and sophisticated presentations to superiors?
Has the ability to train and lead?

Source: Adapted from *Japanese Corporate Personnel Management*, JETRO Business Information Series 10 (Tokyo: JETRO, 1983)

Appendix B
Excerpt from "The Social Responsibilities of Business Leadership," Resolution of The *Doyukai*, 1956

PREAMBLE

The function of management in a modern corporation goes far beyond that of a search for profit. From the moral as well as practical point of view, it is vital that modern corporate managers strive to supply products of highest quality at the lowest possible prices through the most effective utilization of productive resources consistent with the welfare of the whole economy and the society at large. It is indeed the social responsibility of modern executives to serve as an effective instrument to develop a managerial system capable of accomplishing this mission.

KEY POINTS

1. It is acknowledged that a modern corporation was a public instrument. Management was entrusted with the stewardship of the enterprise, not only by the shareholders but by other participants as well—employees, suppliers, customers, and the public; an important responsibility of management, therefore, was to bring about a harmony of interests among the various key participating groups.

2. It emphasized the social responsibilities of modern corporate managers. In a highly complex industrial economy such as Japan's, the overall welfare of the national economic system could no longer be assured merely through the proper functioning of individual firms. It could be achieved only through the concerted, deliberate efforts of the congregate of socially responsible managers of the corporate community. Unless management were willing to fulfill its social responsibilities (as expressed in the above-mentioned preamble), it would face increasing encroachments on its independence and managerial prerogatives by the government. Indeed, the welfare of the whole economy depended, to a large measure, on the effectiveness with which management could fulfill this responsibility.

3. It called for the removal of social and economic imbalances and injustices; specifically, it called for the removal of the evils of monopoly and ills of duality in the economic structure.

Source: Adapted from M. Y. Yoshino, *Japan's Managerial System* (Cambridge, Mass.: MIT Press, 1968).

REFERENCES

Abegglen, J. 1958. *The Japanese Factory: Aspects of Its Social Organization*. Glencoe, Ill.: Free Press.

Adams, R. J., Peterson, R. B., and Schwind, H. F. 1988. "Personal Value Systems of Japanese Trainees and Managers in a Changing Competitive System." *Asia Pacific Journal of Management* 5(3):169–179.

Aoki, M. 1987. "The Japanese Firm in Transition." In K. Yamamura and Y. Yasuba, eds., *The Political Economy of Japan. Volume I*. Stanford, Calif.: Stanford University Press, pp. 263–288.

Asian Productivity Organization. 1984. *Japanese Management: A Forward-looking Analysis*. Tokyo: Asian Productivity Organization.

Billesbach, T. J., and Rives, J. M. 1985 (Autumn). "Lifetime Employment: Future Prospects for Japan and the U.S." *SAM Advanced Management Journal*: 26–46.

Chingin Tokei Soran 1990. [An Overview of Wage Statistics, 1990]. 1989. Tokyo: Sogo Rodo Kenkyujo.

Clark, R. 1979. *The Japanese Company*. New Haven, Conn: Yale University Press.

Cole, R. 1971. *Japanese Blue Collar*. Berkeley, Calif.: University of California Press.

Doi, T. 1973. *The Anatomy of Dependence*. Tokyo: Kodansha.

Doktor, R. 1983 (September). "Culture and the Management of Time: A Comparison of Japanese and American Top Management Practice." *Asia Pacific Journal of Management*: 65–71.

Dore, R. 1986. *Flexible Rigidities*. Stanford, Calif.: Stanford University Press, 1986.

———. 1987. *Taking Japan Seriously*. Stanford, Calif.: Stanford University Press.

Duke, B. 1986. *The Japanese School*. Westport, Conn.: Praeger.

England, G. W., and Lee, R. 1971 (December). "Organizational Goals and Expected Behavior among American, Japanese and Korean Managers—A Comparative Study." *Academy of Management Journal* 425–434.

England, G., and Misumi, J. 1986. "Work Centrality in Japan and the United States." *Journal of Cross-cultural Psychology* 17(4): 399–416.

Focus Japan. 1990. "Welcome to the Working World." 17(3):1–2.

Haire, M., Ghiselli, E., and Porter, L. 1966. *Managerial Thinking: An International Study*. New York: John Wiley and Sons.

"Honda Gets New Driver for the '90s." 1990 (May 11). *Wall Street Journal*.

"Japan Cuts the Middle-Management Fat." 1989 (August 8). *Wall Street Journal*.

Japan Economic Almanac. 1989. Tokyo: Japan Economic Journal.

"Japanese Try Out Job Hopping." 1989 (February 24). *The Christian Science Monitor*, p. 9.

JEI Report, No. 13A. 1990. "U.S.-Japan Competition in Supercomputers."

JEI Report, No. 15B. 1990. "Preliminary Shunto Results Suggest Continued Economic Growth."

JEI Report, No. 18A. 1989. "Women in Japan's Labor Force."

JEI Report, No. 44B. 1989. "Japanese Investment Surge Worries Washington."

JETRO. 1983. "Japanese Corporate Personnel Management." JETRO Business Information Series. Tokyo: JETRO.

Karsh, B. 1984 (June). "Human Resources Management in Japanese Large-Scale Industry." *Journal of Industrial Relations*: 116–245.

Koike, K. 1988. *Understanding Industrial Relations in Modern Japan*. New York: St. Martin's Press.

Lee, S. M., and Schwendiman, G. 1982. *Japanese Management: Cultural and Environmental Considerations*. Westport, Conn.: Praeger.

Lincoln, J. R. 1989 (Fall). "Employee Work Attitudes and Management Practices in the U.S. and Japan: Evidence from a Large Comparative Survey." *California Management Review*: 89–106.

Logan, G. M. 1984. "Loyalty and a Sense of Purpose." *California Management Review* 27(1):149–156.

Lynn, L. H., Piehler, H. R., and Zahray, W. P. 1989. "Engineering Graduates in the United States and Japan: A Comparison of Their Numbers, and an Empirical Study of Their Careers and Methods of Information Transfer." Report of the Department of Engineering and Public Policy, Carnegie Mellon University, Pittsburgh, Pa.

Mannari, H. 1974. *The Japanese Business Leaders*. Tokyo: University of Tokyo Press.

McCraw, T. 1986. "From Partners to Competitors: An Overview of the Period Since World War II." In T. K. McCraw, ed., *America Versus Japan*. Boston: Harvard University Press, pp. 1–34.

McMillan, C. J. 1989. *The Japanese Industrial System*. Berlin and New York: Walter de Gruyter.

Mendenhall, M. n.d. "The Cognitive, Psychological and Social Contexts of Japanese Management: A Review and Critique." Loyola Marymount University.

Nakane, C. 1970. *Japanese Society*. Berkeley: University of California Press, 1970.

Peterson, R. B, and Sullivan, J. 1988. "The Japanese Lifetime Employment System: Whither It Goest?" University of Washington, working paper.

Pucik, V. 1984. "White-Collar Human Resource Management in Large Japanese Manufacturing Firms." *Human Resource Management 23* (3):257–276.

———. 1988. "Strategic Alliances with the Japanese: Implications for Human Resource Management." In F. J. Contractor and P. Lorange, eds., *Cooperative Strategies in International Business*. Lexington, Mass.: D.C. Heath & Co.

Pucik, V., and Hatvany, N. 1983. "Management Practices in Japan and Their Impact on Business Strategy." *Advances in Strategic Management. Volume 1*. Greenwich, Conn.: JAI Press, pp. 103–131.

Reischauer, E. 1977. *The Japanese*. Cambridge, Mass.: Belknap Press.

Rohlen, T. 1975. "The Company Work Group." In E. Vogel, ed., *Modern Japanese Organization and Decision-making*. Berkeley, Calif.: University of California Press, 1975.

Seror, A. C. n.d. "Organizational Control: A Comparative Empirical Analysis of Japanese and American Managerial Strategies." Vanderbilt University.

Shirai, T., ed., 1983. *Contemporary Industrial Relations in Japan*. Madison: University of Wisconsin Press.

———. 1983. "A Theory of Enterprise Unionism." In T. Shirai, ed., *Contemporary Industrial Relations in Japan*. Madison: University of Wisconsin Press.

Sullivan, J. and Taylor, S. 1991. "A Cross-Cultural Test of Compliance-Gaining Theory." *Management Communication Quarterly*.

Suzuki, N. 1981 (Summer). "Spin-Out Employees in Japanese Business Society: Their Problems and Prospects." *California Management Review*: 23–30.

Taira, K. 1970. *Economic Development and the Labor Market in Japan*. New York: Columbia University Press.

Tanaka, H. 1980 (February). "The Japanese Method of Preparing Today's Graduate to Become Tomorrow's Manager." *Personnel Journal*: 109–112.

Taylor, M. S. 1989. "A Transaction Costs Analysis of Japanese Employment Relationships." Unpublished Ph.D. diss., University of Washington.

Trevor, M., Schendel, J., and Wilpert, B. 1986. *The Japanese Management Development System: Generalists and Specialists in Japanese Companies Abroad*. London: Frances Pinter.

Wakabayashi, M. and Graen, G. n.d. "Japanese Management Development in Leading Corporations: Reactions of Line Managers." University of Cincinnati.

Wakabayashi, M., Graen, G., Graen, M. and Graen, M. 1988. "Japanese Management Progress: Mobility into Middle Management." *Journal of Applied Psychology* 73(2): 217–227.

Westney, D.E., and Sakakibara, K. 1988. "The Role of Japan-Based R&D in Global Technology Strategy." In M. Tushman and W. Moore, eds., *Readings in the Management of Innovation*. Cambridge, Mass.: Ballinger Publishing Co.

Yang, C. Y. 1984 (November-December). "Demystifying Japanese Management Practices." *Harvard Business Review*: 171–182.

Yonekura, S. 1988. "Recognizing Potential Innovations: Armco vs. Kawasaki." Working Paper, Hitotsubashi University, Tokyo, Institute of Business Research.

Yoshino, M. Y. 1968. *Japan's Managerial System*. Cambridge, Mass.: MIT Press.

Zimmerman, M. 1985. *How to Do Business with the Japanese*. Tokyo: Charles Tuttle and Co.

13

SOUTH KOREA

Christopher B. Meek and Young-Hack Song

This chapter describes private sector managerial human resource practices in the Republic of Korea (ROK), with a special focus on the member firms of Korea's Chaebol or conglomerate groups. The Chinese ideographic characters used to represent the word "Chaebol" are the same as those used for Japan's pre-World War II conglomerates, the Zaibatsu, which the Chaebol closely resemble in terms of structure and ownership (Hattori, 1989:79–95).

This examination of human resource managers focuses on the policies and practices applied to newly recruited white-collar administrative employees or technical engineering and scientific staff upon completion of their studies at a Korean university or a four-year college. We selected this group first because major corporations have highly systematic human resource management procedures that are very similar across most firms. Second, Korea's 200 largest corporations are responsible for nearly all of the nation's gross national product (GNP), with the revenues of the top ten equal to approximately 70 percent of Korea's GNP and the fifty largest Chaebol contributing 92.6 percent (Amsden, 1989:116; Hamilton and Orru, 1989:43). Finally, although high school graduates are still recruited for entry-level management jobs, this practice is quickly disappearing.

Our analysis is based on a review of previous research as well as primary data from our own ethnograpic study of three Korean firms and a descriptive study of human resource management at eight member companies of Korea's twenty largest Chaebol. The ethnographic study was conducted between 1987 and 1990, and it included a 4,000-person textile firm (KB), an 800-employee mechanical pencil and ceramic ball point pen manufacturer (KM), and a 300-employee wood furniture manufacturer (KF). The eight-company study (K1-K8) was conducted during the spring and summer of 1989.

KOREAN ECONOMIC DEVELOPMENT

The Republic of Korea has become the object of growing international interest because of its swift rise to world industrial prominence. Table 13.1 illustrates precisely how dramatic Korean economic growth has been: the ROK was transformed from an impoverished Third World nation with a per capita income of only US$87 in 1962 to US$4,968 by 1989.

Korean economic growth has been fueled by export development, which rose from 20.6 percent of GNP in 1972 to 45 percent by 1988. More importantly, the composition of Korean exports has changed dramatically from agricultural and simple labor-intensive goods to increasingly more sophisticated value-added products, including steel, petrochemicals, automobiles, consumer electronics, computers, and large shipping vessels (Joo, 1991; Korea Chamber of Commerce and Industry, 1989:3 and 1990:10). This tremendous growth in the volume and increasing sophistication of exports has been made possible by a highly educated workforce that has worked for relatively low wages while maintaining some of the longest working hours in the industrialized world.

The size of Korea's labor force and the quality of jobs available have also changed dramatically. In 1962 the entire national workforce amounted to only 6,615,000 persons, but by 1989 this number had grown by 265 percent to 17,516,000 (Korean National Economic Planning Board, 1963:240–241; 1989: 63). The occupational composition of the workforce also changed dramatically. Professional and technical people represented a mere 2.7 percent of the workforce in 1962 and production workers only 9.1 percent. By 1989 these figures had grown to 6.9 percent and 30 percent, respectively. During this period, the managerial class also grew by 504 percent from only 49,000 managers (0.7 percent of the workforce) in 1962 to 247,000 (1.4 percent) in 1989 (Korean National Economic Planning Board, 1963:240–241; Ministry of Labor, 1990:63).

Korea's world trade success has not been simply the result of entrepreneurial talent and the contribution of high quality but of low-cost labor as well. Indeed, Korea is often referred to as a command capitalist economy. Korean economic development has been planned, directed, and controlled by aggressive government intervention and financed by government-controlled banks.

THE EVOLUTION OF KOREA'S MANAGERIAL CLASS

Management and administration have had a long and honorable history in Korea, but business activity has not. These differential attitudes stem from 3,000 years of Chinese and particularly Confucian influence.

Chinese Confucian philosophy and government practices were first systematically introduced to the Korean peninsula between the third and fourth centuries A.D. when the Three Kingdoms of Paekche, Koguryo, and Silla adopted modified systems of Chinese bureaucratic and dynastic rule complete with Confucian educational academies and degrees. These early systems were riddled with inconsistencies and possessed more of the form than the substance of Confucian

Table 13.1
Economic and Population Growth: Republic of Korea, 1962–89

Year	Population (1,000's)	Growth Rate	GNP (U.S.$ Billion)	Growth Rate (in Real %)	Per Capita GNP - U.S.$
1962	26,513	2.90	2.3	2.2	87
1963	27,262	2.82	2.7	9.1	100
1964	27,984	2.65	2.9	9.6	103
1965	28,705	2.57	3.0	5.8	105
1966	29,436	2.55	3.7	12.7	125
1967	30,131	2.36	4.3	6.6	142
1968	30,838	2.35	5.2	11.3	169
1969	31,554	2.29	6.6	13.8	210
1970	32,241	2.21	7.8	7.6	243
1971	32,883	1.99	9.2	9.4	278
1972	33,505	1.89	10.6	5.3	318
1973	34,103	1.78	13.4	14.0	395
1974	34,692	1.73	18.7	8.5	540
1975	35,281	1.70	20.8	6.9	590
1976	35,849	1.61	28.6	13.4	797
1977	36,412	1.57	36.6	10.7	1,008
1978	36,969	1.43	51.3	11.0	1,392
1979	37,534	1.53	61.4	7.0	1,640
1980	38,124	1.57	60.3	-4.8	1,589
1981	38,723	1.56	66.2	6.6	1,719
1982	39,326	1.53	69.3	5.4	1,773
1983	39,929	1.46	79.5	12.6	2,002
1984	40,523	1.34	87.0	9.3	2,158
1985	41,056	1.25	89.7	7.0	2,194
1986	41,569	1.24	102.7	12.9	2,503
1987	42,082	1.21	128.4	12.8	3,098
1988	42,082	1.21	169.2	12.2	4,004
1989	n/a	n/a	210.1	6.7	4,968

Sources: 1982, Economic Planning Board. 1988, Economic Planning Board, The Bank of Korea; and *Korean Chamber of Commerce and Industry Quarterly Review*, January, 1989, p. 5 and 6. *Business Korea*, September 1989, p. 84.

rule. The Confucian merit system was especially alien to the traditional Korean use of kinship relations and blood ties in defining leadership roles (Han, 1970:51).

After the institution of elementary, secondary, and upper level academies of Confucian learning, the Confucian ideal of a state administered by merit-selected scholar-officials led by a "Sage King" gradually gained acceptance. After the civil service examination system, based on the Confucian classics, was finally instituted in A.D. 958, sentiments developed over several hundred years favoring examination-based appointments over blood ties. With the emergence of Korea's last dynasty in 1392, this transformation was completed, and a new class of scholar-officials and military officers, called Yangban, became firmly entrenched as Korea's leaders for over 500 years. The Yangban also became Korea's principal landlords, and the Confucian feudal ideal became firmly implanted. In theory, the Yangban were best qualified to administer society because their rigorous studies of Confucian writings had enabled them to achieve the high level of moral rectitude necessary to govern societal affairs. In Confucian terms, a virtuous nature was a ruler's most important attribute.

One of the most critical moral qualities associated with the achievement of a virtuous nature was the absence of profit-seeking motives. Consequently, the Yangban were supposed to be benevolent and unconcerned with personal gain. The Yangban were placed at the very top of Korea's class structure, whereas merchants and businesspeople were considered to be near the very bottom because of their obsession with profit making. Yangban therefore became known as gentlemen or great men (*Kunja* in Korean) whereas merchants were referred to as small men (Nahm, 1988:101). This ideal was derived from the Confucian classic, *The Mencius*, and the *Analects* (Legge, 1970:125–127; Waley, 1989:105). To show their adherence to the antiprofit ideal, one Yangban adopted extreme ritualistic behavioral norms such as having the slaves conduct economic transactions and sign contracts for them in order to avoid such "vulgar" and "unethical" activities (Chun, 1980:6)

After more than 500 years of broad societal inculcation, these beliefs and behavior patterns became deeply ingrained at all levels of society. The actions of businessmen that emerged after Korean independence from Japan only served to increase distrust of profit-seeking behavior.

During the period immediately following the Korean War, a group of entrepreneurs became commercial and industrial tycoons by taking advantage of opportunities for profit making during reconstruction. Obtaining access to foreign aid flowing into the country became a central focus of their activities, and the best channel to these funds was through political contacts. The entrepreneurs took advantage of the politicians' need for political finances and the abundant corruption among high-ranking bureaucrats appointed by the regime of President Syngman Rhee. A variety of schemes were devised in which the ruling party, individual politicians, and corrupt bureaucrats received large payoffs in return for preferential granting of loans, foreign aid funds, and government reconstruction projects while simultaneously turning a blind eye to such nonproductive practices as speculation, price fixing, tax evasion, and taking advantage of cumulative inflation. Several firms, which later became some of Korea's largest Chaebol, reaped huge profits from these practices, including Samsung, Lucky, and Ssangyong (Kim, Kyong-Dong, 1985:73).

Such widespread corruption and use of exploitative business tactics resulted in tremendous resentment toward both the government and businessmen, and ultimately led to the downfall of the Rhee regime in 1960. Democratic elections followed, but the nation's economic and social woes eventually precipitated a successful coup d'etat in May 1961 creating the Park dictatorship. Although legal action was taken against some thirty entrepreneurs and their companies, they proved to be the only individuals and companies with the expertise required for undertaking the export-oriented development strategy of government planners. Thus, an unusual deal was cut in which some of the accused convinced the government to help them develop the new industries targeted in national long-range plans (Kim, Kyong-Dong, 1985:72).

The Park regime's initial plan for punishing the business elite actually led to helping them grow into massive industrial empires. However, the Chaebol had to change their image from that of greedy exploiters to sources of national pride and achievement. Corporate profits were plowed back into capital investment for new government-targeted industries, and entrepreneurs donated large sums of money and personal stockholdings to philanthropic foundations. Management philosophies and practices were also adopted which reflected the Confucian ideals of Korea's past.

CULTURAL ROOTS OF CORPORATE HUMAN RESOURCE MANAGEMENT

Korea has been deeply influenced by many religious and philosophical traditions, including Buddhism, Taoism, and the indigenous religion referred to as Shamanism. Even Christianity has roots dating back more than 300 years (Kim, 1963).

Confucianism, however, has been the dominant influence on modern Korean management systems because it directly addresses matters of bureaucratic administration in minute detail in the principal writings that Korea's ancient scholar-officials studied, as well as in a codified law called the Kyungguk-Taejon (Chun et al., 1980; Hahm, 1971:119). In fact, Korean traditional law was essentially a formal exposition of roles and rules for administering government and all other major social institutions from the relationship between the king and his ministers down to the regulation of the individual extended family. Similarly, it prescribed social sanctions for failing to fulfill the moral duties associated with this hierarchy of roles.

In Yi Dynasty Korea this overarching philosophy, together with its codified rules for social behavior, had an especially profound impact on all levels of society because they were introduced through the creation of a thoroughgoing system of national Confucian education. On the one hand, the only route to social prestige and economic security was through study and mastering neo-Confucian orthodoxy. On the other hand, failure to live up to these standards could result in severe group punishment. Entire extended families, villages, and even provinces were often harshly punished, even to the extent of death, for the crime of just one member (Hahm, 1971:63–64).

At the same time that neo-Confucian ideals and norms of social behavior were introduced through education and reinforced through law, Buddhism, which had become highly powerful under previous dynasties, was more harshly suppressed than in any other Asian country, and neo-Confucian orthodoxy and ideology were introduced as a substitute (Kim, 1963:189–190). Where classic Confucian doctrine had provided little spiritual underpinning for justifying its social rules and methods of government administration, much less challenging Buddhist doctrines, neo-Confucianism, particularly the neo-Confucian writings and commentaries of the great Chinese philosopher Chu Hsi (Chuja in Korean), provided a broad overarching metaphysical and ontological framework that tied social behavior and administration of the state to the overall structure and dynamic processes of the universe.

The Confucian virtues and relationships were now seen . . . as manifestations of the nature of the universe itself. To live by the Confucian social and political standards was to live in harmony with the cosmos and. . . . The changeless hierarchical society, governed by a bureaucracy with a monarch at the top, which Confucius envisioned as his ideal, thus came to be seen as ordained by the very nature of reality. (Han, 1970:194)

Thus, neo-Confucianism created a philosophical and religious perspective that ideologically linked the monarchy, government administration, rigid class relations, and family affairs to a mystical interpretation of the relationship between human affairs and the inner workings and physical manifestations of the universe. Today the depth and breadth to which this world-view and its attendant social norms penetrated Yi Dynasty society are broadly manifest in modern Korean social, political, and economic relations.

Inwha-Human Harmony
Historically, the dominant value in the Korean neo-Confucian world-view has been harmony, particularly harmony between human beings or *Inwha* in Korean. The centrality of *Inwha* in the business world is illustrated by Table 13.2, which presents an analysis of corporate management philosophies or mottos, known as *sahoon* in Korean, from eighty-nine of Korea's largest firms. Along with sincerity and diligence (*song* in Korean) clearly harmony is most frequently cited and highly ranked among the values and beliefs espoused in Korean company slogans. These *sahoon* or slogans are intended to evoke an effective response from employees frequently based on their resonance with Korean traditions.

The neo-Confucian concept of harmony was particularly well suited to Korea because its spiritual and metaphysical significance was derived from a world-view that was quite compatible with traditional shamanistic beliefs. From both the shamanistic and neo-Confucian perspectives, human and natural conditions are interdependent parts of a greater unitary cosmic whole called the Great Ultimate. Chu Hsi explained:

Fundamentally there is only one Great Ultimate. Yet each of the myriad of things has been endowed with it and each in itself possesses the Great Ultimate in its entirety. This

Table 13.2
Analysis of Company Sahoon: Percentage Distribution of Values and Principles
for Eighty-nine Major Korean Corporations

Value/Principle	Ranking					
	1	2	3	4	5	Total
Sincerity and Diligence	20	30	5	2	0	57
Harmony, Unity and Cooperation	33	11	7	0	2	53
Creativity and Development	9	15	16	0	0	41
Responsibility	6	8	16	0	0	29
Business Credibility	9	8	7	1	0	26
Service and Sacrifice	5	3	16	2	0	26
Pioneer Spirit	9	7	8	0	0	24
Social Responsibility	1	6	9	0	0	16
Productivity and Quality	2	7	1	0	0	10
Rational and Scientific Management	2	4	3	0	0	9
Employee Self Actualization	5	1	0	0	0	6
Welfare	0	0	3	0	0	3

Source: K.C.C.I. *Sashi/Sahoon Collections*, 1984.

is similar to the fact that there is one moon in the sky but when its light is scattered upon rivers and lakes, it can be seen everywhere. It cannot be said the moon has been split. (Chan, 1987:117)

In an agricultural kingdom such as ancient Korea, the state of the natural environment was of central concern, and it was believed that just as disharmony in nature, for example, storms, drought, and fires, could result in scarcity and misfortune for human and animal life, so also could social discord produce natural disaster. Therefore, the ideal condition was seen as one of harmony between human beings and between human society and the cosmos (Hahm, 1986:319.)

In modern-day Korea, where the proportion of the population engaged in agriculture has declined significantly, this viewpoint is obviously no longer reinforced by a continual sense of dependence on nature. Nonetheless, the preoccupation with harmony still remains, and in the case of the corporate world the international marketplace has become an extension of the natural environment.

Today, harmonious interpersonal relations are considered the fundamental requirement for survival in the marketplace. Similarly, conflict is believed to lead to internal weakness and therefore vulnerability to external competitive forces.

A Vertical Universe and Society

Harmony in the Korean neo-Confucian world-view exists between roles that are hierarchically related within a vertically structured universe. Hierarchy and inequality are the inherent nature of the universe, and at the top of the hierarchy is the cosmos itself or Great Ultimate. Traditionally acting as an intermediary between heaven and earth or between the human and spiritual worlds was the monarch. The king was expected to preserve a harmonious relationship between heaven and earth through his virtuous example as a filial son and as a benevolent sage ruler to the people. The Korean neo-Confucian philsopher Yi Yulgok (1536–84) explained:

> When a Sage King governs the people
> Heaven and Earth are in harmony,
> Bringing wind every five days
> And rain every ten days.
> Because of the ruler's virtue
> There is such a response. (Yi, 1971: 310)

In turn, a hierarchy of duties and relationships from the king's ministers down to individual family roles was recognized as the correct moral structure of society. Indeed, the existence of this hierarchy and observance of proper duties and relationships in this vertical structure were and are still considered to be the defining point that makes human society moral in nature. Known as the Five Relations (*Orhyun* in Korean), this moral structure was first recognized in the *Mencius* as the foundation of human society on which overall societal stability and harmony depend. "[B]etween father and son, there should be affection; between sovereign and minister, righteousness; between husband and wife, attention to their separate functions; between old and young, a proper order; and between friends, fidelity (Legge, 1970:251–252).

Thus, society's critical social relationships are primarily among unequals except in the case of friends, and in Korea even friendships are considered most ideal when they are between a senior and a junior. In modern-day Korea this perspective is strongly reflected in corporate working life. Similar to the kings of old Korea, company founders and CEOs are expected to set the moral tone for the employees of their organizations through their benevolence, impeccable attention to social ritual, hard work, and lack of preoccupation with personal gain and conspicuous consumption. At the same time they should chart a viable but visionary course that brings economic success and social prestige to the firm. Similarly, great care is taken not to violate order between older and younger employees, male and female employees. As was the case with traditional law, the vertically differentiated roles of management employees are carefully delineated in company constitutions.

Collectivism and Dependence

The Korean concern for sustaining harmony within a tightly linked vertical social structure produces a collectivist or group-oriented world-view. Literally, all individuals are linked through a continuous chain of senior-junior and superior-subordinate relationships. Each relationship is necessarily dyadic in nature, composed of one senior member and one junior member. However, all such relationships are ultimately tied together in each organizational context, with a senior member acting as a junior in another relationship and a junior member as a senior in other cases.

Understanding appropriate behavior and attitudes toward being a member of a senior-junior relationship begins in early childhood. In Western society, the goal of socialization is to produce an autonomous individual with a well-defined ego capable of independent action. Such an approach to child rearing is baffling to the Korean parent, for autonomy is not considered to be a virtue. Instead, the Korean parent encourages dependency on the part of the child by maintaining close physical contact at all times and in all situations (Hahm, 1986:322–323).

In the Korean household children are expected to seek a dependent relationship with parents and older siblings. Such behavior is characterized by the Korean words *Origwang* or *Ungsok*, which are quite similar to the Japanese term *Amae*. The individual with whom dependency is sought is expected to respond with generosity, deep affection, and a willingness to invest whatever time, effort, and material or emotional sacrifice is necessary to provide for the junior's needs. In turn, the junior is expected to reciprocate the senior's benevolence and kindness with unconditional obedience to the senior's directives and to show filial respect for the senior's social position and credibility or "face" (*chemyun* in Korean).

This orientation toward social relationships does not end in the household or when the child becomes an adult. Rather, a preference for the senior-junior relationship continues throughout life, with its characteristics of dependency, unconditional obedience, filial respect, and senior benevolence and generosity in all social spheres. In high school and college, older students typically establish senior-junior relationships with younger students. It is quite popular for girls and boys to seek out a junior classmate whom they designate as their younger sister or brother (Koh, 1981). At work, the orientation is the same between seniors and juniors in the same department, in formal superior-subordinate relationships, and informally between employees from the same hometown and especially alumni of the same high school or college. Human resource policies and organizational titles are generally shaped to honor and reinforce these social tendencies, based on the belief that they encourage both loyalty and a dedication to maintaining harmonious working relations.

Filial Piety and Social Ritual

Because of the vertical nature of Korean social organization and its complementary world-view supporting this structure, filial piety (or *Hyo* in Korean) became the guiding doctrine in Korean society for coordinating and directing social interaction within the framework of the "Five Relations." To honor the

Five Relations and remain true to the proper attitudes and behavior associated with each was held up as the ideal of exemplifying filiality. This was often characterized as filial piety toward one's parents and loyalty to the king, but, in reality, familial relations were projected on to society and all its constituent institutions as "the family writ large." Consequently, "the proper relationship between father and son became the paradigm for all hierarchical relationships in a moral society, including that between subject and ruler" (Janelli and Janelli, 1982:50). The king was therefore looked upon as the "parent of the people" following the role idealized in the Confucian scripture the *Book of Documents* (Legge, 1960:283).

In traditional Korean society, this pattern also extended to village elders, government administrators, teachers, older students at school, and the like who became alternatively identified as parents, uncles and aunts, or elder brothers and sisters. Thus, seniors or superiors were expected to demonstrate the appropriate benevolence, concern, and affection, whereas juniors were expected to understand their subordinate and dependent roles and fulfill them precisely and with sincerity.

It was believed that through filial behavior the entire society and its constituent organizations could be held together through peaceful and harmonious, vertically integrated interpersonal relations, or as Confucius explained, "Those who in private life behave well towards their parents and elder brothers, in public life seldom show a disposition to resist the authority of superiors" (Waley, 1989:83).

Similarly, in today's modern corporation filial behavior towards one's superiors and seniors is believed to produce a peaceful and cooperative organizational environment. As was also the case in ancient Korea, filial behavior is demonstrated by adherence to minutely detailed prescriptions for appropriate social etiquette known as *Ye* in Korean or *Li* in Chinese. When literally translated into English, *Ye* means "social rituals" or "rules of ceremony," and they are considered the social equivalent of the eternal cosmological principles that govern the universe (Chai and Chai, 1967, Vol. I:388–389).

Thus, social etiquette in Korea is not regarded as merely cultural refinement, as nice but trivial behavioral proscriptions of the upper class. Consequently, ignorance and/or disrespect for *Ye* are not simply a case of cultural deprivation, but, rather, an outward manifestation of a deeper flaw in moral character. Moreover, failure to know and adhere to *Ye* is considered a very real threat to the stability of any social entity, including the corporation. Rather than a straitjacket that constrains spontaneous and authentic expression of human emotion and ideas, social etiquette in Confucian society was felt to be a positive method for meeting human needs without disturbing social harmony and pitting people against each other in harmful competition (Watson, 1963:89).

In Korea today, *Ye* have not lost their significance in the family, the school, and the workplace, and any individual who fails to recognize and adhere to them is essentially considered an "unperson."

At a Korean dinner table, a young person waits until elders sit down and start eating. It is impolite to pick up his spoon before his father or grandfather begins to eat. In the presence of an elder, he does not smoke or drink. If he happens to be caught smoking, or an elder person comes into his presence, he discreetly hides the cigarettes behind his back. When drinking with an elder, a young man is discreet enough to hide his glass away, turning his body to drink. Even wearing glasses in the presence of an elder is sometimes considered impolite especially in rural areas. (Park, 1979:80 and 52)

In essence, *Ye* provide basic organizing principles that define appropriate role behavior for individuals in the junior or subordinate role of an interpersonal relationship. And they perform the same function in all social relations. Social order and coordinated action are maintained by understanding one's respective role duties in a senior or junior position and, in turn, observing these duties rigorously.

Human Nature and Education

In the neo-Confucian world-view, human beings are considered to be essentially good by nature. The individual's unity with the underlying principles of the universe by definition makes human nature good as part of the broader cosmos. According to Chu Hsi, this innately good or luminous nature can easily become obscured by the corrupting influences in human society (Gardner, 1986:53).

Realization of this good or one's "human nature," in the Korean neo-Confucian world-view, can only be attained through the enlightment that eventually results from personal cultivation through long and rigorous study and adherence to *Ye*. In ancient times it was achieved through scholarly study of *The Four Books*, *The Five Classics*, and the writings and commentaries of Chu Hsi, including *The Elementary Learning*, *The Family Ritual of Master Chu*, *The Great Compendium on Human Nature*, and *Reflections on Things at Hand* (Yi, 1985:142–143). Today, the study of moral teachings is still considered a fundamental part of childhood learning, and Korean children receive a total of 850 hours of formal classroom moral training between the first and tenth grades (Ministry of Education, 1989:53–54, 56). However, rigorous study of all fields has always been supported by Chu Hsi's neo-Confucian teachings (Gardner, 1986:105).

Such an inspiring viewpoint on the significance of education and personal cultivation persists in Korean society today. Just as study of the Confucian classics and commentaries served as the foundation for learning which could be pursued in any field, and the civil service examination system provided the test of one's success in making the effort to learn, today formal education and the entrance exam system provide a modern counterpart to this ancient development process. In ancient times, students who prepared to take the tests that would qualify them to become Yangban spent literally thousands of hours in study, writing, and verbatim memorization of the classic texts of neo-Confucian moral learning. Being intellectually quick or clever was not as valuable in this case as being patient and doggedly determined to internalize the material studied. To persist through this process to "the completion of knowledge" was considered the highest indication of sincerity (Legge, 1971:413–414). Not surprisingly, as Table 13.2 illustrates, sincerity is the most frequently cited quality in Korean company slogans.

Because of the religious awe in which education and learning were held in Yi Dynasty Korea, and the respect and social prestige accorded to individuals who distinguished themselves through scholarly effort, the Korean people enthusiastically embraced universal public education once free from Japanese colonial rule. During the 1950s elementary school enrollment increased by 265 percent, and between 1945 and 1960 the illiteracy rate declined from 78 to 28 percent, while the nation's population of college students increased from a mere 8,000 youth to over 100,000 persons (Joo, 1991:2). As the data in Table 13.3 illustrate, by the early 1970s Korea's literacy rate had grown to nearly 90 percent, and the government ceased to compute this statistic. Today, over 80 percent of all Koreans complete their education through high school, and 26 percent of all college-age youth are engaged in university studies. This rapid growth in education has been essential in Korea's efforts to move toward producing and exporting high value-added products. This is no more clearly illustrated than by the tremendous increase in the number of Korean scientists and engineers from only 4,000 persons in the 1950s to over 361,000 in 1986 (Kim, 1989:3).

In 1989, a total of 166,845 students graduated from college in Korea: 127,350 sought permanent employment; 76,594 individuals, 60 percent of the graduating class, were actually successful; and just 24,056 persons (19 percent) were hired by Korea's fifty largest corporations (Song, 1990:181). Thus, a large pool of highly educated and hard-working candidates from which Korean firms can select an elite cadre of new management recruits has been created. For this reason, it is no longer necessary to recruit commercial high school graduates for entry-level management jobs.

HUMAN RESOURCE MANAGEMENT

Our analysis focuses principally on the human resource management of managers in Korea's major corporations or Chaebol because they are the dominant economic force in Korean society. Moreover, their approach to managerial human resource management is relatively consistent across firms. Korea's management elite are recruited into these companies immediately following their completion of undergraduate or graduate studies where they always begin their careers as either office staff or research and development engineers or scientists. All these recruits enter the firm at the same organizational rank. They then move forward up the management hierarchy based on seniority, with promotions depending on their demonstrated intelligence and ability to lead others with a spirit of harmony and diligence. Thus, although all new college graduate recruits eventually become managers at the section chief level at least, not all reach the highest levels of the company.

Table 13.3
Indicators of Human Resource Development through Formal Education, 1953–86

Dimensions	1953	1960	1970	1980	1986
Literacy Rate (Percent)	22	72	89	*	*
School Enrollment as a Percentage of Corresponding Age Group					
Elementary School (ages 6-11)	60	86	103	101	100
Middle School (ages 12-14)	21	33	53	95	99
High School (ages 15-17)	12	19	29	69	83
College and University	3	6	9	15	26
Graduates of Vocational Training Centers (in 1,000's)	-	-	32	105	51
Total Number of Scientists and Engineers**	4,157	16,436	65,687	174,832	361,330

*   The government ceased to compute the level of overall basic literacy after the mid-1970's because the number of illiterate individuals was so low that this statistic was meaningless.

**   These figures reflect the cumulative number of science and engineering graduates since 1945.

Source: Kim, Lin-Su, *Technological Transformation in Korea and Its Implications for Other Developing Countries* (Seoul: Korea Development Institute, 1989), p. 3.

The Recruiting Process

The modern Korean system of higher education is characterized by rigorous entrance exam competition, with the toughest examinations required for admission to the nation's highest ranked universities. Consequently, the national ranking of universities is universally recognized. The highest ranked university is the state-sponsored Seoul National University, which is heavily subsidized so that any student of merit can afford to attend. Seoul National is immediately followed by two privately funded universities, Yonsei and Korea University, and the ranking continues thereafter in terms of third, fourth, tier schools and so on. Admission to a top-ranked school greatly enhances one's chances for employment at a major corporation. Conversely, the university ranking system provides Korea's top corporations with a valuable prescreening mechanism for recruiting the nation's most talented individuals. The entrance examinations for Korea's top universities cover a tremendous amount of material that must be memorized in great detail, requiring extensive study.

Once Korean companies have determined the total number of people they will hire during a given year and the academic fields from which they will be recruited, a pool of applicants is created from which new management employees will be selected. This is normally done only twice a year, with the principal recruiting conducted in early fall and a smaller effort made in the spring. Hiring as needs arise is carefully avoided because the primary determinant of individual pay increases and promotions is seniority, following the Confucian requirement of "between old and young, a proper order." This pool of candidates is created through advertising in published anouncements, visits made to college campuses by recruiting teams, and, to a lesser extent, personal referrals. Consistent with Confucian tradition, these efforts are directed mainly at male college graduates. For example, of the 24,056 college graduates hired by Korea's fifty largest firms in 1989, only 4.8 percent were female. Recruiting through public notice is called *Kongch'ae* in Korean, a word that denotes individuals who have been hired through a competitive process rather than through personal connections. *Kongch'ae* is the principal method by which Korea's largest corporations recruit and hire new management talent. A 1985 Seoul National University study of 481 firms found that 47 percent of the companies studied with less than 300 employees (128 firms) relied on personal connections for recruiting, whereas 86 percent of the firms surveyed with 300 or more employees (179 companies) used the *Kongch'ae* or public notice method (Seoul National University Management Research Center, 1985:185).

Public notices for corporate recruiting are published in newspaper advertisements, school bulletins, or as advertisements in management and business journals. The information provided in these notices typically includes:

• The number of people needed—sales, engineering, and administration.

• The college majors from which the firm is recruiting new employees.

• All documents that applicants are required to submit.

• The subjects that will be tested, if written tests are required.

• Specification of the applicant age cohort stated in terms of the birth years from which candidates will be selected (normally twenty-six to twenty-eight years prior to the current recruiting year). For example, companies hiring in 1989 indicated that applicants were limited to individuals born in 1962 or after (Yoo, 1989).

When recruiting, major companies also create recruiting teams composed of past graduates of the universities from which new employees have been hired in the past. These teams may be organized at either the group level or the subsidiary level. Firms K2 and K3 from our study exemplify this process. K3 recruiting teams visit major universities in Seoul only, and they do so at four different times, hosting a reception in each instance. Recruiting team members then meet students through class representatives, student job search committees, and department chairs in an effort to identify potential candidates.

K2 also attempts to use the recruiting team for an initial screening, using a group level team. The team members get together after making initial contacts to decide on which individuals they will accept and which they will drop as clearly unsatisfactory. At this stage, the recruiting team is concerned mainly with discerning whether prospective candidates have a personality and interpersonal style compatible with their company culture. Academic ability is not an important consideration at this point, and only those candidates whom team members feel have the best fit are given application forms. In contrast to these face-to-face recruiting techniques used at top universities in Seoul, contact with lower ranked schools is often limited to mailed brochures and applications to other colleges. Thus, applicants from the top universities in Seoul have a considerable advantage. A 1989 study, for example, found that 62.3 percent of all new management employees hired by Korea's fifty largest companies were graduates of colleges located in Seoul (Song, 1990:181). It is especially important for company prestige to recruit from these schools. The personnel manager at KB explained, "We need to recruit graduates from Seoul National University and other top universities for the face of the company.... We need them for our company image when we have to disclose our managers' profiles in the company directory."

The Selection Process

The review process for selecting the final candidates for entry-level management positions is highly competitive. It provides the company with a very fine screening mechanism for ensuring that new management employees are not only capable of performing any technical assignment, but that they will also be able to work effectively as harmonious team members. Similar to management at other firms, the personnel section chief at K6 explained:

We do not want to have a super star in our organization because, even though they may have more ability in their specialty they also may present a greater possibility of breaking up unity.... It is possible to train people in a new job function if they have basic intelligence, but a person's personality characteristics are very hard to change.

Document Evaluation   Evaluation begins with the application and documents submitted, including photographs, college transcripts, military discharge papers, essays on family and personal history, and a report from the Civil Office of the Police Department. This last document describes both any history of criminal activity or involvement in radical student movements or communist organizations. Since democratic reforms were declared in 1987, and labor disputes have risen in number and intensity, Korean employers have reviewed this document carefully.

These documents are scored on the basis of a complex set of criteria. Among the factors evaluated are the applicant's field of study, military career, and age. Individuals who have completed graduate studies in a scientific, technical, or engineering field are usually scored a little higher than applicants with only a bachelor's degree. On the other hand, applicants who have pursued graduate work in the humanities, the social sciences, or business management are actually graded lower than if they had applied with only an undergraduate degree. It is assumed that these candidates chose to pursue graduate studies because they were unqualified for hire after finishing undergraduate work. Their older age also has a negative impact on their score.

Korean companies limit the age groups from which they hire new management employees in order to preserve internal harmony. Older applicants are believed to have a greater potential for disrupting harmony. A one-year difference in age from the average of the applicant cohort is not usually penalized because many students take an additional year to prepare for entrance examinations after high school. However, a candidate who is several years older receives a much lower score.

Applications are also screened according to school ranking, department ranking, and grade point average. Some companies also screen for hometown. In some instances, applicants from the same hometown as the majority of managers in a company are graded higher because these common ties increase the feelings of mutual obligation between managers, thereby also increasing loyalty and harmony.

Another important piece of information evaluated is the *yebi gosa*, which is a preliminary test that graduating high school seniors take before they are allowed to take college entrance examinations. Most firms can easily obtain these test scores as well as the minimum entrance exam score which was required by an applicant's university department in the year of his or her acceptance to college. Applicants are thus scored on the basis of their *yebi gosa* score and how high their entrance exam score was above the cutoff score for their department.

Once all the data have been reviewed and individual items scored, they are analyzed by a computer and the applicants are ranked. Candidates equal to ten times the number of job openings participate in the next step, the written examination.

The Entrance Examination   Most major Korean firms require management applicants to take a written examination. This test evaluates an applicant's knowledge of a major foreign language, college major field, and general knowledge in such subjects as management, economics, law, and current social issues. The foreign language test is particularly important because of extensive export activity. Four of the firms tested which we studied also required that applicants take aptitude and personality tests.

The Interview   The next and the most critical stage in the selection process is the interview. Table 13.4 illustrates that of all the sources of data the interview is weighted most heavily in making final selection decisions. Recruiters believe that the interview provides a window through which they can directly examine candidates' moral nature and character, their personality and interpersonal style, and how effectively they adapt to difficult circumstances. It is considered so important that all the companies we studied used interviewing committees comprised of from three to eight top managers to conduct the process, including the company chairman, the president, a senior vice-president, a senior managing director, a managing director, and the director of the personnel department.

Companies do differ on the interviewing strategies and formats they use; although the majority of companies we studied used at least a two-step process.

Table 13.4

Relative Weighting of Selection Criteria in Small and Large Korean Firms: A Comparative Analysis

Firm Size	Written Test	Interview	Recommendation	Aptitude Test	Document	Other
300+ Employees (n=178)	18.6%	39.9%	9.9%	7.2%	22.2%	2.4%
Under 300 Employees (n=141)	8.0	40.4	15.6	8.0	24.4	3.6
Total (n=319)	12.6	40.2	13.2	7.7	23.4	2.9

Source: Seoul National University Management Research Center. *Hankuk Koip-ui Hyunhwang-Kwa Kwaje/Current Situations and Challenge of Korean Corporations* (Seoul: Seoul National University Press, 1985), p. 191.

Three of the large firms we examined used a two-interview approach. The first interview was used to assess applicants' knowledge in their college major and their English proficiency. During this first interview, applicants are asked to answer questions in English to evaluate their comprehension, pronunciation, and grammar. At the second interview, the focus shifts to evaluating applicants' personal appearance, family background, character or moral nature, bearing, attitude, language, general knowledge, and common sense. During this interview, recruits are often asked about their fathers' occupation and their own family background. Recruits from broken homes are often passed over because they are considered to be more likely to cause problems and disrupt organizational harmony. Individuals who display negative, arrogant, or hostile attitudes are avoided and are dropped from the list.

One of the firms we studied used an interesting combination of group interviews and discussion. In this instance, applicants are first organized into groups of eight people and assigned topics to discuss among themselves in front of the evaluation team. One of the questions asked was, "If you were the company president would you favor adoption of the merit system or a seniority system for promotion?" In this setting the candidates are evaluated as to how well they express themselves and the logic and thought behind their opinions. The evaluation committee also carefully observes how well each applicant listens to the opinions of the other candidates and adapts to other viewpoints. Candidates who hold to their own opinions stubbornly and make few compromises receive a negative evaluation. Next, applicants are interviewed in groups of three by an evaluation committee composed of senior managing directors and executive directors from several affiliate companies.

Final Evaluation Once the interviewing process has been completed, the final evaluation takes place. Candidates are graded on a scale from A to E, with A the highest score. Each interviewing committee member computes his own

individual score. The personnel director then compares all the scores for the
different candidates.

If a serious discrepancy exists between the scores of committee members on
specific candidates, the personnel director tries to determine the reasons for these
differences and to reach some reconciliation between the conflicting opinions.
As a rule, however, the committee members' scores tend to be quite similar.
Thus, candidates who receive all A grades from the evaluation committee members are hired first, and those who receive a mixture of A and B grades are
considered second. Candidates with C grades are usually judged to have failed,
unless the number of people actually needed exceeds the individuals who received
A or B ratings.

Once all the finalists have been selected, a personnel staff member in charge
of recruiting and selection writes up a *p'ummi*. The *p'ummi* is a formal written
statement that receives a stamp of approval from all related managers up through
the chief executive officer, signifying unanimous support for the final decision.
Job offers are extended, and the individuals who accept then take a physical
examination. If a candidate fails the physical, the offer is withdrawn and extended
to alternate candidates.

Vertical Differentiation and Management Promotion

It is impossible to understand management compensation systems and the
function and limitations of performance appraisals in the Korean firm without
first understanding how the promotion process leads to the vertical differentiation
of management ranks. As can be seen in Figure 13.1, the typical Korean corporation has approximately twenty separate management ranks. This diagram
includes only those organizational ranks that apply to employees who start their
careers after college or commercial high school graduation. If blue-collar employees are included, then four to six additional ranks must also be added.

These tall hierarchies are the modern manifestation of the social hierarchy of
age grading created by Korea's Confucian tradition. The Confucian tendency to
vertically structure societal relationships based on age, gender, and social status,
as well as the extreme sensitivity to preserving face inherent in this system,
requires that constant attention be paid to recognizing status differences. Two
factors that are particularly salient in this regard are educational achievement
and seniority. Because individuals who join a company do so after completing
differing levels of education, they require formal recognition of these differences
from the outset. Similarly, because loss of face has such a strong impact on
employee attitudes and motivation, it is necessary to provide regular recognition
of status differences based on seniority to avoid the deterioration of morale.

In status- and order-conscious Korean society, this situation has existed from
ancient times. The Yangban, for example, began their careers as scholar-officials
at different ranks depending on whether they had passed either a higher or a
lower level examination. Furthermore, once an individual entered the bureaucracy, it was expected that his senior status would be officially recognized as
above that of each new wave of Yangban that followed. These conditions initially

Figure 13.1
Managerial Organization Chart in Typical Korean Corporation

1	Isahwe-Board of Directors
2	Hwejang-Chairman of the Board
3	Buhwejang-Vice Chairman
4	Sajang-President
5	Busajang-Vice President
6	Chonmoo-Senior Managing Director
7	Sangmu-Managing Director
8	Isa-Executive Director
9	Isa Daewoo-Director
10	Bujang-General Manager/Department Head
11	Bujang Daewoo-Junior General Manager
12	Cha'jang-Assistant Manager
13	Cha'jang Daewoo-Junior Assistant Manager
14	Kwajang-Section Chief
15	Kwajang Daewoo-Junior Section Chief
16	Kwajang Daeri-Assistant Section Chief
17	* Kyejang-Subsection Chief
18	Chuim/Ch'amsa/Sonim Sawon-Senior Section Member
19 20	Sawon 1-Section Member (college entry) Sawon 2-Section Member (high school entry)

* Kyejang is a position usually restricted to factory operations.

led to the creation of nine bureaucratic ranks or *p'um*. Later, to accommodate growth and save the face of aging Yangban, eighteen ranks were created by dividing the original *p'um* into junior and senior levels. Later, the ranks were subdivided into thirty-six (Han, 1970:236).

The Korean corporation today faces similar pressures to recognize individual seniority and educational achievement. For example, all but one of the firms that we studied had developed company regulations that specified different management levels and sublevels and the normal time period required to move from one level to the next. Actual promotions sometimes vary from the time period specified in company regulations, depending on the development of the individual and especially the availability of positions for promotions. In general, however, most companies try to stay close to the specified time period for the sake of employee morale. A Korea Employers' Federation study of seniority requirements for promotions in major manufacturing firms found that on average 4.4 years were required to move from Sawon to Daeri, 3.2 years from Daeri to Kwajang, 3.3 years from Kwajang to Ch'ajang, and 3.3 years from Ch'ajang to Bujang (Korea Employers' Federation, 1987:115).

As can be seen, several additional management ranking levels are identified in Figure 13.1 beyond those covered in the seniority requirements study of the Korea Employers' Federation. Not all the levels in the figure represent a major change in job duties, but they do signify a clear order in status ranking based on seniority and therefore also an ordering of deference in decision making and interpersonal relations. Thus, among the twenty titles illustrated in Figure 13.1, the titles that are enclosed by rectangular boxes are the principal positions indicating major changes in job responsibilities and scope of authority. The other levels are intermediate points between each of the main levels.

These intermediate titles such as *chuim*, *daeri*, and especially the *daewoo* titles, are created as a corporation becomes older and takes on new employees. As employees that entered the firm in the same year increase in seniority, these new titles must be added for the sake of employees' "face" both with other employees and with their family and friends. If employees do not receive regular vertical promotions, it is considered to be a signal that an individual is inferior and not respected in the company. The *daewoo* system is an even more elaborate scheme for dealing with these issues. The term *daewoo* literally means "to treat as if." Thus, when an individual receives a promotion to a *daewoo* position, although the actual scope of duties has not significantly increased, the individual is otherwise treated "as if" he or she has the new position and enjoys the same increased pay, allowances, and bonuses.

In our own research, although we found that all the larger firms have elaborate systems for evaluating employee performance on at least an annual basis, it was clear that 85 to 95 percent of people who meet the length-of-service requirements specified in company regulations are in fact promoted. Late promotions can be a signal that an individual's job performance is unsatisfactory, and managers who are unable to improve their performance usually leave the company, "self-firing" themselves to escape continued loss of face. On the other hand, early promotions occur because an individual has shown exceptional leadership ability and the company has an urgent need due to growth. This latter case, referred to as a special promotion is very rare, and employees are never promoted by skipping ranks in the same organization. The personnel manager at K1 explains why special promotions are so rare:

I haven't seen anyone receive a special promotion in our company. . . . There is a possibility of breaking up the harmony and unity of the team if someone receives a special promotion. If someone got a special promotion, his colleagues would complain to the company. Also, people themselves are not comfortable with being specially promoted.

Thus, the promotion process is an excellent example of the influence of Confucianism on present-day human resource management. In fact, as Korean companies have matured, these tendencies have actually become more pronounced. A 1987 study found that the adoption rate of the *daewoo* system in all industries grew from 6.4 percent in the 1960s to 62.7 percent in the 1980s (Korea Employers' Federation Labor Economics Institute, 1987:123).

Management Compensation

Seniority is also a critical factor in the calculation and composition of management compensation within the broader Confucian belief that a master (company) is responsible for taking care of a servant (employee) as if a family member. The components of management compensation are base pay, allowances, bonuses, and benefits. Individual performance has an extremely small impact on differentials in management compensation. Indeed, previous research has demonstrated that Korean firms, even more so than Japanese companies, correlate increases in pay and benefits with seniority on nearly a one-to-one basis (Ahn, 1982:61). Even functions such as sales, which in the West are traditionally linked to incentives for performance, are paid on the same basis. Although the company regulations of most firms state that performance appraisal results should be used in compensation decisions, in actuality they have little or no impact on pay grade increases. In the few instances where they do influence bonus allocations, the impact is very small, amounting to a mere 1 to 2 percent differential (Song, 1990:304–305).

Base Pay Base pay is calculated in terms of pay grades called hobongs, and for each year of service an employee's compensation is generally increased by two hobongs. A hobong or pay grade table is developed for each management rank or intermediate rank, and it is adjusted yearly to reflect changes in the cost of living. Each rank or intermediate rank is composed of 20 to 30 hobongs.

Starting base pay for new college graduates is determined by gender, educational level, and military service (for male recruits). Because of the Confucian "Five Relations," which place husband before wife and by implication men before women in general, gender has the strongest impact on initial base compensation. Within each gender, educational level, in turn, determines an individual's base starting salary, and seniority serves as the most important factor in determining increases thereafter. This is clearly illustrated by Table 13.5, which is an English translation of the hobong table for the company K1, a cosmetics and household products manufacturer.

Close examination of K1's hobong tables shows that in 1990 male college graduates received a 27 percent higher base starting salary than female college graduates, with men starting at 430,600 won per month and women at 340,500 won. Similarly, male high school graduates at K1 started at 356,500 won, which was 5 percent more than female college graduates and a full 70 percent more than the 210,100 won per month base starting salary of female high school graduates.

Allowances   Allowances (*sudang* in Korean) first became important in Korea's compensation systems during World War II when the Japanese government passed the Company Finance Control Act which was designed to control labor costs rising due to pay raises. To circumvent this law and provide employees with increased income, some Korean employers began to use allowances as a significant portion of the compensation package. However, it was not until the 1960s that allowances began to assume a generalized pattern in compensation systems.

Added to base pay are two kinds of allowances: legal allowances (*Pobjong Sudang*) and optional or voluntary allowances (*Imooi Sudang*). Legal allowances are those additions to base pay which are required by Korea's Labor Standards Law and include allowances for dismissal, suspension of business operations, menstruation leave, maternity leave, accrued vaction time, and so on. Optional allowances are not required by law and are quite numerous. K1, for example, has eighty-two different types of allowances, and a major study by the Korea Chamber of Commerce and Industry (KCCI) identified 128 different allowances based on allowance purpose (1986:112–113). The KCCI study found that most companies use allowances as a supplement to low levels of base pay. It is obviously impossible to enumerate all 128 allowances in this chapter, but we will briefly describe a few of the most important general categories.

The most common allowances are "job" or "position" allowances and "seniority" allowances. Position allowances are paid in addition to the base pay for the particular management rank which an individual holds above the entry sawon level. One position allowance, called *Chikgup-sudang* is for both principal and intermediate ranks such as *bujang*, *bujang-daewoo*, *ch'ajang*, and *ch'ajang-daewoo*, and the other position allowance, Chikch'aek-sudang, is only for the non-*daewoo* ranks. Many companies pay seniority allowances in addition to hobong increases, based on years of service, with the intent of rewarding employees for loyalty to the firm. For example, employees who have under three years of service receive no seniority allowance, those with three to five years receive an extra 15,000 won per month, five to seven years 21,000 per month, seven to nine years 27,000, nine to eleven years 33,000, eleven to thirteen years 39,000, and over thirteen years 45,000.

Another common allowance for management employees is the overtime allowance. Managers typically receive 10 percent, and clerical staff 15 percent,

Table 13.5
K1's Hobong Table

PAY GRADE	GRADE 1	GRADE 2	GRADE 3	GRADE 4	GRADE 4B		GRADE 4 (Female)		GRADE 5 (Female)			
HOBONG	Bu, Ch'ajang	Ch'a, Kwajang	Deot/ Chuim	Sawon	Hobong	Sawon	Hobong	Hi Grad	Hobong	Hi Grad	Hobong	Hi Grad
1	1,123,800	934,800	704,700	542,000	51	491,800	32	404,200	42	294,300	12	239,300
2	1,109,900	923,900	699,600	535,400	52	486,700	33	400,800	41	292,500	11	236,900
3	1,096,000	913,000	693,100	526,300	53	481,600	34	395,300	40	290,700	10	235,000
4	1,081,800	901,900	686,400	517,000	54	476,400	35	389,800	39	288,800	9	232,600
5	1,067,600	890,800	678,300	508,500	55	471,200	36	388,300	38	287,000	8	230,200
6	1,053,400	879,300	670,000	499,900	56	466,000	37	385,000	37	285,200	7	228,000
7	1,037,400	876,800	660,000	491,100	57	460,800	38	381,800	36	283,400	6	225,600
8	1,021,400	856,400	649,800	482,200	58	454,200	39	378,500	35	281,500	5	222,900
9	1,005,400	845,000	639,800	474,600	59	447,600	40	375,000	34	279,700	4	220,400
10	989,400	831,500	629,400	467,000	60	441,000	41	371,700	33	277,900	3	216,800
11	973,200	818,000	619,200	460,700	61	434,400	42	368,300	32	276,100	2	212,500
12	957,000	*804,400	609,000	451,800	62	427,100	43	365,000	31	274,200	1	*210,200
13	940,800	790,900	598,700	441,500	63	419,700	44	361,500	30	272,400		
14	924,600	777,400	588,300	*430,600	64	412,400	45	358,200	29	270,600		
15	908,300	763,800	578,100	419,600	65	405,100	46	354,900	28	268,800		
16	*892,000	749,400	567,300	408,700	66	399,500	47	351,500	27	267,000		
17	875,800	734,400	557,000	397,800	67	393,900	48	346,000	26	265,100		
18	859,600	719,700	*546,100	387,100	68	388,200	49	*340,500	25	263,300		
19	843,400	705,000	535,200	376,400	69	382,500	50	334,800	24	261,500		
20	827,200	690,300	524,000	365,700	70	375,900	51	329,100	23	259,700		
21		675,600	513,400		71	*369,400	52	323,500	22	257,800		
22		*660,900	502,500		72	362,900	53	317,800	21	256,000		
23		646,200	*491,300		73	*356,500	54	312,100	20	254,200		
24		631,500	480,300		74	349,700	55	306,400	19	252,400		
25		616,800	469,300		75	342,900			18	250,200		
26		602,100	458,400		76	336,100			17	248,400		
27		587,400	447,500		77	329,400			16	246,600		
28		572,700			78	322,700			15	244,800		
29		558,000			79	315,900			14	242,900		
30		543,200			80	309,200			13	241,100		

Note: * refers to starting salary of each grade

calculated as a fixed percent of the base monthly salary. Because this allowance is paid in the same amount every month, managers tend to expect it as part of their normal salary. Many companies treat overtime allowances separately to avoid inclusion in bonus computations.

Most firms also pay a meal allowance for purchasing lunch during working hours and family allowances to aid in the support of employees raising families or caring for aged parents. In the case of family allowances, typical amounts are 5,000 won for parents, 3,000 to 5,000 won for a spouse, and 3,000 to 5,000 won per dependent child. Some but not all companies limit child allowances to two children.

Allowances are also paid to individuals who meet the requirements for special licenses or degrees such as safety specialists, nutritionists, CPAs and Ph.D.s. Similarly, individuals who make an extra effort to assist in international business by developing foreign language competence can also receive special allowances. At K3, for example, individuals with high scores on English (TOEIC) or Japanese (JPT or TOJIC) proficiency tests receive an extra 10,000 won per month for scores of 470 or above and up to 50,000 won for a score of 860 or higher, which is equal to one month's salary over a year. These bonuses are awarded for three years and can be renewed by retesting, thereby encouraging constant study.

These allowances are just a few of the most common examples that are paid on a regular monthly basis. Altogether they can represent a substantial percentage of an employee's monthly salary. A study of 2,169 manufacturing firms conducted by the Korea Chamber of Commerce and Industry, for example, found that allowances account for 18 to 28 percent of monthly earnings (Korea Chamber of Commerce and Industry, February 12, 1990:2).

Bonuses   In the Korean firm, all employees regard bonus payments as part of their regular salary paid on a deferred basis at regular intervals during the year at a fixed rate. Most companies compute bonuses as a fixed percentage of base salary, although a few also include allowance payments in this computation (Song, 1990:339).

The rate at which bonuses are paid tends to be directly correlated with company size, with the largest firms paying the highest percentages. One study of major corporations by the Korea Chamber of Commerce and Industry found that 40.8 percent of firms with 1,000 or more employees paid bonuses of 600 percent or more, and 70 percent of companies with 300 or more employees paid bonuses of at least 400 percent. On the other hand, 52 percent of small companies with fewer than 99 employees paid total annual bonuses of less than 300 percent of monthly salary or wages (Korea Chamber of Commerce and Industry, 1989:92). Our own study showed that among the eight large Chaebol member companies bonuses ranged from 400 percent to 950 percent. In all cases but one, the bonus rates were standard for all employees whether management or labor.

The payment schedule of bonuses differs from company to company, but at least some portion of the total annual bonus is usually paid in each quarter of the year. It is quite common to spread the bonus across several payments, with some timed to coincide with important holidays. At K3, for example, 100 percent is first paid in February for Chinese New Year, two additional 100 percent payments are made in March and June, another 100 percent payment is given in July as a vacation bonus, in September 100 percent is paid for the Korean Thanksgiving (called *Ch'usok*), in October a final 100 percent is paid for preparing winter *kimchee* (called a *kimjang* bonus), and, lastly, a flexible bonus based on profits is paid in December, ranging from 200 to 350 percent during the years of our research.

Additional Benefits   Beyond base pay, allowances, and bonuses, most Korean companies also pay several additional benefits covering a diverse range of issues. These include medical and hospitalization benefits under the recently established national health program, pension benefits, educational support for children, congratulatory and condolence payments for significant events such as births, deaths, and marriages, gifts of company products, discounts on the purchase of company goods, free busing, employee uniforms, and company discount stores.

In education-oriented Korea, educational scholarships for the children of employees are especially important. Most large firms provide scholarships that pay 100 percent of the costs of attending junior high school, high school, and publicly owned colleges and 70 percent of private college costs up to 1.2 million Korean won. As many as three children can be supported similtaneously at a cost to the firm in excess of US$6,000 per year.

Finally, pension benefits are paid in a single lump sum when an employee retires, and like most pension plans these payments are based on both average monthly wage or salary and years of service. The reward to employees for loyalty to the company is not, however, limited to a simple increase equal to multiplying the average monthly salary by accumulated years of service. Typically, an additional incentive is included to encourage long-term employment with the company; it can be worth as much as a doubling of the value of pension benefits for those employees who stay with the firm beyond ten years.

Performance Appraisal

Formal performance appraisal systems first appeared in Korea during the 1960s (Ahn, 1989). In a 1985 study of the human resource management practices of 481 Korean manufacturing companies, it was found that 75.8 percent of large firms (over 300 employees) and 44.4 percent of small companies (under 300 employees) had adopted performance appraisal systems (Seoul National University Management Research Center, 1985:203). In our own study, KB and all eight Chaebol member firms performed regular performance evaluations of their managers, with some also using self-appraisals (K3, K5, and K8) and even peer reviews (K2). In the majority of cases, these evaluations were conducted twice during the year; once in July for the first half of the year and a second in January for the second half.

Most company regulations state that performance appraisals are to be conducted and that the results should be used in determining promotions, transfers, and job assignments, allocating educational experiences such as overseas training, taking disciplinary actions, distributing bonus payments, and determining pay grade increases. Most firms divide their evaluations into three sections, which require an evaluation by the employee's direct supervisor and the department head in relationship to their attitude, ability, and actual achievement of results at work. In all instances the ability section is weighted the most heavily in calculating overall points by a factor as high as two to three times the value placed on attitude and achievement. However, our research found that, although the use of performance appraisals is quite widespread, the actual application of the results in decision making is usually quite limited, especially with regard to compensation. In fact, since the declaration of democratic reforms in 1987 most companies have pulled back even further from using performance evaluations to determine compensation levels and bonuses.

Prior to 1987, many Korean companies determined the actual level of bonus that management employees would receive based on performance evaluations. In the case of increasing job grades (hobongs) however, they have seldom had any influence. Although the majority of people with the same seniority and job rank received exactly the same bonus, a small percentage of people designated as high performers (5 to 10 percent) and low performers (5 to 10 percent) received slightly more or less money than their peers. The percentage of high- and low-performing individuals was exactly the same on both ends of the distribution; therefore, those individuals who received low ratings especially perceived the highly rated group as having taken their money from them. This was particularly the case because Korean employees regard the bonus as part of their regular annual earnings as opposed to special extra income.

Since June 29, 1987, most companies have stopped using this system because it may tend to increase internal disharmony and may increase the possibility of labor-management unrest. Most personnel managers whom we interviewed expressed great discomfort about using evaluation results to determine either bonus or pay grade increases. All the managers stated that performance appraisals are extremely subjective, for management job descriptions describe only the general duties of managers in each rank. Confucianism, eschewed the use of detailed rules and preferred the specification of the more general Ye or rules of etiquette; therefore, using detailed job descriptions for each position based on functions performed is simply considered to be too uncivilized and demeaning. Thus, Western-style performance evaluations are absolutely impossible in the Korean firm, often causing severe morale problems, especially when people are given low evaluations and lose face. Therefore, the evaluations actually decrease motivation, as the personnel manager at K7 explains:

Three years ago, our group tried to create a new atmosphere by adopting an achievement or results approach to calculating bonuses. For example, the top 5 percent received an additional 50 percent added to the basic rate whereas the lowest 5 percent lost 50 percent from the basic rate through the use of the forced distribution system. However, it created a reverse effect. It resulted in a negative atmosphere, not a positive effect. After people received their bonus, they found out that a colleague did not receive very much whereas they had more than the basic rate. Thus, people who received more brought back some of their additional money to the person who got less bonus to make up for it. . . . Our Group, therefore, stopped using it last year because this system would break our harmony and unity.

As this example illustrates, for Koreans even receiving a larger bonus or being recognized for doing a superior job can sometimes be very uncomfortable. A common saying in Korea is, "Don't be the top or first and don't be on the bottom or last." This idea probably originated in the great Confucian text, the *Doctrine of the Mean*. K3's personnel manager pointed out yet another serious problem associated with the use of performance evaluations:

[T]he manager of a department is a father-figure. In this situation if he gives a negative evaluation to his subordinates, there is no alternative for them but to leave the company. When they receive a lower evaluation, they are getting a signal to leave. . . . When a person gets a low evaluation or fails to be promoted, he feels isolated from the other group members, experiences a loss of face, and gets very frustrated. Furthermore, he thinks the company has abandoned him. It is therefore very difficult for managers to give low evaluations. It is the main reason they just give an average grade to most people.

These two examples from companies K3 and K7 provide an excellent illustration of the influence of cultural forces on the managerial behavior of a collectively oriented culture. The issues of harmony, support from group members, dependency on superiors in a paternalistic relationship, and face cannot be ignored in any attempt to adopt evaluation systems, promotion schemes, and merit-based pay systems. Indeed, it simply may be impossible to do so in the Korean case.

In spite of these difficulties, rigorous attention to the performance evaluations on a semiannual basis is beneficial in the long run, at least for high-level promotions beginning with the *bujang* or general manager level. Once an individual is considered for promotion to the *bujang* or higher level, then the company personnel director conducts an analysis of the past ten years of evaluations, or twenty semiannual reviews, to summarize trends in an individual's work performance. An employee who has shown a decline in attitude, ability, and performance will have a more difficult time receiving a promotion on schedule. From the *bujang* level upward, the impact of a manager's attitudes and behavior can be very far reaching because of the large scope of functions and people over which managers are in charge. Therefore, movement from *bujang* and higher is considered very carefully, and these promotions are highly competitive. In addition to past work performance, even an employee's background prior to working is given serious attention. This is particularly the case with regard to educational background.

Employees from the *bujang* level to the board of directors have significant responsibilities in terms of performing boundary maintenance responsibilities and do a great deal of negotiating and networking with officials outside of the company in both government and business. Since most of these individuals, who are also at high levels in other organizations, are graduates of Korea's most highly ranked schools, top company managers must also be able to build strong positive interpersonal relations based on alumni connections. Consequently, as seen in Table 13.6, nearly 47 percent of some 835 top managers (director to chairman levels) at publicly traded Chaebol member firms were graduates of Seoul National University. If the next two highest ranked universities are added, Yonsei and Korea University, 65 percent of top managers are accounted for in this group. And if the top six universities are included, then 74 percent of this top management group has been included. Thus, in Korea, where there are presently 100 universities and four-year colleges, 6 percent of the nation's colleges account for nearly three-quarters of this group.

Management Training and Development

Not surprisingly, in Korea where personal cultivation through education is held in such high esteem, continuous training and development of managers is pursued with considerable seriousness. Some management training is performed by such organizations as the Korea Employers' Federation, the Korean Management Association, the Korea Chamber of Commerce and Industry, and other national or industry-level associations. Training programs sponsored by these organizations have gained increasing importance since President Roh Tae Woo's democratic reforms precipitated the emergence of widespread unionization and increasing labor-management strife. Responding to this new industrial relations environment has required that managers learn how to negotiate and how to deal with an increased union presence in the workplace. National and industry-level associations have provided a natural forum for discussing these issues in which managers from different companies can gain access to new ideas and expertise not available at either the member company or group level. The Korea Employers' Federation (KEF), for example, provides extensive educational programs for top managers and personnel and industrial relations managers in a wide range of issues related to labor-management relations and human resource management at its Socho Training Center in Seoul which opened in 1987 (Korea Employers' Federation, 1987:19). Such multiorganization training centers are often co-sponsored in conjunction with a government agency or ministry. KEF's Socho Training Center, for example, has been certified as a government-authorized National Training Institute. Therefore, management training programs developed and offered at the Socho Center receive heavy government subsidization from the Ministry of Labor. The actual costs incurred by companies that send their managers to the Center are very low. Often no payment is required at all in terms of tuition or fees, especially when the topics and skills dealt with in a program are considered crucial to national economic health (Kim, 1987:1).

In spite of the increasing role which external organizations are beginning to play in the area of management training, the major activities in this sphere are handled internally by the Chaebol themselves. Korean corporations consider the ideological and socialization functions of training to be as important, if not more important, than training in basic technical skills. Consequently, when new man-

Table 13.6
University and College Affiliation of Top Managers: Directors to Chairman Levels at Chaebol Member Firms, 1989

Chaebol Group	Number of Subsidiaries	Seoul Nat'l	Yonsei	Korea	Han Yang	Sungkyun Kwan	Pusan	Other	Total
Hyundai	27	84	25	19	12	6	1	37	184.00
Samsung	28	67	12	9	5	7	5	26	131.00
Lucky-Goldstar	31	50	12	12	4	0	5	28	111.00
Daewoo	28	73	8	5	2	0	1	24	113.00
Sunkyong	13	23	3	3	4	2	0	12	47.00
Ssangyong	21	29	7	7	4	0	0	20	67.00
Korea Explosives	23	22	8	1	1	2	1	14	49.00
Hanjin	15	16	7	3	2	2	1	19	50.00
Hyosung	23	18	4	2	1	1	1	10	37.00
Lotte	25	11	6	2	2	1	2	22	46.00
Total	234.00	393.00	92.00	63.00	37.00	21.00	17.00	212.00	835.00
Percent	100	47.07	11.02	7.54	4.43	2.51	2.04	25.39	100.00

Sources: 1. "Shin Kyongyoung Inmaek," *Maeil Kyongje Shinmoon.* March 25, 27, 29, 31; April 1, 3, 5, 8, 12, 14, 18, 22, 27, 29; May 1, 2, 6, 9, 10, 12, 13, 15, 22, 23, 24, 29, 31; June 1, 3, 5, 6, 7, 9, 10, 13, 14, 16.

2. Council of Korean Companies Listed on Stock Exchanges, *Directory of Korean Companies Listed on the Stock Exchanges,* Seoul, 1989.

agement recruits begin employment at a Chaebol member firm, they are required to participate in an extensive and intensive orientation training program that is intended to remold them into "Samsung men," "Hyundai men," "Sunkyong men" and so forth. Typically, such training is held at a major group-level training center where new recruits prepare to begin their careers at different member firms of a Chaebol group. Since the early 1980s, such training centers have developed and expanded, in both size and curricula, at an increasingly rapid pace as the technical sophistication of Korean products and manufacturing process have also increased dramatically. Hyundai, for example, established a comprehensive human resource development center in 1980 and had all its 21,000 employees participate in a rigorous reeducation program.

Today, Hyundai policy requires that all college graduates, upon entering employment with the member firm, participate in a four-week orientation program that covers some 62 subjects over 184 hours of course participation. This initial orientation course includes moral training involving 36.8 percent of course time, organizational life skills, and physical fitness training for 26.2 percent of the time, plant visits for 21.2 percent, and basic job knowledge 15.8 percent. Before completing this course, all new managers are given a variety of Hyundai products, which they are then required to sell in two-person teams in a remote village area (Chang, 1989:198). Hyundai policy also requires that all college graduates attend a revitalizing course every three years for 70 hours of additional English-language study and 110 hours of job skill training (Chang, 1989:199).

Samsung provides another excellent example of extensive corporate investment in training. In 1989, all of Samsung's 180,000 employees participated in several different types of educational programs, ranging from job skills training at their individual company to graduate-level studies at a major university or technical institute overseas. The expenditures made in that same year amounted to some 3.76 percent of Samsung's total gross revenues.

In the case of the major Chaebol, management training is related to major areas of concern to the entire conglomerate at a central group training center or institute. More specific courses are often held at that level. In the case of the Daewoo Group, for example, all entry-level management recruits fresh out of college participate in new-comers training at the group's central Daewoo Training Center, regardless of whether they begin their career at the group headquarters or any of Daewoo's many affiliate firms. Similarly, all recruits return for follow-up training during their second year. As the managers gain seniority and progress up the management hierarchy, they again return to the Daewoo Training Center for special training that emphasizes the responsibilities of each new management rank all the way up to the level of president. Affiliate company presidents frequently participate in a wide range of training activities, including seminars on corporate strategy and strategic planning, special programs initiated by the Chairman's Office, and advance seminars held at Korea's leading universities. All Daewoo managers also return regularly to the Center each year to participate in functionally related courses such as personnel and industrial relations, marketing management, international business management, and research and development. The Center also sponsors foreign language training. On the other hand, more specialized courses tailored to the special business needs of each affiliate are held at that level, and managers are required to participate in these programs as well. Thus, a great deal of management training is continuously taking place in Korean firms. In 1989, at Daewoo alone 10,462 managers participated in training programs at the Daewoo Training Center. Another 5,580 participated in programs held at the affiliate level totaling 16,042 managers and 89,860 person-days (Daewoo Training Center, 1989:11). Such investment in management training is not unusual among any of the Chaebol, and by no means is Daewoo unique in terms of the investment made in managerial development.

Labor Relations

On June 29, 1987, President Roh Tae-Woo declared major democratic reforms, and tremendous industrial conflict followed. Strikes, which had been outlawed since 1971, increased from 276 in 1986 to some 3,749 in 1987. Unionization levels also climbed rapidly, from 12.3 percent of the workforce in 1986 to 18.7 percent in 1990. Since 1987 strikes have gradually decreased until there were only 322 in 1990.

During this period of turmoil and change, workers secured significant economic gains. Compensation, including base rates, bonuses, and allowances, increased by an average of 10.1 percent in 1987, 15.5 percent in 1988, 21.1 percent in 1989, and 19.3 percent in 1990. Management compensation also rose with that of blue-collar and white-collar clerical workers, but the managers themselves did not become union activists. It is not illegal for managers to join unions. Under both Korea's Labor Standards Law and Trade Union Law, the definitions of a worker or laborer are extremely broad. Thus, virtually all wage or salary earners, including managers, are at least in theory provided with legal protection from arbitrary dismissal or discriminatory employer actions for engaging in union activity (Ministry of Labor, 1988:8–9, 35). However, for junior or middle-level managers to join in the class struggle against their companies is simply too inconsistent with their status as Korea's administrative elite.

CONCLUSION

The practices described here are unlikely to change dramatically in the forseeable future. Indeed, instead of conforming more closely to Western policies and practices, we believe that Korean managerial human resource management is likely to become even more clearly familial and Confucian in nature. Employers will especially need to show even greater concern for the "whole person" in the case of their managerial elite. Although Korean firms adhere to the Confucian ideal of providing "lifetime employment" for their employees, neither younger managers nor workers are hesitant to change companies if they feel that they are not being treated with sufficient benevolence by their current employer. This situation will take on increasing significance during the 1990s especially in relationship to compensation, benefits, and promotions.

Because the Korean economy grew so rapidly during the 1980s, and continues to do so in the 1990s, the basic cost of living has skyrocketed, especially in major cities. Land and housing costs in particular have risen at an incredible rate; the cost of living in Seoul, for example, is rapidly approaching even Tokyo's land prices. Similarly, because of the so-called education mania in Korea, the costs involved in preparing one's children to compete for admission to top-ranking schools are becoming increasingly burdensome. Thus, if the Chaebol hope to develop and sustain a loyal management group in the future, they are going to have to invest substantially more resources in housing and education. These are clearly the two most pressing needs for Korean managerial human resource policies to address, but it is also likely that throughout the 1990s they will have to subsidize an ever widening range of needs of their managers and their managers' families.

The strong Korean concern for face cannot be completely handled simply by adding more compensation levels and additional benefits. Thus, more management ranks and titles will be developed as firms age and promotions take longer. However, ever finer gradations of rank may stifle both innovation and communication, and so Korean companies may be forced to create new firms in order to make promotion possible for many middle managers. If these new firms are to flourish, companies will have to make an even greater investment in training.

ACKNOWLEDGMENT

The Research on which this chapter is based was made possible by the generous support for Chris Meek as a fellow of the Kellogg Foundation's Kellogg National Leadership Program, and through direct research grants from the David M. Kennedy Center for International Studies at Brigham Young University.

REFERENCES

Ahn, C. S. 1982. "Imgumkwalli-ui Kukjebikyo." In Korea Personnel Management Association, ed., *Insakwalli Yongu*. Vol. 5. Seoul: Korea Personnel Management Association, pp. 56–80.

Amsden, A. H. 1989. *Asia's Next Giant: South Korea and Late Industrialization*. New York: Oxford University Press.

Bureau of Statistics. 1987. *Korea Statistical Yearbook*. Seoul: Korea Economic Planning Board.

Chai, C., and Chai, W. 1967. *Li Chi: Book of Rites*. Vol. I. New Hyde Park, N.Y.: University Books.

Chan, W. 1987. *Chu Hsi Life and Thought*. Hong Kong: Chinese University Press, pp. 195–205.

Chang, C. 1989. "Human Resource Management in Korea." In K. H. Chung and L. Hak-Chong, eds., *Korean Managerial Dynamics*. New York: Praeger.

Chu, B, Shaw, W. and Choi, D. 1980. *Traditional Korean Legal Attitudes*. Berkeley, Calif.: Institute of East Asian Studies.

Chun, B. 1980. "Legal Attitudes of the Late Yi Dynasty." In B. Chun, W. Shaw, and
    D. Choi, eds., *Traditional Korean Legal Attitudes*. Berkeley, Calif.: Institute of
    East Asian Studies, pp. 1–14.

Chung, K., and Lee, H. 1989. *Korean Managerial Dynamics*. Westport, Conn.: Praeger.

Daewoo Training Center. 1989. *Education and Training in Daewoo*. Seoul: Daewoo
    Corp.

de Bary, W. T., and Haboush, J. 1985. *The Rise of Neo-Confucianism in Korea*. New
    York: Columbia University Press.

Gardner, D. K. 1986. *Chu Hsi and the Ta-hsueh*. Cambridge, Mass.: Harvard University
    Press.

Hahm, P. 1971. *The Korean Political Tradition and Law*. Seoul: Hollym Corp.

————. 1988. *Korean Jurisprudence, Politics and Culture*. Seoul: Younsei University
    Press.

Hamilton, G. G., and Orru, M. 1989. "Organizational Structure of East Asian Com-
    panies." In K. H. Chung and C. Lee, eds., *Korean Managerial Dynamics*. New
    York: Praeger, pp 39–47.

Han, W. 1970. *The History of Korea*. Honolulu: University of Hawaii Press.

Hattori, T. 1989. *Japanese Zaibatsu and Korean Chaebol*. In K. H. Chung and H. Lee,
    eds., *Korean Managerial Dynamics*. Westport, Conn.: Praeger, pp. 79–95.

Janelli, R. L., and Janelli, D. Y. 1982. *Ancestor Worship and Korean Society*. Palo
    Alto, Calif.: Stanford University Press.

Joo, D. 1991. *Evolution of the Korean Economy and High-Tech Development*. Seoul:
    Korean Academy of Industrial Technology.

Kim, D. 1963. *A History of Religions in Korea*. Seoul: Daeji Moonhwa-sa.

Kim, J. 1985. *Education and Development*. Seoul: Seoul National University Press.

Kim, K. 1985. *Man and Society in Korea's Economic Growth*. Seoul: Seoul National
    University Press.

Kim, L. 1989. *Technological Transformation in Korea and Its Implications for Other
    Developing Countries*. Seoul: Korea Development Institute.

Kim, Y. 1987. *Summary Report: ILO Roundtable for Pan-Asian and Pacific Employers'
    Organizations*. Seoul: Korea Employers' Federation.

Koh, F. M. 1981. *Oriental Children in American Homes*. Minneapolis, Minn.: East-
    West Press.

Korea Chamber of Commerce and Industry. 1986. *Kiop-ui Imgumch'egye Kaeson-
    Banghyang*. Seoul: Korea Chamber of Commerce and Industry.

————. 1989 (May). Korea Chamber of Commerce and *Industry Quarterly*: 3.

————. 1989. *1988 Nyondo Pyojunja Model Imgumjosabogo*. Seoul: Korea Chamber of
    Commerce and Industry.

————. 1990 (October). Korea Chamber of Commerce and *Industry Quarterly*: 10.

————. 1990 (February 12). *Korea Chamber of Commerce Weekly*: 2.

Korea Employers' Association. 1987 (June). *KEF Quarterly Review*. 8:19.

Korea Employers' Federation Labor Economics Institute. 1987. *Urinara Kiop-ui Soongjin
    Jed Gaeson-e*. Seoul: Korean Employers' Federation.

Korean National Economic Planning Board. 1963. *Korea Statistical Yearbook*. Seoul:
    Korean National Economic Planning Board.

Lee, K. 1984. *A New History of Korea*. Cambridge, Mass.: Harvard University Press.

Legge, J. 1960. *The Chinese Classics*. Vol. III. Hong Kong: Hong Kong University
    Press.

320   Managers and National Culture

————. 1971. *Confucius: Confucian Analects, The Great Learning and The Doctrine of the Mean*. Mineola, N.Y.: Dover Publications.

————. 1970. *The Works of Mencius*. Mineola, N.Y.: Dover Publications.

Ministry of Education. 1989. *Education in Korea: 1987–1988*. Seoul: Korean Ministry of Education for the Republic of Korea.

Ministry of Labor. 1988. *Labour Laws of Korea*. Korean Ministry of Labor.

————. 1990. *Yearbook of Labor Statistics*. Seoul: Korean Ministry of Labor.

Nahm, A. 1988. *Korea, Tradition and Transformation*. Elizabeth, N.J.: Hollym International Corp.

Park, M. 1979. *Communication Styles in Two Different Cultures: Korean and American*. Seoul: Han Shin Publishing Co.

Seoul National University Management Research Center. 1985. *Hankuk Kiop-ui Hyunhwang-Kwa Kwaje*. Seoul: Seoul National University Press.

Song, Y. 1990. "Characteristics of Korean Organization and Management: A Descriptive Study of Korean Corporations." Unpublished Ph.D. thesis, Provo, Utah, Brigham Young University.

Waley, A. 1989. *The Analects of Confucius*. New York: Vintage Books.

Watson, B. 1963. *Hsun Tzu: Basic Writings*. New York: Columbia University Press.

Yi, S. 1985. "The Influence of Neo-Confucianism on Education and the Civil Service Examination System in Fourteenth- and Fifteenth-Century Korea." In W. T. de Bary and J. Haboush, eds., *The Rise of Neo-Confucianism in Korea*. New York: Columbia University Press, pp. 125–160.

Yi, Y. 1971. *Yulgok Chonso*. Vol. 1. Seoul: Sunggyun'gwon University Press.

Yoo, D. H. 1989 (August). Recruitment Information: '89 the Second Half Recruitment Plan of Companies." *Monthly Recruitment*: 82–88.

14

HONG KONG

Paul S. Kirkbride and Robert I. Westwood

One of the distinctive characteristics of Hong Kong is the preponderance of small businessmen, owner-managers, and entrepreneurs who are as significant, if not more so, than the managerial cadre in the territory. Among the reasons for this situation are the nonseparation of ownership and control in Chinese enterprises; the predominance of small-scale, owner-managed enterprises within the economy; and the virulent entrepreneurialism present among the Chinese population in the territory. The vast majority of Chinese businesses in Hong Kong are family owned; this family orientation and perspective remains valid even for larger enterprises and those that have supposedly gone public (Redding, 1984). Until quite recently, Hong Kong had a fairly truncated managerial cadre in terms of conventional definitions. However, the last few years have seen substantial growth in the managerial ranks and the concomitant emergence, in both the economic and political arenas, of a new middle class. In this chapter we will therefore operate with an expanded definition of manager—one that includes owner-managers, entrepreneurs, and corporate leaders.

Many of Hong Kong's best graduates go into the civil service rather than into the private sector. Indeed, it could be argued that Hong Kong's success lies in its unique mix of entrepreneurial flair harnessed within the structure of a British colonial (but largely indigenously staffed) civil service and public sector. Since many of the best qualified and most able managers (excluding entrepreneurs) are found within the public sector, we will adopt an expanded view of the managerial category to include both the private and public sectors. Thus, we define managers as any organizational members, whether or not they have an ownership interest in the organization, who have the authority to utilize, coordinate, and direct the work of others in the pursuit of organizational objectives.

In order to describe the terrain against which managers in Hong Kong operate, we need to distinguish between the three basic, and very different, kinds of business organization that exist in the territory. First, the typical Chinese family businesses make up the lion's share, numerically, of the enterprises in Hong Kong, such that the "family business is overwhelmingly dominant as an organizational form" (Redding, 1986: 273). These organizations are usually small-scale enterprises. In 1984, for example, the average number of employees per establishment in Hong Kong was only eighteen, which represents a reduction from fifty-five in 1950 (Redding and Tam, 1985). In the manufacturing sector in 1989, for example, 48,726 establishments employed less than 100 workers (constituting 97 percent of the total), with 503,942 persons engaged in employment (representing 62 percent of the manufacturing workforce).

Second, there are the locally based and largely British-dominated *hongs*, which are long-established large trading conglomerates. Finally, there are the multinational corporations and other businesses from the United States, Western Europe, and Japan that have increasingly opened subsidiaries in Hong Kong or used the territory as a base for China, Far East, or Pacific Rim operations.

Hong Kong is currently a separate entity as a British dependent territory, but we should not lose sight of either its past or its immediate future. Since the midnineteenth century, Hong Kong has been a British colony. Obviously, much of its organizational behavior has been influenced by British systems and attitudes, particularly in the *hongs* and the public sector. Yet, increasingly, major influences are coming from another quarter. Under the 1984 Sino-British Joint Declaration on the Question of Hong Kong, the territory will revert to the sovereignty and jurisdiction of the People's Republic of China (PRC) from July 1, 1997 in the form of a Special Administrative Region. Hong Kong is thus facing a unique transition. The territory is also a complex mix of Western and Eastern cultural influences. It is populated mainly by Chinese refugees from the mainland and as such is a typical example of a Nanyang Chinese (Chinese of the Southern Ocean) community (Redding, 1986).

THE MANAGERIAL CONTEXT

Economic Background

Hong Kong is an extremely small territory with little arable land and a lack of resources other than its location, harbor, and population. Hong Kong has transformed itself during the last 150 years from a tiny British enclave into an international commercial and financial center, with a visible trade of $1,135 billion (gross value, 1989), a stock exchange ranked fourth in the world, and the world's busiest container port in terms of throughput. The population also grew from a mere 23,817 in 1845 to 5.8 million in 1989. Even though in many ways it is cosmopolitan and international, Hong Kong has always been numerically and culturally dominated by ethnic Chinese who currently make up about 98 percent of the population.

Hong Kong has also sustained an incredible annual average growth in gross domestic product (GDP) of 9.9 percent from 1961 to 1981 and 6 percent from 1981 to 1986. This growth has fluctuated in the last few years and was at a low

Table 14.1
Average Annual Growth Rates of GDP and GDP per Head (percentage)

Year(s)	GDP	GDP per head
1961–1966	10.9%	8.0%
1966–1971	7.6%	5.4%
1971–1976	8.8%	6.8%
1976–1981	12.4%	9.5%
1982	3.0%	1.4%
1983	6.5%	4.9%
1984	9.5%	8.4%
1985	−0.1%	−1.2%
1986	11.9%	10.3%
1987	13.8%	12.2%
1988	7.3%	6.0%
1989	2.5%	1.1%

Source: National Income Branch, Census and Statistics Branch, 1989.

2.5 percent in 1989, with an estimated 3 percent for 1990. Its economic growth has been well ahead of all the advanced Western industrial economies and only a little behind Japan. Table 14.1 shows Hong Kong's annual growth rates of both total GDP and GDP per head. From the data we can note both the impressive sustained growth throughout the period, despite the usual downturns associated with world economic conditions, and the capacity of the Hong Kong economy to recover more rapidly than most and bounce back to continued growth.

How has this phenomenal economic performance been accomplished? Given limited domestic resources, the answer clearly lies in Hong Kong's trading capacity and in its vigorous, adaptive, export-led industrialization in the postwar period. It has been argued that several factors contribute to Hong Kong's industrial development (Chen, 1980). First, it has been the beneficiary of successive postwar inflows of labor, capital, and entrepreneurial flair from the mainland.

Second, external events such as the Korean War and the Sino-Soviet alliance forced Hong Kong to shift its economic orientation towards industrialization and away from the earlier entrepôt focus. Third, Hong Kong has benefited from a benevolent colonial administration that has enabled economic expansion through the creation of political stability. Finally, the government has been consistently committed to a policy of positive noninterventionism and thus provides the opportunity and freedom for people to pursue economic goals in a largely unfettered manner. This combination of opportune historical developments; relatively efficient, equitable, and laissez-faire government; abundant supply of relatively cheap and productive labor; and dynamic entrepreneurial talent has spawned some of the most impressive economic growth ever witnessed over the past 150 years.

The labor force has grown markedly and steadily over the period and currently stands at about 2.8 million. Participation rates have averaged over 64 percent in the last decade, and unemployment is traditionally low, with a level of just over 1 percent in 1989. Hong Kong presently has an extremely tight labor market. Indeed, in some areas it is suffering from labor shortages that have been made more acute by the increasing rates of emigration as nervousness about 1997 is converted into tangible action. These issues are posing significant problems for Hong Kong enterprises and challenges to management.

Organizational Context

The emergence and growth of a managerial and entrepreneurial class and the development of a managerial/entrepreneurial ideology are influenced by a host of environmental factors, including the political, economic, legal, and sociocultural contexts. Of immediate relevance is the dominant organizational context.

The export-led nature of Hong Kong's industrialization and economic development has resulted in manufacturing activity which is in the form of production to order for buyers and producers in the export markets. Thus, its economy frequently amounts to little more than offshore production, assembling, processing, and subcontracting work for mainly U.S. and European clients. There has been, and still is, little indigenous design and product development, sparse domestic branding, and limited direct knowledge of foreign markets. Thus, the key success criteria are adaptability and flexibility so as to respond to the rapidly changing demands of their clients and the overseas markets. This form of industrial activity has clear implications for a general business ethos, the form and structure of enterprises, and the nature of the managerial task in Hong Kong firms.

Redding (1986) has argued that small Chinese businesses are centralized, implicitly structured, paternalistic, and nepotistic organizations that tend to rely on personalistic networks of business contacts for external linkages and exhibit little systematic planning or organization. It has been argued that such firms are best seen as molecular business units within wider networks of related firms, which enables flexible responses to be made to changing customer demands (Redding and Tam, 1985). One implication of this structure is that Chinese managers in such organizations face extremely simple internal environments that are easily mastered. Thus, more attention can be given to the extremely complex external environment (Tam, 1987). The result is a system that nurtures entrepreneurs rather than managers. The prevalent nepotism leads to the "bifurcation of managerial career pathways" whereby promotion is only for relatives, while others have to search for advancement outside the company, often by starting a small business. For both internal and external reasons, then, Chinese businesses lean toward "fission" and instability rather than "fusion" and growth (Tam, 1987: 5–6).

Managerial Ideology

What kind of managerial ideology arises from this organizational context? It has been persuasively argued that the "essence of Chinese economic organisation is familism" (Wong, 1985: 58). Family unity has traditionally been at the heart of Chinese culture, and the central tenets of Confucianism prescribe an ordered hierarchical structure for society with the family at the heart. Both the family system and societal structure are based on dependence, conformity, and respect. Traditional family values and structures transported into the business organization provide a built-in legitimizing framework and the core of a distinctive managerial ideology.

The family structure of these businesses entails an owner-father position, and the owner as father is entitled to exert fatherlike authority over the business. Leadership is autocratic, paternalistic, and highly personalized. Although the father has authority over the business, the assets are not his to do with as he wishes. They belong to the family (*jia*), and so the father-owner is like a trustee on behalf of the family (Wong, 1989). His managerial role, mirroring his fatherly role, is to run the business so as to maintain, extend, and perpetuate the family interests. This is the guiding rationale for business—a rationale that is different from the rationality and impersonality of the West and that implies a different managerial ideology and practice. Redding (1987) has argued that Chinese societies have therefore not developed legitimized systems, such as the Western business corporation, outside those provided by the family and the state.

The strengths of familism in the organizational context lie in its adaptiveness and flexibility, in the cohesiveness provided by family ties and interests, and in the ability to pool resources. However, it does have some potential drawbacks in the organizational setting. It has been argued that it provides a general built-in limitation on the growth and size of organization (Redding, 1986; Wong, 1989) despite some limited counterevidence (Lassere, 1988). A related problem concerns succession. The traditional patrilineal inheritance system under which sons receive an equal share of the inheritance places a natural strain on the coherence of family assets. Other potential weaknesses include an inability to make long-term plans, inattention to personnel planning and development, a responsive posture, and a lack of loyalty from nonfamily members. Allied to this traditional familism are a set of widely held normative orientations, which include pragmatism, materialism, desire for order, and the short-term time orientation that forms such an important part of the refugee mentality. In conclusion, we can employ Lau's (1982) depiction of the ethos of the Hong Kong people as "utilitarianistic familism" to summarize the more widely prevailing social orientation and the managerial ideology of Hong Kong.

Of course, the role of management also depends on the general politicoeconomic context or milieu within which it has to operate, as well as the more specific organizational context. In many countries, the prevailing managerial ideology is simply a particular representation of a broader and more general capitalist ideology; this is the case in Hong Kong. The territory represents a remarkably strong version of a capitalist society. This orientation, in part, stems from the postwar influx of economic and ideological refugees from the People's Republic of China.

Hong Kong's economy is thus built on strong capitalist principles of free trade, open business systems, and the relatively unfettered pursuit of profit and personal wealth. Personal wealth is prized, sought after, conspicuously displayed, and is a considerable mark of status and prestige. Business activity, and the wealth it may bring, is seen as the most legitimate and plausible route to security and mobility. The impermanence of Hong Kong, with its "borrowed place on borrowed time" (Hughes, 1976) syndrome, has been identified as the single most important factor in accounting for Hong Kong's managerial style and philosophy (Chung, 1975). Chung has argued that the perceived transitory nature of Hong Kong leads people to focus on the present, to have strong materialistic tendencies, and to have feelings of rootlessness. There is thus little identification with Hong Kong itself, and, as Chung noted (with remarkable prescience), key members of the population will leave if they cannot readily pursue their economic interests.

The economic inequalities inherent in Hong Kong's economic system seem to be largely accepted and legitimized. Indeed, the openness of the system is seen as providing opportunity (Lau, 1982). In two recent surveys, Hong Kong people did not view the business success of others as deriving from exploitation and did not endorse any redistributive intervention (Lau and Kuan, 1988). Broadly speaking, wealth and wealth-seeking activities are legitimized. People appear to support the strong capitalist values of unfettered pursuit of wealth, private accumulation, open competition, success built on individual initiative and effort, and nongovernment interference. As Lau and Kuan note from their extensive empirical work on attitudes in the territory, "the capitalist system of Hong Kong is founded upon solid normative orientations" (1988, 63).

These attitudes have, of course, been molded in a particular political and legal context. The colonial administration has provided a stable politico-legal framework in which entrepreneurial and business interests could flourish. The laissez-faire policies of the government have provided an enabling setting for the full-blown pursuit of capitalistic goals such that Hong Kong is probably the ultimate free market economy. This environment, as we have seen, has been generally welcomed by the Chinese population who see it as providing the opportunities they desire as well as considerable freedom in business and managerial practice. It is also seen as a necessary environment to enable managers in Hong Kong to pursue flexible and adaptive strategies in coping with their particular international trading environment.

CULTURE AND MANAGERIAL BEHAVIOR

Hong Kong is a society in flux and transition. As Lau and Kuan note, "Hong Kong is geographically a part of China, but for more than a century and a half it has developed apart from China as an increasingly distinctive social entity" (1988: 1). Thus, the "Hong Kong ethos represents a mixture of traditional Chinese culture and modern cultural traits fostered by the particular nature of the Hong Kong society itself and the changes it has experienced in the past, particularly since the Second World War" (1988: 2). As we have already outlined some of the more modern orientations and the political, legal, and economic contexts, we can now turn to the key cultural traits or values that are derived from traditional Chinese culture and that still inform and influence behavior today (Bond, 1986). In each case we will endeavor to demonstrate the implications for managerial behavior.

Causality

It has been suggested (Redding, 1980) that the Chinese have a distinctive paradigm of causation characterized by nonlinearity, multiple and mutual forces, and a relational conceptualization. Events or objects are situated in a complex "field of force" that is the result of mutually influencing and related elements rather than a single cause-effect chain. In contrast, the West has developed a linear, mechanical, unicausal conception of causation. Related to this Chinese conception of causality are three associated elements; contextualism, holism, and probability. Chinese society has been described as a high-context society; that is, people apprehend elements (events, relationships) in relation to the context in which they occur. Holism refers to the cognitive predisposition to perceive stimuli as being part of a greater whole rather than as individual elements. Finally, while the Western causal model lends itself to probabilistic thinking where past and present events can be extrapolated into the future according to the logic of sequential, linear, cause-effect relations, the Chinese cognitive system with its nonlinear, multicausal, and holistic tendencies makes for differences in conceiving probabilistically (Wright, 1977).

The implications for managerial perception and behavior are consequential and far-reaching. First, while the modern Western corporation is built on the impersonal and abstract foundations of Weberian bureaucracy, Chinese organizations are structurally more simple and less formalized (Pugh and Redding, 1985; Redding and Wong, 1986). Second, problem-solving and decision-making styles are likely to be different, with less reliance on formalized information systems. Third, the differences noted above naturally lead to the absence of systematic, long-term, quantitatively based planning (Graham and Tuan, 1988). Instead, a Chinese manager is more likely to attempt to stay tuned in to concrete events around him through informal and personal contacts and intuition. Fourth,

Chinese organizations are less likely than those in the West to view control and coordination abstractly and impersonally and thus develop formal control systems. In the Chinese case, control and coordination will be viewed in specific concrete terms, be contingent on context, and be personalistic and relationship-specific, utilizing implicit, even moralistic, mechanisms. Finally, Kirkbride, Tang, and Westwood (1991) have argued that contextualism and holism have a bearing on Chinese conflict and negotiation behavior with the adoption of less assertive and less competitive orientations.

Time

In contrast to the Western notion of time as linear and monochronic, the Chinese conception is polychronic and cyclical, with little differentiation between past and present so that time "stretches" in an indefinite manner between past and present. Polychronic conceptions stress the involvement of people and completion of transactions rather than adherence to preset schedules. The major managerial implication of these temporal differences has to do with planning. The Western conception of time lends itself to formal planning and to detailed scheduling of activities. The indications are that the Chinese manager is less inclined to engage in such formal planning activity and scheduling. Furthermore, Redding (1980) has argued that the absence of a structuring time frame leads to the increased need for centralized control and to a reliance on more personalistic and particularistic methods of coordination.

The Self Concept

While the Western conception of the individual has associations with uniqueness, separateness, free will, and self-determination, the Chinese conception of self connotes relationships and interconnections. In the Chinese view, the self cannot be separated from the relationships and the situation in which the individual is embedded. As Jackofsky, Slocum, and McQuaid put it, "the 'jen' philosophy states that to describe a person, one must describe not only the personality but the intimate social and cultural environment that makes his/her existence meaningful" (1988: 47). The major implications of this view of self is that notions like self-actualization and individual self-achievement may not be meaningful in a Chinese context. Empirical research has revealed distinctively Chinese patterns of need, with higher scores on social and pecuniary needs and lower scores on self-actualization compared with Western patterns (Graham and Leung, 1987; Redding, 1977). There are clear implications for reward systems and training and development in this self-concept and the motivational evidence. It also has major implications for how individuals define themselves and how they view interpersonal relationships. This colors the managerial role and how managers conduct themselves in relation to others.

Harmony

Harmony is a key element in Chinese culture, and the preservation of harmony is a key responsibility of actors in all social relationships. This is to be achieved by avoiding any extreme behaviors that would upset the relationship. Although the Chinese have evolved elaborate mechanisms to prevent conflict from developing and becoming manifest, they have rather fewer social mechanisms for coping with and resolving conflict once it has surfaced. Generally speaking, open confrontation is not acceptable; this concept takes on even greater significance when linked to hierarchical structure and respect for authority. This focus on harmony may lead to what would be seen in the West as suboptimal decision making. For example, in a conflict situation, the Chinese may seek to optimize harmony at the expense of a suboptimal decision, whereas Westerners may seek to optimize the decision output at the expense of group harmony (Tang and Kirkbride, 1986). Indeed, Evans, Sculli, and Yau (1987) have suggested that Chinese organizations may well put harmony before efficiency in terms of overall objectives.

Li

In Chinese philosophy there is a pervasive injunction that one must always conduct oneself within the norms of propriety (*Li*). This is accomplished by behaving in line with the five hierarchical relations (Wu-Lun) and the five cardinal virtues of Confucianism (loyalty, filial piety, faithfulness, caring, and sincerity). The maintenance of order in East Asian societies is based on moral norms and self-restraint in contrast to the legalism of the West. It is suggested, then, that "the source of authority in the Chinese case is eventually moral" (Redding, 1984: 15), and thus rests on the shared normative legitimacy of unequal but reciprocal relations, on mutual obligation, and on the behavioral requirements of the five virtues and rules of propriety. Managers who enact their role in accordance with these precepts can expect to have their authority accepted and legitimized.

Thus, in Chinese organizations, an elaborate, informal system of behavioral norms and mutual expectations and obligations maintains the order. Consequently, a significant part of the management task is to remain mindful and true to these principles and to behave appropriately in any relationship. A further consequence is the relative absence of the need for more explicit, formal, and impersonal control systems. This is one reason for the low formalization reported in Chinese enterprises (Pugh and Redding, 1985; Redding and Wong, 1986).

Face and Shame

While "face" is universal, it takes on particular significance in the Chinese case. Chinese people are highly sensitive to saving face and will conduct themselves in social settings in order to gain, protect, give, or take face. Losing face is a social sanction of the greatest force and represents a major means for regulating and controlling social behavior. Chinese culture is also described as a "shame" culture as distinct from typical Western "guilt" cultures. People evaluate their behavior and are judged by others with reference to *social* approval or disapproval. In constructing a piece of behavior, people will ask themselves whether or not it will be viewed by others as right and proper and will receive social approval. Shame is created if others see the behavior as improper. In guilt cultures, the individual internalizes general moral or behavioral principles. It is to this internal referent that they turn in constructing their actions and in judging their own and others' behavior.

Managers in Chinese societies have to be mindful of the implications of face and shame in all interactions but particularly in the areas of negotiation (Kirkbride, Tang, and Westwood, 1991; Tang and Kirkbride, 1986), performance appraisal (Redding, 1982), training and development (Kirkbride, Tang, and Shae, 1989a), and discipline. These cultural orientations may lead to conflict avoidance, a reluctance to surface important issues, and a fear of exposure to criticism. In the case of discipline, it appears that shame is the key mechanism (Ho, 1986). Managers in Hong Kong may avoid taking disciplinary action for a long time because of the implications of face. Yet it would appear that the cultural imperatives of shame and collectivism are likely to lead to discipline being administered in public rather than the more frequent yet private acts of discipline favored by more individualistic Western managers.

Particularism

Chinese culture is extremely pragmatic and tends toward the particularistic (as opposed to the universalistic). Such pragmatism is heightened in the Hong Kong Chinese case given their precariousness and marginality (Evans, Sculli, and Yau, 1987; Redding, 1984; Redding and Casey, 1976). Westerners, who are more universalistic, tend toward absolute norms and rules that apply in all circumstances and to all persons. In contrast, the Chinese are less likely to seek abstract and all-embracing rule systems and will consider each case in terms of the particular situation, especially in terms of the prevailing relationships. The practice of nepotism is partially explained by this cultural value. The pragmatic/particularist orientation has strong implications for the management task in terms of control systems and the specific areas of manager-employee relations, selection, and performance evaluation.

Collectivism

Hofstede (1980) has noted that Hong Kong scores low on individualism and is thus a collectivist culture. Collectivist societies are socially oriented, and the frame of reference is collectivity; individualistic societies value individual performance and achievement. In the Western work context, the individual is the focus for the design of jobs; standard and target setting; performance evaluation; rewards allocation and motivational techniques. None of this, nor the organization and management practices that go with it, may be applicable in a collectivist culture. In collectivist cultures, persons subsume their personal interests to collective interest and display loyalty to the collective in exchange for security and protection within the collective.

Hierarchy, Status, and Power Distance

Chinese society is sharply hierarchical, even in family relations. These hierarchical relations are marked by status and involve clear mutual obligations and behavioral norms and standards. They have been readily transferred into the organizational context. This marked and legitimized disparity in power and authority is reflected in the high power distance scores of Chinese societies on Hofstede's (1980) instrument. An acceptance of authority and a cultural norm militate against challenging authority, further reinforcing the authority of management and the centralization, authoritarian, and paternalistic management style outlined here. Lower managers have little scope for discretion and initiative and are not much consulted before decisions are made. Managers show less inclination to share information or objectives with subordinates and are averse to participative systems (Redding and Casey, 1976).

We have now traced how certain traditional Chinese values and orientations continue to affect the managerial behavior of the Hong Kong Chinese. However, we have also seen how aspects of a distinctive managerial ideology have emerged in Hong Kong from the mixture of traditional values and modern circumstances. These determinants and resulting behaviors are summarized in Figure 14.1.

HUMAN RESOURCE MANAGEMENT IN HONG KONG

Having identified the various cultural and environmental factors that influence managerial behavior in Hong Kong, we can now turn to more practical concerns. In this section we describe how managers in Hong Kong are recruited, selected, trained, compensated, and appraised, and we also consider the extent of managerial unionization and managerial attitudes toward trade unions.

Managerial Demographics

It is difficult to specify precisely the size of the managerial cadre in Hong Kong. This is partly because the expanded definition with which we are working includes entrepreneurs and partly because the available statistical data are limited. An examination of labor force distribution by occupation reveals that 11 percent belong to either the administrative and managerial category or the professional and technical category. Of course, not all members of these two groups will be managers in any real sense. However, both categories grew over the 1978–88 decade, as have other tertiary occupations at the expense of manufacturing and production (Census and Statistics Department, 1990). Another method of estimation is to consider the labor force by activity status. Here we can note that 4.8 percent of the labor force comprises employers and another 6.1 percent are self-employed, although not all of the self-employed will be classifiable as managers. It is equally clear that large numbers of managers will be subsumed within the 86 percent of the labor force who are employees. It thus appears that the total managerial cadre including entrepreneurs may be somewhere in the region of 10 percent of the labor force.

With regard to the sex distribution of managers, we can note that, although

Figure 14.1
Hong Kong Chinese Values and Their Implications for Managerial and Organizational Behavior

CULTURAL VALUES/ORIENTATIONS	IMPLICATIONS FOR MANAGERIAL/ ORGANIZATIONAL BEHAVIOUR
Causality - Contextualism - Holism	Managers in Chinese organizations are not reliant on formalized information systems and long term plans.
	Organizations are less formalized and rationalistic.
	Managers are less likely (than Western counterparts) to use assertive and competitive conflict styles.
Polychronic and cyclical view of time	Managers unlikely to engage in formal planning and detailed scheduling.
	Increased use of personalistic and particularistic methods of co-ordination and control.
Relational view of Self	Managerial implications of Western motivation theories may be inappropriate and ineffective.
	Extensive use of pecuniary rewards.
Harmony	Managers are not likely to engage in open confrontation and conflict with subordinates or peers.
	Group harmony preferred as an 'end' to optimal decisions.
Norms of propriety - 'Li'	Tendency for organizational order to be maintained by internalized means.
	Less need for formalized and externalized means of control.
	Managerial decisions regarding employees often judged against moral rather than technical or rationalistic criteria.

Figure 14.1 (continued)

CULTURAL VALUES/ORIENTATIONS	IMPLICATIONS FOR MANAGERIAL/ ORGANIZATIONAL BEHAVIOUR
'Face' and 'Shame'	Managers tend to avoid situations which could lead to loss of face or shame. Conflict avoidance prevalent. Employees tend to fear criticism. Tendency to use shaming mechanisms to control and discipline subordinates.
Particularism and Pragmatism	Systems of nepotism commonly used. Managers may show lack of 'fairness' and 'consistency' in decisions regarding employees such as selection, appraisal, promotion and discipline.
Collectivism	Western managerial techniques built on individualistic assumptions (eg MBO, performance evaluation, appraisal) may not be appropriate or effective.
High power distance	Employees willing to accept managerial authority. Union activity less likely. Lower incidence of collective bargaining. Authoritarian and paternalistic managerial styles common. Participative management rare.

the total labor force is split 63 percent male/27 percent female, higher relative concentrations of males are found among employers, the self-employed, and the administrative and managerial echelon (Census and Statistics Department, 1990). In terms of levels of educational attainment, less than 30 percent of both the administrative and managerial and professional and technical occupational categories are qualified to degree level. In both cases, large numbers are qualified at the upper secondary level, which in Hong Kong includes craft skill courses at technical institutes. Although no data are available on the ethnicity of managers in Hong Kong, we can note that the territory is predominantly (98 percent) Chinese. Most of the entrepreneurs in the territory are Chinese apart from a small Indian community. The overwhelming majority of managerial employees will also be Chinese, but there is a sizable and growing expatriate managerial cadre.

It is equally difficult to specify the demographics of managers in the public sector. Burns and Scott (1984: 17) report that the total size of the Hong Kong civil service in 1983 was 173,633, which represented a 65 percent increase over 1973. Of these, 1,850 (or 1 percent) are either administrative or executive grade, which would mean that they were certainly managers (1984: 21). Taking a wider definition, we find that 12 percent of civil service is on a salary grade (Master Pay Scale 30 and above, including Directorate) which would normally indicate possible managerial status (1984: 24). The sex distribution of the civil service (as of 1983) was 73 percent male and 27 percent female, although more women appear to be represented at higher levels.

Managerial Recruitment

Obviously, the major source of Hong Kong's managers is the education system and, increasingly, the tertiary level of that system which produces graduates at subdegree and degree levels. The tertiary education sector in Hong Kong is administered by the University and Polytechnic Grants Committee (UPGC) which advises the governor on higher education policy. At present, seven institutions are funded via the UPGC: the University of Hong Kong (founded in 1911); the Chinese University of Hong Kong (1963); Hong Kong Polytechnic (1972); the City Polytechnic of Hong Kong (1984); Hong Kong Baptist College (1956); the Open Learning Institute (1989); and the Hong Kong University of Science and Technology (1991). In total, all the existing institutions produced a total of 3,380 graduates, 809 postgraduates, and 4,345 subdegree diploma holders in 1989 (Census and Statistics Department, 1990).

Owing to both the high demand for higher education in the territory and the historical restrictions on the supply of tertiary places, many local students have had to go abroad for their higher education. While no precise figures exist, the Educational Commission Report No. 3 estimated that annually 1,600 undergraduate students went to the United Kingdom, 3,900 went to the United States or Canada, 5,400 to the University of East Asia (or allied East Asia Open Institute) in Macau, and smaller unspecified numbers to Australia, Taiwan, the PRC, and Singapore (Educational Commission, 1988: 19).

All the existing tertiary institutions in Hong Kong offer undergraduate degrees in business and management areas. MBAs are offered at Hong Kong University (part-time), the Chinese University (full and part-time), City Polytechnic (part-time), and Hong Kong Polytechnic (part-time). The Hong Kong University of Science and Technology will also offer postgraduate degrees in business and management disciplines and will reportedly specialize in management science. The expansion of MBA-type management education is of very recent origin. The two established universities have offered MBAs for some time, but the number of graduates has been rather small. The demand for MBAs in the territory has been so great that many students have gone outside the UPGC institutions (or even the territory) to find a place.

Of course, another source of supply of managers is from outside the territory in the form of expatriates. Until recent years, the trend had been for a reduction in the use of expatriates owing to pressures for localization. This has occurred in both the private and public sectors, where the government has had a civil service localization policy since 1946. However, even by 1983 over 50 percent of Civil Service Directorate posts were still held by expatriates (Burns and Scott, 1984: 30). Since the signing of the Sino-British Agreement on the future of the territory post–1997, Hong Kong has experienced an increasing emigration problem caused by political and economic uncertainty. A recent survey of 361 private sector organizations reported that around 16 percent of all managers were expatriates (Kirkbride and Tang, 1989). As a result of the emigration problem, 29 percent of companies were recruiting more expatriates. These increasingly came from elsewhere in the South East Asian region as well as from the advanced Western economies. In addition, 73 percent of companies with localization plans reported a shortage of suitable local candidates to replace expatriates.

The final source of supply is from the existing Hong Kong labor market, but this source is proving increasingly difficult. Demand for managers is increasing, fueled by economic growth and foreign investment, at a time when there is an acute labor shortage (Joint Associations Working Group, 1989). The results are high levels of managerial labor turnover and an increasing salary spiral as companies chase talented and experienced managers (Kirkbride, Tang, and Gilbert, 1989b).

Managerial Selection

In the private sector, it is difficult to specify exactly what criteria are used to select managers. However, small Chinese businesses are well known for operating nepotistic selection systems for both entry and promotion, which systematically favor family members over outsiders (Redding and Wong, 1986; Tam, 1987). It is difficult to specify the criteria in use in larger organizations because there is a lack of research, but both the particularism mentioned earlier and the general Chinese tendency to value formal academic qualifications should be noted. However, the extent to which this latter criterion is as important to employers as it appears to be to employees and potential employees is open to doubt.

The situation in the public sector is somewhat clearer. Recruitment to the core administrative officer class is predicated on formal academic qualifications such as the possession of a good honors degree. Candidates are then exposed to a formal written examination followed by two interviews and a medical test. During these interviews, the interviewers are attempting to determine whether the candidates have the basic qualities required for an administrative officer. These qualities are deemed to be "a critical and analytical mind, a sound education, common sense, a determination to get results, a potential ability to command and lead others, a tolerance of the opinions of others when fundamental principles are involved, a sense of proportion, a broad outlook, and versatility and adaptability" (Mushkat, 1984: 101).

The systems of selection used for managers in the private sector are fairly standard. For direct recruitment they involve the usual filters of application form/curriculum vitae, interviews, and tests. Even in larger organizations such procedures rarely involve scientific testing and rely heavily on multiple or panel interview processes (Kirkbride and Tang, 1989: 22–23).

Management Development

With the growth of the service sector and managerial activity in Hong Kong, management development has become an increased priority. In an attempt to increase levels of management development in the territory, in 1984 the government set up the Management Development Centre of Hong Kong (MDC) under the auspices of the Vocational Training Council. The main purpose of the Centre is to improve the quality and quantity of management in Hong Kong, ensuring that it is capable of meeting changing needs, in both the short and long term.

The MDC has four principal functions: (1) it operates as a research center undertaking or commissioning research projects concerning management training and development; (2) it is charged with developing new teaching programs and materials and management information that can be used by academic institutions and companies; (3) it collaborates with training boards, educational and training institutions, and professional associations in the design and use of an overall management development and training system to meet Hong Kong's needs; and (4) it seeks to promote effective management programs to encourage entrepreneurs and managers to participate in relevant activities and to promote the use of management information.

Very few companies in Hong Kong currently provide any formal Western-style management development for their staff (Kirkbride and Tang, 1989). Such management development that does occur is generally confined to the larger organizations and to subsidiaries of MNCs or foreign firms. Much of the development that does take place takes the form of individual employees deciding to follow part-time courses of study at educational institutions at their own cost and during their own time. Where organizations provide management development for their staff, they tend to use low-cost providers such as the academic institutions and bodies such as the Hong Kong Management Association rather than consultancies. However, the absence of Western-style management development should not be seen as an absence of management development per se. Small Chinese family businesses do develop entrepreneurial and managerial talent but not by formal management development methods. Instead, they use an indigenous approach that focuses on socialization, coaching, and a form of action learning (Redding, 1986).

In the public sector, training and development are often regarded as a "poor relation" to other functions. As a result, this function has traditionally been underfunded, neglected, and lacking in official recognition. As Scott and Burns have noted, prior "to 1980, management training in the Hong Kong government did not receive much support from senior officials" (1984: 130). However, since 1977 there has been a great expansion in management training provision, and the Civil Service Training Centre now offers a wide portfolio of management courses for officers at higher levels on the master pay scale. Another major development in recent years in the public sector has been the setting up of the Senior Staff Course Centre, which is primarily charged with the design and delivery of a three-month, full-time senior management training program called the Senior Staff Course.

Managerial Compensation

Unfortunately, there is a dearth of information in Hong Kong regarding the levels, methods, and forms of managerial remuneration. It may be suggested that traditional Chinese business secrecy, allied with a laissez-faire government, has led to a lack of detailed statistics in this area. Using what little data are available, we will endeavor to flesh out a basic picture of managerial compensation in this section.

In 1988, the average salary (for nonmanual supervisory, technical, and clerical workers) was HK$61,788, or approximately US$7,921 (Census and Statistics Department, 1990: 46).[*] Turning our attention to entry-level positions, we can note (Hong Kong Institute of Personnel Management, 1990b: 24–25) that the mean starting salary for a business administration degree holder in 1990 was HK$98,088 (US$12,575), while a new MBA could expect to earn HK$112,017 (US$14,360). It is, of course, much easier to provide data on remuneration levels in the public sector. Using the previous cutoff of Master Pay Scale (MPS) point 30 and above as indicative of managerial status, we observe that in 1990 this was set at HK$241,980 (US$31,023) per annum, while the top point (MPS 49) represented HK$534,060 (US$68,470). The higher Directorate Grades ranged from HK$595,200 (US$76,300) for D1 to HK$1,392,000 (US$178,460) for D10 (Hong Kong Institute of Personnel Management, 1990a: 73–74).

Eighty-six percent of companies reviewed managerial salaries annually, while 11 percent did a salary review on a six-month basis (Kirkbride and Tang, 1989). Formal systems of job evaluation to determine managerial salaries were not

---

[*] All conversions have been made at the rate of US$1 = HK$7.80, which is the rate at which the Hong Kong rate is pegged to that of the U.S.

common, with only 35 percent of companies currently using such systems and over 50 percent neither having a system nor planning to have one in the near future (Kirkbride and Tang, 1989: 55). The most popular method of job evaluation appeared to be job classification or grading, followed by use of the Hay points assessment method (Kirkbride and Tang, 1989: 56). These findings fit with an aspect of the cultural context mentioned earlier. The rules of *Li* mean that management may decide rewards unilaterally without recourse to formalistic performance appraisal and job evaluations, but they must do so within the spirit of the moral code. Similarly, ethical factors such as loyalty, trust, and good behavior are likely to be valued and reflected in rewards more than harder performance indicators.

Large numbers of Hong Kong organizations use forms of incentive payment system. Kirkbride and Tang (1989: 50) report the usage of different forms of incentive system for managerial staff, with the most popular form being discretionary bonuses (found in 70 percent of companies), followed by profit sharing (23 per cent) and individual systems of payment by results. The use of discretionary bonuses was more prevalent in indigenous than in foreign companies.

The most common fringe benefits in the areas of pensions/insurance, leave, and financial provision for both local managerial staff and expatriates are also reported by Kirkbride and Tang (1989: 52–54). The most usual benefits were medical insurance plans, contributory provident funds or retirement plans, personal accident insurance, permanent disability insurance, and death-in-service benefits. The most common leave benefits were paid annual leave, maternity leave, paid medical appointments, paid compassionate leave, and marriage leave.

The most common financial benefits available to staff appear to be a Lunar New Year Bonus, discounts on products and services, housing allowances, subscriptions to professional bodies and clubs, and mortgage facilities. Finally, a wide range of other benefits may be provided, including company cars, medical facilities, education allowances, long service awards, and subsidized meals.

Managerial Appraisal

Redding (1982) has argued that Western performance appraisal systems are culturally inappropriate for Hong Kong because they rest on assumptions that do not transfer to the Chinese culture. Such systems focus on individual accountability and control, which are not accepted in the more collectivist Chinese culture. As Redding notes, ''Chinese managerial systems, when practised in their indigenous form, such as that of the Chinese family business, tend to avoid the measurement of individual performance by managers. Their lower levels of structure do not allow for it, their more personalistic and paternalistic styles run counter to it'' (1982: 16). The universalistic notions of fairness and objectivity implicit in formal systems of performance appraisal also run counter to the more particularistic Chinese culture. Finally, some of the design aspects of appraisal systems, such as two-way communication and rights of appeal, which are based on the premise of low ''power-distance'' (Hofstede, 1980) between superior and subordinate, are negated by the high power distance culture of Hong Kong.

Thus, we would expect to find little use of such systems among the smaller Chinese organizations in the territory. Elsewhere, in the larger organizations and the public sector, Western influences have ensured that such systems are adopted, although we would have reservations about the extent to which such systems operate effectively.

Some recent survey data reveal the extent of performance appraisal penetration in the private sector (Kirkbride and Tang, 1989: 35–39). Seventy-two percent of the sample of 361 companies reported that they had formal systems of performance appraisal. Usually, managerial appraisals were done annually, and the most widespread appraisal methods were results-oriented systems (used in 53 percent of companies), written reports (46 percent), and alphanumeric ratings (42 percent). The use of alphanumeric systems was more prevalent in larger organizations with specialist personnel functions and in U.S., Australian, and British organizations than in either smaller organizations or Hong Kong or Japanese firms.

Appraisals in the larger companies (over 200 staff) were usually made by the immediate superior, with quite high use of "grandfathers" (older, respected employees/managers who look after younger staff members) but little evidence of personnel department involvement. Virtually all companies conducting managerial appraisal used interviews, yet only 20 percent provided training in interviewing and 55 percent provided no appraisal training at all. Such training was more likely to be provided by foreign companies than by indigenous firms (Kirkbride and Tang, 1989: 35–39).

The Hong Kong civil service has traditionally had a system of staff reporting rather than performance appraisal (Terry, 1984). In essence, this system involves two activities: the annual completion of a staff report form and an interview with the member of staff concerned. In the last few years the government has been gradually introducing a new system of performance appraisal. This goes beyond staff reporting to encompass performance analysis and counseling. It involves the measuring of actual performance on the job and the setting of performance targets for the future. Attention is paid to both the negative and positive aspects of performance, and the appraisal interview has become a two-way communication process.

Despite these changes, there are doubts as to how effective the new system of performance appraisal in the civil service will prove to be. One problem concerns the cultural backdrop against which the system operates. Performance appraisal systems rely on a degree of trust and openness, which are generally not present in low-trust Chinese cultures. As Terry has noted:

[The] new approach to performance appraisal requires an element of *trust* between management (the appraiser) and staff (the appraisee). Although the creation of such an element is precisely the object of the new philosophy of staff management, it is easier said than done. . . . Hong Kong is essentially a Chinese society, and the vast majority of civil servants are Chinese. Despite their Westernized education and way of life, they still hold various Chinese values and beliefs. There is a fairly strong belief in the concept of hierarchy, meaning that the subordinate is and always should be "subordinate" to the superior. What this amounts to in terms of performance appraisal is that management and staff may not easily communicate on an equal and collaborative basis. To those working under him, the "judicial" role of the manager is bound to overshadow his "coach" role. Although the same phenomenon is a dysfunction of hierarchy which may appear in other countries, the cultural peculiarities in Hong Kong have certainly compounded the problem. (Terry, 1984: 166; emphasis in original)

Labor Relations

The labor relations scene in postwar Hong Kong may be said to have three significant features (Ng and Levin, 1983): the relative weakness and fragmentation of the trade union movement and the low density of trade union membership; the low incidence of collective bargaining arrangements between workers and employers; and the comparatively low levels of strike activity by international standards.

As England and Rear have noted, the "particular circumstances of trade union development in Hong Kong have produced a form of trade unionism largely characterized by weakness, fragmentation, and a concern for political rather than job-related questions" (1981: 140). Despite recent consolidations, the trade union movement remains both fragmented and divided. In 1988 there were 472 trade unions in Hong Kong, of which 430 were employee unions, 29 were employers associations, and 13 were mixtures of both (Registrar of Trade Unions, 1989). The employee unions represented a total of 416,136 members and were split between civil service unions (169) and private sector unions (261). Hong Kong trade unions are also divided by ideological orientation with 81 unions (173,956 members) aligned to the pro-Beijing Hong Kong Federation of Trade Unions (FTU), 71 unions (17,835 members) aligned to the pro-Taiwan (Kuomintang) Hong Kong and Kowloon Trades Union Council (TUC), and 278 unions (224,345) members who declare no allegiance.

Overall union density is around 15 percent, with a low of around 7 percent in manufacturing and over 50 percent in the civil service (Arn, 1984; Ng, 1986). White-collar unionism is relatively weak in the private sector but is strong in the public sector where, despite the recent aggregate decline in union membership, white-collar trade unionism has enjoyed sustained growth over the last twenty years. Managerial unionization is virtually unknown outside of the public sector.

A corollary of the weakness of the trade union movement has been the relative neglect of formal systems of collective bargaining. Trade unions have, by and large, tended to focus on political issues and neglect economic issues. Recent survey research has empirically quantified this neglect in respect of the methods used to determine salary levels, with only 1 percent of companies using collective negotiations with trade unions or staff associations (Kirkbride and Tang, 1989: 49). Both employers and managers in Hong Kong are generally antithetical to organized labor and would see the recognition of trade unions as a diminution of the managerial prerogative and a loss of face.

The weakness of the trade union movement and the lack of collective bargaining lead us to consideration of the final characteristic of the local industrial relations scene: the comparatively low levels of industrial action. For example, 1988 saw only eight strikes, which involved around 800 workers and resulted in a total of 2,345 working days lost. The trend in terms of industrial action also appears to be downward over recent years.

Recent survey data (Kirkbride and Tang, 1989:39–44) on industrial relations practices confirm the picture outlined above. Eighteen percent of responding companies did not have written contracts for managerial employees. Only 25 percent of companies reported having any collective bargaining procedural agreements covering managers, and only 49 percent had discipline and grievance procedures covering managerial employees.

CONCLUSIONS

As we have noted, Hong Kong has experienced a long period of almost unparalleled economic growth since World War II. Until very recently, the territory, together with the other members of the so-called four little dragons of East Asia (Singapore, South Korea, and Taiwan), was still exhibiting strong economic growth and increasing prosperity. However, the long-term continuation of this success story is far from certain. It has been suggested that the factors leading to the success of Hong Kong in its initial stage of exporting labor-intensive products may actually be negative factors as it moves into the second stage of exporting capital and technology-intensive products (Ho, 1988). And there remains the unresolved question of the economic and political impact of the takeover of Hong Kong in 1997 by the People's Republic of China. Organizations in Hong Kong currently face three related problems that stem from the issues of structural change and 1997: increased skilled labor emigration from Hong Kong because of fears surrounding 1997; a severe labor shortage as a result of continued economic growth; and the need for skill upgrading to meet the new technological demands in manufacturing. We may briefly consider each of these in turn.

The period since the signing of the Sino-British Joint Declaration has witnessed a marked expansion in emigration from the territory. From a situation of a net outflow of around 20,000 in the late 1970s and early 1980s, the territory has seen increases to 30,000 in 1987, 45,000 in 1988, 42,000 in 1989, and a provisional figure of over 55,000 in 1990 (following the Tiananmen Square incident). A recent study reported average organizational emigration turnover rates of 1.45 percent, but this overall figure hides great disparities among different industries, occupations, organizational grades, and individual companies (Kirkbride, Tang, and Shae, 1989b; Kirkbride, Tang, and Ko, 1989c).

Particularly hard hit have been managerial grades, with another survey reporting emigration turnover rates of 6.5 percent for managers and 7.0 percent for senior managers (Hong Kong Institute of Personnel Management, 1988). Emigrants are predominantly young graduates drawn from professional, managerial, and technical ranks (Kirkbride, Tang, and Ko, 1989b), and this is causing a worrying loss of skilled personnel from the territory at a time of increasing demand for such services. As a result, many larger organizations are suspending localization programs; recruiting more expatriates; increasing the training and development of junior managers for succession; and offering increased reward packages that tie staff to the territory ("golden handcuffs").

One early result of the emigration pressure has been an inflationary wage and salary spiral as organizations chase dwindling stocks of skilled personnel in key functions. The emigration problem has forced human resource management issues to the top of large organization's agendas in Hong Kong, and we would suggest that managers will be dealing with this problem for some time to come.

At the same time as the emigration problem, Hong Kong has been grappling with a more general labor shortage caused by the period of recent strong economic growth and a reduction in the population growth rate. A recent study suggested that the overall shortfall in 1988 was 200,000 vacancies (Joint Associations Working Group, 1989). Both this general labor shortage and the emigration problem are causing a series of negative effects for the Hong Kong economy, including rising inflation; limitations on GDP growth; declining quality of services and products; and, increasingly, the threats by multinational companies to move regional bases and production facilities elsewhere in East Asia.

Finally, there is the need to remedy a perceived weakness in technological upgrading. The Hong Kong government's policy of positive noninterventionism has increasingly been questioned by calls for the government to be more proactive and to provide active support and facilitation to help Hong Kong industry move toward the use of higher technology and thus the production of higher quality goods (SRI, 1989). These calls have been prompted by the recognition of the need for Hong Kong industry, beleaguered by labor shortages, rising wage bills, and a decline in competitiveness, to retrack its industrial direction. It may be argued that managers in Hong Kong need extensive technological upgrading if they are to cope with such changes.

Two key issues on the human resource agenda for the territory in the 1990s stem from the factors outlined here. First, increasing labor turnover, whether as a result of emigration or increasing job opportunities in Hong Kong, naturally leads to increased replacement by both external recruitment and internal promotion. In both cases this produces a need for induction training, job performance training, and training for promotion. In addition, the need for the skill upgrading necessary for technological growth generates massive training demands. Hong Kong organizations are currently attempting to respond to these trends, with the greatest priorities being accorded to middle management, administrative, and supervisory levels which are being most seriously affected by emigration (Kirkbride and Tang, 1989: 30).

A major challenge for personnel management in Hong Kong in the 1990s is thus to increase both the volume and quality of management training and development against a backdrop of traditional neglect, paucity of current provision, and general shortage of experienced management development specialists and management trainers (Kirkbride and Tang, 1990; Ng, 1983). Only 37 percent of Hong Kong companies have a training department, and even fewer (14 percent) have specialist training staff (Kirkbride and Tang, 1989: 25). Where training and development are provided, they often appear to be very traditional and didactic (Kirkbride and Tang, 1989: 28; Ng, 1983). While this could be partly a result of the use of inexperienced and untrained training staff, it may stem largely from Chinese learning and teaching dynamics (Kirkbride, Tang, and Shae, 1989a).

Second, if emigration continues at present levels and the government resists labor importation, companies will increasingly be unable to secure adequate replacements in the marketplace. One result will be that attention will inevitably turn to the levels of overmanning and organizational inefficiency in the use of labor which exist in the territory. While this assertion may surprise the outside observer given Hong Kong's reputation for efficiency, it can easily be explained by the historic low-wage economy and the lack of penalty for labor inefficiency. As a senior government economist has noted, "there appears to be scope for Hong Kong to continue to achieve above average growth through improved output per manhour within the limits of existing technology" (McLean, 1986).

It may therefore be argued that another major challenge for personnel managers in Hong Kong in the 1990s will be learning to live with the reduced labor supply through structural reorganization and a focus on individual productivity (in managerial and administrative ranks) and organizational efficiency. In this respect, it is worrying to note that personnel managers in the territory currently enjoy little discretion and influence over such topics as organizational development and work-restructuring and thus spend little time on them (Kirkbride and Tang, 1989: 61). Even more bothersome is the fact that the personnel managers themselves see such issues as being relatively unimportant in the future. While this perception may change with a deepening labor crisis, it is not clear that it will change early enough to avoid major problems.

Turning our attention to more general matters, we can note that predicting the future of management in Hong Kong is exceedingly difficult given the political and economic uncertainties facing the territory. If the "one country, two systems" concept enshrined in the Joint Declaration is not adhered to after 1997, then we can expect the breakdown of the "Hong Kong economic miracle" and an extremely difficult time for the managerial cadre in the territory. More optimistically, if the Joint Declaration is honored, then the challenges to management may continue in broadly current directions. We would thus expect trends toward the adoption of more sophisticated technology; higher quality production; further advances in the service sector; more educated managers with significant exposure to Western management practices and ideas; and an increased emphasis on professional management skills and competencies. If foreign direct investment continues to grow at current rates, we would expect the local management cadre to be further exposed to a variety of management and business approaches from Europe, the United States, Japan, and possibly from other countries in the region.

Despite this latter trend, there are few signs that small family businesses are in decline or that all larger Chinese businesses have lost their family orientation. The Chinese entrepreneurial drive and the desire for one's own business, together with the persisting cultural values, will probably mean that owner-managers of family business will continue to predominate, at least in the short to medium term. But shifts are taking place, and some commentators (Bangsberg, 1987) have pointed to clashes between older patriarchs and younger, often Western-educated, sons over how the business should be run, with the new generation pushing for modern, professional management techniques. Current management students in Hong Kong clearly prefer to work in the multinationals and not in the traditional Chinese businesses.

Some observers have suggested that Hong Kong may only be experiencing a surface westernization, with Hong Kong Chinese organizations and managers pragmatically selecting certain managerial systems, processes, and practices from the West, which are then embedded in Chinese structures and value systems. Bond and King (1985) have argued that the Hong Kong Chinese cognitively and emotionally separate modernization from westernization, remaining Sino-centric and able to conceive of themselves as being modern without losing their Chineseness. Furthermore, as Deyo (1976) cogently suggests, even if increasing organizational size and complexity and the internationalization of business do bring about changes, those changes need cause neither a Western homogenization nor a perpetuation of traditional practices and values. Instead, they may lead to the emergence of new organizational practices, perhaps forming the basis for the phenomenon of a new Asian capitalism (Berger and Hsiao, 1988).

REFERENCES

Arn, J. 1984. "Public Sector Unions." In I. Scott and J. P. Burns, eds., *The Hong Kong Civil Service: Personnel Policies and Practices*. Hong Kong: Oxford University Press.

Bangsberg, P. 1987 (January). Bridging the Generation Gap in Hong Kong's Family Businesses." *Asian Business* 40–41.

Berger, P. L. and Hsiao, M.H.H., eds. 1988. *In Search of an East Asian Development Model*. New Brunswick, N.J.: Transaction Books.

Bond, M. H., ed. 1986. *The Psychology of the Chinese People*. Hong Kong: Oxford University Press.

Bond, M. H. and Ambrose, Y.C. King. 1985. "Coping with the Threat of Westernisation in Hong Kong." *International Journal of Intercultural Relations* 9:351–364.

Burns, J. P., and Scott, I. 1984. "A Profile of the Civil Service." In I. Scott and J. P. Burns, eds., *The Hong Kong Civil Service: Personnel Policies and Practices*. Hong Kong: Oxford University Press.

Census and Statistics Department. 1990. *Hong Kong Annual Digest of Statistics*. Hong Kong: Government Printer.

Chen, E.K.Y. 1980. "The Economic Setting." In D. Lethbridge, ed., *The Business Environment in Hong Kong*. Hong Kong: Oxford University Press.

Chung, S. Y. 1975. "Management Styles of Hong Kong: Their Strengths and Weaknesses." *The Hong Kong Manager* 11(1):10–16.

Deyo, F. C. 1976. *Decision-making and Supervisory Authority in Cross-cultural Per-*

spective. Sociology Working Paper No. 55, Department of Sociology, University of Singapore.

Educational Commission. 1988. *Report No 3: The Structure of Tertiary Education and the Future of Private Schools.* Hong Kong: Government Printer.

England, J. and Rear, J. 1981. *Industrial Relations and Law in Hong Kong.* Hong Kong: Oxford University Press.

Evans, W. A., Sculli, D. and Yau, W.S.L. 1987. "Cross-cultural Factors in the Identification of Managerial Potential." *Journal of General Management* 13(1):52–59.

Graham, R. G., and Tuan, C. 1988. "An Empirical Analysis of Manpower Planning in Hong Kong." *International Journal of Manpower* 9(1):21–27.

———, and Leung, K. 1987 (February/March). "Management Motivation in Hong Kong." *The Hong Kong Manager:* 17–24.

Ho, D.Y.F. 1986. "Chinese Patterns of Socialization: A Critical Review." In M.H. Bond, ed., *The Psychology of the Chinese People.* Hong Kong: Oxford University Press.

Ho, H.C.Y. 1988. "Views on Hong Kong's Past Growth and Future Prospects." In H.C.Y. Ho and L. C. Chau, eds., *The Economic System of Hong Kong.* Hong Kong: Asian Research Service.

Hofstede, G. 1980. *Cultures' Consequences: International Differences in Work-related Values.* London: Sage.

Hong Kong Institute of Personnel Management. 1990a. *Pay Trend Survey.* Hong Kong: HKIPM.

———. 1990b. *Pay Level Survey.* Hong Kong: HKIPM.

Hughes, R. 1976. *Borrowed Place, Borrowed Time: Hong Kong and Its Many Faces.* London: Andre Deutsch.

Jackofsky, E. F., Slocum, J. W., and McQuaid. S.J. 1988. "Cultural Values and the CEO: Alluring Companions?" *Academy of Management Executive* 2(1):39–49.

Joint Associations Working Group. 1989. *A Report on Hong Kong's Labour Shortage.* Hong Kong: Joint Associations Working Group—Griffiths Management Limited.

Kirkbride, P.S., and Tang, S.F.Y. 1989. *The Present State of Personnel Management in Hong Kong.* Hong Kong: Vocational Training Council, Government Printer.

———. 1990. "Training in Hong Kong: The Missing Link in Industrial Development?" In J. Ben Shaw, J. E. Beck, G. R. Ferris, and K. M. Rowland, eds., *Research in Personnel and Human Resource Management—Supplement on International Human Resource Management.* Greenwich, Conn.: JAI Press.

Kirkbride, P.S., Tang, S.F.Y., and Ko, G. 1989b. *Emigration from Hong Kong: Evidence from Organisations.* Hong Kong: Hong Kong Institute of Personnel Management.

———. 1989c. *Emigration from Hong Kong: Evidence from Professionals.* Hong Kong: Hong Kong Institute of Personnel Management.

Kirkbride, P.S., Tang, S.F.Y., and Shae, W. C. 1989a. "The Transferability of Management Training and Development: The Case of Hong Kong." *Asia-Pacific Human Resources Journal* 27(1):7–20.

Kirkbride, P.S., Tang, S.F.Y. and Westwood, R.I. 1991. "Chinese Conflict Preferences and Negotiating Behaviour: Cultural and Psychological Influences." *Organization Studies* 12(3).

Lassere, P. 1988. "Corporate Strategic Management and the Overseas Chinese Groups." *Asia Pacific Journal of Management* 5(2):115–131.

Lau, S. 1982. *Society and Politics in Hong Kong.* Hong Kong: Chinese University Press.

Lau, S., and Kuan, H. 1988. *The Ethos of the Hong Kong Chinese*. Hong Kong: Chinese University Press.

McLean, A. 1986. "Symposium on Hong Kong's Economic Growth." *Hong Kong Economic Papers* 17:111–128.

Mushkat, M. 1984. "Staffing the Administrative Class." In I. Scott and J.P. Burns, eds., *The Hong Kong Civil Service: Personnel Policies and Practices*. Hong Kong: Oxford University Press.

Ng, S. 1983. "Training Problems and Challenges in a Newly Industrialising Economy: The Case of Hong Kong." *International Labour Review* 126:467–478.

———. 1986. "Labour." In Joseph Y.S. Cheng, ed., *Hong Kong in Transition*. Hong Kong: Oxford University Press.

Ng, S., and Levin, D.A. 1983. "Editors' Introduction." In S. Ng and D. A. Levin, eds., *Contemporary Issues in Hong Kong Labour Relations*. Hong Kong: Centre of Asian Studies, University of Hong Kong.

Pugh, D. S., and Redding, S.G. 1985. "A Comparative Study of the Structure and Context of Chinese Businesses in Hong Kong." Paper presented at the Association of Teachers of Management Research Conference, Ashridge, England.

Redding, S. G. 1977. "Some Perceptions of Psychological Needs Among Managers in Southeast Asia." In Y. H. Poortinga, ed., *Basic Problems in Cross Cultural Psychology*. Amsterdam: Swets and Zeitlinger.

———. 1980. "Cognition as an Aspect of Culture and Its Relation to Management Processes: An Exploratory View of the Chinese Case." *Journal of Management Studies* 17:127–148.

———. 1982. "Results-Orientation and the Orient: The Role of Individualism as a Cultural Determinant of Western Management Techniques." Paper presented to the Ninth Annual Conference of the Asian Regional Training and Development Association, Hong Kong.

———. 1984. "Varieties of the Iron Rice Bowl." *The Hong Kong Manager* 20(5):11–15.

———. 1986. "Developing Managers Without 'Management Development': The Overseas Chinese Solution." *Management Education and Development* 17:271–281.

———. 1987. "The Study of Managerial Ideology among Overseas Chinese Owner-Managers." *Asia-Pacific Journal of Management* 4(3):167–177.

Redding, S.G., and Casey, T. W. 1976. "Managerial Beliefs among Asian Managers." In R. L. Taylor, M. J. O'Connell, R. A. Zawacki, and D. D. Warwick, eds., *Proceedings of the Academy of Management 36th Annual Meeting*. Kansas City: Academy of Management, p. 355.

Redding, S.G., and Tam, S.K.W. 1985. "Networks and Molecular Organisations: An Exploratory View of Chinese Firms in Hong Kong." In K. C. Mun and T. S. Chan, eds., *Proceedings of the Inaugural Meeting of the Southeast Asia Region Academy of International Business*. Hong Kong: Chinese University of Hong Kong.

Redding, S.G., and Wong, G.Y.Y. 1986. "The Psychology of Chinese Organisational Behaviour." In M. H. Bond, ed., *The Psychology of the Chinese People*. Hong Kong: Oxford University Press.

Registrar of Trades Unions. 1989. *Annual Report*. Hong Kong: Government Printer.

Scott, I., and Burns, J. P. 1984. "Training." In I. Scott and J.P. Burns, eds., *The Hong Kong Civil Service: Personnel Policies and Practices*. Hong Kong: Oxford University Press.

SRI International. 1989. *Building Prosperity: A Five-Part Economic Strategy for Hong Kong's Future.* Hong Kong: Hong Kong Economic Survey Limited.

Tam, S.K.W. 1987. "The Making of Chinese Managers in Hong Kong." Paper presented at the Hong Kong Institute of Personnel Management Tenth Anniversary Conference, Hong Kong.

Tang, S.F.Y., and Kirkbride, P.S. 1986. "Developing Conflict Management Skills in Hong Kong: An Analysis of Some Cross-cultural Implications." *Management Education and Development* 17:287–301.

Terry, L. 1984. "Performance Appraisal." In I. Scott and J. P. Burns, eds., *The Hong Kong Civil Service: Personnel Policies and Practices.* Hong Kong: Oxford University Press.

Wong, S. 1985. "The Chinese Family Firm: A Model." *British Journal of Sociology* 36(1):58–72.

Wright, G. N. 1977. Cultural Differences in Probabilistic Thinking: An Extension into Southeast Asia." *Technical Report 77–1*, Decision Analysis Unit, Brunel University.

15

PEOPLE'S REPUBLIC OF CHINA

Oded Shenkar

The managers treated in this chapter include a great variety of people who occupy supervisory positions in organizations within the People's Republic of China (PRC). Because of the special nature of the political and economic system in the PRC, such managers, or "cadres", include both conventional supervisors in business units and supervisory personnel in regulatory agencies within the state and party apparati who indirectly manage enterprises in this still centrally planned economy. Here, unless otherwise noted, we define managers as individuals holding at least a first-line supervisory position in either state-owned or collective enterprises in the nonrural sector of the Chinese economy. In the urban, industrial sector, state enterprises are still dominant, although during the reform period (1978–89), the proportion of collective-owned enterprises in the urban sector gradually increased. Many collectives are in fact joint ventures of domestic state firms rather than associations of individual entrepreneurs. We do not refer to managers in private businesses that are strictly limited in terms of size and scope of activities.

Following the Tiananmen massacre in early June 1989, the Chinese leadership has decided to further curtail private enterprises and to close a significant number of such ventures. However, we do refer briefly to managers in foreign affiliates operating in the PRC (international joint ventures and wholly owned foreign subsidiaries). Although the number of executives employed in foreign-owned ventures remains minuscule, their impact as a reference point for PRC managers has been remarkable. PRC managers have been employed in an economy that grew quite erratically during the 1949–89 period. During relatively pragmatic periods, such as 1949–52 and 1953–57 (the first Five-Year Plan), the economy registered impressive gross national product (GNP) annual growth rates of 22.1 percent and 6.7 percent, respectively. The same was true for the 1961–65 and 1977–83 periods, which registered annual GNP growth rates of 8.1 percent and

10.7 percent, respectively. However, during the political campaigns of the Great Leap Forward (1958–61) and the Cultural Revolution (1966–76), GNP actually declined at the rates of –6.6 and –2.5, respectively (Henley and Nyaw, 1987). Table 15.1 reports annual GNP figures for the PRC.

A word of caution: China is an enormous and extremely diversified country, with a multitude of dialects, subcultures, religions, and economic conditions, as well as various organizational forms (state-owned enterprises, collectives, private firms, foreign joint ventures, and wholly owned foreign affiliates). Generalizations regarding "China" must therefore be made with extreme prudence. Another word of caution has to do with the reliability of Chinese statistics. A combination of politically cynical use of such statistics and periodic purges of people employed in statistical agencies produced statistics that are sometimes distorted or contradictory. Although we applied special care to the problem and report what in our judgment were fairly accurate estimates, the reader should approach those numbers with caution.

EVOLUTION OF THE CHINESE MANAGERIAL CLASS

The Chinese Imperial bureaucracy that governed China for 2,000 years until 1911 was an autonomous status group closely associated with the literati (scholars) stratum, with whom it shared similar status criteria and symbols. This helped the bureaucracy to defend its position vis-à-vis the emperor and other strata, and enabled it to withstand their pressures for nepotistic recruitment while retaining such privileges for its own members.

In Confucianism, China's state orthodoxy, there was a pronounced hierarchical ranking of different occupations, with the bureaucrat, or the learned man, at the top. Since the bureaucrat enjoyed the highest status, as well as considerable earnings opportunities, members of other strata were always eager to join the bureaucracy. The pressures came particularly from those with economic resources who wished to convert them to the power, prestige, and revenue associated with bureaucratic service, from those already in service who wished to control the access to bureaucratic positions, and from the emperor, who wanted to staff bureaucratic positions with his own protégés. The high status of the bureaucrat was expressed in various symbols, for example, the use of an official carriage or the colors that differentiated among the various ranks. Officials who were not initially recruited through the ideologically approved channel of the examination system but, for example, through purchase of positions were not entitled to ride the official carriage that served the other bureaucrats. A strong effort was also made to tie the status symbols of bureaucratic service with the powerful kinship framework. An official's family could display banners announcing "here resides a successful candidate of the government examinations," and families of high-ranking examination candidates were invited to have an audience with the emperor.

During the Republican period (1911–49), attempts were made to form a new managerial stratum to replace the crumbling imperial officialdom. Such a stratum

Table 15.1
GNP, People's Republic of China, 1949–87

Year	GNP[1]	Year	GNP[2]
1949	49	1967	173.00
1950	59	1968	164.60
1951	69	1969	188.10
1952	82	1970	224.00
1953	87	1971	241.50
1954	91	1972	248.40
1955	100	1973	269.50
1956	108	1974	272.90
1957	115	1975	290.90
1958	137	1976	282.00
1959	129	1977	307.20
1960	129	1978	350.20
1961	99	1979	389.10
1962	113	1980	429.30
1963	125	1981	457.50
1964	142	1982	504.70
1965	163	1983	565.20
1966	177	1984	679.20
		1985	832.20
		1986	937.20
		1987[3]	1085.90

[1] *Source:* CIA, People's Republic of China: *Handbook of Economic Indicators*, August 1976, p. 3; CIA, *Handbook of Economic Statistics,* September 1977, p. 31. In units of billion 1975 dollars.

[2] *Source*: World Tables, Data files of the World Bank, pp. 192–193. Unit: Billions of current Chinese yuans.

[3] Estimate.

evolved out of Western-educated officials staffing the Nationalist bureaucracy (1927–35), but it failed to achieve any meaningful cohesiveness. The deterioration of both the internal situation (the struggle with the communists) and the external one (the Japanese aggression) prevented the further development of an effective management group in Republican China.

With the establishment of the People's Republic, the managerial group of the Republicans was effectively neutralized. Although managers with highly technical skills, such as finance, remained in service for several more years, they were eventually replaced by political trustworthy managers with a record of revolutionary struggle and an "appropriate" class background.

Because of Mao's opposition to the creation of a bureaucratic class (see later discussion), a cohesive managerial stratum has not developed in the PRC. Instead, a stratum of Chinese Communist party (CCP) cadres has emerged. These people shared, or at least appeared to have shared, the Maoist ideology of egalitarianism. In reality, CCP officials constituted an elite group, entitled to special perks that were not available to the broader population. Later on, Mao would severely criticize them as being extravagant and wasteful, who "the more they devour, the more they want" (see Shenkar, 1983).

In many instances, CCP cadres did not occupy management positions in state enterprises or even regulatory posts in state agencies. Instead, they staffed the parallel superimposed party hierarchy that looked over state organizations at every level, and frequently yielded the real decision-making power. Managers in state enterprises were not always CCP members, but they never developed into a cohesive status group. Unlike cadres in the CCP apparatus, managers in state units lacked the support of key social groups, such as the military, which enabled the party to achieve superior status. And while party cadres derived their legitimacy from the ideology of the regime and from their past contribution to the revolutionary struggle, managers in state and collective enterprises lacked any such bases and as a result were subject to challenge and even removal, especially during political campaigns.

During the reform period (1978 on), a genuine attempt was made to anchor the legitimacy of the managerial group in its technological skill which by now was recognized as vital to the achievement of the "Four Modernizations." In 1988, an American news network that interviewed a Chinese youngster heard that his aspiration was to become a manager and thereby contribute to China's progress. By the time the network returned for a followup (in late 1989), the youngster had changed his mind. Apparently, in post-Tiananmen China, being a manager involves too few benefits to outweigh the risk.

CHINESE TRADITIONAL AND MODERN IDEOLOGIES

Chinese tradition is a heterogeneous system of values and beliefs. The imperial state philosophy, Confucianism, coexisted with other philosophies and religions—among them Taoism, Buddhism, Legalism, and Mohism—whose values greatly differed from those of Confucianism. Rival schools of Confucian thought emphasized different values as representing the true Confucian tradition. Nevertheless, Confucianism may be considered as the backbone of a Chinese tradition whose values continue to influence the Chinese people.

Confucius placed the bureaucrat, the gentleman in his words, highest on the social ladder, not because he was more knowledgeable in administration, but because he possessed some broad virtues: "The Master gave Ch'i-tiao K'ai leave to take office, but he replied, 'I have not yet sufficiently perfected myself in the virtue of good faith'. The Master was delighted" (Confucius, Book 5: Article 5). It is therefore suggested that "once a man has contrived to put himself aright, he will find no difficulty at all in filling any government post" (Confucius 13:13). Confucius opposed the idea that the ideal official should possess technical skills:

Fan Ch'ih asked the Master to teach him about farming. The Master said, you had much better consult some old farmer. He asked to be taught about gardening. The Master said, "you had much better go to some old vegetable-gardener.... A gentleman.... What need has he to practice farming?" (Confucius 13:4)

The opposition to technical training is also apparent in this statement:

A villager from Ta-hsiang said, Master K'ung is no doubt a very great man and vastly learned. But he does nothing to bear out this reputation. The Master, hearing of it, said to his disciples, what shall I take up? Shall I take up chariot-driving? Or shall it be archery? I think I will take up driving. (Confucius 9:2)

Technical skills were not denounced; rather, Confucianism was opposed to technical skills being acquired by the bureaucrat: "Just as the hundred apprentices must live in workshops to perfect themselves in their craft, so the gentleman studies, that he may improve himself in the way" (Confucius 19:7).

Once the bureaucrat was recruited and in office, he did not have to concentrate on a limited area. What Confucius wanted were officials with broad interests: "He who is broad wins the multitude" (Confucius 17:6), adding that a "High office filled by men of narrow views . . . are things I cannot bear to see" (Confucius 3:26). In addition to his opposition to technical specialization in the bureaucracy, Confucius discounted the importance of directives issued from above: "If the ruler himself is upright, all will go well even though he does not give orders. But if he himself is not upright, even though he gives orders, they will not be obeyed" (13:6). Furthermore, Confucius saw rules as degrading: "Govern the people by regulations . . . and they will flee from you and lose all self respect" (2:3).

The application of Confucian ideology to the Chinese Imperial bureaucracy was relatively smooth. The successful candidates of the examination system were able generalists capable of filling many positions that did not require much technical knowledge. This was particularly true in local posts, such as that of a district magistrate, who performed multiple functions in huge areas merely on the basis of some general policy guidelines. A problem, however, arose in areas such as finance, public works, and the military, where technical knowledge was pertinent. The Chinese, unwilling to lose efficiency in these important domains, yet unwilling as well to deviate from the Confucian framework, found some solutions. The military, for example, was designated separately from the civil bureaucracy, and therefore was not subject to Confucian prescription. Fiscal and technical functions in the localities were performed by individuals with no official status. These solutions enabled the Imperial administration to utilize bureaucratic principles such as specialized division of labor and regulations without violating the Confucian mode (Shenkar, 1984).

In the twentieth century, modern ideologies emerged in China. One such ideology was that of Sun Yat-sen, as summarized in his famous Three Principles of the People and Fundamentals of National Reconstruction. This ideology provided the basis for the Chinese Nationalist bureaucracy (1927–35) and later for the Taiwan Republic of China (ROC) government. It sought to adopt Western principles of technical expertise while preserving certain traditional principles, especially those pertaining to the importance of the family.

In 1949, Maoist ideology, adapted from Marxism-Leninism and Mao's own revolutionary experience in Yanan, became the central ideological pillar of the PRC. As Marx before him, Mao suspected that managers and experts could be easily tempted to establish a new ruling class. He also shared Marx's view that since narrow specialization was not the wave of the future, the need for technical experts was only temporary. Mao insisted that formal training and practical experience were the two components of "complete knowledge" (1967:33–41). He suggested the following criteria for the recruitment of cadres: "Whether or not a cadre is resolute in carrying out the Party line, keeps to Party discipline, has close ties with the masses, has the ability to find his bearings independently, and is active, hard working and unselfish. This is what is meant by "appointing people on their merit" (1966:202).

Mao also opposed strict directives, because of their inability to cope with changing situations, as well as being harmful to the initiative of the lower echelons. Directives were considered harmful mechanisms that higher echelons utilized to enhance private gain, as well as a means of "control, restriction and suppression." It was only logical, therefore, that the amount of authority and decision-making power assigned to the lower echelons be increased. This was also a response to the extreme variations among localities and the resulting need to improvise from the central guidelines, with adaptations for local conditions. An example of this adaptation is seen in Yanan, with the Campaign for Crack Troops and Simple Administration. Writes Selden (1971:222): "The tasks of the official involved more than routine enactment of policies handed down from above; he was required to modify and adapt policy." Mao emphasized that the lower and local echelons were always to be consulted: "We should encourage the style of work in which the local authorities are consulted on the matters to be taken up . . . first confer with the localities on all matters concerning them and issue no order without full consultation."

Inherent in the Maoist position is the perception that the lower levels be more knowledgeable at times or at least as knowledgeable as the higher ones. Therefore, each should learn from the other: "There must be mutual instruction . . . between officers and soldiers . . . the masses of the soldiers should be roused to discuss how to attack and capture enemy positions and how to fulfill their combat tasks."

In an effort to prevent the principle of consultation from becoming merely a ritual, Mao also specified that the upper echelons should not affect the opinion of the lower levels by expressing their own thoughts first: "Ask your subordinates about matters you don't understand or don't know, and do not lightly express your approval or disapproval" (1977:378).

Mao opposed economic incentives. Economic incentives for managers and workers, he suggested, encouraged an orientation toward possessions, lack of initiative, and required an immense control apparatus to prevent inefficiency (Andors, 1974:26). Instead, Mao encouraged moral motivation through a system of model workers (1977:86), a pattern already introduced in Yanan (Selden, 1971:211). Further based on the system of moral motivation was the Maoist opposition to impersonality and social distance among managerial levels and between cadres and their clientele:

As if you had never been an official at all . . . you must stop putting on the airs of an overlord, of a bureaucrat, you must put aside your airs and go among the people and your subordinates. Don't let the close relations between the higher and lower levels, between officers and men . . . be impaired as a result of the adoption of the system of military ranks and other systems. It goes without saying that the higher levels should maintain close relations with the lower levels and that these should be comradely. (1977:438,439)

To Mao, personal relations were not only an ideological matter but also an integral part of an organizational system that assumed a distribution of knowledge among different levels: "If you stay in your office, you will never get a clear idea of how factories, cooperatives and shops are run. The higher the office, the less the knowledge. To tackle problems, you must go down personally or invite people to come up."

In the early 1950s, the Soviet influence pushed China away from the Maoist model, but the model was enforced during the Great Leap Forward of 1958–60, which had disastrous consequences. From the early 1960s to 1966, China maintained a state of compromise between the Maoist prescription and the technical demands of specialization. Then, the Cultural Revolution was launched.

The Cultural Revolution started in 1966 with the seizure of government, party, and industrial organizations by the Red Guards following Mao's directives. Although the upheaval ended in 1968, the Cultural Revolution continued to affect China until 1978, when the Third Plenum of the Central Committee of the Chinese Communist party was convened. Years later, the Chinese press acknowledged the devastating impact of the Cultural Revolution: The economy was brought to "the brink of collapse" and to "semi-anarchism," companies' profits went down sharply, rural production stagnated, and irreparable damage was inflicted on the basic infrastructure.

China's potential for scientific progress was undermined during the Cultural Revolution, with the number of colleges and universities substantially reduced and numerous individuals missing opportunities for higher education. The young generation of Chinese managers became smaller and less qualified than their predecessors. At the end of 1978, about 200,000 scientists and technicians were out of work, a staggering figure for a country so short of technical expertise. Many had been assigned to lower posts or moved to other fields altogether. Only after 1978 were specialists reappointed to senior posts carrying substantial decision-making power.

Following the death of Mao Zedong and the rise of Deng Xiaoping to power, the PRC has embarked on an ambitious modernization program announced during the Third Plenum of the Eleventh Central Committee in December 1978. Although initially confined to rural areas, the reform program has been gradually expanded to urban regions, a shift that gathered further momentum after the 1984–85 period.

Work-Related Values

The data reported here are based on a 1982 study of 163 PRC managers (Shenkar and Ronen, 1987). The findings help to elucidate the values held by managers in the PRC as well as the impact of the traditional and modern ideologies described earlier.

Table 15.2 shows standardized scores and rank order for twelve work goals, while Figure 15.1 presents a Smallest Space Analysis (SSA) of those goals. Table 15.2 shows some results that are unique to China. For instance, in contrast to the findings obtained in other countries, the goal of promotion receives a very low ranking. How can this ranking be explained?

One explanation is ideological. Mao was fiercely opposed to strict hierarchy, claiming that "to each according to his worth" and "the contest for rank" were "remnants of bourgeois ideology" (Starr, 1979:125). He attempted to abolish hierarchy by denouncing the use of special clothes and managerial titles by highly ranked individuals. The low ranking of promotion, however, does not necessarily signal a triumph of Maoist ideology over the Confucian preference for an hierarchical order. No less important is the reality that, in the PRC, nominal promotion did not always result in enhanced authority, and brought only meager financial rewards; but it did increase the risks involved in assuming responsibilities in a politically volatile environment. The low importance assigned to promotion may have serious repercussions for the drive to promote young technical managers to positions of authority.

When compared with plots of other countries, the SSA plot of the PRC (Figure 15.1) also displays some unique aspects. First, unlike the maps of countries that have been studied, the plot for the People's Republic includes the training goal in the Team (IV) region. Second, the goal of having co-workers who cooperate is not situated between low- and high-order need categories, which is also a

Table 15.2
Standardized Scores and Rank Order of Work Goals for PRC Managers

	PRC
Co-workers who cooperate	635(1)
Automony	603(2)
Training	583(3)
Challenge	515(4)
Working relationship with manager	483(5)
Earnings	454(6)
Security	450(7)
Recognition	446(8)
Benefits	439(9)
Favorable physical conditions	433(10)
Promotion	364(11)
Time for non-work activities	345(12)

Source: Based on O. Shenkar and S. Ronen, "Structure and Importance of Work Goals among Managers in the People's Republic of China," *Academy of Management Journal 30*, no. 3 (1987):564–576.

departure from the SSA maps of other countries. The prominence of the collective in both traditional and modern Chinese ideologies may explain this finding. Third, the efficiency goal appears not only in the Actualization region (III), but also in the Team region (IV). This implies that, although respondents regarded efficiency as a high-order goal, they perceived its achievement to be tied to a team effort.

Fourth, the goal of having a good working relationship with one's manager appears not only in the Team region (IV), but also in the Progress region (II), hinting that the managers served as "linking pins." A concept ingrained in Confucian ideology, a linking pin refers to a manager's role in mediating the effects of work environment on employees. Elton Mayo (1949) observed that Chinese managers played that role in a plant in prerevolutionary China where,

An SSA Plot of Workgoals for Managers from the People's Republic of China, 1949–92

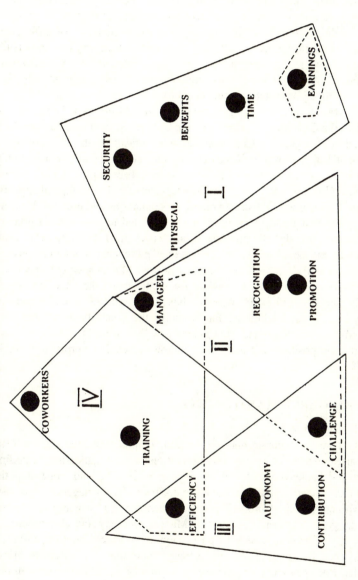

[a] Points are a geometric representation of the work goals positioned in Euclidean space. Distances between points are inversely related to the similarity coefficients among them.

[b] N = 163

Coefficient of Alienation = .17

Source: O. Shenkar and S. Ronen, "Structure and Importance of Work Goals among Managers in the People's Republic of China," *Academy of Management Journal 30,* no. 3 (1987):564–576.

during World War II, unsatisfactory relations between workers and supervisory officers led to general discontent despite other positive aspects.

Fifth, although SSA maps for West Germany, Canada, Britain, and France show the goal of higher earnings on or about the borderline between intrinsic and extrinsic goals, thus representing both a basic need and a symbolic value, in the SSA plot for the PRC it is clearly an extrinsic goal. Unquestionably, economic conditions influenced this finding. For many years, wage differences had had little impact in China, for all necessities were priced very low and luxury goods, if available at all, were priced very high (Eckstein, 1978). However, cultural and ideological factors also probably played an important role (see Managerial Compensation later in this chapter).

Although Maoist ideology was greatly emphasized during some periods in the PRC (such as the Great Leap Forward and the Cultural Revolution, during which cultural tradition, especially Confucianism, was attacked), in other periods a more pragmatic approach dominated. During the reforms, many (but certainly not all) proponents of the Maoist line seem to have been replaced by "technocrats": practical persons who were not only less sensitive to ideological appeals, but who had also learned to distrust volatile proclamations and policies. Lindsay (1983) suggests that frequent changes in the PRC led to so much uncertainty that they undermined the effectiveness of any proclaimed ideology. The result was a return to traditional values, which remained entrenched among the masses. This was particularly true for interpersonal norms. Maoist ideology has challenged only some of these norms, while frequently using the very practice of kinship allegiance it officially opposes, thus leaving intact a major basis of traditional interpersonal relations. Furthermore, the volatility associated with applying Maoist ideology and subsequently withdrawing it seems to have strengthened the position of traditional Chinese values and norms as a stable "anchor."

HUMAN RESOURCE MANAGEMENT

Managerial Selection

While systematic, accurate data on the demographic characteristics of PRC managers are hard to come by, several observations may be made, first, regarding the nature and background of Chinese managers and, second, regarding the process of their selection. It appears that a majority of PRC managers still consists of those who possess the "proper" political orientation, with senior-level posts occupied by party members. Because of Marxist ideology and also because it was frequently difficult to assess the possession of "correct" political attitudes, family and class background became primary determinants of ascent to managerial ranks. Poor peasantry or proletarian origin was particularly useful in this regard. Although nonparty members rose in the managerial ranks between 1978 and 1989, current trends suggest at least a partial return to the former mode.

Because of the "iron rice bowl" (guaranteed job security) and seniority policies, most PRC managers do not reach senior posts until a fairly advanced age.

Most of them are males, which is consistent with Chinese tradition, although women have made strides in advancing to management positions. Women now account for 8.9 percent of the population of Chinese managers (Hildebrandt and Liu, 1989). Education is an important criterion for advancement, although during the political campaign periods of the Great Leap Forward and the Cultural Revolution, education was played down to the point of becoming a liability.

Most senior managers in the central bureaucracy and major national organizations appear to be ethnic, "Han" Chinese, although at the local provincial level, an effort has been made to promote local minorities as well. The Chinese media frequently emphasize the promotion of minorities to senior managerial posts, but lack of ethnic staffing has been a source of friction in a number of localities.

Beijing University enjoys a prestige probably similar to that of Tokyo University in Japan. However, it does not serve a similar role as the basis for the country's senior bureaucracy. This has to do with the ambivalent and sometimes hostile attitude in political circles towards intellectuals, and with the potential danger seen in university education as a catalyst of new ideas. The Tiananmen massacre has made that danger look quite real.

While many of China's senior communists have been educated abroad (mostly in the former Soviet Union or Eastern Europe), the practice of sending promising Chinese students to major foreign universities was practically suspended between 1958 and 1978. As a result, there are few foreign-educated people in middle management echelons. In the last decade, a significant number of students were sent to Western countries and to Japan, but their impact has been fairly limited. Many have not returned, and those who have come back have found that their knowledge is hardly applicable in the Chinese system and, in many instances, has branded them as politically nonreliable. Recently, the Chinese leadership decided to drastically curtail the number of students who study in the West so as to limit the "damaging influence" of foreign ideas. Thus, it seems that PRC management is once again becoming insular to the outside world.

Despite the recent reforms, most PRC employees are still assigned to their work units by the central authorities (Von Glinow and Teagarden, 1988). Many still inherit their parents' job, a practice that draws more criticism with the worsening employment situation. The exceptions are employees joining foreign joint ventures and wholly owned foreign subsidiaries; those joining collective and private enterprises; and those working under a contract system, a growing but still not a very common phenomenon. The contract workers found their positions through their own personal initiative, connections, word of mouth, advertisement, and job fairs. An increasingly important role was played by 240,000 labor service companies that claim to have placed over 14 million employees over the past decade (FBIS-CMI–89–201). These were the exception, however, rather than the rule. Following the Tiananmen massacre, it appears that even these limited exceptions are about to be curbed, with the dismantling of many collective and private enterprises.

Chow and Shenkar (1989) found that none of the state firms in their study considered recruitment and selection to be major responsibilities of the personnel department. In contrast, collective enterprises considered staffing an important personnel function and used job analysis to identify their recruitment needs. Some state enterprises also conducted job analysis for their workers and managers, but this was done strictly for assignment of employees who were on the firms' staff and were about to be promoted or transferred to other jobs within their organization.

In the politicized PRC environment, staffing was never a question of a simple match between an employee and his or her organization, as much as a question of control of a huge number of people whose mobility was perceived to potentially cause serious dislocation or even chaos. The assignment of managers serves as a mechanism of social control that has been somewhat loosened during more pragmatic periods.

Career planning is still a rarity in PRC enterprises; none of six state units in Chow and Shenkar's study had career planning in 1989. The collective enterprises had career counseling and planning "when necessary" rather than in regular intervals, and sessions did not amount to much more than informal discussions of job prospects.

Foreign joint ventures face a significant problem in this context of regulated staffing. Skilled staff is in short supply, and when it is available, the Chinese parent is often reluctant to transfer such talent to the venture and would prefer instead to transfer superfluous and less qualified personnel. Overcoming personnel shortages by means of an expatriate workforce is difficult, and is not due only to legal constraints and the Chinese insistence on supplying and controlling the staffing and promotion process in the ventures. As Tung (1986) notes, expatriates in the PRC face numerous hardships. More than in other countries, expatriates in China tend to be single or at least not to have children, and, with the possible exception of Beijing, lack supportive national communities. Cohen and Valentine (1987:40) add that many expatriates in the PRC "feel they are being consciously and systematically discriminated against in daily life because they are foreigners."

Management Education

Because of Marxist and Maoist suspicions of technical expertise, management education was not emphasized before 1978 except during the brief Chinese-Soviet honeymoon of the 1950s. During the Cultural Revolution in particular, the educational system as a whole suffered gravely, producing graduates with substandard skills in all domains.

To rectify that, the PRC leadership embarked on an ambitious management education program in the late 1970s. Today, much of the responsibility for management education rests with the Chinese Enterprise Management Association (CEMA) which was set up in 1979. Until early 1988, CEMA reported to the State Economic Commission, and from then on it came under the State Commission for the Restructuring of the Economy. CEMA oversaw the training of cadres of the State Economic Commission and also provided courses for managers of large and medium-size enterprises. Actual training was provided by a network of over 100 Economic Management Cadre Institutes and 10 Senior Economic Cadre Training Centers (Warner, 1986, 1989).

Warner (1989, 1990), who studied Training Centers in a number of major Chinese cities, found considerable variations in both the content and process of the programs. He also notes that the Management Training Centers are worried about their future. Having trained most of the senior managers available, they now have to deal increasingly with lower level personnel who cannot always attend for prolonged periods. Following the Tiananmen massacre, the Centers probably have more to worry about. Many of them have been associated with foreign influences which are likely to be labeled dangerous once more. Even prior to Tiananmen, some Chinese managers were quite critical of some of the centers. Such centers, for example, Dalian, taught Western management principles (e.g., motivation, leadership) by the faculty of U.S. or European business schools, principles that in some instances were hardly applicable to the Chinese environment. Warner (1990) reports that in 1987 there were 312 higher education organs offering management training courses in China, with more than 100,000 students—roughly 5 percent of the total in higher education. It has recently been reported that enrollment in institutes of higher education has been cut. This is particularly true for some leading Beijing universities, whose students were actively involved in the demonstrations. If such a trend is established, China will face an even greater shortage of qualified managers.

So far, China is moving ahead with another ambitious undertaking: the International On-the-Job Training Program, orchestrated by the United Nations Center on Transnational Corporations (CTC). The program will allow PRC middle managers to work in U.S., Japanese, and Western European firms with expenses covered by both the CTC and the host corporations. It is too early to judge whether this program will go on as scheduled, and it is not yet known how many Chinese managers will enroll, if any.

Managerial Compensation

The compensation system in state and collective enterprises consists of three major components: monetary wages, social wages, and nonmaterial incentives. These components have been variably applied between 1949 and the present. In recent years, there have also been increasing differences between the compensation systems of state and collective enterprises. (This section is based on Shenkar and Chow, 1989.)

The monetary wages of managers include (1) basic (or standard) wage—the wage earned by all PRC employees, but with regional cost-of-living adjustments; (2) seniority wage—based on length of service; (3) position wage—determined by industry and position; (4) floating (or flexible) wage—differential pay awarded according to contribution to the enterprise; (5) time rate wage—determined by the amount of time spent at work; (6) piece rate wage—awarded on the basis of productive efficiency or individual merits and in the case of managers, determined by the efficiency of the (sub) units in which they are employed; and

(7) bonuses—that is, payments based on such criteria as above-quota output, superior product quality, cost reduction, waste elimination, on- or before-schedule completion, safety improvement, and technical innovation.

Social wages include (1) labor insurance, which covers paid sick leave, disability payment, paid maternity leave, funeral allowance, relief payment for family dependents, retirement benefits, free annual medical checkup, paid vacation, leave for visiting immediate family members and hardship allowance; (2) collective welfare, which covers subsidized housing; subsidies for grain, oil, and nonstaple foods; subsidies for personal services (e.g., haircuts) and transportation; and various kinds of community services, such as nurseries, kindergartens, homes for the aged, and medical and recreational facilities.

Nonmaterial incentives are provided in the form of recognition offered at various levels, from the work unit and up to the nation. Model workers and managers are praised as role models for other employees to follow. Other forms of nonmaterial incentives are democratic management, which allows employees and subunit managers to participate in decision-making processes (but is frequently a ritual orchestrated from above); workers' congresses and various job enrichment strategies, for example, rotation; and, more recently, election of managers.

New practices, such as termination or limited employment contracts, stock ownership, and increased autonomy for enterprise directors, have been tried on an experimental or limited basis, but are likely to be held back in the current political climate.

Ideological and Political Trends Material incentives have always been somewhat suspicious in Chinese tradition. The Chinese term for incentive, as Andors suggested in 1977, "has the connotation of inciting or provoking into action; behind the definition is a morality or state of mind embodying one's inclinations, even in the absence of external stimuli, which is only a trigger for doing what one is anyway disposed to do." Confucius, while not objecting to material remuneration for administrative officials, emphasized that pay should not serve as a prime motivator: "In serving one's prince, one should be intent upon the task, not bent upon the pay" (15:37), and "A gentleman (an ideal official) takes as much trouble to discover what is right as lesser men take to discover what will pay" (4:16). Instead, Confucius trusted the internalization of organizational values (13:20) and the moral example of leaders (*The Analects*, 13:6, 13:11, 13:19) to provide motivation for subordinates.

Maoist ideology was even more opposed to material incentives than Confucianism, suspecting them of encouraging individual interest, power, and privilege; reducing personal initiative; and necessitating massive control. Like Confucius, Mao also emphasized the motivating power of emulation, with labor heroes setting an example for others to follow (Mao, 1977). In sharp contrast to Confucianism, however, Mao sought to establish an egalitarian society, although he saw "absolute equalitarianism" as being counterproductive to the revolutionary struggle (Starr, 1979).

To neutralize public disenchantment and because of an ideological conviction that unemployment was a capitalist malady, the PRC leadership sought to provide universal job security. This led to the development of the infamous "iron rice bowl," making firing in state-owned enterprises virtually impossible. The employment security policy forced enterprises to overstaff, dragging wages down in the process.

The initial consolidation period (1949–52) of the PRC represents a confusing application of various compensation systems, including some inherited from the Nationalist regime (see Figure 15.2). During the first Five-Year Plan (1953–57), material incentives (wages, piece-rate bonuses, and even rewards for work improvement) were common in Chinese industry. At that time the ideological environment was relatively supportive of individual achievement. McClelland (1963), who studied PRC children's fiction between 1950 and 1959, found it fairly strong in need for achievement. Following the expulsion of the Soviet advisers, however, the PRC leadership moved to adopt a more egalitarian compensation scheme, conforming to Maoist principles. Until its formal alteration in the wake of Mao's death, that system was intermittently adhered to or neglected.

During the Great Leap Forward (1958–60) and the Cultural Revolution (1966–68, and, in a milder form, 1969–77), material bonuses were denounced and were labeled revisionist stuff and capitalist restoration. Bonuses were criticized for causing inequality, and those who supported their use were accused of putting money in command and taking the capitalist road. Bonuses were therefore canceled in most enterprises: everyone was paid regardless of whether one did a good job or bad, did more or less, or even if one did not turn up for work. Slowdowns and absenteeism reportedly increased substantially during that period. (Exact figures are unavailable, however.)

In pre-reform PRC enterprises, performance was not perceived as being a product of one's effort, since the overstaffed enterprises were assigned very low performance levels. At the same time, employees did not expect performance to lead to such desirable outcomes as higher pay (especially when bonuses were canceled) or promotion (which was based on either seniority or political background and connections). Furthermore, managers received continuously changing ideological signals regarding which outcomes were supposed to be more or less valued.

Compensation systems were at the heart of reforms during the last decade. They were expected to generate superior motivation and hence improve the notoriously low productivity of the PRC workforce through accelerated shifts in the relative weight of the various compensation components. Between 1978 and 1985, the proportion of time wages decreased from 85 to 59.5 percent. At the same time, the proportion of piece-rate wages increased from 0.8 percent in 1978 to 9.9 percent in 1985 and that of bonuses rose from 2.3 percent in 1978 to 12.9 percent in 1985. Penalties for inefficient performance were introduced as well.

The changes encountered stubborn opposition. Socialized with a strong collective spirit and unaccustomed to performance-based pay, employees lobbied vigorously against its use. Managers used bonus funds towards other endeavors or distributed them among all employees indiscriminately. Overtime payments also got out of hand and were used to supplement the wages of employees and

Figure 15.2
Prevalence of Various Compensation Components in the People's Republic of China, 1949–92

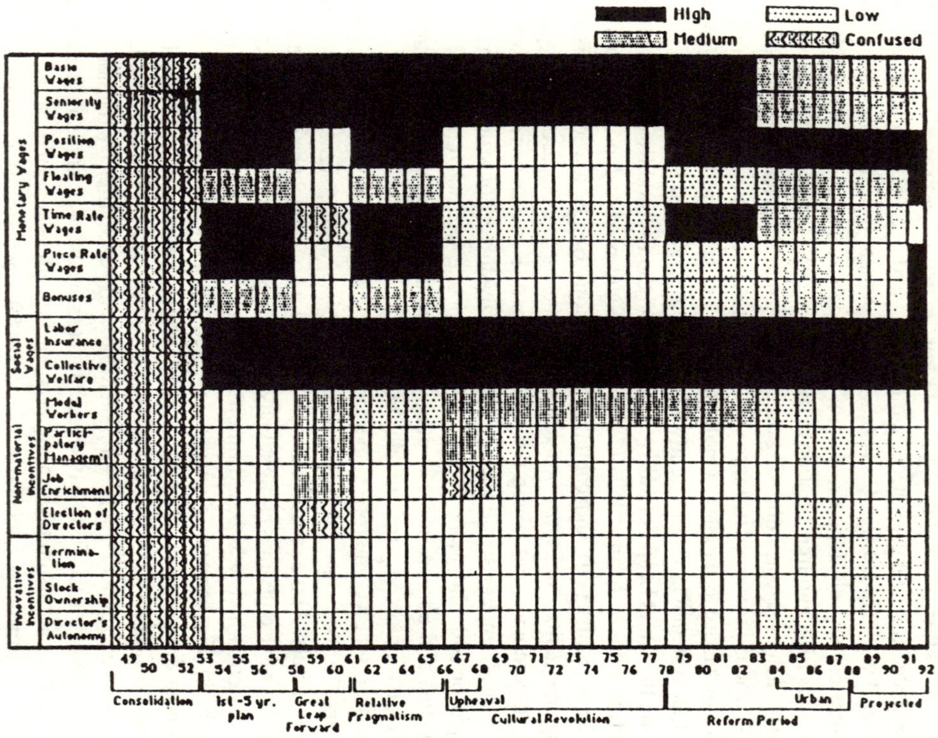

Source: Reprinted from Oded Shenkar, and Irene Hau-siu Chow, "From Political Praise to Stock Options: Reforming Compensation Systems in the People's Republic of China," Human Resource Management, 28 (1990): 65–85. Copyright © 1990. Permission granted by John Wiley & Sons, Inc.

middle managers who did little during regular working hours, and managers were pressured by envious employees to forfeit their bonuses. About two-thirds of the respondents in a recent survey believed that factory directors should not take home all their bonus if that exceeded "a reasonable amount."

Managers in foreign joint ventures have their own problems. First, downward pressure on expatriate salaries is generated by Chinese demands for parity of pay to foreigners and Chinese executives holding similar titles, even though in many cases the locals are virtually trainees with no skills (Cohen and Valentine, 1987). Second, foreign exchange regulations initially limited repatriation to 50 percent of after-tax pay. Third, the Chinese insistence on replacing expatriate personnel within a few years make start-up costs for such personnel much higher.

The Chinese managers, on their part, feel deprived, since a parity in wages has only a partial impact on their actual paychecks. Rank-and-file workers suffer less because their reference group is likely to be state enterprises where workers usually make less. However, they may feel frustrated that only a fraction of this relative advantage does indeed reach their pockets, and they sometimes have a hard time adjusting to a competitive wage system instead of the egalitarian system of the Maoist period. Nowhere is this Maoist heritage more apparent than in Article 93 of the Joint Venture Law, which states that "the salary and bonus systems of joint ventures shall be in accordance with the principle of distribution to each according to his work, and more pay for more work," a principle that would be self-evident in most countries.

Although such data for indigenous PRC enterprises were not available, foreign firms in the PRC today appear to make effective use of both material and nonmaterial incentives. In Henley and Nyaw's (1987a) study of foreign joint ventures in Shenzhen, six of the thirty-one ventures responding to that question argued that the material incentives in their enterprises were very effective, while fourteen reported moderate effectiveness and eleven average effectiveness. At the same time, out of twenty-four ventures responding, one reported that moral stimuli were very effective, while fifteen reported moderate effectiveness and eight average effectiveness. No venture has reported "ineffectiveness" or "extreme ineffectiveness" in regard to either material or moral incentives. It should be noted, however, that, unlike state firms, foreign enterprises are relatively free to determine how these incentives are used.

Figure 15.3 shows that wage levels in the PRC remained relatively stable until the reform period, except for downward trends during the Great Leap Forward and the Cultural Revolution. With relatively stable prices, subsidized food and housing, and with very few consumer goods available, wages served as a fairly effective hygiene factor, limiting dissatisfaction among PRC employers. In 1985 the average monetary wage of staff and workers in state-owned units was more than 2.5 times the 1952 figure, but this represented only 1.5 times in real terms. If one suspects the official inflation figures, the real growth of wages becomes marginal.

Much of the improvement in living standards came through population control. The average PRC family continued to shrink throughout the 1960s and 1970s. In 1983 the average urban employee supported merely 1.71 persons compared

Figure 15.3
Wage Indices of Staff and Workers in State-Owned Units (1952 = 100)

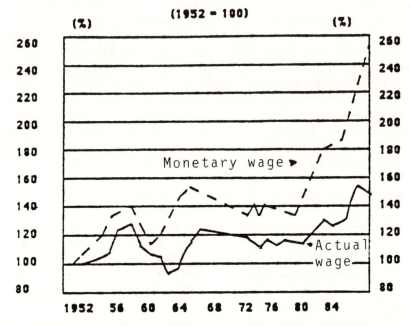

Note: Calculated from The Statistical Bureau, PRC, *Statistical Yearbook of China*, 1986.

Source: Reprinted from Oded Shenkar, and Irene Hau-siu Chow, ''From Political Praise to Stock Options: Reforming Compensation Systems in the People's Republic of China.'' *Human Resource Management* 28, no. 4 (1989):65–85. Copyright © 1989. Permission granted by John Wiley & Sons, Inc.

to 3.29 in 1957 (Yue, 1985). Failure to control population growth will endanger some of these gains. In 1987 the PRC population grew at the alarming rate of 1.44 percent, up sharply from the 1.1 percent rate of 1985, although still below the 2 percent annual increase of the 1960s. In the near term, continued population growth will lower living standards by increasing the number of dependents per wage earner, bringing about demands for higher wages to cover increased expenses, and therefore inflationary pressures. In the longer term, excessive population growth will increase the number of job seekers beyond the ability of even a growing economy to accommodate. This could lead to either widespread unemployment or rampant overstaffing, which would greatly reduce the incentive for increased productivity-based pay. The Chinese now admit that unemployment, previously considered a capitalist malady, exists in China, although the figure quoted, 3.39 million as of September 1989, is probably greatly understated.

In the early 1980s, wage earners became more dissatisfied with the inflationary erosion in their pay (see Figure 15.3). In the first half of 1988 alone, retail prices increased 13 percent, but actual inflation for urban consumers was believed to be at least double. The rise in inflation has led the PRC leadership to increase subsidies as well as to ponder an index-linked wage system. At the enterprise level, such increased outlays mean that the proportion of wages that can be linked to performance remains limited.

Although PRC employees seem to be very concerned about wages (Henley and Nyaw, 1987b; Nevis, 1983), managers appear to have different opinions. For the seventy-seven managers in their study, Henley and Nyaw found that increase in basic wages ranked in only eighth place, while bonuses ranked fourteenth in the twenty-goal list. These lower rankings for cadres are quite consistent with Shenkar and Ronen's (1987) study of 162 PRC managers. In that study, the possibility of having higher earnings was ranked eighth, while benefits were ranked eleventh out of a fourteen-workgoal list. The lower standing of wages among cadres vis-à-vis rank-and-file employees is puzzling, since Mao accused them at the beginning of the Cultural Revolution of "paying a great deal of attention to wages." Mao had expressed his disappointment with that state of affairs in his famous speech titled "Twenty Manifestations of Bureaucracy," in which he talked sarcastically about "those who work as officials and barely make a living." "The greater an official becomes," Mao said, "his demands for supporting himself become higher and higher, . . . his home and its furnishings become more and more luxurious, . . . [and] . . . his access to things become better and better" (Mao, 1970). Mao was alluding to a situation in which senior party and state officials made good use of their status to accumulate various nonmonetary privileges, from chauffeured limousines to special-access stores. It can therefore be argued that pay is not important to cadres because most of their compensation is received through other means. Another possibility is that cadres are more likely to have internalized, or at least express, a party line that is still suspicious of material rewards. Indeed, when managers were asked about their satisfaction with (rather than importance of) pay, the result was different. Alutto and Coleman (1986) thus found that satisfaction with pay for PRC managers in two surveys (1984 and 1985) was the lowest of all items listed.

According to a recent proposal by Li (1986a) in *Jingji Guanli* [Economic Management], the fixed wage system will be supplemented by a floating, performance-based component. In addition, workers and staff will receive a relative proportion of a variety of subsidies and welfare benefits. Technical skills and position pay will account for 30 percent and 20 percent, respectively, while floating wages will account for 20 percent (Li, 1986a). A similar wage system has been tested in a Beijing leather manufacturing company with promising results (Li, 1986a; Survey Group of Beijing City, 1988).

Interestingly, Li's proposal allows for merely 20 percent of compensation to be distributed by the enterprise, which seems to be in contradiction with the trend toward greater enterprise autonomy. Perhaps this is an attempt to alleviate the pressures directed at managers to practice egalitarianism by enforcing a unified system with fixed criteria.

Growing Disparities The PRC leadership's desire to downplay economic disparities was anchored in ideological grounds, yet it also sought to minimize pressure for mobility across provincial and industry boundaries by reducing the differentials among them. Such mobility pressures were considered harmful to the policy of provincial self-sufficiency and would have reduced the party's grip on human resources.

In 1984, however, the Chinese authorities adopted a different developmental strategy. Richer provinces no longer had to subsidize the poorer ones, thereby bringing about substantial wage differentials. In 1985 workers in Guangdong Province received an average wage of 2,219 yuan, while workers in Anhui received an average wage of 748 yuan. Wages in the Special Economic Zones (SEZs) are even higher than in the wealthier provinces. In comparison, the average monthly salary in Guangzhou, the capital of the richest province, Guangdong, was equivalent to HK$200. The gap has probably widened since, because salaries in the SEZs have been rising more rapidly than in the rest of China. Figure 15.4 presents wage levels in the various provinces and SEZs.

Foreign-owned enterprises, which are disproportionately concentrated in SEZs and in the coastal provinces, have been a major factor in the growing variability of wages. Although they constitute a tiny fraction of the PRC workforce, employees in these enterprises have become a reference point for millions of Chinese managers and workers who make much less doing similar jobs. The Joint Venture Labor Management Provision requires that the wage rate for joint venture staff and workers be at least 120 to 150 percent of the prevailing rate for comparable jobs in state-owned enterprises. Thus, although the average annual salary in state-collective joint enterprises across China was 1,110 yuan, the average wages paid by foreign joint ventures ranged from 2,048 to 2,437 yuan (*Statistical Yearbook of China*, 1986). The actual difference may be larger because some foreign companies pay bonuses in Foreign Exchange Certificates, which are worth substantially more in the open market. At the same time, workers in some foreign companies stand to have part of their wages withheld in case of company losses (Oborne, 1986).

The increasing disparity has created, for the first time in the history of the PRC, a widespread feeling of relative deprivation based on the creation of diverse reference groups within China. In motivational terms, equity (Adams, 1963) has suddenly become an issue, and, while many state unit employees recognize that the "input" required in the foreign ventures is also much higher, others resent the emergence of a "two-layer" system of compensation. This "red-eyed disease" (envy) has created a potentially explosive situation whereby workers in less well-to-do enterprises might challenge the growing disparity.

Figure 15.5 shows that the wage level is substantially higher in collective enterprises than in state units. Also, while wage inequality in state-owned units

Figure 13.4
Average Annual Wage—Staff and Workers, 1985

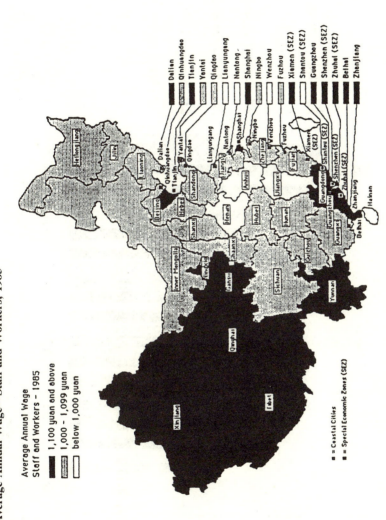

Average Annual Wage
Staff and Workers — 1985

▰ 1,100 yuan and above
▨ 1,000 – 1,099 yuan
☐ below 1,000 yuan

Dalian
Qinhuangdao
Tianjin
Yantai
Qingdao
Lianyungang
Nantong
Shanghai
Ningbo
Wenzhou
Fuzhou
Xiamen (SEZ)
Shantou (SEZ)
Guangzhou
Shenzhen (SEZ)
Zhuhai (SEZ)
Beihai
Zhanjiang

■ = Coastal Cities
■ = Special Economic Zones (SEZ)

Source: Reprinted from M. Barnard and Oded Shenkar, ''Variations in the Economic Development of China's Provinces: An Exploratory Look,'' *Proceedings of the International Symposium on Pacific Asian Business*, Pacific Asian Management Institute, and the Academy of International Business Pacific Region, Honolulu, Hawaii, January 1989. *Geo Journal* 21. Reprinted by permission of Kluwer Academic Publishers.

Figure 15.5
Wage Levels—Collectives versus State and Combined

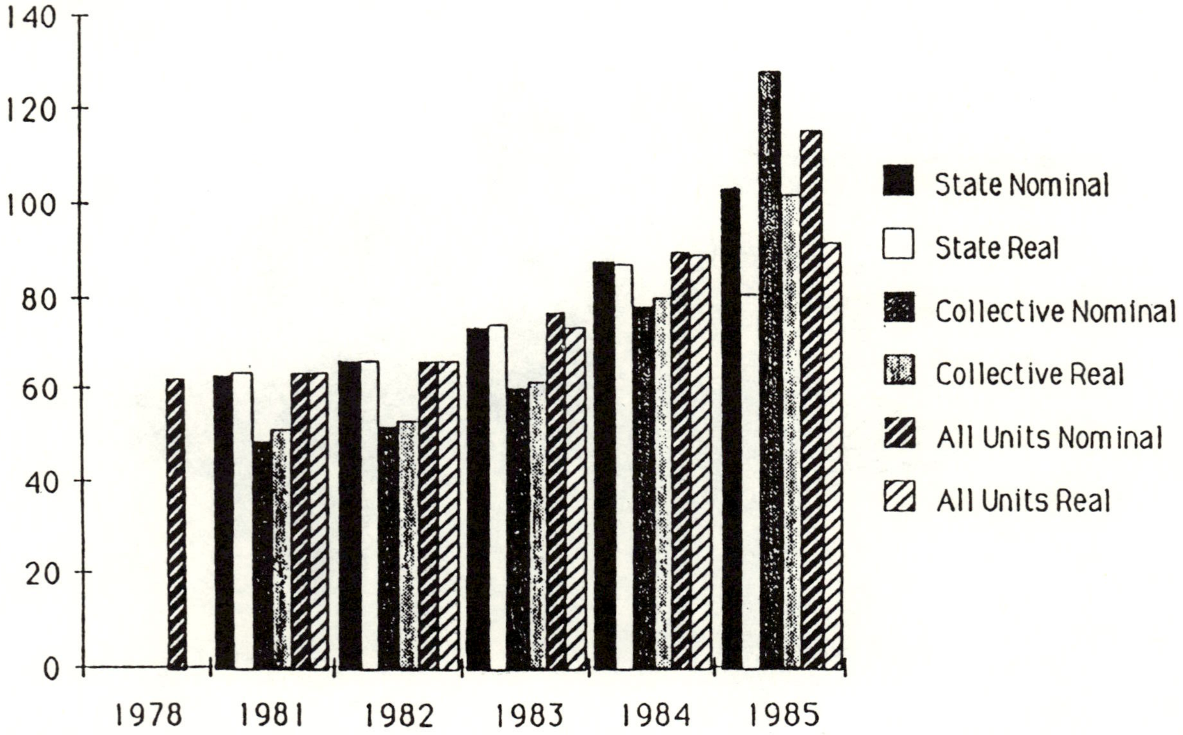

Source: Reprinted from M. Barnard and Oded Shenkar, "Variations in the Economic Development of China's Provinces: An Exploratory Look," *Proceedings of the International Symposium on Pacific Asian Business*, Pacific Asian Management Institute, and the Academy of International Business Pacific Region, Honolulu, Hawaii, January 1989. Reprinted by permission of Kluwer Academic Publishers.

decreased after 1984, variance among collectives increased substantially. Under the economic reforms, collectives had fewer restrictions on planning, pricing, marketing, and budgeting and more freedom to set wages, producing wage differentials between efficient and nonefficient enterprises.

Managerial Performance Appraisal

Performance appraisal has been the subject of controversy in the PRC, where the slogan "to each according to his work" was legitimized only during more pragmatic periods. The very definition of performance and the operationalization of performance criteria were debatable, and the debate was carried out in both ideological and practical terms. Dogmatic Maoists argued, for instance, that political behavior was a relevant part of performance and had to be appraised too. For them, however, there was no contradiction between the two, since they believed that politics contributed to economic performance. If performance was emphasized at all, it was mostly done in output terms, so as to meet production quotas. Quality, for instance, was hardly an issue.

The 1978 reformers emphasized the importance of performance evaluation as a prerequisite for economic growth and modernization, but it is difficult to estimate the extent to which this had been implemented. In the study by Chow and Shenkar (1989), three out of six state units and the two collective units in the sample had a performance evaluation system in place. Two of the state units conducted such evaluation on an annual basis, while the other units conducted more frequent evaluations. In only one of the eight organizations studied was performance evaluation used to determine bonuses, although such evaluations were taken into account by other enterprises in determining promotion/transfer and in identifying training needs.

Further expansion of performance appraisal in Chinese enterprises is impaired by the lack of progress on the price reform front and the reemphasis on central planning in the wake of the June 1989 events. Without an increase in their decision-making leeway, managers cannot be judged on the basis of task performance over which they have little control. Indeed, this is one of the major paradoxes in the current attempt to ensure macro-centralization while pressuring individual firms to increase productivity.

Labor Relations

Unions in China operate at the national (industry-based), regional (provincial, local), and company level, and normally include both blue- and white-collar employees. Union representation exists in virtually all PRC enterprises. It is based on both ideological reasons (the workers as "masters" of the enterprise) and political necessities (as a means of social control) and is controlled by the party through the All-China Federation of Trade Unions rather than by nationally independent craft unions (Helburn and Shearer, 1984; Hoffman, 1981). Chinese trade unions are expected not only to protect employees' welfare, but also to safeguard the party position in the enterprise. In their party capacity, Chinese unions are frequently engaged in political and ideological education in addition to employee training, cultural and welfare activities, and the handling of grievances. Union membership is voluntary, but only a small minority of Chinese workers are not union members (Helburn and Shearer, 1984; Hoffman, 1981).

In their capacity as an outlet for the workers' will, trade unions are expected to facilitate employee representation in the enterprise's affairs. Another vehicle for such participation is the Workers' Congress, which has the right to scrutinize managerial resolutions on subjects ranging from production plans to budgeting. According to Henley and Nyaw (1986; Nyaw, 1990), the Congress has the power to

(1) examine and adopt resolutions submitted by factory directors on production plans, budgets, etc.; (2) discuss and decide on the use of funds, regulations for awarding or penalizing workers and staff; (3) approve reforms on management structure and wage adjustments; (4) recommend leading cadres for commendation or promotion; and (5) elect administrators, subject to approval and appointment by the appropriate higher authorities. (Nyaw, 1990: 110)

The Congress also has broad powers, at least in theory, to affect the election of factory directors. This role, implemented only recently after a brief attempt in 1958–60, is particularly important but may eventually prove a mixed blessing. Fearing for their popularity, directors may rely on state directives so as to minimize possible errors of judgment and ensure reelection. This, in turn, will jeopardize the intended benefits of the increased autonomy granted to factory directors, which is one of the cornerstones of the reform.

Trade union committees are another vehicle for employee representation in Chinese enterprises. Such committees are expected to implement the decisions of Workers' Congresses and, in addition, to protect employees' rights and welfare as well as to perform other functions of the Congresses when they are not in session.

In addition to their prevalence in domestic enterprises, trade unions can also be found in many foreign joint ventures in the PRC. The Joint Ventures Law stipulates that union officials can attend board meetings as observers, but some reports (e.g., Nyaw, 1990) suggest that this right is not always included in the venture's documents of incorporation and is not carried out in practice. As a whole, joint ventures' unions tend to be less militant than their counterparts in state enterprises. Experience suggests that unions have not taken an adversarial role in foreign-PRC ventures, but were generally supportive of efforts directed at greater productivity. Furthermore, unions proved indispensable in interlocking such ventures with relevant state and party apparati.

Strikes, though legal, are extremely rare in China, which partially explains the alarm of the leadership when such work stoppages occurred during the spring 1989 events. Slowdowns do occur, although one might cynically say that they are hardly noticeable in the not-so-productive PRC firms.

CONCLUSION: IN THE AFTERMATH OF TIANANMEN

It is doubtful whether there is another group of managers who experienced as many changes in their lifetime as the PRC managers. The Chinese manager of the early 1950s enjoyed a special role as a vital participant in a massive reconstruction effort, only to be later told during the Great Leap Forward that the masses, and not expert managers, held the key to China's development. His previous role was resurrected in the early 1960s, but then came the Cultural Revolution and the manager became a prime target for attack and abuse. Under these circumstances, the willingness of the Chinese manager to once again shoulder the burden of reconstruction and reform was almost miraculous, but was no longer shared by everyone. And just when it seemed that China had reached a point of no return in its reform program and managers became at least partially convinced that "this time it was going to be different," came the Tiananmen massacre and confirmed the old saying that the only predictable thing in China was unpredictability.

The events in Beijing in the spring of 1989 and the consequent backlash against many components of the reform program raise many question marks regarding the future of PRC managers. Political criteria of party loyalty and a "correct" political line are again becoming determinants of managerial promotion. Collective and particularly private enterprises are being curbed, depriving managers of the opportunity to work for those organizations that have been the boldest in introducing organizational reforms such as performance-based pay. The same is true for foreign affiliates which provided PRC managers with a chance to learn at first hand from their foreign counterparts. The new limits on PRC students allowed to study abroad (particularly in the United States) will also deprive Chinese enterprises of potential change agents who could apply their foreign-acquired skills to those firms.

If China reverts back to a full-fledged centrally planned economy, the hard-won measure of autonomy achieved by enterprise managers will be gone, and enormous frustration is likely to ensue. The last decade has taught Chinese managers that they can make significant contributions to the success of their enterprises and to the modernization of the country. If they are deprived of that opportunity, a new generation of passive, more apathetic managers is likely to emerge.

REFERENCES

Adams, J. S. 1963. "Toward an Understanding of Inequality." *Journal of Abnormal and Social Psychology* (Fall):422–436.

Alutto, J. A., and Coleman, D. F. 1986. "An Initial Examination of Changes in Managerial Job Perceptions as a Result of Economic Reform in the People's Republic of China." Unpublished manuscript.

Andors, S. 1974. "Hobbes and Weber vs. Marx and Mao: The Political Economy of Decentralization in China." *Bulletin of Concerned Asian Scholars* 6:19–34.

Barnard, M., and Shenkar, O. 1989 (July). "Regional Inequality in China: Managerial Implications." Paper presented at the Colloquium on Selected Issues in International Business, Pacific Asian Management Institute, University of Hawaii.

Chang, C. Y. 1980. "The Modernization of Chinese Industry." In R. Baum, ed., *China's*

Four Modernizations: The New Technological Revolution. Boulder, Colo.: Westview Press.

Chau, W. L., and Chan, W. K. 1984. "A Study of Job Satisfaction of Workers in Local
Factories of Chinese, Western and Japanese Ownership." *The Hong Kong Manager* 20: 9–14.

Chen, P. W., and He, X. Q. 1984. *Gongye gi-ye gongzi guanli* [Wage management in
industrial enterprises]. Shanxi renmin chubanshe (Shanxi People's Press).

Chen, P. W. 1980. "Rising Prices and Wages in Mainland China: An Analysis." *Issues
and Studies* 20(2):3–45.

Chow, I.H.S., and Shenkar, O. 1989. "Emerging Human Resources Management in
PRC Enterprises." Proceedings of the Second International Conference on Personnel and Human Resource Management. Hong Kong: December.

Cohen, J. A., and Valentine, S. T. 1987 (May). "Foreign Direct Investment in the
People's Republic of China: Progress, Problems, and Proposals." *Roundtable on
Foreign Direct Investment in the People's Republic of China.* Beijing, China: 25–
26.

Confucius, 1938. *The Analects.* Trans. A. Waley. New York: Vintage Press.

Ding, J. Z. 1987. "Reforming the Industrial Wage Structure Is a System Engineering."
Economic Management 4:27–29.

Eckstein, A. 1978. *China's Economic Revolution.* Cambridge, Mass.: Cambridge University Press.

FBIS (Foreign Broadcasting Information Service). 1989 (October 19). *Labor Service
Companies Assist Jobhunters.* CHI–89–201.

Helburn, I. B., and Shearer, J. C. 1984. "Human Resources and Industrial Relations in
China: Time of Ferment." *Industrial and Labor Relations Review* 38 (1): 3–15.

Henley, J. S., and Nyaw, M.K. 1986. "Introducing Market Forces into Managerial
Decision Making in Chinese Industrial Enterprises." *Journal of Management
Studies* 23 (6):635–656.

———. 1987a (June 1–2). "The Management System and Organizational Functioning
of Joint Ventures in China: Some Evidence from Shenzhen SEZ." Paper presented
at the Chinese Enterprise Conference, Manchester Business School, United Kingdom.

———. 1987b. "The Development of Work Incentives in Chinese Industrial Enterprise—
Material Versus Non-material Incentives." In M. Warner, ed., *Management Reforms in China.* London: Frances Pinter.

Herzberg, F. 1968 (Winter). "One More Time: How Do You Motivate Employees?"
Harvard Business Review: 53–62.

Hildebrant, H. W., and Liu, J. W. 1989 (Fall). "Chinese Women Managers: A Comparison with Their U.S. and Asian Counterparts." *Human Resource Management*
27 (3): 291–314.

Hoffman, C. 1964. "Work Incentive Policy in Communist China." In C. M. Li, ed.,
Industrial Development in Communist China. New York: Praeger, pp. 92–110.

———. 1981. "People's Republic of China." In A. A. Blum, ed., *International Handbook of Industrial Organizations.* Westport, Conn.: Greenwood Press.

———. 1988. *Work Incentive Practices and Policies in the People's Republic of China
1953–1965.* Albany, N.Y.: New York State University Press.

Hofstede, G. 1980. *Culture's Consequences: International Differences in Work-related
Values.* Beverly Hills, Calif.: Sage.

Howe, C. 1973. *Wage Patterns and Wage Policy in Modern China: 1919–1972*. Cambridge, Mass.: Cambridge University Press.

Laaksonen, O. 1988. *Management in China during and after Mao*. Berlin: de Gruyter.

Lawler, E. E., III. 1981. *Pay and Organizational Effectiveness: A Psychological View*. New York: McGraw-Hill.

Lee, P.N.S. 1986 (Spring). "Enterprise Autonomy Policy in Post-Mao China: A Case Study of Policy Making." *The China Quarterly* 105:45–71.

Li, J. Y. 1986a. "A Proposal on a Structural Wage System and the Preliminary Wage Relations." *Jingji Guanli* [Economic management] 5:35–38.

Li, P., ed. 1986b (July). *Gongzi dawen* [Questions and answers on wages]. Xuelin chubanshe. (Xuelin Press).

Mao Zedong. *Selected Works*. Vols. 1–5. Beijing, China: Foreign Languages Press, 1970–77.

McClelland, D. 1963 (Winter). "Motivational Patterns in Southeast Asia with Special Reference to the Chinese Case." *Journal of Social Issues* 19:12–13.

Nevis, E. C. 1983. "Using an American Perspective in Understanding Another Culture: Toward a Hierarchy of Needs for the People's Republic of China." *Journal of Applied Behavioral Science* 19:249–264.

Nyaw, M. K. 1990. "The Significance and Managerial Roles of Trade Unions in Joint Ventures in China." *International Studies of Organization and Management*.

Oborne, M. 1990. *China's Special Economic Zones*. Paris, France: OECD.

Redding, G., and Wong, G.Y.Y. 1987. "The Psychology of Chinese Organizational Behavior." In M. H. Bond, ed., *The Psychology of the Chinese People*. Hong Kong: Oxford University Press.

Richman, B. 1971. "Ideology and Management: The Chinese Oscillate." *Columbia Journal of World Business* 6:23–33.

Riskin, C. 1973. "Maoism and Motivation: Work Incentives in China." *Bulletin of Concerned Asian Scholars* 5(1):10–24.

Shenkar, O. 1983. "The Cultural Revolution Against the Chinese Bureaucracy: An Ideological-Structural Analysis." *Asian Profile* 11(4):323–337.

———. 1984. "Is Bureaucracy Inevitable? The Chinese Experience." *Organization Studies*.

Shenkar, O., and Chow, I.H.S. 1989 (Summer). "From Political Praise to Stock Options: Reforming Compensation Systems in the People's Republic of China." *Human Resource Management* 28(2):65–85.

Shenkar, O., and Ronen, S. 1987. "Structure and Importance of Work Goals among Managers in the People's Republic of China." *Academy of Management Journal* 30(3):564–576.

Skinner, G. W., and Winckler, E. A. 1969. "Compliance Succession in Rural Communist China: A Cyclical Theory." In A. Etzioni, ed., *A Sociological Reader of Complex Organizations*. New York: Holt, Rinehart and Winston, pp. 410–438.

Starr, J. B. 1979. *Continuing the Revolution: The Political Thought of Mao*. Princeton, N.J.: Princeton University Press.

State Statistical Bureau, 1986. "People's Republic of China." *Statistical Yearbook of China*.

Survey Group of Beijing City. 1988. "A Survey Report on the Trial of Industrial Structural Wage System in a Beijing Leather Manufacturing Factory." *Jingji Guanli* [Economic management] 3:19–25.

Tung, R. 1986. "Expatriates in China." *Columbia Journal of World Business*.

U.S. Congress, Senate Committee on Government Operations. 1963. Subcommittee on
     National Security Staffing and Operations, Staffing procedures and problems in
     Communist China.
Von Glinow, M. A., and Teagarden, M. B. 1988 (Summer). "The Transfer of Human
     Resources Management Technology in Sino-US Cooperative Ventures: Problems
     and Solutions." *Human Resource Management* 21(2):201–229.
Wang, C. 1985. "Strengthen Political Ideology in the Economic Reform." *Jingji Guanli*
     [Economic management] 2:33–39.
Warner, M. 1986. "Managing Human Resources in China: An Empirical Study." *Or-
     ganization Studies* 7(4):353–366.
————. 1989 (January). "Senior Executive Training in China." Research Paper 1.89,
     Cambridge University Engineering Department.
————. 1990 (June). "Developing Key Human Resources in China: An Assessment of
     University Management Schools in Beijing, Shanghai and Tianjin in the Decade
     1979–1988." *International Journal of Human Resource Management* 1(1):87–
     106.
Yue, G. 1985 (Summer). Employment, Wages and Social Security in China." *Inter-
     national Labor Review* 124(4):411–422.

16

MALAYSIA

Diane J. Garsombke and
Thomas W. Garsombke

Throughout the world, effective international management depends on many factors, such as political risk, financial stability, cultural adaptation, and technological sophistication. Of these elements impacting on company performance, cultural factors are among the most significant. Because people's actions and behaviors are molded by culture, good managers need to study the many cultural differences in their workforce and utilize this knowledge to formulate strategies that will enhance productivity and performance. This chapter illustrates the importance of culture with a study of managerial practices in Malaysia, a country with several culturally divergent peoples—Malays, Chinese, and Indians.

MANAGER DEFINED

Manager as defined in this chapter includes all administrative and managerial positions in Malaysia. This is distinct from the classifications of workers such as professional and technical positions, sales positions, service positions, and production workers.

ECONOMIC BACKGROUND

The postwar growth of the Malaysian economy has been very strong as evidenced by the gross domestic product (GDP) and GDP per capita figures. World Bank estimates for 1990 and 2000 of Malaysia's GDP per capita figures are US$2,100 and US$3,154 (1989). This compares to US$1,400 per person in 1980, US$1,018 in 1970, US$781 in 1960, and US$550 in 1950 (Mehmet, 1986; Young, Bussink and Parvez, 1980) (see Figure 16.1). The GDP for Malaysia has risen steadily at about a 7 percent annual growth rate in the past forty years,

Figure 16.1
GDP per Capita, Malaysia, 1950–90

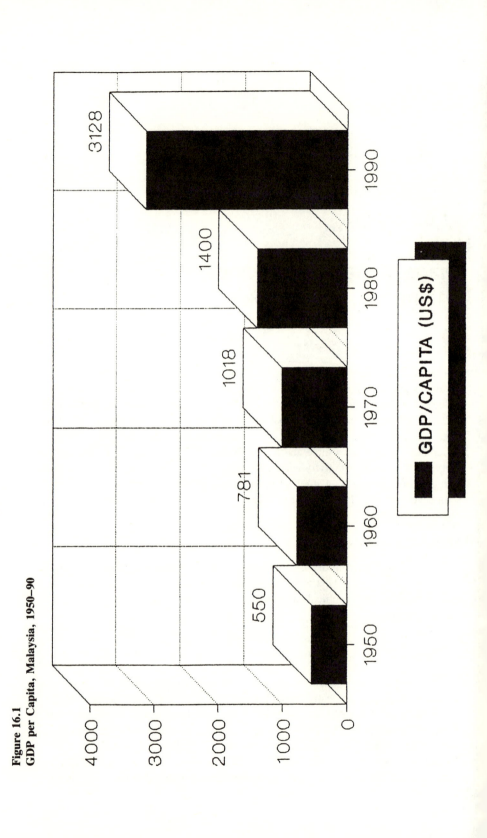

increasing from $0.2 billion in 1950 to $56.7 billion projected for 1990 (see Figure 16.2).

With a ratio of merchandise exports to GDP of almost 50 percent, Malaysia is heavily dependent on the export sector. While in the early 1960s its economy was heavily dependent on two exports, namely, rubber (50 percent of merchandise exports) and tin (16 percent), in the 1970s these percentages fell to 25 percent and 11 percent, respectively. By 1976 Malaysia successfully diversified 85 percent of its exports to palm oil, timber, and crude oil. In the past two decades, there has been a large increase in the growth of manufactured exports, particularly in the areas of electronics, machinery equipment, and textiles.

Malaysia has progressed through a series of economic plans to guide its economic development. The first economic plan was formulated in 1966. At that time, manufacturing comprised only 10 percent of gross national product (GNP). Dualism between agriculture and the other sectors characterized the economy. In addition, within the agricultural sector there was a dual economy, with the modern highly productive estate on the one hand and the traditional smallholder sector with low incomes and productivity on the other (Young, Bussink and Parvez, 1980). In the 1960s the income distribution and economic position of the Bumiputras (native-born Malays) was significantly inferior to that of the non-Malays (Chinese, Indian, or Westerners). One of the major reasons was that the majority of Malays lived and worked in the rural areas, primarily in agriculture.

The representation of native Malays in the 1960s in most economic sectors, but particularly in managerial, professional, and supervisory occupations, was poor (Young, Bussink, and Parvez, 1980). In 1970 Malays held 47 percent of all professional and technical positions, with the Chinese and Indians having approximately 50 percent; Malays held 22 percent of administrative and managerial positions, and non-Malays 73 percent. The percentages of Malays in these two job categories increased somewhat in 1980: 55 percent professionals and 26 percent administrators were Malays; 44 percent professionals and 70 percent administrators were non-Malays. The projections for 1990 are 56 percent Malays in professional and technical positions and 49 percent Malays in administrative and managerial; non-Malays are projected at 43 percent professional positions and 49 percent administrative jobs (Onn, 1986).

Although the representation of Bumiputras in the more professional job classifications has improved somewhat in the past thirty years, wage rates are still lower overall when compared to those of non-Malay groups. The 1967 figures show that average monthly income for professionals was $298 for Malays, $434 for Chinese, and $462 for Indians; the administrator's average income was $415 for Malays, $494 for Chinese, and $576 for Indians. In 1970 there was again a racial differential in average monthly income for professionals: $319 for Malays, $459 for Chinese, and $567 for Indians. Although in the administrative category Malays fared better than Indians ($574 versus $411), they still trailed Chinese ($740) in average monthly income for 1970. However, when compared to the overall population, the professional and administrative ranks are paid a relatively

Figure 16.2
GDP, Malaysia, 1950–90

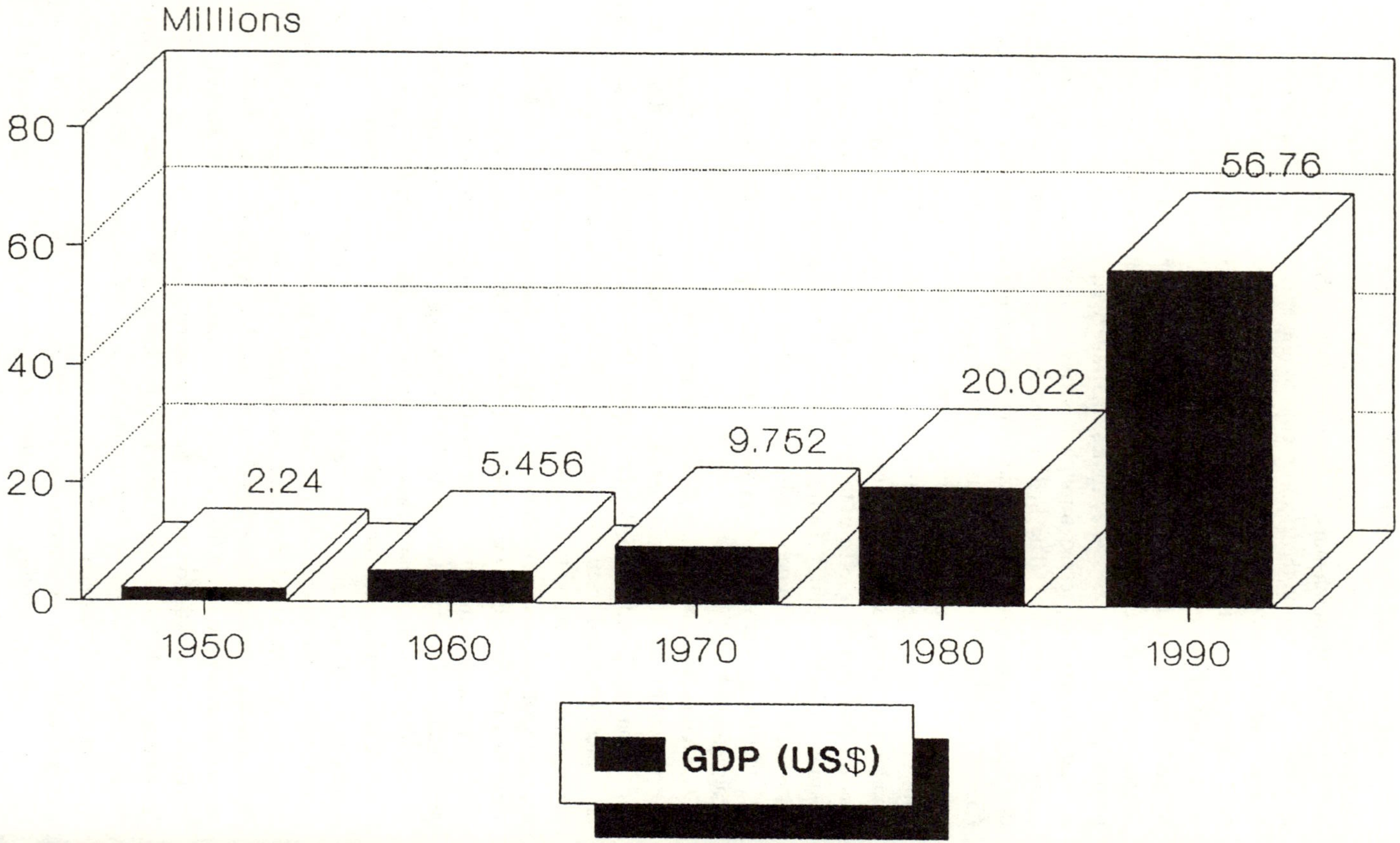

Millions

80

60

40

20

0

56.76

20.022

9.752

5.456

2.24

1950   1960   1970   1980   1990

GDP (US$)

affluent wage. In 1970 the average monthly income of all Malays was $172, Chinese $394, and Indians $304 (Young, Bussink, and Parvez, 1980). Although the average monthly wage in the last twenty years has increased steadily, the racial differential in wages still exists for professionals and administrators.

The sectoral changes in the economy have improved the native Malay's economic status. From 1950 to 1990 the contribution of the agricultural segment to GDP decreased from 45 to 15 percent, while the manufacturing sector's contribution to GDP rose from 8 to 25 percent (see Figure 16.3).

Malaysia is a country in transition, gradually moving from the "less poor" to the "well-to-do" category. (Group cutoffs are US$500 and US$2,000 GDP per capita, respectively.) The rapid changes in the economy have induced changes in the society, sometimes challenging the social traditions and existing business practices in the country. Although this chapter describes the past and present cultural values, it should be noted that these values are changing as the society changes.

Employment Trends

In the early years of its independence (1957–70), Malaysia had extreme inequities in employment for Malays compared to non-Malays. For example, 80 percent of the Malays, but only 50 percent of non-Malays, worked in the rural agricultural sector. In urban areas, which totaled about a third of overall employment, non-Malays had over 75 percent of all jobs. Imbalance in ownership of assets was another area of inequity, with Malays having 2 percent, the Chinese and Indians 31 percent, and foreigners the remaining 67 percent of capital. Because of these inequities, the Malaysian second Five-Year Plan (1971–75) was based on economic as well as social and political criteria. The planner set targets for Malay ownership of shared capital, proportion employed in the manufacturing sector, enrollments in the universities, and managerial position quotas. Under the Malaysian Infant Industry Program, Malays were granted state subsidies, favorable treatment under licensing and franchising, concessional loans and grants to enter industry, and privileged access to capital markets (Mehmet, 1986).

In 1970 Malays made up 52 percent of the labor force but only 29 percent of the manufacturing sector because of their tendency to reside in the rural areas. Their share of the income was relatively lower since wages in the rural areas tend to be lower. In addition, unskilled and semiskilled occupations are largely Malay, with relatively few (7 percent) of industrial managers being Malay. The two sectors of food processing and wood employ Malays since they are typically located in the rural areas close to raw materials.

The expansion of manufacturing for export purposes was largely responsible for the 108,000 additional jobs created in the manufacturing sector during 1971–75, the period of Malaysia's second plan. During this time, the greatest number of employed workers were in the sectors of rubber (724,000) and trade, transport, and private services (595,000) (Pyatt and Round, 1978). Unemployment has been fairly steady at 8 percent. The fifty-year employment trend (1940–90) shows

Figure 16.3
GDP Composition by Sector, 1950–90

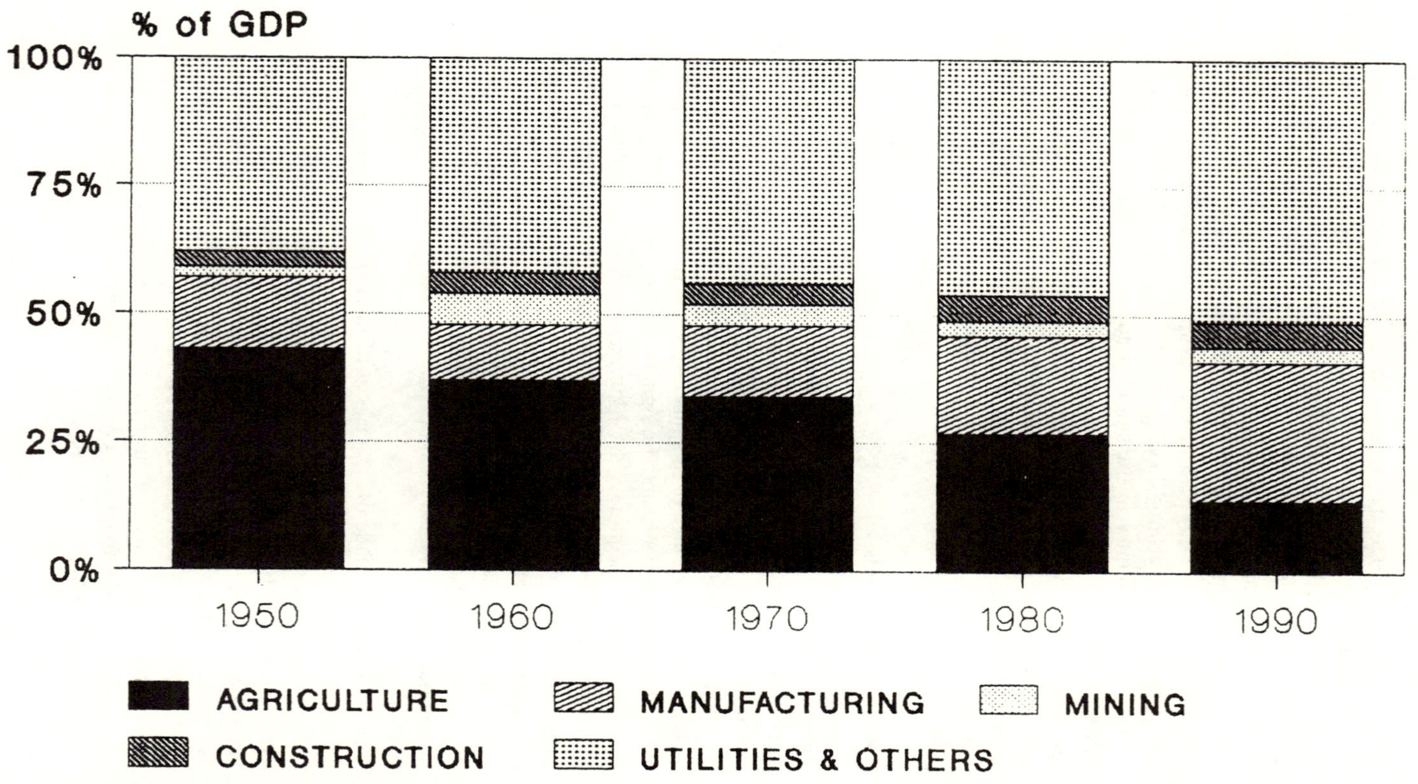
% of GDP
100%
75%
50%
25%
0%
1950
1960
1970
1980
1990
AGRICULTURE
MANUFACTURING
MINING
CONSTRUCTION
UTILITIES & OTHERS

decreases in agriculture, forestry, and fishing, stability in mining, quarrying, building, and construction, and increases in manufacturing, services, and re- tailing (see Figure 16.4). In the third Malaysian Five-Year Plan, targets for Malay employment were set for 1990; presently, the overall Malay share of nonagricultural employment has increased to 44 percent, with a parallel decline of the Chinese share to 46 percent (see Table 16.1).

EVOLUTION OF THE MANAGERIAL CLASS

Status in Society

As in other former British colonies, Malaysia's managerial class has evolved out of the strongly developed civil servant class. British rule gave rise to a mediating middle class of "clerks, lawyers and school-teachers first, and later other professionals" (Subramaniam, 1970). British influence in Malaysia spanned over a century, with the British establishing trade in Penang and Malacca in the late 1700s and indirect rule in 1880. The British rule was severed in 1957 when the Federation of Malaya secured its independence. In fact, today's man- agerial group is very likely to be the descendant of a civil servant father or grandfather who worked in a government post under British rule. Malaysian managers are usually university graduates who have achieved first-class degrees (passed standardized test necessary for university admission).

With only five universities located in Malaysia, there is intense competition for those places and for scholarships to foreign universities. The Malaysian government has employed the largest percent (83) of these graduates, with many holding administrative positions. However, the granting of university scholar- ships has been made most frequently to students from the richest families in Malaysia, including Chinese, Indian, and Malay ethnic groups within the coun- try. The educational system that has emerged is elitist (Mehmet, 1986). In fact, the society covets higher education in general, and university graduates have a privileged status. Since managers are some of the highest paid positions available for university graduates, they hold an extremely prestigious status in Malaysian society.

Ideology of Managerial Group

Malaysian managers have an elitist attitude owing to their status in the society; they are from the richest and most influential families and believe they are entitled to the privileges this status affords them, such as membership in social and sports clubs, expensive houses and cars, and perks that add prestige to their affluent life-styles. In some cases, managers use their contacts, influence, and networks to gain privileges for themselves, their families, and their friends. To sum up, managers as a group highly value protocol, rank, and status (Harris and Moran, 1987).

In addition, managers are usually very politically astute, have well-developed relationships with the ruling political parties, and, in the case of nationalized or government-controlled industries, are politically appointed. Native Malaysian

Figure 16.4
Employment Composition by Sector, 1950–90

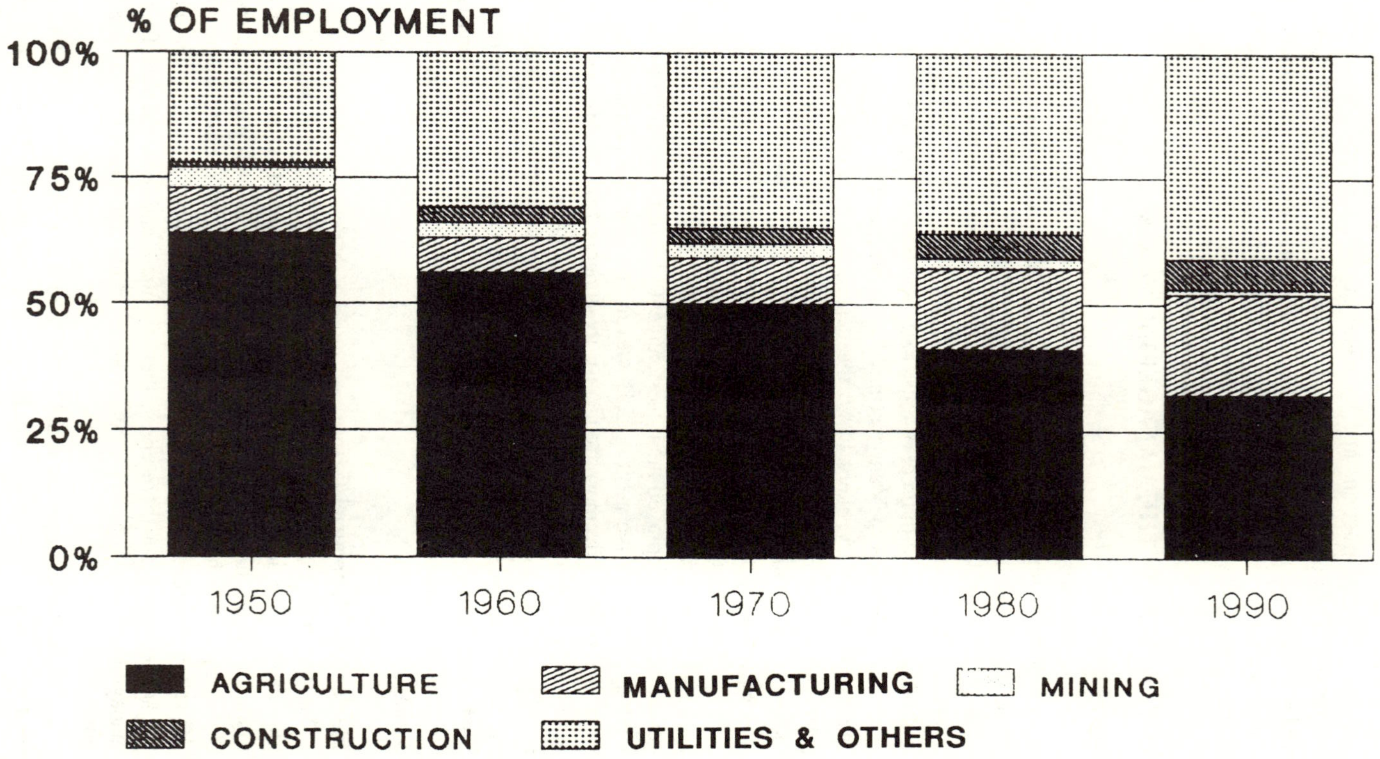

% OF EMPLOYMENT

AGRICULTURE   MANUFACTURING   MINING

CONSTRUCTION   UTILITIES & OTHERS

100% 75% 50% 25% 0%

1950 1960 1970 1980 1990

Table 16.1
Employment Restructuring in Malaysia: Targets and Actual Performance, 1970– 90 (in percent)

EMPLOYMENT	MALAY	CHINESE	INDIAN	OTHERS	TOTAL
1970					
Agricultural	67.6	19.9	11.5	1.0	100.0
Non–agricultural	38.0	51.3	9.6	1.0	100.0
1980					
Agricultural	66.3	19.9	13.0	0.9	100.0
Non–agricultural	43.7	45.9	9.6	0.8	100.0
1990 Targets (a)					
Agricultural	(59.0)	(29.4)	(10.8)	(0.8)	
Non–agricultural	(48.4)	(40.2)	(10.7)	(0.7)	
Achievement rates 1970–1980(b)					
Agricultural	41.9	0	c	33.3	
Non–agricultural	96.6	85.7	c	66.7	

a Figures are from the Fourth Malaysian Plan.
b Rates are calculated as follows:

$$At = A - \frac{(T-B)}{2} \times 100$$

where At = achievement rate

A = actual achievement in employment restructuring 1970–80

B = employment share in 1970

T = 1990 target as set out in TMP

c Indicates a negative achievement.

manager-owners are often hired to fulfill the legal requirement of partial Bum-iputra ownership. In addition, if these managers have political ties, their firms are rewarded government funding for "Bumiputra" firms, or are able to gain access to specially earmarked "Bumiputra" capital and loans. This is particularly true for managers selected from the native Malaysian ethnic group who have active ties with the United Malays National Organization (UMNO), the dominant political party in Malaysia.

The common values that influence successful managerial behavior across ethnic lines throughout Malaysia are change, cooperation, creativity, and energy (Dwivedi, 1970). For Malaysian managers, the most important quality of a leader is confidence and the ability to understand people. Moreover, Malaysian cultures in general are considered "high context," which means that managers depend more on nonverbal communications and are more group-oriented (Harris and Moran, 1987). Trust and strong personal relationships serve as a basis for all long-lasting business relationships. Intraracial relationships are easily achieved, whereas interracial relationships take more work owing to some differences, inequalities, and jealousies between ethnic classes.

Bases of Legitimacy

The basis of legitimacy for Malaysian managers comes from their educational and family background as well as the influence of religion and political activity (which often reinforces religious beliefs). Managers are linked to coalitions based on different political parties and religions. Businesses are often handed down to family members or friends sharing party and religious affiliations. Industries are traditionally aligned along ethnic groupings, although this is changing somewhat with the new economic reform policies. In addition, wealth forms a basis of legitimacy for many managers in Malaysia. Managers develop ties with other Malaysian managers through cultural, educational, professional, and sporting affiliation.

The path Malaysians have chosen for growth and development as well as the solution for their country's problems has been economic expansion, greater industrialization, and new business development. With greater diversification and modernization of industry, Malaysia is placing its future in the hands of its business leaders, managers, and administrators who will spearhead the economic restructuring to make it a strong independent nation.

CULTURAL AND EMOTIONAL BEHAVIOR

Cultural Background

Examining the cultural makeup and fabric of the Malaysian people provides a greater understanding of the values that influence the way managers in Malaysia behave and think (Garsombke and Garsombke, 1986). Experts believe that cultural factors are key determinants of strategy and provide insights into managerial value system comparisons (Hofstede, 1980; Kanugo and Wright, 1983; Kaynak, 1984; Lugmani, Quaraeshi, and Delene, 1980; Ricks, 1983). See Figure 16.5.

Figure 16.5
An Organizational Effectiveness Model: Cultural Factors Influencing Worker Behavior and Goal Achievements

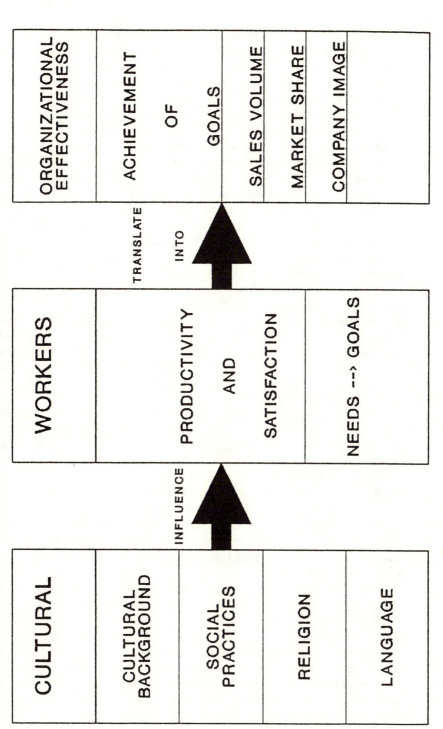

In Malaysia, three cultures exist. The racial distribution of the workforce is as follows: Bumiputra Malays 53.9 percent; Chinese Malays 34.9 percent; and Indian Malays 10.5 percent. (Others account for the remaining 0.7 percent.) Presently, ownership of business is largely by Chinese Malays (nearly 40 percent), with the Bumiputras' share of corporate assets about 12 percent. In addition, each culture is identified by its historical role. Chinese have long been restaurant and business owners, bankers, and mining developers; Indians small shopkeepers, government administrators, and laborers on palm oil/rubber plantations; and Bumiputras rice farmers, policemen and military, and workers in small cottage industries, like batik painting in the rural areas (Hirschman, 1983).

The Malays are less aggressive and less experienced in business than the Indians and Chinese. In fact, outsiders would probably characterize Malays as humble, shy, or even lazy. This passive personality has made it difficult to change the cultural disparities in economic status between Malays and non-Malays. But as more Malays become leaders and managers in the society, the role models for shifts in behavior will become more common, and the Malay personality will be characterized differently. All three cultural groups believe in strong ties to family and friends; business is based on these networks of social ties. Because of the historically based tensions among the three ethnic groups, people tend to want harmony and avoid personal conflicts as much as possible. Malays, who are probably the most conservative or traditional in this regard, are prone to voice their disapproval of an action or program through a third party rather than face to face. Or they may just avoid any comment to a third party or contact with a protagonist at all.

With growing nationalism in the country and political control of the government by the majority group of Bumiputras, managers in Malaysia face increased pressure to hire Bumiputra Malays as employees generally and in managerial positions specifically. In fact, the New Economic Policy of 1970 mandates that all companies must be 70 percent locally owned (30 percent Malay, 40 percent non-Malay) by 1990 (Mulliner, 1986). Although these targets are being revised in the short term because of economic shortfalls caused by a recession and falling export product demand (i.e., foreign investors applying before 1990 have been permitted to retain 100 percent control if they export 50 percent or more or employ over 350 full-time Malaysians), such goals will be reached in the long-term future of the country.

A major implication of these goals is the increased need for the training and development of Bumiputras. Affirmative action programs incorporating a quota system similar to those pursued in the United States for minority groups (i.e., blacks and women) are presently being adapted to the Malaysian experience, opening up hiring, promotion, and training of Bumiputras. Managers who are flexible enough to share local management control over critical parts of the business and think of business in Malaysia in terms of long-range results are emerging as the most successful. Non-Malay managers, instead of being threatened by and resisting such programs, should find proactive ways to enhance their business growth while adapting to the changes in the society. Joint ventures and licensing with Malay majority start-ups are options that non-Malay managers have chosen in order to overcome their cultural differences.

Religion

Religious Beliefs Religious beliefs also influence human behavior, for they are the basis of many actions and are sometimes difficult to separate from social customs. The predominant religions in Malaysia are Islam for Bumiputra Malays, Buddhism for Chinese Malays, and Hinduism for Indian Malays. To attest to the importance of religion in the context of business, a marketing research firm, conducting a demand study in the international environment, found that the clusters (grouping of countries) are almost uniformly characterized by the size of the religious groups. Just as the United States' values have been influenced by Protestant beliefs, Malaysia's cultural groups have been impacted by their religious convictions. Hinduism, Buddhism, and Islam should not be thought of as just religions, but as ways of life complete with social structures, legal systems, and bodies of art, philosophy, and science. It is not the intent of this chapter, however, to give a complete description of each of the dominant religions in Malaysia. Rather, the purpose is to illustrate how religion has influenced the way managers think and act.

For example, the Indian Malay culture has been shaped by the Hindu belief that the soul is immortal and reborn into another body upon death. The fortunes of a soul in its present life are determined by the soul's actions in previous lives. This belief justifies the caste system since the person born into a high caste is perceived to have earned this reward from actions in previous lives (Schweitzer, 1952). One drawback to the rigid structure of Hinduism is that social innovation and experimentation are rarely encouraged (Dube, 1965). Managers themselves are likely to resist managerial practices that could improve their firm's productivity, especially such American-oriented techniques as participatory management and the delegation of more authority to subordinates. These new management practices promote values opposite to the Indian Malay's traditional norms and, hence, are unlikely to be readily accepted (Copeland and Griggs, 1985). "Conformity, often of a ritualistic order . . . characterizes the value system" (Dube, 1965).

Another indirect effect of Hinduism concerns the low aspiration levels of workers (Dube, 1965). McClelland (1961) compared the achievement motive in several different castes and found that the higher the caste, the greater the achievement motive. The lower castes seem unable even to dream about increasing their lot in life. In Malaysia, this has translated to a steady group of Indian Malays who have remained the major labor force of rubber and oil palm plantations. The rigid social structure has resulted in a lot of power being held by certain small groups in the higher castes. They have been the small shop-keepers and, in some cases, the middle-level management of the rubber and oil palm plantations.

Religious Symbols Conducting business in multicultural Malaysia is especially tricky because each religion has its own set of symbols, which sometimes can conflict with one another or cause difficulty in managerial decision making. For instance, Hinduism has many religious symbols that a manager might use inadvertently. These include such venerated animals as monkeys, cobras, and peacocks. Particular Hindu sects worship various of these animals, but there is an almost universal veneration of cows, which are supposed to represent the earth. Obviously, a company should never show steak or other beef products in an advertisement for kitchen appliances. Other religious symbols are the banyan and pipal trees and the trident, a symbol of Siva. For followers of Islam, any reference to a pig or pork in promotional materials or company brochures would be very inappropriate. Most native Malaysians consider such a reference profane. However, in Buddhism, the pig is a symbol of prosperity, and Chinese Malays favor pork over other meat choices.

Religious Traditions   In addition to carefully using symbols, Malaysian managers are sensitive to any company violation of religious principles in their activities. For example, one company made the mistake of using a photograph that had an executive exposing the soles of his shoes. This is considered unclean in Malaysia, and, as part of religious and social tradition, shoes are removed before entering the mosque or someone's home. In Ricks's (1983) account of business blunders, a classic Indian example is the Binoca Talc incident. The company ran an ad in all the major newspapers that showed an apparently nude woman with the strategic parts of her body covered with the slogan "Don't go wild—just enough is all you need of Binoca Talc." The public was outraged and thought the ad highly indecent. In a similar fashion, Doublemint Gum promotions showing a young man and woman kissing were reviled in Malaysia by Islam fundamentalists who felt such behavior in public was indecent.

Besides problems with selecting symbols with religious meanings, there are also inherently negative symbols that Malaysian managers avoid. Owls are thought to bring bad luck, much like the U.S. black cat superstition. Sunsets are connected with death and sickness (Copeland and Griggs, 1985). Crossing a river has strong religious connotations to crossing into another world, and white, analogous to the color black in America, is associated with mourning and death ("Beware," 1976).

Such blunders, besides being embarrassing to managers, can cause economic ruin for a company. Smart managers form interracial and interdepartmental teams to create marketing plans that are consistent with ethnic and religious norms in Malaysia.

Social Practices

Social Values   The social fiber of Malaysia is largely a result of historical influences. The Chinese population in Malaysia is an emigrant one. In order to prosper, Chinese businessmen migrated to Southeast Asia, often leaving family and friends. They became "joiners" of clubs and associations. The contacts in these clubs and associations provided access to credit based on personal relationships. Because of this social practice, business on credit thrived. Business based on trust among group members was and still is the norm. The Chinese

Malay manager considers formal debt to be positive, a sign of a person's trust and creditworthiness. Since the Bumiputra Malays are indigenous, they do not have the same historically based feelings about loaning money. In fact, formal debt is seen as a source of shame to them. It signals an inability to manage one's business and indicates a dangerous lack of friends or business connections (Gosling, 1985a).

Progressive Malaysian managers, aware of the difference in the Chinese and Bumiputra attitudes to debt, adjust their incentives to meet the approval of each social grouping. Offering low interest loans or credit purchasing to Chinese employees is a strong incentive for productivity and increased sales. But for indigenous Malays the most effective incentive program used has been oriented toward assets rather than debt. Malay employees usually prefer options such as a savings plan, use of a company car, stock options, granting of discounts for surplus items, or free "giveaway" promotions over credit or loan-based benefits.

Malaysian managers try to foster a family atmosphere. Since Bumiputras are the majority group, the link to Islam is an important one. An excellent place to solidify business relations is at the prayer sessions at the local mosque on Fridays during business hours. Flextime allows employees this freedom and is widely practiced throughout the business community. Some Indian and Chinese non-Muslims even go so far as to convert to the Islam religion to enhance their business relationships in Malaysia, and they conduct business meetings at the mosque. Through weekly business meetings at the mosque, Malaysian managers seek to bring workers together with a set of shared beliefs and experiences. In this way they forge a corporate culture in much the same fashion as is done at the Friday afternoon "beer busts" of the Hewlett-Packard Company or the daily "coffee klatches" at Delta Airlines practiced in the United States.

Aside from the mosque, other nonreligious organizations and clubs are also important tools for shaping a strong organizational culture and employee commitment in firms. Membership in golf, badminton, tennis, and polo clubs is the most popular form of indirect compensation benefits, particularly for managers. The Royal Selangor Golf Club, for example, is a sports club known throughout Malaysia and is frequented by businessmen of all nationalities (Rafferty, 1985).

Personal Relationships Malaysians are somewhat taciturn upon first meeting. When approached in a friendly manner, they expect a deep reciprocal friendship to evolve. If this does not happen, they become distrustful of the person involved. Most Malaysians do not attempt to become friendly too fast, for they believe that genuine friendships can grow only over time. Unlike some foreigners who tend to ask personal questions too early in the friendship, Malaysians never ask or discuss personal issues except with very close friends.

Although many Malaysian managers have lived and studied in the United States or abroad and have acquired a very modernized appearance and demeanor, they generally still respect and adhere to their traditional cultural values. For instance, Muslim Malaysian students while in a foreign country may eat pork, drink, or gamble, all of which are forbidden by their religion. When they return to Malaysia, however, they may reject these activities as unacceptable. Societal pressures to conform are still very strong, even for westernized or highly educated and worldly Malaysian managers.

This situation extends to relationships between men and women. By religious custom in Islam, men and women are separated in the mosque. Society follows this religious custom by tabooing physical contact between men and women in public. Malaysian women educated overseas may be very liberal when studying, training, or conducting business in a foreign country, but find they too must conform to the separation of the sexes when they return to Malaysia or they will face ostracism.

Malaysians also expect different actions from their friends than do other cultures. For example, in the United States, when people perform favors for friends, they unconsciously expect their friends to realize that they have now incurred a debt that they must pay back sometime in the future. Hinduism holds the opposite belief. Therefore, for Indian Malays, the "friend's role is to sense a person's need and do something about it. The idea of reciprocity as we know it is unheard of" (Chowdhry, 1971). Indian managers will not show gratitude for favors because the Indian believes that "what he does for others he does for the good of his own psyche" (Dube, 1985).

As mentioned earlier, the norm in Malaysian relationships is not to be open and direct, but rather to go to a third party to discuss problems or always to agree with a colleague when confronted directly. This approach can cause problems in cross-cultural managerial relationships, since Westerners like to ask direct questions about the performance and capabilities of the firm (Illman, 1980). Malaysian managers will not state that things are going badly or that they cannot fulfill an executive's request, since this would make them lose face. However, once they have become close friends, Indian and Chinese Malays will be honest and even critical in a relationship (Reeder, 1987). Management in Malaysia is characteristically paternalistic. Along with this more directive and authoritarian leadership style, organizations are structured more centrally, with decision making resting primarily with proprietors (Chow, Andres, and Szalay, 1987). Owner managers feel responsible for their employees' well-being, much as most heads of households feel responsible for their own family members. When employees make mistakes, Malaysian managers point out the mistakes or have a friend tell them, and then they take time to show them the correct way of doing the job. In addition, most managers do not dismiss employees for poor job performance but will not hesitate to fire employees who cannot be trusted (Choy, 1987).

Language

Spoken and Written Languages   Malaysian is the official language in the country, but English is a widely spoken second language and the acceptable language for business. In addition, Chinese and Indian dialects are spoken by nearly half of the population. Because of the emphasis on nationalism in the 1970s and the subsequent law changing all primary and secondary schools to the Malay medium by 1982, the Malay language is gaining importance in all business dealings and customer promotions. The primary language for films and television programming as well as media advertisements is Malay, with subtitles usually in Tamil. For films produced in India or Chinese-speaking countries, the spoken language is the Indian or Chinese dialect, and subtitles are given in Malaysian. Labeling and directions on product packaging are normally given in Malay, English, Tamil, and Mandarin.

The majority of managers in Malaysia are fluent in at least two languages— English and their native tongue. Many younger managers who are Chinese and Indian are becoming fluent in three languages because proficiency in both English and Malay is now required to pass university entrance exams. Translators or local managers who are facile in local languages are vital in business to ensure successful communications. Business documents, publications, contracts, product labeling, and packaging are often multilingual, depending on employee and customer makeup.

Naming Traditions Each culture in Malaysia has its own distinct naming traditions. Bumiputras use the Arabic Muslim naming system, with the given name, usually of Arabic origin (e.g., Hassan), followed by the kin designation *bin* (son of) or *binte* (daughter of), followed in turn by the father's given name (Ismail). In the United States, John Smith, son of Peter Smith, would be called John bin (son of) Peter following the Muslim naming system. The bin or binte may be eliminated changing his name to simply John Peter. Titles or honorifics may also precede the name, such as Tunku (prince or princess), Tan Sri (honored by the government), Datuk (knighted by a state sultan), Doctor (medical doctor or with a doctoral degree), and Haji (one who has made a pilgrimage) (Gosling, 1985b).

For the Chinese, the surname comes first and the given name follows (e.g., Tan Kah Seng). Kah is a generational name used by all siblings and cousins in the same generation, and Seng is the individual's first name. Our John Smith would be called Smith John, with no equivalent for the generational name found in English. Chinese dialects complicate the picture further with their distinct sounds and spellings; Mr. Wong Lam Poh (Cantonese) is the same person as Mr. Huang Lin Pao (Mandarin) (Gosling, 1985b).

Indians use the initial of the father's name rather than a complete surname first. For example, V. Rajaratram may stand for the father's name of Veurasamy. John Smith's name would be changed to S. John. The Indians also adopt the use of names that indicate their religion and family relationship. Gurmit Singh s/o (son of) Jo gindar Singh indicates Gurmit's father is Jo gindar and that the family follows the Sikh religion (shown by "Singh") (Gosling, 1985b). These cultural differences change the behavior of Malaysian managers in three ways: (1) they ask how people wish to be called—family, given, or a nickname (shortened and Anglicized versions are common); (2) they obtain a person's full name and supporting information (address, telephone number) to avoid errors; and (3) they realize that "first-name basis" has very little meaning since names are juxtaposed by Chinese and Indians. Figure 16.6 summarizes the cultural factors that influence successful management in Malaysia.

Figure 16.6
Summary Chart of Cultural Factors and Managerial Implications

Cultural Factors	Managerial Implications
Cultural Background	
1. Bhumiputra Malays comprise over 50 percent of the population but are a minority in the workforce; historically each race has played a distinct role in society.	1. Training and development of Bhumiputra Malays; affirmative action programs; local ownership, partnerships and joint ventures.
Religion	
1. Predominant religions are Islam, Buddhism, and Hinduism; some religious customs and traditions clash with Western managerial practices.	1. Managers may be slow to adopt Western managerial practices such as participatory management and decentralization.
2. Religious symbols and meanings are diverse and conflicting.	2. Inter-racial and inter-departmental teams are used to create promotional materials for the firm.
Social Practices	
1. Different views of debt are seen (ie. Chinese use debt widely; Malays see debt as shameful).	1. A "cafeteria" of incentives (ie. low interest rates, credit purchasing, "giveaways".
2. Sports are widely accepted social practice among all races.	2. Offer sport's club memberships or participation in organized sports.
3. Muslims attend Mosque prayer sessions every Friday.	3. Mosque as a meeting place for business.
4. Management is paternalistic.	4. Employees are dismissed only if not trusted.
5. Malaysians take problems to third party.	5. Managers are not confrontational.
Language	
1. Four major languages are spoken (English, Malaysian, Chinese, Indian) with variations of dialect.	1. Fluency in English foremost; Malaysian is second.
2. Not all people in country are fluent in more than one language.	2. Language training of employees; documentation and addresses are made in most appropriate language.
3. Different naming systems and use of titles indicating marital status, social position and religion are part of the special vocabulary.	3. Managers take care in addressing people properly; "first name basis" is meaningless.

HUMAN RESOURCE MANAGEMENT PRACTICES IN MALAYSIA

Managerial Selection

Administrative positions in Malaysia are usually filled by graduates of the nation's five major universities and Malaysian graduates returning from colleges and universities in the United States and other Western countries. A university diploma is often a passport to well-paid jobs. The universities in Malaysia are the University of Malaya (UMJ), the National University of Malaysia (UKM), the Science University of Malaya (USM), the University of Technology Malaysia (UTM), and the Agricultural University (UPM).

Located in the capital city of Kuala Lumpur, UMJ (1982 enrollment of 2,487) is the oldest university in Malaysia. It is the largest in terms of basic degree graduates and postgraduate students, and it has the largest science and engineering faculties of all local universities. In Bangi, Selangor, UKM (1982 graduates of 1,737) has been earmarked by the government to be the main university of Malaysia. To reach that goal, UKM has increased its science faculty and doubled its graduates with science degrees, while retaining their lead in the humanities and social sciences. Much smaller than UMJ and UKM, USM (a 1982 total of 764 candidates) concentrates on science, educational science, pharmacy, housing planning, and applied science and is located in Penang. To serve the technical and professional personnel needs of the country, UTM (total 1982 graduates of 1,021) has diploma programs in the technical areas of engineering, surveying, architecture, and land management. Finally, UPM (739 total graduates in 1982) serves the agricultural community with degrees and diplomas in agriculture, forestry, veterinary medicine, and animal science. For subprofessional and technical level training, the two colleges of MARA Institute of Technology (ITM) and Tunku Abdul Rahman College (TAR) provided training for 2,780 and 506 students, respectively, in 1983 (Onn, 1986).

Presently, 20,000 Malaysian students attend higher educational institutions in the United States. In 1983 there were 58,000 Malaysian students enrolled in foreign universities in the United States, Great Britain, Canada, and India. For 1990, over 100,000 Malaysian students were projected to be enrolled overseas. Traditionally, administrators and managers have been from the economics and humanities areas. At UM in 1982, there were a total of 1,065 graduates in economics and 36 in business administration. The humanities students in 1982 at UKM numbered 848. The total graduates from the universities and colleges in Malaysia were 9,631 (0.06 percent of the total population) in 1982. Experts predict that there will be an ample supply of graduates to fill present and expected future positions well into the 1990s ("*Malaysia*," 1988).

Recruiting Techniques Managers in Malaysia are most commonly recruited through newspaper advertisements. For top-level professionals, firms search through intermediary consulting firms or head-hunting organizations, which use newspaper advertisements and personal contacts. Another option is the public Professional Employment Bureau which lists the qualifications of new graduates and those seeking to move up. The Bureau registers only those with degrees/ diplomas from local/overseas universities and colleges. Proven skills of managers are given the most weight in selecting or promoting employees to managerial jobs in most sectors. In more rural areas and in smaller organizations such as family-run businesses, nepotism and family background weigh heavily in decisions for promotion and selection. Nepotism is most rampant among the Bumiputras, the most traditional ethnic group in Malaysia.

Dominant Selection Techniques and Criteria   Interviewing is the favored selection technique for choosing candidates for managerial and administrative positions. Firms are also aware of the government's affirmative action emphasis which seeks to place more native Malaysians in mid- and top-level management positions. From 1970 to 1980 the proportion of Malays employed in administrative and managerial jobs increased from 23 to 26 percent, while the proportion of Chinese decreased from 65 to 64 percent and the Indians from 8 to 6 percent (Onn, 1986a). (See Table 16.2 for a breakdown of the experienced labor force by occupational group and ethnic group.)

In his research on white-collar occupations, Hirschman (1983) found that ethnic inequities still exist: Chinese and Indian men were, respectively, 6 and 5 percentage points more likely to be selected for white-collar jobs than Malay men. Educational level (those with at least an LCE credential, which is achieved by passing an exam after lower secondary schooling) also had a strong selection effect—40 and 60 percentage points above lower secondary schooling alone and no schooling, respectively.

Hirschman (1983) also discovered a 10 percent Indian and a 17 percent Chinese differential over Malays in retailing and wholesaling. In manufacturing, Malays and Indians were at the same level, but the Chinese had a 12 percentage-point edge. Another factor that influences employment is location. In urban areas, Chinese are most likely to have a white-collar job, but in rural areas Malays are almost as prevalent as Chinese in professional positions.

Another selection consideration is that many Malaysian managers who are trained overseas often receive educational grants from government-sponsored agencies such as the MARA Institute. In return for these monies, students sign a contract agreeing that they will serve in governmental organizations or nationalized businesses. Private firms try to attract the best candidates from the returning student pool by buying off these contracts when hiring. In addition, they offer higher salaries and greater career ladder mobility as incentives over the public employer.

Training and Development of Managers
The key managerial training institution in Malaysia is the University of Malaya, which provides advanced managerial education. Managers are also sent to centers in the United States, Singapore, and Britain for managerial training. Formal business training is available through in-country business programs sponsored by foreign universities. (The University of Bloomsburg in Pennsylvania, for example, provides an MBA program in Singapore.) Executive development

Table 16.2

Percentage Distribution of Experienced Labor Force by Occupational Group and Ethnic Group, Peninsular Malaysia, 1970 and 1980

Occupational Group	Number (thousands)		Malays		Chinese		Indians		Others	
	1970	1980	1970	1980	1970	1980	1970	1980	1970	1980
Professional, technical, and related workers	129.4	261.9	46	55	39	34	13	10	3	1
Administrative and managerial workers	30.3	38.2	23	26	65	64	8	6	4	4
Clerical and related workers	133.3	304.5	36	50	48	39	15	10	1	1
Sales Workers	236.7	357.3	23	29	66	63	11	8	--	--
Agricultural, animal husbandry and forestry workers, fishermen and hunters	1322.1	1256.3	69	70	21	18	9	11	1	1
Service workers	225.4	331.2	46	59	39	29	13	12	2	1
Production and related workers, transport equipment operators and labourers	542.8	993.5	34	42	55	46	11	12	--	--
Occupation not adequately described or not stated	126.3	250.2	56	54	33	35	10	10	1	1
Total	2736.4	3793.1	52	54	36	35	10	11	1	1

seminars are also offered by private consulting firms, the MARA Institute, and the National University of Malaysia. Language and cross-cultural training is available at both UMJ and UKM, as well as the University of Singapore and private language institutes such as Berlitz in Singapore and abroad. The National Industrial Training and Trade Certification Board (NIITCB) sets trade standards and provides tests for trade certification, while the goal of the Center for Instructor and Advanced Skill Training (CIAST) is to upgrade skills in vocational training institutions and to provide advanced training to skilled workers seeking managerial and supervisory positions (Onn, 1986).

Technical seminars in such areas as computer technologies, logistics, and production scheduling and design are given at the Science University of Malaysia, the MARA Institute, and Tunku Abdul Rahman College. Computer software vendors also provide technical training to managers and staff as incentives for purchase of their products. Many multinational and large firms located in Malaysia have their own training and development programs, led by in-house staff as well as outside consultants. In small- and medium-sized firms, the top managers train junior managers on the job, or former/retired managers are used as training and development consultants. For example, when foreign-owned rubber and oil palm plantations were nationalized in the early 1980s, European managers were replaced with Malaysian managers, but they were retained as consultants to provide technical and managerial training and development for several years to make the transition successful.

Compensation of Managers

Wages in Malaysia are substantially below Western standards but when compared to salaries in neighboring countries, except Singapore, are substantially higher (Bedlington, 1978). Wage differentials exist between unskilled (US$95/month), semiskilled (US$250/month), and skilled (US$380/month) workers. Government employees have a good pension plan and preferential interest rates on housing and car loans. They received substantial pay increases in 1988 after eight years without any increments (*Labor*, 1989). Private sector wages increased an average of 5.6 percent in 1989, with top managers earning an average of US$1,900 per month, midlevel management making US$1,200 per month, and managers in production and sales having average monthly salaries of US$1,350. Workmen's compensation, disability and survivor benefits, and old age benefits programs are provided through government programs and legislation. Retirement pensions are mandated by law, with the employee's share at 9 percent of monthly wages and the employer's share at 11 percent.

One specific incentive scheme that is practiced by Chinese Malay managers is called Pok Chow. The industries that commonly use this incentive package are saw milling, plywood manufacturing, goldsmith shops, and tin mining. The firms are normally smaller sized. "Pow Chow" is a form of gang contracting that focuses on profit sharing. The gang contractors agree voluntarily to be part of a team whose size is mutually decided on. Many of the team members are related by family ties. The more the group produces, the more earnings each person receives; the proportion is negotiated with company management. Individual team members negotiate among themselves for work content, hours, and earnings. Earnings can vary from 17 to 28 percent of output, depending on the skill level and contribution of each team player.

The members of a Pow Chow system are considered part-time employees who are not entitled to the Employees Provident Fund, Social Security, and Workmens' Compensation Scheme programs contributed to or paid for by the company. In addition, these workers are not entitled to medical leave, paid holidays, pension plans, and vacation leave, but they normally do receive the year end bonus payment. Because of the loss of these benefits, trade unions are widely opposed to this incentive system (Thong, 1987).

Incentives such as medical and vacation leave, paid holidays, pension plans, life insurance, yearly bonuses, merit raises, and profit sharing are the most prevalent for managerial positions. Added benefits such as housing, company car (or the financing to purchase one), and sports club memberships are becoming more widespread, particularly for upper middle and top management positions (*Doing Business*, 1982). These fringes can range from 20 to 200 percent of the administrator's yearly salary.

Managerial Performance Appraisal

Professional managers in Malaysia use performance appraisals on an annual basis. The methodologies include interviews and setting performance goals. Some organizations prefer formal performance appraisals for managers. Although in other firms the "old boys network" is very strong and reinforced by the social and sports clubs, the network influences managerial evaluation.

Formal performance appraisals are usually practiced in large Malaysian firms, multinational firms, or Malaysian firms with Western ownership, where Western management techniques are more visible. Higher levels of training, inter- and intrafirm mobility, and competitive managerial practices are the hallmarks of the largest and dominant firms in Malaysia.

In a study of East Asian managers, Danandjaja (1987) showed that successful managers valued their human resources more than unsuccessful managers. That is, 65 percent of successful managers (measured as a higher income/age ratio) versus 47 percent of unsuccessful administrators placed primary value on their subordinates. The successful manager group valued achievement of success for their employees, and performance appraisal programs give the structure needed to implement this value system.

In evaluating work roles and activities in Malaysia, Zabid (1987) found that the most highly rated roles were entrepreneur, leader, and administrator. The top three work activities were staff requirements such as hiring and firing, evaluating the performance of subordinates, and reviewing the reference data of new applicants. The importance of performance appraisals for retaining and recruiting the "best" job applicants is becoming more self-evident. Malaysian managers are gradually changing from systems that reward employees on the basis of sex and family ties to more objective systems evaluating the individual's performance.

Labor Relations

The labor force in Malaysia has been slow to unionize, with the number of union workers decreasing from 10.4 percent in 1987 to 10.1 percent in 1988 (*Labor Developments*, 1989). Unions are generally organized along the lines of a company or industry grouping. The majority of in-house unions are in the public sector. Union membership is primarily male, with only 25 percent female representation of the total union membership, approximately 550,000 members. The ethnic representation in unions is 51 percent Malay, 22 percent Chinese, and 23 percent Indian (Onn, 1986). Partly because managers have a favorable role from labor's perspective, union membership is poor. Administrators do not usually participate in any unions, although some lower supervisory positions may. Executives are more likely to be members of trade associations and local chambers of commerce.

Collective bargaining is the norm in Malaysia, but the government (i.e., the Industrial Court) plays an active role in promoting conciliation and arbitration to settle disputes. Strikes are relatively rare and end quickly. Recent labor laws have excluded bonuses from wage figures, reduced the maximum overtime rates payable on holidays from 4.5 to 3 times basic pay, and officially declared unions legal (e.g., the Trade Union Act).

As mentioned previously, affirmative action programs in education and employment encourage companies to have an employee mix parallel to the country's ethnic mix; reserve an equitable share of university places for Bumiputras; and promote Bumiputra entrepreneurship (i.e., favored access to government contracts; favorable licensing and franchising treatment; state subsidies; and new business loans) (Snodgrass, 1980). Potential discontent among university graduates who are unable to find professional and administrative positions because of the economic slowdown currently threatens the country. Women account for 35 percent of the workforce and 31 percent of the administrative and managerial positions, but these are primarily in the teaching and nursing professions.

CONCLUSION—FUTURE MANAGEMENT

The heterogeneity of cultures, religions, languages, and social practices in Malaysia creates a challenging environment for managers. In this multicultural setting, managerial practices are evolving to maximize employee motivations and to help create more dynamic organization cultures, which are truly results oriented. In such a rapidly growing economy as Malaysia, the relative power, influence, and status of managers will be enhanced in the 1990s. There is much evidence showing that the professionalism of managers has made a dramatic rise over the past fifty years, and there is every reason to believe this trend will continue into the next decade. As the country has developed and grown, so too have its people. The trend has been away from agricultural managers and administrative positions in the public sector towards administrators in manufacturing and the private sector. This privatization and shifting sectoral trend will grow, and greater export trade is predicted for the next ten years. Profit motives and an international perspective will characterize future Malaysian managers.

Inequities in the ethnic proportion of managerial jobs have been improving, with percentages coming closer to the ethnic mix of the society in general. Although more remains to be accomplished, the managerial scene is becoming more equitable. The gap between rich and poor still exists among rural and urban employees, but the gap in income levels attributable to racial differences will be closing considerably as the target from the Third Malaysian Plan is implemented in the early 1990s.

The economy has been diversified into a wider mix of industries and greater exportation of products (Neff, 1985). New technologies have been imported through licensing and joint venture agreements ("Investing," 1982). The trend will be to import even more sophisticated technologies and professional managerial practices from the West. Younger Malaysian managers will be technically oriented and more adaptable to these changes.

The biggest future threats to managers are economic downturns, depression of export prices and product demand, social changes such as the American consumer demand for healthier low fat and no cholesterol oils in their diets, new technological developments, making their electrical and mechanical products obsolete, and natural disasters such as oil spills and monsoons.

Future managers will be highly trained, with undergraduate and graduate degrees in business and economics. Entry-level managers will be young and fresh out of universities, with mid- and top-level managers proving their skills through on-the-job experiences. In addition to greater racial equity, the authors believe that Malaysia will be taking steps to bring more women into the ranks of managerial positions in the future.

Because of their higher educational experiences and greater competition, managers will institute more formalized human resource systems such as performance appraisals, job classification schemes, and strategic planning techniques. Although the paternalistic and centralized decision mode is still predominant in Malaysia, there will be a slight shift to decision making lower in the hierarchy. Top Malaysian managers will learn to place greater trust and responsibility further down the line as managerial behavior becomes more sophisticated. The reduction of ranks in managerial levels does not appear to be an immediate term forecast but will build in momentum as the larger and more multinational firms adjust to greater competition from lower cost manufacturers in Asia and Africa (Sharma, 1984).

For some industries, the competitive threat is from local firms. As the country faces problems of labor shortages in the more skilled and technologically advanced areas and increased urbanization, managers need to be more flexible and willing to adopt more modern management techniques in automation, computerization, and improvement in the image and presentation of the business products/services to suit a younger, more progressive generation of customers, or lose them to new start-ups managed by younger, more aggressive entrepreneurs (Thong, 1987).

In addition, as Malaysian firms grow, increase their exports, and compete more directly with foreign firms, they will need technological skills and innovative professionals to develop creative products. More Malaysian multinationals will be formed to compete on a global basis. World-class competition requires that Malaysians train and develop world-class managers in the future.

ACKNOWLEDGMENT

Special acknowledgment for outstanding assistance in computer graphics and library research is given to Roy Ulrichson III, a business undergraduate and work study student at the University of Maine.

REFERENCES

Alpander, G. 1984. "A Comparative Study of Motivational Environment Surrounding First Line Supervisors in Three Countries." *Columbia Journal of World Business* 19:95–103.

Bedligton, S. S. 1978. *Malaysia and Singapore: The Building of New States*. Ithaca, N.Y.: Cornell University Press.

"Beware When Bearing Gifts in Foreign Lands." 1976 (December). *Business Week* 6, pp. 91–92.

Chow, I. H., Inn, A., and Szalay, L. B. 1987 (May). "Empirical Study of the Subjective Meanings of Culture Between American and Chinese." *Asia Pacific Journal of Management* 4:144–151.

Chowdhry, K. 1971. "Social Cultural Factors and Managerial Behavior in Organizations." In I. Nakayama, ed., *Social and Cultural Background of Labor Management Relations in Asian Countries*. Tokyo: Japan Institute of Labor.

Choy, C. 1987 (May). "History and Managerial Culture in Singapore." *Asian Pacific Journal of Management* 4:133–143.

Copeland, L., and Griggs, L. 1985. *Going International*. New York: Random House.

Danandjaja, A. A. 1987 (September). "Managerial Values in Indonesia." *Asia Pacific Journal of Management* 5:1–7.

Doing Business in Malaysia. 1982. New York: Price Waterhouse.

Dube, S. C. 1965. "Cultural Problems in the Economic Development of India." In R. Bellah, ed., *Religion and Progress in Modern Asia*. New York: Free Press.

Dwivedi, R. S. 1970. "The Relative Importance of Personality Traits among Indian Managers." *Indian Management* 9:30–35.

Fisk, E. K., and Osmanrani, H. 1982. *The Political Economy of Malaysia*. New York: Oxford University Press.

Garsombke, D., and Garsombke, T. 1986 (Summer-Fall). "Cultural Disparity in International Marketing Management: A Framework for the Overseas Agent's Selection and Supervision Processes." *Issues in International Business* 3:19–26.

Gosling, P. 1985a (Spring). "Both a Borrower and Lender Be." *Southeast Asia Business* 5:27–30.

———. 1985b (Summer). "What's in a Name?" *Southeast Asia Business* 6:30–38.

Harris, P. R., and Moran, R. T. 1987. *Managing Cultural Differences*. Houston: Gulf Publishing Co.

Hirschman, C. 1983 (October). "Labor Markets and Ethnic Inequality in Peninsular Malaysia." *Journal of Developing Areas* 18:1–20.

Hofstede, G. 1980. *Culture's Consequences: International Difference in Work-Related Values*. Beverly Hills, Calif.: Sage Publications.

Illman, P. 1980. *Developing Overseas Managers and Managers Overseas*. New York: AMACOM.

"Investing, Licensing, and Trading Conditions Abroad." 1982 (September). *Business International Corporation*: 21–24.

Kanugo, R. N., and Wright, R. W. 1983 (Fall). "A Cross-cultural Comparative Study of Managerial Job Attitudes." *Journal of International Business Studies*:115–129.

Kaynak, E. 1984 (January). "Marketing in the Middle East and North Africa." *Management Development* 22:23–29.

Kessler, C. S. 1978. *Islam and Politics in a Malay State Kelantan 1838–1969*. Ithaca, N.Y.: Cornell University Press.

Labor Developments in Malaysia. 1989. Washington, D.C.: U.S. Department of Commerce.

Lugmani, M., Quraeshi, Z. A., and Delene, L. 1980 (Summer). "Marketing in Islamic Countries: A Viewpoint." *MSU Business Topics*:17–25.

Malaysia: Background Notes. 1988 (August). Washington, D.C.: U.S. Department of State, Bureau of Public Affairs.

Malaysia's Good News for Foreign Investors. 1984. New York: The Conference Board.

McClelland, D. 1961. *The Achieving Society*. Princeton, N.J.: D. Van Nostrand Co.

Means, G. P. 1987 (April). "The Politics of Ethnicity in Malaysia." *Current History* 36:168–183.

Mehmet, O. 1986. *Development in Malaysia*. London: Croom Helm.

Mulliner, K. 1986 (Spring). "Malaysia: Economic Muddling and Political Meddling." *Southeast Asia Business* 9:11–15.

Nagata, J. 1984. *The Reflowering of Malaysian Islam: Modern Religious Radicals and Their Roots*. Vancouver: University of British Columbia.

Neff, R. 1985 (November). "Indonesia's Biggest Importer Cultivates Exports." *International Management*:69–70.

Onn, C. F. 1986. *Technological Leap: Malaysian Industry in Transition*. Oxford: Oxford University Press.

Pyatt, G., and Round, J. I. 1978. *The Distribution of Income and Social Accounts*. Washington, D.C.: World Bank.

Rafferty, K. 1985. "Malaysia." In *Asia and Pacific Review*. Essex, England: Ballantine Books, pp. 223–232.

Raymond, C. 1972 (December). "Predicting Demand for Consumer Products in Foreign Countries." Academy of International Business Conference, Toronto.

Reeder, J. A. 1987 (January-February). "When West Meets East Asia." *Business Horizons* 30:69–74.

Ricks, D. 1983. *Big Business Blunders: Mistakes in International Marketing*. Homewood, Ill.: Dow Jones-Irwin.

Schweitzer, A. 1952. *Indian Thought and Its Development*. Boston: Beacon Press.

Sharma, B. 1984 (June). "Multinational Corporations and Industrialization in Southeast and East Asia." *Contemporary Southeast Asia* 6:159–170.

Snodgrass, D. R. 1980. *Inequality and Economic Development in Malaysia*. Oxford: Oxford University Press.

Subramaniam, V. 1970. *The Managerial Class of India*. New Delhi: All India Management Association.

Thong, G. T. S. 1987 (May). "The Management of Chinese Small-Business Enterprises in Malaysia." *Asian Pacific Journal of Management* 4:178–186.

Young, K., Bussink, W.C.F., and Parvez, H. 1980. *Growth and Equity in a Multiracial Society*. Washington, D.C.: World Bank.

Zabid, A.R.M. 1987 (September). "The Nature of Managerial Work Roles in Malaysian Public Enterprises." *Asia Pacific Journal of Management Studies* 5:16–27.

17

INTEGRATION AND CONCLUSIONS

Richard B. Peterson

We have examined the influence of cultural values on managerial behavior in fifteen countries covering the United States, Europe, the Middle East, and Asia. The authors of each country chapter have also discussed how managers are recruited, selected, appraised, compensated, and trained, and the role of unions in the work life of the managerial group. Finally, the authors have looked at trends that may affect managers in the coming years.

In this final chapter, we begin by pointing out both the commonalities and differences found in a comparison of managers across the fifteen countries. In some cases, we discuss similarities among a group of countries, while in other cases the comparison is between two or three countries. We also draw some broader conclusions regarding the role of the managers in the late twentieth century, and we briefly discuss questions raised by this project that should be addressed by future researchers.

COMMONALITIES AND DIFFERENCES

The authors of each chapter were asked to follow a common outline in discussing managers in the particular country they wrote about, and in large part, they accomplished this goal. Table 17.1 provides some summary information on the major issues covered for each of the fifteen countries. This summary proved easier to do for some countries than for others. For example, what is said about the role of managers in the former Soviet Union and Poland relies largely on the system that existed in those countries prior to 1989 when the dominant role of the Communist party and the central planned economy were facts of life. Since both countries are undergoing important changes, much of what these authors report may be less relevant five or ten years from now. This is particularly true for the Commonwealth of Independent States (CIS). To this

Table 17.1
Summary of Information about Managers and HRM Activities Regarding Them across Fifteen Select Countries

MALAYSIA

Definition of Managers	Managers are defined as all administrative and managerial personnel in private and public sector organizations. The managerial class evolved out of the civil service class.
Managerial Status, Ideology, Legitimacy	The managerial group has high status and first-class degrees. Strong elitist ideology characterizes the highest social background families. Education, religion, and political connections are strong backgrounds for managers. Emphasis is on high trust.
Dominant Managerial Values	Value in cooperation, confidence, and interpersonal skills. High context communication. Strong paternal and family roots. In reality, cultural traditions are somewhat different depending on whether the manager is Chinese, Malay, or East Indian. Strong role of traditional values.
HUMAN RESOURCE MANAGEMENT	
Recruitment	Recruitment is largely from graduates of the five major Malaysian universities or from Malays returning from colleges and universities in the United States or Western Europe. Mostly through newspaper advertisements or "head-hunting" firms (experienced).
Selection	Primary use of interviews. Existence of employment contracts.
Compensation	Salary and yearly bonus given most managers. Special pok chow incentive scheme in Chinese Malay communities in certain industries. Pay low by advanced industrial country standards, but high in that area of Asia.
Performance Appraisal	Formal annual performance appraisals, particularly in large Malaysian firms, multinationals, and Western-owned Malaysian firms.
Training and Development	In-company training complemented by attendance at managerial and technical courses run by universities. Managers sent abroad to United States, Singapore, and Britain.
Labor Relations	Few managers belong to unions.
Future Trends	Expected further professionalism of managers. Trend toward selecting higher percentage of managers from Malay ethnic group, also more women managers. More managers will be trained in business and economics.

MAINLAND CHINA

Definition of Managers

Managers include a great variety of people occupying supervisory positions in private and public sectors plus foreign staff in joint ventures.

Managerial Status, Ideology, Legitimacy

A managerial elite in the Western sense does not exist in the post Mao period. Ideology influenced by Confucianism and Maoism. Recent strengthening of traditional values.

Dominant Managerial Values

Managers influenced by such Confucian values as emphasis on kinship, respect for elders, and hierarchy.

HUMAN RESOURCE MANAGEMENT

Recruitment

Recruitment during most of the Mao Period (1949-76) heavily influenced by political considerations. Bias against those managers with technical training (1949-76).

Selection

Lack of professional selection criteria. Job assignment determined by state rather than company or government agency.

Compensation

Pay consists of monetary wages and nonmaterial incentives. Post Mao leadership has recognized the need for greater pay incentives of managers, but there is strong pressure in society for retaining egalitarian stance. Considerable disparity exists between the pay of Chinese and joint venture firms.

Performance Appraisal

Performance appraisal system not well developed because of stress on pay not being related to individual or organizational performance.

Training and Development

Present emphasis on International On-the Job training program orchestrated by United Nations Center on Transnational Corporations.

Labor Relations

Virtually all employees and managers belong to trade unions that are affiliated with the All-China Federation of Trade Unions.

Future Trends

Since the Tiananmen Square confrontation, the trend has been to reduce managerial autonomy and freedom to run the firm or government agency. The shift is already away from recent reforms.

Table 17.1 (continued)

HONG KONG

Definition of Managers	Managers include owner-managers, entrepreneurs, and corporate leaders in both private and public sectors. Most business organizations are family-owned firms; many are characterized as autocratic, implicitly structured, paternalistic, and nepotistic.
Managerial Status, Ideology, Legitimacy	"Familism" as the managerial ideology based on dependence, conformity, and respect. Father seen as steward of the business. Strong belief in capitalism.
Dominant Managerial Values	Nonlinearity, multiple and mutual forces, and relational concept to causation. Contextualism, holism, and nonrational probability. Sense of time in polychronic and cyclical sense. The self cannot be separated from relationships. Harmony, propriety, particularistic collectivistic. Sense of shame and importance of face. Hierarchical.

HUMAN RESOURCE MANAGEMENT

Recruitment	Recruitment from Hong Kong universities and students who have gone to Britain, the United States, and Macao. Recruitment of expatriates.
Selection	Applications, interviews, and written examinations (public sector) are used for initial selection.
Compensation	Limited information available on pay of managers, but university graduates receive starting pay that is low by advanced industry country standards.
Performance Appraisal	Formal PA systems often using alphabetical rating system. "Staff reporting" system in civil service consisting of completing a staff report and meeting with subordinate.
Training and Development	Few companies provide in-house training courses. Management Development Center of Hong Kong's is a major source of management development, but is complemented by universities and H.K. Management Association.
Labor Relations	Managerial unionism virtually unknown outside public sector.
Future Trends	The overriding question is what will happen in 1997 when China takes over control of Hong Kong. The great worry is that there will be a flood of emmigration of most talented managerial group.

SOUTH KOREA

Definition of Managers	Managers refer to those individuals who are initially recruited to work as white-collar administrative employees and as technical engineering and scientific staff by major private sector firms upon completion of undergraduate and graduate studies, most of whom are later promoted to managerial positions.
Managerial Status, Ideology,	
Dominant Managerial Values	Confucianism and neo-Confucianism strongly influence managerial and societal behavior. Its basic elements include harmony, emphasis on hierarchy, collectivism and dependence, filial piety, social ritual, people "good" by nature, and high value of education.
HUMAN RESOURCE MANAGEMENT	
Recruitment	Directly from Korean university system with preference for graduates of Seoul National University, Yonsei, and Korea University. Admission to such universities based-on scores in entrance examinations. College recruiting and personal connections and help-wanted ads used.
Selection	Initial screening interviews for determining "fit" with company. Other selection tools include document evaluation, written examinations, and particularly the interview with multiple interviewers scoring the candidates. Promotion based on education and seniority.
Compensation	Starting pay based on gender, educational level, and military service. Compensation consists of base pay, bonuses (2-4 times a year), numerous special allowances, and fringe benefits. Seniority largely determines base pay increase.
Performance Appraisal	The common practice is to give twice yearly appraisals of the manager's performance, but especially since 1987, Korean firms have been reluctant to tie such appraisals to compensation decisions, in contrast to trends in the United States.
Training and Development	Continuous training and development of managers is pursued. Large chaebols (e.g., Hyundai) use induction course to socialize new hires to values of the firm. There is much training and updating of skills both internally and externally sponsored.
Labor Relations	Managers, by law, can form unions and be union members, but only a small number have chosen to do so.
Future Trends	If anything, Korean firms will become even more Korean and Confucian in their concern for unity, harmony, and the view of the whole person. There will be increasing pressure on companies to increase pay and benefits, given higher costs of land, housing, and education.

Table 17.1 (continued)

JAPAN

Definition of Managers

Managers are defined as including section chiefs, assistant department heads, assistant section chiefs, and department heads in large firms.

Managerial Status, Ideology, Legitimacy

High status, legitimacy, and power.

Dominant Managerial Values

Dominant cultural values of managers include groupism, harmony, acceptance of hierarchy in work relationships, sense of obligation, and debt of lower level personnel and superiors. Consensual decision making.

HUMAN RESOURCE MANAGEMENT

Recruitment

Future managers recruited from university-trained pool of graduates with technical and non-technical education. Increasing use of midcareer hiring but still the exception.

Selection

Selection criteria based on the university and academic major and "fit" with firm. Popular techniques include an interview, employment test, and background (reference) check. Recommendation by university professor important. Best companies prefer graduates of most prestigious universities (e.g., Tokyo).

Compensation

Manager's salary mainly determined by rank in the company, but some firms now factoring merit into salary determination, but seniority is still most common criterion. Base salary and sizable twice yearly bonuses.

Performance Appraisal

Implicit performance feedback handled through individual feedback. Systematic appraisal involving two-way communication.

Training and Development

Initial training of recruits into management track emphasizes socialization. Emphasis is usually on generalist training by firm.

Labor Relations

Managers early in their career often involved in enterprise (firm-based) unions. Considerable information-sharing between managers and union employees.

Future Trends

Trends include restructuring of economy toward service sector; tight labor market; increasing number of women in the labor force; and shifting values of the younger workforce toward favoring leisure.

SAUDI ARABIA

Definition of Managers	
Managerial Status, Ideology, Legitimacy	
Dominant Managerial Values	Strong collective sense. Importance of honor, pride, and dignity in interpersonal relationships. Loyalty to work group. Focus on people rather than task. High risk avoidance. Centralized decision making. Shame culture. Strong influence of religion in work.
HUMAN RESOURCE MANAGEMENT	
Recruitment	Considerable recruiting of foreigners in certain parts of the labor force. Preference for graduates who have attended prestigious universities in the West (Britain and Egypt earlier, now more from the United States).
Selection	Interviews most common. Nepotism and connections important for Saudis.
Compensation	High managerial pay by international comparison. Egalitarian treatment of managers at same organizational level.
Performance Appraisal	Formal performance appraisals more common in foreign-owned firms. Informal appraisals with emphasis on positive and timely feedback common in Saudi firms and government sector.
Training and Development	
Labor Relations	Unions are outlawed.
Future Trends	Difficult to predict but clear that there is a dichotomy between traditional tribal-based values and those of a modern wealthy country. Changes are most apparent in foreign-owned firms.

Table 17.1 (continued)

ISRAEL

Definition of Managers	Managers, while not uniformly defined, usually refer to those persons occupying middle to top-level organizational position in the private or public sector.
Managerial Status, Ideology, Legitimacy	Relatively high social status.
Dominant Managerial Values	Informality in work and interpersonal relationships. Tendency toward centralized decision making. Emphasis on improvisation and ingenuity. Willingness to make decisions. Support teamwork, group responsibility, work involvement, and sense of belonging. High organizational commitment.
HUMAN RESOURCE MANAGEMENT	
Recruitment	Roughly half of all Israeli managers have completed university studies. The dominant number were born in Israel or from American or European roots. Important source of managers is retired military personnel.
Selection	Interview is most common selection tool. Testing using aptitude, skills, and personality inventories. Widespread use of graphology (handwriting analysis). Head-hunters and assessment centers also used.
Compensation	Salaries considerably higher in private sector than in either Histadrut or government. Payment in kind not uncommon as supplement. High level of fringe benefits.
Performance Appraisal	Formal performance appraisals used widely in medium and large organizations. Employee-traits, behavioral, and MBO systems most common. Shift is toward using Performance Appraisal for training and development purposes.
Training and Development	Wide use of in-company training programs and external management development centers and university programs within the country.
Labor Relations	No managerial union or association exists, but individual managers can join the Histadrut on an individual basis.
Future Trends	Increased emphasis in recent years on managerial professionalism. Emerging trends that will affect managers in the future include: globalization; recession; the role of women; possible greater job insecurity; changing technology; and greater social standing of managers.

POLAND

Definition of Managers	Managers are confined to middle and higher supervisory personnel in state-owned industrial enterprises.
Managerial Status, Ideology, Legitimacy	Low prestige of managers since World War II. From late 1970s to late 1980s political criteria often used for selecting executives and managers.
Dominant Managerial Values	Strong sense of individualism and dignity of individual. Egalitarianism, particularly at lower managerial levels. Low risk-taking propensity.
HUMAN RESOURCE MANAGEMENT	
Recruitment	About one-third of managers have university education. Most recruits to management have had engineering training, followed by education in economics. Closed selection system based on party loyalty.
Selection	Open selection system (after 1980) run by competition committees to choose best person for the managerial job based on job analysis.
Compensation	Uniform pay scales where managers not paid commensurate with their training and responsibility. Often paid less than workers. Base pay, supplemental pay, and bonuses included.
Performance Appraisal	Use of a variety of PA systems consisting of a mixture of personal traits and job behaviors, done by committees in firm, union, and party. Poor feedback on performance.
Training and Development	Traditionally, little concern for training managers, but more recently new management institutes and business school programs have been established.
Labor Relations	Labor union membership before Solidarity was 100 percent but not independent, organizations until recently.
Future Trends	Predicting the future role of managers is difficult now because Poland is in the process of shifting from a socialist to a free market economy. The likely trend is that Polish managers will be more like their Western European counterparts if the shift is successful.

413

Table 17.1 (continued)

CONFEDERATION OF INDEPENDENT STATES

Definition of Managers	Managers are defined as administrative functionaries who are clearly subordinate to macroeconomic planners.
Managerial Status, Ideology, Legitimacy	Ideology of managers since 1917 was Marxism-Leninism. Relatively low status of managers as viewed by the leadership of country and the public. Viewed as administrative functionaries.
Dominant Managerial Values	A communitarian, egalitarian ethic mixed with authoritarian ethic of centralized controls.
HUMAN RESOURCE MANAGEMENT	
Recruitment	Engineering the most common educational background.
Selection	Strong political control over business and managerial selection since the 1930s. Political loyalties helpful in being selected for managerial jobs. Use of personality tests and some assessment centers.
Compensation	Decline in recent years in managers' real salary. Bonuses for managers who fulfill the economic plan.
Performance Appraisal	Formal appraisals based more on personal traits and bureaucracy than as evaluation or development tool. Performance Appraisals have little influence on careers.
Training and Development	Only 42 percent of managers have some years of higher education. More have secondary education. Newly emerging system of postgraduate training courses offered by colleges and institutes.
Labor Relations	No real independent trade union organization.
Future Trends	Clear trend towards post-diploma education centers. Great need to professionalize HRM activities like performance appraisal and compensation.

414

AUSTRIA

Definition of Managers	Managers include both small entrepreneurs (owner/-managers) and those employed by larger firms to supervise the carrying out of major functional areas.
Managerial Status, Ideology, Legitimacy	
Dominant Managerial Values	Low power distance. Fairly high uncertainty avoidance. Medium scores on collectivism. Formal participation arrangements. Emphasis on compromise and consensus in making decisions.
HUMAN RESOURCE MANAGEMENT	
Recruitment	Recruitment from commercial high schools or university (mainly economics and business) Increasing use of head-hunters. Newspaper advertisements most common recruiting vehicle.
Selection	Interviews the primary basis supplemented by detailed resumes, psychological tests, and sometimes assessment centers. Candidates may be asked to critique case studies during interviews.
Compensation	Manager salaries rank in the middle among European managers. Extensive use of bonuses (ranging from 12 - 28% of annual salary).
Performance Appraisal	Formal annual performance appraisals. Emphasis on evaluation more than development.
Training and Development	Most management development done by specialized programs run by the labor market parties, Chamber of Commerce, universities, and institutes.
Labor Relations	No separate unions for managers, but many retain membership. Social Partnership provides guidelines for bargaining and pay increases.
Future Trends	Possible value changes in broader society towards individualism may cause considerable changes in Austrian management system.

Table 17.1 (continued)

SWEDEN

Definition of Managers	
Managerial Status, Ideology, Legitimacy	Managers enjoy considerable prestige and respect - in both private and public sectors. Egalitarian ideology based on competence. Belief in free market system.
Dominant Managerial Values	Egalitarianism and informality. Leadership by competency and authority of knowledge and expertise. Teamwork. Consensual decision making.
HUMAN RESOURCE MANAGEMENT	
Recruitment	Potential managers recruited from technical institutes and universities. Most prestigeous include Stockholm School of Economics, the Gothenberg School of Economics, Royal Technical University and Chalmers Technical University.
Selection	Interview the most common vehicle. Increasing use of employment consultants. Use made of aptitude, skills, and personality tests in evaluating candidates.
Compensation	Managers generally poorly paid by international comparisons, particularly in light of high taxation. Narrow pay structure.
Performance Appraisal	Formal performance appraisal systems are not common. Slight tendency to favor development and training over evaluation.
Training and Development	In-house training. Attendance at various management training centers in Sweden, Scandinavia, and Europe.
Labor Relations	Managers may belong to unions affiliated with professional union confederation (SACO).
Future Trends	Future difficult to discern, but Swedish competitiveness weaker today than before. Possible trend toward strong personal leadership style.

GERMANY

Definition of Managers	German law and tradition define upper and middle managers (vice-presidents and department heads) as at the level of <u>Leitende Angestellte</u>.
Managerial Status, Ideology, Legitimacy	High status of managers as they contribute to the state. Strong commitment to free market economics.
Dominant Managerial Values	Sense of professional calling. Belief in the sanctity of private property in communitarian sense. Paternalistic commitment to the country's welfare. Strong sense of pride in work. Tendency towards authoritarian leadership style.
HUMAN RESOURCE MANAGEMENT	
Recruitment	Recruited more recently from universities and <u>fachhochschules</u>. Other sources include newspaper advertisements and professors' recommendations. Increasing use of executive search firms at higher managerial levels.
Selection	Person's qualifications and skills are paramount. Interviews also paramount, supplemented by letters of recommendation, school records, and telephone references. Assessment centers for promotion to managerial level jobs.
Compensation	Above average pay for Common Market managers. Christmas and annual bonuses beyond regular salary. Pay discretion granted in private firms that are not unionized.
Performance Appraisal	Formal, quantitative-style, performance appraisals. However, fairly heavy use of informal feedback and coaching too.
Training and Development	On-the-job training. Company training programs and being sent to INSEAD or other prominent management development centers in Germany and Europe.
Labor Relations	Separate union of managerial employees. Managers have voice through codetermination, works councils, and union movement.
Future Trends	Likely to move toward more professional HRM, but often retaining paternalistic style of management. Big question is how smoothly the former East Germany will be integrated into the united Germany.

Table 17.1 (continued)

FRANCE

Definition of Managers	Manager is defined as supervisory staff above the foreman level, but does not include executives, professional employees, higher ranking sales staff, and senior technical staff also included in managerial cadre. Early sense of cadres as "technocrats" (Saint-Simon).
Managerial Status, Ideology,	Presently high status based on the model of competence and elitism.
Dominant Managerial Values	High power difference. High uncertainty avoidance. High emphasis on individualism. Low on masculinity. Low on cooperation across organizational levels. Authority based on absolutism, omnipotence, and universalism. Uncomfortable with face-to-face conflict.
HUMAN RESOURCE MANAGEMENT	
Recruitment	Recruitment of future managerial staff favors those who have elitist education from the major grand e'coles - preferably after work in the civil service. Younger managers are likely to have university degrees and have fathers who are cadres.
Selection	
Compensation	French managers are well paid by international comparison.
Performance Appraisal	Many firms use a formal performance appraisal system involving a meeting between the manager and his or her subordinate.
Training and Development	
Labor Relations	Low extent of unionization of private sector cadres (managers), but higher in the public sector. Cadres, though, are covered by labor law and collective bargaining agreements.
Future Trends	Likelihood is that the future will largely be a continuation of the recent past.

BRITAIN

Definition of Managers	Manager is defined as all employees above the first-line supervisory level (foreman) who are involved in the control of a company.
Managerial Status, Ideology, Legitimacy	Managers have relatively low status in British society. Strong influence of class system; managers highly likely to have fathers who were in white-collar occupations.
Dominant Managerial Values	Low to medium power distance. Low to medium uncertainty avoidance. High on masculinity scale. High on individualism. Authority vested in the person, not the position. Stability and tendency towards authoritarian style of leadership.
HUMAN RESOURCE MANAGEMENT	
Recruitment	Higher managerial staff recruited largely from upper middle class who have gone to public (private in U.S.) schools. Lower managerial positions recruited from middle class who have attended comprehensive schools and red-brick universities. Preference for promotion from within.
Selection	Interview is the most common approach; panel interview is fairly commonly used in very large firms. Applicants submit resumes with copies of recommendations.
Compensation	British managers paid poorly in comparison to managers in other advanced industrial countries. Salary and bonus common. Traditional value of seniority, but in 1980s shift to merit and company performance emphasis.
Performance Appraisal	Use formal PA programs. Emphasis of evaluation is on performance and interpersonal skills.
Training and Development	Before World War II there were few training centers, because of the belief that leaders were born to succeed. Multiplicity of training programs within and external to company at the present. London and Manchester Business Schools most prestigious.
Labor relations	Managers in private sector not unionized.
Future Trends	British business still strongly influenced by tradition and unwillingness to change ideas and values.

Table 17.1 (continued)

UNITED STATES

Definition of Managers

Managers usually include all supervisory staff beyond the level of foremen, but not including top level policy-making executives (e.g., VPs, president, or chairman of the board).

Managerial Status, Ideology, Legitimacy

Managers generally enjoy high status because of pay level, importance of firms to the country's economic success, and power. Managers generally share an ideology centering on the rights of private property and the benefits of the "market". Private property is the basis of legitimacy.

Dominant Managerial Values

Includes achievement and success, belief in hard work, pragmatism, optimism, puritanism, rationality, impersonality in interpersonal work relationships, equality of opportunity, acceptance of competition, and individualism.

HUMAN RESOURCE MANAGEMENT

Recruitment

Managers are usually initially received from colleges and universities, but there is also a fair amount of midcareer recruitment.

Selection

Primary reliance is on selection interview (individual or panel). Other selection techniques include psychological evaluation, testing, and assessment centers.

Compensation

All managers receive base salary, but the salary may also include yearly bonuses and other incentives (e.g. stock options). Benefits represent 30 to 40 percent of base salary, many provided by the firm rather than through law. Largest spread in pay in industrial countries. Recent emphasis on pay for performance and team incentives.

Performance Appraisal

Almost all managers are exposed to performance appraisals using MBO, graphic rating scales, behavioral ratings, or essays.

Training and Development

Most of managerial training and development is learned on-the-job. Wide use of auxiliary development through interval training programs, enrollment in MBA and Executive MBA programs, and so forth.

Labor Relations

Few, if any, managers belong to labor unions because of their socialization, lack of legal coverage to organize, and employer resistance.

Future Trends

Growth in number of managers to the year 2000, but largely in women and in small, service sector organizations. Downsizing in large corporate managerial staffs. Declining loyalty by and to managers by their employers.

point, the government of Poland has committed itself to a rapid transfer over to a market economy. Whether this will continue to be the case is still unclear. We will have a much better idea of the changes in the two countries by the end of this decade, because it will take time for them to develop managerial cadres with sufficient authority and risk-taking propensity to operate effectively in a market economy. Similar changes, no doubt, will be required in other Central and Eastern European countries like Hungary, Czechoslovakia, Rumania, Bulgaria, Yugoslavia, and Albania.

Saudi Arabia represents another example that varied somewhat from our outline. Robert W. Moore spends considerable time discussing the role of the Islamic religion and the Qur'an in explaining the behavior of Saudi managers today. While the Saudis have borrowed elements of human resource management from the West, it is also evident that religion and traditional cultural values have created a system that varies from that of both Western and Asian industrialized nations.

We shall follow our outline in discussing both similarities and differences between individual countries and groups of countries. In so doing, we can offer a more integrative way of viewing managers across the diverse countries. Most of the discussion of managers in particular countries has focused on the private sector, because of the interests of the author(s) and the strong role of the private sector in the economies of those countries. However, this has not been as true in countries such as the former Soviet Union, Poland, and, to a lesser extent, Israel.

Definition of Manager

The definition of manager varies across the selected countries. For example, managers in the United States and Britain are often defined as those personnel in the private sector who are placed above the role of foreman, but do not include high-level policy makers such as vice-presidents and presidents (or managing directors, or chairmen of the board). In some cases, a person can be given a managerial title without necessarily supervising one or more subordinate managers, supervisors, and/or staff. Hence, professional staff are sometimes included.

The authors of the chapters on Sweden, Israel, Mainland China, and Malaysia use a more encompassing definition of the term to include both governmental and private sector managers in their discussion. Polish and CIS managers, on the other hand, have largely been restricted to lower- and middle-level supervisory and administrative functionaries who have clearly been subordinate to those higher level government officials in central planning offices.

German (West German) managers, according to Rick Molz, are generally seen as limited to middle and higher level officials, including the equivalent of vice-presidents. Supervisors are treated as a more encompassing separate group. In cases such as Austria and Hong Kong, the definition given includes owner-managers as well. Such entrepreneurs are a dominant group in the economies of both Austria and Hong Kong.

France offers a slightly different concept of the managerial role. The French term *cadre* is similar to the term *managers* in the United States and Britain, but it also includes professional employees, higher ranking sales staff, and senior technical (engineers) staff. This definition is explained in part by the importance that engineers and technocrats have played in France since the days of Saint-Simon.

Thus, like Roomkin (1989), we find no universal definition for managers in our sample of countries. This is not really surprising because of the variance in historical experiences, political ideology, and economic systems.

Social Status

In general, today managers in most of the countries have relatively high status in their society. Some of this high status can be attributed to their high level of competence (e.g., France, Sweden, and the United States). Elitism (e.g., France and Malaysia) is another possible explanation. The fact that managers in most of these countries are paid quite well fits in with studies of social stratification where the highest paid occupations are often viewed as also having the greatest prestige.

High social status of managers is not universal, however. For instance, Oded Shenkar points out that a managerial elite, in the Western sense, does not exist in post–Mao China, nor for that matter, did it exist during the Maoist period. The authors of the chapters on Poland and the Commonwealth of Independent States observe that enterprise managers have had low status in their respective societies during the postwar period. Much of the explanation rests with their subordinate role relative to leaders of the Communist party and higher officials of the centralized planning ministries (e.g., Gosplan in the Soviet Union).

Managers in Great Britain also have relatively low status, but for different reasons. For many decades "the best and brightest" from Oxford and Cambridge chose to enter careers in the civil service and the professions. In addition, the educational level of lower- and middle-level supervisors and managers was not particularly high. Some change is taking place, however. Former Prime Minister Margaret Thatcher gave considerable attention to strengthening the private sector by denationalizing a number of public corporations. At the same time, university graduates were attracted to the financial opportunities available in such private sector industries as financial services. How solid the shift is remains to be seen.

Ideology

Ideology also plays an important role in explaining the role of managers in the various countries. For example, Bendix (1956) discusses its historical role in the early stages of industrialization in Britain, the United States, Germany, and the former Soviet Union. Granick (1972) compares managers in the four countries (using West Germany) as of the early 1970s. Today we find that most of the countries surveyed are solidly committed to capitalism and the market economy, although some countries are more comfortable with industrial policy and an important role for the state in directing financial resources among industrial sectors (e.g., France, Japan, and South Korea).

We can see that the rights of private property are still strongly held in countries like Austria, South Korea, Malaysia, and the territory of Hong Kong where ownership, rather than managerialism, is strongly entrenched. As an illustration, most of the firms in Hong Kong are owned and controlled by extended families using the ideology of familism based on dependence, conformity, and respect according to Paul S. Kirkbride and Robert I. Westwood. Unlike the present situation of Japanese *keiretsu*, most of the largest South Korean *chaebols* are led by the founding families who believe they retain property rights beyond those accorded managers who have minimal share ownership.

The concept of leadership based on being chosen by God, as in pre-World War II German executives (Hartmann, 1959), has given way in recent years to managerial values based on responsibility to the state (society). Present-day managers in most of the advanced industrial countries realize that they are hired for the position to carry out fairly well-defined duties in accord with the company's needs. They expect to be given commensurate power and authority to carry out such duties within the identified boundaries. We discuss managerial values below, because they are related to the broader cultural values that prevail in a given society.

Cultural Values and Managers

It is not easy to offer a set of similarities and differences in cultural values, because there is considerable variance across the fifteen countries. There are also important differences within a country like the United States which has such a heterogeneous population. Other more heterogeneous populations in our sample include those in Britain, Israel, the CIS, and Malaysia. In contrast, Japan, Hong Kong, and Mainland China represent very homogeneous populations from which the managerial ranks are drawn.

Hofstede (1980) identified four factors that differentiated the employee and managerial populations of a large American multinational corporation operating in approximately forty countries. Some of the authors made use of his findings in reporting on managerial behavior in their particular nation. To the degree that Hofstede's findings are representative of managers in the host country as well, we can make some generalities. The United States, Britain, Germany, and Austria share more in common in terms of lower power distance, greater individualism, lower uncertainty avoidance, and stronger masculinity. The situation tends to reverse itself in countries like France and Saudi Arabia, except that individualism is given considerable weight in France.

Research by Hall and Hall (1990) and others points out that managers in countries like Britain, Germany, and the United States operate in low-context cultures where the language is clear and direct. On the other hand, French, Saudi Arabians, Japanese, Chinese, and Malaysians perform their duties within a high-context culture in which language and mannerisms are much more indirect and complex.

Individualism versus communalism offers another useful typology in differentiating cultural and managerial behavior across various countries. Put quite simply, individualistic-oriented societies place considerable stress on the role of the individual agenda in accomplishing national and managerial goals. Communitarian societies place greater stress on group and societal commitment. Lodge and Vogel (1987) link these terms to national growth in gross national product (GNP) over a recent twenty-year period. They find that, on average, the communitarian countries have recently surpassed the economic achievements of those nations that have generally preferred stress on individualistic goals and priorities.

Based on our sample, the United States, Britain, Israel, Sweden, and possibly Poland would fit more closely with the individualistic orientation. The communitarian model guides the behavior of managers in such countries as the former Soviet Union, Japan, South Korea, Mainland China, Malaysia, and the territory of Hong Kong. Cultural values of groupism and hierarchy are very much evident in the way that managers operate in most of Asia.

Leadership styles and views of authority also vary across our national samples. Moshe Banai and Dennis J. Gayle, for example, see British managerial authority as vested more in the person than position. Jacques Rojot argues that authority in French management is based on absolutism, omnipotence, and universalism. Swedish managerial authority resides in their knowledge and expertise, according to Jan Selmer.

According to a number of our authors, it appears that the tendency towards authoritarianism can be found in a number of countries (e.g., Britain, France, Germany, Israel, the CIS, South Korea, and the territory of Hong Kong). In contrast, consensual tendencies are more noticeable in Austria, Sweden, and Japan. Paternalistic managerial styles may be found in countries like Germany, Japan, and Malaysia, but there is variance within each of these countries. For instance, in Malaysia we find important differences based on whether the manager is Chinese, Malay, or East Indian.

Egalitarian values are also important in understanding managerial behavior in such countries as Sweden, the former Soviet Union, and Poland, but for very different reasons.

One often thinks of American management as a haven for participative management, but in terms of formal arrangements a number of countries seem to be more in the forefront than the United States. Notable among them are Austria (through the Social Partnership), Germany (codetermination), Sweden (works councils, joint councils, and employee participation on the board of directors), and Japan (consensual decision making). Perhaps one of the reasons is that some of these countries prefer compromise and consensus (e.g., Sweden, Austria, and Japan) over decisions made by individuals that may generate conflict and ill-will (e.g., France).

Managerial values seem to be only moderately influenced by religion and deep philosophical systems in most of the countries covered in this book. However, this may be less true than is commonly thought, because of the indirect impact that religion has in some countries. For example, Weber (1958) believed that Protestantism played an important role in the rise of capitalism in parts of Europe and the United States. Today some of those links are taken as givens and are rarely mentioned.

We can see, however, that religion and philosophy have played important roles in some of the countries. For example, the Puritan work ethic is very crucial to understanding managerial behavior in the United States, as Richard B. Peterson and Jane George-Falvey note in their chapter. Many centuries after it was formulated, Confucianism still helps to explain managerial behavior in Mainland China, the territory of Hong Kong, South Korea, Japan, and the Chinese segment of business in Malaysia. Islam is an encompassing part of Saudi Arabian society, as Moore reports. Judaism, no doubt, plays some role in present-day Israeli management, although it probably is most obvious in the kibbutzim movement.

Clearly, a variety of cultural values are represented in the fifteen countries we covered. There are also links between broader cultural values and the behavior of managers in a particular country, but this relationship, at times, is not obvious. Now we turn our attention to comparing and contrasting the various human resource management systems that apply to managers in the various countries.

Human Resource Management and Managers

What are the similarities and differences across the sampled countries in how managers are recruited, selected, compensated, appraised, trained, and represented? We will begin our discussion by focusing on recruitment.

Recruitment In reality, most managers are originally hired into nonsupervisory or professional positions upon graduation. Only later are they promoted into managerial posts. The trend in recent years has been to hire people with either technical or nontechnical education at the university level (e.g., Britain, France, Germany, Sweden, Japan, and South Korea). French managers, and especially executives, are very likely to have attended one of the *grand écoles*. Saudi Arabia, Malaysia, and Hong Kong hire a number of future and present managers who are foreigners, or who have attended colleges and universities abroad.

Newspaper advertisements are the primary recruiting approach used in many countries. Yet college recruiting is heavily used in such countries as the United States, Japan, and South Korea. Engineering, economics, and business majors form the most popular educational backgrounds for entry-level staff in many of the countries.

It appears that executive search firms are being used more often than before when hiring managers from outside the organization (e.g., Austria and Germany). Japan is beginning to make use of such firms, even though most managerial positions are filled through internal promotion. Itzhak Harpaz and Ilan Meshoulam mention that in Israel retired military personnel represent an important midcareer recruiting source.

Selection The interview is almost a universal part of the selection process for managers across the fifteen countries. Mainland China, where political loyalty and state decisions largely determine who receives such jobs, is an exception.

Psychological tests seem to be more common in Austria, Sweden, Israel, and the former Soviet Union. Such tests may include aptitude, skills, and/or personality inventories. The use of written examinations as part of the initial selection process is fairly common in South Korea and Japan. Such examinations are often part of the selection process for governmental agencies in Hong Kong. Some firms use assessment centers for choosing people to be promoted or hired into managerial positions (e.g., the United States, Austria, and Germany). Letters of recommendation and reference checks are used in many of our sampled countries. Personal recommendations from key professors are especially important in Japan. An interesting point is that some firms in Germany and Israel use graphology, the study of the person's handwriting.

In Poland, during the 1980s there was both an open and closed selection system. The closed one was based on political loyalties, while the open process used job analysis to pick the most professionally qualified person for a given managerial position. Moore comments that nepotism and connections are important criteria for managerial selection in Saudi Arabia.

Both Japan and France are examples where selection from the most elitist universities is given considerable weight in determining who will be finally hired. However, the prestige of the university is also important in a number of other countries (e.g., Britain, Sweden, South Korea, and Malaysia).

Compensation   Some broad generalities can be made about managerial compensation across the fifteen countries. All managers receive a base salary plus a set of fringe benefits. The amount and variety of benefits vary across country. Bonuses, usually paid twice a year, are an important part of pay in Japan, South Korea, and Malaysia. Managerial bonuses, based on meeting or exceeding economic planning targets are used in the former Soviet Union and Poland. Mainland China has experimented with such bonus plans periodically since the Communist Revolution in 1949. Interestingly, Israeli managers sometimes receive payment in kind as a supplement to their regular salary.

Traditionally, we find that egalitarian values regarding differences in managerial salary have been the norm in Sweden, Saudi Arabia, and Mainland China. Pay increases for managers in Britain, according to the authors, were weighted primarily in terms of seniority, but in the 1980s more attention was given to individual merit and company performance. Japan and South Korea give greater attention to seniority in managerial pay increase decisions than is true in the United States.

How does managerial pay compare across the various countries? It is likely that the pay of managers in the United States is generally quite high in a real sense as well as relative to other salaries in the organization. The pay of German and Saudi managers is also high by international comparisons. Apparently, the pay of Austrian managers is in the middle among European managers. British managers receive relatively low pay by international comparisons.

Managerial pay in the Commonwealth of Independent States, Poland, and

Mainland China has generally been low. According to the authors of the chapter on Poland, managerial pay has at times been lower than that of blue-collar workers. The Chinese government has shifted back and forth on pay incentives for managers over the past forty years. Most recently, the government has been more receptive to improving the pay of managers.

If we look at Asia, the pay of Japanese managers is somewhat closer to that of managers in the Western industrial countries. The situation is less true in South Korea, Hong Kong, and Malaysia. However, it should be noted that the first two countries are part of the newly industrializing countries (including Taiwan and Singapore). Malaysia, on the other hand, is one of the emerging countries that may well follow the course of the "Four Tigers" in the 1990s. Continued economic growth may bring managerial pay closer to that of the wealthy nations in ten to twenty years.

What is lacking here is any real international comparison between total managerial compensation (including base salary, bonuses, supplements, and fringe benefits). According to many of our authors, such meaningful comparisons are also difficult to find for pay data within nations.

Performance Appraisal A review of Table 17.1 shows that formal performance appraisals for managers are fairly commonplace among the surveyed countries. However, there are exceptions. According to Selmer, appraisal systems are not common in Sweden. They are more likely to be found in foreign-owned than in native-owned firms in Saudi Arabia. Formal performance appraisals have not received much use in China.

A wide variety of performance appraisal techniques are used with managers in the United States and Israel, including trait, behavioral, and MBO systems. German firms apparently prefer quantitative instruments. More informal or indirect ways of providing feedback to managers are used in countries like Japan, China, and South Korea where face saving is given considerable importance.

Variance exists across these fifteen countries in terms of the primary purpose for such appraisals. A number of Western firms use performance appraisal primarily for evaluation purposes, but the trend in Sweden and Israel is toward greater weight being given to development and improvement of the manager. The authors of the chapters on Poland and the former Soviet Union state that performance appraisal has not been used very effectively in those countries.

Training and Management Development The trend in recent years in many of these countries is to give more attention to the training and development of managers. All fifteen countries use internal or in-house training programs for potential and present managerial staff; Japan is perhaps the best example of this approach. Most university graduates, with the exception of some technical specialists, are recruited into the company as generalists. They are given a series of generalist assignments to learn about the breadth of the firm's activities as a preparation for eventual promotion into a managerial position. Such managers in large Japanese firms are socialized to think of themselves as representatives of their company ("I work for Hitachi") rather than the manager of a particular functional department like accounting.

Not surprisingly, in-house management development programs in many countries tend to be found most often in larger companies where training staff is
sufficient to carry out such training sessions. On-the-job exposure to management
is more common in smaller and medium-size organizations.

External management development programs have grown considerably in most
of our sampled countries in recent years. Many of these are training centers,
institutes, and college- and university-sponsored programs. Consultants are
brought in for specialized training as well. Managers may be sent to such programs in their own country, region, or abroad. In the case of smaller countries
like Austria, the courses may be operated by the labor market parties, the chamber
of commerce, or institutes specializing in economics and business administration.

Countries like the Commonwealth of Independent States and Poland are de-
voting more attention to postgraduate training courses for managers as a step in
improving the international competitiveness of their economies. Shenkar men-
tions that the present emphasis in China is on the International On-the-Job
Training Program orchestrated by the United Nations Center on Transnational
Corporations.

Enrollment in special programs, like INSEAD and IMEDE in France and
Switzerland, respectively, is designed to expose managers from various countries
to broader international ways of understanding the management function. Finally,
we find that managers are being sent back to school to attend executive MBA
programs in countries like the United States and Britain. In reviewing the chapters
of this book, we note that employees with high potential for managerial careers
in Hong Kong, Malaysia, Japan, and South Korea are being sent to the United
States and some Western European countries for MBA degrees. The Eastern
European countries will probably do the same in the coming years, given their
need to learn about the operations of a market economy.

Labor Relations   The role that labor relations plays for managers in most of
our surveyed countries is more likely to be as members of the management side
in contract negotiations and grievance handling. Exceptions are where close to
half or more of the labor force in the particular country are represented by a
union or employee association (e.g., Sweden, Norway, Austria, and Denmark).

When we look at the private sector only, we observe that managers in most
of the surveyed countries are not usually members of labor unions or employee
associations involved, in part, in collective bargaining. For example, federal
labor law in the United States does not require companies to negotiate with their
managerial staff. This is not the case in Mainland China where virtually all
employees and managers are affiliated with unions belonging to the All-China
Federation of Trade Unions. In Sweden, a manager may belong to the confederation representing professional staff (SACO). There is a separate union for
managerial employees in Germany. Managers in that country also have a voice
through their participation in the codetermination scheme, works councils, and
the labor movement itself.

In some of the countries (e.g., Austria and Israel), the employee may retain union membership after becoming a manager, but there is no union that bargains for him or her directly. In Saudi Arabia all unions are illegal. Government in many of the Asian countries has not encouraged union membership (e.g., South Korea and Singapore).

We will not comment here on possible trends in the individual countries in the coming years, but some of those trends are mentioned in summary in Table 17.1. The comments of the authors of the various chapters tend to be country-specific, so it is difficult to say much about the similarities and differences across the fifteen countries. What seems to be happening, though, in many of the countries mentioned here is that increasing internationalization of the economy is placing greater pressure on the countries to professionalize their managerial staff.

CONCLUSIONS

What broad conclusions can we draw from this study of management in the fifteen selected countries? It seems that several points can be made. First, and perhaps foremost, our insights provide only limited support for the universality of management behavior. Over thirty years ago, Harbison and Myers (1959) argued in favor of a logic of industrialization that would lead towards a common path of managerial behavior among those countries that shared a common level of industrialization. The assumption was that the United States, as the leading industrial power at the time, was exhibiting the appropriate management behaviors for its stage of industrialization.

No doubt, there is some borrowing of managerial ideas, techniques, and approaches across nations. For example, many Western European managers have been exposed to U.S. management and techniques since World War II. And yet, we do not often find French and German managers behaving in the same way as their American counterparts (Hall and Hall, 1990). We also find differences in the ways managers are recruited, selected, compensated, appraised, trained, and whether or not they are represented by a union. We even find differences within Western Europe (e.g., elitism versus nonelitism).

We can discern even greater differences when comparing Asian management with that in the United States or Western Europe. For instance, Japan is at the same level of industrialization as the United States or Germany, but it has chosen a different model of management in its large firms. Culturally, and for historical reasons, it is difficult to equate all three geographical groupings as having common streams. What is known about managerial behavior in China, South Korea, Malaysia, and the territory of Hong Kong so far suggests that they may choose routes to industrialization that are more appropriate to their values and experience than the route taken by the West. The importance of familism in Hong Kong offers one illustration of a cultural value drawing on Confucianism that is not found in either the United States or Western Europe.

We are not arguing that there are no commonalities or overlaps between so-called Eastern and Western countries. What we are saying is that whatever common ties there may be, there are also important differences that argue against the universality principle of management.

A second conclusion is that there is no common agreement across these nations regarding the definition of management itself. Some of this difference may be due to the fact that the word "manager" itself does not always have a common term for it in another language. However, in addition, we find that the law has clearly defined the term one way in one country (e.g., the Wage and Hours Act in the United States), but differently in another nation. Sometimes we find that the common usage of the term is more encompassing (e.g., using "manager" for all supervisory personnel or including professional and technical staff as well) than the legal definition.

Finally, this review shows that most of the authors concentrated on managers in large, and sometimes medium-size, firms but gave limited or no attention to managers in small companies. An example is Japan, where Sully Taylor restricted most of her remarks to the large Japanese corporation. She would have had to qualify some of her remarks had she included smaller size firms. On the other hand, Kirkbride and Westwood remind us that the overwhelming number of native-owned private firms in Hong Kong are owned by extended families and employ small staff. Thus, we must be wary of generalizing the managerial situation in large firms to the entire business community.

We have concentrated on native-owned firms in the private sector in our sample of countries. Much less has been said about intercountry joint ventures or foreign-owned firms operating in these countries. Part of the reason is the space limitation given the authors. However, much less is known about managerial behavior and human resource management in such firms than is true of the native-owned firms. Furthermore, the authors were not expressly asked to address those companies with partial or full-foreign ownership. Now let us briefly discuss what steps future research might take in this area to help us better understand cross-national management.

FUTURE DIRECTIONS

Future writers and researchers on national and cross-national management behavior and human resource management might take several steps. First, the inclusion of a section on foreign-owned firms and management behavior could provide the reader with an interesting comparison. We could even compare managerial behavior and human resource management between home country management and the behavior of managers in the same firm's foreign subsidiaries. Another possibility would be to study managers in international joint ventures.

Second, researchers might wish to look at managers in the public sector. This book did not really give equal attention to the management of governmental agencies in the various countries. More was said about it in those countries where the public sector is a sizable part of the total labor (and managerial) workforce, such as in Sweden, Israel, and China, but it was lightly covered or not covered at all in other chapters.

Third, in the future it would be desirable to use a longitudinal perspective to discern any noticeable shifts in managerial behavior. The greatest changes may well take place in the former Communist Bloc countries and in Saudi Arabia in the next ten to twenty-five years, but we should not rule out important changes in the major industrialized nations like the United States, Japan, or a number of advanced Western European nations either.

Finally, we would encourage others to broaden the number of countries covered in the study of managers. Our country sample was representative primarily of the industrialized nations. We know much less about the developing world as represented by many countries in Africa, Asia, and Latin America. Previous books and articles suggest that culture, history, economics, and politics have led to different managerial experiences from those in the industrialized world.

In closing, it has been an enriching experience for the editor of this book. I trust that the same holds for the authors of the country chapters and the readers as well.

REFERENCES

Bendix, R. 1956. *Work and Authority in Industry: Ideologies with Management in the Course of Industrialization.* New York: John Wiley.

Granick, D. 1972. *Managerial Comparisons of Four Developed Countries: France, Britain, United States, and Russia.* Cambridge, Mass.: MIT Press.

Hall, E., and Hall, M. 1990. *Understanding Cultural Differences. German, French, and American.* Yarmouth, Me.: Intercultural Press.

Harbison, F., and Myers, C. A., eds. 1959. *Management in the Industrial World.* New York: McGraw-Hill.

Hartmann, H. 1959. *Authority and Organization in German Management.* Princeton, N.J.: Princeton University Press.

Hofstede, G. 1980. *Culture's Consequences: International Differences in Work-related Values.* Beverly Hills, Calif.: Sage Publications.

Lawrence, P. 1980. *Managers and Management in West Germany.* London: Croom Helm.

Lodge, G. C., and Vogel E. F., eds. 1987. *Ideology and National Competitiveness: An Analysis of Nine Countries.* Boston: Harvard Business School Press.

Roomkin, M. J., ed. 1989. *Managers as Employees.* New York: Oxford University Press.

Weber, M. 1958. *The Protestant Ethic and the Spirit of Capitalism.* New York: Scribner's.

INDEX

Korea, 291; and view of industry,
Sweden, 119–20; Western-oriented,
Israel, 218
Culture and management: cadre, France,
71; Commonwealth of Independent
States, 167–69; hierarchies, South
Korea, 304; Hong Kong, 322–27;
Malaysia, 394; social status of, France,
84; training for, Great Britain, 60, 62
Culture and managerial behavior: Austria,
143–45; France, 73–78; Hong Kong,
327–28; Japan, 259–63; motivation,
Sweden, 122; Saudi Arabia, 235;
South Korea, 313–14; social context of
managerial attitudes, Austria, 152;
summary, 423–25; Sweden, 123–29
Cultural values of: Germany, 94–98;
Great Britain, 56–57; managing
uncertainty, China, 358; Poland, 186–
93
Currency control, Israel, 231
Czechoslovakia: anticipated changes in,
421; opening up of, 6

Daewoo, South Korea, 306
Daewoo Training Center, 316–17
Debate as a decision-making tool, Israel,
214
Decentralization, trend toward, Malaysia,
400
Decision making: centralized, France, 76;
centralized, Japan, 263; centralized,
Saudi Arabia, 252; collective, Sweden,
123; in the Commonwealth of
Independent States, 168; by consensus,
Sweden, 126–28; consultative, Austria,
143; in Israel, 214; Japan, post-World
War II, 4; participative, China, 353–
54; participative, Saudi Arabia, 254;
public challenges to managerial,
Germany, 99–100; and religion,
Malaysia, 390; Sweden, 121
Democracy in America (de Tocqueville),
19
Demographic characteristics: general, and
trends in Austria, 152–53; of the labor
force, Israel, 209–10; Poland, 193–95
Demographic characteristics of managers:

Austria, 145–46; Hong Kong, 331–34;
Sweden, 114, 129–31
Depression, due to change, Poland, 180
Deprivation, relative, China, 368
de Tocqueville, Alexis, United States, 19
Deutsche Bundesbank, 92–93
Developing countries, need for research
on, 431
Development centers, Austria, 147
Dignity, value of, Poland, 193
Direktor, 120
Discrimination: country-of-origin of
Israeli managers, 217; against women,
Israel, 231–32
Dissent, Austria, 144
Diversification: economic, Saudi Arabia,
239, 254; Malaysia, 386, 401; and
management recruitment, Japan, 269–
70
Diversity: in China, 349; cultural, of the
American workforce, 11; management
of, Japan, 280
Doctrine of the Mean, 313
Document evaluation for management
selection, South Korea, 301–2
Downsizing, elimination of middle
management positions, United States,
29
Doyukai, Resolution of, 282, 284
Drucker, Peter, 2
Dual economy, Malaysia, 379
Due process, France, 75
Dunlop, John, 2
Durkheim, Emile, 1

East Asian Union, 7
Eastern Bloc, 11–12
Eastern Bloc, opening up of, 6–7
École Centrale, 72
École des Arts et Métiers, 72
École Nationale d'Administration, 72
École Polytechnique, 72
Economic development: Commonwealth
of Independent States, 158–59; pay-as-
you-go, Japan, 257–58; role of actors
in, 2–3; Saudi Arabia, 240–41; South
Korea, 288; after World War II,

ABOUT THE CONTRIBUTORS

MOSHE BANAI is an assistant professor at Baruch College, City University of New York. He received his training at Ben Gurion University (B.A.), Tel Aviv University (M.Sc.), and the London Business School (Ph.D.). His academic work focuses on organizational behavior in multinational corporations and comparative human resource management, and includes studies in several countries such as Britain, Belgium, Germany, France, Israel, the Netherlands, and the United States.

DIANE J. GARSOMBKE is an associate professor of management at the University of Wisconsin—Superior. Her present research interests include international competitor analysis, business in the Pacific Region, and corporate culture.

THOMAS W. GARSOMBKE is an associate professor of marketing and management at the University of Wisconsin—Superior. His current areas of research are strategic marketing in exporters, advertising overseas, and globally competitive strategies.

DENNIS JOHN GAYLE is director of international affairs and associate professor of business environment at Florida International University, Miami. He is a graduate of the University of California at Los Angeles, the London School of Economics, and the University of the West Indies, Jamaica.

JANE GEORGE-FALVY is a Ph.D. student in human resource management and organizational behavior at the University of Washington. She received a B.A. in psychology from Whitman College in 1987. Her research interests include goal setting, accountability in organizations, and group dynamics.

PETER R. HAISS is with the Secretariat to the Managing Board at Z-Landerbank, Austria AG, and a lecturer at the Institute of European Studies, Vienna, Austria. His research interests include cultural influences on planning and human resource management, banking strategy, and the adjustment of the financial services industry to the European Common Market, to the opening of Eastern Europe, and to the green value change.

WILLIAM E. HALAL is a professor in the Department of Management Science at George Washington University in Washington, D.C. His research interests include the changes currently taking place in capitalist and socialist economic systems.

ITZHAK HARPAZ is an adjunct professor at the organizational behavior department, School of Management, Brigham Young University and earned his Ph.D. in industrial relations at the University of Minnesota. His areas of interest include work values and behavior, and cross-cultural comparisons of work, management, and organizations.

PAUL S. KIRKBRIDE holds a senior faculty position at Ashridge Management College in the United Kingdom. From 1984 to 1989 he taught and researched in Hong Kong. His research interests include strategic human resource management, power and influence in organizations, and cross-cultural and comparative management.

JÓZEF KOZIŃSKI is assistant professor at the Faculty of Management and Computer Science, Wroclaw Academy of Economics, Poland. His research fields include general management, managerial economics, and personnel management.

TADEUSZ LISTWAN is professor of human resource management and vice-dean of the Faculty of Management and Computer Science, Wroclaw Academy of Economics, Poland. His research interests include management problems in general and human resource management in particular.

CHRISTOPHER B. MEEK received a Ph.D. in industrial relations from Cornell University. He is associate professor of organizational behavior at Brigham Young University. His research interests include the impact of national culture on organizational behavior and business strategy, and he has also done extensive research on worker participation, empowerment, and ownership.

ILAN MESHOULAM is associate professor of human resource strategy and management in the Faculty of Industrial Engineering at Technion–Israel Institute of Technology.

RICK MOLZ is an associate professor in the School of Commerce and Administration, Concordia University, Montreal, Canada. His research interests are in the area of management adaptation to privatization of government enterprise, the response of corporate strategy to public policy initiatives, and the relationship between forms of enterprise ownership and the generation of national wealth.

ROBERT W. MOORE is professor of international management and strategy at the University of Nevada, Las Vegas. He holds an MBA in finance from the University of California, Los Angeles, and a Ph.D. in business strategy from Claremont Graduate School. Besides extensive overseas business and academic experience, he has over fifty publications and proceedings.

RICHARD B. PETERSON is professor of management and organization at the School of Business Administration at the University of Washington. His Ph.D. in industrial relations is from the University of Wisconsin. His primary research interests are in the fields of international management and labor and industrial relations. He has authored or edited six books and some sixty journal articles in these and related fields.

VLADIMIR S. RAPOPORT is deputy director of the Institute for Systems Studies of the Soviet Academy of Sciences in Moscow. He is interested in human resource management and the management of economic systems, both macroeconomic policy and the management of enterprises.

JACQUES ROJOT is professor of management and industrial relations at the Sorbonne in Paris. His doctorate is in industrial relations from UCLA. He previously taught at INSEAD, the University of Main at Le Mans, and the University of Rennes. His interests are in the fields of labor law, industrial relations, and HRM.

VALERIA RYSSINA is research scholar at the Institute for Systems Studies of the Soviet Academy of Sciences in Moscow. She is interested in human resource management and the design of educational programs for training enterprise managers.

WERNER SCHICKLGRUBER is head of the research department at Z-Landerbank, Austria AG, Vienna, Austria. His research interests include human resource management, structural and historical industry paradigms, risk management, economic, fiscal, and banking policy.

JAN SELMER is docent (associate professor) in business administration at the University of Stockholm, Sweden. Presently, he is principal lecturer and head, Department of Management, School of Business, Hong Kong Baptist College, Hong Kong. He has been engaged in cross-cultural management research in Asia for a decade. He is currently completing a project on expatriate business managers in the Far East.

ODED SHENKAR received his Ph.D. from Columbia University and is senior lecturer, Faculty of Management, Tel-Aviv University, and professor of Management, College of Business Administration, University of Hawaii-Manoa. His main research interests are in comparative and international management, with a special emphasis on East Asia.

YOUNG-HACK SONG received a Ph.D. in organizational psychology from Brigham Young University. He is a fellow at the National University of Singapore where he teaches courses in organizational behavior and human resource management. His research interests include the comparative study of Asian management systems and the role of national culture in shaping organizational behavior.

SULLY TAYLOR is an assistant professor of International Management at Portland State University, where she teaches courses on international management, international human resource management, and the Japanese business environment. Her research areas are international strategic human resource management, the selection and training of expatriates, and the management of Japanese research and development.

STUART A. UMPLEBY is a professor in the Department of Management Science at George Washington University in Washington, D.C. His research interests include the psychological and cultural foundations of economic systems and interactive planning methods.

ROBERT I. WESTWOOD is senior lecturer in the Department of Organization and Management at the Chinese University of Hong Kong. His research interests cover cross-cultural and comparative management, power, language, and organizations, and gender issues in management and organizations.